The Norton Introduction to Literature

SEVENTH EDITION

Instructor's Guide for the
Regular and Shorter Editions
and
The Norton Introduction to Poetry

The Norton Introduction to

Literature

SEVENTH EDITION

Instructor's Guide for the
Regular and Shorter Editions
and The Norton Introduction to Poetry

Kelly J. Mays
New Mexico State University

Gayla McGlamery
Bryan Crockett
Loyola College in Maryland

W. W. NORTON & COMPANY
NEW YORK • LONDON

The text of this book is composed in Optima and Stone Serif,
with the display set in Optima and Stone Serif.
Composition by Binghamton Valley Composition.
Book design by Joan Greenfield.
Cover illustration: By David Hockney, "The Road to Malibu," 1988 (detail).
Oil on 3 canvases, 24"×96". © David Hockney.

ISBN 0-393-97203-8 (pbk.)

W. W. Norton & Company, Inc., 500 Fifth Avenue, New York, NY 10110
http://www.wwnorton.com
W. W. Norton & Company Ltd., 10 Coptic Street, London WC1A 1PU

1 2 3 4 5 6 7 8 9 0

Contents

Exploring Contexts 94

Understanding the Text 218

Exploring Contexts 340

Teaching Drama 490

Drama: Reading, Responding, Writing 492

Understanding the Text 498

Exploring Contexts 524

Evaluating Drama 587

Introduction

In putting together this latest edition of the *Instructor's Guide to The Norton Introduction to Literature*, I have often been led to wonder, uneasily, about the connotations of the word "guide," which to me calls up rather disturbing images of experienced natives or park-service employees in intimidating uniforms taking curious tourists into realms unknown. But if the title carries unfortunate connotations, the volume itself is not written or organized in such a spirit. While it has certainly been the effort of all who have contributed to this and earlier editions of the *Guide* to speak from and about our own experiences (both bad and good) with teaching the materials, concepts, and skills covered in the *Introduction to Literature*, the goal of the *Guide* is to highlight options and questions for readers whom the *Guide* envisions and speaks to as colleagues. In this regard, I see the polyphony of voices and personalities present in the *Guide* as one of its real strengths, since it ensures that the *Guide* contains a wide variety of approaches, and that it takes some account of the equally wide variety of pedagogical situations in which the *Introduction to Literature* and the *Guide* are used. By the same token, the *Guide* complements the *Introduction to Literature* by suggesting different and even dissenting points of view on, or approaches to, particular texts, pedagogical situations, and readerly and writerly strategies or concepts, while also providing some suggestions on how to use the material in the *Introduction to Literature* in a way that differs from that suggested by the organization of the anthology itself. Again, the goal throughout has been to multiply rather than to close off possible strategies and points of view.

As in past editions of the *Guide*, the bulk of each chapter is devoted to discussion of the individual reading selections included in the *Introduction to Literature*. Such discussions typically include a commentary, a list of questions one might use to spark in-class discussion, and a list of questions one might use for student writing assignments. Though many of the commentaries argue for a particular interpretation, often offering a way of approaching a selection in terms of the concepts or approach covered in the particular chapter of the *Introduction to Literature* in which the selection appears, others focus instead on articulating the variety of interpretive angles one might take or on interpretive questions or problems rather than answers or solutions. Some commentaries also include biographical or historical information and/or short excerpts from relevant secondary sources, such as historical or literary critical studies, and/ or from historically, generically, or thematically related literary texts not included in the *Introduction to Literature*. The commentaries themselves embody the eclectic quality of the *Guide* as a whole, and users of the *Guide* may well find some of these commentaries more helpful and/or more amenable to their own views and approaches than others. I hope that you will find this eclecticism a strength rather than a weakness, and that you will find these commentaries as helpful when you (and/or your students) disagree with them as when you agree.

In addition to such commentaries, each chapter of the *Guide* begins with a brief introduction to the chapter and a list of "Planning Ideas," both of which suggest possible ways of using the materials in the *Introduction to Literature*, of incorporating works that aren't included, and of handling the issues and questions raised in the chapter, while also offering actual reading and writing assignments that might prove helpful. Throughout, the focus is on highlighting various possibilities and discussing the costs and benefits of particular approaches.

Each chapter of this edition of the *Guide* also includes a new section entitled "Reading/Writing Ideas" that I hope will prove especially helpful to those teachers who use the *Introduction to Literature* in composition-focused literature courses or literature-focused composition courses—that is, courses that focus, in one way or another, on writing about literature and especially on writing essays about literature. Each of the "Reading/ Writing Ideas" sections treats the concepts in the *Introduction to Literature* from a writerly point of view in a way that complements the readerly point of view offered in the *Introduction to Literature* itself. Though many of these sections include specific essay assignment suggestions not unlike those offered in the *Introduction to Literature* and elsewhere in the *Guide* itself, they aim, on the whole, to discuss writing issues, assignments, genres, and tasks in a more general and/or conceptual way. Thus each section discusses the kind(s) or genre(s) of essays that are suggested by the concepts discussed in the corresponding chapter of the *Introduction to Literature*, examines (in a subsection called "Troubleshooting") some of the problems or challenges that such genres typically pose for student writers and/or their teachers, and offers several writing exercises to help student writers meet those challenges by breaking the essay-writing process itself into manageable steps. Many of these sections also demonstrate the genres and strategies discussed by incorporating excerpts from actual student essays.

Thus, for example, the "Reading/Writing Ideas" section for Chapter 5 ("Characterization") begins by discussing four common types of character-focused essays and illustrates those types with sample thesis statements and topic sentences from student essays; next, a brief "Troubleshooting" section considers one key conceptual problem that often keeps students from thinking and writing effectively about character; the section concludes by outlining two writing exercises, the first designed to help student writers identify evidence and counterevidence for essays on character and the second to suggest how student writers might move or build from one type of character-focused essay to another. Again, however, each "Reading/Writing Ideas" section varies somewhat from the others depending upon the kind of concept or approach it engages.

Though the *Guide* is organized to ensure that it complements the format of the *Introduction to Literature*, I also hope that the commentaries on particular selections, as well as the "Reading/Writing Ideas" sections, will prove equally useful to you even if—like many teachers—you do not format your course in accordance with the format suggested by the *Introduction to Literature* itself. I also hope that you might consider allowing the *Guide* to spark your students' thoughts as well as your own by directly sharing some of the materials in the *Guide* with them. To that end, the *Guide* speaks directly to students rather than to instructors in some discussion questions and writing assignment suggestions.

Finally, I hope that the *Guide* proves helpful to you and to your students not by "guiding" you down any one path, but by both embodying and becoming a part of the ongoing conversation between teachers and students about the multiple ways in which, and reasons why, we read, write about, and teach literature. For that reason, I would very much welcome any suggestions you have about how future editions of the *Guide* might be improved to better facilitate that conversation and that work.

Kelly J. Mays
New Mexico State University

Acknowledgments

Many of the best ideas in the *Guide* come directly or indirectly from the many wonderful colleagues and students I have had the great privilege of working with at Stanford, Harvard, and New Mexico State universities. I owe special thanks to Jerome Beaty, Shaleen Brawn, Stephen Donatelli, Kelly Hager, Gordon Harvey, Cheryl Nixon, Diane Price-Herndl, Nancy Sommers, and to all the students of the Expository Writing classes I taught at Harvard between Fall 1994 and Spring 1996 and of the Writing about Literature classes I taught at New Mexico State in Spring and Fall 1997. I am especially grateful to the talented student writers who have graciously allowed me to reprint excerpts from their work—Sonesh Chainani, Scott Cundy, Sebastian Fuhrer, Marian Hennessy-Fiske, James Martinez, Shia Sin, and Paul Todgham—and to Kerry Walk for providing me access to the work of Shia Sin. For allowing me to use excerpts from the essays of Montira Horayangura, Lauren Marie Kim, Mary Rose Kwaan, Matthew Light, Jeannette Y. Louh, Janet S. McIntosh, and Elaine Yeung, which originally appeared in the Harvard Expository Writing Program's magazine, *Exposé*, I am also heavily indebted to the program, to its director, Nancy Sommers, and to the magazine's editor emeritus, Stephen Donatelli. The *Guide* would have been much impoverished without the contributions of these exceptional student writers, just as it would have been impossible without the consistently thoughtful input of Jerome Beaty, J. Paul Hunter, and W. W. Norton's Peter Simon. Finally, I am deeply grateful to the authors of earlier editions of the *Guide* for setting a wonderful example for me to follow and to try to live up to.

Using the Instructor's Guide

The materials in this guide offer informal, nonprescriptive assistance to teachers using *The Norton Introduction to Literature,* Seventh Edition Regular or Shorter, or *The Norton Introduction to Poetry.* New features expand the range of suggestions offered in each chapter; almost every chapter in the *Guide* has six sections, as follows:

- An introductory headnote treats the chapter topic, often including teaching strategies and suggestions.
- "Planning Ideas" is designed to be helpful for teachers as they prepare for class. Among the planning ideas are suggestions for constructing a syllabus, assignments to be given before class, and possible in-class activities.
- Discussions of individual texts take up the bulk of each chapter. All of the stories and plays included in the chapters of *The Norton Introduction to Literature,* Seventh Edition, are discussed; approximately 30 percent of the poems in the book are either discussed in depth or addressed through a series of questions.
- "Questions for Discussion" follow each story, play, and many of the poems.
- Text-specific writing assignments, different from those in the text, are provided in "Suggestions for Writing."
- A new section, "Reading/Writing Ideas," discusses element-, concept-, and approach-specific writing assignments; typical student problems; and strategies for helping students avoid or solve those problems.

The Norton Introduction to Literature

SEVENTH EDITION

Instructor's Guide for the
Regular and Shorter Editions
and
The Norton Introduction to Poetry

Teaching Fiction

The materials that follow offer teaching suggestions of two kinds.

First, the notes to particular stories and the "Planning Ideas" sections suggest ways to approach teaching the stories in the fiction portion of *The Norton Introduction to Literature*. Almost invariably some information reinforces or extends the guidance offered in the text itself; but this is not done systematically, nor is it the primary function of the Guide. Instead, I have aimed to share my thoughts on and experience in teaching the stories.

Thus sometimes the commentary offers a reading or interpretation of the story, or alternative interpretations. When I have a firm opinion about the reading of a controversial story I will say so—not to close the issue but to avoid the false permissiveness that all of us fall into from time to time and that is the worst sort of intellectual bullying ("What am I holding in my hand?"). At other times I will discuss what worked best for me in opening and directing discussion about a particular story. Occasionally I warn against pitfalls that I have found in teaching a story or in teaching fiction in general.

I have not tried consciously to impose any fixed system of pedagogy, and I have tried to make the comments such that anyone teaching any selection of these stories in any order would find them helpful (if only by provoking argument). Methods of teaching fiction are as various as the personalities and preferences of the teachers of fiction. I have tried to touch on various methods, reader-response, aesthetic, historical, sociopolitical, among others, without emphasizing any one unduly.

In sections called "Reading/Writing Ideas" I've described reading and writing assignments focusing on the concept, element, or approach covered in the relevant chapter of the anthology. Here I've tried to describe essay assignments that have worked for me personally or types of essays that seem to be commonly assigned or produced in the kinds of courses for which *The Norton Introduction to Literature* is typically used. Each of these essay assignment descriptions is followed up by a discussion of the problems that student writers typically face in writing them, as well as strategies and techniques that can help you help your students avoid or deal with such problems. Since one of those techniques involves helping students build their essays step by careful step, each "Reading/Writing Ideas" section ends with a description of one or more short writing exercises that I've found useful in guiding students through the steps involved in writing a particular kind of essay. Where appropriate, I've also tried to explain how I use those exercises in class, whether as a way to spark and focus discussion among the class as a whole or as the basis for small-group work of various kinds. I've found it useful and often necessary to use my own and my colleagues' experiences as a basis for these ideas; however, I've also tried as much as possible to focus on alternatives, on the questions that particular assignments may raise for you and your students, and on the costs and benefits involved in various assignments and approaches.

The first section, *Fiction: Reading, Responding, Writing*, is designed to be discussed as it stands, and I have not offered alternative approaches there. *Reading More Fiction*, on the other hand, belongs entirely to you, and I offer only minimal guidance.

Fiction: Reading, Responding, Writing

- Instead of assigning "The Zebra Storyteller" to be read outside class, read it aloud the first day, pausing at key moments to ask students what sense they make of the story and what they anticipate will happen next. This exercise can provide a good introduction to a discussion of literary conventions and reader expectations. (See commentary on "The Zebra Storyteller" below.)
- When I assign Maupassant's "The Jewelry," I sometimes ask students to prepare for class discussion by marking the specific points in the story at which their feelings toward M. Lantin begin to change. I ask them to be ready to provide the class with reasons for their shift(s) in perspective.

SPENCER HOLST

The Zebra Storyteller

Discussing this short, whimsical story is a good way to begin talking with students about what short stories do and why it is worthwhile to read them. I think the selection works well both as an introduction to the genre and as an object lesson in how to engage a text. Rather than assigning it to be read outside class, I like to read "The Zebra Storyteller" aloud the first day, pausing after each paragraph to ask students what they're thinking. I ask students to note which aspects of the story seem familiar and conventional. Someone almost always mentions the fairy-tale opening "Once upon a time" and the one-sentence "moral" at the end. Sometimes a student observes that the story is structured as a fable.

As I read, I prompt the class to tell me when the story has startled them or upset their expectations in some way. I do this in a very forthright manner by pausing after each paragraph and asking, "Any surprises? Is this what you thought would happen? Why or why not?" It can be useful to record these responses on the blackboard to provide a visual record of how reactions are shaping up.

Once we've finished reading through the story, I turn to the lists on the board. The list we've compiled of "Conventional Aspects" gives me an opening to talk about the relationship between reader and author. For example, when an author begins a story with the opening "Once upon a time," I ask, what expectations about the kind of story we are reading has he or she created? In talking about the conventions the students have listed, I ask them to name types of narrative that depend heavily on conventions, on the implicit agreement between author and reader that the story will take a certain form—in effect, that there will be a limited number of surprises or only (if I may be forgiven the phrase) "expected" surprises. Most classes are able to come up with several examples from their own reading—the stories of Agatha Christie, Stephen King, John Grisham, Barbara Cartland, Sidney Sheldon, etc.

Discussing conventions usually makes it easy to move on to talking about the points in the story at which the author ignores or subverts them. A good example is the phrase "Here now" at the beginning of the third paragraph. You may want to ask the students why this phrase sounds wrong or, to use Holst's word, *inappropriate*. Under the heading of "Unexpected Elements," someone will probably mention the cliché about the zebra's reaction to the cat—"he's just fit to be tied"—and the author's literal use of the phrase in the action of the story. If you have a bright group, someone may notice that the cat is guilty of using trite, cliché-ridden language in his greetings to the zebras.

Eventually, of course, the class will want to tackle the "moral" of the tale. As mentioned in the text headnote, the story suggests that one function of the storyteller is to prepare us for the unexpected. I sometimes ask the class if the story implies that the storyteller has other functions as well. A good way to explore this question is to ask about the cat's "inappropriate language"—his use of clichés. If the cat uses language poorly, then the storyteller might be said to be one who must stamp out poor usage (storyteller as teacher?). Because the storyteller knows a lot about language, he or she is not easily manipulated by it.

Clearly the story also emphasizes the power of the imagination. By imagining himself to be a lion, the cat accomplishes lion's feats. By imagining a story, the zebra storyteller arms himself against attack. If you are feeling particularly brave—or if student comments open the door—you may want to discuss the notion that the storyteller's function may have an ethical component as well.

AUDRE THOMAS

Kill Day on the Government Wharf

A good way to begin discussion of "Kill Day" might be to have students extrapolate on the ideas expressed in the anthology, particularly the suggestion that the unnamed wife in this story represents a somewhat "romantic" "yearning for the primitive and the natural" and her husband, Tom, an "unimaginative," perhaps "realistic," "appreciation" of civilization and all its conveniences (see discussion following the story). In this way, one can also begin to encourage students to understand and explore the ways in which characters in fiction function not only as individuals but also as individuals who are meaningful to us precisely because they represent or embody particular worldviews, attitudes, and/or values: in liking, disliking, or rooting for a particular character, in other words, we are also taking a stance in regard to the worldview that character embodies, usually by implicitly comparing that worldview with those represented by other characters in the story. And point of view is one of the key ways through which texts encourage us to take up certain stances, something that "Kill Day" does in a particularly interesting fashion.

If, then, the very first page of "Kill Day" sets up a comparison, contrast, and/or conflict between the romantic worldview of the wife and the realistic worldview of her husband, how does the rest of the story develop and/or resolve that conflict? By adopting the point of view of the wife, the body of the story encourages us to sympathize with her efforts to adopt a more primitive and more natural way of life, a life that is "simple and uncluttered" (par. 55), by learning to bake bread, to treat wasp stings, to build a fire, and to understand the nature and uses of "various weeds and plants" (par. 30–31). And that process seems to culminate somewhat successfully in the moment she becomes part of the "cacophony of sound and smell and pure sensation" on the wharf, "part of" the "strange Sunday morning ritual of death and survival" that is "Kill Day" (par. 46–48).

But is her effort ultimately as successful as this scene might make it seem? After all, the story makes clear to us that the wife's yearning for a "simple and uncluttered" life comes out of a vivid sense of her own disconnection from, and unfitness for, that life, particularly in comparison to her husband. As she recognizes, "*He* was the one who could really have survived here without complaint. . . . He was the one who had the strength to drag up driftwood . . . and the knowledge that enabled him to mend things or to start a perfect fire every time" because "he had grown up in the country and by the sea," whereas "She was a city girl" (par. 29), "shy" about "physical things" (par. 28). Thus, from his point of view, a point of view that the beginning and end of the story encourage the reader to adopt, she is only "playing at being primitive" (par. 54), doomed to remain "the Missus" (par. 28), "simply another of the summer folk" rather than a native like the Indian who uses her telephone (par. 28), an interpretation perhaps supported by the fact that the Indian fisherman tries to clean up the bloody traces of his own world that he tracks into hers.

And because her husband and the Indian fisherman represent to her the kind of "knowledge" and "strength" she doesn't and possibly can't have, it is possible to read her yearning as quite literally "romantic," in the sense that it is ultimately as much about her relationship with her husband as it is about her relationship to nature. After all, she describes herself as "jealous" more than once (par. 27, 29), and that "jealousy" seems to conflate her desire to possess the "knowledge" and "strength" that she sees her husband and the Indian fisherman as possessing with her emotional and/or physical desire to possess these men physically and/or emotionally. Ultimately, reading the woman's "jealousy" in this way might help to make sense of the ending, particularly the husband's feeling that in "the violence of her lovemaking" "somehow she was trying to possess him, devour him, maybe even exorcise him" (par. 88).

The story, however, does not end on that note or with the husband's or the wife's point of view. Instead, as the husband falls "into a deep, cool, dreamless sleep" (par. 88), the story ends with an omniscient narrator's view of the whole scene. What stance, then, does this ending ultimately encourage us to take toward these two characters, their relationship, and the conflict of worldviews embodied in that relationship?

QUESTIONS FOR DISCUSSION

1. The anthology suggests that the female character in this story is a "romantic," her husband a "realist." What evidence from the story might you use to support this interpretation of each of these characters? Is there any evidence in the story that might suggest a different or more complex interpretation?
2. How does the rest of the story develop and/or resolve this conflict between "realistic" and "romantic" worldviews?
3. How do the other characters in the story contribute to the exploration of this conflict? What, for example, is the significance of the wife's encounter with the Indian fisherman? The fact that she paints her face with his blood? How does this encounter serve to develop the central conflict?
4. Does the final paragraph of the story offer a resolution to this conflict? What is that resolution?
5. How would you describe the point(s) of view in "Kill Day"? How do shifts in point of view affect our attitudes toward the two central characters and the worldviews they represent? What are the effects of the shift to a third-person omniscient point of view at the very end of the story?
6. What might be the significance of the fact that the story takes place on a Sunday? That the killing is described as a "ritual"? Are there other religious allusions or images in the story? How might they complicate or broaden our interpretation of the story and of the conflict it explores?

GUY DE MAUPASSANT

The Jewelry

Part of the pleasure of reading "The Jewelry" comes from the significance the details of the story assume when we think back over the story or reread it. When assigning this selection, I encourage students to read very slowly and carefully (as suggested in the introduction); then I ask them to go over the text again, noting the new or additional shades of meaning that play about certain phrases ("the slight smile . . . seemed a reflection of her heart," "finally she yielded, just to please him," "You would swear it was real jewelry"). A second reading (or third, or fourth) will also help students chart their shifting sympathies in regard to M. Lantin. When his wife suddenly dies, we pity him. When do his feelings toward his wife begin to change? What are the stages of Lantin's emotional reactions, and why do his grief and shame disappear so quickly? How are our feelings about him related to these changes? Had he known how much money was at stake, would he have prevented her from going "out on the town"?

Sometimes just to shake things up a bit, I pause in the midst of discussion and ask the class if infidelity is the only explanation for Mme. Lantin's possession of the jewelry. After all, the author never spells this out. If the class agrees that Mme. Lantin probably was in some sense a "kept" woman (who thereby managed to keep her husband in comfort), I might ask why the author doesn't come right out and state this. What, if anything, is gained by leaving Mme. Lantin's activities a mystery? I'm not sure I can answer all these questions with certainty—and I let the class know this (but not too soon). Does our being led on by the narrator—we suspect something is wrong, but don't know just what—make the story more effective? More pleasurable? More meaningful? If so, in what ways?

You might ask students whether they believe the story considers adultery a sin, and if so, how serious a sin—and whether it is better for the victim of infidelity to know or not to know. In the story itself, are we given any hint as to why Mme. Lantin might cheat on her husband? If so, are we offered any justification for the wife's behavior—or does she need justification?

No discussion of "The Jewelry" can come to a satisfactory close without addressing the last paragraph, one of Maupassant's "surprise endings." Some students will want to interpret M. Lantin's ill-fated second marriage as a case of the sinner receiving his just deserts. Others may note that, after having his fling, M. Lantin tried to settle down to a decent life with an "upright" spouse and was repaid with a life of misery.

QUESTIONS FOR DISCUSSION

1. Does the narrator seem to suggest that virtue and conventional morality are overrated?
2. Does the ending simply supply a neat twist, or does it suggest that this is the way the world really works?
3. Does anything about Mme. Lantin's supposed infidelity and her husband's reaction to it seem strange or foreign? What, on the other hand, is recognizable and familiar about the characters' reactions?

SUGGESTION FOR WRITING

Write an analysis of "The Jewelry" discussing which events in the story fulfilled your expectations and which plot developments surprised you. Did the surprises seem to have a purpose in the story—other than providing entertainment? Explain.

Understanding the Text

1

PLOT

As the text suggests, a good way to stress the difference between plot structure and mere chronology is to compare a story's plot to a criminal plot—the criminal's plan for committing a crime. I tell students to assume the author has a plan for each story (just as a jewel thief makes specific plans to pull off a particular heist) and that the author has some purpose in arranging the elements of the story in a particular order. In a traditional short story, if the author has plotted well, the casual reader won't be aware of the way the author manipulates plot to create emphases or build suspense; the reader won't "catch" the author plotting but will simply enjoy the result. (This is where my analogy of criminal and crime breaks down!) Of course, careful, analytical readers will pay special attention to the way authors arrange the materials of their stories and will thereby gain a better understanding of the craft of fiction. In less-traditional stories, like Margaret Atwood's "Happy Endings," the author may raise questions about the nature of fiction by handling plot(s) in ways that are contrary to our expectations. In such stories, getting "caught" in these manipulations is part of the point.

PLANNING IDEAS

- If you have a fairly sophisticated group of readers, you may want to dive right into Atwood's "Happy Endings" and discuss the issues it raises concerning the nature of plots in particular and fiction in general. If you believe your students would benefit from a more gradual introduction to plot, you might begin this section by studying a story with a more straightforward suspense structure—Connell's "The Most Dangerous Game" or Poe's "The Cask of Amontillado"—using the simpler plot as a basis for comparison with the more complex plot structures of the stories offered here.
- Assign a nineteenth-century novel published serially: *Great Expecta-*

tions, perhaps, or *David Copperfield*. This will provide an opportunity to examine how plot can be structured to meet the demands of the readership, the marketplace, and a particular mode of production. (For example, *Great Expectations* was issued in weekly installments, and the ending was changed to make it more audience pleasing. If you assign this novel, be sure to order an edition that provides both endings.)

- Before class, ask students to imagine that they are writing several versions of their life stories: one in which they emphasize their educational history; one in which they emphasize the importance of their relationship with a family member; and one in which they construct their story as a comedy, a tragedy, or a romance. With what event, description, and details would each begin? How would each story end? Have students bring to class a brief sketch or outline of each story, and ask several volunteers to share their plot outlines with the class.
- If you assign "Sonny's Blues," bring in recordings of Louis Armstrong and Charlie Parker to play during class so that students can hear the difference between Armstrong's fairly close adherence to the melodic line and Bird's freer interpretations.

MARGARET ATWOOD

Happy Endings

Some students will recognize that Atwood's story is a *metafiction*—a story that comments on the nature of fiction itself. Others will be completely puzzled by it. One way to approach this work is to begin with a discussion of short story conventions and reader expectations, drawing on Atwood's "stories" A through F. (If you have spent some time discussing these issues in regard to Holst's "The Zebra Storyteller," you may want to refer back to that discussion as well.)

Students likely will find stories A–F lacking in a number of ways. It may prove fruitful to discuss what seems to be missing in *all* of the stories—then to draw some distinctions among them. Atwood suggests at the conclusion of "Happy Endings" that the "how" and "why" are missing from these plots—but I try to nudge students to see that Atwood hasn't really supplied plots at all. If you revisit the definition of plot provided in the anthology, students should quickly recognize that in "Happy Endings" Atwood has simply provided several histories or chronologies—merely the raw material of plot structure.

Once we reach this stage in the discussion, I ask students to imagine why Atwood might write such a story: what does "Happy Endings" suggest about the nature of fiction? The nature of life? Several possible answers occur to me, although my list is certainly not exhaustive:

A. The story suggests that fictions lie about life if they don't end in death—as all lives do (see first three paragraphs after F)—or at least it wants to provoke thought about the relationship between fiction and "real life."

B. Atwood is poking fun at the notion that writing fiction is just a matter of putting together so many plot elements (see especially the endings to stories E and F). Perhaps this is the response of a writer who's been handed too many such elements by strangers, with the comment: "I've got a great story you should write."

C. The grab-bag structure of the work—and particularly the cafeteria menu ending of E—is purposely unsatisfying, implying that readers welcome, and even need, the direction of the author—that readers *want* to experience someone else's worldview. By implication, this structure devalues so-called interactive fictions, which ask the reader to choose among alternative paths and alternative endings to create a story free (or relatively free) of *authority*.

D. A and D seem to ask whether virtuous people make interesting subjects for fiction and perhaps even whether happy, conflict-free stories are worth writing. (Students often complain that the short stories they read are depressing and too few have happy endings. This story provides an opportunity to discuss that perception and evaluate it.)

You may want to lead the class in reexamining the endings of other short stories they have read, using the implied criteria provided at the end of "Happy Endings": (1) Are the endings "fake"? (In terms of the narrator's standards, do they end with the deaths of the characters or not?) (2) Do they seem "deliberately fake"? (3) Do they appear "motivated by excessive optimism"? Ask the class to defend the stories against the charges they imagine the narrator would level against them.

QUESTIONS FOR DISCUSSION

1. Analyze the language of the last sentence of story F. What type of fiction might Atwood be satirizing?
2. In what sense are all endings the "same"? Is this true in life? In art? What is the relationship between life and art in regard to endings?
3. Has the narrator of "Happy Endings" indeed said "about all that can be said for plots" by the end of the story? Are plots *just* "a what and a what and a what"? If not, then what else are they?
4. Is Atwood the narrator of "Happy Endings"?

JOHN CHEEVER

The Country Husband

The problem I find with "The Country Husband" is not that my college-age students don't understand the neighborhood. If you add a few divorces and lots of working mothers, many of them come to school from suburbs like Shady Hill. Even among students from very different neighborhoods, I find the problem is the character, not the place. Perhaps Francis Weed is in some sense too close to their experience or their dreams—a man near their fathers' age, someone they might someday marry, or become. Despite his goofiness, Francis is desperately unhappy, and it is always disconcerting—but particularly so in our success-oriented, money-driven society—to confront the notion that we may find a mate, establish a family, buy a nice house, accomplish all our career goals, and suddenly find ourselves, as Francis does, trapped and woefully dissatisfied.

Some students, particularly those who are social activists, may be uncomfortable with the story for a different reason—because they find it hard to sympathize with Francis's plight. Why should we care about this whiner, this aging Lothario, this wife-abuser? they sometimes ask. The guy lives in a relative paradise within commuting distance of people who don't have enough to eat. What is his problem, and why should it make any difference to us? I have the feeling that Cheever would chuckle ruefully to hear such questions. Clearly he doesn't expect us to take Francis entirely seriously, and this is where I generally start. I ask the class whether "The Country Husband" is a serious story, and I try to get them to characterize the tone in which it is written. If your students don't pick up on the comedy of the narrative—and sometimes they don't—you might try asking them about the many literary, historical, mythological, and military allusions peppered throughout the work. Do they find anything incongruous about Mr. Nixon using the language of Shakespeare to chase off a dog? About Francis comparing his retreat from his children's squabble to returning to "headquarters company"? What about Francis thinking to himself that he was "meant to be the father of thousands"? Once we've established that Francis is a comic figure—an ordinary middle-class American male who is suddenly engulfed by longing for youth, for a life without constraint, for a more heroic time, which he and the narrator express through excessive, elevated language—we can move on to taking Francis's plight seriously, or at least semiseriously.

One way to talk about Francis's crisis is to talk about the events that brought it on. Cheever's plotting is a good place to start, and he provides the perfect hook, since he opens the story with the sentence "To begin at the beginning, the airplane from Minneapolis in which Francis Weed was traveling East ran into heavy weather." I like to ask students to explain in what sense the plane crash is the "beginning" of Francis's story. Why does Cheever start here? These questions often lead to some discussion of near-death experiences and the ways that such adventures can affect the actions and perceptions of those who survive them.

As we focus on plot structure, someone will mention that a seemingly random series of events appears to throw Francis off his stride and to feed his dissatisfaction with his life in Shady Hill: the plane crash, the unexpected appearance of the woman Francis had seen punished at the cross-roads in France during the war, Francis's sudden attraction to Anne Murchison (hard to say whether this a cause or effect of the crisis), his glimpse of the golden "Venus" on a passing train. As these events occur, Francis begins to feel less and less comfortable with his life in the present. In effect, each event takes Francis, either actually or imaginatively, backward in time. Both the plane crash and recognizing the Farquarson's maid recall France during World War II. Meeting Anne Murchison and visiting her neighborhood, Francis also has the sense of visiting an earlier time. (When Anne holds his hand as he walks her to the door, he's a young man again on a date.) Seeing the beautiful, naked woman on the train from the station platform affirms Francis's awakening sense of youthful romance; but she travels past him, and he is left standing alone, savoring his secret vision.

You might want to ask your students why Cheever describes these scenes in such detail. Or, to get at the same issues another way, what do these scenes have in common? If all goes well, someone will observe that all share the quality of being exciting and/or forbidden; that all are associated in some way with an earlier, more youthful part of Francis's life; and that Francis, for one reason or another, cannot share them with anyone he knows. (No one understands or even seems to care about the plane crash, for example.) In effect, all these experiences set up barriers between Francis and the world he inhabits. They make him long for a world of adventure and romance—half-glimpsed, half-remembered, half-imagined.

At some point in class discussion I like to ask students whether they approve of Francis's actions in the story before he seeks the help of a psychiatrist. This is really a throw-away question because their disapproval is usually fairly strong, although Francis always has defenders who sympathize with his feelings of frustration and entrapment. I ask the question to get us on to the next topic, which is to find out what students disapprove of most. Usually hitting Julia wins out by a few votes over sabotaging Clayton Thomas's job opportunity or grabbing Anne Murchison for a kiss, but not always. Then I like to ask students whether they are satisfied with the final picture of Francis in the basement of his Shady Hill home doing woodworking for therapy.

If the class has trouble articulating a response to the story's ending, you might call their attention to the final, panoramic vision of Shady Hill and the lyrical language the narrator uses to describe it. I'm not entirely sure I know what to do with the tone of the ending myself. Certainly there's a difference between the boisterous, boastful (too-boastful?) tone of the proud host who says his wife makes him feel like Hannibal crossing the Alps and the narrator's magical evocation of kings in golden suits in the last line of the story. What I can't say for certain is exactly how we are to read the latter statement. It could be the concluding line of the artist/alchemist, who creates a comic world, then waves a wand and wishes it away like Oberon clearing the magical mist in *A Midsummer Night's Dream*. The words seem otherworldly, enchanted. The narrator could be trying to tell us that anything is possible—even in Shady Hill—that on a night like this, anything can happen. On the other hand, these words, like several other examples of elevated language in the story, could be used satirically in humorous contrast to the insignificant or ho-hum doings in the neighborhood (see the footnote tracing this allusion to Sinclair Lewis's *Main Street*).

Note: According to Cheever, when he was growing up in Boston, E. E. Cummings befriended him and gave him some advice. Cummings said, "Boston is a city without springboards for people who can't dive. Get out! Get out!" Cheever claimed that the poet's words influenced him to leave home and move to New York at seventeen to try his chances as a writer (*Southwest Review*, Autumn 1980, 344). I like to save this anecdote for the end of class, because it seems to me that students are all too prone to read stories through the author's lives, as veiled biography. Nevertheless, I find it too appropriate not to mention. To keep students from drawing too-facile parallels between Cheever's experience and Francis's, I like to remind them that Cheever's purpose in leaving Boston was to become a writer and ask them, if Francis left home, what his purpose in leaving would be.

QUESTIONS FOR DISCUSSION

1. Why, if Shady Hill is still the same old peaceful suburban neighborhood he's lived in for years, does Francis begin to see it as a trap? What has changed Francis's perspective on Shady Hill?
2. Why does the narrator describe Francis's comfortable, polished living room in the words Julius Caesar uses to describe Gaul in *The Gallic Wars?* (At some point along the way, you may need to stop and talk briefly about point of view. Are there times when the narrator seems to be seeing through Francis's eyes and speaking for him? Times when the narrator's perspective diverges from Francis's?)
3. Students who don't think the rest of the story is funny almost always find Francis's rudeness to Mrs. Wrightson (notice the name) more amusing than reprehensible. Why?
4. Do you believe the narrator when he says Francis is happy? Does Francis seem at home in his shop in the basement? Why or why not?
5. What does Cheever's ending reveal about his worldview? What are we to make of the frolicking Babcocks? Of the cat trussed up in doll's clothes? Why does the story close with the vision of Jupiter holding a lady's slipper in his mouth?
6. If Francis is happy in the fictive present of the story, do you believe he will remain so? Why or why not?
7. How would you describe the tone of the last line? Is it different from the tone of the line alluding to Hannibal earlier in the story—when

the Weeds' host declares that his wife makes him feel like "Hannibal crossing the Alps"? (See the footnote regarding Sinclair Lewis's *Main Street*.)

SUGGESTION FOR WRITING

Write an essay defending or at least explaining Francis Weed's actions and provide evidence from the story.

JAMES BALDWIN

Sonny's Blues

Students from Harlem will know; African-American students, especially those from the inner city, will pretty well know; other students from wherever will recognize and will usually at least try to empathize with this story of black experience. Many African Americans in college or university, as well as some second- or third-generation Americans, will understand the narrator's uneasiness, aloofness, and guilt about having made it and being proud of it and his guilt about those he left behind. A great many in each generation and in every ethnic group ought to be able to empathize with the narrator's plight. That the death of his child has sensitized him to his brother is a kind of wound that makes us recognize our common humanity, perhaps. The story is a relatively recent one; the setting is familiar indirectly to all of us and directly to a fair number; the emotions are accessible.

"Sonny's Blues" is a story with an intricate and significant time structure and could be profitably studied alongside "A Rose for Emily." I like to begin discussion by asking students how the story would be different if Baldwin had begun with the scene in which the narrator's mother tells about the death of the narrator's uncle at the hands of drunken, careless white men. If need be, I try to jostle the students' thinking by asking them why the narrator's mother has waited all these years to tell him the story. What would be the effect if the story began here? What would it suggest the story will be about? I sometimes use this to discuss the relevance and importance of how the story begins.

The way Baldwin crafts the opening of the story can also be a useful topic for discussion. As suggested in the text headnote, his repeated use of the pronoun *it* without antecedent draws us into the narrative. We want to find out what "it" is. Students pick up on this fairly quickly. I like to ask them what other purposes the use of *it* serves. Someone usually comes up with the notion that the narrator won't give a name to what Sonny has done because he wants to distance himself from Sonny's involvement with drugs. He finds the mere thought of Sonny's trouble disturbing, hateful, even frightening. From here we can go on to talk about how Sonny and his brother differ and how their differences create distance and eventually estrangement.

To launch into this topic you may want to ask how the first-person narrator is identified or characterized in the first sentence of the story, in the first paragraph, in the first couple of pages, and in the story as a whole. We learn about Sonny through the narrator. What effect does this form of presentation have on our view of Sonny? How does the narrator let us see more than his own judgment? When does our judgment of Sonny vary from the narrator's? At what point are his judgment, the story's judgment, and our judgment of Sonny identical or nearly identical?

Although some of your students may be jazz aficionados, I find that many of mine don't understand the musical references. A quick explanation of the differences between Louis Armstrong's style of jazz and Charlie Parker's will suffice, but if you have the resources, you might bring in brief recordings from each to play for the class. (See "Planning Ideas" at the beginning of this chapter.) At the close of the story, Sonny invites his brother to hear him play. When the brothers arrive at the nightclub, the older musician Creole welcomes the two, and it becomes clear to us—and to Sonny's brother—why Sonny had once acted as if his friends in the Village were more his family than was his brother. The musicians act like a family. They understand what Sonny cares about; they applaud his faltering return to the music; they know what he's been through; they welcome him home. You may want to ask your students how Baldwin's writing style changes in the nightclub section of the story. As Creole, Sonny, and the others play, something happens to the words the narrator uses to express himself. How are they different? Why this change? What does the change tell us about the narrator's state of mind?

Toward the end of the discussion, I often ask the class to tie the musical references of the story together—for example, to tell me whether the woman singing gospel songs on the sidewalk earlier in the story has anything to do with the men making music at the nightclub. I find that the narrator's thoughts about his family and his heritage don't always make sense to students until they stop to think about the history of African-American music—that behind jazz lies the blues, behind the blues lies the spiritual, and behind the spiritual lie the songs of slaves. You may want to use the last four paragraphs of the story to open up the question of the transmutation of life or emotion into art, as a theme of this story and an explanation of its title.

The ending of "Sonny's Blues" is so intricately tied up with African-American experience and African-American music that it may be useful to ask, if the issue hasn't already come up, whether white readers can really understand the story (can men really understand stories by and for women). It is difficult to avoid having the discussion get to the point of "Can," "Can't," "Can," "Can't," either in an obvious or subtle way. One way I've found to break the magic circle is to ask to whom the story is addressed. Is it aimed at whites, either as a plea or demand for understanding and sympathy or as an indictment? Is it aimed at blacks, giving a voice to their long-silent experience and, if so, for what kind of response? Is it directed to educated, more or less successful, upwardly mobile blacks, both to show understanding and sympathy for their plight and to remind them not to abandon their brothers and sisters?

I rather think the last, but not with real confidence. There is only one instance of white persecution in the story, and that incident is narrated about the somewhat distant past and is placed in the South. I must admit I was a bit more confident of my reading before I looked up the "cup of trembling" passage in Isaiah. "Sonny's Blues" is a fine story about relationships, but it also raises questions about sociohistorical context and its importance in understanding as fully as possible the meaning, the methods, the tone, and other aspects of fiction—even conjectural questions about what students think readers a hundred years from now will get and what they will miss, or how this story might be read in India or Australia, or what the relevance of the date of publication is and how things or our perceptions have changed. Such questions might be especially effective if the story is taught with other stories that raise questions about cultural contexts: "A Souvenir of Japan," "Sánchez," "A Rose for Emily," "A Pair of Tickets," "The Management of Grief," "Young Goodman Brown," "Love Medicine," "The Rain Child," "Holiday."

QUESTIONS FOR DISCUSSION

1. How do you react to Baldwin's change of prose style in describing the scene at the nightclub? How does the change of style contribute to his message? In what ways does it make his message harder to decipher?
2. How should we read the reference to the "cup of trembling" in the last paragraph of the story? Should we read it to mean that trembling and fury will be visited on whites ("them that afflict thee")? Or pushers? Or is the full biblical passage not relevant? Would whites or blacks be more likely to recognize Baldwin's allusion?

SUGGESTIONS FOR WRITING

1. Rearrange the scenes of "Sonny's Blues" into chronological order, and explain how this rearrangement would alter the meaning and effect of the story. Supplement your analysis by describing how other orders might affect the story.
2. Evaluate the endings of "The Country Husband" and "Sonny's Blues" using the implied criteria for endings supplied in "Happy Endings."

READING/WRITING IDEAS FOR CHAPTER 1

ESSAYS ABOUT PLOT

Though a basic understanding of how plot works is obviously crucial to the analysis of literary texts and though student writers obviously need to learn to use facts about plot in making arguments about literature, it is extremely rare in my experience that instructors ask students to write essays solely or wholly on plot. (Asking students to write about what a story such as Atwood's "Happy Endings" says about plot is a whole different can of worms.) One of the only truly workable plot-related essay assignments that I know of involves asking students to focus on a particular event or moment in the plot of a story and to write an essay in which they argue that this moment or event is pivotal, showing how this moment foregrounds, complicates, and/or resolves a central (thematic) conflict in the text (which, in the language of the anthology, means showing why and how a particular event is key to the "rising action" or constitutes a "turning point" or "climax"). One of my students, for example, recently wrote a very successful essay on *Pride and Prejudice* that focused on Elizabeth Bennett's visit to Darcy's estate, showing precisely how it complicates Austen's portrayal both of the heroine and of the ideal marriage. (This type of thesis or argument is a version of a very common type, which basically involves arguing that "this thing [event, character, word, image] that seems trivial is really important.")

In the case of the stories included in this chapter of the anthology, the moments or events about which students might write such essays include the plane crash that opens "The Country Husband"; Francis's wartime encounter with his neighbor's French maid, with Mrs. Wrightson on the train platform, or with the girl he mistakes for Anne on the train; or the death of the narrator's uncle or of Little Grace in "Sonny's Blues."

You might also ask students to concentrate on the narrative timing and mode of telling, as well as on the nature of, the action. Students might, for example, write terrific essays about the effects of the way Baldwin (and his characters/narrator) delays telling the stories of these two deaths and/or the way that Baldwin has characters serve as mediators who tell these stories during his story rather than showing them directly to the reader.

TROUBLESHOOTING

I generally have to work at guiding students toward formulating thesis statements that put the focus on the significance of a particular event or moment in the plot of a story; otherwise, it's all too easy for them to home in on claims about how events make a story more "interesting" or "engaging," how they make the reader more "curious," or how they heighten suspense. Such claims are usually true enough and can often be quite insightful, but they aren't the kind of arguable claims that most often lead to engaged or engaging analytical essays.

PLOT-FOCUSED WRITING EXERCISES

1. Summarizing the Plot

Even when I am not asking students to write essays that analyze the plot of a fictional text per se, I still often find it very useful to have students write short plot summaries as a writing exercise in preparation for writing essays about some other facet of a text. For example,

In five sentences or less, describe the plot of "Sonny's Blues." In doing so, try to make the story vivid and interesting to your own reader, to *show* as well as tell that reader what Baldwin's story is all about.

This exercise can be used in multiple ways for multiple ends. First, writing plot summaries is often quite easy for students and can sometimes be a good startup technique for nervous or inexperienced writers. Second, as the "showing" versus "telling" vocabulary of the assignment emphasizes, it also allows me to begin highlighting for students the kinds of basic writing strategies that make for effective, vivid, descriptive prose. Often, I have students bring their plot summaries to class where they then exchange and discuss them (or I discuss one with the class as a whole and then have them break into groups so that everyone's gets looked at).

I also use the plot summary exercise to begin talking more generally about just what an argument about literature is and about how a writer begins to formulate one. On the one hand, since inexperienced writers often tend to substitute plot summary for argument in writing essays, one can use the plot summary exercise to discuss the differences between pure description and analysis or argument. The key difference, of course, lies in the fact that arguments include inferences about facts in addition to the facts themselves, and I find *inferences* a tremendously important vocabulary word when teaching writing, one that this plot summary discussion helps me to get on the table. On the other hand, it's also helpful for students to understand that even the most basic and seemingly objective descriptions or summaries of a plot almost necessarily begin to imply a certain interpretation of, or argument about, a story, if only by virtue of including some things and excluding others. As a result, writing and comparing plot summaries can become a good technique for students to use to generate topics and theses for essays, to figure out what their individual "angle" on a particular text is.

Since students often have trouble with introductions (that aren't of the "throughout human history" variety), I also encourage them to begin to use very short plot summaries in their introductions, as a way to give, or at least remind their reader of, the information about a story that he or she needs to understand an argument about it and as a way to "build up to" the thesis.

Finally, I find discussion of plot summaries and of their uses in argumentative essays a really good place to open up questions about audience and about the amount and kinds of information student writers should feel called upon to provide in their essays. Obviously there aren't right or wrong answers to such questions, but I always find it necessary to answer them somewhat early in the course, because my ideas about audience and those of my students tend to be very different. While they tend to assume that their classmates and I are their only readers and that they can, therefore, assume intimate knowledge of the text(s) they're writing about, I simply think that essays read a lot better if they are written to be intelligible to a wider audience, including readers who haven't read the text in question. (And because I often allow or even require students to write about texts that the class as a whole hasn't necessarily read or discussed, it's often literally the case in my classroom that their essays need to include certain basic information to be intelligible to the classmates who actually do read the essays.) Whatever your assumed audience, it's helpful to give students a clear image of their reader; in my case, that means suggesting that they envision their reader as a classmate or roommate who is familiar with, and interested in, literary analysis but who hasn't read this particular text (or at least hasn't read it as recently or as closely as the writer has).

2. Summarizing the Plot in Terms of a Key Event or Moment

If you do give students the essay assignment about plot described above, you might want to have them do a preparatory exercise in which they write a short summary of the story that places particular emphasis on the event or moment on which they are going to focus in their essay. Then discuss with students how—in doing so—they have necessarily begun to imply the kind of arguments about why that event or moment is pivotal that they will need to make explicitly in their essays. You can use this exercise as a follow-up to the first exercise (in which case students are essentially and quite self-consciously revising their summaries with an eye toward homing in on their "moment"), or you can use it in lieu of the first exercise (so that from the very beginning, writers are summarizing with an eye to argument). Doing both has the advantage of making students more aware of the process by which one can move from summary to argument, while the latter obviously saves time and encourages students to begin focusing on argument from the very beginning.

3. Comparing Chronological Order and Actual Plot Structure

If students' essays will focus wholly or in part on the author's timing of events in the narrative, then it's also useful to have them write a summary that reorganizes those events into chronological order. Then have them generate ideas about the effects of the differences between this chronological ordering and the actual order in which events are narrated in the story.

4. Recording and Commenting on Readerly Expectations

Another fun and helpful plot-related exercise asks students to keep a record of the expectations that develop during their reading. Having students record expectations and what happens to those expectations as they read seems to work best for me when I assign specific points at which they should stop their reading and when I have them conclude the exercise by writing a paragraph or so on the overall significance of the ways the story raises and then defies particular expectations.

In addition to the stories included in this chapter of the anthology, the stories "Souls Belated," "Lamar Loper's First Case," and "The Cask of Amontillado" lend themselves especially well to this exercise, and the notes to those stories suggest possible stopping places.

2

POINT OF VIEW

Just as perspective and focus influence the way a play in a baseball game is viewed (did the runner touch second base before he was tagged? Did the batter swing? Was the pitcher really guilty of a balk? Coach, player, and various umpires probably have different answers), perspective and focus influence the way we view the events of our lives and the way we tell stories. Sometimes we distort (consciously or unconsciously) in reporting our triumphs and failures. Sometimes we simply don't know all the facts—or don't remember them clearly. Sometimes we are distracted or confused. The author's choice of focus, of point of view, imitates this reality; the decision to tell a story from one perspective or another puts a spin on the action—creates a perspective from which the truth is revealed and concealed to greater and lesser degrees and encourages us to feel and think about characters in particular ways. The purpose of raising to consciousness the way narration distorts experience is not to belittle narration; on the contrary, it suggests to students that learning how to read stories, how people tell stories, and what's involved can make them aware of how they make stories out of their own experiences and how they try, through narrative, to make sense of their own lives.

PLANNING IDEAS

- Along with "The Cask of Amontillado," assign Robert Browning's "My Last Duchess," a poem published just four years before Poe's story was first published, and discuss first-person murderous narrators, character types, literary tradition.
- Ask students to rewrite a page of a story in this chapter from a point of view different from the original (for example, retelling part of "Sonny's Blues" from Sonny's perspective or retelling part of "The Cask of Amontillado" from the third-person omniscient point of view). Use these exercises as the bases for talking about the effects of

point of view when you take up the stories for discussion.

• If you assign "An Occurrence at Owl Creek Bridge," ask students, in advance, to keep a brief record of their expectations as they move from paragraph to paragraph through the story.

EDGAR ALLAN POE

The Cask of Amontillado

I like to discuss a story like "The Cask of Amontillado" fairly early in the course because it is familiar—many students will have read it in high school and almost all will have heard of Edgar Allan Poe; it is brief—instructor and students, after a couple of readings, can hold the story in mind almost in its entirety and virtually isolate details with a mental pointer—and its devices and structure are rather obvious (one might say that Poe lays it on with a trowel, but of course one wouldn't). The story is useful in talking about point of view because it is told entirely in first person by an at least partially unreliable narrator who reveals only at the end of his tale that the events he describes happened a half a century ago. Many of Poe's plot devices hinge on Montresor's first-person narration—upon Montresor's early revelation that he hates Fortunato and is determined to get revenge. Most of the suspense is founded on the reader's expectation that Montresor will gain revenge and on the reader's curiosity (even anxiety?) about how he will attempt to do so.

The plot structure seems fairly obvious here, with the exposition largely in (but not wholly confined to) the first three paragraphs; the rising action continuing until the climactic chaining of Fortunato to the wall (his recognition scene corresponding to that of many readers' recognition of precisely what Montresor has in mind); the action falling to the last paragraph's conclusion, and the leap of fifty years to the time of the narration (a gap we previously did not know existed, but which might allow us to conjecture just why Montresor is narrating—or confessing).

There are only two characters here, and Fortunato will be able to tell no tales, so only Montresor or an omniscient narrator can tell the story. It might be profitable to ask some or all of the students to try rewriting this story in the third person to see what's lost (see "Planning Ideas"). Early on, I like to ask students what effect(s) an author might expect to create when choosing to tell a story in first-person. You might point out to them that it is our tendency in reading fiction to take high moral ground and to damn all characters who are imperfect (for not being like ourselves). The first-person pulls us closer to the narrating character, makes us cheer for him or her, as it were. When that narrator is a murderer, as here (and in Graham Greene's *Brighton Rock* or in Burgess's *A Clockwork Orange*), or even just a snob, like Pip in *Great Expectations*, our emotions are more complicated. Is it that we understand or sympathize with the "sinner" more? Or is it that we say, "There but for the grace of God go I" and so think about our own fallibility (not yours, of course)? Or both?

This might be a good story to introduce the notion of character types or stereotypes. Why Italy? What period is the story set in? What do the students know or feel about the kinds of people and kinds of actions that took place then and there? You might want to bring up Machiavelli or pair this story with Browning's "My Last Duchess" and get at the issues raised by setting through discussion of Browning's dramatic monologue.

The macabre story is almost a fable for readers, a paradigm of the relation between writer and reader, with Montresor as author and Fortunato as the unfortunate reader. So, you can tell your students, if they don't want to get pinned to the wall, they'd better pay attention. Montresor as author of the plot begins by announcing that there is a plot—as authors implicitly do by writing a story—and he announces, too, that he considers a good plot one in which the perpetrator–author doesn't get caught. This challenges the reader to try to catch him, to try to guess what will happen next. The author challenges the reader's pride just as Montresor's dubious amontillado challenges Fortunato's pride in his knowledge of wine; the cask as wine and "The Cask of Amontillado" as title are thus central to both plots. (You might not want to call attention to the fact that Fortunato is dressed as a fool.)

The first thing a story must do, then, is to arouse a certain amount of expectation or anticipation, to get the reader to follow the story—to read on—and to try to guess what is going to happen next with the story or how it is going to happen. For there to be suspense or anticipation, there must be some doubt or alternative possibilities; and for there to be more than one possibility, at least one possibility must turn out to be wrong. Using a first-person narrator contributes to this effect because a narrator can purposely (or unconsciously, as in the case, for example, of someone who is self-deceived) mislead us about the action. False leads are inherent in plotting, and being aware of them (but not necessarily aware that they are false) is essential to participating in the story.

I like to ask students if they believe Montresor is a dependable narrator. We usually discuss whether Montresor really has a legitimate complaint against Fortunato and then talk about whether Montresor as a narrator is unreliable in a way that confuses readers and/or interferes with the story's building suspense. Usually students observe that, whether or not Montresor has a legitimate beef with Fortunato (the vagueness of his charges raises the possibility that Fortunato is entirely innocent), Montresor does appear single-minded in his pursuit of revenge. We feel we can count on him to carry out his plot—whatever it is—and this certainty is the basis for the suspense about what he will do and when.

Because I think such alertness important, I often ask students to stop at certain points in reading a story and to write down what they think might be going to happen next. Perhaps the first reasonable stopping place would be as Montresor and Fortunato are about to enter the vaults. A later one might be just after Fortunato's first coughing fit. You might even want to have the students stop reading as late as Montresor's stapling Fortunato to the wall, to see if they picked up the significance of the trowel (not too well buried in the mason joke). After discussing these scenes, we might ask what would be lost if the story were told from a third-person omniscient perspective.

If there are false leads, there must also be true leads; and you might want to suggest that even Montresor "plays fair" with Fortunato by ironic indications of his intentions, such as his agreeing that Fortunato will not die of a cough, his drinking to his victim's long life, his producing the trowel. These spots might make good stopping points, too; or you might want to ask, once the story has been read, just when it becomes clear just what Montresor is up to.

I like to call attention at this point, or at least early in the discussion of point of view, to how much of the reader's guesswork is based on cause-and-effect, on the reader's assumption that there is logic in the sequence of events and in the characters' motivations. We assume Montresor is leading Fortunato into the catacombs for a reason; in searching the story and our minds for the reason, we notice the cough; when Montresor agrees that Fortunato will not die of a cough, we either discard that possibility or believe the narrator to be a liar, or keep both possibilities in mind; if we notice the trowel and take it seriously, we have an answer. In one sense, plot and suspense seem to depend on logic—how could you guess what's to happen next in a wholly irrational universe? In what we can call the non-Western tradition, however, there is the suspense of expectation of sheer wonder, as in *The Arabian Nights* (The Thousand Nights and a Night) or tales of magic.

There's another way of guessing with an author, of course, and that is by the conventions of the kind. Though you may want to hold off any lengthy discussion of this until you get to "Literary Kind as Context," there's no reason not to acknowledge that some of our guesses come from what we are used to in the way of stories on the page, screen, or tube.

QUESTIONS FOR DISCUSSION

1. Who (if anyone) is the narrator talking to at the end of the story?
2. Why do you think the narrator has waited fifty years to tell what he has done? Under what circumstances is he reporting his deed?
3. How would you assess the mental stability of the narrator?
4. Why does the narrator call for Fortunato after he has walled him in? Why does he report that his "heart grew sick"?

AMBROSE BIERCE

An Occurrence at Owl Creek Bridge

As suggested in the text headnote, this story scarcely could exist were it not for the focus shifting in section three to Peyton Farquhar's consciousness for much of the rest of the story. Indeed, between the sergeant's stepping aside at the end of the first section and the final paragraph nothing much happens: Farquhar merely hangs.

You might want to ask students about the second section and what would happen to their expectations if it were removed. This is not exactly a false lead, but like a false lead it distracts the reader from anticipating correctly or certainly. Of course, it does something else: by characterizing Farquhar as patriotic, dedicated, and daring and by revealing that his crime was an entrapment, the reader's sympathies are entirely enlisted on his side. You might ask how many students basically side with the Union and whether any of them wanted Farquhar to be "caught." If not, you may ask, why not? Getting us on Farquhar's side, to cheer him on and to hope for his escape is, of course, an important element in the strategy of the story.

There are a number of clues in the story pointing to what is actually happening. You might ask the students to identify them. You might also ask them in advance to keep a brief record of their expectations as they read through the story.

I often call attention to some of the minute, realistic details in the first section, and then have the students identify others and ask them why there are so many and what they do. One of the functions seems to be to slow down, almost stop the fictional clock—there's so much description that we seem to be looking at a tableau or still picture. Why? Where's the focus? What's going on?

There is a fairly common feeling among many of us and many of our students that this is essentially a story with a gimmick and, therefore, not "serious" fiction. Though it may seem contrived to us, it is very likely that when first published, like the stories of Guy de Maupassant, this story was considered "realistic." For adventure stories and romances, the popular fiction of the time, usually ended happily, and heroes did miraculously escape. That Farquhar did not, that he was misled by the fiction his mind made up, may, in context, appear bitterly realistic. The story, then, may ask us to contrast wishes, wish-fulfilling fantasies—including the kind of heroism suggested in section two—with the cold external realities. Just as Poe makes us for a time identify with a villain, here we emotionally identify with a hero who doesn't make it.

QUESTIONS FOR DISCUSSION

1. Both "The Cask of Amontillado" and "An Occurrence at Owl Creek Bridge" are stories that rely on gimmicks. Should these stories be considered serious works of literature? Why or why not? Do you rank one story above the other? If so, why?
2. How would you film "An Occurrence at Owl Creek Bridge"? What technique might you use to convey the experiences Farquhar imagines?

SUGGESTION FOR WRITING

Write a comparison/contrast essay discussing the function of point of view in "The Cask of Amontillado" and "An Occurrence at Owl Creek Bridge."

TIMOTHY FINDLEY

Dreams

Findley's "Dreams" is a wonderful story with which to conclude and to complicate any discussion of point of view precisely because it deftly and rather quietly calls into question so many of the assumptions and beliefs about individuality, consciousness, and reality that underlie our notions of point of view (and, for that matter, of character). The very concept of point of view, after all, depends on the idea that individuals have unique ones; the idea that, in the language of the anthology, it is "more realistic" to narrate a story "through the filter of an individual . . . consciousness" (see introduction to "Point of View") presumes (as most of us do) that each individual has a distinct consciousness and also, therefore, a point of view that is unique to that person and that this consciousness and point of view are in essence inviolable, never fully accessible to anyone else. Yet by the very fact of making individual consciousness accessible to us, as readers, fiction tends simultaneously to affirm the uniqueness and inviolability of individual consciousness even as it, in a sense, violates it by virtue of taking us inside characters' heads. One of the unique pleasures of so much fiction is, in other words, that it allows us a unique kind of access to other people's thoughts, dreams, and points of view, yet part of the reason this is such a pleasurable process is that this is something we can't (or think we can't) do in the "real world," because (we believe that) in the real world, as opposed to the fictional ones we temporarily occupy, we can't achieve such access to other consciousnesses. In a sense, then, much fiction affirms for us that, in the words of Joseph Conrad, "We live, as we dream, alone," even as fiction also allows us to temporarily and imaginatively both live and dream with, or as, others.

Because this is precisely what happens in a peculiarly frightening way in "Dreams," it may well be possible to read the story as drawing our attention to this very readerly process and to the similarities between that process and that of psychoanalysis. In so doing, however, the story necessarily challenges the assumptions both psychoanalysis and fiction ironically affirm by so often undermining them.

Obviously, however, to get students to this point, one has to begin with more basic and more familiar questions, and I would suggest that questions about character, and particularly the character of the Drs. Menlo, may well be the best or easiest starting point. Both Mimi and Everett are, above all, scientists who believe or want to believe that everything about the world and about people can be rationally analyzed, explained, resolved, and controlled. Mimi herself refers to her husband at one point as one of "the gods of reason" (par. 42); Everett looks on the task of rationally "explain[ing]" his patients' seemingly irrational dreams as both "His job and his pleasure" (par. 59); Mimi "watche[s] her husband's silent torment . . . with a kind of clinical detachment," "the result . . . of her training and her discipline" (par. 144); and Everett struggles valiantly "to marshal the evidence" that would allow him to solve the mystery of Allbright's dreams, "to put it all in order—bring it into line with reason" (par. 173). (And, indeed, I would suggest that the story at least initially presents itself as a detective story in which the reader is as much a detective as Everett figures himself to be.) Even in their dreams, Mimi and Everett remain somewhat clinically detached: she describes her dreaming self as "nothing more than an observer," "unable to participate" (par. 190), while he witnesses "this scene from several angles, never speaking, never being spoken to" (par. 99).

From the very outset, however, the story sets up a conflict between the Menlos' rational, scientific, detached worldview and the irrational, uncontrollable, and mysterious. By the second paragraph, Mimi's own efforts to, in the imagined words of Everett, "gai[n] control of [her]self" (par. 4) by "prescrib[ing] herself a week's worth of Dexedrine," prove to be of "no avail" (par. 2). And through their patients, Brian Bassett and Kenneth Allbright, both of the doctors come face to face with mysteries that defy their efforts "to put it all in order." As Mimi herself suggests, the "unexplained and inexplicable" seems to win out here completely over the rational at the moment when "Her husband—after all, the sanest man alive— . . . suggest[s] something so completely mad he might as well have handed over his reason in a paper bag and said to her, *burn this*" (par. 96, 182).

Interestingly enough, however, the two patients represent mysteries of very different, indeed seemingly opposite, kinds. On the one hand, Brian Bassett seems to represent, in an odd way, an extreme version of the very detachment that characterizes the Drs. Menlo, an idea underscored by the fact that Mimi links Everett and Brian together in her thoughts, "watch[ing] her husband through the night" "in the light of

Brian Bassett's utter lack of willing contact with the world around him—his utter refusal to communicate" (par. 52). On the other hand, Kenneth Allbright seems to represent the very opposite; far from being isolated and detached, he insists from the very outset on the possibility of the most intimate, and to Everett impossible, kind of human entanglement, that "a person" might "really dream someone else's dreams" (par. 57), a possibility that obviously seems to come true as the story unfolds.

At a deeper level, however, and as Everett's dreams suggest, Allbright is ultimately less Everett and Mimi's opposite than he is an extreme version of another facet of the scientific worldview they represent. After all, isn't it Everett and Mimi's job to, in essence, do to people precisely what Allbright does in Everett's dream, "pulling" their patients open psychically "the way a child will pull a Christmas present open—yanking at its strings and ribbons, wanting only to see the contents" (par. 99)? Certainly Everett's hopes of "break[ing] the barriers in Anne Marie" and his attraction to her very "fragil[ity]" suggest a kind of violence that might also be inferred from the fact that, for all her compassion, Mimi understands Brian Bassett's refusal of her help as his "win[ning]" (par. 67–68, 120).

What such a notion of struggle takes for granted, however, is precisely what we, along with Everett and Mimi, assume, that there are hard-and-fast barriers not only within the human psyche but also and more important between different psyches, precisely the assumption of individuality and integrity of consciousness that, as I've suggested, underlies the very notion of point of view. And it is precisely such notions that the story, ultimately, calls into question. Obviously, this questioning occurs most profoundly through the way in which the characters in the story do seem to dream each other's dreams and think each other's thoughts, most subtly, perhaps, when Mimi is "startled" "by the fact that" she and Edward are "thinking of dreams" simultaneously (par. 156). But once we've discovered or experienced that extraordinary possibility alongside the characters in the story, it becomes possible to see the much more subtle, pervasive, even ordinary ways in which the whole story throws individual identity into question. In the very first paragraph, for example, Findley's narrator invites us into such confusion by ostentatiously referring to "Doctor Menlo" and "the other Doctor Menlo," encouraging us to see that the only way that we as readers (or he, as narrator) can distinguish one from the other is by designating one "Doctor Menlo" as the one "whose name was Mimi." And Mimi herself, of course, again calls our attention to the (in)significance of proper names when she looks at "the words BRIAN BASSETT" and realizes they "were nothing more than extrapolations from the alphabet—something fanciful we call a 'name' in the hope that, one day, it will take on meaning" (par. 132), by which I think she means, among other things, that we "hope" that our individual names "take on meaning" because they serve as signs of an identity, a consciousness, that is purely ours and no one else's. And this notion of individuality may be one of the many "dreams" that come to mind when

Mimi says *"We dreamed him"* (par. 135). Mimi's reveries gain their true meaning and significance, however, only if we attend to all of the ways in which the story suggests that ordinary, everyday life can be seen to constantly pose these questions once we become aware of them: as when Mimi's thoughts about what her husband "would have said" in a given situation reveal the way in which all of us always have other people in our heads (par. 4); when Mimi experiences herself as fragmented into parts who speak in different voices inside her head (par. 137) and/or refers to "the lover in her" and "the psychiatrist in her" (par. 144); when Everett "spoke as if in someone else's voice," a practice that "was not entirely unusual" (par. 152); and when Mimi notes that she is "playing wife" (par. 138).

Obviously one way to interpret the story is to turn it into a version of "An Occurrence at Owl Creek Bridge" by interpreting Mimi's ultimate question as indicating at least the possibility that it was all, after all, a dream, her dream. And as the anthology's questions indicate, one could thus read the entire story as representing, in essence, Mimi's point of view, an interpretation perhaps legitimated by the fact that it is undoubtedly Mimi's consciousness that we are most often inside in the story. Findley's story, unlike Bierce's, however, refuses to allow us such clarity and in so doing at the very least forces us to recognize that we are making a choice if we do choose to interpret the story in this way. And by insisting, however subtly, on the similarity between us, as readers of the story, and Everett and Mimi as "observers" or even detectives trying desperately "to put it all in order—bring it into line with reason," to interpret the text of their patients so that they make rational sense, Findley's story draws our attention to the reading process and to our readerly choices. For this and a host of other reasons, Findley's story differs from Bierce's in being much more self-consciously and relentlessly a metafiction, as well as a series of quite delightful, because ultimately unsolvable, puzzles.

QUESTIONS FOR DISCUSSION

1. How would you characterize the worldview of the two Drs. Menlo?
2. Why and how do the encounters with Brian Bassett and Kenneth All-bright challenge the Menlos' worldview? What might each of these characters represent?
3. The word *dream* has many different connotations. Which connotations of the word seem to be used in, or relevant to, this story?
4. What exactly does Mimi mean when she says names are "nothing more than extrapolations from the alphabet" and that she and the other doctors "dreamed" Brian Bassett? Might the story be saying or asking something about what it means to be an individual person, a distinct self? If so, what do you think it's saying or asking?
5. What do you make of the ending of the story, particularly Mimi's final comment? Do you think it's possible that someone in the story is

dreaming these events? What's the effect of our not knowing?

6. Everett and Mimi are described in the story as observers who, some-what like detectives, are trying "to put [their experiences] all in order—bring [them] into line with reason." To what extent is what they do with their patients like what we, as readers, do with this or any text? Might you read Findley's "Dreams" as a metafiction, a story that is in some ways about fiction? If so, what do you think it says or asks about fiction?

7. Why do you think this story is in the "point of view" chapter? How does Findley's use of point of view contribute to the meaning of the story? Might the story be about point of view just as Atwood's "Happy Endings" is about plot? If so, what do you think the story says or asks about point of view?

READING/WRITING IDEAS FOR CHAPTER 2

ESSAYS ABOUT POINT OF VIEW

I find that point of view, like plot, is less often the focus of student essays on literature than it is a component of such essays. For that reason, I tend to assign exercises about point of view, like those described below, rather than actual essays. With some work and thought, however, I think that either or both of these exercises could lead to full-length essays focusing on questions about how particular point(s) of view and/or shifts between different points of view contribute to the meaning of a particular text.

TROUBLESHOOTING

I find that my students are usually very good at seeing how point of view affects the reader's sympathy for, and knowledge of, particular characters, guiding the reader to take certain stances in regard to those characters. But what I find they are not so good at is recognizing or talking and writing about the ways in which point of view affects the text's portrayal of particular issues—the way, for example, that Poe's making "The Cask of Amontillado" a first-person, confessional narrative complicates the picture of revenge offered within the story or the way that the multiple narrators of *Heart of Darkness* compound and re-create for the reader the questions posed in the text about the relationships among language, elo-quence, and truth. And a text such as *Heart of Darkness* or "Why I Live at the P.O." brings up another dimension of the workings of point of view that students can also at times ignore or underrate—the way in which the occasion of the narration itself shapes a text's overall meanings. I've discovered, however, that I seem to be able to be more helpful to students in this regard if I encourage them to make what might seem like some-what simplistic distinctions between form and content, talking first about interpretations of content and then about how form either supports or complicates particular interpretations.

POINT-OF-VIEW-FOCUSED WRITING EXERCISES

1. Rewriting Texts from Different Points of View

Having students rewrite all or a selected portion of a given text from a different point of view (or two) is a wonderful exercise for generating discussion about a particular text and/or about point of view in general; and I find that it always works best when I assign them a particular section of the text to rewrite, assign them particular points of view, and ask them to conclude the exercise by writing a paragraph about what's lost or at least fundamentally changed by altering the point of view. One might, for example, have students rewrite the first few paragraphs of "The Cask of Amontillado" from a third-person-omniscient point of view and the end or middle of the story from Fortunato's (who knows? maybe there was a pen and a piece of paper in there).

In addition to the stories in Chapter 2 of the anthology, other stories that lend themselves especially well to this exercise are the first-person stories, such as "Why I Live at the P.O.," "My Contraband," and "The Yellow Wallpaper," and third-person stories in which there is a single central consciousness, such as the O'Connor stories in Chapter 8 or "Without Benefit of Clergy."

2. Recording and Analyzing Readerly Expectations in Light of Point of View

Another good point-of-view exercise is a version of the expectations exercise described in "Reading/Writing Ideas for Chapter 1" (exercise 4). You might, in other words, have students keep exactly the same kind of record of expectations, but this time ask them to pay special attention to the way in which point of view and/or particular shifts in point of view affect those expectations. Again, I find that the exercise works best if I tell students exactly when and where to pause in their reading and ask them to conclude the exercise with a paragraph or so summing up their conclusion about the way the text uses point of view to play with readerly expectations.

In addition to the stories in Chapter 2 of the anthology, other stories that lend themselves especially well to this exercise are "Kill Day on the Government Wharf" and "Souls Belated."

3

CHARACTERIZATION

In some sense we judge characters in fiction much the way we judge the real characters in our lives, the people we meet day to day. Our responses are based on what the characters say and do, how they say and do it, and what others say about them. Our job in analyzing fiction is to read characters carefully—to try to understand who, in all their individualities, they really are. "Fenstad's Mother" and "Our Friend Judith" provide opportunities to talk about the influence of cultural stereotyping in fiction and in life. Both stories suggest that human character doesn't lend itself very readily to pigeon-holing; Fenstad's mother and Judith are complex personalities, reacting according to type one moment and the next, confounding all expectation.

How close we get to a character in a story is, at least in part, a function of point of view. First-person narration—the perspective of three of the four stories in this section—provides a close encounter, a kind of intimacy and proximity to one character's thoughts and experience that may cause us to respond more sympathetically than we otherwise might to the character's situation—or to feel a greater sense of outrage or betrayal if the character lets us down.

PLANNING IDEAS

- If you have not assigned Maupassant's "The Jewelry" and Chekhov's "The Lady with the Dog" earlier in the semester, assign these stories as background reading for Grace Paley's "A Conversation with My Father."
- Have each student bring to class an analysis of a single paragraph from one of the stories that reveals something important about the main character. Ask volunteers to share these at the appropriate time, and encourage students who have written about the same character, but

with different results, to confront the conflicts between their perceptions.

- Assign a student who is a good actor to practice and then read a key section of "Why I Live at the P.O."—perhaps the first page or so—during class. This is often a useful way to prompt thinking about Sister's character and to help students appreciate the story's humor.
- If your students are keeping journals as part of their classwork, ask each to write a paragraph characterizing themselves as honestly as they can, mentioning at least four major character traits—both positive and negative. Then have them write characterizations of themselves as they imagine might be written by (1) a parent, (2) a sibling, (3) an instructor with whom they get along, (4) an instructor with whom they do not get along, (5) a good friend, or (6) a rival.

EUDORA WELTY

Why I Live at the P.O.

Surely Welty's Sister is one of the great comic characters in American short fiction, although Sister's is not a voice students always appreciate at first exposure. (In my experience, many students have difficulty "hearing" the comedy in fiction unless it comes directly from puns or overt jokes.) To help the class tune into Sister—some are ready to dismiss her as "stupid" and the story as equally so—I like to have a student with some acting ability read aloud the first dozen paragraphs. (If I don't have a talented student reader, I do the reading myself, striving for the rapid-fire, sharp Southern twang of a Holly Hunter—or a female Ross Perot—as opposed to the slow drawl so often assumed by non-Southern actors playing Southerners without regard to character or background.) The reading, if it goes well, will prompt some chuckles and provide an opening for talking about Sister's character and her role as narrator of recent events in China Grove.

Discussion might start with a close analysis of the first paragraph and with questions about what it reveals about Sister as a character and as a filter for the story. Students immediately will note that Sister's resentment over losing Mr. Whitaker to her younger sister, Stella Rondo, taints her testimony and causes us to question Sister's reliability almost from the first sentence. Fairly detailed analysis of Sister's vocabulary, sentence structure, tone, and emphasis in the opening paragraph helps the class to sketch out some notions of her character. The melodrama of such phrases as "a deliberate, calculated falsehood," Sister's willingness to recount Stella Rondo's crudely intimate lie—she "Told him I was one-sided"—to whomever will listen, the tawdriness of her meeting with Mr. Whitaker when he came to town to take "Pose Yourself" photos, the non sequiturs, and her fragmented style of delivery all help to flesh out her portrait.

Since the story is Sister's explanation of why she's living at the post office instead of at home (why, by the way, the P.O. instead of the post office?), I sometimes ask students to give *their* analyses of why she lives at the post office—that is, to explain what we reader/listeners understand about Sister that she seems not to understand about herself.

QUESTIONS FOR DISCUSSION

1. How much of what Sister reports can we believe? Does she appear to have good reasons to resent Stella Rondo?
2. Why does Sister insist that Stella Rondo's daughter is not adopted? What point is she trying to make? Why? Why does Mama accept Stella Rondo's story that Shirley T. is adopted?
3. How would you characterize the other members of Sister's family? Stella Rondo? Mama? Papa-Daddy? Uncle Rondo? Which characters in the story are most fully fleshed out?
4. Is there a realistic way to account for the melodrama of Sister's family life, or is Welty merely exaggerating for comic effect?
5. What do you make of Sister's revelation at the end of the story that she has been living at the P.O. "for five solid days and nights"? What does her choice of words convey about the way she views this self-imposed exile?
6. What do you make of the bigotry the characters display? Is this a racist story?

SUGGESTION FOR WRITING

Do some library research on Eudora Welty and discover what she has said about "Why I Live at the P.O." Write an essay evaluating the contribution of her comments to your understanding of the story.

CHARLES BAXTER

Fenstad's Mother

One of the delightful things about the experience of reading this story is the way that Baxter flirts with stereotypes. Repeatedly he tempts us to press Fenstad and his mother into neat little boxes marked "milk-toast son" and "domineering mother," or "well-meaning Christian" and "lefty activist," and then he makes it impossible for us to do so. An action occurs, a gesture is made, a phrase is uttered, a thought is revealed, and the characters overflow their boxes—gradually revealing themselves to be too complicated, too unpredictable, and too humanly perplexing for such neat and dismissive packaging.

Such an approach to characterization can make students uncomfortable. Those who typically read stories hoping at the end to distill a hard, gold nugget of wisdom—or at least an unambiguous theme or two—may not know what to do with "Fenstad's Mother." This type of student may simply "resolve" the characters' inconsistencies by ignoring evidence that doesn't conform to stereotype. To counter this tendency, I like to call the class's attention to several passages in the first twenty paragraphs of the story in which at first we are tempted to embrace a stereotypical view of Fenstad or his mother, and then find the stereotype overturned.

Baxter creates the first temptation at the beginning of the very first paragraph:

> On Sunday morning after communion Fenstad drove across town to visit his mother. Behind the wheel, he exhaled with his hand flat in front of his mouth to determine if the wine on his breath could be detected. He didn't think so.

I ask the class what sorts of expectations these three sentences create. One normally imagines that a mother would be proud of an adult son who gets up on Sunday morning to attend church and take communion, but Fenstad doesn't want his mother to detect that he's been drinking wine—even communion wine. Could Fenstad be an alcoholic, covering up his weakness for morning drinking with an early visit to church? Is his mother an old-fashioned teetotaler who disapproves of the use of wine even in the communion service? Is Fenstad a Jew who has provoked his mother by converting to Christianity? As it turns out, the third guess is the closest to the truth—and yet still far off the mark; the truth is both less expected and more complicated. Fenstad's mother appears to think of Fenstad's churchgoing as a mild form of rebellion against her life-long socialism. But, as the story unfolds, we realize that she is also amused at her son's attempts to be "good" in some vague Christian sense and dismayed at how ineffectual he is at it, how often he fails to make the essential human connections that goodness requires.

Later, in paragraph eight, Clara Fenstad questions the necessity of Fenstad's divorce, now a decade past, and wonders aloud why he and his former wife Eleanor couldn't live together. This exchange seems a reprisal of many such conversations between elderly, conservative parents and their grown-up children, but Clara is politically more liberal than her son, and so her seemingly stereotypical reaction is the one that is unexpected here. Of course, things are never quite so simple as they seem. In the next several paragraphs, Clara reveals a rather tough-minded, unromantic view of marriage, one that values companionship as a stay against loneliness over romantic attachment. It is a response that reveals her own situation, as well as her concern for her son's happiness. She doesn't want him to end up, as she has, alone and lonely.

Clara Fenstad's desire to get out of her apartment leads to her son's invitation to attend the night class he teaches in English composition and sets us up for other surprises. When Fenstad's mother responds to his invitation with the statements, "They'll notice me. . . . I'm too old," we scarcely expect that she will virtually take over Fenstad's class and demonstrate a talent for teaching that her son cannot begin to approach. When we are told that Fenstad teaches the course, not because he needs the money but "because he liked teaching strangers and because he enjoyed the sense of hope the classrooms held for him," we imagine that he will be a far better teacher than he turns out to be.

Only later do we reexamine this notion that Fenstad likes to teach strangers and realize that it is, sadly, literally true. He doesn't connect with his students. He lacks the personal touch that his mother so abundantly exhibits, and that is why his well-meaning Christianity gets him nowhere. Fenstad embraces a religion based on the idea that the divine entered human history to show love for mankind by becoming intimately human, but Fenstad gives so little personal attention to his fellow human beings that his Christianity becomes a joke. From this perspective, his mother's gentle mockery of his beliefs seems almost too generous.

QUESTIONS FOR DISCUSSION

1. Why does Clara Fenstad hate "niceness"? What does this attitude suggest about the way she prefers to interact with people?
2. What kind of architecture would you expect a socialist to approve? What is Clara Fenstad's reaction to the architecture of the school where her son teaches? Does she like what you would expect her to like?
3. What is wrong with Fenstad's approach to teaching? Why is his mother a more effective teacher than he is? Is her approach more political or personal?
4. Why is Fenstad so upset by the encounter with the homeless woman in the all-night restaurant? Why does his mother excuse herself and go to the restroom after the encounter? What is her reaction to the scene? To her son?
5. Why does Fenstad's mother risk her health to go out and watch Fenstad skating with his girlfriend? What reason does she give? What reason(s) would you add?
6. What draws Clara Fenstad to York Follette and him to her? Why does York Follette visit the ailing Mrs. Fenstad and bring jazz recordings for her to hear?
7. What are these "glimpses" Fenstad's mother keeps referring to? Glimpses of what?

DORIS LESSING

Our Friend Judith

This is one of those stories about which some students are likely to say, "nothing happens," so it might be a good idea from the beginning to ask them to list all the things that do happen in the story. In a sense the students are right—many of the things that happen do not happen in the story but are told about by the narrator or Betty or Judith herself. It's probably important for students both to know that a good deal happens and to understand why it doesn't seem that anything happens. It might be useful, then, to have them show how the interesting things in the story—Judith's affair with Luigi, the young cat's labor and delivery—are distanced by being reported. This is an aspect of focus—a kind of mediated mediation—not directly treated in Chapter 3, that might be useful to discuss at this point: its effect, its relation to the play-within-the-play or "embedded" narration, perhaps its relation to dialogue. (A return to Baldwin's "Sonny's Blues" might prove enlightening in regard to the narrative filter.) There is little sense of suspense; the major question we ask while reading the story is not "What's going to happen next?" And that's probably what the students mean by "nothing happens."

If it is going to take so much of the anticipation away, why, then, have the friend narrate and why have so many things told to her? What's gained? To what questions, what other centers of interest, is the reader's attention shifted?

Of course, if you ask the questions that way and if you are following the chapters in the text, the brighter students will put two and two together and come up with Judith's character as the center of interest, following with the question, "What's Judith like?" Good enough, but you will have to look out for—or hope for?—the reductive readings: she's this cool-seeming, intellectual, respectable type who's really all fire and like that underneath; she lives one kind of life in the open and another in secret. With any luck, you'll get a more contemporary and subtle but perhaps equally reductive reading—Judith is her own woman, who does not need a man to lean on or depend on but lives in the world, has her profession, and does her own thing in a liberated way that used to be thought of as only the province and right of men. If both those readings come up—or if you can provoke the other once one comes up—your problem will not be to arouse discussion but to keep things in hand.

To pursue another direction, it may be useful to suggest that this is a detective story in which the detection seeks not the solution of a crime but the understanding of a character. You might want to start with the narrator's rejection of the two smug assumptions in the first two paragraphs—that Judith is a typical English spinster and that she has given up. The narrator's experience of other spinsters, her aunts, suggests first that Judith does resemble them but that they are not fossilized, conventional old maids and suggests then that the narrator may have to change her "pitying" attitude toward women without men. The narrator then sadly confesses that through her own stupidity she lost her chance to find out what Judith and her life are really like. We need to get on the table what the lost opportunity was and whether the narrator really blundered. But suppose we can read through the story, beyond the stupid blunder in a way the narrator cannot? Imagine a detective story in which Holmes or Ellery Queen is stumped but the reader is left with what seems to be a sufficient number of clues to solve the crime.

The narrator sets forth some clues in the three revelatory incidents: the dress that Judith refuses to wear (Judith says, "One surely ought to stay in character, wouldn't you say?"), the refusal to castrate the tomcat ("It's the nature of a male cat to rampage lustfully about, and therefore it would be morally wrong for Judith to have the cat fixed"), and Judith's ultimate "apology" to the young man who damaged her flat (". . . having chosen that you should have it, it was clearly an unwarrantable infringement of your liberty to make any conditions at all"). "The facts about Judith, then, are all in the open," the narrator says, "unconcealed, and plain to anyone who cares to study them" or, as it becomes clear she feels, to anyone with the intelligence to interpret them. The challenge is thrown in the reader's face: Are we intelligent enough to interpret the facts with any certainty? (I'm not sure I am, by the way.) Perhaps students should be asked to stop reading the story at this point, as they have been asked to stop reading suspenseful stories at certain points, and to use their intelligence to "interpret" Judith's character as they were earlier asked to predict plot developments. Then they might compare their conclusions here with what they think of Judith at the end of the story. Regardless of how successful the predictions are, this should show students that as readers they collect, recollect, and project as they read in areas other than plot.

When I teach Lessing's story, much of the discussion is shaped by the questions for discussion listed below. I use these not as a pedagogical device—though I do think these and similar questions ought to stimulate discussion—but because I feel they are real questions—that is, they are without single, simple answers. Or, to put it another way, I'm not sure I understand exactly what we are to make of Judith or whether what we are to make of the story is the difficulty of making anything about people's characters. One of the reasons I like Lessing so much is that she, like Lawrence, gets the reader to make human judgments about human actions and character, and that there is no one "literary" answer planted symbolically or structurally in the story. This is not to say that Lessing and Lawrence have not made judgments, but that the judgments are complex, variable, individual; your judgments of the human issues in the story define your character, not your moral or intellectual worth necessarily but what you are "like." Since our egos make us to some extent want to "like" the creator of the fiction we are reading, we try to understand and intuit that vision. In inviting us into their worlds such writers "teach" us not judgments or maxims but how to judge.

As I have earlier suggested, students are often uneasy with this kind of openness—not just a paradox or literary irony or structural ambivalence but an openness that tests the readers' characters rather than their intelligence alone. They're especially uneasy when you can't or won't give them some answers to write in their notebooks. So it might be best in some classes to hold off on this story until you're well into the course. On the other hand, if you have a sharp, articulate, aggressive group, it would be well to throw this at them early—and not let them off the hook with modish, ready-made answers.

QUESTIONS FOR DISCUSSION

1. This story, as the narrator suggests, should modify our notions of the typical English spinster, largely through our knowledge of Judith. How is our stereotype modified? Is it wholly reversed? Drastically changed? Changed in all superficial aspects (celibacy, prudery) but retaining some of its inner nature?
2. What sort of image do the students have of the narrator? She calls herself stupid yet sees and interprets much evidence convincingly (the two rows of books from Judith's former lovers, for example), but at the same time she seems to fall into such banalities as saying oh, yes, Judith would have a cat, and she must be lonely sometimes. Is the narrator "interfering" when she asks Judith about her leaving Italy?
3. Do we agree with Judith that the narrator is "stupid" for using the word *interfere*? What do the students make of Judith's failure to understand why the narrator, Betty, and the Rinieris "care"?
4. Who is right about why the cats gather to watch the painful labor of Judith's pregnant kitten? What do your students make of Judith's reaction to Luigi's killing the kitten?
5. Why, you might ask, are the other women friends involved in the story at all? Why is it *our* rather than *my* friend Judith? Why is Betty involved? (How much do we learn about her?)

SUGGESTIONS FOR WRITING

1. According to the stereotype, spinsters like and keep cats. Write an essay about Judith and the cats. What role(s) do the cats play in "Our Friend Judith"? How does Judith's treatment of, and interaction with, the cats help to characterize her?
2. Write a personal essay about a time when you felt that someone was viewing you stereotypically instead of seeing you as you really are or were. What stereotypes did the other person impose on you? Did you

challenge his or her perception of you in any way? If so, did you get a reaction? What sort?

GRACE PALEY

A Conversation with My Father

Paley's brief but richly nuanced story offers a number of perspectives from which to talk about characterization. Since the story focuses on two versions of the framed tale the narrator writes for her father—and since students usually pay close attention to these when they read—it may be helpful to begin discussion with the differences in the ways the two characters judge a story's merit, focusing on the two tales the narrator constructs. As the footnote points out, one of the father's favorite writers, Turgenev, is best known for his novel *Fathers and Sons*, a work treating conflicts between generations. Mentioning this detail can provide an introduction to discussing the differences between the kinds of stories the narrator likes—and prefers to write—and the stories of which her father approves.

The father says he wants a "simple" story with "recognizable people," but those familiar with the literary models he cites will realize that this is an oversimplification of his requirements. Maupassant and Chekhov (both writers represented in this anthology) wrote stories that are straightforward but also sophisticated and characterized by somewhat bleak realism. (If you have assigned Maupassant's "The Jewelry" and Chekhov's "The Lady with the Dog" earlier in the semester, you may want to refer back to discussions of those works as a means of identifying the type of story to which the father is attracted.) Both writers are capable of great humor and remarkable insight, but they are associated with a vision of reality more dark, fate-ridden, and cynical than optimistic. The daughter has always despised the kind of plot to which her father is attracted "because it takes all hope away." "Everyone, real or invented," she says, "deserves the open destiny of life." Still, she wants to please her father—and he is dying—so she makes an effort to write the kind of story he has requested.

Probably no one in the class will approve of the story the narrator first constructs, an "unadorned and miserable tale," as she describes it. I like to ask students what they make of this first story and of the narrator's aims in writing it. Someone, quoting the father, will observe that the narrator has "left everything out." If the class has read Atwood's "Happy Endings," someone may note that the narrator's first story is similar to the stark plots Atwood constructs. The narrator doesn't describe the characters or create a real background for them, and we have no sense of their lives unfolding over time. She appears to have left out almost "everything" that provides interest in a story—or, to put it another way—meaning in life. The brevity of the first story also suggests the narrator's lack of enthusiasm for writing it. Her description of the tale she has produced appears to be a judgment on the kind of story her father likes, perhaps even an (unconscious? semiconscious?) form of retaliation against the parent who doesn't approve of the stories she normally creates.

When we take up discussion of the second version of the narrator's story, I ask students to explain how this tale is an improvement over the last. I also ask why it doesn't fulfill the father's request. At the heart of the matter, of course, are the differences in the two characters' perspectives. The father is old; he has a damaged heart and is dying. Both a former doctor and a former artist, he unflinchingly confronts the reality of his situation—"Despite my metaphors, this muscle failure is not due to his old heart, he says, but to a potassium shortage"—and he yearns for stories that imbue human life—and the end of life—with resonance and meaning. His daughter, differently situated, believes she has "a different responsibility"—a responsibility to maintain hope. Rejecting the father's characterization of her second story as a "tragedy," she imagines a scenario in which the drug-addicted woman reclaims her life and lives on. Her father recognizes in his daughter's rejection of fictional closure her attempt to deny his approaching death and the inevitability of her own, and his final question implies that some day—perhaps some day soon, when he dies—she will have to "look it in the face."

QUESTIONS FOR DISCUSSION

1. What do you make of the jokes in Paley's story? Of the jokes in the narrator's second story? Are jokes out of place in a story about someone facing death?
2. Why is the father impatient with the daughter's statement that sometimes "you have to let the story lie around till some agreement can be reached between you and the stubborn hero"? What is the difference between her conception of characterization and his?
3. In the second, comic version of the narrator's story, the young man at first sees life through the perspective of drugs. Drugs create the meaning in his life. Eventually he meets a woman who sees life through the perspective of health food and is converted to her perspective. Through what perspective does the father see the world?
4. What characteristics do you value in a short story? Why? Do the stories you like reflect your interests? Your age? Your experiences? Your attitudes toward life?

SUGGESTION FOR WRITING

Compare and contrast the relationships between parent and child in "Fenstad's Mother" and "A Conversation with My Father"—or in another parent/child story—for example, "Everything That Rises Must Converge."

READING/WRITING IDEAS FOR CHAPTER 3
ESSAYS ABOUT CHARACTER

Whether we are aware of it or not, student writers are often most experienced at writing, because we so often require them to write, essays that focus on character, and the following are the types of essays on character that my students most often produce:

1. Essays that show that and how a particular character embodies a particular worldview or value system and/or that show that, how, and why a character suffers a particular problem or dilemma (because of their worldview or value system).

Though being able to argue that a character embodies a particular worldview is crucial to almost any kind of literary essay, I find that assignments that ask students to write essays that do only this tend to encourage rather flat essays. One way to jazz up such essays is to encourage students to focus on what a (shallow) reader might expect such a character to represent and how that character defies such readerly expectations or interpretations. Such an essay might thus be governed by a thesis that goes something like, "While character X seems to be a Y, he or she is really a Z."

2. Essays that show how and why a particular character *or* our vision of that character (and/or his or her worldview or values) develops or changes over the course of a narrative.

Students often produce very good essays of this type, and one way to ensure that they are good is to encourage students to come up with an outline that clearly articulates claims about each of the stages a character or our perception of that character goes through, for example, "At the beginning of the story, character X is (or seems to us to be) a Y"; "When A happens, character X begins to see Z (or "When A happens, we, as readers, begin to see Z about character X"); "By the end of the story, character X has become (or seems to us to be) a D." Doing so can help students to avoid letting the body of their essays devolve into plot summaries and, again, can encourage them to focus on the attitudes an author embodies in a character rather than on the character per se.

Here are examples of how two writers organized such essays on James Joyce's "The Dead" (which is not in the anthology) and Flannery O'Connor's "Everything That Rises Must Converge" (which is).

Sample Thesis: Gabriel Conroy in Joyce's "The Dead" is loquacious, but his words are empty. He is empty, one of the living "Dead." But he is not doomed to remain so, for through a series of highly-charged encounters, the soul of Gabriel awakens to truth.

Sample Topic Sentences
- The story opens at the Misses Morkan's annual dance, a scene of apparent cheer and high spirits. . . . Yet Joyce begins weaving in the spectre of death from the beginning.
- In the midst of this gathering of spectres, it is only appropriate that Gabriel should in a sense be dead himself.
- Yet both the narrative itself and his encounters with people subvert Gabriel's desire to pass neutrally through the world.
- [H]e flees from the conflict and withdraws himself into more empty talk. This emptiness is the result of his inability to be honest with himself.
- With bitter irony, Gabriel realizes that he is still essentially a failure. Accepting this truth about the limitation of his capacities opens the way to other realizations.
- Gabriel thus experiences a reversal of his earlier paralysis. He experiences the onset of spiritual passion, triggered by sexual passion.

From Montira Horayangura, "Awakening the Dead." In *Exposé:
Essays from the Expository Writing Program, Harvard University, 1993–1994*
(Cambridge, Mass.: Expository Writing Program, 1994). Reprinted by permission.

3. Essays that show how a central conflict in the narrative is dramatized through the comparison of and/or opposition between multiple characters.

Sample Thesis: As a girl raised in the fading glory of the Old South, amid mystical tales of magnolias and moonlight, the mother [of "Everything That Rises Must Converge"] remains part of a dying generation; surrounded by hard times, racial conflict, and limited opportunities, Julian, on the other hand, feels repelled by the provincial nature of home, and represents a new Southerner, one who sees his native land through a condescending Northerner's eyes.

Sample Topic Sentences
- Throughout the story Julian and his mother constantly look to the values and circumstances of their early environments as anchors, as references points in guiding their speech, thoughts, and actions. For the mother, her era consists of an archaic past. . . . In stark contrast, Julian's experience is that of the depressing present.
- They wage much of this tireless fight over issues of proper etiquette. As a Southern "lady," Julian's mother is naturally preoccupied with an overriding concern for appearance. . . . Like a practical sensible Yankee, [Julian] feels no meaningful attachment to articles of clothing.
- Such an ironic juxtaposition of contesting views indicates deeper philosophical rifts between the mother and son; the contrast points to a conflict ages-old in literature . . . : the clash of the idealist versus the realist.
- But these issues . . . seem like skirmishes against the pivotal issue that creates the backdrop for the ugliest showdown between mother and son. They fight with weapons of racism, using blacks as the fodder for their respective ideological cannons.

From " 'On Their Own Side of the Fence': Mother and Son
in 'Everything that Rises,' " unpublished student paper.

4. Essays that show exactly why and how a seemingly minor character, a character who isn't obviously either a protagonist or an antagonist or foil, plays a crucial role in a given text (a version of the "this seemingly unimportant thing is really central" essay).

TROUBLESHOOTING

One of the key problems my students face in writing about character is the tendency to treat characters as individual people rather than as embodiments of certain worldviews, values, attitudes, ways of being, or whatever vocabulary you choose to use. Another, perhaps less reductive, way to phrase this would be to say that characters in fiction function both as individuals and as representatives of certain worldviews just as a given object in a fictional text can be simultaneously that object and a symbol for something else. With character, as with other fictional elements, in other words, I find that my students need help learning to move back and forth between the concrete and the abstract, the specific and the general, and learning to recognize and understand that readerly/writerly process.

CHARACTER-FOCUSED WRITING EXERCISES

1. Identifying Evidence and Counterevidence

To make students aware of how many different kinds of evidence can be used by a writer to support a particular interpretation of a character, I often give them a list of several types of evidence and ask them to identify at least one piece of evidence of each type with which they might support a particular claim about a character. That list usually looks something like this:

Something that the character says or thinks
Something that the character does
Something that another character or the narrator says about the character
Something that the character wears, owns, etc.

With every essay assignment I give students, I try to incorporate at least one exercise that asks them to think about counterevidence and/or counterarguments, because I have found that doing so encourages students to produce much more complicated and sophisticated essays. You can do that easily here by asking students to follow-up their list of different kinds of supporting evidence with a list of at least two pieces of evidence that undermine (or that might seem to undermine) their claim about the character and a paragraph that either shows how and why this piece of evidence doesn't really or necessarily contradict the claim or shows how this piece of evidence may require the student to broaden or complicate his or her interpretation of the character. An extension of this assignment that is less evidence oriented asks students to articulate the most powerful counterargument that they can imagine, as if, for example, they were lawyers preparing for court.

Whichever version of the assignment I use, I find discussions of this part of the exercise a perfect opportunity to hammer home once again the distinction between facts and inferences and the necessity of always having both working together to have an argument: as my students quickly tire of hearing me say, yet never stop needing to hear, facts don't support any argument unless or until one infers something from them, and inferences only make sense if you show the facts they derive from. (To stress these ideas, I actually tend in my classes to use the word *evidence* to refer to only facts plus inferences, not to facts alone.)

2. Using Essay Type 1 to Prepare to Write a Type 2, 3, or 4 Essay

It might be very useful to have students write a few paragraphs that sketch out an argument like that described under essay type 1 above that they might then use as part of a type 2, 3, or 4 essay, especially since it is exactly the kind of thing that they will need to do to move from exercise 1 to an essay on character development or character opposition.

4

SETTING

Each of the stories in this chapter takes us to unfamiliar places—whether the Sierra Nevada Mountains, war-torn China during the Japanese invasion of World War II, or Moscow in the late nineteenth century. The chapter focuses attention on three questions: (1) When does the story take place—at what hours of the day, what seasons, over what period of time? (2) Where does the story take place—in what rooms, buildings, places, regions, countries? and (3) What part does the setting play in the experience and meaning of the story? It may be well to set out these questions very simply before beginning your study and to ask that students underline the answers they discover as they read. I find that, while students have little problem grasping the significance of setting in abstract terms, they have a tendency to skip over descriptions of setting when reading, and they often lack the geographical and historical knowledge to make settings foreign to them come alive. For the latter reason, it may also be helpful to bring maps into class and supply abbreviated historical backgrounds when appropriate.

PLANNING IDEAS

- Ask students to write and bring to class a description of the scene they would show during the opening credits of their film version of "Sánchez," "A Pair of Tickets," or "The Lady with the Dog." Use the descriptions as a jumping-off point for talking about the importance of setting.
- Show students the film *The Joy Luck Club* (or portions of it) after they have read Tan's "A Pair of Tickets." Discuss how particular settings are portrayed in the film and how those portrayals work to evoke particular feelings, expectations, or attitudes in viewers.
- Have students write a description of a friend's bedroom and discuss what this "setting" might reveal about this person if he or she were a

character in a short story; or before discussing "Sánchez," have them write about a particular place and time that is meaningful to them, discussing why and how it is meaningful to them and then imagining how it might mean something different to someone else—a parent, someone native to a place they visited on vacation, etc.

RICHARD DOKEY

Sánchez

Because the story opens in Stockton and because most students will have had the experience of seeing their parents react negatively to something to which they are attracted or about which they are proud, I like to start discussion by asking about the different reactions Juan and Jesús Sánchez have to the town. Jesús clearly sees in his new situation an opportunity for independence, adventure, and economic advancement. He guides his father proudly through the place he envisions as the site of his future success. But Juan sees Stockton differently. He sees the squalor of Jesús's rented room, the ugliness of a place where all seems uprooted. Ultimately, he declines to visit the canning factory where his son will work, his disappointment in his son's vision of the future as palpable as his love for him.

Students who have read closely will remember that Juan knows Stockton, has visited the town repeatedly in the past. If no one brings it up, I ask what memories Juan has of the town (see par. 43). Responses to this question usually lead us to talk about Juan's dreams and ambitions as a young man and to contrast these to the hopes of Jesús. At this point, I ask students to explain the reasons for Juan's disappointment in Jesús's choices.

We are told that Juan left his parched homeland when he was a young man "because he feared the land, believed almost that it possessed the power to kill him—as it had killed his mother and father, his aunt, was, in fact, slowly killing so many of his people." He felt he was compelled to change his situation as a matter of survival. In comparison, his son's motivations for moving to Stockton—independence, the chance to work in the canning factory and make money—must seem woefully inadequate. In addition, Stockton has unpleasant associations for Juan. When he was a much younger man, he traveled to the town in the company of other immigrant workers who got drunk, visited whores, and fought. He didn't join in their revels, however, but instead stood on the corners of Stockton's skid row and thought about what he had lost. At the time his dearest hopes for the future had been cast down by the tragic outcome of his wife's most recent pregnancy. Desperate to ensure that she would not become pregnant again, he had recently had a vasectomy and given up, as he then believed, all hope of ever having a family.

Stockton's ugliness, both remembered and observed anew during the tour with his son, contrasts sharply with the beauty of the Sierra Nevadas where Juan doggedly pursued his own dreams as a young man. It must seem to him, when his son rejects that place for a rented room in Stockton, that his struggle to establish a home in the midst of loveliness for his family has come to nothing. The son whose life was so costly to La Belleza and to Juan remains Juan's *querido*, his dear one, but Jesús's rejection of all his father has labored to attain breaks the older man's heart and makes him realize that the home he established first for his wife, and later for his child, is no longer home to him either.

QUESTIONS FOR DISCUSSION

1. Have you ever tried to share something that you are proud of with a parent and found him or her unable to appreciate what you appreciate? How do you account for the differences in your perceptions?
2. In paragraph 47, Juan Sánchez gets up in the night and looks at the stars, and "as always he was moved by the nearness and profusion of their agony." Why does Juan associate the stars with agony? What do the next few lines tell us about Juan's view of life?
3. Richard Dokey spends a good portion of the story suggesting how beautiful the area in the Sierra Nevada Mountains is where Juan eventually makes his home. Why does he begin the story by describing the ugliness of Stockton, where Jesús will work for the Flotill Cannery?
4. How does Juan account for the racism of the people of Twin Pines? What does Juan's explanation tell us about him? How is this racism expressed?
5. What do you believe happens to Juan at the end of the story? Does he go home to Mexico, called back to his homeland by the "embracing love" that he felt "lowing across the mountains from the south"? Or does he commit suicide, seeking out the love that "must all still be alive somewhere" by joining La Belleza in death?
6. Define the two kinds of love Juan discovers that are described in paragraph 71. What is the love that "wanted him for his own"? Does this kind of love have anything to do with the way the story ends?

AMY TAN

A Pair of Tickets

The first five paragraphs of "A Pair of Tickets" provide the seeds of the story. I like to start discussion by asking the class to notice the clues the opening offers about what will be important as the narrative unfolds. The first paragraph situates the narrator in the fictive present, crossing from Hong Kong—symbolic gateway between East and West—into China. The second paragraph reaches back through memory to a time twenty-one years before when the narrator, a high-school sophomore in San Francisco, told her mother that she didn't feel Chinese and made it clear she didn't particularly want to feel Chinese. Paragraphs three through five project foward into the future—first the humorously awful future the narrator imagined when she was young (her transformation into a "mutant" with all her mother's Chinese behaviors), then the unknown future of the journey to China, which the narrator makes carrying the dreams (the hoped-for future) of her dead mother. Students will probably mention that the opening paragraphs suggest the story will concern itself with the relationship between the narrator and her mother, the narrator's perspective on her heritage, and the interrelations of past, present and future.

You might want to ask how the style of narration and the temporal arrangement of the narrative reflects the movement of memory. Jing-mei, the narrator of "A Pair of Tickets," reports from the narrative "present." Her journey becomes our journey. We piece together the facts of her mother's past and discover the narrator's heritage as she does. What is the effect?

One good way to talk about setting is to start with the many names and references to names in the story. Jing-mei's sense of dislocation from her ethnic origins and her parents' physical dislocation from their homeland find expression in places and place names and, of course, in the narrator's two names: Jing-mei and June May. (Someone may note that neither name is "purely" of one nationality. Jing-mei is a Chinese name written in Roman—"American"—letters, and June May seems a Chinese notion of an American name.) The name of Jing-mei's San Francisco school is Galileo High. An Italian name, of course, is perfect to suggest cosmopolitan, melting-pot America.

When Jing-mei visits 1980s China, the old, Westernized city names have been replaced by more authentically Chinese names approved by the postrevolutionary leadership. This China both is and is not the country her mother knew. With its luxury hotels stocked with Western products, it is certainly not the China Jing-mei expected. (Only the hotel shampoo, "the consistency and color of hoisin sauce," seems to her sufficiently, authentically Chinese.) The landscape she has read and heard about has changed, just as the landscape had changed when her mother returned with her new husband to look for her twin daughters and the rest of her family in 1945, after the Japanese invasion.

Mr. Woo's description of her mother's trek from Kweilin during the invasion is vivid, and with it we move to yet another landscape. Little topographical detail is given, but the description of the roads filled with people, the trucks passing by, the mother's agony, and the children make it easy to visualize the scene. The landscape particular to China is unimportant because we are really in "War Land," that zone where separation and tragedy occur despite all best intentions.

At some point in class discussion, I like to ask why Jing-mei goes to China. The obvious answer is that she goes to meet her newly discovered sisters, but I think, perhaps, that she also goes out of a sense of guilt—feeling that she didn't appreciate her mother sufficiently (Are there children who do?), that she somehow should have shared her mother's secret pain and compensated for the loss of her sisters. She goes to China thinking that the least she can do is accomplish her mother's dream of recovering her children, however inadequately, by proxy. In some sense, perhaps inadvertently, she also goes to China to meet the mother she never knew—the woman who hid her hopes and deepest grief from her husband as well as her daughter.

If you are lucky, someone will mention that this is a story of self-realization—if not, you may want to bring it up. An aspect of Jing-mei's character or soul has been obscured, and this odyssey enables her to uncover it; she discovers her Chinese self. But there are other people, other discoveries about the nature of family and identity. (It is significant, I think, that Jing-mei's mother is certain all the people in the family house are dead because she knows how they as a family behave—that they would all be together.) You might ask the students what they make of all the activity with the Polaroid and the narrator's observations about physical resemblances.

The miracle of this story is, for me, the "rightness" of its resolution. I like to ask my students to tell me what Jing-mei needs in order for her story to have a happy ending. What are the shapes of her fears? The sources of her grief? One possibility is that Jing-mei fears she will be insufficient for her sisters, as she was insufficient for her mother (through no real fault of her own). She fears her mother never loved her as much as she loved her lost children. She grieves over the loss of the mother she knew and over the loss of the mother she has come to know during her journey. Like all of us who lose loved ones, she has regrets. She wishes her mother had lived to see her hopes rewarded, and she feels unworthy to meet her sisters in her mother's place.

Near the end of class, I like to ask how the meeting at the airport satisfies Jing-mei's longings. Her mother will never come back to say, "You're wrong; I always loved you," but in her sister's expression—"the back of her hand pressed hard against her mouth"—her mother is returned to her with evidence of her love. Recalling her mother's gesture of tearful relief when she discovered the five-year-old Jing-mei was safe and not dead as she had feared provides the necessary affirmation. In the faces of her sisters, Jing-mei recognizes her lost mother and her lost self. The important part of her that is Chinese is her family. In finding her sisters, she finds not only what her mother wanted for herself, but what she also wanted for her three lost daughters.

QUESTIONS FOR DISCUSSION

1. What does it mean to be a member of a family, even when you've grown up without ever seeing them?
2. What are "blood ties" and what is their power? Does being Chinese by blood and family expand or modify what we mean by "self"?
3. Why is Jing-mei reluctant to go to China? What are her fears? How are these fears resolved?
4. What is the meaning of the Polaroid photo at the end of the story? Why does Tan describe it coming into focus?

SUGGESTIONS FOR WRITING

1. Analyze the photographs in Tan's "A Pair of Tickets." What do they represent? Do photographs represent the same things each time they are mentioned in the story? How is the significance of the photographs influenced by setting?
2. Write a personal essay about (a) visiting a place in which the prevailing standards and values seemed very different from your own *or* (b) visiting a place that holds significance for an older family member—parent, aunt, uncle, grandparent.

ANTON CHEKHOV

The Lady with the Dog

For the average student this story does not seem to have immediate appeal, perhaps because the setting seems so unfamiliar, perhaps because it doesn't seem much like a "story." If this objection comes up, you might be able to use it. In what ways do stories perform that this one does not? I try to lead the discussion toward the point that in most stories emotions such as love are explained, defined, understandable, whereas here the love seems simply to happen for no good or obvious reason at all. At this point I try to lead them to move away from fiction and "stories" to their own experience. Can they explain how or why they fell in love with the person they love or loved? Is he or she the most beautiful or handsomest? The most intelligent or kind? The "best" person they have ever met? In real terms, not just in romantic hyperbole? Did the circumstances of their meeting have anything to do with why they fell in love?

If the class is made nervous by the intimacy of such questions, I shift ground and ask if they've ever found themselves in a setting—at the beach, for instance, or in a foreign city—where they felt free to behave in an uncharacteristic manner. (I find if I probe a bit that some students will admit going off to college has offered this kind of liberation.) From this discussion, it is easy to turn back to Gurov and Anna in Yalta and the circumstances of their meeting. Before they meet, what has Gurov been doing with his time? How has Anna spent hers? What are the circumstances of their everyday lives? Both Gurov and Anna seem genuinely, not fashionably bored, both are in Yalta alone, and both have unhappy marriages. You may want to ask your class at what point in their reading they discovered Yalta was a beautiful place. The descriptions that make the resort sound appealing begin only after the two meet and stroll by the sea. It is as if meeting Anna opens Gurov's eyes to the beauty around him, even though he believes that his relationship with her is nothing special. The relationship between characters and setting thus works in two directions at once—the setting prompts their relationship and is itself simultaneously transformed by that relationship.

To Anna the relationship is from the first something "very special, very serious," a reaction Gurov finds "disconcerting." There are two widely separated scenes in which Gurov sits beside Anna while she suffers. I like to ask students to compare his reactions in the two scenes and account for the differences. How are the connections between the scenes related to the structure of the story? At some point I like to call attention to the four divisions of the story and ask the class to outline briefly what happens in each.

Gurov thinks of Yalta and vacation time as unreal and Moscow and snow as real, yet somehow the unreal becomes his real reality. You might ask your students to speculate about what causes this change in perception—whether Chekhov offers us any clues ahead of time that Gurov's affair with Anna will surprise him.

I have to watch myself in teaching this story because it is one of my two or three favorite stories in the volume, and I cannot let my enthusiasm show too soon. (When I have done so it has the effect of dictating responses, or appearing to do so.) I like this story in part because it surprises convincingly: Gurov begins a routine and even somewhat sordid vacation affair and surprisingly falls in love with Anna. The story does not say why or how, does not show Anna to be in any way remarkable, yet I am convinced that Gurov is in love with her, that love can happen this way, and that human actions are often inexplicable, not in any final way to be analyzed or explained.

It does more, too, because it is about more than love. It shows the depths beneath even ordinary experience: it suggests something about the relationship between inner and outer reality (or appearance and reality) and, both in some expository sentences describing the beauty of the world Gurov begins to notice and in the way that Gurov and Anna act and express their feelings toward each other, it suggests that life retains meaning, even in the face of what seems like an indifferent universe.

When Gurov seeks out Anna in S., they stand together in a theater staircase under a sign inscribed, in some translations of the story, "To the upper circle." (In the translation used in the anthology, the sign reads

"To the Amphitheatre" [par. 93].) The allusion to Dante's Inferno seems obvious, if not entirely clear in its implications. Does their meeting present a last chance to avoid the hell of a clandestine relationship, or are they offered no more than a choice between one circle of hell and another (the pain of separation versus the misery of an affair)? If Gurov and Anna are already imprisoned in one of the lower circles of Hell, what kind of hell might it be? Dante consigned the lustful to the second circle of the inferno, but Chekhov is writing in a different time and culture. His lovers forgive one another instead of seeking absolution from a priest.

Since translation makes a world of difference here, this could also represent a good opportunity for discussing questions about how translation itself functions as a kind of literary criticism or interpretation and about what it means to analyze or interpret such translations/interpretations. Just be prepared, if you do so, for students who claim that one can't effectively analyze a story in translation!

QUESTIONS FOR DISCUSSION

1. How does the weather and season described in each section relate to the action? If Gurov's and Anna's affair heats up under the hot sun in Yalta, why doesn't it cool down, as we would expect, in the snow of a Moscow winter?
2. Compare and contrast Gurov's reaction to the pomeranian in Yalta and later in the town of S. where he travels to see Anna. Why are his reactions different?
3. What do you make of the house in S. where Anna lives? What does Gurov make of it?
4. What hope does Gurov hold out for Anna and himself as the story closes? How would you describe the tone of the last two lines?

READING/WRITING IDEAS FOR CHAPTER 4

ESSAYS ABOUT SETTING

I often teach the "Symbols" and "Setting" chapters in conjunction, precisely because the two elements often, though obviously not always, become intertwined as my students read and write about texts, both facets of the setting (furniture or buildings, for example) and settings themselves (Stockton in "Sánchez," for example) coming to function in essence as symbols. I also try to talk about setting by alluding back to our conversations about character, for quite often students write most effectively about setting when they analyze it in relation to, or as a part of, characterization; in terms of its role in creating conflicts within or between characters (or forcing such conflicts into the open); and/or almost as if it were itself a character of sorts within a given story. Giving students essay assignments that ask them to analyze setting in relation to character in one of these ways both ensures that their essays have a real point (and aren't just random observations about setting) and gives them a vivid sense of building on past accomplishments as they begin to produce writing that interrelates elements rather than treating them singly.

TROUBLESHOOTING

What my students (and I) can too often ignore is the way in which setting is as much about time and history as it is about particular places: the setting of "The Country Husband" is as much post–World War II as it is the suburb of Shady Hill, just as the Civil War and the Renaissance are crucial facets of the setting of "An Occurrence at Owl Creek Bridge" and "A Cask of Amontillado." An even less obvious facet of setting may well be the time frame of the text itself—the long time span of "Sonny's Blues" or the very compressed one of Bierce's "Occurrence," for example. As a result, I find that I often have to place especially heavy emphasis on these facets of setting in discussion and in writing assignments, and I find that doing so has the added benefit of paving the way for our later discussions of cultural context.

SETTING-FOCUSED WRITING EXERCISE

Answering Setting-Focused Questions and Generating Setting-Focused Theses

To prepare students to write the kind of essay described above, I generally have them start by reading and/or re-reading the story they're going to write about, paying special attention to descriptions of setting and/or characters' remarks or thoughts about a particular setting. Then I ask them to consider the following questions about the way setting operates in the story, making notes both about their answers and about the evidence from the story they would use to support their answers:

- What qualities are associated with the setting or settings of the story? What's the "character" of the setting(s)?
- Do the setting(s) seem to serve as symbols? If so, for what?
- Do the setting(s) seem to have different meanings for different characters? How do the characters' attitudes toward the setting(s) help characterize each of them and/or inspire or bring into the open the conflict between the characters?
- Do some or all of the characters' attitudes toward the setting(s) change? If so, what does this change reveal about the character(s)? Would you say that the setting plays a role in the character's or characters' learning process? If so, how so?
- Do particular aspects of the setting seem to have specific symbolic significance? If so, what are those aspects and what do you think their particular significance is?

I ask students not only to answer these questions but also to use the questions to generate thesis statements that suggest how the setting, settings, or some particular aspect(s) thereof either

- contribute(s) to the characterization of a particular character or characters;
- help(s) bring out a conflict within a character or between characters; or
- help(s) dramatize the change within a character or within the reader's perception of a character over the course of the story.

5
———————

SYMBOLS

Among the stories in this chapter, "Young Goodman Brown" seems to offer the most straightforward approach to symbolism. The semi-allegorical form employed by Hawthorne tempts the reader to draw simple equations between names or objects and ideas, which is one reason I like to assign this story first. Discussing the allegorical aspects of "Young Goodman Brown" helps lay the groundwork for exploring the more complicated symbolism of "Janus" and "A Hunger Artist." Yet a close analysis of Hawthorne's conditional phrasing can also explode easy assumptions about matching symbol and meaning. After first guiding the class through a fairly narrow allegorical reading of the story (assuming that student comments stay within those bounds), you might want to go on to the other stories in this chapter and then revisit "Young Goodman Brown" afterward, urging the class to look more closely the second time around at the way Hawthorne plays with the allegorical form.

PLANNING IDEAS

- Bring in an American flag and ask students to imagine what the flag might symbolize to different people in different contexts: a World War I veteran on Veterans Day, a grandmother on the Fourth of July, a teenager at a ball game, a French student protesting NATO exercises, a Russian politician up for reelection, an Iraqi soldier on guard duty at one of his country's borders.
- Assign a straightforward allegory—part of *Everyman* or *Pilgrim's Progress*—along with Hawthorne's "Young Goodman Brown" so that students can see more clearly how Hawthorne manipulates the allegorical form for his own purposes.
- Before coming to class, have students
    a. Underline the ambiguous words and phrases in "Young Goodman Brown" as a prelude to talking in class about the differences

between traditional allegory and the symbolism in Hawthorne's story.

   b. Write a paragraph explaining the symbolic meaning of the bowl in "Janus."

- Before discussing "Janus" in class, photocopy and hand out a description of the god Janus (see commentary) or ask students to find out who or what Janus is for themselves and bring a description to class.

NATHANIEL HAWTHORNE

Young Goodman Brown

This deceptively simple story works well in class, I find, and is particularly useful fairly early in an introductory course. There may be a few students who will see none of the allegorical implications and little if any of even the more conventional aspects of the initiation theme. Most, however, will see some of the "clues," and classes often come to life as they pile on detail after detail; even those students who saw nothing at first will get into the act before the discussion is turned to the less obvious elements in the story. There will be an initial sense of accomplishment and contribution; then a deep breath; further discussion; and one hopes, greater illumination.

The initial stage of the class discussion, if you are lucky, may wind up with something like this: The innocent hero learns that there is evil even in the best of us, that all men are sinners, that we all partake of original sin. This participation in sin is represented in the story by the townspeople's participating at night and in the woods in a satanic version of their daytime religious services and rituals. Salem, the scene of the notorious witch trials, is thus an appropriate setting. Though *goodman* is a title merely meaning "husband," the allegorical weight of "good man" is clearly appropriate; *young* clearly suggests "innocent"; *Brown* is so common a name that, like Tom Jones, perhaps, it can suggest "Everyman." Other events, phrases, objects point to the struggle with evil: when Brown says, "What if the devil himself should be at my very elbow!" the traveler suddenly appears; Goodman says, "Faith kept me back awhile"; the stranger's walking stick has a snake carved on it and looks alive.

The story seems to work best in class when the allegorical reading comes out piecemeal but rather fully and without nagging doubts. If it goes on long enough someone in the class is bound to react, relieving you of the responsibility. There are bothersome details. Why does Faith wear pink ribbons? What's the innocent Brown doing going into the woods at night in the first place? Clearly, he's up to no good, and he even feels guilty about it. So maybe he's not quite so innocent, at least about himself. Why does he undertake the meeting soon, but not immediately, after he's married? Why is it that Faith's participation in the rites is more crushing to him than his father's or even the preacher's?

Students are used to discussions in English class turning to the subject of sex, and clearly that's where this one is leading. It could also lead to the subject of sexism, however, and this might be a good point to distinguish between what a story shows and what attitude it takes toward what it is showing.

QUESTIONS FOR DISCUSSION

1. How can we take seriously, and treat as meaningful for our own problems and experience, a story about Satan and witches and people who lived a couple hundred years ago and had problems other than our own?
2. Is the story acceptable simply as "allegory," as "message-bearing," or are we more concerned with the questions it raises about human actions and attitudes than with the precepts or adages that it might offer?
3. Should this story be read as a straight allegory? What do you make of the conditional language in which the action is sometimes described?
4. If the "sin" has to do with sex and sexuality, and if the hero accepts his own share of sin, no matter how guilty he feels, but is traumatized by seeing his bride's complicity, does all that add up to a sexist attitude? Is the story sexist for showing it or antisexist for doing so?
5. Does it make any difference in your understanding of the story to know that one of Hawthorne's ancestors was a judge involved in the Salem witch trials?

SUGGESTION FOR WRITING

Read *Pilgrim's Progress* and explain the differences between Bunyan's use of allegory and Hawthorne's.

FRANZ KAFKA

A Hunger Artist

Kafka's "A Hunger Artist" is and always has been one of my favorite stories to teach simply because it both appeals to "symbol-hunting" students and allows me to complicate their sense of how symbols particularly and literary texts more generally work by showing them how our reading of literature (and of life!) can be enriched by formulating interpretations that allow for multiplicity or that are what I call "yes-and" rather than "either-or" interpretations. At the same time, however, "A Hunger Artist" is also incredibly accessible even to the most inexperienced or most literal-minded of students because, as the anthology indicates, it simply doesn't make any (or at least much) sense on a literal level or on the pop-psychology level, where inexperienced students often want to take up permanent residence. Another way to say this is that, in the case of "A Hunger Artist," it is well-nigh impossible for students to really argue that there is one and only one interpretation of just what the artist symbolizes or, for that matter, that there is one and only one interpretation of just what the story says about him. Yet the story also isn't particularly shy about advertising what the most obvious of those interpretations are.

One of the most obvious, of course, is that suggested by the title itself, which, if we remove the "hunger," pretty much tells us that the main character or hero here is "an artist" in the general sense, an idea underscored by the fact that he has no other name. (Thus this story provides a great opportunity to point out to students that any literary text that features an artist as a character or discussions of art is almost certainly at least in part about literature and/or art more generally, an idea that may seem obvious to us but that comes as something of a revelation to many of my students.) Less obvious, but still eminently appropriate and suggestive, I think, is the idea that the hunger artist represents a religious figure of some sort or, in slightly different terms, the spiritual side of humankind, the soul, as opposed to the sensual or animalistic side, or the body. This other side is most obviously represented in the story by the panther, "his noble body, furnished almost to the bursting point with all that it needed," "the joy of [animal] life stream[ing] with . . . ardent passion from his throat," and it is also less obviously represented by the spectators who are so entranced by the panther that they "did not ever want to move away" from his cage (par. 10). Obviously, these interpretations work eminently well together both in terms of this particular story and in terms of our more general (Romantic) conceptions of art and of the (starving) artist who does (or, we believe, should) disdain the idea of concerning himself with any merely physical or material needs or desires to pursue his heavenly vision and quasi-religious mission. Thus the hunger artist in Kafka's story has such a strong sense of, even "zeal" about (par. 6), "the honor of his profession" (par. 2) and is so "fanatically devoted to fasting" (par. 5) that he would, and eventually in fact does, willingly fast himself to death.

By virtue of its characterization of the hunger artist, then, and because of its emphasis on the "markedly diminished" "interest in professional fasting" in the "world now" (par. 1), "A Hunger Artist" has been said by many to symbolically consider the fate of the artist, of religion, and of man's soul in the twentieth century, contrasting an earlier time in which all three were revered and appreciated by an admiring public with a modern world in which reverence for such things has given way to indifference to them and to interest in "bread and circuses" (a phrase that becomes quite literal here). According to this reading of the story, then, the artist's final words can be interpreted as a commentary on what has killed him and all that he represents: there is, symbolically, no longer in the world "the food" that sustains art, religion, or the soul. The hunger artist can only die in a world in which his values, his beliefs, his art simply aren't appreciated, when children can ask only, "what did they care about fasting?" (par. 7).

Yet this interpretation, while satisfying in some ways, doesn't make a lot of sense in others—after all, starving was his art—and it ignores the judgment the artist passes on himself when he says that his art isn't admirable because it is easy. Here, then, is where interpretation of the story and its commentary on art, religion, and/or the soul becomes a great deal more complicated, sending us (with any luck) back to the story with the following questions in mind. Are the "good old days" of the story really so different from the new? Is the hunger artist really so admirable and sympathetic a figure as the noble-artist-in-a-fallen-world reading might suggest? To my mind, the answer is both yes and no. On the one hand, it is certainly true that, as the narrator tells us again and again and as the hunger artist himself ultimately discovers, there has been a dramatic change in the public's attitude toward the hunger artist, his art, and whatever a reader takes them to symbolize. And it is equally true, I think, that the hunger artist is, in his own way, rather noble in his self-sacrificing dedication to his art. But, on the other hand, it is not true that the artist's situation in the circus is fundamentally unlike the situation he enjoys in his heyday. For whatever his sense of the nature and ends of his art, the hunger artist's past success rested in great part on the efforts of "the impresario," efforts that seem to be just as much driven by the desire for material profit as those of the circus manager are. It is, moreover, this very impresario who portrays the hunger artist as a "suffering martyr," a portrayal that the narrator tells us was simultaneously true and distinctly false advertising (par. 3). What, ultimately, is the difference between a crowd clamoring to see a panther and a crowd clamoring to see a hunger artist? Is the hunger artist's grim fate in any sense his own fault? What does the story ultimately suggest about what art, religion, and/or the relationship between body and soul should be? After all this time, I don't have answers yet, which is precisely why I find that the story works so well in the classroom.

QUESTIONS FOR DISCUSSION

1. The anthology suggests that the hunger artist in Kafka's story symbolizes the artist in a more general sense. What evidence from the story might you use to support this argument? If the hunger artist does represent "the artist" in a general sense, then how does the story characterize "the artist" and his relationship or attitude to his art? To his audience? What other attitudes toward the artist and toward art are represented through other characters in the story?
2. What are the usual connotations of, or reasons for, fasting in our cul-

ture? What might the fact that the hunger artist's art is fasting suggest about the other things he might symbolize in addition to "the artist"? What evidence in the story would you use to support this interpretation? How might this interpretation complement and/or contradict the argument that the hunger artist symbolizes "the artist" in a general sense?

3. What attitude do you think the text as a whole encourages us to take toward the hunger artist and his art? Toward his audience? Do you think the text treats the hunger artist as an ideal whose death we should lament? If so, why and how? If not, how are we to take the death of the artist? Who or what do you think is being criticized in Kafka's story?

4. What do you make of the artist's comment that it is easy to fast? That he fasted because he couldn't find any food that he liked?

5. What is the symbolic significance and/or role of other characters in the story, especially the impresario and the panther?

ANN BEATTIE

Janus

Like "Our Friend Judith," this is a story that resists simple answers and tidy interpretation. It is also a story without a plot. Before you tackle the one-hundred-million-dollar question—"What on earth does that bowl represent?"—you might want to ask the class the same question that sometimes comes up with "Our Friend Judith"—whether "Janus" really qualifies as a short story. Does something actually have to happen in a short story, or can something else substitute for action?

Some students are uncomfortable with the story because it lacks a traditional plot, but I find many more are disturbed by what we might call its symbolic latitude. We are never able to state with finality, "The bowl represents X," nor are we able to say with any real assurance what we are to think of Andrea, the protagonist. Students sense that the bowl symbolizes something about Andrea and the life she has chosen, but many will be frustrated in their attempts to move beyond that basic observation. Those who have managed some comparisons may be hard-pressed to pull them together coherently. If the class has discussed "Young Goodman Brown" or "A Hunger Artist," you might get things rolling by asking students to compare the way symbols operate in each story.

Clearly Beattie's story is more oblique. While the bowl is described, it remains essentially mysterious to its owner and to us. (I like to suggest at some point in the discussion that with a different ending "Janus" could have been turned into "The Story of the Magic Bowl: A Modern Fairy Tale.") The impersonal third-person narration tells us something about the bowl, what it looks like, how people react to it. We also learn something about Andrea and the way she feels about the bowl, but when we try to set up parallels between the two, we flounder. Although the narrative offers information of apparent significance (the bowl is cream colored, like some flesh; Andrea believes it "was meant to be empty"; she has "never talked to her husband about the bowl"; she has had an affair), it is remarkably free of indicators about which pieces of information are important. We need a reference point or some voice of authority to tell us what to pay attention to.

After we establish that "Janus" lacks the reference points and relatively clear parallels Hawthorne offers in "Young Goodman Brown," I like to ask the class if "Janus" offers reference points of another sort. Are there elements in the story that seem more significant than others, elements that might be used at least as guides to reading, if not keys? I think there are at least two—the title of the story and our delayed discovery that the bowl is the present of Andrea's former lover—and with a little probing, a bright class will come up with them.

It seems to me noteworthy that Beattie never mentions Janus in the story itself. (Andrea's lover calls her "two-faced," but he doesn't use the term in the way that it's commonly used: to label one who is deceptive.) The title remains "outside" the narrative, and it is up to us to establish its connection with the tale. We've got to fill in the blanks. For this, a little background may be in order, and you may want to give your students something like the following description on a handout so they can consider possible applications:

Janus was the Roman door god, and each ancient Roman household had its own Janus. The Romans thought there were gods everywhere and in everything and that the most important feature of successful living was getting along with these myriad gods. Good relations with the gods was known as the *pax decorum*, and the Roman politician/literatus/philosopher Cicero could claim, quite seriously, that the Romans owed their success in conquering the world to their exceptional care in religious matters.

The Roman state also had a temple in the forum dedicated to the god Janus that was open when they were at war (most of the time) and closed (rarely) when they were at peace. It was the "religious door" of the Roman people and the Roman state. As the door god, Janus was also, appropriately, a god of beginnings, transitions, and even of exclusion. Hence, the month January, the first month, the month of transition, is named after Janus. Janus was conventionally depicted with two faces pointed in opposite directions (going in the door and going out). By extension, someone who was perceived to be "two-faced," duplicitous, or deceptive came to be called a Janus.

The second element students will want to consider—the narrator's revelation that the bowl is a gift from a lover—is significant not only because it provides an emotional background, if you will, for the bowl but also because the narrator so clearly saves this piece of information for last. We feel, whether it is true or not, that this is the piece of the puzzle we've been waiting for.

At some point you might want to get students talking about how Andrea uses the bowl in the first part of the story to manipulate potential real estate buyers. It is one of the "tricks" she uses to "convince a buyer that the house is quite special." It is a deceptive practice, but one we may not think too much about until the word *trick* pops up again near the end of the story (and until we ponder the title). I like to ask the class what is different about the way the word *trick* is used the second time. In the first instance, the real estate tricks are cited simply as common practice, and Andrea is portrayed as one who uses them with exceptional success. In the second instance, such practices appear to have convinced Andrea that she lives in a world where you can't trust anything to be the way it seems—"a world where people set plants where they did not belong, so that visitors touring a house would be fooled into thinking that dark corners got sunlight—a world of tricks." Ironically, her own deceptions have made her profoundly mistrustful of the rest of the world.

In the paragraph immediately following, we discover that Andrea has participated in another kind of deception. Several years earlier she has had an affair—judging from the details, a fairly extended one that must have required her to deceive her husband repeatedly. In leaving Andrea, her lover hopes to "shatter her intransigent ideas about honoring previous commitments." I like to ask students whether they think Andrea has a real commitment left to honor. How close does Andrea seem to her husband? Has she already broken her commitment to him by having the affair? How completely should we trust the lover's assumptions about Andrea? Is she "always too slow to know what she really loved," as he has told her, or does she simply find it hard to love? Is she "two-faced" in the sense of being pulled in two directions, as he seems to think, or is she simply deceptive?

At this point, I like to go back to Andrea's relationship with the bowl and ask the students to characterize it. They usually mention that she says she loves the bowl, that she is obsessed with keeping it safe, that she even compares the experience of leaving it behind for a few minutes to a parent forgetting a child. In the second paragraph after the section break in the middle of the story, Andrea tries to analyze her feelings toward the bowl and becomes confused. I like to ask students what else she expresses confusion about in that paragraph. Someone will always note that she's at least as confused about her marriage ("people who lived together and loved each other . . . [b]ut was that always so clear, always a relationship?") as she is about the bowl. The bowl is always kept empty, and Andrea doesn't let her husband put his keys in it. (If you want to go Freudian at this juncture, I think the story invites it. Empty bowl = empty womb/woman = empty heart/life, and so forth.) If Andrea believes she loves this bowl, then what is her definition of love? (As we've already noted, Andrea is disturbed about this question herself.) What is the difference between loving a person and loving an object?

It may be, as I have suggested in the introduction, that the bowl symbolizes the empty half-life Andrea has without her lover, that she has somehow transferred her love for him to the bowl he gave her, that she cannot talk to her husband about the bowl, not only because her feelings about it are tied up with her former lover but also because her response to the bowl is so complex and mysterious. Andrea, we are told, is attracted to ironies, but her husband grows "more impatient and dismissive when matters [become] many sided or unclear." On the other hand, a less romantic interpretation might be that Andrea is a deceiver—perhaps even a self-deceived deceiver. Incapable of real love, loyalty or commitment, she attracts people (a husband, a lover) as the bowl attracts admirers, but she remains essentially untouched, "smoothly empty," safe and alone.

QUESTIONS FOR DISCUSSION

1. If the bowl is a symbol, what does it symbolize? How many possibilities can you come up with?
2. What is your view of Andrea's marriage? Does the fact the she has had an affair mean that she doesn't value her husband? Why do you think she refuses to choose her lover over her husband?
3. What symbolic significance would you attach to each of the gifts Andrea receives from her lover?
4. How should we interpret the ending of "Janus"?

SUGGESTION FOR WRITING

Analyze the symbolism of the sweatshirt Andrea receives from her lover.

READING/WRITING IDEAS FOR CHAPTER 5

ESSAYS ABOUT SYMBOLS

Quite frankly, I have a little trouble with teaching students to talk and write about symbols, simply because if one reads literary texts actively anything and everything can be a symbol in the sense that it has both literal and figurative significance. Nonetheless, I persist because it's obviously a necessary and useful concept, however much I struggle with it.

Students often come into my classes quite comfortable with writing essays that analyze the symbolism of a particular text, whether by tracing the changing or possible meanings of a single, particular symbol or analyzing how various symbols work together. And these are the two basic symbol-focused essay types that students typically produce and/or are asked to produce.

TROUBLESHOOTING

While some students tend to share my confusion about just what counts as a symbol and what doesn't, by far the most common symbol-related writing problem I've encountered is the tendency to construct essays that don't really come together as unified arguments but instead devolve into lists of symbols or of the various occurrences of a single symbol. Sometimes, the student writer even has trouble making inferences along the way; more often particular inferences are there, and the problem is that there aren't really any big ideas toward which those inferences lead or through which the writer can link together particular inferences. The challenge for me, then, is to help students tie together their various observations, weaving them together into a single argument rather than allowing them to remain a list of "cool observations."

One technique that helps students avoid the "list" problem involves simply talking with them about that problem (either in the abstract or with reference to particular examples) and about the way thesis statements that only identify the symbol, such as "In 'The Yellow Wallpaper,' the wallpaper is an important symbol," can encourage such problems. I then try to point out how much easier it is to create substantive and coherent arguments if one creates thesis statements that are themselves more substantive, indicating not just what the symbol is (or symbols are) or saying something about the symbol(s) being "important" or "interesting" but also indicating why or to what end the author uses the symbol(s) and what the author communicates through it or them. Again, I find a kind of thesis formula along the lines of "The author uses X as a symbol to explore or illustrate or ask Y" very helpful to students, and it is exactly the sort of thesis statement that drives the student essay by Geoffrey Clement included in Chapter 5 of the anthology.

Like Clement's essay, most essays that analyze the changing meanings of a single symbol end up being structured very like the second type of essay described in "Reading/Writing Ideas for Chapter 3" (on character), and you might encourage students writing this type of essay to craft versions of the kinds of topic sentences described there as they plan their essay, since doing so can, again, potentially head off the list problem.

Finally, for reasons I can't be very articulate about, I find that my students tend to write better, more interesting symbol-focused essays when I have them write about stories that are less obviously or relentlessly symbolic, allegorical, or mythic than are "Young Goodman Brown" or "A Hunger Artist." So I tend to use these stories to generate discussion about symbolism and then to ask students to write about other stories in the anthology. While many of the stories included in earlier sections of the anthology work well for that assignment, there are also several especially good ones in the "Reading More Fiction" section, including "The Yellow Wallpaper," "Cathedral," and "Shiloh."

SYMBOL-FOCUSED WRITING EXERCISE

Symbol Hunting and Gathering

When asking students to write symbol-focused essays, I generally have them start by reading the story and simply identifying everything in it that might be said to function as a symbol, underlining each occurrence of each symbol. In giving them the instructions, I remind them of how the Clement essay focuses not on a thing literally present in the text but on a recurring metaphor, and I encourage them to look for these kinds of symbols as well as the more obvious kinds. (And, in fact, I usually ask my students to read the story at least twice, trying to find new symbols each time they read it.)

If the essay assignment asks them to focus on a single symbol, I then ask them to look over their list and choose the symbol they want to focus on, encouraging them to choose the one that seems most puzzling to them at first rather than the one that they think they "get" right away and/or the symbol that they began to see as a symbol only on a second or third reading of the story. Then I ask them to go to work analyzing the symbol, encouraging them to do one of two things, depending on which seems to best fit their story and its symbolism. The first is to break the story down into at least three stages that correspond roughly with the beginning, middle, and end; to make clear, topic-sentence-like statements about what they infer from or about the symbol's meaning and significance at each of these stages; and then to begin crafting a thesis statement that captures the overall significance of the symbol and serves as a kind of "umbrella" for their various inferences. The second is to come up with a series of possible topic-sentence-like claims about just what this symbol might symbolize and to identify the evidence from the story that supports each claim. Essentially, I'm asking students to come up with three or four different answers to the question "What might this thing symbolize?," but I also ask them to conclude the exercise by saying a little about the effects of ambiguity itself, of the fact that the story allows for several different answers. By asking students to decide which of these two approaches best fits the particular text they're working on, I'm trying to emphasize the way in which certain texts—such as "Janus," "A Very Old Man with Enormous Wings," or "Our Friend Judith"—depend on ambiguous, nonallegorical symbols whose figurative significance cannot be easily paraphrased or pinned down. As a result, such texts demand the second approach rather than the first, as my students tend to discover for themselves as they tackle this exercise.

If the essay assignment asks students to focus on multiple symbols, I have students look at their list and choose what they see as the three or four most important, yet least obvious, symbols. I then ask them to generate claims about how each of these symbols works in the story, collecting evidence to support each, and then to develop claims about how the symbols work together, about how a given symbol adds to, or complicates, the meaning of another, etc. Here I emphasize, too, that students need to begin thinking about how they will organize or order the discussions of each symbol in their essays, suggesting that this organization needs to be logical and climatic, that it shouldn't be possible to simply lift out a section of the essay and move it somewhere else. So at this point they need to begin asking themselves, what order will I discuss the symbols in and why does this order work the best, seem the most logical and climactic? And the answers usually have to do with levels of obviousness or complexity and/or with the extent to which the meanings of a given symbol depend on other symbols, etc.

Regardless of the kind of essay or the particular exercise I assign, I devote class time to discussing the exercise. Usually, I break students up into groups for this, encouraging them to be tough on each other in evaluating ideas and essay plans, which means, among other things, generating as many counterarguments and/or counterinterpretations for each writer as they can. When time allows I conclude class by having each student write a paragraph or so summing up the criticisms and counterarguments of their peers and brainstorming about how their essay plan might change to address these. I've found that doing so helps ensure that students truly remember the ideas generated in their groups. Finally (and, again, if time allows) I collect both the exercises and this in-class writing to add my own criticisms, comments, and suggestions before the students begin actually drafting the essays.

6

THEME

Somewhere along the way, many students have gotten the impression that reading literature is a bit like panning for gold. You sift through the work looking for bright glints of meaning. When you find the meaning, the gold at the bottom of the pan, you extract it and tuck it safely away—maybe in a quiz or exam; then you dump the rest of the story or poem out like so much sand into a riverbed and move on. To disabuse students of this notion, it is sometimes helpful to return to a work taken up earlier in the course for a brief discussion of themes. If your class has read "Sonny's Blues," for example, constructing a list of even a half-dozen themes will not be difficult, but the list will probably fail to satisfy everyone as an appropriate distillation of the story's meaning. It shouldn't take much prompting from you—"What important things about 'Sonny's Blues' are missing from this list?" I sometimes ask—for someone to complain that none of the elements that make Baldwin's story so profoundly moving and absorbing is on the list. Other stories that work well for this exercise include "The Country Husband," "Fenstad's Mother," "Our Friend Judith," and "A Pair of Tickets." This approach works best with a story that students like and have responded to on multiple levels.

PLANNING IDEAS

- Assign "A Souvenir of Japan" to be read along with Atwood's "Happy Endings," another story that calls attention to the process of writing fiction and imagining stories.
- Divide the class into four groups. Ask one group of students to bring to class a one-sentence statement of the theme(s) of "Her First Ball." Ask one group to bring in a two-sentence statement, another to bring a three-sentence statement, and the other to bring in a four-sentence statement of theme. Work through the statements, using elements from student contributions, to gradually create a complex statement

of the themes of the story. Then discuss what important aspects of the story are left out. This exercise—like the one suggested in the head-note—can help combat the misconception that a story's theme is simply a one-line moral or message that one extracts from the interaction of characters and events.

- Have students bring to class a one-page description of the souvenirs they imagine the narrator of "A Souvenir of Japan" taking away with her after she leaves the country. Encourage them to think in both concrete and abstract terms.

KATHERINE MANSFIELD

Her First Ball

Like "Young Goodman Brown," this is a rather subtle story that at first appears to be quite simple and obvious. The apparent initiation is rather conventional: time flies, youth is fleeting, or as Leila wonders to herself, "Was this first ball only the beginning of her last ball after all?" Even eighteen-year-old students may respond to the passage of time—remember how long summers were when you were nine?

Neither the story nor Leila stops there, of course. The music starts again, a young man asks her to dance, and she is once more enthralled. Youth may respond to thoughts of the ephemeral nature of our lives, but it is swept up again by living in the moment as if that moment will go on forever.

What seems to be the attitude of the story toward Leila's shaking off serious thoughts? Are we to see her as blithely vacant, incapable of taking the older man's warning to heart? Is she merely young and vibrant—after all, what can be gained by sitting around lamenting that time is passing by? These questions may be interesting in themselves, but they are also interesting in terms of the focus and voice. We see in the story only what Leila sees, and hers are the only inner thoughts we're privy to. Clearly some of the language that is not in quotation marks is nonetheless hers ("Oh, how marvelous to have a brother!" for example). Are there words and expressions that seem not to be hers? What is the effect of keeping the story entirely or almost entirely within her mind, eyes, and range of knowledge and emotions? Does it help us to judge her responses? Does it shift emphasis and attention to some aspect other than the questions about youth and seriousness raised earlier? This might be one of those stories in which all or part may be rewritten from another point of view— say, that of the elderly partner, or a more "omniscient" view.

You might want to use this story also to discuss the possibility of distinguishing the attitudes of the characters and the society from those of the author.

QUESTIONS FOR DISCUSSION

1. Why—some students, particularly some women students, may ask—
   are male initiations usually presented in terms of hunting or sailing
   or journeys or incidents in the "real" or "outside" world, whereas
   female initiations are most often presented in terms of such trivialities
   as dances and other social occasions?
2. Is it the writer, male or female, who is to blame or is this the material
   his or her (sexist) society gives the writer to work with?

JAMES JOYCE

Counterparts

Because it is one of the more vignette-like and enigmatic of the *Dubliners*
stories, "Counterparts" may well prove more difficult for students than
for instructors who come to this story with a sense of typically "Joycian"
themes or issues such as the antagonism between the English and Irish;
the pettiness and monotony of everyday Dublin life; and the role of
Catholicism, especially in terms of the spiritual paralysis induced by
adherence to a moral code that Joyce portrays as rigid and puritanical.
But while they may not know Joyce and may not at first have much
patience with Farrington, I've found that students ultimately get a lot out
of this story, in part because its portrayal of abuse often proves both compelling and highly relevant to them.

One way to begin opening up the story in terms of these issues is to
focus on the title. Though you may want to start with what students
themselves know about the term, another good tactic is to start with the
definition they don't know and then move into more familiar territory.
The definition they probably won't know is the first entry for the term
in *Webster's New Collegiate Dictionary:* "one of two corresponding copies
of a legal instrument: DUPLICATE." Producing such "counterparts" is, of
course, Farrington's job, a mind-numbing task that turns Farrington into
a fairly anonymous, faceless, and largely powerless drone, an idea underscored by the fact that, as Robert Scholes notes in " 'Counterparts' and
the Method of *Dubliners"* (*Dubliners*, New York: Viking Critical Edition,
1968), "[i]n the office scenes we learn Farrington's name through its use
by Mr. Alleyne. But to the narrator—and hence to us—he is just 'the
man.' " As a result, Farrington's overwhelming "thirst" is at once literally
and symbolically meaningful, and what he yearns for is not only the
escape offered by alcohol but also the sense of individual identity and
importance he gains in the pub, even from a narrator who, as Scholes
notes, "for the first time" in the pub scenes gives him "the dignity of
being referred to as 'Farrington.' " In the pub, Farrington also becomes

not a mere copyist, dutifully repeating other men's words, but an author and a narrator of his own tale: "As he walked on [through the pub] he preconsidered the terms in which he would narrate the incident to the boys" (par. 42).

But the other and undoubtedly much more familiar definition of the word *counterparts* comes into play in the way Joyce peoples the story with characters who are themselves symbolic counterparts of, or parallels to, each other (and other characters in *Dubliners*) and with scenes that are counterparts to each other. The two most important parallels—that between Farrington and his wife and that among Farrington, Mr. Alleyne, and the "little boy"—are not fully revealed to us until the very end of the story. As Scholes notes, Farrington and his wife are "well-matched counterparts," not only because she "bullied her husband when he was sober and was bullied by him when he was drunk" (par. 60) but also because she seems to seek "at the chapel" the same thing that Farrington seeks at the pub (par. 66), a parallel underscored by the fact that the narrator refers to a waiter as a "curate" (par. 24). And just as the futility of Farrington's efforts are revealed when his night at the pub merely leaves him "humiliated and discontented" and "not even" "drunk" (par. 57), so the futility of the wife's is suggested by the fact that the "little boy" isn't saved from a beating by invoking the Virgin Mary. (Underscoring that sense of futility is the fact that in other stories Joyce continually highlights the idea that adherence to Catholicism itself helps produce such abusive, unhappy marriages.) At the same time, in taking out his own frustrations on his nameless "little boy," Farrington obviously becomes the counterpart of his own abusive boss, Mr. Alleyne, even as he turns his son into a nameless victim of exactly the sort he has been earlier in the story. In the process, of course, "the man," "the little boy," and the "wife" are made to seem part of an endless, repetitive cycle of violence and brutality, and it is at this point in the discussion that you will probably need or want to entertain students' ideas about just what this story says through Farrington about the nature and causes of both physical abuse and the abuse of alcohol. To what extent or in what specific ways might Joyce's story help us understand, if not sympathize with, the abuser?

Obviously the ultimate namelessness of "the man," "the little boy" and the "wife" universalizes Joyce's portrait of the cycle of abuse, yet "Counterparts" and *Dubliners* as a whole also insist on the particularity of the Irish situation and on the machinery of colonialism that has created it. In this story, we get a glimpse of that machinery through the character of Weathers and through Farrington's brief, enthralled glimpse of the "striking" young woman in the pub (par. 47). As Scholes insists, Weathers represents "an alien London world which challenges and in some sense defeats Dublin," just as Weathers himself adds to Farrington's humiliation and defeat by literally beating him in a game of arm wrestling. The exoticism and appeal of that "alien" world is embodied in the colorful garb and sexually frank gaze of the young woman in the pub, even as the irony of that appeal is made clear to the reader through Joyce's emphasis on the vulgarity of both her dress and her Cockney "London accent" (par. 47). To what extent, then, and in what specific ways, are the problems and questions explored in "Counterparts" specific to Dublin and/or Ireland? To colonized places and peoples (like those also portrayed in Kipling's "Without Benefit of Clergy")? And to what extent and in what specific ways are those problems and questions more universal?

QUESTIONS FOR DISCUSSION

1. What does the story, particularly the characterization of the office, suggest about why Farrington is such an unhappy or frustrated character? What cues do we get that his thirst is symbolic or spiritual as well as physical? What does the pub seem to offer Farrington that his office (and his home) does not?
2. How does the ending of the story and the introduction here of Farrington's wife and son change, qualify, or broaden our view of Farrington?
3. How is our view of Farrington and of his actions informed by the fact that he is referred to only as "the man" in the beginning of the story and again at the end? That his wife remains nameless and his son is referred to as "the boy"?
4. What does the word *counterparts* mean? Who and/or what are "counterparts" in this story? How and why is this a fitting and/or revealing title?
5. How would you articulate the theme(s) of "Counterparts"? To what extent are those themes particularly relevant to the Ireland of Joyce's day? To what extent are these themes "universal"? What exactly does Joyce's story suggest, for example, about the nature and causes of child and/or spousal abuse? Of substance abuse?

ANGELA CARTER

A Souvenir of Japan

Since students are sometimes unsure what to make of this story—another of those about which someone is likely to complain "nothing happens"— I like to open discussion by mentioning the narrator's confidence that she can read her lover's thoughts and that she understands his motivations. Sometimes I introduce the topic directly, asking if students take the narrator's word for what is going on in her lover's mind. Sometimes I simply read paragraph five aloud and ask for reactions. Students who have had romantic relationships, as well as those who haven't, will recognize in the narrator the not uncommon tendency to interpret a loved one's unspoken thoughts. And while sensitivity to another's wishes is laudable, she seems to go overboard. I ask students to consider what circumstances might drive the narrator so thoroughly to supply desires, motivations, and excuses for her lover. Is he uncommunicative? Is she trying to create a story to justify her involvement with him? Is she supplying reasons for his behavior that, while disturbing, are not as disturbing as other possibilities? (For me, these are real questions.)

The narrator of the story is a Caucasian woman who has been involved for at least a year with a Japanese man several years her junior. On the face of it, the relationship seems to offer her very little, so I like to ask students what they think of the relationship as she reports it and why they think she has stayed in it. What is the attraction of her Japanese lover for the narrator?

The lover, as the narrator portrays him, appears to use her only for sex—and that in an apartment she pays for. She says he fancies they have a unique and sublime passion, but he spends much of his time at night away from her, never lets her know if or when he's coming home, and seems to take her out only from a sense of duty. He emerges from her description seeming like a sullen, bored adolescent. The narrator provides no evidence of shared interests or experience, no suggestion that their interactions—sexual or conversational—are especially passionate. In fact, strong undertones of resentment at the beginning of the story become overtones by the end. And yet there is something almost magically obsessive about her attraction to this young man and—again, as she describes it—about his for her.

What *is* the attraction here? If comments are not forthcoming, I like to call attention to the paragraph beginning "Sometimes he seemed to possess a curiously unearthly quality." If part of the attraction of one gender for the other is an attraction to "difference," then perhaps there can be a particular *frisson* of pleasure to be derived from extreme difference—from the exotic, the "other" who is very much of another world. Students, may note that the narrator describes her lover as appearing "almost goblin," seeming like "a weird visitor." And this alien quality is clearly desirable to her, for at the end of her extended physical description of him she says she would like to "have had him embalmed and been able to keep him . . . in a glass coffin." (You may want to pause over this statement and ask students to do a little psychological analysis!)

A friend of mine who has long been married to a man from a culture very different from her own believes that people who are attracted to such unions don't want to get too close to their mates. They are people who value their privacy and who find cultural and linguistic barriers to intimacy reassuring. I tell students what my friend has observed and ask them whether the story provides any support for her theory. Certainly the Japanese lover appears to have little interest in knowing the narrator or being known by her. What about the narrator's desire to know and be known?

As I suggested earlier, the narrator's undertones of dissatisfaction early in the story seem to come to the fore as the story progresses. What complaints are mentioned? Students will notice that the narrator's benign descriptions of Japanese life give way to more critical comments as the story nears its conclusion. I ask them to what degree they believe these dissatisfactions with the country are primarily dissatisfactions with her lover. Can the two be separated? Are the narrator's criticisms of Japanese life fair? (Is it possible to find neutral ground from which a culture can be criticized?)

Depending on the way you are using this story, you may want to wait until late—as I have—to talk about the "writerly" issues that emerge near the end, or you may want to discuss these issues much earlier. Near the conclusion of her narrative the speaker reveals that she has fabricated the name Taro for her lover and made up the story about Momotaro, the peach baby. She also says that she doesn't want to provide "enough well-rounded, spuriously detailed actuality that you are forced to believe in [the story's characters]." She means to offer only "glimpses of outlines." I ask students whether they believe these observations constitute a statement on the way the narrator thinks fiction should operate—or just the way she wants this particular story to operate. If students believe the statements are general ones about the way the narrator thinks fiction should work, I ask them to restate the narrator's view of her role as writer in their own words. Then I ask whether the same statements might also tell us something about the narrator's interactions with others—whether these statements might not also suggest an unwillingness to be known—or to be known only in outline. Or perhaps the narrator means to suggest that—however we wish to write or however well we wish to be known—the reality is that we can be known only in "glimpses of our outlines"—whether we share with our readers and lovers the same gender and culture and language or not.

QUESTIONS FOR DISCUSSION

1. Does it make any difference that the narrator is a woman instead of a man? Is it only a stereotype or does it seem true that women pay more attention to nonverbal signals and are more likely to seek clues from these signals about the thoughts and motives of those close to them? Is the attempt to read another's thoughts a positive or a negative thing?
2. If the narrator is attracted to her lover partially because he is exotic to her, is there also some pleasure for her in being exotic to him? Of being an exotic in the culture? Are there elements of pain involved as well?
3. In talking about gender bias in Japan, the narrator observes, "At least they do not disguise the situation. At least one knows where one is." What do you make of this observation? Does it provide another possible reason for the narrator's attraction to Japan and to her lover?

4. How much of what the narrator says about her lover and his wishes and motivations might also be applied to her?
5. What do you make of the story of the peach baby? Of the narrator's description of the old, senile woman placed outside the shop in her neighborhood each day?
6. What does the title suggest about the future of the narrator's love affair? Does the narrator suggest a reason or reasons she might leave her lover and leave the country?

SUGGESTION FOR WRITING

Compare Carter's handling of the conflicts between people of different cultures in "A Souvenir of Japan" with Mukherjee's in "The Management of Grief," Kipling's in "Without Benefit of Clergy," or Porter's in "Holiday."

READING/WRITING IDEAS FOR CHAPTER 6

ESSAYS ABOUT THEME

Essay assignments that ask students to write about the theme, or a theme, of a given text are very familiar to students, rivaling the character-focused essay in their affections. Thus, with the following provisos in mind, I find that theme-focused assignments tend to encourage truly fine student writing.

TROUBLESHOOTING

Though the concept of theme is obviously crucial to reading and writing about literature, I find that the concept and the word can create several problems for students, particularly when it comes to writing. On the one hand, student writers quite often conflate theme with what we might call a topic or subject, producing theses along the lines of "The theme of 'X' is love or alienation." Such theses often produce boring essays simply because writers avoid saying what a text says about "love" or "alienation" or whatever the noun of choice is or even, quite often, what "love" or "alienation" means. On the other hand, student writers often go to the opposite extreme, conflating theme with something very like "moral," and usually a moral that is little more than a cliché. While such an approach has the advantage of at least forcing student writers to say something more substantive about what a text says, I find that substantive all too often comes to mean simplistic.

To help students avoid both of these problems, I work not only to bring these problems into our discussion of theme but also to discourage students from using the word *theme* in their writing. Instead I encourage them to use the same words I tend to use in the classroom (and in this

Guide), words such as *conflict, issue,* and/or *question,* producing theses such as " 'Kill Day on the Government Wharf' explores the conflict between a 'romantic' desire to live a simple life in harmony with nature and a 'realistic' desire to enjoy all that civilization offers" and " 'Dreams' explores the question of whether there is any such thing as an individual consciousness or point of view." I simply find, in other words, that students' thinking of texts in terms of "conflicts" or "questions" rather than "themes" makes for more complex arguments, arguments that allow for the ways in which texts tend to explore problems rather than offer simplistic solutions. Another technique involves building on, or working from, students' tendency to conflate theme with moral, a technique described under "Theme-Focused Writing Exercises."

Finally, students tend to think of stories as having *a* single theme and to think that writing about theme requires that they discover and focus solely on that biggest of big ideas. In discussions and writing assignments, then, I do everything I can to encourage students to look for multiple themes or at least multiple ways of articulating the same theme. Again, I find that having students focus on issues, questions, or conflicts can help in this regard, because they simply seem more able to adjust to the idea that stories can explore multiple questions or issues simultaneously. And the emphasis on questions and "exploring" discourages easy answers and premature closure. Writing exercise number 2 (below) can also prove helpful in this regard.

THEME-FOCUSED WRITING EXERCISES

1. Identifying and Complicating "Morals"

To work from, rather than against, students' tendency to conflate theme with moral, I sometimes assign them the task of coming up with and bringing to class a moral "tag" or cliché—such as "To thine own self be true" or "Appearances can be deceiving"—that to their mind fits a given story. In class, I have one or two students put their clichés on the board and have the students talk about them one at a time as a class, discussing how they might lay out an argument to support the case for each, what evidence they would use, etc. Often in the process of doing so, students become dissatisfied with the clichés. If so, then I can simply encourage the conversation to move in the direction of complicating the clichés, coming up with evidence that refutes them. If not, I do it myself, simply waiting for an opportune moment to introduce a piece of contradictory evidence.

This technique has the added advantage of modeling a certain kind of essay, in which the thesis might be something along the lines of " 'Young Goodman Brown' examines our belief in the old adage Appearances can be deceiving" and which would proceed by showing, first, why the story seems to fall in line with the cliché and then showing how it complicates the idea conveyed in the cliché, perhaps—in the case of "Young Good-man Brown"—by showing how the story reveals the havoc that comes of seeing appearances as *only* deceiving.

2. Generating Theme-Related Theses

To avoid some of the problems described above when asking students to write about theme, I often assign them the task of coming up with multiple theses (usually three to four), each of which must focus on a distinctly different issue, question, conflict, or theme. Though not terri-bly inventive, this and other thesis-generating exercises I use have been among the most productive for, and helpful to, student writers. Having to come up with multiple theses simply makes them dig deeper and think about the text and their essay from different angles; often they discover that the best essay results not from the first thesis they come up with, but the third or fourth.

Usually I devote a class meeting or part of a class meeting to discussing what they came up with, having a few students put their first and last theses on the board for the class as a whole to discuss and critique. The goal of that discussion is both to help this particular writer pick his or her most promising thesis and improve it by targeting potential problems (either with the thesis itself or with the essay it predicts) *and* to help the class as a whole identify the qualities of a "good" thesis, in this case a good theme-related thesis, and the problems potentially created by cer-tain types of theses.

7

THE WHOLE TEXT

The focus of this chapter is on the whole text—the way the elements of fiction we've been talking about in isolation fit together and make up a whole that is somehow more than the sum of its parts. Each story—"The Secret Sharer," "Love Medicine," and "The Watcher"—is sufficiently complex to reward more than one class period's worth of study, and I generally allow a longer period of discussion than usual for at least one of them. As a departure from my procedure with earlier stories, sometimes I begin discussion by talking about the interplay between certain words or images in a given work—about the network of associations that establish a story's meanings and effects: the references to watching or snooping in "The Watcher" that tie into scenes involving sexuality and/or violence, for example, or the series of anecdotes involving the nexus of love, death, magic, and a "higher power" in "Love Medicine."

PLANNING IDEAS

- "The Secret Sharer," "Love Medicine," and "The Watcher" are placed in the text where they are because any of the three stories would work beautifully as part of a number of different chapters. For example, each would fit nicely into the chapter on initiation that follows. "Love Medicine" would of course work equally well in Chapter 2 on point of view, Chapter 5 on symbols, or Chapter 9 on cultural contexts.
- Since Guy Vanderhaeghe's "The Watcher" has certain affinities with Flannery O'Connor's fiction, pair "The Watcher" with the O'Connor stories for a week-long comparative study, paying particular attention to dramatic irony and the characters' use of key phrases that attain heightened meaning as the stories unfold.
- "Love Medicine" is in one guise a short story, in another part of a novel. All the characters in the story have histories in the novel. You might want to assign the novel and open up a can of worms called

"When Is a Story a Story?" How independent are stories? *Love Medicine* forms one kind of whole of which "Love Medicine" is a part; "The Country Husband" appears in an interrelated volume of stories—not a novel—titled *The Housebreaker of Shady Hill;* and "Counterparts" is itself a part of the *Dubliners* collection. All stories are part of an author's canon. What are the boundaries? This discussion might lead neatly into Chapter 8.

• Before class discussion of "The Secret Sharer," "Love Medicine," or "The Watcher," ask students to locate and then diagram (in whatever way each finds most appropriate) a pattern of images or a series of related statements that they believe are vital to the meaning of the whole text. Have two or three students reproduce their diagrams on the blackboard and explain them. Use these presentations as a starting point for talking about how issues of character, theme, symbol, point of view, etc., interrelate.

JOSEPH CONRAD
_____

The Secret Sharer

Depending on the personality of the class and how closely I believe they've been reading, I sometimes open discussion of "The Secret Sharer" by calling three or four people up to the blackboard to draw the layout of the captain's cabin, his bath, and the saloon. (If, following the arrangement of the text, the class has been reading a number of fairly heavy, serious selections, this can be a way to lighten the mood—even though "The Secret Sharer" itself is not an especially light story. If your class is anything like mine, you will get some amusing blueprints. Once the drawings are complete, you can ask members of the class to critique them, using their texts as guides.) The exercise is not meant to suggest, by the way, that one has to "know" the captain's cabin to understand the story, although certainly knowledge of the cabin arrangement contributes to the narrative suspense. I use it to call attention to Conrad's careful handling of detail and to remind the class how attentively they must read if they are to make sense of this rather long and somewhat difficult story.

In some ways "The Secret Sharer" is an old-fashioned, straightforward narrative, a simple chronology of events told by a veteran ship's captain, who recounts the story of his first voyage in command. His description of setting and character, his recreations of dialogue and thought seem clear, vivid, and meticulous. I sometimes ask my students if they find anything surprising about this. Why might the captain remember this particular journey so clearly and vividly? I also like to ask them if they are surprised that the voice and focus of the story (the seasoned veteran looking back on the adventures of his younger self) impinge on the narrative as little as they do. Don't we expect the older narrator to reveal more about how we should judge the story he's telling us than he does? Why does the narrator do so little of this?

Despite its apparent simplicity and clarity of presentation, "The Secret Sharer" is a complex and morally ambiguous work. Students usually come to class eager, not to draw the layout of the captain's cabin, but to grapple with the moral and psychological issues the story offers. Since I want to channel this eagerness, I start discussion pretty near square one. (I find that the length of the story and the seeming simplicity of the "double" motif sometimes encourages students to read skimmingly and to jump to interpretive conclusions without basing them firmly in evidence.) I like to ask them, harking back to a question posed in the text headnote, if the opening section of the story provides any clues to the nature of the problems that lie ahead for the protagonist. Because I want the class to piece together in some fairly systematic way the details that inform their interpretations, I often write these "clues" on the blackboard as the class comes up with them.

Frequently the first comment they offer is that the setting evokes a sense of stillness, isolation, and profound loneliness. Someone will mention the fact that the narrator is a stranger to the ship—and that he has confessed to being "somewhat of a stranger" to himself. Someone else— often a student familiar with other Conrad works—will remark that the words *mysterious* and *crazy* create anticipatory caution. Generally we also discuss the last sentence of the opening section in which the narrator makes clear that he viewed the voyage as a personal challenge and a test of character. (I sometimes mention the opening of *David Copperfield* and use the stated focus of David's narrative—"Whether I shall turn out to be the hero of my own life, or whether that station will be held by anybody else"—as a point of comparison.) If it doesn't come up in discussion, I also call attention to the fact that the narrator seems to feel that everyone is watching and judging him: his new officers, even the stars in the sky. (After we've completed our list, I ask students to check their assumptions against the rest of the narrative to confirm that the intimations of the opening are borne out in the rest of the story.) Then, keeping in mind the aspects of the narrator's situation listed before us, we're ready to tackle the secret sharer and his mysterious influence over the narrator.

I find that using the list on the blackboard, we can move pretty swiftly through the more obvious aspects of the story, outlining the similarities between the captain and his secret guest (size, age, training, sense of etiquette, position as strangers aboard their respective ships . . .), the aspects of the captain's situation that prompt him to identify with Leggatt and hide him (his loneliness, his lack of self-confidence, his lack of leadership experience . . .), and the consequences of the captain's "decision" to hide Leggatt (profound uneasiness, the sense of having a divided self, questioning his own sanity . . .). Then I ask the class what effect Leggatt's visit has on the captain. Does the experience leave him a better or worse captain? A better or worse man?

In terms of the action of the story, the narrator is successful, a hero. He pulls off the trick of hiding Leggatt until he gets the fugitive close enough to shore to swim safely away from the ship (no mean feat), and he executes a dangerous maneuver the crew did not believe he could complete without wrecking the ship, thereby proving his skill. In terms of pure narrative, the story reaches a satisfying closure. Leggatt is not recaptured by the captain of the *Sephora* or discovered by the crew of the ship where he hides. He escapes to the life he has chosen, and the captain sails on with his ship, having gained confidence in his ability to command it. I like to ask the class if the ending answers all their questions about the action of the story. Then I ask if the ending answers all their questions about the meaning of the story and the story's moral perspective. In some sense the captain has passed his test, but we are still left wondering whether he has lived up to the "ideal conception" of himself mentioned in the opening section. In fact, we are also left wondering what his ideal conception was. The narrator never tells us, so that the story resists moral closure, even if in some ways it reaches a satisfactory conclusion on other levels.

You may want to ask your students how Conrad injects this element of moral ambiguity into the story. A number of answers may surface. The nature of Leggatt's crime is one area of ambiguity. You might ask students to prepare a defense for him, imagining him brought before, as he says, "an old fellow in a wig and twelve respectable tradesmen." While it is clear Leggatt strangled a man on board the *Sephora*, one could argue that the circumstances mitigated the crime. After all, if what Leggatt reported was true, his rapid, instinctive action saved the *Sephora* when her captain was too frightened to give orders. The man he killed ignored naval discipline during a horrific storm; and when Leggatt (his superior officer) struck him down, out of the way, the man jumped up and made it a fight. (You may want to call attention to how often Leggatt is associated with instinctive, almost animal action. For example, he says if the *Sephora's* crew had tried to haul him back "Somebody would have got killed for certain" and he "did not want any of that"; but his comment makes clear he'd have killed again, however much he might have regretted it. He is, figuratively, the body; the young captain, the head.)

Another troubling aspect of the story is the young captain's almost immediate willingness to side with Leggatt—not only to see the crime his way but also to act as if he understood and sympathized with Leggatt's action before he's spent even an hour with the man or heard his version of the story (" 'Fit of temper,' I suggested confidently"). We can understand from a psychological perspective why the young captain allies himself with the stranger. You may want to ask your students whether it is appropriate or right that he does so.

Closely linked with this question is the issue of the captain's responsibility as the leader of a ship. Once the captain of the *Sephora* comes aboard and is allowed to leave without Leggatt, the narrator commits himself to keeping Leggatt hidden and helping him to escape. Clearly the strain of this commitment drives him nearly crazy. I like to suggest to the class that he is torn between his duty to his crew and his impulse to help Leggatt. I like to suggest this and then hope that someone will argue with me because it seems that another disturbing thing about the captain's story is that he's not consciously torn between two loyalties. He simply identifies and sides with Leggatt as a matter of course. Just before he helps Leggatt escape, he realizes helping him may end his own career. Just after he maneuvers the ship near land, he realizes he doesn't know the ship well enough to ensure they can avoid shipwreck. But these are not issues he ponders. He seems willing to sacrifice himself and his crew to get Leggatt, not just within swimming distance of land, but as close as possible.

QUESTIONS FOR DISCUSSION

1. To what do you attribute the narrator's successes at the end of the story? Skill? Luck? The "righteousness" of his cause? To what does the narrator attribute his success?
2. Does Conrad point to a moral in this story? If so, what is it?

LOUISE ERDRICH

Love Medicine

It is virtually impossible to talk about this story without discussing its narrator, Lipsha Morrissey; so I like to start by asking the class to characterize him. To the traits mentioned in the text—his kind heart, lack of education, thoughtfulness, naïveté, unintentional wisdom, etc.—which will come up immediately, you might ask students to add what they know of Lipsha's biography. According to Grandma Kashpaw, Lipsha's mother didn't want him, and so he's an orphan of sorts, a "took-in" like some of the other children Grandma and Grandpa Kashpaw have reared. Lipsha is at least part Chippewa; in his middle to late teens (having flunked out of school previous to the time of the narrative); and up until the time of the story, he appears to have spent many of his days playing video machines, killing time ("the thing I been training for all my life . . . is to wait"), and occasionally putting "the touch" on people.

"Love Medicine" sometimes confuses students because it seems to mix serious topics and comic topics indiscriminately and because Lipsha's voice ensures that no somber subject will come across to us entirely straight. In talking about Lipsha's "voice," you might want to ask students how many malapropisms, solecisms, and colorful colloquialisms they can come up with. At what points in the story does Lipsha's unintentionally humorous language undercut the seriousness of a scene he's trying to convey soberly? (My favorite example is when he mournfully commands his grandfather's ghost to "Go back" beyond the "wall of death," then whispers, "Look up Aunt June.") Does Lipsha's comic narrative prevent us from taking the story seriously? If not, why not?

Lipsha says that his grandfather told him he'd been "chosen" for his second childhood and "couldn't say no." I like to ask my students to respond to this statement. Does Grandpa really have any control over his increasing senility? Why might he say such a thing to Lipsha? You may want to ask what kind of world we have entered when a statement like Grandpa's is reported uncritically. (Lipsha believes Grandpa made the choice. He only questions briefly whether Grandpa knew what he was doing by saying yes to the "call.") It may be well to take a few minutes to discuss the cultural and social milieu of Lipsha, Grandma, Grandpa, Lulu Lamartine, and the others: their mixture of tribal belief, Catholicism, and superstition; their poverty; their history of hardship; and their lack of education.

And yet "Love Medicine" isn't really a story about oppression or failure, though both topics surface. Despite poverty, alcoholism, exploitation by whites, and the decimation of their tribe through white disease ("outfight germ warfare"), some of Chippewa blood have endured and succeeded. Many of the children the Kashpaws have reared—blood kin and took-ins—return from the funeral to jobs that are "numerous and impressive."

"Love Medicine" is a story about love and grief and death and magic and searching for "Higher Power." Many of the anecdotes of the story (Lulu's experience with the parakeet, Grandma's prediction about the car wreck, the story of Wristwatch) and the central story of Lipsha's efforts to create a love medicine are narratives about love (or sex) and death. I like to call students' attention to the many spiritual references that accrete in the course of the story—the anecdote about Grandpa yelling his prayers because he believes God is going deaf, Lipsha's references to reading the Bible, his attempt to have the turkey hearts blessed, his inadvertent reference to the "paraclete" instead of the parakeet. I ask them why these stories are part of the narrative, what they contribute to the theme. All suggest the human need for some sort of help and the search for some sort of consolation with which to confront the hardships of life and the mysteries of death.

Lipsha tries to cure Grandma's grief by concocting a "love medicine" that will bring her straying husband back to her side. This may be the time to ask your students to talk about the other ways the title can be interpreted. Whether or not tribal magic is effective, whether or not God listens, in this story of the Higher Power, the one thing one can count on is love. Love, embodied in the Kashpaws, rears a family of children, all of whom are "wanted," whoever or wherever some of their parents may be. Love draws these grown children back from their numerous and impressive careers to mourn the passing of Grandpa. (As Lipsha suggests, their common grief—an expression of their common love—gives them a "rock" or anchor in time of trouble.) Love, in the shape of Lipsha, tries, however ineptly, to cure Grandpa's waywardness. And love, through Lipsha, comforts Grandma when Grandpa dies.

Near the end of the story, Lipsha observes, "Your life feels different on you, once you greet death and understand your heart's position." You might want to ask your students what Lipsha means—and what love and death have to do with one another in this story. You might also want to ask what they think Lipsha is suggesting when he says of his life, "you have the feeling someone wore it before you and someone will after."

Whether or not we're supposed to believe in the magical/mystical things that Lipsha believes in (and I think Erdrich leaves this issue open), what are we to make of the conclusion to the story? After Grandma listens to Lipsha's confession, she puts her rosary beads inside his hand and clasps her hands tightly around his. It is clearly a gesture of love; it may also be a gesture of blessing. When she releases his hand, he goes outside to do what his grandfather used to do—weed dandelions. There, feeling the sun on his back like a "hand," the "touch" seems to come back to him, and instead of healing others, it seems to heal him. (If the "touch" is magical, it is also the touch of love and concern. No wonder those Lipsha treats feel better.) As he pulls up the weeds he observes, "with every root I prized up there was return." What does he mean by this? One answer is that he realizes the seeds of the dandelions will ensure their "return" in a season—that the life of even the uprooted dandelions will go on. Another answer might be that in some sense his grandpa's life/love continues through him because all loving life is, like the globe of seeds, "frail" but "indestructible." These suggestions by no means exhaust the possibilities of the conclusion. I find that students are eager to discuss other parallels between Lipsha's life and the way he describes the dandelions.

QUESTIONS FOR DISCUSSION

1. What does Lipsha mean when he observes at the funeral "how strong and reliable grief was, and death"? What does he mean when he says "death would be our rock"?
2. How do you think we are to respond to the magical/mystical aspects of Erdrich's story? How are they part of the story? Does Erdrich expect us to believe that Lipsha has a healing touch? That Grandma can predict the future?
3. Is this a comic story or a tragic one? Explain your answer.
4. Why do you think Erdrich chooses to tell this story through Lipsha? How might it be different if it were told from another perspective? Through another character?

SUGGESTIONS FOR WRITING

1. Read Erdrich's book *Love Medicine*, of which the story "Love Medicine" is only a chapter. Write an analytical essay in which you show how "Love Medicine" works differently or has different meanings as a short story and as part of the larger book.
2. Write an essay comparing the ways ritual, religion, and magic (and love?) are portrayed in "Love Medicine" and Kipling's "Without Benefit of Clergy."

GUY VANDERHAEGHE

The Watcher

"The Watcher" is, among other things, an initiation story. As is true of most initiations, the one Charlie goes through the summer he is eleven reveals the world to be a nastier and harsher place than it had been for him theretofore. A good place to start discussion is with Charlie's voice. I might ask students to what degree the language and attitude of the narrator are a re-creation of the language and attitudes of the eleven-year-old Charlie—and to what degree they are a reflection of the older and wiser Charlie of years later. Charlie is a character with whom many students are reluctant to sympathize. "He's a peeping Tom," they say. "He's spoiled." "He doesn't care about anyone but himself." In a story as long as this one, students may lose track of some elements, so in response to the criticism of Charlie that usually arises, I like to call their attention to a couple of passages that indicate that the older Charlie recognizes some of the weaknesses of his younger self. (One occurs in the section of the story shortly after he arrives at the farm, with the paragraph beginning "Most days it was so hot that the very idea of fun boiled out of me and evaporated." Another occurs near the end of the story, when the narrator explains his unwillingness to identify the Ogden brothers on Thompson's behalf in the paragraph beginning "He had no business begging me.")

Once we've established who Charlie is and from which perspective the story is being told, we can begin looking at what happens to him during his eleventh summer. While Charlie's father tries to make the prospect of a summer with his grandmother seem enticing, the reality is not very appealing. The farm turns out to be a ramshackle operation with not one hoped-for dog or pony but only a few chickens and a nervous rooster. His father's car hasn't yet faded from view when Grandma lets Charlie know she's willing to "belt" him if he misbehaves. His grandmother's profanity, her disrespect for his mother, and her apparent lack of concern for his comfort and entertainment are all a shock. Until recently, Charlie has been a much-favored mama's boy. But Charlie's real initiation doesn't begin until Aunt Evelyn and her boyfriend, Thompson, show up.

Most of the important threads of the story after this arrival are revealed in a series of observation or "snooping" scenes. It may be helpful for students to make a list of the various things Charlie sees and hears that he is not supposed to know about. Working from this list, students will be able to identify some common threads in each of the scenes and recognize that all of them involve a sex/violence/power nexus of some sort. By snooping, Charlie learns that his aunt, according to her mother, has "elevator panties." Charlie also witnesses Thompson's abuse of Aunt Evelyn while he's following the two on a walk. Awakening in the night to loud sounds that he mistakes for sounds of violence, Charlie goes to his aunt's room and sees Thompson and Aunt Evelyn making love.

After discussing these scenes, I like to turn to the passage in which Charlie kills the rooster and ask students to explain why he does so. Some will mention the dreadful heat that clearly works on everyone's nerves that day. Others will mention how bored Charlie is and how frustrated that the rooster is afraid of him and will not act like a pet. If all goes well, prior discussion of the snooping scenes will enable students to recognize Thompson's influence on Charlie—despite the fact that Charlie "has his number" in most respects—and the sense in which Charlie's experiences on the farm have prepared him to kill the rooster.

Charlie is a self-acknowledged "watcher"—an observer more than a doer. I like to ask students why the narrator, the older Charlie, is so adamant about labeling himself in this way. It is true that Charlie's only real action in the story is the killing of the rooster. His other significant action—his refusal to identify Thompson's assailants—is really only a passive denial. Perhaps one purpose of the story is for the narrator to explain—to his audience and to himself—why he killed the rooster and why he lied about Thompson's attackers. It may be that the summer he spent with his grandmother has changed him in ways that he is still struggling to understand.

QUESTIONS FOR DISCUSSION

1. Does the older narrator ever revise Charlie's initial harsh judgment of his father?
2. Do you like the young Charlie or the older narrator by the end of the story? Why or why not? Do you sympathize with either?
3. Why does Charlie kill Stanley the rooster? What feelings and experiences have led up to this act? It is a violent act. Is it in any way a sexual act?
4. In the end, the grandmother resorts to violence to get Thompson out of the house and away from Evelyn. Is the grandmother justified? Do you think Thompson has, in some sense, corrupted her—tempted her to sink to his level—or does her hiring of the Ogden brothers simply show that she is more than a match for Thompson in the end?

5. Were you surprised when Charlie refused to testify for Thompson? Why does he say he does so? Why do *you* say he does so?

6. Thompson has a goatee like a stereotypical portrait of the devil. Is there some sense in which he tempts people at the farm to do evil? (Is he *really* a "goddamn freak," as the grandmother calls him?) Do you think Thompson believes in evil? In sin? What role does Thompson's interest in psychoanalysis play in the story?

7. What is your characterization of Evelyn? What part does she play in the summer's events? To what degree, if any, is she responsible for her own troubles? For Thompson's beating?

8. What do you think Charlie learned during his summer at the farm?

SUGGESTIONS FOR WRITING

1. Write a personal essay about someone who has had an influence on you but about whose influence you have had doubts.

2. Do some library research on Allen Ginsberg, the Beat Generation, and the word *beatnik*. Then write an essay arguing whether it was silly for Grandma to call Robert Thompson a "beatnik" or not.

READING/WRITING IDEAS FOR CHAPTER 7

ESSAYS ON THE WHOLE TEXT

Whereas earlier chapters of the anthology provide great opportunities to focus student writers on element-specific types of essays and to thereby expand their repertoire of readerly and writerly techniques and strategies, I find that this chapter is very useful for helping my students to develop strategies for dealing with open-ended essay assignments of the type often assigned in upper-division courses. As a result, my whole-text essay assignment often asks students to choose the text that they want to write about (from this chapter or from the anthology as a whole) and to develop their own topic from scratch. I use the writing exercises to help them develop strategies for developing the kinds of questions that lead to effective topics and theses and to help the class as a whole focus on general writing issues that aren't dealt with in the kind of element-specific exercises described in earlier chapters. (For obvious reasons, however, there is some overlap between the exercise assignments for this essay and those described in earlier chapters.)

Often, I add an additional requirement, asking that somewhere and somehow in their essay each student address at least three of the elements that we've covered and preferably address all of them: an essay on "Janus" that primarily focuses on the symbolism of the bowl, for example, would also need to consider how the bowl functions in the characterization of Andrea, how the bowl functions as part of the conflict or theme of the story, and how the reader's view of character, theme, and symbol is affected by the use of a third-person point of view and by the plot structure.

TROUBLESHOOTING

Some of my students are intimidated by open-ended assignments, but frankly it's precisely because they're intimidated and because the assignment is so common that I feel students need to learn strategies for coping with it. And many of my students have the opposite response, reveling in the freedom to write about exactly what they want.

On occasion, I find that whether intimidated or not students have a tendency to return to what is most familiar in tackling such assignments, half-forgetting everything we've done since they came into the class and writing the kinds of essays they wrote before taking my course. On the one hand, that tendency is natural for all of us; and many students produce good writing when they write from their strengths and from within their "comfort zones," as it were, while doing so in the context of a composition-focused class allows them to build on those areas of strength. On the other hand, returning to the same kind of essay they've always written can also be counterproductive for many students. That's why I organize the exercises for this assignment so that they both help students cope with the open-ended assignment and require that they do so by at least considering the full range of options available to them.

WHOLE-TEXT WRITING EXERCISES

When giving students an open-ended assignment, I usually start by describing the assignment and then encouraging questions and discussion about it. If the question of how to pick a text doesn't come up, then I introduce it. Invariably my students will argue that you should write about a text you "like," and I try to push them to explain exactly what this means, why and in what way "liking" the story makes for a more effective essay and why not liking a story might itself be productive. Though I encourage students to seriously consider writing about stories that puzzle or challenge them in some way rather than stories that they "get" right away, my main goal here is to simply get students thinking about the costs and benefits involved in such choices: if you choose a story you immediately like and get, what might your challenges be in trying to write effectively about it? If you choose a story you don't like or get immediately, what might your writerly challenges be?

After that, I simply let them have at it and (depending on the class) either have them begin working on the exercises outlined below or start off with one or two of the more basic exercises described in earlier chapters (such as the plot summary exercise described in Chapter 1). In the case of several of these exercises, I reproduce here the actual text of my assignments rather than descriptions of them. As some of the assignments make clear, I devote class time to each exercise after the students have completed it, having the whole class discuss thesis types with reference to particular students' theses the day after they've done exercise 1, having the class break up into small groups to discuss counterarguments, etc.

1. Formulating Theses

Below, I describe four types of theses common to literary-critical or analytical essays, and I give you one or two examples of each type. Your assignment is to craft at least one thesis of each type that you might use as the basis for your essay.

A. As we've seen, one genre of literary essay focuses on **character**. One could, for example, make an argument about the development of a particular character, or one could, to take another example, make an argument comparing two or more characters and showing how a central conflict in the text is embodied in the differences and direct conflict between those two characters.

Example:
Though David Leavitt's "Family Dancing" is primarily, as its title suggests, about the way in which family members "dance" both with and around each other, it also explores the ways in which these and all human interactions are shaped by gender. Leavitt explores this issue by focusing on three female characters of three different generations, each of whom seems to represent a different notion of women's roles. From the old-fashioned Pearl to the confused Suzanne to the defiantly feminist Lynette, these three characters seem to each embody a step in the historical process of women's liberation. Since the seemingly liberated Lynette is ultimately portrayed as no happier than the old-fashioned Pearl, however, Leavitt's story ultimately refuses to allow us to see the process of liberation as straightforward and simple, instead drawing our attention to the problems *and* possibilities entailed in each generational type of female role.

B. As we've seen, one genre of literary essay focuses directly on **a central theme or conflict.** Such an essay would have a thesis that made a claim about the, or a, central theme or conflict in the text. While great essays can be written about theme, don't forget the potential problems with theme-focused essays that we discussed earlier.

Example:
Kate Chopin's "The Story of an Hour" explores the conflict between a woman's desire to be loved and taken care of by a man and her desire for independence.

C. Yet another genre of literary essay focuses on posing and exploring possible answers to **a difficult question** about a literary text. Such a question can focus on a particular action (Why does character X do such and such?) or about theme (Is the author saying this or this?) or about character, etc. As the second example below demonstrates, a question essay can offer an answer or answers to the question and/ or it can explore the effect of ambiguity itself, the significance of the fact that the question *isn't* really answerable. Just remember that even if your essay will ultimately answer your question, you can argue effectively that this answer is right only if you explore other potential answers along the way.

Examples:

1. In portraying a family torn apart by divorce, Leavitt's "Family Dancing" would at first glance seem to be an exploration of a dysfunctional family and of a society in which the intact nuclear family has become the exception rather than the rule. Such a reading would suggest that what Leavitt ultimately offers the reader is a defense of the traditional nuclear family or a lament for its disappearance. On a second reading, however, the story and its attitude toward the family doesn't seem that simple, especially since it's not at all obvious that the story encourages the reader to wish that Herb and Lynette hadn't gotten divorced. To what extent, then, is Leavitt's story really about the problems entailed in the breakup of the traditional nuclear family and to what extent is it about the problems entailed in the breakup of the traditional nuclear family and a what extent is it about the problems inherent to the nuclear family?

2. Early in David Leavitt's "Family Dancing," Lynette recalls what is obviously a fond memory of her father pushing her on a swing. At the very end of the story, however, Lynette recalls the same memory in much less fond or idyllic terms. What, then, is the truth about Lynette's relationship with her father, both in the past and in the present? And what might be the point or significance of our not knowing the truth?

   D. Among the many, many other types of essays about literature and one that is sometimes very like type C is one in which one shows why some **detail or element in a text that seems insignificant** is, in fact, of crucial importance. One might, for example, focus on a particular, seemingly minor character, a particular word or phrase, a particular action or moment in the text, a detail of setting or any other element.

Examples:

1. David Leavitt's "Family Dancing" focuses primarily on the interactions of three generations of a single, divorced family, and most of the characters are either family members—Suzanne, her husband, her ex-husband (Herb), her son (Seth), her daughter (Lynette), and her mother (Pearl)—or "significant others"—Herb's new girlfriend, for example. Interestingly enough, however, there is one character who is neither of those things and whose role seems puzzling—Lynette's friend John. The fact that John is the only character of this type featured suggests, however, that he is much more important to the story than we might at first guess. What, then, is John's role in the story?

2. David Leavitt's "Family Dancing" is primarily, as its title suggests, about the way in which family members "dance" both with and around each other, yet throughout the story there are continual references both to food and to the weight of the various characters, particularly Suzanne and her daughter, Lynette. Though a seemingly minor detail, such references are, in fact, crucial to the story because they are one of the ways in which Leavitt explores the issue of appearances and perception, posing questions not only about our perceptions of ourselves but also about the complex ways in which our self-perception is shaped by our perceptions of how others perceive us.

2. Gathering Evidence

Once you've developed a thesis, the next step is to gather the facts you will use to support and develop that thesis in the body of the essay.

   In class, we will talk about the various kinds of facts in and about a literary text that one can use as evidence. To prepare for that discussion, you should re-read the student essays in your anthology. As you do so, highlight or underline the facts that the writers refer to, whether those facts are taken from the text or are about the text or the author. Which facts are used as evidence? What *kinds* of facts are used as evidence here? What other kinds of facts might one use as evidence in a literary-critical essay? What specific techniques do these writers use to gracefully incorporate facts into the essay?

Facts alone are simply facts; they aren't evidence for anything. To turn a fact into evidence, then, you have to both present the fact itself to readers and tell readers what you infer from the fact, showing them how and why it is evidence for your idea. Usually, every paragraph in the body of an essay should begin by articulating a particular subidea, and everything "inside" the paragraph should be either an inference or a fact that contributes directly to supporting and developing that idea. Look at the student essay again; this time, mark the ideas and the inferences. What specific techniques does the writer use to turn facts into evidence for particular ideas, to link facts directly to inferences? Are there moments in the essay when the use of evidence seems weak? Is it because there aren't enough facts? Because there aren't enough inferences? Because the two aren't linked clearly?

Now that you've closely examined the way another student writer presents facts and turns them into evidence, it's time to begin the work of gathering facts for your own essay. Doing so will require that you decide on your thesis. Remembering what we discussed about the function of literary-critical essays (for authors and for readers), which of the theses you formulated in the last class or came up with since then seems to you to promise the most interesting and effective essay both for you and for your readers? Type that thesis out; then look back over your story with that thesis in mind. Underneath your thesis, make a list of the facts from and about the text that you think will be most necessary to supporting and developing that thesis. That list should include at least one or two passages from the novel. Beside each fact (including passages), brainstorm about that fact, paying attention to diction, syntax, etc., and about the ways you might use it in your essay. What idea might this fact be good evidence for? What are the inferences that make it evidence?

I find it useful when possible to spread this exercise across two days, first having students concentrate on the use of evidence in general and then on the use of evidence in this particular essay. Sometimes I've found it useful to handle the former discussion by breaking the class up into groups, each group being assigned a particular student essay to concentrate on; being asked to generate lists of kinds of evidence, of techniques for using evidence effectively, and of problems with the use of evidence; and being asked to illustrate their points with examples from their essay. At the end of class, we discuss what they've come up with, and I collect their lists and examples, compiling them to make up a handout on the use of evidence that they can all use in crafting this and future essays.

3. Identifying Counterevidence and Imagining Counterarguments

Since you don't want to oversimplify the literary text to make your argument persuasive, to make your argument overly simplistic, or to undermine your credibility with your reader, you always want to consider possible objections to your argument, counterarguments, alternative interpretations, etc.

One way to do that is to look for evidence that seems to contradict or at least complicate your initial thesis. So, come up with one or two facts from your story that might seem to contradict your thesis, that suggest a different answer to your question, etc. Comment briefly on how you might use the fact or facts as evidence in your essay: How might you interpret this fact in a way that shows that it does not, ultimately, contradict your thesis? Conversely, how might you use this fact to build on and complicate your argument?

Another way to accomplish the same goal is to imagine that you are a defense attorney preparing for an upcoming trial in which you will have to persuade a jury to accept your interpretation of your story. To prepare your case effectively, you're going to have to imagine the counterarguments that the prosecutor might come up with to undermine your argument. What's the prosecutor's most powerful argument? How will you defend your argument against that possible counterargument in your essay? If the counterargument is more persuasive than your own argument, how does your argument need to change?

4. Critiquing Body Paragraphs

I've found that a good way to follow-up on the evidence/inference discussion generated by exercise 2 (and to make draft day productive) is to have each student exchange drafts with a colleague. I then ask each student to turn to page 3 of the draft and carefully read the first full paragraph on that page, identifying the main idea or topic sentence, each fact, and each inference. I then ask them to look over their markings to evaluate the paragraph, discussing their evaluation with the writer. Do all the facts and inferences here relate to, and help support, the main idea? Are there enough facts to support the main idea? Are the inferences ample and clear enough to show exactly how particular facts support the idea?

As with other small-group work, I conclude class by bringing everyone back together to discuss what they've learned, and I frankly never cease to be amazed at how productive this exercise always turns out to be. Sometimes, students discover that they really don't understand the concepts well enough to distinguish ideas, facts, and inferences, giving us the opportunity to discuss and clarify. More often, students discover that they can identify them just fine, and what surprises them are the problems they discover in their writing by doing so: paragraphs that don't have clear main ideas or stray from them, paragraphs that consist almost entirely of facts or of inferences, etc.

Exploring Contexts

8

THE AUTHOR'S WORK AS CONTEXT: D. H. LAWRENCE AND FLANNERY O'CONNOR

While this text is designed to introduce students to a number of different writers and a variety of ways of looking at the world and responding to it, this chapter narrows our focus to two authors and offers an opportunity to explore in some depth the unique vision of each. Three stories by D. H. Lawrence and three stories by Flannery O'Connor provide the basis for such discussion, and passages from the writers' essays and letters at the end of the stories offer insights into their ideas about life and art. Teachers may chose to teach both authors and all six stories as a way of introducing students to the uniqueness of a writer's vision by way of comparison. (A D. H. Lawrence story is emphatically *not* a Flannery O'Connor story, and students who study the stories of each offered here will readily see this.) Teachers who prefer to focus on one of the two authors exclusively may want to add a novel or short story collection to their syllabus and spend more time fitting these stories into the larger context of the author's oeuvre.

PLANNING IDEAS

- Assign Lawrence's *Sons and Lovers, Women in Love,* or *Lady Chatterley's Lover* or O'Connor's *Wise Blood* to be studied in conjunction with the stories or to serve as the subjects of analytical essays that students work on independently.
- Assign Lawrence's "The Blind Man" in conjunction with Raymond Carver's "Cathedral," using a comparison of the two stories to bring out ideas about the uniquely "Lawrentian" qualities of "The Blind Man." Or assign Faulkner's "Barn Burning" or "A Rose for Emily" in conjunction with the O'Connor stories to help students get a vivid sense of what's unique about O'Connor's vision of the South.

D. H. LAWRENCE

Odour of Chrysanthemums

In my experience students like this story a great deal, though they find it, and properly so, strangely moving and even disturbing. They have a tendency—confirmed, alas, by many critics—to insulate themselves from the applicability of the story to their own lives by overparticularizing the situation, that is, by attributing the isolation of Mrs. Bates from her husband only to the infelicity of that particular marriage. Though this may be true to a degree—inferring the reasons for the unhappiness of the marriage can be an interesting classroom exercise—it seems to me the implications are broader than that, and that's what makes the story greater and more disturbing: Lawrence may well be suggesting that we are all ultimately alone, separate even from our loved ones. This may not be a very startling or original truth, but it is given great impact in the story. Moreover, he seems to infer something about proper behavior from that truth: the recognition of our separateness, our individuality, should prevent us from defining for others their role in relation to ourselves—if they, whether spouse or child, are other, they must be free. This does not mean, of course, that there cannot be love and relationship, but rather that it is relationship between free, independent selves. (See the quotations from *Women in Love* included in the discussion of "The Blind Man," below.) We're all willing to accept this freedom for ourselves, but it gets a little sticky when our parents or children, husband, wife, girlfriend or boyfriend want to stand alone. (Students may want to push this to mean only sexual freedom, but the Lawrence story clearly involves fuller kinds of ultimate integrity.) That, and the loneliness of separateness, might be what some readers find disturbing here.

But who's Lawrence to say? It is true that he won't let us disengage ourselves from his fiction very readily, that we have a hard time talking about Lawrence stories in terms of focus or symbol or structure, but why should we pay any more attention to him than we do to Ann Landers, say? It is here that Lawrence's power of observation, particularly of natural detail, and his ability to describe that detail in words count. His presentation and control of sensory detail convince us he knows what he's talking about, and if he knows what he's talking about when it comes to trains and flowers, the reader tends to feel that he's more likely to know what he's talking about when it comes to love and marriage. That's why it might be useful to tell the class about how Lawrence was "discovered," especially since the anecdote involves the opening of "Odour."

Before World War I, a young woman sent to Ford Madox Ford, then editor of the *English Review*, three poems and a short story written by a schoolmaster friend of hers, the then-unknown D. H. Lawrence. Ford's comments are reprinted in the anthology.

It should be mentioned that the final paragraph in the story as Ford read it was later replaced, by Lawrence, with a new conclusion (the final seven paragraphs in our version). That paragraph puts Elizabeth in a less favorable light than the final version seems to: originally she seemed to have preferred her husband dead—dead, beautiful, helpless, like a baby. She can then possess him, have power over him. (Some living men want to regress, Lawrence says elsewhere—Gerald Crich in *Women in Love* and the paralyzed Sir Clifford in *Lady Chatterley's Lover*, for example—and certain kinds of women, or certain "lesser" drives in all women, want men to regress, just as there are comparable men or drives within all men that would reduce women to objects or slaves. Again, see the discussion of "The Blind Man," below, for more on this.)

I've always had trouble with the final sentence of the story, for I'm just not sure what it says or implies. Elizabeth tidies up the room because she submits to the necessities of living, of everyday life; she winces or shrinks from death, the idea of her own death, with fear. But why shame? The "and" makes it difficult to read this as shame of the fear of death. Perhaps, though, the sentence says that death is her ultimate master. It is not primarily or immediately the thought of her own death that she winces from in fear and shame, but the whole concept of death, even the death of another. Or she might be ashamed of the fact that another's death, particularly that of her husband, is really a convenience to her and that she feels something like relief.

Some instructors, in courses in which novels are assigned in addition to short fiction, will want to read *Sons and Lovers*, and of course the relationship between the Morels in that novel is quite close to that of the Bateses here (as well as, apparently, quite close to that of Lawrence's parents—see some of the excerpts from Lawrence's nonfiction in the anthology). In the novel, Mrs. Morel dies before her husband, though he is injured more than once in mine accidents. To read the story in the light of the novel or vice versa raises an issue: is the author's canon cross-referential or interdependent (with or without regard to time of composition, development, etc.)? I do not think there are right or wrong answers to this question, though I think all critics, teachers, and students ought to face the question, answer it for themselves, and make the answer clear. So I'll start: I think there is a story called "Odour of Chrysanthemums" that exists in approximate isolation, separated from Lawrence and all his works (but not, of course, from the English tradition—thus "approximate"), just as a frieze can exist as a work of art separate from its building, a song from its play, a short story like "A Pair of Tickets" outside its context in *The Joy Luck Club*. Perhaps the first stage of reading should or must be to see works as free-standing forms, as isolated on the page. But whether you want to or not, you cannot read Lawrence or "Odour" for the first time twice, and once you read *Sons and Lovers*, you cannot read "Odour" as if you have not read it. Works exist in relation to other works, the most obvious relation being to other works of the same author, and there is a kind of literary ecology or ecological balance in which every work to a greater or lesser degree affects every other work. . . . Now it's your turn.

I must add, finally, that I am embarrassed to have to admit that I don't fully understand the final sentence of "Odour," a story I've read countless times, and taught a number of times, by an author whose works I've based whole courses on. There are many things about many of these stories that I do not fully understand or have not finally made up my mind about. In my experience it's good, though it may be initially embarrassing, to admit these gaps and uncertainties, publicly, in class. It may shock the students at first—"You're not omniscient? What are you doing posing as a teacher then?"—but not only does it get the students to participate more actively and seriously in discussion (so much so that it's tempting to fake it, even when you have decided about a story, but I've found that disastrous) but I think it ultimately gives them greater respect for you and your subject matter and opens them up to education as opposed to, or in addition to, mere "training."

QUESTIONS FOR DISCUSSION

1. What sensory details do you find in the opening paragraph? Later in this story? In later Lawrence stories? What expectations are aroused by the opening paragraph of the story? How are they fulfilled? Do the first four paragraphs of detailed description lead you to expect something other than a story of outcome? When do you first begin to suspect that Walter Bates is not off drinking somewhere? How does Elizabeth's assumption that he is in a pub affect expectation? Tone?

2. What is the focus of narration? How does Elizabeth respond to her father's intention to remarry? How do we know? Can we conjecture more confidently after having read the rest of the story? On what basis? At what point do we first enter Elizabeth's mind? What shifts of focus are there? How does the movement from preponderantly dramatic presentation to Elizabeth's centered consciousness and into her mind relate to the development of the action?

3. What is the major dramatic irony in the story? What related ironies are there? What other ironies? In a Greek tragedy the audience knows the outcome in advance and so can immediately identify ironic statements and actions; the irony seems, therefore, directed primarily against the character, with the audience having something of the advantage of the gods. Here, however, when Elizabeth says, "I won't wash him. He can lie on the floor," or "they'll bring him [home] like a log," though you may already have suspicions, you are no more certain of the outcome than she is. What is the effect, then, of such passages? Does the insistence on or repetition of such phrases create certain expectations or a range of expectations? Do you recall the phrases when you learn about the accident, realizing that they have

lingered somewhere in your mind? What seems to be the purpose of such potentially ironic hints? What is the effect of such hints when you read the story a second time? (The answer to this last may be more complex than it seems at first. Is there any difference, for example, in watching films of a game you know ended 14–13 and one that ended 42–0?) What is the difference in effect between the earlier ironies and Elizabeth's telling her awakened daughter that her father has been brought home and is asleep downstairs?

4. How do the numbered sections structure the story?

5. How is Walter's mother's selfishness indicated? Elizabeth "fastened the door of the little parlor, lest the children should see what was lying there." What is implied by the use of *what* rather than *who*? Faced with the dead body of her husband, what failures of her own in their relationship does Elizabeth come to recognize? Was Walter's isolation and separateness the result of their inadequate relationship? Does this final passage suggest something beyond the particularities of the Bateses' marriage relationship, something more universal? Does it imply a view of proper human relationships, including love and parenthood? What is Elizabeth's attitude toward her husband's death? Toward death itself? What does the last sentence of the story mean? Lawrence is often accused of being a didactic writer, of preaching. Would this story substantiate such a charge? Compare the presentation or embodiment of meaning or of a view of reality in "Odour of Chrysanthemums" and "Love Medicine."

6. Compare the use of chrysanthemums here with that of photographs in "A Pair of Tickets." Are the chrysanthemums ever used figuratively or nonliterally? How do they gain or accrete meaning?

D. H. LAWRENCE

The Blind Man

For various reasons, I like to teach Raymond Carver's "Cathedral" in conjunction with Lawrence's "The Blind Man," even when I'm asking students to write solely on Lawrence. Both stories focus on a couple whose life is temporarily disrupted by the visit of the wife's male friend; and in both stories, the literal visit entails a symbolic confrontation between a man who is physically blind and one who is in some sense spiritually blind, a confrontation that culminates in a moment of physical intimacy and spiritual enlightenment. While a comparison of the two stories would thus make for an interesting essay in its own right, simply reading and discussing the two stories together might also help students who are writing solely about Lawrence to grasp the uniquely Lawrentian elements and qualities of "The Blind Man."

At the center of Lawrence's story lies the contrast and/or conflict between the qualities and values represented by Maurice Pervin and by Bertie Reid. On the one hand, Bertie Reid represents "the intellectual type," who is at once "ironical" and "sentimental" rather than truly emotional (par. 8), a lack underscored by Bertie's being "chivalrously fond" of "a few good women" rather than passionately, "physically" intimate with any one of them (par. 138–139). "[A] brilliant and successful barrister" and a "littérateur of high repute" (par. 139), Bertie is a man of ideas and words rather than feelings and touch, a man who lives in his mind rather than his body. On the other hand, Maurice Pervin is wholly a creature of touch, feeling, and body, representing the "blood-prescience" Lawrence so admired because he saw it as so rare (par. 86). Maurice's very blindness puts him in constant, intimate, "pure contact" with the "world of things" and gives him a knowledge of that world that is immediate, physical, and emotive rather than analytical (par. 86): "He did not think much or trouble much. So long as he kept this sheer immediacy of blood-contact with the substantial world he was happy, he wanted no intervention of visual consciousness" (par. 86); "He was passionate, sensitive, perhaps over-sensitive. . . . For his mind was slow, as if drugged by the strong provincial blood that beat in his veins" (par. 8). As at home with the horses in the stable as he is with his wife, Maurice is not merely in constant, intimate contact with nature, but inseparable from it, as Isabel emphasizes when she "feel[s] the . . . strong contact of his feet with the earth" and sees him as "ris[ing] out of the earth" (par. 69). Thus Maurice also represents a man fully in touch with his primitive connection to the earth, whereas Bertie represents a modern man alienated from that primitive earthy essence: "a great social success," "[a]t the center [Bertie] felt himself neuter, nothing" (par. 139).

As a result, Maurice and Bertie come to represent the conflict or estrangement between "mental" and physical knowledge most explicitly thematized in Lawrence's *Lady Chatterley's Lover* (New York: Bantam, 1968, pp. 37–38):

> Real knowledge comes out of the whole corpus of the consciousness; out of your belly and your penis as much as out of your brain and mind. The mind can only analyse and rationalise. . . . [W]hile you *live* your life, you are in some way an organic whole with all life. But once you start the mental life you pluck the apple. You've severed the connection between the apple and the tree: the organic connection. And if you've got nothing in your life *but* the mental life, then you yourself are a plucked apple . . . you've fallen off the tree.

But at this point one is, I think, led to ask why Maurice Pervin is so often and so desperately unhappy, given that he enjoys both the "rapture" of "blood-prescience" and (par. 86), because of that, an equally rapturous "almost incomprehensible peace of immediate contact in darkness" with his wife (par. 2). After all, it is precisely those fits of unhappiness that bring Bertie Reid to the farm in the first place. Why, too, is

Isabel so contented when Maurice is not, so happily looking forward to "luxuriat[ing] in a rich, physical satisfaction of maternity" (par. 6)? Why, in other words, do the men seem in this story to be just as "freakish and unreasonable" as Isabel at one point insists that they are (par. 10)? Such questions not only are important to a thorough understanding of the story but also, I think, are more easily answered in "the context of the author's work," a context that in fact suggests two different, but related, answers.

The first lies in the typically Lawrentian emphasis on the need to balance the mental and the physical to achieve "real knowledge" and real happiness. According to this reading, Maurice's unhappiness derives from the fact that he utterly lacks "the mental life" that is all Bertie enjoys, whereas Isabel's happiness derives from her ability to enjoy "the whole corpus of the consciousness," an ability symbolized by the very fact that she appreciates and loves both of these two disparate men.

The second possible answer depends on recognizing another of the typically Lawrentian themes present in "The Blind Man"—the insistence on the difference between men's and women's attitudes toward marriage and on men's need for relationships with other men (a difference that may make not merely these particular men, but all men in Lawrence seem "freakish and unreasonable.") Indeed, one effective way to push forward the discussion of "The Blind Man" might be to share with your students some or all of the following excerpts from Lawrence's *Women in Love* (New York: Penguin, 1976), the first being the dialogue between Birkin and Ursula that ends that novel, the second and subsequent excerpts representing Birkin's thoughts on the same issue:

> "Aren't I enough for you?" she asked.
> "No," he said. "You are enough for me, as far as a woman is concerned. You are all women to me. But I wanted a man friend, as eternal as you and I are eternal."
> "Why aren't I enough?" she said. "You are enough for me. I don't want anybody else but you. Why isn't it the same with you?"
> "Having you, I can live all my life without anybody else, any other sheer intimacy. But to make it complete, really happy, I wanted eternal union with a man too; another kind of love," he said.
> "I don't believe it," she said. "It's an obstinacy, a theory, a perversity."
> "Well—" he said.
> "You can't have two kinds of love. Why should you!"
> "It seems as if I can't," he said. "Yet I wanted it."
> "You can't have it, because it's false, impossible," she said.
> "I don't believe that," he answered. (pp. 472–473)

> What it was in him he did not know, but the thought of love, marriage, and children, and a life lived together, in the horrible privacy of domestic and connubial satisfaction, was repulsive. He wanted something clearer, more open, cooler, as it were. The hot narrow intimacy between man and wife was abhorrent. The way they shut their doors, these married people, and shut themselves into their own exclusive alliance with each other, even in love, disgusted him. It was a whole commu-

nity of mistrustful couples insulated in private houses . . ., always in couples, and no further life, no further immediate, no disinterested relationship admitted. (p. 191)

[I]t seemed to him, woman was always so horrible and clutching, she had such a lust for possession, a greed of self-importance in love. She wanted to have, to own, to control, to be dominant. Everything must be referred back to her, to Woman, the Great Mother of everything, out of whom proceeded everything and to whom everything must finally be rendered up.

It filled him with almost insane fury, this calm assumption of the Magna Mater, that all was hers, because she had borne it. Man was hers because she had borne him. . . . [Woman] was only too ready to knock her head on the ground before a man. But this was only when she was so certain of her man, that she could worship him as a woman worships her own infant, with a worship of perfect possession. (p. 192)

Understanding Maurice's moments of despair as an indication of a thirst for what Birkin calls the "further life" and for "eternal union" with a man can, I think, help students to more fully grasp the symbolic resonance, as well as the pathos and irony, of the conclusion of "The Blind Man." For, with Maurice "filled with hot, poignant love, the passion of friendship" and Bertie longing only "to escape from this intimacy, this friendship," "like a mollusc whose shell is broken" (par. 221, 235), "The Blind Man" ends much as *Women in Love* does, attesting to the need and desire for "mortal friendship" even as it suggests how very "impossible" and impossibly frightening that intimacy seems to be for modern men who are, as it were, "plucked apples."

QUESTIONS FOR DISCUSSION

1. From the first, according to Isabel, Bertie Reid and Maurice Pervin "did not like each other." Why? What worldview, values, lifestyles, and/or way of knowing does Lawrence embody in Maurice Pervin? In Bertie Reid? Why and how exactly are the two incompatible and/or in conflict? What stance does the story encourage us to take toward these two characters and the values they embody?
2. Is the conflict between Bertie and Maurice resolved or merely brought to a climax in the conclusion of the story? Why do the two men react so differently to the same encounter? What do you think provokes that encounter? How might this encounter and/or "The Blind Man" as a whole embody the ideas about relationships articulated in Lawrence's "Morality and the Novel"?
3. What is Isabel's precise role in the story, particularly in terms of the central conflict between the worldviews represented by the two male characters? Why do you think that she seems happier than her husband and/or Bertie Reid?
4. How specifically is Lawrence's "The Blind Man" like "Odour of Chrysanthemums"? What commonalities do you see in terms of char-

acter types and themes? In terms of style or imagery?

5. How specifically does Lawrence's characterization of Maurice Pervin and Bertie Reid echo his characterization of his father and other work- ing-class men in "Nottingham and the Mining Countryside" and "Autobiographical Sketch"? To what extent might "The Blind Man" be interpreted as exploring the class differences Lawrence describes in these essays?

6. How is Lawrence's "The Blind Man" like and unlike Raymond Carver's story "Cathedral"? What seems typically Lawrentian about "The Blind Man" compared to "Cathedral"?

D. H. LAWRENCE
_____

The Rocking-Horse Winner

This is an oft-anthologized story, one of Lawrence's most popular. More than one person has told me that it is the only story they remember from their introductory fiction class of ten or fifteen years ago. And yet it is not a typical Lawrence story.

Achsah Barlow Brewster remembers hearing Lawrence tell the story (quoted by Edward Nehls, *D. H. Lawrence: A Composite Biography*, Madi- son: University of Wisconsin Press, 1959, 3:43–44):

> Out on the terrace of Quattro Venti [on the Isle of Capri], sitting in the spring sunshine, we were talking about the curse of money. He related his story of "The Rocking-Horse Winner," bringing money, but the little boy's death. The tale was told of a woman's inheriting a fortune, whereupon she bought herself a close collar of pearls; soon afterward a bee stung her on the throat, which swelled before the collar could be removed, choking her to death. Someone else recounted that a poor farmer inherited forest land which he sold for ten thousand dollars. When he was told it should have brought twenty thousand, he was so chagrined that he hanged himself on one of the trees. There seemed no end of such tales. Lawrence decided at once to write a volume of them under the title of *Tales of the Four Winds* [*Quattro Venti*] from which the proceeds should be divided equally among us, that the curse of the riches should be shared by us all.

The story was first published in Lady Cynthia Asquith's *The Ghost-Book: Sixteen New Stories of the Uncanny* (1926). The story might be read, then, as something of a jeu d'esprit, more at home among the collected ghost stories then in the collected Lawrence.

For just this reason, however, it may be a good story to use to discuss canon or the author's style or fingerprint. Here, in this most atypical story, Lawrence cannot help but write like Lawrence. The flat, fairy-tale- like or late-Tolstoy opening can be found in other Lawrence stories of the period, like "Two Blue Birds." Vintage Lawrence, too, is the reality that lies beneath appearances, beneath words, even beneath actions: "Everybody else said of her: 'She is such a good mother. She adores her children.' Only she herself, and her children themselves, knew it was not so. They read it in each other's eyes." You might ask the students about their own experiences: whether there are things they know without words, despite appearances, underneath actions. The theme of money or materialism versus love and life is also familiar in Lawrence's work, as is the perception that the lust for money is insatiable, that even too much is not enough. Family tensions, deftly handled, are common in Lawrence's "Odour of Chrysanthemums" and *Sons and Lovers*—even though the suburban setting may seem unfamiliar.

The idea that this story is about masturbation for some reason has great currency—better not to inquire about the reasons, perhaps. Riding even a rocking-horse may, it is true, be assumed to involve a certain amount of genital excitation; Paul's frenzy may be translated sexually, and getting the secret name of the horse may suggest for some sexual climax. But a Freudian reading of this story is a reading out of the story. That is, the masturbation is not in the story, part of the story, demonstrable in detail in the story: it is a translation of the details of the story according to another formula or system than that contained within the story. This may be legitimate if you want to talk about Lawrence's sexuality or attitudes toward sex—conscious or, especially, unconscious. It may be legitimate, too, in trying to explain reader response. Readers may respond to this story because it parallels or embodies the rhythms or structures of masturbation; maybe that's why some students remember it more vividly than other stories. But that's a study of responses and the reasons for them, conjectural and fascinating, and it seems to me that this is quite a different thing from saying that this story is about masturbation.

QUESTIONS FOR DISCUSSION

1. If you did not know that this and the preceding two stories were by the same author, what internal evidence (elements, views, language within the story) might suggest it? How does this 1932 Lawrence story differ from his earlier ones? Describe the continuity and the change or development in his work, assuming these stories to be typical of that work at the time of publication.
2. Compare the opening sentences of the Lawrence stories. In what ways might the opening of this story prepare you for the surreal or supernatural events later in the story?
3. What expectations are aroused by what precedes the first dramatic scene? By the divulging of Paul's luck? By the "secret within a secret"? When did you first guess how Paul learned the names of the winning horses? When did you first begin to suspect the eventual outcome of the story? Why is Paul's mother anxious about him? What is implied about feeling and common sense? Is Paul's mother's anxiety part of

the realistic or of the supernatural aspect of the story? What are the implications? Tone? Emotional effect? Of Oscar Cresswell's final remarks?

4. What is the focus of narration? How would you characterize or identify the narrator?

5. The "center" of Paul's mother's heart is cold and hard; she is incapable of love, but other people think she is a loving mother; she knows it isn't so, and she knows her children know it isn't so because they "read it in each other's eyes." What does this suggest about appearance or behavior and reality? About different kinds of reality? About different kinds of knowing? To what extent does this prepare you for the strange nature of the events that follow? How does the vagueness, for example, the absence of names on the first page or so, prepare you for those later events? How does the relationship between inner and outer reality here resemble or differ from that relationship in the other Lawrence stories? In "The Lady with the Pet Dog"? How do the different kinds of reality here compare to those implied in "A Souvenir of Japan"?

6. What kind of literal sense do you make out of the children's hearing the haunted house whispering? Their seeing in each other's eyes that they all hear it? That the rocking-horse hears it? What does Paul's mother mean by luck? How does he interpret it? Why doesn't Paul want his mother to know he's lucky? What happens when he does tell her? What is the irony of Paul's claiming luck? What does the story imply about luck?

7. Why do the voices in the house get louder or more insistent after Paul's mother gets the five thousand pounds? What is the effect on Paul? What does the story suggest about monetary needs?

8. In what sense may this story be considered symbolic or mythic? If mythic, and if myth is social or communal, of what social group or community is this a myth?

SUGGESTION FOR WRITING

Carter's "A Souvenir of Japan" and Lawrence's "Odour of Chrysanthemums" have in common female protagonists who feel alienated from their mates. Write an analysis of the way each author handles this topic.

FLANNERY O'CONNOR

A Good Man Is Hard to Find

One good potential starting place for a discussion of "A Good Man" is the title itself. What might students make of this phrase if they hadn't read the story? Students can often immediately identify the ways in which the title echoes familiar laments about the difficulty of finding good employees or servants, eligible husbands, or fit soldiers. What do all such laments have in common? They all imply that the present is both different from, and worse than, the past. And the initial appearance of the phrase in the story itself clearly plays on and reinforces those associations: the words first appear in Red Sammy's lament for the passing of those "better times" when you "could go off and leave your screen door unlatched" and "kn[e]w who to trust" (par. 43–44, 34).

Having noted this, however, one might then ask students if O'Connor's story is endorsing the view that the past was better than the present. Obviously this view is most relentlessly advocated by, and embodied in, the character of the grandmother, so that answering this question will necessarily entail analyzing and evaluating both her character and O'Connor's characterization of her. That the grandmother represents not only a figure from the past but also a person obsessed with the past is suggested by the mere fact that she desires, from the very outset of the story, to journey back to the past, to the place of her own origins. Even after agreeing to go on the journey to Florida, she remains so obsessed with the past that she tries to imagine the trip as itself already safely in the past, carefully keeping track of the mileage because "it would be interesting to say how many miles they had been when they got back" (par. 11). That the grandmother does imagine and represent the past as a safer place is suggested by the fact that she introduces the threat of the Misfit as part of her argument against the journey and, in so doing, clearly implies a necessary connection between the violence and criminality the Misfit represents and the journey to the present and future that she doesn't want to take (par. 5).

But what is the exact character of the past that the grandmother so yearns for? Why and how precisely was it safer? Why and how exactly did one "know who to trust" then in a way one doesn't now? As in many O'Connor stories, the past is, as the grandmother wittily remarks in *Gone with the Wind*, a place where one knew who to trust because everyone dressed and behaved (and evaluated everyone else) according to clearly marked social distinctions: a woman dressed herself so as to ensure that anyone "would know at once that she was a lady," even if a dead one (par. 12); Negroes were "pickaninn[ies]" who could be presumed not to "have things like we do" (par. 18–20); and people were "nice" because people were "more respectful" of their betters (whether those betters were parents, whites, or gentlemen and ladies of "good" family) (par. 18). And such "nice" social distinctions are, at least initially, at the very heart of the grandmother's notion of a "good man," for, as she says to the Misfit, "I know you're a good man. You don't look a bit like you have common blood. I know you must come from nice people!" (par. 88).

Two facts may help students to begin to question O'Connor's attitude toward this picture of the romanticized Old South past: (1) the meeting with the Misfit comes about precisely because the grandmother has mis-remembered the past, forgetting that the plantation she yearns to see one more time isn't where (or, perhaps, what) she remembered it to be (par. 65); and (2) the Misfit, the very embodiment of the violent present, him-self seems to be as obsessed with, and as confused about, his own past as the grandmother is and, indeed, as insistent on social "niceties," apolo-gizing, for example, for not being dressed as he should be in the presence of "ladies" like herself, even though he plans to shoot her all along (par. 99). And might not this man who is a misfit in the present have been quite at home in the violent slavery-era South? Ultimately the Misfit, who at first glance seems to represent everything the grandmother isn't, a violent present she refuses to embrace, is revealed to be very like her, a fact underscored by her final words—an avowal of their kinship (par. 136).

If violence in O'Connor forces characters and/or the reader to glimpse an uncomfortable truth that lies beneath the surface, then perhaps one of the truths revealed here is the simple fact of this essential human kin-ship that lies beneath surface differences, the impossibility of drawing lines between a "good man" and a bad one. Yet, if this is so, why at the end of the story does the Misfit persist in using the term *good* to describe the woman the grandmother might have been (par. 140)? How exactly has the meaning of the term *good man* or *good woman* been revised by the end of the story? To what extent does the action of the story itself support or challenge the Misfit's own view of religion and of crime and punish-ment?

QUESTIONS FOR DISCUSSION

1. What values or worldview is represented by the character of the grand-mother in "A Good Man Is Hard to Find"? How specifically do her own words and those of the narrator contribute to our understanding of her character? What stance does the story encourage us to take in regard to the grandmother? How or why might the grandmother be one of the people O'Connor describes in "The Fiction Writer and His Country" as having "little—or at best a distorted—sense of spiritual purpose"?

2. The grandmother is associated with the past from the beginning of "A Good Man." What was the past like, according to the grandmother and Red Sammy? How exactly was it different from, and better than, the present?

3. How does the encounter with the Misfit change the grandmother and/ or our view of her? In what way might we see the encounter with the Misfit as, in O'Connor's own words, "returning" the grandmother "to reality and preparing [her] to accept [her] moment of grace" ("On Her Own Work")? How does O'Connor characterize the Misfit? What is the significance of the fact that the grandmother recognizes or mis-

takes the Misfit for "one of [her] own children" right before she dies? What does the Misfit mean when he says the grandmother "would of been a good woman . . . if it had been somebody there to shoot her every minute of her life"?

4. During their brief encounter, both the Misfit and the grandmother talk a great deal about religion and morality. What do you think the story ultimately says about either or both of these issues? To what extent and how specifically might "A Good Man" embody the belief, expressed in "The Fiction Writer and His Country," that "the meaning of life is centered in our Redemption by Christ"? That, as O'Connor says in "The Grotesque in Southern Fiction," "life is and will remain essentially mysterious"?

5. From its title right through to the Misfit's comments about the dead grandmother, this story clearly explores the question of what it means to be a "good" man or woman, contrasting at least two different definitions of *good*. What are those definitions? What, if any, definition, do you think the story ultimately embraces?

FLANNERY O'CONNOR

The Lame Shall Enter First

College students are a difficult group to startle these days. If they haven't experienced all manner of shocking things before they arrive on campus, they have certainly seen them on television and at the movies, often from a very young age. They are a tough group to shake up, and yet many of my students admit to being shaken up by this story. I must admit that I, too, find it deeply disturbing. Like O'Connor's "A Good Man Is Hard to Find," it's not a story one easily forgets and not just because of the ending.

Perhaps it's the implacable bluntness with which O'Connor presents her flawed and troubled characters: the smugly self-righteous Sheppard, his woebegone and neglected son, and the fiendishly malign but often amusing Rufus. Maybe it's that there is no one in the story to like. All of the characters are in some degree grotesques, "large and startling figures," as O'Connor would have it, created—as she says—as a means of speaking to the "almost blind" ("The Fiction Writer and His Country"). We sympathize with Norton, and we sometimes applaud Rufus's actions out of our own malice toward Sheppard, but we find no one with whom we want to identify, nor can we feel completely comfortable with our own reactions. By leaving us so much outside the story, O'Connor forces us into the position of judges. It is easy—perilously easy—for example, to recognize Sheppard's self-righteousness and to condemn him, but in the process we may be lured into an uncomfortable smugness of our own.

O'Connor's handling of Rufus's club foot is surely another reason the story disturbs us so profoundly. Ours is a culture deeply ill at ease with physical disability, and I have found students reluctant to talk about Rufus's foot, even though its ugliness is something he clearly enjoys flaunting. Sheppard observes that Rufus is "as touchy about [his] foot as if it were a sacred object." Rufus doesn't want the clerk to touch his foot, but he makes certain when Sheppard interviews him that the counselor cannot avoid looking at it. In O'Connor's work, bodily disability almost always accompanies spiritual disability. (Students familiar with her "Good Country People" will note the parallel to Hulga's false leg.) Talking about what Rufus's foot represents moves the discussion quickly into some key issues in the story because both for Sheppard and Rufus and for O'Connor it is a symbolic as much as a physical entity.

Sheppard, secure in his training as a counselor ("his credentials were less dubious than a priest's"), believes Rufus's club foot "explains" the boy's destructive behavior. In a rather Adlerian way he concludes that Rufus is trying to compensate for his handicap when he gets into trouble. On the contrary, as we discover near the end of the story, because of the training Rufus has received from his fundamentalist grandfather, he takes literally the biblical proclamation that at the gates of heaven "the lame shall enter first." He doesn't see his foot as a disability (as Sheppard does) but as a special admission ticket to paradise—even though Rufus realizes he will have to repent of his sins before he can take advantage of his position of privilege. In the story, the foot represents Rufus's pride in his ability to carry out evil acts and get away with it. His bodily disability is emblematic of his spiritual disability. He flaunts his leg as he flaunts his sin. Like the Misfit in "A Good Man Is Hard to Find," Rufus understands the basic teachings of the Christian faith, but in him the knowledge has become twisted and ugly. Unlike the Misfit, who wishes he knew for certain whether Christ is worthy of his belief (a fact that may make him somewhat like Sheppard, the empiricist), Rufus believes Christian teachings are true. But for him they offer the opportunity to enjoy being evil for a while before he repents and is saved.

O'Connor does something very clever with point of view in this story. She keeps us very close to Sheppard, making us privy to his thoughts and offering us ample opportunities to criticize him and feel superior. We recognize that Sheppard is wrong about Rufus, but we may not suspect how tragically wrong until the very end of the story because we're hearing Sheppard's thoughts, not Rufus's. A smug do-gooder who ignores and abuses his son makes a fine target for our dislike (I'm reminded of Mrs. Jellyby in *Bleak House*), and while we know Rufus isn't the boy Sheppard imagines him to be, we may wonder if he might not be a better influence on Norton than is his father. O'Connor plays fair with us; she doesn't turn Rufus into a child of Satan suddenly at the end. From the very beginning of the story, Rufus overtly allies himself with evil ("Satan," he says, "He has me in his power"). He combs his hair "Hitler fashion." He "hisses" like a snake. Yet most of us, I think, are shocked to discover the depths of Rufus's evil. Perhaps we are so busy enjoying the many ways he frustrates Sheppard's plans that we ignore O'Connor's characterization. Perhaps it is that our imaginations can scarcely encompass the evil of which he is capable, which may be one of the points (at us) of the story.

One exercise I like to use with O'Connor stories works especially well with "The Lame Shall Enter First." The eyes in her works are almost always windows to souls. You might have your class skim through the story, marking all the references to eyes, sight, seeing, etc., then ask them to talk about how these references provide insights into each character's way of viewing the world. You might want to ask them what they make of Sheppard's eagerness to buy Rufus a telescope—and then a microscope—and of Norton's fascination with the former.

In the world of O'Connor's fiction we confront ultimate issues—love and hate, truth and falsehood, sin and redemption, life and death. O'Connor makes it clear she sees these issues from the perspective of orthodox Christianity. I like to ask students whether they believe a reader must share O'Connor's beliefs to appreciate her vision. Is O'Connor's vision comprehensible to an agnostic? To someone outside Judeo-Christian culture?

QUESTIONS FOR DISCUSSION

1. At the beginning of the story, we see the world from Sheppard's perspective. When does your sympathy begin to move away from Sheppard and toward Norton? Why do you think O'Connor has Norton prepare such a disgusting breakfast? What do you make of Sheppard's diagnosis of why Norton threw up? What name does Norton use for his father?

2. Sheppard believes Norton sells seeds because he's greedy, materialistic, and selfish. Can you provide another explanation? What might the seeds symbolize? Why is Norton described as looking like a larvae?

3. How does having Rufus in the house change things for Norton? Why does Norton become absorbed in using the telescope? Why does Sheppard refuse to tell Norton that his mother has gone to heaven? Why does Norton want to believe she has?

4. Rufus spends a lot of his free time reading encyclopedias. What is Sheppard's reaction to this activity? Why do you think O'Connor describes Rufus as ravaging each subject that he reads about? When Sheppard uses the words *truth* and *light*, what does he refer to? When Rufus uses these words, what does he mean?

5. O'Connor says each of her stories depends on the success of a "gesture"—"some gesture of a character that is unlike any other in the story, one which indicates where the real heart of the story lies" ("On Her Own Work"). Is there such a gesture in "The Lame Shall Enter First"? If so, can you explain its importance to the story?

6. Why, at the end of the story after Rufus and Sheppard have their last confrontation, does the policeman say, "Well, they seen each other now"? Why does Rufus allow himself to be caught?
7. Why does Sheppard repeat to himself, "I did more for him than I did for my own child"? Do you find any significance in Sheppard's name?

FLANNERY O'CONNOR

Everything That Rises Must Converge

Among all O'Connor's stories, this one contains some of her funniest dialogue and reveals O'Connor's fine ear for the rhythm, nuance, and banality of everyday speech, particularly southern speech. After talking about the devastating conclusion of "The Lame Shall Enter First," I find the class needs a little comic relief, so I like to begin discussion of "Everything That Rises" with language. O'Connor always pays particular attention to the ways the language we use reveals us. If you've discovered some talented readers in your class, you might want to have two of them read a passage from the story (just the dialogue)—perhaps the section from Mrs. Chestny's comments at the end of paragraph 10 through Julian's comment—"Doubtless that decayed mansion reminded them." Mrs. Chestny's cliché-ridden conversation shows her to be unreflective, uninventive, and unable to escape either the verbal locutions or the mental landscape of the past. (Yet occasionally she speaks the truth, however unintentionally, as when she observes that what Julian calls "true culture" is "in the heart.")

Students will often note that Julian's use of language is no less revealing of character than his mother's. He doesn't converse with his mother so much as emit exasperated retorts more appropriate in tone to those of a sulky adolescent than a grown man. Because O'Connor presents the story from Julian's perspective, we are also privy to the "language" of his thinking. I like to ask students what they make of the way Julian is described in paragraph 2—what they make of the perspective presented in paragraph 10.

O'Connor's use of point of view in "Everything That Rises" is very similar to that in "The Lame Shall Enter First," so you may want to ask your class to compare O'Connor's presentation of Julian's perspective and Sheppard's perspective in each story. Both men have great faith in their own judgments, although one is wrong about the others he judges and one is basically right. Both men are also portrayed in such a way as to prompt readers to judge them harshly. Do we in a sense condemn ourselves by adopting the same role as O'Connor's protagonists? Or is there a distinction between the judgments Shepperd and Julian make about others and our own about them?

In "Writing Short Stories," O'Connor emphasizes the importance of conveying the social idiom in which her characters move: "When you ignore the idiom," she writes, "you are very likely ignoring the whole social fabric that could make a meaningful character." This comment can provide a neat entry into a discussion of the social milieu of "Everything That Rises" and its importance to our understanding of Julian, his mother, and the African-American woman Mrs. Chestny angers. Julian claims his mother doesn't understand where or who she is. He believes that she lives in the past, that she ignores the changes in her status and in the status of African-Americans and pretends that little has changed since her great-grandfather owned "a plantation and two-hundred slaves." I like to ask half of the class to provide support for Julian's contention that his mother doesn't face the world as it is and the other half to offer evidence that Julian can't face the world either.

O'Connor wrote that she used violence to wake her characters up, to return them to reality and prepare them "to accept their moment of grace," and to reveal who they really are ("On Her Own Work"). The conclusion of "Everything That Rises" reveals who Julian is, a man-child still deeply dependent on his mother. Whether his mother's stroke will cause him to see himself clearly is left indeterminate, as is the question of his ability to confront his "guilt and sorrow." The final paragraph of the story has the surreal quality of a nightmare: Julian runs, but he seems to be getting nowhere. I must confess that the final sentence of the story remains something of a mystery to me—perhaps as O'Connor intended. It would appear that the "tide of darkness" that seems to pull Julian back to his mother would cause him to make "his entry into the world of guilt and sorrow." Instead, somehow this tide allows him to postpone it, "moment to moment."

QUESTIONS FOR DISCUSSION

1. Describe as fully as possible what you believe Mrs. Chestny feels when she recognizes that the African-American woman on the bus is wearing the same hat she is. Describe the other woman's feelings. Why is she so enraged when Mrs. Chestny offers her son a nickel?
2. What does Julian think about when he is inside his "bubble"? What do you understand the bubble to represent?
3. Julian considers himself far more enlightened in his attitude toward African-Americans than his mother. What do you think?
4. What do you make of the change in language Julian uses with his mother when he realizes she may be dying?
5. Examine the references to eyes, sight, etc. in "Everything That Rises." What do these references tell us about Julian's perspective through most of the story? At the end of the story? What do you make of O'Connor's description of Julian's mother's eye raking his face?

6. Does Mrs. Chestny's encounter with violence prepare her "to accept her moment of grace"? Or is Mrs. Chestny simply doomed because of her bigotry?

7. How specifically is "Everything That Rises Must Converge" like "A Good Man Is Hard to Find"? "The Lame Shall Enter First"? What commonalities do you see in terms of character types and themes? In terms of style or imagery? In terms of plot? How specifically is the grandmother in "A Good Man" like Mrs. Chestny? How specifically are the Misfit, Sheppard, and Rufus like Julian? If the author's name were missing from these stories, how would you know that Flannery O'Connor wrote them?

SUGGESTIONS FOR WRITING

1. Write a personal essay describing an encounter with racism. The essay could be about racism directed toward you or toward another person. It could even be about racist impulses you have had yourself. What prompted the incident? How did it end? How did it make you feel? Were there any "aftershocks"? What sense did you make of it?

2. Using the appropriate parts of "Passages from Essays and Letters," write an essay about either the three Lawrence stories or the three O'Connor stories, exploring the degree to which the author's statements about writing conform to the author's practice.

3. Research the background of either O'Connor or Lawrence and write an essay discussing the influence of the author's background on the situations and settings of his or her work.

4. Write an essay comparing and contrasting Lawrence and O'Connor's use of characterization, setting, or symbolism.

READING/WRITING IDEAS FOR CHAPTER 8

ESSAYS ABOUT AN AUTHOR'S WORK

Among my favorite assignments, one that I have found both very useful and very enjoyable for students, is the assignment that asks them to write about "the author's work as context" or to produce what I call "multiple-text, single-author" essays. Students find this assignment both instructive and gratifying for a number of reasons, not least the sense of accomplishment they get from feeling that they have become experts on something. Requiring students to make some use of the O'Connor and Lawrence nonfiction excerpts included in the anthology adds even greater depth to the assignment because it allows students to begin to use primary source material in a relatively painless way, allowing them (and you) to focus on questions about why and how writers use such material to make arguments before getting caught up in questions about how researchers locate it.

The multiple-text, single-author essay presents a series of very useful challenges for student writers, especially when it comes to theses and structure. For that reason, I always begin this assignment sequence by having students read multiple sample student essays to address questions about why one writes such essays, about what kinds of theses and structures tend to work, and about how writers decide which structures "fit" their arguments.

I have discovered over the years three types of workable structures for such essays, and I generally try to provide students with sample essays that represent each of these types. Though I have yet to come up with satisfying names for these three structures, I can offer the following rough characterizations:

1. **The "side-by-side" or "simultaneous" structure** in which a writer discusses all of the works by his or her author simultaneously. Within the body of the essay, topic sentences tend to be claims about the author and his or her work in general and paragraphs include evidence from all or most of the texts under discussion. Obviously, this structure tends to work best when the writer has one overarching interpretation that fits all of the texts under discussion, when the stories all seem to fall into a single, basic pattern.

Sample Body Paragraph Beginnings

> Here [Pam] Houston's male and female characters [in *Cowboys Are My Weakness*] begin to appear as separate species that inhabit entirely different worlds, making peace of any kind nearly impossible. Houston represents this polarity of the sexes within her stories as promoting the notion that "a man desires the satisfaction of desire, a woman desires the condition of desiring" ("How to Talk to a Hunter"). Houston's men and women not only harbor different desires, but they also want entirely different things out of relationships. This distinct separation is evident in the narrator's struggle in "Selway" for control over Jack.
>
> From Marian Hennessy-Fiske, "Even Cowgirls Get the Blues," unpublished student paper.

> Leavitt's stories also demonstrate that it is not possible to choose between these two desires of equal fortitude without paying a heavy price. Having taken a risk, the characters are now pressured by their loved ones into deciding between security and passion; however, each of these competing desires is accompanied by una-voidable losses. In "When You Grow to Adultery," Andrew's choices are to either remain with Allen or with Jack. . . . In "Houses," Paul cannot live with Ted unless he accepts the loss of his wife and a secure home.
>
> From James Martinez, "Passion vs. Love in David Leavitt's
> *A Place I've Never Been*," unpublished student paper.

2. **The "serial" or "one-text-at-a-time" structure.** Here, the body of the essay is divided into text-specific sections, the challenge being to craft very clear and careful transition paragraphs. This structure tends to work best (or only) when students can show that and how one text

somehow complicates the view of an author's work that might be suggested by another text.

Sample (Transition) Paragraph Beginnings

> In a sense, one could think of [Joyce's] "A Little Cloud" as representing the logical conclusion of "The Boarding House." In this other story the object of Joyce's scrutiny is, in part, a marriage very much like that which Mrs. Mooney concocts for her daughter.
>
> > From Matthew Light, "Staying Home and Leaving Home in *Dubliners.*"
> > In *Exposé: Essays from the Expository Writing Program, Harvard University, 1990–1991* (Cambridge, Mass.: Expository Writing Program, 1991).

> The word "home" does not always have [the] oppressive, stifling connotations of financial success and narrow-minded morality [that it does in David Leavitt's "A.Y.O.R."]. Although she tries to escape to Europe from the memories of her childhood poverty, Celia in [Leavitt's] "I See London, I See France" finds herself inextricably linked to the warmth and familiarity of her childhood home.
>
> > From Sonesh Chainani, "Where the Heart Is: The Promise and Problem of the American Home in David Leavitt's *A Place I've Never Been*," unpublished student paper.

3. **The "lens" structure** in which a writer focuses primarily on one text, using it as a "lens" through which to look closely at the entire canon of the author's work, using references to other texts merely to support or amplify points about the focal text. This structure tends to work best when students see one text as particularly typical and/or revealing of an author's work.

TROUBLESHOOTING

Careful, thoughtful discussion of structure is key to helping student writers to write truly successful multiple-text, single-author essays because the real danger is that such essays prove to be either incredibly repetitive (again in this text we see . . .) or incredibly incoherent, rambling through a series of similarities without really making connections between them or indicating their overall significance.

AUTHOR'S-WORK-AS-CONTEXT WRITING EXERCISES

1. Identifying and Describing Patterns in the Author's Work

The following is an exercise that has proved very helpful to my students as a way to generate ideas for essays about multiple texts by a single author. Indeed students often comment on this exercise in their end-of-term evaluations, citing it as their favorite.

Read your author's stories at least once, underlining passages that seem significant to you. As you read, work not only to understand the individual stories but also to look for patterns across these stories, similarities that link them together into a coherent whole, make them part of a unified canon. Once you have finished, think more about these similarities, working to answer the following questions as if you were trying to capture for someone who hadn't read your author the essence of that author's work. You may well also want to make notes about which of the passages might serve to illustrate or support the claims you make.

- How would you describe your author's typical **heroes or heroines**? What makes them alike? What (internal and external) characteristics do they tend to share?
- Which hero or heroine seems most typical in light of your description? The least typical? Why?
- How would you describe and/or categorize the **other characters** whom the heroes or heroines encounter, or interact with, in the stories? Are there similar types? Do the stories tend to present characters who are foils to the main character, clear antagonists?
- Which character(s) seem the most typical? The least typical? Why?
- How would you describe the **problems or conflicts** that the heroes or heroines of these stories typically face?
- How would you describe the typical **plot** of your author's stories?
- In terms of plot, conflict, etc., what's the most typical story? The least typical? Why?
- How would you describe the **narrative structure** of the stories—i.e., the way the plots, conflicts, etc., are narrated?
- In light of this description of structure, which story is the most typical? The least typical? Why?
- How would you describe the **setting** of these stories? The significance and role of the setting or environment (social, cultural, and/or physical) in the stories?
- In light of setting, which story is most typical? Least typical? Why?
- How would you describe the **style** of your author in terms of diction, syntax, etc.? What quotations might you use to illustrate this author's style or the range of the author's style(s)?
- What's the overall **tone** or **mood** of these stories—the feelings they tend to evoke? How do they do so?
- What do you think are the themes, concerns, problems, or issues articulated or tackled in these stories?

Taking all of these factors into account and without referring to any particular story, narrate, outline, script out, or draw a map or flowchart that captures the basic features, action, elements, etc. of your author's short stories.

Here's a very fun (as well as astute) example of such a schematic outline (actually excerpted from an essay on "cyberpunk," a popular contemporary science-fiction subgenre):

> . . . a self-destructive but sensitive young protagonist with an (implant/prosthesis/ telechtronic talent) that makes the evil (megacorporations/police states/criminal underworlds) pursue him through (wasted urban landscapes/elite luxury enclaves/ eccentric space stations) full of grotesque (haircuts/clothes/self-multilations/rock music/sexual hobbies/designer drugs/telechtronic gadgets/nasty new weapons/ exteriorized hallucinations) representing the (mores/fashions) of modern civilization in terminal decline, ultimately hooks up with rebellious and tough-talking (youth/artificial intelligence/rock cults) who offer the alternative, not of (community/socialism/traditional values/transcendental vision), but of supreme, life-affirming *hipness*, going with the flow which now flows in the machine, against the spectre of a world-subverting (artificial intelligence/multinational corporate web/evil genius).

From Istvan Csicsery-Ronay, "Cyberpunk and Neuromanticism,"
Mississippi Review 47, n. 8 (1988). Reprinted by permission of Istvan Csicsery-Ronay.

2. Generating Theses and Describing Structures

Because multiple-text, single-author essays do represent such a challenge to student writers in terms of structure, etc., I almost always have students who are writing such essays do an exercise before they start drafting in which they articulate at least two different possible thesis statements for the essay, describe exactly how they would structure each essay, and say a little bit about why and how each structure fits each particular thesis/argument. I usually leave it up to the students themselves to decide whether it would be more helpful to them to write an informal discussion of the essay for us to discuss or whether they want to write actual topic sentences, transition paragraphs, etc. Though students may well complain about having to plan more than one essay, I strongly recommend requiring them do so; they usually appreciate it later. With any assignment, I find that students almost always write better essays if they are forced to try out different thesis statements rather than settling for the first that comes to mind. And with this assignment in particular, outlining different essays can help students to really get why and how different theses suggest different structures.

Because certain kinds of thesis statements simply work better for this kind of essay, I often give the students a formula for this thesis, requiring that their thesis statement be something like, "In (titles of stories), (author's name) explores the conflict between X and Y." Though this may seem ridiculous and reductive (to you and/or to your students), it is helpful to them, especially in terms of helping them avoid the problems described in the "Troubleshooting" section.

9

LITERARY KIND AS CONTEXT: INITIATION STORIES

Students seem to respond well to initiation stories, perhaps because student life is a series of initiations—or because many students are not so very far from the initiation experiences of childhood—or (more mundanely) because initiation stories are a genre they are familiar with from high school literature courses. I think of this chapter as one that can be used rather late in the course, as placement in the text indicates, or quite early in the term. Some classes respond better to literature when their first engagement with it is familiar (and thereby reassuring), and—if I sense that I have a group of such students (science majors uncomfortable about their verbal and literary skills?)—I sometimes teach these stories before moving on to the chapters that focus on particular fictional elements.

PLANNING IDEAS

- Ask students to bring to class a short personal essay (1–2 pages) in which they describe an initiation experience—either an experience of first love, an experience of disillusionment, or an initiation into a different sense of self. Ask several volunteers to read their essays as an introduction to the initiation theme.
- Supplement the readings in this chapter with other initiation stories in the anthology, such as "Her First Ball" and "The Watcher." (I find that my students truly enjoy and benefit from re-reading stories they've dealt with earlier in the course in light of their new insight into initiation stories. Among other things, it gives them a vivid sense of the difference between reading a text on its own terms and in terms of its relation to other stories of the same literary kind.) And/or assign them stories that aren't classic initiation stories, but that nonetheless also deal with the relationships between children and adult family

members (O'Connor's "Everything That Rises Must Converge," for example) or with definitions of proper adult roles (Kincaid's "Girl," for example).

- Ask students to compare these initiation stories with any of the stories they've already read that focus on the learning process of a particular character but that aren't initiation stories. What's the difference? What are the distinguishing features of an initiation story?
- If students have read "The Secret Sharer," have them compare it with "Pants on Fire." Though the two stories are obviously dramatically different, they both to some extent revolve around the central character's confrontation with his ideals of heroism or manliness. Why is one story so funny and the other so serious and dark? How might an adventure story like Conrad's help us imagine the "Pants on Fire" narrator's sense of what a real man and his daily life should be?

TONI CADE BAMBARA

Gorilla, My Love

One might say there are at least two initiations—or perhaps better, transformations—going on in Bambara's story, and I like to begin discussion by asking students to describe them.

1. Hunca Bubba plans to get married, and as part of this new beginning, he changes his name. Changes of name often accompany such initiations in our society. (For example, when Catholics are confirmed—that is, when they ritually confirm their faith and accept the obligations it entails—they take on a new name. Marriage in our society often entails a change of name for the bride and, more recently, sometimes for the groom.) Hunca Bubba's change of name—or return to his official name—indicates an impending change in his status. In a sense, the new name suggests that he is taking on a new identity.

2. Scout/Hazel also experiences an initiation. She had already been aware of the duplicity of adult society, as the movie theater anecdote tells us. The anecdote also tells us that she is willing to fight such mendacity through means simultaneously comical and alarming. But there is something particularly disturbing to her about the "change-up" Hunca Bubba pulls on her, and I like to ask students why this is so. The text seems to suggest that her previous experience of adult lying has been outside the family. But Hunca Bubba is an *uncle* who deceives her, a member of the us-versus-them club. (It is revealing that when Baby Jason joins Scout/Hazel in crying, it is in part "Cause he is my blood brother." Blood is thicker than water and should be, correspondingly, more reliable. But from a child's point of view this, heartbreakingly, turns out not to be the

case.) Beyond lashing out verbally at her uncle, there is little Scout/Hazel can do.

This experience is for her an initiation into the breadth and depth of adult mendacity; it is also an occasion for the acquisition of transformative wisdom. Appropriately, she marks this transformation with a change of name. Henceforth, she will go by Hazel, her proper, even adult, name. And she will not permit Hunca Bubba, the betrayer, to call her by any of the pet names that she has acquired within the family. Hazel has moved into a new phase of life, a phase initiated (like so many others in the process of growing up) by a painful realization and the dispelling of the comforting illusions and fantasies of childhood.

QUESTIONS FOR DISCUSSION

1. We do not know for sure that the narrator is a girl until well into the story. Did you assume from the first that the narrator was a girl or a boy? Explain your assumption. On what evidence or impressions was it based? Discuss your assumptions in terms of the text and in terms of gender expectations.
2. Do you find the children's reaction to the religious movie somehow irreligious or even blasphemous? How is the fact that the narrator and her companions are children relevant to this question? Can we discern anything about the narrator's religious convictions from this story?
3. Are comforting illusions and fantasies, no matter how untrue in the adult world, essential to childhood? How painful has the dispelling of childhood illusions and fantasies been for you? (Will you tell your own children that Santa Claus exists or not? Why?)
4. What do you make of Hunca Bubba's reaction to Hazel's sense of betrayal? Why does he apologize for misleading her?

SUGGESTION FOR WRITING

"Translate" a page of "Gorilla, My Love" into standard, academic English prose. Then write an essay describing what is gained and lost in the translation.

ALICE MUNRO

Boys and Girls

If, in what my students call "the present day and age of these modern times of today," you have trouble getting a discussion started on this story, you'd better call for an investigation by the narcotics squad or hang up your mortarboard. In my perverse way, if I detect the proper intensity of seethe and the lid of indignation about to blow, I try to get their noses (in or out of joint) back into the text. I sometimes start them off with the second sentence: what's going on there with beautiful silver foxes besides killing and skinning them? Does this have anything to do with that more central killing, the killing of the horse, and with the more central concern of differentiation of the sexes? (No, no, don't get too far ahead of me. We'll talk about that issue more fully a little later.) And now the third and fourth sentences: the heroic calendars sent by fur companies (irony anyone?), and what does one of those calendars show? European heroes with "savages" serving as beasts of burden, all against a background of a rather hostile nature. Are we getting a picture of where the narrator stands on social, political, economic issues? Any relation to. . . . Well, we'll get on to that in a minute.

Now, in the second paragraph, there's the girl's mother, who doesn't like the killing and skinning or the gruesome play of the hired man, or the smell. But the girl finds the smell "reassuringly seasonal, like the smell of oranges and pine needles." How could she associate those? Would this be the time to begin to talk about responses "innate" and "learned" or "acculturated"? The "feminine" responses of the mother and the "masculine" responses of the girl here and through much of the story may be looked at in these terms, mightn't they?

It might be impossible to keep "the issue" out of the discussion, but one good in-class written or oral exercise might be character descriptions of the mother and of the father, of Laird, of the hired man. Can the students sketch the character of the narrator as a girl as well? An alternative assignment would be an analysis of the relationship between the girl and her father, the girl and her mother, her brother. You might want to call attention as well to the age as well as sex division, to child versus grown-up and the narrator's perception of grown-up versus child.

But sooner or later, and quite properly, the discussion will turn to the subject indicated in the title, the subject that dominates even if it does not exclude other subjects in the story. This may be a good story in which to stress "development" or the sequential and temporal ordering of the material, for the first and second halves of the story may suggest different emphases, and to "spatialize" the story or take evidence without regard for its place in the story may be misleading. To show the differences, you might want to ask the students to look at the contexts and implications of the two appearances of the phrase "only a girl." You might want to call attention to the narrator's differing roles in her earlier and later dreams. The turning point comes when she is eleven and involves the horses, yet that section is introduced by "I have forgotten to say what the foxes were fed." How could so significant an element in the story be "forgotten"? There would be no initiation story—at least not in these terms—without the horses, you might suggest. You might point out that the trigger to the memory is the father's bloody apron, as if she were just remembering her childhood up to that point. You might ask the students whether this suggests anything about the older narrator's—the voice's—attitude toward the innocence of her childhood (the first part of the story), and toward her initiation into youth if not adulthood. Do these attitudes tell them anything about why certain details were included in the first part of the story, why they were treated the way they are there, and why quite different details are selected and treated quite differently in the second half of the story?

There is no sense in denying the force of theme in determining much of the content and structure here, so I find it just as well to get it out on the table—though not necessarily first. You might want to ask in what sense the characters are representative: Father, Mother, Little Brother, Average Male, Girl? Do the students see any thematic relevance in the different characterizations of the two horses? Would the girl have opened the gate wide for Mack? Is there any theme wider than the sexist theme implied by the burdened savages, by Henry's Stephen Foster song, by the slaughtered foxes and horses?

Still, you might want to ask to what degree the particulars of the story transcend the theme in interest and import. Are the details of fox farming and of life in rural Canada only interesting in their thematic implications? (You might here want to relate childhood and rural life—innocence/Eden/garden—as a common American theme.) Putting up the curtain between her brother's bed and hers may have thematic import, but are all the specific details of the unfinished upstairs bedroom, its contents, the children's superstitions about security, their songs interesting only in terms of the theme? (And, by the way, to what degree is "boys-and-girls: childhood" just as good a rendering of the implications of the title, as "boys-versus-girls: sexism"?) Why does the girl put her brother on the rafter in the barn, endangering his life? How is that act like and unlike the freeing of Flora?

Since in some ways this story may give women students a bit of a hard time, if that's the way your class goes, you may want to ask the question (for discussion or paper) whether there is any significance in the fact that the initiating act here—regardless of outcome—is the liberating of an animal.

QUESTIONS FOR DISCUSSION

1. What is the nature of the initiation in the story? Is there more than one initiation?
2. How do you read the final paragraph of the story?
3. What kind of story might this have been *without* the horses?

SUGGESTION FOR WRITING

Write a personal essay about a time when you felt that assumptions about gender created discomfort or restrictions for you or when you discovered your own gender-based assumptions about someone else to be true or false. Whose assumptions were they? How did you or the other person respond?

Pants on Fire

Baker's "Pants" is a great story to read and discuss after, and in light of, the other initiation stories in this chapter because it is so very different from them, opening up for discussion the similarities between the Munro and Bambara stories, which, at first glance, seem so different from each other.

One thing that I think "Pants on Fire" opens up to view for us is how initiation is figured in the Bambara and Munro stories in terms of the growth, change, and transformation of the protagonists, a growth that comes about through their interactions with others. "Pants on Fire" brings that to light by figuring for us a very different kind of initiation, the narrator himself suggesting that adulthood is less about change or transformation than about discovering that one has already become the kind of person one will always be or, in the narrator's own words, that "I had finished with whatever major growth I was going to have as a human being, and that I was now forever arrested at an intermediate stage of personal development" (par. 10). And in this story the process of initiation is relentlessly internal; the only interactions this narrator has are with shirts, deodorant, and toast (and the toast is even imaginary!).

Nevertheless, "Pants on Fire" is similar to "Gorilla, My Love" and "Boys and Girls" in the way it hinges on a conflict between the protagonist's expectation and reality, in this case the conflict being between "the magnitude of man [the narrator] had hoped to be" and the man the narrator suddenly realizes that he already is (par. 10). And this is where I would focus students in discussion, asking them what the details of the story imply about what kind of man the narrator is and about what kind of man he—and, perhaps, we—wish he were. (The word *hero* might come in handy here, and you might also want to have students dwell on the significance of the word *man* as opposed to *adult, person,* etc.) In this way, I think, one can begin to suggest how the experience of reading the story—the precise ways in which the story plays with, and defies, our expectations—becomes part of the conflict the story itself explores between what is and what might be. And you might here even take up larger questions about how literature in general and particular literary kinds (including initiation stories) inform our vision of what we and our lives might or should be, revisiting—in very different terms—issues that you may have first asked students to consider in relation to "The Zebra Storyteller."

QUESTIONS FOR DISCUSSION

1. What do you think the narrator means when he says that he is "forever arrested at an intermediate stage of personal development," "a man, but not quite the magnitude of man I had hoped to be"? What kind of man do you imagine he hoped that he would be? What kind of man is he and how do all of the details in the story contribute to our sense of what kind of man he is?
2. The narrator opens this story by announcing to us that it is the tale of "the day that my life as an adult began." What exactly does that mean here? How does this narrator define what it means to be an "adult"?
3. Baker's title seems to allude to the childish chant or taunt, "Liar, liar, pants on fire." What do you make of the title? Does it suggest that the narrator is lying? If so, when and where and about what is he lying?
4. How is this story's representation of adulthood and of the process of initiation like and unlike that presented in the Bambara and Munro stories? How might initiation stories like Bambara's and Munro's (as well as stories of other kinds) help form our ideals of adulthood (and of life), ideals such as those the narrator of "Pants on Fire" finds he doesn't live up to?

READING/WRITING IDEAS FOR CHAPTER 9

ESSAYS ABOUT LITERARY KINDS

I find this chapter of the anthology a perfect opportunity to work with students on the techniques and strategies involved in crafting effective comparative essays, and the assignments I use for this unit are, therefore, of two kinds. The first is fairly open-ended and comes closest to the standard comparative essay assignment with which we're all familiar, simply asking students to compare two initiation stories from the anthology in terms of a particular issue, question, theme, element, or point of interest in the texts. The second is a bit more defined and demanding and is a more specifically literary kind-focused assignment, asking students to compare multiple initiation stories to make some general argument about this literary kind, showing—for example—what initiation stories tend to imply about the passage from childhood to adulthood; or how initiation stories with male and female protagonists tend to differ; or following up on the comments in the anthology itself, tackling the question of whether and how initiation stories can really be distinguished from other kinds of short stories.

To prepare students to comfortably and authoritatively make the kind of generalizations required by the second type of essay, I usually require them to read and consider other stories besides the three included in this chapter of the anthology. (I often do the same thing, however, when assigning the first type of essay simply to give students more options and, for some, a chance to analyze a story from a different angle than they did the first time around.) Stories in the "Reading More Fiction" section of the anthology that could be considered initiation stories include "Great Falls," "Personal Testimony," and "Lamar Loper's First Case" (which might be said to be a play on the initiation story rather than a genuine initiation story), while those in other chapters include "Her First Ball," "The Watcher," and "Barn Burning." (I also can't resist the temptation to suggest that "Girl" could make for a very interesting comparison, even though it is obviously not an "initiation story" in any conventional sense.) If you want to go beyond the bounds of the anthology, you're undoubtedly familiar with plenty of appropriate stories, but some of the ones that my students have really enjoyed working with are Michael Chabon's "The Lost World" (*A Model World and Other Stories*); Ellen Gilchrist's "Revenge" (*In the Land of Dreamy Dreams*); Elizabeth Graver's "The Body Shop" (*Have You Seen Me?*), James Joyce's "Araby" (*Dubliners*); and two short but wonderful novels, Jamaica Kincaid's *Annie John* and Carson McCullers's *The Member of the Wedding*.

Essay assignments that ask students to consider the difference between initiation stories and other kinds of short stories might allow or require students to use any stories in the anthology as test cases, but especially good, I've found, are stories such as Bobbie Ann Mason's "Shiloh" that clearly focus on the learning process of the, or a, central character, forcing us to ask whether, how, and why such "learning" differs from what we typically think of as "initiation."

TROUBLESHOOTING

Over the years I have found that comparative essays pose challenges to student writers that are very similar to those posed by the multiple-text, single-author essays described in the last chapter, the key challenges in both cases being the crafting of effective theses and effective argumentative structures. (In terms of structure, I find that—with the exception of the "lens"—the same options tend to hold for this essay, though it's much more often the case in comparison essays that the side-by-side or simultaneous structure proves most workable and effective. And the lens structure in fact can work well for the more kind-focused essay described above) For these reasons, I tend to use versions of the exercises described in the last chapter for this assignment as well, and I also tend to refer to these essays as multiple-text, multiple-author essays in order to insist on the connections between them and the kind of essay described in the last chapter.

KIND-FOCUSED WRITING EXERCISES

1. Identifying the Function and Form of Comparative Essays

I find that the challenges entailed in writing comparative essays are best tackled by focusing students first on questions about *why* one writes comparative essays and then on questions about *how* one writes effective ones. Such "why" questions will be answered very differently, depending on which of the two types of essays sketched out above you're interested in having students write. Essays of the first type—the straightforward comparison of two or more texts in terms of some theme or issue or element—tend to be written (I think?) to show exactly what differentiates two similar texts, what makes each unique. Essays of the second type, however, tend to be much more focused on the similarities that define a given literary kind, what makes a given set of texts alike enough to be considered members of a certain group or part of a certain whole (in this case called "initiation stories"). For this reason, I think such essays tend to be or look a bit more like the multiple-text, single-author essays described in "Reading/Writing Ideas for Chapter 8." Though I have been successful in having discussions about such issues in the abstract, I find it very useful when possible to have students discuss such abstract issues in the light of specific examples, sample essays (by students or scholars) of the type they are being asked to produce. Again, the point of such discussion is to generate ideas about the purpose of comparative essays first and then about the form such essays need to take to fulfill those purposes (which also means discussing what form specific elements of the essay, such as the thesis, need to take).

2. Asking Comparative Questions

Whichever of these two multiple texts essay types I'm assigning, I generally get students started writing by asking them to do a version of the "pattern" exercise described in Chapter 8 (exercise 1), giving them a list of questions to help jump-start their comparison of the texts they're writing about.

In the case of the straightforward comparison assignment, this exercise assignment ends up looking something like this:

Read each of your stories at least once, underlining quotations in each that seem significant to you. As you read, work not only to understand the individual stories but also to identify the similarities and differences among them, identifying both the things that link them together and make them "initiation stories" and the things that distinguish and individualize each. Once you have finished, think more about these similarities and differences, working to answer the following questions as if you were trying to capture for someone who hadn't read your stories the essence of each. You may well also want to make notes about which of the quotations you underlined in reading the stories might serve to illustrate or support the claims you make.

- How would you describe each author's **hero or heroine?** What makes them alike? What (internal and external) characteristics do they share? What makes them different? What (internal and external) characteristics differentiate them?
- How would you describe the role played by the **other characters** whom the heroes or heroines encounter, or interact with, in the stories? How specifically are the roles played by these other characters in the stories alike? Different?
- How would you describe the **problems or conflicts** that the heroes or heroines of these stories face? How exactly are the problems and conflicts alike in the different stories? Different?
- How would you describe the **resolutions** to these conflicts offered in these stories? In what ways are those resolutions alike? In what ways are they different?
- How would you describe the **plot** of the two stories? What's alike about them? What's different?
- How would you describe the **narrative structure** of the stories, i.e., the way the plots, conflicts, etc., are narrated? What's alike about the structure of the stories? What's different?
- How would you describe the significance and role of the **setting** or environment (social, cultural, and/or physical) in the stories? How is the role setting plays alike and different in the two stories?
- What's the overall **tone** or **mood** of these stories—the feelings they tend to evoke? How do they do so? How specifically is the tone or mood of your stories alike? Different?
- What do you think are the **themes**, concerns, problems, or issues articulated or tackled in these stories? How specifically are the themes of the two stories alike? How specifically do they differ?

Taking all of these factors into account and without referring to any particulars (such as character's names), use this sheet of paper to narrate, outline, script out, or draw a map or flowchart that captures the basic features, action, elements, etc., of each of your short stories and/or of the relationship between them. Where do your flowcharts overlap and where do they part ways?

On the whole, what seem to you to be the most significant similarities and differences here? How is each story alike and different in terms of its portrait of "initiation" and/or its definition of "childhood" and "adulthood"? How do the stories compare in terms of the questions or issues they portray as being integral to initiation or that they consider in addition to initiation?

If I'm asking students to write the second, more kind-focused essay, then the questions look even more like those in the exercise described in Chapter 8. Indeed, the only real difference here is that rather than referring to the author's work, I refer, depending on the exact nature of the prompt, to "initiation stories" and/or "initiation stories with female protagonists versus initiation stories with male protagonists" and / or "initiation stories versus other kinds of stories."

Note, too, that the cyberpunk outline (p. 115) reproduced at the end of that exercise description is an especially fitting example for this assignment because it comes from an essay that is itself of this "kind-focused" variety, making claims about the literary kind called "cyberpunk" of precisely the kind that this essay assignment asks students to make about the literary kind called "initiation stories."

3. Generating Theses and Describing Structures

Since this exercise looks exactly like the exercise of the same title described in Chapter 8, I won't bore you by reproducing it again. I will say, however, that I haven't developed a workable "thesis model" for either of these essays, and what's more I don't want to, hoping that students by this point in the course have successfully completed their own initiation process and can fly on their own, especially when they've already tackled multiple-text essays of a different sort.

10

FORM AS CONTEXT:
THE SHORT SHORT STORY

As the anthology suggests, this chapter can provide occasions for exploring and even celebrating the marvelous flexibility of the short story form and, despite the brevity of its selections, can test the analytical abilities of even the most seasoned and sophisticated reader. The "short shorts" provided here can also very usefully be assigned at the beginning of the term, perhaps in conjunction with the short selections that make up the "Reading, Responding, Writing" chapter. I find that if I have a class of students relatively untutored in the methods of literary analysis, it can be helpful to assign a number of very brief works during the first week or two of the term and to spend a significant amount of time (at least a week or two) showing students how to read closely and effectively. When I use these stories in this way, I pay more attention to conveying ways to glean significance from the text than to studying particular elements, imparting terminology, or suggesting theoretical approaches. In these sessions, we tend to study a story's opening paragraph(s) for hints about its conflicts and concerns, to look closely at the possible implications of the title, to note repeated patterns, and to jot down questions that the text provokes. In other words, we work to gather the raw material of analysis and then try to make sense of it. After several such sessions, I find that the class has a better understanding of what it means to read a text, and students are ready to tackle the work of the semester with some degree of confidence.

PLANNING IDEAS

- Show the class a videotape of the BBC film *Five Stories of an Hour,* which offers a straight reading and four film renderings or "translations" of the work in a mere thirty minutes. Divide the class into groups and have each group analyze one of the translations of the story, taking

care to comment on which parts of the story the filmmaker emphasizes, which parts are changed, and to what apparent purpose and
effect.

- If you are using poetry in your course, you might pair one of these very
  short stories with a narrative poem of about the same length and use
  the pairing as a basis for discussing the similarities and differences
  between reading a poem and a very concentrated short story.

- Assign different stories from this chapter to different groups of students. Have the students draft a plan for expanding the story into a
  longer work—a full-length short story, a novel, or a screenplay. Ask
  each group to share the plan with the class, to explain what additions
  would be made, why they chose to expand the story as they did, and
  what they see as the strengths and weaknesses of the expanded form
  in comparison to the original.

- Bring in a copy of *Life's Little Instruction Book* so that you can compare
  some of the father's suggestions to his son in that work with the
  mother's suggestions to her daughter in "Girl." You may also want to
  discuss why one work is classified as a nonfiction "how to" book and
  the other is called a short story (i.e., is labeled literature). You might
  also have students read short stories that use the how-to format, such
  as those in Lorrie Moore's *Self-Help* or Pam Houston's "How to Talk to
  a Hunter" (*Cowboys Are My Weakness*).

KATE CHOPIN

The Story of an Hour

Chopin's story concludes with what has come to be called an "O. Henry
ending," and so I sometimes ask students how the author sets us up for
this ending. Since we know from the beginning of the story that Mrs.
Mallard suffers from heart trouble, how is it that we are surprised (if we
are—and I was the first time I read the story) when her husband unexpectedly returns and she dies of a heart attack? Clearly Chopin takes
particular care to put us off the scent. Early on the narrator assures us
that a family friend, Richards, has inquired closely into the matter of
Brently Mallard's death and convinced himself by way of "a second tel-
egram" that Mallard truly has perished in the railway disaster. He goes to
this trouble because he wants to make absolutely sure of the truth before
bearing the news to the ailing Mrs. Mallard.

Such careful craft is evident throughout the work: in the upstairs/
downstairs, private/public dichotomies Chopin sets up and in the way
she sustains suspense as she gradually allows Mrs. Mallard—and the
reader—to discover her own possibly "monstrous joy" at her husband's
apparent demise. One way to examine Chopin's masterly use of suspense

is to read the story aloud, pausing at several junctures to imagine what revelations might be up ahead. (If you show the videotape suggested above, you can simply stop the tape at several points during the actress's reading.) For example, the glorious spring day so beautifully described in paragraphs 5 and 6 might be expected in a more conventional story to suggest the tragic contrast between the liveliness and beauty of the season and the desolation and loss that are Mrs. Mallard's lot. However, as we soon discover, the birds twittering and the mottled vista of clouds and sky suggest, less predictably, that a new, freer life is opening up for Mrs. Mallard. Similarly, when we read that the lines of Mrs. Mallard's face "bespoke repression and even a certain strength," we may at first believe that she is repressing her grief, trying to be strong and maintain her composure despite the loss of her husband. Later we realize that she is probably repressing recognition of her joy—and perhaps that the lines of repression also suggest something about her history within the marriage.

Some students may jump to the conclusion that Chopin's is a story about a woman subdued and perhaps abused by her husband—a story implicitly critical of the "Western patriarchal hegemony." But a closer look at the text suggests that assessing blame is not the story's aim; and in this regard, of course, paragraphs 12 and 13 are key. (Of course for some of us, critiquing patriarchy and assessing blame are not quite or necessarily the same thing.)

In paragraph 13 the narrator describes the husband's hands as "tender" and acknowledges that his face "never looked save with love upon her." More important, in paragraph 14 the narrator suggests that the repression Mrs. Mallard has felt is experienced by women *and* men: "There would be no one to live for her during those coming years; she would live for herself. There would be no powerful will bending hers in that blind persistence with which men and women believe they have a right to impose a private will upon a fellow-creature. A kind intention or a cruel intention made the act seem no less a crime."

Chopin here seems to suggest that, by its very nature, marriage encourages people to impose their wills on one another. To explore this idea a bit more pointedly, I like to ask my students to think about their dating experiences. I ask them if they *always* get to go to the movie they most want to see when they go out on a date. (And I suggest some serious self-examination may be in order if they answer in the affirmative!)

QUESTIONS FOR DISCUSSION

1. What examples of irony do you find in the last five paragraphs of the story?
2. Why is it appropriate that Richards try to screen Brently Mallard from his wife's view?
3. Do you believe the Mallards' marriage was a loveless one? How would you describe the marriage, based on what the story tells you?

SUGGESTION FOR WRITING

Compare the portrait of marriage in "The Story of an Hour" with that in Lawrence's "Odour of Chrysanthemums."

GABRIEL GARCÍA MÁRQUEZ

A Very Old Man with Enormous Wings

The best defense, we're told, is a good offense, so I like to be offensive in teaching "A Very Old Man" and ask students whether they can take a story like this seriously. If credibility doesn't come up, I ask if they believe the story. Then, do they "believe" the people in "Sánchez" or "Boys and Girls" ever really existed or if the events happened as they are told? With luck, we're off and running on issues like probability and telling the truth by lying. Why should a probable fiction be better or more serious or more valuable than an improbable one? Aren't they both, after all, fiction— i.e., false? Well, of course you can learn about people and life from probable fiction, but how often do you run into a very old man with enormous wings? But do you learn anything about Pelayo and Elisenda? About provincial culture and provincial Latin American culture? About crowd behavior? About human response to the unknown or extraordinary? Indeed, you can argue, you may be able to learn more about response to the unknown here than in, say, "Everything That Rises Must Converge." There you know about the limited perspectives of Julian and his mother and can feel superior to them, but here the extraordinary man is as strange to you as he is to the villagers.

This may be a good time to bring up symbol once more: is the old man a symbol? As a symbol, if he is one, does he "stand for" something? If so, what? If not, can he still be a symbol? We're back to symbols as nonparaphrasable units of meaning.

As usual—or perhaps more than usual—you, of course, must be prepared to handle quite different responses and to bring them back to areas you want to discuss at this point in the course. If credibility doesn't come up right away, you may want to listen for interpretations of what the old man stands for, begin with symbol, and work around to meaning in terms of the way people in the story act. Or someone may begin by saying that what García Márquez is doing is recounting a folk tale straight, as if the narrator were as credulous as the villagers, and that it is a kind of patronizing tale whose subject is human credibility. How do we deal with folk tales? Do we dismiss them? Interpret them psychologically or anthropologically? Accept them as a vision of reality from an angle quite different from ours but more or less common to a significant number of people in the world? You might want to compare the folklore element here with that in "Love Medicine."

At some point in the class discussion the realistic (some would say disgusting) detail in the story is sure to come up. It's easy to dismiss this merely as a device for achieving credibility or willful suspension of disbelief in an evasive half-truth, I think. I'd rather think of the details as part of the imagination or vision of the story, as if García Márquez had said to himself, "What would happen if a very old man with enormous wings were found here in the village?" and had then imagined the consequences as precisely as he could.

One hopes someone will mention the humor—the neighbor woman who knows everything about life and death and who identifies the old man as an angel; Father Gonzaga's testing him with Latin; the villagers' plans for him, including his being "put to stud in order to implant on earth a race of winged wise men." I hope you don't have to explain why such details are funny; or why funny details don't disqualify the story from serious consideration.

QUESTIONS FOR DISCUSSION

1. The story is full of rather off-putting realistic details, cruelty, greed, humor: what is it we feel reading this story? Does the mixture of real and fantastic have its analogue in the potpourri of emotions?
2. And what, finally, do we feel about the old man—pity? fear? disgust? wonder? Do we want him to turn out to be a hoax? Stay and play with the children and make Pelayo and Elisenda rich? Die (to rid the world of monstrosity)? Soar off into the sun?
3. How are we to take the subtitle, "A Tale for Children"?

ERNEST HEMINGWAY

A Clean, Well-Lighted Place

I confess Hemingway's "A Clean, Well-Lighted Place" has never done much for me personally. But I persist in teaching this story anyway because it is always a favorite of students, perhaps because we are all, at a certain age, would-be existentialists. Despite its appeal to students, however, I find that my students have a hard time "unpacking" the story in any meaningful way. As a result, I have found that posing (and often reposing) very specific questions is the only way that I can provoke a meaningful discussion. And even before I get to questions I tend to open discussion by asserting that this story, in a fashion not unlike Kafka's "A Hunger Artist," really makes sense only as a kind of parable or allegory in which "a clean, well-lighted place" refers to much more than a late-night café.

To get at what else a "clean, well-lighted place" might be, however, I find that I have to first get out ideas about why that place is so meaningful to some, but not all, of the characters in the story, which means starting with questions about those characters and the kinds of attitudes, values, worldviews, or ways of life they each represent. The two key figures in this regard are obviously the waiters, and students are quick to note that the older of those waiters is closely allied with the old man. It is they who appear to most appreciate, even need, the "clean, well-lighted place." But why? What differentiates them from the young waiter? What do the young waiter's remarks suggest about the kind of person he is? For one thing the young waiter has a wife and, as the older waiter points out, "youth, confidence, and a job" (par. 64). For all this, however, the young waiter is obviously presented as the less admirable character. Why? Among other things, the young waiter lacks sympathy, imagination, and compassion, caring more about his own creature comforts than about the old man or anyone else, not even wanting "to look at him" (par. 44). And in this case, the notion of "looking" carries deeper connotations, for one might say that what the older waiter and the old man share is a willingness both to see and to experience the "fear" that comes of seeing (par. 76). But, as the older waiter asks himself, "What did he fear?" The answer and the reason why the old man, according to the waiter, tried to kill himself is, of course, "nothing," "nada," the realization that "It was all a nothing and a man was nothing too" (par. 6, 76).

At this point in the conversation, I always have to pause to make students really think and talk about exactly what this means. What is "it" and what does it really mean to see or accept that "It was all a nothing and a man was nothing too"? For without a clear understanding of what "nothingness" in the story refers to, it's simply not possible to understand how "a clean, well-lighted place" functions as a kind of temporary resting place, "a lighted island" in which, as literary critic Earl Rovit puts it in *Ernest Hemingway* (New York: Twayne, 1963), "those without the illusions of belief (religion, youth, confidence, family ties, insensitive indifference) can come, can sit, can drink with dignity; can find a small surcease or point of rest from their constant awareness of the meaninglessness of life and their struggles to oppose that meaninglessness" (pp. 114–15).

As a result the young waiter and the two older characters represent, respectively, the two orders into which, as Rovit argues, Hemingway's fiction constantly divides the human race: on the one hand, those "who are too flabby in their self-indulgence, too susceptible to a variety of illusions concerning themselves and life to be allowed to take over the responsibilities of creating their own lives," "who 'have' wealth, security, position, and the protective comforts which these possessions erect as a barrier against the elemental struggle of life," and, on the other hand, those who "cannot countenance [such] illusions . . . because their knowledge . . . forces them to accept the reality of life as a grim, relentless struggle" (pp. 117–18), a struggle in which the honest fearfulness and the "dignity" in the face of it that characterize the old man and the old waiter become the highest and in some ways the only positive values (par. 51).

QUESTIONS FOR DISCUSSION

1. How is each of the waiters characterized? What worldview or values does each represent? Why is the older waiter more sympathetic to the old man? What makes the older waiter similar to the old man? What makes them both different from the young waiter? When the older waiter remarks that the difference lies in the fact that the young waiter has "youth, confidence, and a job," what is he suggesting about how these things make the young waiter different from him and the old man? What do these qualities or things give him that they don't have?
2. *Nothing* is a word invoked by the older waiter at the beginning and end of the story to explain why he is afraid and why the old man tried to commit suicide. Why? What does this mean? In what sense is "nothing" something to be afraid of or in despair about?
3. What does the clean, well-lighted café mean or represent or symbolize to the two older characters in the story? Why exactly is such a place so important to them? Why and how specifically is it important that the place be clean? Well lighted?
4. What do light and dark symbolize in our culture? How does this story build on and/or complicate that symbolism?

SUGGESTIONS FOR WRITING

1. Do some library research on Hemingway's theories of fiction and write an analysis of "A Clean, Well-Lighted Place" in which you measure his success in following his own precepts with that story.
2. Write an essay comparing "A Clean, Well-Lighted Place" to Kipling's "Without Benefit of Clergy," two stories that seem to explore questions about how people cope with a world in which "Our nada . . . art in nada."

JAMAICA KINCAID
_____

Girl

It might be interesting to approach this story as an example of "wisdom" or "didactic" literature. The earliest wisdom literature we know of is the

Sumerian "Instructions of Suruppak," parts of which date to as early as 2500 B.C. We know of Egyptian, Aramaic, Hebrew, African, Greek, Irish, and Norse versions, among others. The genre is as old and widespread as literature itself. Generally, wisdom literature offers advice about conduct and supports this advice with truisms and general pronouncements usually offered in a fictitious setting wherein a father addresses his son.

Traditional "didactic" literature—and there is much that feels and is traditional in "Girl"—offers practical advice on some aspect of life. For example, the Greek poet Hesiod in his *Works and Days* and Thoreau in *Walden* offer practical suggestions about farming and rural life. Yet, almost invariably, mixed in with this practical advice and/or subtly suggested by the advice are ethical admonitions as well. These authors are interested in teaching people not merely how to farm but how to live and what to value.

It can be useful to give this background information to students and then ask them to what degree "Girl" fits in with the genres of wisdom and didactic literature and to what degree it departs from them. Is it, in effect, an antiwisdom or antididactic work in which the advice harms rather than edifies? The most obvious difference between "Girl" and the works I have mentioned is its brevity. I sometimes ask the class whether a series of suggestions of this length can hope to impart much (positively or negatively) or whether so short a story, because it *does* consist of a series of straightforward admonitions, is likely to be more effective than a story that tells a tale. And one of the questions you'll probably want to pose to students at some point is how we might interpret the story differently if we read it as representing a single "conversation" (that is largely a monologue) and if we read it as representing a grown-up or adolescent girl's memory of years' worth of accumulated advice. What significance does the timing of certain remarks take on, for example, if we read the story in each of these ways? What is the effect of Kincaid's inclusion of at least two responses by "girl"?

One of the aspects of "Girl" that may distinguish it dramatically from traditional wisdom literature is its obvious concern with gender issues, with what is considered appropriate wisdom for "girl." (And in raising this issue, one might want to ask students to consider all of the ramifications of Kincaid's title, not just the fact that it is gender-specific, but also the fact that it isn't *"A Girl"* or *"The Girl."* What are the effects of the very brevity of the title and its obvious lack of articles?) In fact, one could teach "Girl" as a distinctly different sort of female initiation story, comparing it, for example, to a much more conventional, yet also gender-interested, initiation story such as Munro's "Boys and Girls." What conception of female roles is suggested by the kind of advice being given here? The relentless focus on buying, growing, preparing, and serving food; making medicine; making and caring for clothing; keeping a house and one's body clean; behaving properly toward, and caring properly for, others, but especially men? The concern with appearances and reputation? The obvious anxiety about sexuality? What does this adviser end up communicating to "girl" about what "kind of woman" she should and should not be? About what's valuable and important in life? About what adult life is like?

QUESTIONS FOR DISCUSSION

1. How might the advice be different if the addressee were a boy or young man? What advice might a mother give to a young man? What advice might a father give?
2. Why, amid all the practical advice about how to iron, set table, etc., does the speaker include the admonitions about not becoming a slut? Does the inclusion of these admonitions suggest that not becoming a slut is no more or less important than ironing correctly, or does it suggest just the opposite? Is there an inner coherence or logic to these pieces of advice and/or to the order in which they are given?
3. Who is speaking? How can you tell?
4. Is this really a story? If so, why do you say so? What makes it a story? If it is not a story, what is it?
5. Why does "Girl" end with dialogue about feeling bread? Is this somehow a conclusion to what has come before? Why does the author end where she does? With a question?

SUGGESTION FOR WRITING

Write your own short story "Boy" modeled on "Girl" or write your own version of "Girl," accounting for your inclusions and omissions. Do this either from your own point of view or from that of an unwelcome adviser.

YASUNARI KAWABATA

The Grasshopper and the Bell Cricket

The narrator's approach to the events of "The Grasshopper and the Bell Cricket" transforms a rather simple, children's adventure into a lovely prose poem about love, the assessment of value, and the gifts of memory and innocence. The story also presents a parable about art and artistry, and it is with that aspect of the story that I like to start. In paragraphs 3 and 4, the narrator explains the origins and evolution of the beautiful lanterns that the children carry each evening in their search for grasshoppers. The lanterns, which were first bought or made as practical tools for the hunt, have become over time lovely and elaborate works of art, with each child vying to produce a more beautiful version than the last. I encourage students to discuss what views of art and the artist the narrator seems to suggest in his telling of this part of the tale.

The last half of the story introduces the subject of youthful attraction. The boy who has found a grasshopper keeps offering it to the children at large, but he waits until the girl he fancies expresses her wish for the insect before making a present of it to her. Students are sometimes puzzled by this introduction of young love into the story. I like to provoke their thinking about this element in a somewhat roundabout way, by asking why the narrator feels "slightly jealous" of the boy. In the course of exploring this question, students often come to perceive that the narrator envies the boy and the other children their innocence, their naive pleasure in the grasshoppers, the bell cricket, and each other. He knows that time will change all this—that, figuratively speaking, they will probably catch common grasshoppers more often in their adult lives than they will catch rare bell crickets—that life will be full of disappointments as yet unimagined. When he sees the names of the boy and girl projected by serendipity on each other's clothes, he appreciates the chance beauty and rightness of the picture before him. He imagines that if each could carry that picture into the future, it would provide pleasure and solace in the midst of adult dissatisfactions and failures.

QUESTIONS FOR DISCUSSION

1. What does the part of the story involving the artistry of the children have to do with the ending of the story—the narrator's desire that the boy and girl remember the beauty of their names projected onto each other's clothes? In what sense is this part of the scene, which is temporary and which only the narrator observes, a work of art?
2. Why do the children make new lanterns every day? What are their motives?
3. What do the narrator's musings reveal about his experience of life and love? Would it make any difference to your interpretation of the story if you found out that the narrator only imagines the creation and evolution of the lanterns, building this part of the story on the evidence of the lanterns with which he sees the children playing?

SUGGESTION FOR WRITING

Write an essay comparing representations of the artist in "The Grasshopper and the Bell Cricket" and "A Hunger Artist," "The Zebra Storyteller," or "The Real Thing."

READING/WRITING IDEAS FOR CHAPTER 10

ESSAYS ABOUT FORM

Though there are obviously a multitude of ways to use this chapter and an equal number of appropriate writing assignments, one possibility is to have students tackle a different version of the kind of essay assignments described in Chapter 9, this time focusing on a formally, rather than thematically, defined literary kind. Again, then, you might either have students write a straightforward comparison essay, showing how two or more short short stories differ in terms of the way they use the "short short" form, or have them write an essay that focuses on several texts and that makes more general claims about the qualities inherent to the short short form or about the range of possibilities within the short short story form. If you choose either of these options, you may well want to use versions of the exercises described in Chapter 9 to get students started.

If, on the other hand, you decide to use this chapter early in the semester, as the headnote suggests, you will undoubtedly want to handle the essay assignment very differently, using it to deal with more basic "writing about literature" issues. One possibility might be to have students write what some instructors refer to as an "explication" of one of the short stories here rather than an essay proper, asking them to walk through the text step by step and to analyze details at each step. This assignment can be useful both for honing inexperienced students' skills at close reading and as a basis for a discussion of the differences between explication and the kinds of argument that demand organizing one's analysis in terms of one's own ideas about it rather than in terms of the chronological order of the text itself. The short short stories on offer here work well for this simply because they are compact enough to reward such a careful, step-by-step analysis. And, in fact, this assignment might, as a result, prove effective even if you teach this chapter later in the term, particularly as a bridge between fiction and poetry, which—I find—students typically approach in an explication-type way.

Yet another possibility would be to use this chapter to begin having students think about the relationship between fiction and poetry by having them write an essay on the differences between one of these short stories and one of the more narrative poems in the poetry section of the anthology. (If you do so, I recommend choosing a poem that doesn't rhyme, simply because this helps students avoid seeing the differences in simplistic terms.) Poems that might work well for this assignment include Pound's "The River-Merchant's Wife: A Letter," Wayman's "Wayman in Love," Mouré's "Thirteen Years," Piercy's "Barbie Doll," Knight's "Hard Rock Returns to Prison from the Hospital for the Criminal Insane," Olds's "I Go Back to May 1937," and Song's "Heaven," among many, many others. One of the questions I face in giving this assignment is whether it would be more helpful for students to compare texts that treat the same or similar issues or to compare texts that have absolutely no similarities in terms of content. Obviously, the first option can make for more interesting comparisons in terms of what students say about particular texts, but the latter forces students to focus completely on form and on the general question of what differentiates short fiction from narrative poetry.

TROUBLESHOOTING

Obviously, the challenges students face here will be very different depending on the kind of writing you assign. To some extent, I find that the exposition assignment can potentially create the most problems because it invites students to walk through a text step by step in a way that it is usually necessary to encourage them *not* to do in tackling other essay assignments. But because students are tempted to take this approach anyway (especially, but by no means exclusively, when they begin to write about poetry), the assignment can provide a great opportunity to tackle the issue head-on and to help students figure out how to work from, rather than against, this tendency. At the very least, identifying such a step-by-step analysis as an "exposition" assignment and thus distinguishing it from your other "essay" assignments suggests to students that the two kinds of writing are fundamentally different. To reinforce that point, you might consider using the exposition assignment as an exercise, having students then revise their exercises into more conventional, thesis-driven essays.

11

CULTURE AS CONTEXT

When I first read the title for this chapter of the anthology, I was sure it was going to focus on the strategies involved in analyzing fictional texts as artifacts informed by their particular sociohistorical contexts. And the chapter does deal with such methodological issues, the story "Pierre Menard" foregrounding them in an especially intense and funny way. But the chapter also deals with culture as context in a different, more thematic manner as well, the first two stories here—Porter's "Holiday" and Laurence's "The Rain Child"—exploring what happens when individuals encounter cultural groups different from their own or when individuals and families live across or between cultures (as many of my students do). Thus the chapter focuses both on cultural-context reading strategies and on fictional texts that themselves thematize the ways in which culture shapes individuals and their "readings" of, and interactions with, each other, while also asking questions about the very nature, origins, and meaning of "culture." As a result, I think the chapter lends itself to being used in at least two different, if also potentially quite compatible, ways, one more thematic, the other more methodological.

PLANNING IDEAS

- If you're going to use this chapter to introduce methodological issues, you might want to consider saving it for after you do the "Critical Contexts" chapter, using Dillon's essay on styles of reading to pave the way for introducing this cultural context style of reading to your students. Or you might consider building your discussion of cultural-context reading directly out of your work with canonical-context reading by introducing the idea that authors are themselves products of particular cultural contexts. If you take this approach, you might want to give students biographical information on Porter and Laurence, as well as some pertinent historical information and/or primary materials, to read in conjunction with "Holiday" and "The Rain Child," discussing how personal biographies and history interrelate and how both can speak through stories and inform our interpretations of them. Or you might use this opportunity to get students into the library to identify and collect such information on their own. Then you might use "Pierre Menard" as a way to introduce questions about what is lost and gained through such an approach.

- If you want to supplement the stories in this chapter with others that lend themselves to cultural-context analysis, I frankly find that "The Yellow Wallpaper" is by far the easiest to work with in this way, not only because it is informed by its cultural context in ways that are easy for students to see and exciting for them to think, read, and write about but also because there happens to be a wealth of primary and secondary material available to help students with such work (see note to "The Yellow Wallpaper"). Or you might want to allow students themselves to identify stories that they've already read that present contexts they would like to learn more about.

- If you decide to also or instead use this chapter to focus on culture in a more thematic way, you might want to have students read "The Rain Child" in conjunction with a story or a novel by an African writer that deals with similar issues from a different perspective. Collections containing stories that might work well for this include Christina Ama Ata Aidoo's *No Sweetness Here* and Ngugi wa Thiong'o's *Secret Lives*, while Chinua Achebe's *No Longer at Ease* (a "sequel" of sorts to his more famous *Things Fall Apart*) and Tsitsi Dangarembga's *Nervous Condition* are each wonderfully teachable novels that would work very well in this context. (Jamaica Kincaid's novel *Lucy* also works well for this, though Kincaid is West Indian rather than African and her novel set in the United States.

- On the other hand, the thematic approach might also work well if you instead supplement the texts on offer here with texts that deal with such issues in a setting more familiar to your students. Teaching, as I do, on the border between Mexico, Texas, and New Mexico, I find that my students respond very enthusiastically to the short stories of Denise Chavez (*The Last of the Menu Girls*), Sandra Cisneros (*Woman Hollering Creek*), and Benjamin Saenz (*Flowers for the Broken*). But I highly recommend that you try seeking out appropriate texts by local writers, since for my students this approach has the added advantage of allowing us to read, think, and write about the work of writers who are virtually our neighbors; living, breathing people whom students can see and even talk with at local readings, rather than simply read about or experience only as words on a page.

- Have students read "Holiday" in conjunction with Robert Frost's "Stopping by Woods on a Snowy Evening," a poem that one critic argues informs the ending of Porter's story (see "Questions for Discussion," below).

KATHERINE ANNE PORTER

Holiday

"Holiday" is a wonderful text for a discussion of "cultural context" precisely because, like so many Porter stories, it is a tale of cross-cultural encounters narrated from the point of view of the outsider whose marginal position allows her insight into the workings of that culture that might not be available to insiders, even as it also prohibits her from truly understanding this way of life as only insiders can and do. (As a result, the story also works well in conjunction with the anthology's "Point of View" chapter or can provide a good opportunity to revisit the issues raised there from a slightly different angle, allowing you to emphasize how points of view can be cultural, as well as individual.)

The character of the narrator may, in fact, be a good place to start discussion. For like other Porter characters (in, for example, the well-known "Flowering Judas"), the unnamed narrator of "Holiday" is an outsider by choice, who comes to the Texas farm of the Müllers not so much to experience another culture as to escape her own, to "run away" from her "troubles" and even from the "tradition, background, and training" that taught her that running away was wrong (par. 1). And what she appreciates about the Müller household is precisely that she cannot, at least at first, understand their language or their ways, enjoying the freedom that came of knowing "they were not talking to me and did not expect me to answer" (par. 26): "it was good not to have to understand what they were saying. I loved that silence which means freedom from the constant pressure of other minds and other opinions and other feelings, that freedom to fold up in quiet and go back to my own center" (par. 27). It is only when she is first shown the private attic room (a symbolically fitting setting for this observant outsider) that the narrator first begins to think that she's "going to like it here," "it's going to be all right" (par. 25).

At this point, you might want to discuss the ways in which that desire to escape defines the meaning of *holiday* at the beginning of the story and, perhaps, in our culture more generally (though, perhaps, *vacation* might be the more appropriate term in today's language). Indeed, you might even want to discuss how often we associate holidays or vacations not only with escaping our own everyday lives and environments but also with temporarily escaping to other, more exotic, cultures and/or settings, to experience places and peoples that—in Lucy's words, "you'd hate to live with but [are] very nice to visit" (par. 4). And it does, in fact, seem to be true that an exotically or romantically pastoral setting is exactly what the narrator hopes for and expects, largely because of Lucy, the romantic novel-reader, and her depictions of the Müller farm.

What she finds instead, of course, is not a pastoral idyll, but a grim landscape and the in some ways equally grim way of life of the people who make their living from it. That life is, above all, defined by an unremitting cycle of work in which "one" day was "like the other" (par. 41). That focus on work is perhaps brought out most vividly when the narrator observes the children "kneading mud into loaves and pies and carrying their battered dolls and cotton rag animals through the operations of domestic life" (par. 42), even in their play performing precisely the same tasks the adults around them perform every day. For, as the narrator remarks when observing Hatsy "on her knees in the dining room, washing the floor" as she does every night, "She would always work too hard, and be tired all her life, and never know that this was anything but perfectly natural; everybody worked all the time, because there was always more work waiting when they had finished what they were doing then" (par. 46, 48). Ironically or not, then, the narrator has come on holiday to a place where there seem to be no holidays except for the weekly trips to the *Turnverein*, where even meal times are themselves a time of work for at least some female members of the family.

As a result, the narrator comes to see the Müllers as people whose "enormous energy and animal force" makes them in some ways very like the farm animals that they care for (and that Porter describes quite vividly in the story) (par. 33), people whose very work-driven, "muscular life" lends their daily lives a kind of mental "repose," an "almost mystical inertia" of mind different in kind from that enjoyed by the kind of people who go on holidays (par. 40). (And, in this regard, Porter's characterization of the Müllers comes startlingly close to Lawrence's portrayal of Maurice Pervin in "The Blind Man.")

Here you might want to bring out the ways in which the story thereby to some extent associates the Müllers and the culture they represent with the physical and/or sensual and with nature and the narrator and the culture she represents with the mental and/or intellectual and with culture in the sense of civilization (a good chance to re-engage the anthology's discussion of the different meanings of *culture*). This might also be the place to draw out the ways in which, in turn, the mental life is associated with individuality, since it is precisely a sense of her own individual identity that the narrator seeks to affirm through the "freedom" granted her by her outsider status, "to fold up in quiet and go back to my own center, to find out again, for it is always a rediscovery, what kind of creature it is that rules me finally," "the one thing I cannot live without" (par. 27). And, obviously, one of the things that immediately and continuously strikes the narrator about the Müllers is how nonindividual they are, how nearly indistinguishable each is from the others, "every face" having the same "pale, tilted eyes, on every head that taffy-colored hair, as though they might all be brothers and sisters" (par. 23). This physical likeness merely symbolizes the deeper sameness created by a way of life or a culture that grants to individuality little room or value: "They were united in their tribal scepticisms, as in everything else. I got a powerful impression that they were all, even the sons-in-law, one human being divided into several separate appearances" (par. 39). (One might also see the Müllers' disregard for individuality as being supported or suggested, too, by Father Müller's rather paradoxical affinity for Marxism.) Rather than honoring individuality, the Müllers exemplify a culture that prescribes roles for people based on their gender and/or on their physical capabilities, an idea aptly illustrated through the carefully organized seating (and standing!) arrangements at the family dinner. And, interestingly enough, the narrator seems also to recognize that it is this very insistence on familial roles rather than individuality, even the drive and ability to absorb new members into itself as the Müller family does its sons-in-law (par. 35), that has allowed the Müllers and the German immigrant community they represent to maintain their distinct cultural identity, the very same mealtime decorum illustrating that "three generations in this country had not made them self-conscious or disturbed their ancient customs" (par. 32).

And while, in the end, the Müllers' treatment of Ottilie brings this particular, nonindividualistic, and/or somewhat utilitarian ideology to the fore, she at first seems like a glaring exception to it. For Ottilie to the narrator at first "seemed" "the only individual in the house," more "whole" by virtue of her utter nonbelonging than even the narrator herself (par. 39). It is obviously this quality that simultaneously repels and attracts the narrator to Ottilie, even as it also—I think—complicates the narrator's vision both of the Müllers and of the meaning and value of both individuality and nonbelonging. For in a somewhat ironic fashion, it is Ottilie's nonbelonging that the narrator seems to want to save her from by taking her to join her family at Mother Müller's funeral, even as it is also Ottilie's individual grief that the narrator seems to want to force the Müllers themselves to recognize. And both of these contradictory impulses are already present, in a sense, in the narrator's initial reaction to the photograph of Ottilie,

> which connected her at once somehow to the world of human beings . . .; for an instant some filament lighter than cobweb spun itself out between that living center in her and in me, a filament from some center that held us all bound to our unescapable common source, so that her life and mine were kin, even a part of each other, and the painfulness and strangeness of her vanished. (par. 58)

Obviously at this or some point, students are bound to want to talk about the Müllers' treatment of Ottilie and to assess it for themselves. While I try to let them have their say, I also insist that they work to understand, if not to accept, the sympathetic, even positive assessment ultimately offered both by the narrator and by the text as a whole (par. 60–61), especially since such cross-cultural judgments are, to a very large extent, precisely what this story and this chapter are all about. Be warned that the conversation can, at this point, quickly turn into a forum on moral or cultural relativism itself with students arguing about the degree to which one should try to understand and respect the values and practices of other cultures on their own terms and the degree to which one should apply absolute moral standards. (If you want to go there, and you really want to mix things up, just try saying the word *clitoridectomy*.)

Though I tend to let the conversation go there, as it were, at least for a while, precisely because I think such questions are genuinely part of Porter's story and of the narrator's particular ambivalence about Ottilie, I eventually try to bring students back to the story itself by focusing them on the wonderfully ambiguous ending. As the anthology suggests, one obviously valid argument interprets it as suggesting that "what the narrator, the stranger from the wider world comes to realize is that for all of the differences, human life is the same" (see introduction to "Culture as Context"). I tend to begin the discussion of the ending with that statement (since students have undoubtedly read it), asking them both to explain what they think the statement itself means, what the ending might say about how and why "human life is the same," and what details in the story support that interpretation. Then, if the students themselves haven't begun to critique that interpretation (which they sometimes do), I point them to evidence that suggests another, very different possibility—that the narrator's "ironical mistake" in fact involves assuming that she can bridge the gap between herself and Ottilie, that there is some essential humanity that transcends or cuts across cultural difference. Thus, according to this interpretation, the story might in fact end up affirming that others can be so different from us as to be, in certain senses, "beyond" "reach" (par. 83). What I like about the story is that it seems to support both of these utterly opposed interpretations, as well as others that sometimes come out at this point in discussion. Thus our discussion of this ending can very vividly illustrate for students what I mean when I talk about "yes-and" rather than "either/or" interpretations.

QUESTIONS FOR DISCUSSION

1. How would you characterize the narrator of "Holiday"? What values and/or worldview might she represent? How do her expectations about, and initial reactions to, the Müllers help to characterize her? Why is she taking this "holiday" and what does *holiday* seem to mean to her and to us early in the story?
2. How does the narrator herself characterize the Müllers and the culture or way of life they represent? How specifically does she see the Müllers and their way of life as different from and/or in conflict with her own? Does her attitude toward the Müllers change? If so, when, how, and why? Do you think these changes reflect a kind of learning process? If so, what might the narrator learn?
3. How do the narrator's responses to Ottilie change over the course of the story? How does she first interpret Ottilie and her relationship to the family? What, perhaps symbolic, significance does Ottilie have for

her at this point? How does her interpretation of Ottilie and/or Ottilie's significance change when Ottilie shows her the photograph? Why
does it change? How does her interpretation of Ottilie and/or Ottilie's
significance change after Mother Müller's death? Why does it change?
Why does she start to take Ottilie to the funeral and what do you think
she's trying to accomplish by doing so? How does her interpretation
of Ottilie and/or Ottilie's significance change at the very end of the
story? Why does she ultimately not take Ottilie to the funeral?
4. The anthology argues that the ending of the story suggests that "what
the narrator, the stranger from the wider world comes to realize is that
for all of the differences, human life is the same." What precisely does
the ending suggest about how and why "human life is the same"?
What evidence from the story supports this interpretation? How else
might you interpret the ending of the story and/or the messages the
story as a whole conveys about cultural difference and human sameness?
5. Literary critic George Hendrick argues in *Katherine Anne Porter* (New
York: Twayne, 1965) that the ending of "Holiday" can be interpreted
as a rewriting of, or allusion to, Robert Frost's "Stopping by Woods on
a Snowy Evening," a poem you can find in the "Reading More Poetry"
section of your anthology. Do you agree that this is a valid interpretive
possibility? If so, how specifically does Porter rewrite Frost's poem?
How might this comparison affect your interpretation of Porter's
story? Of Frost's poem?

SUGGESTION FOR WRITING

Rewrite some or all of "Holiday" from the point of view of Hatsy or Ottilie. Then write an essay describing what is lost and gained by changing
the point of view, particularly in terms of the story's central conflict or
theme.

MARGARET LAURENCE

The Rain Child

Laurence's "The Rain Child" might be said to explore in a particularly
vivid and emotional way an idea that is only mentioned in Porter's "Holiday"—that one shouldn't "confuse nationality [or culture] with habitation" (par. 26). Laurence's story complicates our vision of the relationship
between nationality, culture, and habitation, in part, by simply exploring
the real and quite complex effects of colonialism upon all three.

And though the story works perfectly well for students if read on its
own terms, I find that I like to share with my students some information

on African colonialism either before they read the story or at a convenient point during our discussion of it. For those of you who (like me before I studied up in preparation to teach a postcolonial literature class!) don't know a lot about this issue, here are some facts that might be pertinent in giving students a larger context for the story (and that will be especially so if you follow up on the "Planning Ideas" strategy of pairing the story with African texts). Though one could trace the history of African colonialism as far back as recorded history itself, the first serious, large-scale efforts by Europeans to explore and colonize Africa began in the late nineteenth and early twentieth centuries as part of what is now generally referred to, fittingly enough, as "the scramble for Africa." The primary scramblers, as it were, were Belgium (under the rather notorious King Leopold, whose particular exploits serve as the background for, and focus of, Conrad's *Heart of Darkness*), Portugal, France, Germany, and Britain. (The extent to which African interests drove foreign relations in these years, as well as the brazenness of this process is suggested by the fact that the Berlin Conference of 1884–85 was utterly devoted to establishing the ground rules by which these European nations would carve up the African continent.) Resistance to European rule was almost coterminous with that rule, but it began in earnest across Africa in the 1920s; and in the words of Jonathan A. Peters ("English-Language Fiction from West Africa," A *History of Twentieth-Century African Literatures*, Oyekan Owomoyela, ed., Lincoln: University of Nebraska Press, 1993), "the achievement of political independence within the national boundaries arbitrarily set up by the Europeans began in earnest with Ghana in 1957 (a generation after Egypt's Independence in 1922), and was soon after followed by territories elsewhere" (p. 11).

Nigeria, the West African nation in which "The Rain Child" is set (and which was the birthplace of novelist Chinua Achebe), essentially became Nigeria when the British finally succeeded in gaining full control of the area in 1914 and continued as such until Nigerians gained independence and self-rule in 1960, just three years before Laurence's story was first published. (Students are often surprised by how recently Nigeria and other African nations gained independence.)

The policies of each European nation toward its African colonies differed dramatically, however, and in one way that is especially relevant to Laurence's story: for the British (and French) policies were dramatically distinguished from those of other nations by virtue of their basis in the drive to essentially and quite systematically Westernize the natives of the areas they controlled, imposing in or, in the colonizers' language, bringing them the gift of, their languages, systems of education, law, and government, as well as various forms of Christianity. As "The Rain Child" itself makes clear, the education of many Nigerians both under colonialism and to this day was and is "British" not only in terms of form and personnel but also in terms of content, British literature, for example, being equivalent to literature itself in the colonial curriculum. (And it's revealing that many literary texts that deal with the ironic effects of this policy focus on precisely the same example that Laurence does—the teaching of Wordsworth's "Daffodils" to students who will most likely never see a daffodil and are daily surrounded by some of the most beautiful flora in the world. I suppose it's because this example so wonderfully captures the way in which students are thus taught implicitly and explicitly to identify and locate beauty of all kinds in both cultures and landscapes other than their own.) The end of that educational process for the best Nigerian students thus has historically been and continues to be advanced study in the "home" country, which in the case of Nigeria is England, and scholarships encourage the best students to work toward this end exactly as Laurence's Dr. Quansah has done, the idea being that they will eventually return to Nigeria to put their education to work as part of the country's Westernized governing elite.

Such policies and practices have obviously complex, contradictory, and often quite painful effects on all people caught up in them, particularly in terms of cultural identity, and it is precisely these effects that Laurence's story so wonderfully captures and explores through the characters and events of "The Rain Child." And what I both love and intensely respect about this story is how deftly it manages both to point out the way that *everyone*, "colonizer" and "colonized" alike, experiences that pain and confusion equally, if differently, and to encourage us to treat all of its characters (with the possible exception of Miss Povey) with both respect and empathy.

A good way to begin exploring those issues is to begin where the story itself begins—with the character of Miss Povey. For Miss Povey essentially embodies the very traditional British policies and attitudes toward African peoples and African culture that I've just described. Miss Povey is as relentless about retaining her own British identity, despite her twenty-seven years in Africa, as the Germans in Porter's story are about remaining German after three generations in America, an idea underscored by Miss Povey's attempts to cultivate a traditional English garden in the midst of the jungle (par. 35). And that sense of identity is obviously continually reinforced by her experience of Africans as both different and inferior, as well as—quite simply—all alike: "Twenty-seven years here, to my twenty-two, and she still felt acutely uncomfortable with African parents, all of whom in her eyes were equally unenlightened. The fact that one father might be an illiterate cocoa farmer, while the next would possibly be a barrister from the city—such distinctions made no earthly difference to Hilda Povey" (par. 5). Miss Povey's educational ideals obviously derive directly from these attitudes, as is revealed when she "took decided umbrage" at the narrator's decision to teach traditional Akan poetry rather than "Daffodils" (par. 5), a poem celebrating the very "English flowers" she grows in her own garden.

Yet Miss Povey's values and ideas are clearly brought out in the story precisely because they differ so dramatically from those of the narrator,

Violet, who has—at least to some extent and to use a term that Miss Povey herself would undoubtedly approve—*gone native*, being both physically and culturally transformed by her long residence in a country whose people, culture, and landscape she has clearly come to respect, appreciate, and love on their own terms rather than in (negative) comparison to a British standard. Indeed, by the end of the story, Violet herself is forced to confront just how thorough that transformation has been and just how inevitable it is that she will be "a stranger" whenever she returns to her English "home," "that island of grey rain where I must go . . . when the time comes" (par. 226).

What forces Violet's own confrontation with her "nonbelonging," to use Porter's term, is, of course, watching the events that unfold when another "native" "stranger," Ruth Quansah, returns to a "home" she has never known. And though students will undoubtedly pick this up and be able to run with it with little coaxing from you, you may want to focus especially on the way that Ruth ironically comes to resemble Miss Povey, even, perhaps, to out-Povey Miss Povey in her disdain for her African peers. As a result, one could interpret the text as hinging on a parallel between Violet–Hilda and Ruth–Kwaale, though the word *parallel* doesn't even begin to capture the complex ways in which the various characters' situations mirror and intersect each other: in relation to "Englishness," Violet is in much the same position that Ruth is in relation to "Africanness"; in relation to "Africanness" she is, as her interactions with Ruth's father suggest, in much the same position that Ruth is revealed to be in relation to "Englishness" when David remarks that "You're almost—almost like a—like us" (par. 188). One might also say that Miss Povey defines "Englishness" for Violet much as Kwaale defines "Africanness" for Ruth, so that the irony and complexity of all of this is underscored by the fact that, in some key ways, Violet is herself more culturally "African" or "Nigerian" than Ruth is.

And what is incredible about the story is that its complexities multiply and probe even deeper into the African, and specifically Nigerian, situation through the characters of Ayesha and Yindo, both of whom together problematize the very notion of a coherent "Nigerian" cultural identity, being as much transplants and strangers in this particular setting as any of the other characters are, despite the fact that their travels, unlike those of Violet and Ruth, have been within their own country.

QUESTIONS FOR DISCUSSION

1. How would you characterize the narrator and her relationship to, or attitude toward, Nigerian people and culture? How is Violet characterized by being juxtaposed with her colleague Miss Povey? What do you make of Violet's name? Her handicap and its origin? What might the symbolic significance of these facts be?
2. By the end of the story, Violet refers to herself as a "stranger" to her

own homeland. Why and how do the events in the story, and the situation of Ruth Quansah in particular, prompt Violet to see this about herself? How is Violet's situation like Ruth's?

3. What role do the other characters, particularly Kwaale, Ayesha, Yindo, and Ruth's mother, play in the story?

4. The descriptions of Violet and Hilda Povey's gardens tell us much about each of these characters, but there are many other references to plants and flowers in the story. What other such references do you see here, and how might these references work together to create an interconnected web of symbols in the story?

5. Laurence could have focused the climatic scene of this story on any number of traditional Nigerian rituals. What's the effect of her choosing the specific ritual that she does? Why might this ritual seem particularly fitting to this story?

6. What do you make of the title?

SUGGESTIONS FOR WRITING

1. Write an essay explaining why one of the seemingly minor characters in "The Rain Child"—either Ayesha, Yindo, or Ruth's mother—in fact plays a pivotal role in the story.

2. Write an essay analyzing the symbolism of "The Rain Child."

JORGE LUIS BORGES

Pierre Menard, Author of the Quixote

At first glance, "Pierre Menard" is a rather straightforward parody, and questions about just what genre is being parodied here might well be the best way to launch discussion. That genre is, of course, the literary critical essay, but since this genre will undoubtedly be more familiar to you than to your students, you may want to consider waiting to teach this story until after students have read the sampling of literary criticism in the "Critical Contexts" chapter of the anthology. And, given the nature of the "essay" Borges presents here, the story might also work well as a bridge between that chapter and "Evaluating Fiction."

If your students have read some literary criticism, then genre questions are a good place to start, especially in terms of working to draw out the fact that Borges's "essay" is a peculiar and in some ways peculiarly dated sort in which the emphasis is less on analyzing an author's work than on memorializing an author by establishing his or her claim to respect and to fame and immortality. Thus the carefully compiled list of Pierre Menard's extant work, complete with publication dates and annotations, thus the biographical explanation of the origins of his greatest work, and the hilariously implausible exegesis designed to prove not only that Menard's *Quixote* is better than the original of which it is an exact copy but also that it is "the most significant [work] of our time" (par. 5).

If students aren't so familiar with the genre, you might want to focus simultaneously or instead on questions about the character of the "narrator" and about his characterization of Menard. A decidedly polemical literary critic whose effort to establish his "true friend" Menard's reputation is inseparable from an effort to establish his own, this essayist begins that effort in the very first paragraph with an *ad hominem* attack on Madam Henri Bachelier and her "Calvinist, if not Masonic and circumcised" circle of critic-readers and with a heavy-handed depiction of the "approval" and "authorizations" his work has received from the unfairly "slandered" Countess de Bagnoregio (par. 1–2). Chivalrously defending the honor of an aristocratic lady thus becomes part and parcel of the effort to defend the reputation of the writer Menard and the essayist's own, ironically by establishing the modernity of Menard's *Quixote*.

But it is precisely this analysis of Menard's *Quixote* as a modern work that makes "Pierre Menard" a much less dated and simple parody than it might at first appear. For by arguing that Menard's *Quixote*, as opposed to Cervantes's, displays "the influence of Nietzsche," William James, and Bertrand Russell (par. 12, 15), the essayist performs a kind of analysis uncomfortably close to certain kinds of contemporary historical criticism that see the text as a reflection or instantiation of ideas current at the time of its writing, which—in other words—read a work in terms of its "cultural context." And the potential ironies of such criticism are wonderfully pointed up through the narrator's discovery of a "new technique" of reading in terms of "deliberate anachronism" and "erroneous attribution" (par. 21). By the same token, Menard's seemingly mad project of reproducing without copying a well-known literary work from the past is itself not utterly unlike modernist and postmodernist projects such as Joyce's *Ulysses*, Kathy Acker's *Great Expectations*, or even Jane Smiley's *A Thousand Acres* (which rewrites *King Lear*).

Thus what I try to push students to see are the serious issues about literary production and about reading and literary analysis that are brought into the open by a story that at first glance seems like a painfully elaborate joke. In so doing, I also try to use the story to engage questions that I think students in introductory literature courses themselves struggle with. What is the difference between reasoned analysis and sophistry of the kind this critic seems to engage in when he justifies his interpretation by saying that Menard was known to express "the exact opposite of his true opinion" (par. 4)? At what point does the attempt to read a text in terms of its cultural and historical context or in terms of an author's biography become a kind of sophistry? What, if anything, would be lost or gained by reading "the *Odyssey* as if it were posterior to the *Aeneid*" (par. 21)? By reading "A Good Man Is Hard to Find" as if it were written by D. H. Lawrence or "Odour of Chrysanthemums" as if it were an O'Connor story? By the same token, what does constitute originality in art? What does make Joyce's *Ulysses* different from Pierre Menard's *Quixote*? How does our own cultural and historical moment inform our interpretations of a given text? Doesn't *Don Quixote* mean something different to us than to Cervantes's contemporaries?

QUESTIONS FOR DISCUSSION

1. Borges's short story is clearly a parody of another genre of writing. What is that genre? What specific features of that genre are recognizable and what exactly does Borges suggest is laughable about them?
2. How would you characterize the "narrator" of the story? What clues do we get about his attitudes, values, etc.? What do his characterizations of Menard tell us about him?
3. How would you characterize Pierre Menard and his literary efforts? Though the narrator clearly wants us to admire and respect both, do we? Why and why not? Do Pierre Menard and his writings remind you of any other authors and/or texts?
4. Parodies are usually only funny if they are also more than funny, bringing to our attention serious issues in a comic way. What serious issues do you think Borges tackles in "Pierre Menard"?
5. Why do you think that this story is included in the "Culture as Context" chapter of the anthology? To what extent is "cultural context" important to the story and to what extent is the story commenting on literary criticism that focuses on cultural context? What does the story ultimately say or ask about such criticism?

READING/WRITING IDEAS FOR CHAPTER 11

ESSAYS ABOUT CULTURAL CONTEXT

Your decisions about writing assignments for this chapter will obviously depend on just how you've decided to use the chapter.

The more methodological approach suggests an assignment that asks students to write essays that interpret a text by relating it to its cultural context, showing, for example, how "The Yellow Wallpaper" is informed by nineteenth-century notions of "the rest cure" for women or how "The Rain Child" is informed by the colonial and postcolonial situation in Nigeria. If you do choose to go with this assignment, you might use this as an opportunity to get students into the library (if that's a requirement or need of your particular course, as it is of mine), asking them to identify and locate both primary and secondary materials relevant to their text and/or topic, rather than, or in addition to, providing them with such information as the "Planning Ideas" section of this chapter suggests. If you choose to go that route, however, you might want to consider saving this chapter and assignment until after students tackle the "Critical Contexts" chapter and assignments that follow.

Another version of this assignment might ask students to consider the ramifications of such an analytical approach, showing what is lost and gained by reading the story on its own terms and by reading it in terms of its cultural context, perhaps taking into account in the process the questions about such analysis suggested in "Pierre Menard" or even using those questions as a framework.

The more thematic approach obviously suggests more thematically driven assignments, assignments that ask students, for example, to analyze what a particular story says about how culture informs individual identity and/or relationships between individuals or that compares what two or more stories say about this issue. Since such an assignment would likely be a more focused version of the theme-focused essay assignment, you might consider getting students started with versions of the exercises described in "Reading/Writing Ideas for Chapter 6."

TROUBLESHOOTING

Obviously the more methodology-focused essay assignments described above will be much less familiar and much more challenging to student writers than the more thematic assignments, particularly if your assignment includes a research component. My students often tend to be both very excited and engaged by assignments that require them to incorporate source materials of various kinds and to read a text in terms of them, but they are also often uncertain about how to go about doing so effectively. One of the biggest challenges they face in tackling assignments that involve analyzing a text in terms of its cultural context is the temptation to let their essays turn into reports on that information or on that context, rather than crafting essays that use such information in the service of analysis. Thus from the beginning of our work on such an assignment, I simply try to emphasize the similarities between this kind of essay and the kinds of analytical essays they've been writing all semester, to insist that analysis and the text should remain the focus. I also use the exercises below to try to ensure that students approach outside sources from the very beginning with an eye toward questions that arise from, and return them to, the text they're analyzing. And, again, I find that it's very helpful to start students off by having them read and discuss essays of the kind that they are being asked to write with an eye toward generating and answering questions about *why* and *how* writers successfully tackle this kind of essay.

CULTURAL CONTEXT–FOCUSED WRITING EXERCISES

Since the more methodology-focused essay assignment described above is the more challenging and differs most from those discussed in previous chapters, the exercises below are by and large meant to suggest ways to get students started on that particular assignment. And, again, you might want to save the assignment until after students have tackled the "Critical Contexts" chapter, perhaps merging chapters and assignments into a longer research paper that includes primary and secondary sources.

1. Identifying the Nature and Function of Primary and Secondary Sources

As with so many essay assignments, I tend to begin this one, as I've already suggested, by having students read sample essays of the type they are being asked to write—either not-too-intimidating scholarly essays or essays by students—and asking them to answer a series of questions as they read. In the case of this assignment, this reading exercise tends to look something like this:

Mark the places where each writer mentions source material of any kind. Then, when you've finished, go back and look at your markings, working to generate answers to the following questions:

- Which of these sources are primary?
- Which of these sources are secondary?
- How would you define the difference between primary and secondary sources? To what extent are the two kinds of source materials themselves different and to what extent does the difference seem to have to do with the way the writer uses the materials?
- What function do each of the references to primary sources seem to serve in this essay? Why does this writer use primary sources? Make a short list of what you see as the primary functions of primary sources. Might primary sources serve purposes other than those for which they seem to be used in this essay? If so, add those to your list.
- What specific techniques does the writer use to incorporate primary source material effectively? When and why, for example, does the writer quote from the sources? Paraphrase? How does the writer introduce sources?
- Does source material ever seem to get in the way of, rather than contribute to, the argument here? If so, why and how do you think it interferes? What might this writer have done differently or better?

2. Generating Contextual Questions

One way to get students started on writing their own contextual analysis of a text and to ensure that they focus from the outset on the text itself is to have them reread the text in question and to generate research questions along the way, to note when, and where, and how in the text questions arise for them about the cultural context of this story that they can only answer by acquiring more information about that context and/or about the author's particular relation to it. Students reading "The Rain Child," for example, might discover in rereading it that they want to know why there are English teachers in Nigeria; whether the situation of Ruth and Dr. Quansah was or is a common one; what the precise relationship between England and Nigeria was before and during the time that the story was written; what Laurence's cultural identity is (was she English? Was she ever in Nigeria?); or they might want to know something more about the ritual described in the story or about what "Akan poetry" is, etc. You might have students conclude the exercise by looking over their list of questions, grouping related questions together to generate a list of bigger topics (such as "native Nigerian peoples and cultures" or "English colonial policy toward and in Nigeria" or "education in Nigeria"), and choosing which of these large topics interests them most. Or you might simply wait and have this "homing in on a topic" part of the exercise be part of the in-class work you do with the exercise after students have completed it.

Have them bring their list of questions and topics to class and have them discuss both the questions and topics themselves and strategies for identifying and locating sources that might help them find out the things they want to know about their topic. With this exercise, as with many others, I find it helpful to first use one student's questions as an example for the whole class to discuss and then to break the class up into small groups so that everyone's exercise gets thoroughly discussed and every student leaves the class with a rough idea of where to go next.

12

CRITICAL CONTEXTS: A FICTION CASEBOOK

Offering students an opportunity both to read, discuss, and write about a story that they always tend to love and to engage with the arguments about that story written by another student and several scholars, this chapter allows students a chance to hone their own analytical skills by actively participating in a lively, ongoing conversation about a wonderfully enigmatic text. Students can, at least at first, feel intimidated when confronted with the polish and sophistication of scholarly essays and with the prospect of having to find something to say that the critics haven't. But I find that such feelings prove to be extremely short-lived if I encourage students to open their eyes to just how diverse the criticism is and yet how incomplete and if help them see for themselves that scholarship is, indeed, a kind of never-ending conversation in which there is always more to say, always another angle to take or another question to ask or another detail to take into account. In figuring out how best to help students make those discoveries, I encounter such big questions as just how late in the reading and writing process to have students read and write about the critical essays. Should I have students read and talk about the story only briefly at first and then jump straight into the criticism, allowing students to tackle writing topics suggested by the criticism? Or should I have my students begin to craft their own arguments about the story first and only then have them try to place that argument within the critical conversation or context? These questions remain questions for me, however, precisely because answering yes to either question works, and in the "Reading/Writing Ideas" section of the chapter, I've tried to discuss the different ways these two approaches can work, as well as the costs and benefits of each.

PLANNING IDEAS

- Before class, have students write a paper or draw up a chart for class discussion of the time scheme in "A Rose for Emily." Ask students to bring those papers and charts back to class when you're ready to discuss the Moore essay on the chronology of the story.

- At least one film version of "A Rose for Emily" is available on videotape. Showing the film and discussing how the director and actors interpret Faulkner's text—by portraying the setting in a particular way, rearranging the order of the story, and/or representing the characters and their behavior and action in certain ways—can be a good device for helping students articulate their own interpretations and prepare to compare their own interpretations with those of other readers, including not only the filmmaker but also the critics whose essays are included in the chapter.

- If you're not having students keep a reading journal throughout the term, you might want to have them start something of the sort now to record their responses to the critical essays in this chapter, encouraging them to use their journal as a place to pose questions about the essays as they read them, to talk about what bugs them about particular essays and/or what points they agree and disagree with, to make notes about aspects or elements or moments of and in the story that aren't discussed in the essays or that they interpret in a different way than a particular author does, and even about writing techniques used by these writers that they might want to try out in their own writing. I find that doing so is a way to help students feel that, even as readers, they are active participants in, rather than passive witnesses to, scholarship.

WILLIAM FAULKNER

A Rose for Emily

The most striking and memorable thing about "A Rose for Emily" is its shocking revelation at the end, and that, naturally is what most students—even those who have read the story before—will want to talk about. In this case, it is probably advisable to give students their heads. For one thing, it is rather easy to turn such a discussion to the recuperative aspect of reading—that is, how later elements in a story make us selectively recall and reconsider earlier ones. I often ask students to compare Faulkner's surprise ending with Maupassant's; I then point out how the typical structure of detective stories, a kind most students are familiar with, forces you by the revelation at the end to go back over the story recalling "clues." In "Emily," of course, you don't know that you are working toward a revelation—or do you? Isn't there a kind of expectation based on the very lack of an obvious "plot," an obvious sense of suspense or curiosity? Doesn't the fact that you are reading a story mean that you have to expect something—or otherwise it would not be a story? (Such a discussion has the added advantage of paving the way for the essay by

Lawrence R. Rodgers that deals with precisely this topic.)

When you are talking about later events in the story recalling earlier ones, you are really talking about sequence, not necessarily chronology—for one of the more obvious characteristics of this story is its elaborate and complex treatment of historical time. (This manipulation of the history of Emily, you may want to point out, is a dramatic example of structure.) It may be useful to have the students write a paper or draw up a chart for class discussion of the time scheme in the story (see "Planning Ideas"). Such an exercise highlights the structuring, draws attention to how many time signals and specific dates there are in the story, ensures careful reading, and results in enough differences to ensure a lively class discussion, and one that sets the stage for later discussions of the essay by Gene M. Moore, which works to establish an exact chronology of events in the story.

Why so unorthodox a time scheme? (If one of your students does not, with more or less exasperation, bring this up, you just may have to do so yourself.) I always have at least one student who believes authors are deliberately, even perversely, obscure, and another who thinks "obscurity" is a sign of "art" or "modernity" or both. I'm afraid I usually put such students off and say, "Well, let's talk about this story for a while, and I'll come back to that question." If I don't do that, I find myself forced into giving my "reading" of the story to "justify" its structure. It is possible, however, to deal with the issue of plot manipulation, which often arises at this point. Isn't the purpose of the complicated time scheme to delay the revelation or to put the reader off the scent? Probably so. We cannot know whether manipulation is good or bad unless we explore what the relationship is between the structure and the meaning of the story. If some students attack the story hard enough, others are sure to leap to its defense, and one fairly obvious defense is more than likely to come up: the time shifts are mimetic; this is the way people tell stories, and this is the way memory and gossip and oral narrative generally work. Now you're forced to be the devil's advocate. That reasoning may explain shifting time in general, but it does not help with these shifts, these particularities.

If the world, or the world of the classroom, were an orderly place, you would always reach exactly this point and turn to the second paragraph of the story. I want to talk about structure and time scheme and all that I've mentioned, but I also really want to get to that second paragraph and a discussion of setting, so I get there one way or the other, even if it means saying, at some irrelevant point, "Speaking of the second paragraph, . . ." What is there in this paragraph that suggests that the narrator, the voice, is not just spinning a yarn, happening to tell the story in this seemingly casual way?

It usually does not take too long for someone to point out that the description of Emily's house "lifting its stubborn and coquettish decay" is not entirely innocent or accidental, that the noun and both adjectives relate to more than just Emily's house. And, if the class has brought up the time element, it should not be too long before someone mentions that there are the three specific times suggested in the paragraph: the 1870s, when the house was built; the more-or-less present with garages and gasoline pumps, probably the 1920s; and the 1860s, the time of the battle of Jefferson in the Civil War. Emily is joining the Civil War dead in the cemetery. It is at this point that I like to look forward to the next paragraph—"Miss Emily had been a tradition, a duty, and a care"—and back to the first—"the men [went to her funeral] through a sort of respect-ful affection for a fallen monument"—and ask what the title means.

The narrator offers only glimpses of Miss Emily, standing behind her father at the house door, riding next to Homer Barron in his carriage, waiting at the druggist's counter to purchase poison, presiding over a class of young would-be china painters, sitting upright in the window. We are limited to what the townspeople can see of Miss Emily's life and to what they guess about her thoughts. From mere glimpses of her over the years, they construct a life for her and envy, pity, marvel, or disapprove largely according to what they imagine. What we and the narrator find out at last is that their imaginations are too small to take in Miss Emily as she really is. In her imagination—unbalanced as it may be—she creates and holds a world in stasis.

The standards and beliefs of this world are implied in the story, but it may be useful to make the implications explicit by listing some of them on the blackboard.

With the list as backdrop, we can then discuss not only the focus of the story but also the voice. Who is speaking? What is he like? To what extent are we supposed to share his values? The answer to the first ques-tion is easy—he's a (self-appointed) white male representative of the townspeople. The answer to the second question is just a bit more com-plicated. The narrator tells us that men go to the funeral out of affection and respect, the women out of curiosity, wanting a peek inside the house; only a woman would believe Colonel Sartoris's gallant lie; the very title suggests a male tribute to a "lady." Sexism in "A Rose for Emily" could be a good place to now try to take the discussion, for the question of the narrator's attitude toward Emily and ours toward the narrator is central in our reading of the story, and sexism is another issue taken up by the critics whose work students will encounter later in the chapter, particu-larly in the essay by Judith Fetterley.

Questions about voice, however, involve not only gender roles, of course, but also the values of the whole town or society (and the attitude of the story toward the attitude of the town). To what degree are these values a function of time and place or cultural context? How are we sup-posed to feel about Colonel Sartoris? He gallantly remits Emily's taxes and protects her pride by telling her that the town owed Emily's father money. Yet it was Colonel Sartoris's edict that decreed that "Negro" women should not appear on the streets without an apron. How are we supposed to feel about Emily's proud refusal both to lie and to obey the law when she purchases arsenic? Matters of sex and race and class permeate the story, bringing a whole bygone society back to life. Good or bad, it's gone, and not even Emily can pretend that it is not dead.

QUESTIONS FOR DISCUSSION

1. Can this story really be a tribute to someone whose gray hair is on the pillow next to a skeleton? What are we supposed to think of Miss Emily Grierson? Who is Emily? What is she a monument to, and why does she deserve a rose?
2. Is the narrator's opinion of Miss Emily at all influenced by the place and time in which he lives? By his gender, class, and race? By Emily's? If so, how?
3. Does Miss Emily's status as a town monument suggest a reason for the manipulation of time sequence, a spatializing of the fifty or sixty years following the Civil War?
4. Can your students imagine this story told any other way, perhaps as a Poe story, "The Casket of Homer Barron," beginning, "The dozens of insults of that low-born Yankee I had borne as best I could, but when he ventured to injure my good name before all the town I vowed revenge"?

SUGGESTIONS FOR WRITING

1. Write an essay comparing and contrasting the use of the southern setting in "A Rose for Emily" and "Everything That Rises Must Converge," "A Good Man Is Hard to Find," and/or "Why I Live at the P.O." What vision of the South and of changes within southern society does each story offer?
2. Write an essay analyzing the treatment of societal values in "A Rose for Emily." Does "A Rose for Emily" ultimately affirm the values of Jefferson society? Describe them objectively and noncommittally? Treat them ironically or critically? Nostalgically? Some combination of these? Do we need to distinguish between "the story" (i.e., Faulkner, or even the reader) and the narrative voice? Is the reader obliged to evaluate the narrator's values and those of the society he represents? If so, how?

READING/WRITING IDEAS FOR CHAPTER 12

ESSAYS ABOUT CRITICAL CONTEXTS

In my experience, both literature-based composition courses and composition-focused literature courses tend to require students to write at least one essay over the course of a term that incorporates secondary sources, usually literary criticism of one sort or another. Such assignments have proved both beneficial and enjoyable to my students for a host of reasons, not least the fact that "research essays" are so commonly assigned in all types of courses, yet my students often feel very uncertain about their skills in this area. But such assignments can also be rewarding to students because they suddenly begin to see their essays not just as responses to assignments that have value only in the context of a particular classroom, but as real contributions to real scholarly debates, their chance to be part of a conversation that includes, but extends well beyond, this particular classroom.

I have begun to require my students to write two research essays, providing them with the secondary source material for the first assignment and requiring them to identify and locate some or all of their source material for the second. This arrangement works well for me because it allows me to focus separately on the very different issues of research per se and of writing with sources, focusing first solely on the techniques and strategies involved in actually incorporating source material into one's writing, as well as questions about why one bothers to do so, and then and only then on actual research strategies and techniques. Thus for my purposes and for those of you who—like me—aren't blessed with an extensive university library, the "Critical Contexts" chapter of the anthology works really well for the first kind of essay assignment, saving me the time and labor that I usually put into assembling packets of secondary source material.

With this essay assignment, as the headnote indicates, I find that a central question I face is when and how exactly to introduce the critical essays; and this question for me raises all kinds of methodological issues, some of which I tackle here and some of which I discuss when describing the "Drafting without Sources" exercise. Ironically, I find that one way that I can sometimes begin to answer this question is by first asking and answering another question, which is just how specific I want the assignment to be: do I want to give students a very specific topic to write about or to simply require that they make an argument about the text that somehow incorporates material from the provided literary criticism? This question is related to the ones about when to introduce the criticism, because I find that while the open-ended assignment works well regardless of when and how the critical readings are introduced, the specific topic assignment tends to work best when the topic or topics come directly out of the critical readings. In the case of the materials provided in the "Critical Contexts" chapter of the anthology, for example, a specific topic assignment might ask students to tackle one of the following topics or questions (or to choose one from a list):

Chronological and narrative order: Though Moore's essay purports to establish an exact chronology of events in the story, he doesn't really say a great deal about how this chronology might affect our interpretation of the story. If you accept Moore's chronology, what is the significance of the dating of events in the story? Conversely, what is the significance of the ambiguity about time in the story and/or of the order in which Faulkner relates the events of the story?

Motives for, and meanings of, the murder: Both Fetterley and Rodgers see Emily's crime as a triumphantly defiant act, though each reads just how it is defiant and who Emily defies here somewhat differently. How else might one interpret the significance of the murder?

Homer Barron: All of the literary critics seem to agree in seeing Homer Barron as a fitting victim, a man who—according to the logic of Faulkner's story—essentially deserves to die. How else might one interpret Homer Barron's character, significance, and/or role in the story? Or how might one interpret the story from a standpoint more sympathetic to Homer?

Central conflict: Several of the critics suggest that the main conflict in Faulkner's story is between the Old and New South, a reading that Fetterley counters by arguing that the real conflict is between women and patriarchy. Is there a way to reconcile these two readings or is there a different way to understand the central conflict in the story?

Race, class, and gender: While the Fetterley essay clearly argues for the centrality of gender issues to "A Rose for Emily," neither Fetterley nor any of the other critics have a great deal to say about how Faulkner's story deals with, or is informed by, the issues of race or class, or how gender issues interrelate with these other issues. What do you think?

A slightly less-specific assignment, building on the Dillon essay, might ask students to make an argument about the story that employs one of the three readerly "styles" he identifies, producing a "Character-Action-Moral," "Diggers for Secrets," or "anthropological" argument.

After much trial and a lot of error, I have pretty much settled on the loosest form of assignment for this kind of essay, one that simply asks students to make some argument about the text in question and, in so doing, to incorporate material from the secondary sources. I do so because, as I've said, one of the real benefits that my students derive from the "Critical Contexts" essay assignment is a feeling of being real participants in an ongoing scholarly conversation about a text, and I have found that being allowed to formulate their own topics and questions, while making the assignment more difficult in certain ways, makes it easier in other ways by encouraging that feeling. I find that this more open-ended assignment, unlike the specific topic assignment, tends to leave open for me the question of when and how to introduce the critical readings. Sometimes I have students do the sourceless draft exercise described below before reading any of the critical essays and sometimes I have them jump straight from the story into the critical essays, using our discussion of those essays and the source-related exercises described below to help students generate their own essay topics and questions from their reading of the secondary material.

Thus, your decision about how specific you want the assignment to be—as well as other factors that I've tried to describe below—will necessarily affect decisions both about which, if any, of the following writing exercises to assign, which order to assign them in, and how exactly to phrase them. Whichever option you choose, however, you might well want to also assign a version of the thesis-generating exercise described in the "Reading/Writing Ideas" section of the "Whole Text" chapter at some point in the process.

TROUBLESHOOTING

One of the main challenges that my students face in writing "Critical Contexts" essays (or "research essays" of any sort, for that matter) is the tendency to let sources dominate the essay and drown out their own ideas. I've found that this problem tends to take one of two forms in my students' essays: first is the essay that simply reiterates the argument of a source; second, the essay that spends all of its time arguing with a source or sources, yet "forgets," in a sense, that the only way to make such an argument is to provide an alternative interpretation of the text and to support that interpretation with textual evidence. Such problems are precisely what has led me so often to assign the sourceless draft exercise described below, despite my reservations about it, because it at the very least does ensure that students have their own argument to make about the text and that sources come second, contributing to that argument rather than overtaking it. But regardless of whether I assign that exercise or not, the main thing I try to do is insist from the beginning that (and how and why) the text itself must be the focus, that even arguments with sources can only be substantiated by interpretation of evidence from the text. Though it doesn't always serve to head off such problems, the function and use of sources exercise described below and the discussion I build out of it helps me a great deal in terms of at least getting such issues on the table and giving students the kind of vocabulary they need to diagnose and cure such problems when they do come up.

CRITICAL CONTEXTS–FOCUSED WRITING EXERCISES

Because using sources effectively in their own writing requires that students have an understanding of the uses of sources, have an accurate understanding of the sources they plan to use, and have their own independent argument about the text in question, I've found it helpful to require my students to do exercises that ensure that they master each of these steps one at a time, though I vary the exercise assignments and the order in which I assign them to fit specific essay assignments.

1. Identifying the Functions and Uses of Sources

To prepare students to write essays that use secondary sources, I almost always begin by having them read one or two essays that do so. Though I often use student essays from past courses, it seems to me that the essays on "A Rose for Emily" in the anthology could serve this purpose just as well, particularly the Rodgers essay, which uses secondary sources in rather interesting ways. My goal in having students read and then discuss such essays is to begin to ask questions not only about *how* writers use secondary sources but also about *why* they do so, the idea being that one can't do something effectively unless or until one knows what the purpose of doing so is. In preparation for discussion, then, I ask students to read the essays very carefully and to pay particular attention to the use of sources, asking them to formulate answers to the following basic questions as they read.

- Mark the places where each writer refers to secondary sources. How does the writer introduce source material? What does the writer tell you about each source? Are there any places where you feel the writer doesn't give you enough or gives you too much information about a source?
- What function does each reference to a source seem to serve in the essay? Why does the writer refer to each source? What precise contribution does it make? Are there any places where you feel the purpose of source material isn't clear? Where source material doesn't seem to make much of a contribution?

In discussion, I allow students free rein, while making sure that we focus at some point on the three issues that I see as key to using sources effectively:

- Specific techniques for incorporating source material effectively (use of signal phrases to introduce source material, for example).
- Specific functions that secondary sources serve, among them to establish the essay writer's
  —motive (my essay is interesting because it does something that others haven't, because it solves a problem raised by others, etc.);
  —expertise (I know about, and can indicate my precise relationship to, an ongoing conversation about a text);
  —authority (my argument gains credibility because other people agree with me *or* because I can persuasively make an argument that disagrees with other scholars).
- Specific ways in which writers manage to use secondary sources without having them take over their argument. (To get this issue on the table, I sometimes assign one essay that doesn't do a very good job of staying focused.)

2. Summarizing Critical Conversations

Because using source material requires that students can understand and effectively describe not only individual arguments but also the relationships between different arguments and because I've discovered—much to my chagrin—that these tasks often prove difficult for students, I always have my students write short summaries of source material. I usually ask them to first write very short summaries (say, three sentences long) of the argument of each source and then to write what I call a "synthetic summary" that brings those arguments together in two or so paragraphs, showing how they all fit together as parts of one argumentative "conversation." Doing so requires that they define the main issues of the conversation and that they define a spectrum of possible stands on those issues, indicating what place each source occupies on that spectrum. Sometimes I also have students conclude their summary with a paragraph or two in which they evaluate the sources, pointing out weaknesses in the arguments, identifying questions or details ignored by critics, etc.

The following is an example of such an assignment for a class that was working with the Norton Critical Edition of Conrad's *Heart of Darkness*. It could quite easily be modified to work with the readings in the "Critical Contexts" chapter or any other select body of source material.

For this assignment, you are asked to read both Guerard's "The Journey Within" and the essays by Achebe, Singh, and Sarvan that deal with the issue of race in *Heart of Darkness*. After you've read all four essays, write a one- to two-page mini-essay in which you first summarize the "conversation" or "debate" about *Heart of Darkness* taking place between these critics and **then** establish your own place within that conversation. What is or are the main issue or issues under debate here and what position do the various critics occupy in that debate? In what particular ways do some or all of these critics agree? In what ways do some or all of these critics disagree? (In writing your summary you will have to pay particular attention to where and how Guerard's essay fits in here, since it does not deal explicitly with race.) With whom do you agree and disagree? How and why?

The following questions, which pertain to the particular essays included in the "Critical Contexts" chapter of the anthology, might help you tailor the above assignment to this material and/or guide class discussion on it:

- What is the thesis and basic argument of each of these essays?
- In addition to, or in the process of, forwarding his or her own argument about "A Rose for Emily," each of these authors mentions other possible arguments or interpretations, whether to agree or disagree with them. While arguing that "A Rose for Emily" is a detective story, for example, Rodgers mentions that the story also has been read as "a dark parable of the decline of Southern sensibility." What other implied thesis statements do you see here?
- On what points do Fetterley, Rodgers, and Moore agree with each other and with the other implied theses they note in passing? On what points do they disagree? To what extent are these interpretations or arguments compatible with each other and to what extent are they incompatible or mutually exclusive?
- What events within, or aspects of, the story do each of these authors see as central to the story? What questions about those events or aspects does each take to be central to interpreting the story? To what

extent do some or all of these critics agree about which events, facets, and/or questions are important, even if they interpret or answer them differently?

- What aspects of the story or what questions about the story do these critics ignore or consider only briefly?

- Dillon's essay is less an argument about, or interpretation of, "A Rose for Emily" than it is an argument about, or interpretation of, interpretations of "A Rose for Emily"; and Dillon explicitly labels Fetterley's argument an example of the "anthropological style" of reading. According to Dillon's definitions, what style of reading might the arguments of Rodgers and Moore represent?

- Dillon's essay implies that different styles of reading are incompatible with each other because they are based on very different assumptions about texts, life, etc. To what extent does that seem to be true and to what extent untrue in the case of these arguments?

3. Drafting without Sources

As the anthology points out, all of us, but especially student writers, often have a hard time figuring out what we think or want to write about a text once we've read other arguments about it. For this reason, I quite often have students write notes toward, or even an actual draft of, an essay on a text before I have them read or begin to discuss and work with sources. Only after that do I have them do exercise 2, substituting the generic evaluation paragraph(s) with paragraph(s) in which they begin to articulate the relationship between the argument they've been sketching out and the arguments of the sources and to articulate their plans for incorporating material from specific sources into their essays.

The obvious advantage of this approach is that it ensures that students have their own arguments and don't allow their essays to devolve into reportage on the arguments of sources. The disadvantage is that it tends to convey the message that our initial close readings of a text are in some sense "pure" rather than uninformed until we "contaminate" ourselves by reading secondary sources and that conversations about a text are ancillary to our individual experience of it rather than a potentially productive part of the experience of reading, thinking, and writing about literature. Even though I find myself conveying that message in subtle ways all the time, I am also troubled by it, finding it a rather odd and even contradictory message to convey in courses that are all about teaching students how to participate effectively in both written and oral conversations about literature. Such courses by their very nature seem to assume that such conversations are an integral part of the experience of literature and that literature itself is an integral part of a host of ongoing conversations, an assumption or message somewhat undermined by this kind of exercise, even thought it also, quite frankly, works.

Evaluating Fiction

For most students, a "good" story is a story that they enjoy—good literature is literature that entertains them—even though they sometimes suspect that their teachers' notions of "good" literature are just the opposite (literature that doesn't entertain but instead bores, depresses, or confuses them). Part of the job of courses like this and teachers like us is to expand students' horizons and enlarge the realm of literature that students are *able* to enjoy. But, along the way to doing that, I find I can't push too hard when it comes to evaluation. I find, for example, that many students respond enthusiastically to Connell's "The Most Dangerous Game" and are extremely resistant to analyses that would devalue the story because of its formulaic qualities. I have had much more success with stressing the positive aspects of the very best stories we read, realizing that many students will come to a more sophisticated understanding of literature as they learn to read closely and to understand works of greater complexity.

As far as my own evaluative standards are concerned, I try to mention them repeatedly during the term but in an unobtrusive way. I often talk about how certain stories have grown in richness for me over the years, standing up to repeated rereading and yielding new insights over time. I talk about the difference between a book or story that one reads merely to find out what happened and the work that rewards one's attention long after one *knows* what happened. I also stress the degree to which writers offer new ways of looking at age-old problems, the degree to which the best literature offers the unpredictable, the unexpected.

PLANNING IDEAS

- Show the PBS American Short Story film version of "Barn Burning" (with Tommy Lee Jones as Abner) and ask students to (1) compare and contrast the written and the film versions, and (2) evaluate which version is "best," taking care to define what they mean by "best."
- Spend some time asking the class to evaluate the selections on your syllabus they have read thus far. Which stories did they find most memorable? Least? Which stories do they think will still be anthologized and read one hundred years from now? Why? Which stories would they recommend to someone else? Why?

RICHARD CONNELL

The Most Dangerous Game

Many students will have read this story before, perhaps in high school, and in my classes the vast majority still like it a good deal. As a matter of fact, it fairly consistently scores in the top three or four when I ask students to rank the stories they've read in order of preference. For many instructors this will be a little surprising, and for some more than a little disappointing. But it is a "rattling good" adventure story with a good plot that is well structured. I have to be very careful in teaching this story not to be patronizing or off-putting. This is not, after all, a poor story.

Assuming considerable student response, then, you can plunge right in, discussing the structure or the means by which the excitement of the story is controlled and heightened. Students who have not read the story before might be asked to stop reading at the first break and write down their expectations about how the story will develop and what in that section gives rise to such expectations. It may be well at this point to suggest that almost all plots involve false expectations as well as "true" ones, or fore-shadowings, just as a good mystery story will involve false clues leading to false suspicions. The "true" expectations make the ending of the story appear, when looked back on, "inevitable," and the false ones, cleverly used, make that inevitable ending appear nonetheless "surprising." As I suggest in the anthology, the best reader is not necessarily the one who guesses the outcome correctly, but the one who is most sensitive to all the possibilities, all the expectations—a point that bears repetition.

There are two common, related, widely held, and often unexpressed assumptions that might be challenged in discussing this story. One is that "mere adventure" stories or slick stories are devoid of themes or thematic scope; the other is that "real literature," as opposed to popular literature, is cerebral or intellectual—literal detail in such stories being only the embodiment of the abstract "idea" of the story. "The Most Dangerous Game" has a rather clear theme that is announced in the first few paragraphs; if its call for sympathy for the "huntee" in a world divided between hunters and huntees is not necessarily an outright condemnation of hunting or killing for any purpose, it is surely an appeal for sympathy for the underdog and a condemnation of violence, urging the reader to put himself in the place of the victim. That the story is set just after World War I and the Russian Revolution, and that Zaroff and Ivan are Cossacks (the most ferocious and loyal of the adherents to the czar) does not seem wholly accidental. The story thus has political and moral thematic scope. Indeed the plot is almost too contrived to illustrate that theme, too pat: Rainsford, the hunter who believes in his total difference from, and superiority to, the game he hunts, is forced literally to put himself in the position of the hunted. If this story falls short of "literature," one might argue that it is not because of its lack of "ideas," but because it is too cerebral: the fiction or fable, the plot and characters, being too dominated by theme, too abstract and unlifelike.

The precise detail, including details of character and characterization, and the precise language in which the story is written are not highly significant here. That's why the story can be (and repeatedly has been) made into good movies and TV plays, and why it can be retold in other words with relatively little loss of power. This is not necessarily a flaw, of course. It is, for one thing, testimony to the strength of the story line. And in this respect it is typical of the yarn or tale, a story that can be retold, can be transmitted orally with great variation in words and sentence structures. It is, in fact, an excellent illustration of history existing in large measure independent of structure and might be useful in class for just that purpose.

QUESTIONS FOR DISCUSSION

1. What expectations are aroused by the first few sentences of dialogue in the story? How is each of these expectations continued or reinforced, fulfilled or disappointed? Once the nature of Zaroff's "game" is clear, how is suspense maintained? Do you ever really doubt the outcome? If you are reasonably sure who is ultimately going to win the "game," how do you explain the "excitement" or appeal of this story and others like it? Is *suspense* or *expectation* a better word for describing your responses? How do you know (by what means do you know) who is going to win in this story? (How do you know who will win in a John Wayne movie?) Can you tell with the same certainty who is going to win an election? A football game? An Olympics competition? Does your relative certainty about the outcome of this story imply a "view of reality" that you detect here? Can you discover any specific evidence within the story of that view? How much of your certainty of outcome derives from evidence within the story and how much from previous reading or film-watching experience?

2. Are there any details or actions in the story (such as Rainsford's falling overboard) that seem hard to believe? How do these affect your enjoyment of the story while you are reading it? Your judgment of the story afterwards? Have you ever seen a film which you enjoyed until you thought about it later? Until you saw it a second time? To what extent are "second thoughts" and second viewings or readings valid criteria for judging a work?

3. The first scene is presented almost entirely through dialogue. Are there any passages there that seem unnatural as conversation, as if they were clearly intended for the reader and not for the person spoken to? What is gained and what lost by this dramatic presentation?

4. In the first scene the discussion of hunting, the actual purpose of the trip, seems to be introduced casually into the conversation. Did it alert

your expectations? In the light of later events, should it have? How is that discussion related to what happens later in the story? To what extent does the conversation define the specific theme of the story? How does Rainsford's dismissal of superstition and of "mental chill" as "pure imagination" relate to his theories of hunting?

5. Zaroff says that "instinct is no match for reason" and that "life is for the strong." How do these statements relate to Rainsford's earlier description of hunting? What are his reactions to Zaroff's statement? Is Zaroff's position logical? Are Rainsford's objections logical? Is there any significance in the fact that Zaroff's clothes fit Rainsford?

6. What does "game" in the title mean? To what extent is Zaroff's hunting a sport? Could he make the hunt more "interesting" by evening the odds, by giving the quarry more weapons or advantages? Does the fact that he does not do so throw any question on the validity of his arguments?

7. Zaroff is a Cossack and considers the overthrow of the czarist regime by the communists a debacle; he is a gentleman, a gourmet, a connoisseur. How do these details relate to his "game"? To his arguments? To the theme? Are there, then, political implications in the hunting-hunter theme of the story?

8. In a story that involves a considerable amount of action, the climatic action, the final fight between Zaroff and Rainsford, is not described. Can you think of any reasons for this omission? For in the paragraph leading up to the fight, the focus of narration shifts for the first time from Rainsford; why?

WILLIAM FAULKNER

Barn Burning

This is a good story to use late in the semester with students experienced in analysis who have the basic elements of fictional presentation firmly under their belts. "Barn Burning" works well in the sections of the course emphasizing point of view, characterization or setting, or as part of a study of the initiation theme. I find it works best—and I'm most pleased with class discussion—when I teach it after students have the tools in hand to appreciate its richness and complexity. Since the introduction in the text focuses on style of presentation, I like to start discussion by asking the class to compare Faulkner's narrative presentation in two paragraphs of "Barn Burning" to the "suspended time/animation" scene in Ambrose Bierce's "Occurrence at Owl Creek Bridge." I sometimes read aloud (or ask a good student reader to read aloud) the passage in which Faulkner uses something between a freeze-frame and a slow-motion technique similar to Bierce's to describe Sarty's sensations in the pause between the judge's question and Harris's response (par. 10–11).

In "Occurrence at Owl Creek Bridge," Bierce suspends time to call attention to the differences between imaginative wish fulfillment and reality, and in doing so, he experiments with an early type of psychological realism. Faulkner's use of psychological realism is similar in that the scene in the make-shift courtroom juxtaposes the "reality" of the pause between the judge's question and Mr. Harris's answer and the simultaneous imaginative sensation Sarty has of swinging helplessly out over a ravine. Some members of the class, I hope, will see a qualitative difference between the ways Bierce and Faulkner employ this technique. If you can get your students to talk about this difference—one accomplishes little more than an interesting plot twist, the other helps to create the portrait of a deeply divided soul—the class will be well on its way into an evaluation (and, I hope, an appreciation) of "Barn Burning."

Once we've begun to talk about Sarty and Faulkner's portrayal of his conflict, I like to ask how the story would be different had Faulkner made Sarty the narrator. Clearly the boy isn't capable of telling a story nearly as complex as the one Faulkner presents through the shifting focus of a third-person perspective—and it's not just that he's a boy, or that he's ill-educated. Sarty neither knows nor understands a number of important things about his father's history and motivations—for example, Abner's activities during the Civil War and his attitude toward fire—that we learn about through the third-person narrator. Much of the social context of "Barn Burning"—the suggestion that the old southern hierarchy of plantation aristocrat over poor tenant farmers and slaves remains intact after the war—would be lost without this outside, authoritative voice. Much of the irony of the ending—Sarty's despairing, desperate attempt to assert his father's bravery as a counter to all his father's wickedness—would be lost without the authoritative voice.

As it is, Faulkner manages to have it both ways; and after stating this, I sometimes ask students to speculate about what I mean. What I'm getting at is that Faulkner's shifts in perspective, however confusing, enable him to present Sarty's plight with all its personal urgency and to present the larger context in which Sarty's struggle is only one of many struggles. By taking us into Sarty's mind, Faulkner causes us to feel the powerful tug of war within the boy between the pull of "blood" (product of genetics, nurture, loyalty of kinship?) and the pull of justice. He does this both through the narrative description of Sarty's feelings and through the italicized words that convey Sarty's thoughts in his own words. The details about setting and history (par. 15) fashion a much larger perspective. And the curious statement near the end of the story, "The slow constellations wheeled on," simultaneously suggests the vastness of the new world Sarty faces alone and the insignificance of his decision (and even of all human endeavor) in the face of an indifferent, impersonal universe.

If style hasn't come up in our discussion of focus and narrative technique, I like to get the class to look at a couple of passages from the story in which Faulkner uses some of his notoriously long sentences: perhaps the paragraph describing Sarty's fight with the older boys after the first trial and the paragraph near the end of the story describing his wild flight away from De Spain's house after he's carried the warning. While Faulkner is deeply concerned with the inward life of his characters, his prose is often extremely cinematic. You might ask your students to describe the way they would film both these scenes using whatever techniques of filmmaking—montage, jump cutting, voice-over, etc.—seem appropriate. If your library has the PBS film version of "Barn Burning" from The American Short Story series, you might have the class watch the film and critique it. If your students have thought about filming the two scenes mentioned above, they will probably be eager to suggest how the film they've seen could be improved to convey more of Faulkner's vision. I find this approach very effective as a way to call attention to Faulkner's narrative virtuosity (students can see how much he packs in that the film leaves out) without seeming to preach about it.

Faulkner's characterization of Sarty seems to me quite different from his characterization of Abner. Students usually find Abner a somewhat mysterious character, as Sarty himself does. You might want to instruct half of the class to write a paragraph explaining why Sarty finally breaks away from his father—providing evidence from the story about what events lead up to his decision—and instruct the other half to write a paragraph explaining why Abner Snopes habitually burns barns. Which group is able to come up with the most definitive explanation?

QUESTIONS FOR DISCUSSION

1. Why do we feel we know Sarty better at the end of the story than we know his father? What does Faulkner gain by characterizing Abner as he does?
2. To what degree does the end of "The Most Dangerous Game" offer closure (a sense that all loose ends are accounted for and tied up)? What about the ending of "Barn Burning"? If a story ends somewhat inconclusively, is this good or bad, or does your answer depend on the story? Which story leaves you with more to think about?

BHARATI MUKHERJEE

The Management of Grief

When Judith Templeton asks Shaila Bhave to help her communicate with the other Indian people in Toronto who have lost relatives in the airplane bombing, she does so because Mrs. Bhave is reported to have responded to the accident "more calmly" than the others. Indeed, in the first half of the story, the narrator seems reliable and steady—especially in contrast to her neighbor Kusum, who threatens suicide and makes it cruelly clear that her older daughter is a burdensome responsibility in contrast to the beloved younger daughter who has been killed. I like to ask students whether at any point in the story they begin to question Mrs. Bhave's reliability. Students usually come to class wanting to know what they are to make of the mysticism in Mukherjee's story, and this question gets us into the issue. When midway into the narrative Mrs. Bhave reports that her dead husband Vikram appears to her in a temple, we may question whether this is a mystical experience or a delusion brought about by grief and longing. You might want to ask your students whether the story seems to support one interpretation over the other.

"The Management of Grief" is a story about how one group of people responds to loss. It is also about being different or "other"—about living outside the dominant culture. Pretty early in the discussion I like to get students to talk about the cultural groups represented in Mukherjee's story. There are the Hindu Indians who have settled in Canada, like Mrs. Bhave; the Sikhs, represented not only by the elderly couple in Agincourt but also by the radicals accused of bombing the airliner; the native Canadians, represented by Judith Templeton, the provincial representative, and the white neighbors who attend Satish's and Kusum's housewarming; the Irish men and women Mrs. Bhave and the others meet during their trip to the crash site; and perhaps also the Americans, represented by the white-haired TV preacher and his audience. Conventional wisdom would have it that universal experiences, especially tragedies like death, transcend cultural differences. You may want to ask your students if Mukherjee's story supports this view.

Who, besides the other relatives of the deceased passengers, offers sympathy that Mrs. Bhave is able to believe and accept? Why are the gestures of the Irish welcome while Judith Templeton's best efforts ultimately are not? It may be a question of proximity to the tragedy. Judith Templeton is an ocean away from the bombing site. The TV preacher and his audience are also miles away, seemingly oblivious to suffering amid "potted palm trees under a blue sky." But the Irish are intimately involved in dealing with the gruesome aftermath of the disaster. They see grieving relatives wandering their streets and haunting their shores, and they mourn with them.

On the other hand, it is hard to avoid the suggestion that the gulf between the Canadians and Americans and the immigrant Indians exists because those who are part of the dominant Western culture refuse to accept the Indian way of handling grief, to admit the validity of another way of mourning. Could it be that the Irish are more accepting, not just because they are close to the scene of tragedy, but because historically they have always been outsiders, too?

Perhaps at some point someone will suggest that cultural differences are not the only barriers to accepting another's way of grieving and that cultural similarity does not necessarily guarantee understanding. (If no one does, I bring it up myself.) One recurring motif in the story is the idea that "a parent's job is to hope." Mrs. Bhave, her neighbor Kusum, Dr. Ranganathan, and the elderly Sikh couple share this belief. It is perhaps the main thread that links them as Indians in their response to the tragedy, but it is notable that the experience of loss itself is their strongest tie. The granddaughter of a devout Hindu and the daughter of rationalists, Mrs. Bhave has no firm spiritual or cultural anchor. When she goes to India, she travels for months with her family "courting aphasia," but as Dr. Ranganathan says, the survivors have "been melted down and recast as a new tribe." Only those who have suffered this particular loss can share its particular anguish—yet even those in the "tribe" cope with grief in very individual ways.

At some point in discussion I like to bring up the implications of the title. The coldness of the term *management* would seem to hark back to Judith Templeton's well-meaning but rather clinical approach to helping the bereaved immigrants. Although I'm tempted to dismiss the idea that Mukherjee's story is an indictment of white/Western/American/Canadian insensitivity toward minority cultures—especially given the discussion above—I'm not certain the notion will go away. What are we to make of Mrs. Bhave's defection from Ms. Templeton's crusade? Of Judith Templeton's name and its associations with Judeo-Christian culture?

QUESTIONS FOR DISCUSSION

1. What of the ending? Does the story seem incomplete? Does Mrs. Bhave receive instructions from the spirits of her family—and if so, what do we make of them—or does she descend into utter madness? If we believe the latter, do we do so out of Western skepticism?
2. Is the ending in some sense a means of confronting and frustrating readers who reject mysticism? Readers who like pat endings? Do you believe any audience would find the ending completely satisfying? If so, what kind of audience?

SUGGESTION FOR WRITING

Both Laurence's "Holiday" and Mukherjee's "The Management of Grief" focus, at least in part, on the way in which people from different cultures cope with grief and the way in which people from one culture view the coping strategies of people from other cultures. Write an essay comparing the two stories in terms of what they each say about these issues.

READING/WRITING IDEAS FOR EVALUATING FICTION

EVALUATIVE ESSAYS

As the headnote to the "Evaluating Poetry" section of the guide suggests, evaluation has become a rather vexed issue among contemporary literary critics and theorists. But this headnote also suggests one quite viable way of steering through those rough waters. The following assignment would work very well as a supplement to, or substitute for, the writing suggestions in the anthology.

Imagine that you are the fiction editor of a good periodical, one that appeals to a broad spectrum of well-educated readers (*The New Yorker*, say, or *The Atlantic*). You have space in the upcoming issue for only one short story, and you have narrowed the choices from a field of several dozen to two, both of which should be included in the anthology. Write a three-page rejection letter to the author of the runner-up. Explain in precise terms why you ultimately decided on the other story. If you wish, spend a paragraph or two on the chosen story's strengths, but the bulk of your letter should describe the weaknesses of the second-place finisher, while saying enough about its strengths so that writer isn't discouraged from trying again. Be careful here not to short-circuit your argument by deciding ahead of time which sorts of stories are appropriate and which are not. Don't say, for example, "Our readers like uplifting stories, and yours is depressing" or "Your story is very long, and our readers like short short stories." Are *all* depressing stories artistically inferior to uplifting ones? Short short stories always superior to longer ones? Assume that your readers would answer no to both questions; they enjoy all sorts of fiction, as long as it is carefully crafted and somehow compelling. Your rejection letter, then, should point out in as much detail as possible why the story is not quite successful in fulfilling its goal, in doing its job.

If you, like me, prefer to have students write essays, one option that works well here is to have students write an evaluative essay by reworking an essay that they wrote earlier in the semester. If a student wrote an essay on the symbolism of "A Hunger Artist," he or she could now rewrite that essay so that it not only analyzed but also evaluated, Kafka's use of symbolism. Or students could go back and evaluate the work of Lawrence or O'Connor.

Regardless of the specific assignment, however, I encourage students to think and write in less absolute terms, concentrating more on showing what's good *and* what's bad in their evaluation. Doing so is important for me because I feel it is a great deal more consistent with the model of writing I've been advocating throughout the course, a model that emphasizes the exploration of an issue, problem, or question from various angles (as I believe literature itself does) rather than the "position paper" type argument that insists on a single, iron-clad view, solution, or answer (if only because airtight answers can only be argued for effectively if a writer shows that he or she has considered others).

EVALUATION-FOCUSED WRITING EXERCISES

1. Developing Definitions and Criteria

To get students started on this assignment and to ensure that they understand that effective evaluation depends on the carefully, thoughtful articulation (and even defense) of explicit criteria, I generally have them do a version of an exercise that my class as a whole usually does together in the very first few days of the class. That exercise entails giving students a chart something like the following to fill out and/or asking them to make such a chart themselves. My basic chart looks like this (only it takes up a whole sheet of paper, turned sideways).

Purposes or Functions of a "Good" Short Story

For Writers: For Readers:

Formal Elements or Features that a "good" short story needs to have to fulfill those functions:

In the case of this particular version of the exercise, I often put this model of the chart on the board and then encourage each student to adapt it as he or she does the exercise in order to fit the exact approach to evaluation he or she is going to take. Thus students who want to focus on a particular element or aspect of a story or stories, such as symbolism or endings, might want to substitute words referring to those elements for the words *short story* (though I also point out to them how much their evaluation of a particular element may depend on their evaluation of others).

Once students have completed this exercise, I then have them work with each other in small groups to compare and critique charts, giving each other feedback about potential problems, areas of disagreement and/or possible counterarguments, etc.

2. "Charting" Other Writers' Definitions and Criteria

Another option here is to have the students do exercise 1 only *after* they've done a version of that exercise that asks them to read sample student and/or scholarly essays that evaluate a text and to make a chart that lists the definitions and criteria stated and implied in those essays. The sample student essays in the anthology work well for this, but I find that reviews of fiction from newspapers and magazines often prove even more helpful and provocative to students.

Reading More Fiction

LOUISA MAY ALCOTT

LOUISA MAY ALCOTT

My Contraband

My students almost invariably know Louisa May Alcott as the author of
Little Women and, as a result, bring to her work certain quite limited and
limiting assumptions. For that reason, when I teach Alcott I often introduce into the conversation at least some biographical information in an
effort to expand students' notions of what an "Alcott story" might be
about.

To start with, Alcott published *Little Women* very late in her quite successful literary career and only when her publishers requested a "girls'
story." Though such stories were certainly a staple of Alcott's career precisely because they paid well (an important consideration since Alcott,
along with her mother, supported her entire extended family for many
years), Alcott also wrote both realistic fiction and a good deal of sensation
and fantasy fiction for adults. Indeed, Alcott's first real success came with
Hospital Sketches in 1863, a volume based on her six weeks as an army
nurse at the Union Hotel Hospital in Georgetown, an experience that
lasted only six weeks because Alcott came down with typhoid fever. The
same experience also informs "My Contraband," also known as "The
Brothers," which first appeared in print in *The Atlantic Monthly* in the
same year that *Hospital Sketches* was published.

What students may not appreciate is just how radical it was for a
respectable middle-class woman like Alcott or her fictional alter-ego
Nurse Dane to serve as nurses, especially since an army nurse's duties
required constant and quite intimate physical contact with men. As a
result, Alcott's decision to volunteer as a nurse was part and parcel of her
life-long efforts to defy the limits imposed on women in the nineteenth
century, efforts that also included joining the New England Woman Suf-
frage Association in 1868 and taking quite openly feminist stances in
much of her fiction (including *Little Women*). As Alcott wrote in her journal just before volunteering as a nurse, "I've often longed to see a war.
. . . I long to be a man; but as I can't fight I will content myself with
working for those who can" (in Elaine Showalter, ed., *Alternative Alcott*,
New Brunswick, N.J.: Rutgers University Press, 1988, p. xviii).

What this information (or at least some of it) may help students to see above all are the underlying connections between Robert and Nurse Dane in "My Contraband." For, as Elaine Showalter comments in *Alternative Alcott*, it is possible to see "The character of Nurse Dane [a]s another contraband, the independent woman, who vicariously shares the ex-slave's revenge against the white men who have enslaved and betrayed him" (p. xxix). This parallel is suggested in multiple ways within the story, among them the fact that Robert adopts the nurse's name and the fact that she initially blames herself for the attempt on Ned's life, describing how she "sprang up" from her nap "to see what harm my long oblivion had done" (par. 53). This may also be one way to understand the significance of the story's title and Nurse Dane's constant reference to Robert as *her* contraband, as well as the fact that Nurse Dane describes herself as "hat[ing] [Ned] as only a woman thinking of a sister woman's wrong could hate" (par. 85).

Attention to this parallel between the characters and to the deeper parallel it suggests between the situations of blacks and of women in nineteenth-century America (both of which are combined in the plight of Lucy) obviously gives a distinctly different cast to Nurse Dane's repeatedly emphasized "sympathy" not only with Robert's plight but also with his murderous longings. And I think attention to Nurse Dane's vicarious violent feelings is important to bring to students' attention because it lends so much power and depth to what might otherwise seem to them a quite conventional, even sentimental, tale of divine retribution. Indeed, Nurse Dane's inability to "love [her] enemies" is emphasized from the outset of the story (par. 7) and constantly disrupts any view of her as a simplistically pious character.

Alcott seems in fact to go to great lengths to distance her tale from the more sentimental abolitionist fiction of, among others, Harriet Beecher Stowe. In this regard perhaps even more important than the radicalism of her characterization of Nurse Dane is that of Robert himself, whom Alcott explicitly contrasts to Stowe's "saintly 'Uncle Tom' " (par. 100). And, again, this facet of the story may be one that students need more background to appreciate. To that end, you might both work to draw out their understanding of the phrase "Uncle Tom" and consider sharing with them the following scene from *Uncle Tom's Cabin* (New York: Bantam, 1981), the scene in which the long-suffering, all-forgiving Tom meets his death at the hands of the notorious Simon Legree:

> Legree drew in a long breath; and, suppressing his rage, took Tom by the arm, and, approaching his face almost to his, said, in a terrible voice . . . "You've always stood it out agin' me: now, I'll *conquer ye, or kill ye!*—one or t'other. I'll count every drop of blood there is in you, and take 'em, one by one, till ye give up!"
>
> Tom looked up to his master, and answered, "Mas'r, if you was sick, or in trouble, or dying, and I could save ye, I'd *give* ye my heart's blood; and, if taking every drop of blood in this poor old body would save your precious soul, I'd give 'em freely, as the Lord gave His for me. O Mas'r! don't bring this great sin on your soul! It will

hurt you more than 'twill me! Do the worst you can, my troubles will be over soon; but, if ye don't repent, yours won't *never* end!"

Like a strange snatch of heavenly music, heard in the lull of a tempest, this burst of feeling made a moment's blank pause. Legree stood aghast, and looked at Tom; and there was such a silence, that the tick of the old clock could be heard, measuring, with silent touch, the last moments of mercy and probation to that hardened heart.

It was but a moment. There was one hesitating pause . . . and the spirit of evil came back, with seven-fold vehemence; and Legree, foaming with rage, smote his victim to the ground. (pp. 410–11)

What such a passage may allow students to appreciate is just how much less pious and simplistic Alcott's hero, narrator, and story as a whole are. Even if he does not, finally, kill his brother/enemy directly, Robert's desire to do so, as well as Nurse Dane's tremendous sympathy for, and vicarious fascination with, that desire, are in themselves fairly radical when compared to the much more traditional *Uncle Tom's Cabin*. And, in light of the way in which Uncle Tom dies more concerned with his master's soul than his own, so is the fact that Robert's decision not to kill his brother, as well as Nurse Dane's persuasive arguments to that effect, rest almost solely on concerns for Robert's own worldly and spiritual welfare. From beginning to end, both Nurse Dane and the reader find themselves in quite un-Christian fashion "Feeling decidedly more interest in the black man than in the white" (par. 13). However seemingly pious its conclusion, then, Alcott's story never for a moment asks Robert or anyone who suffers oppression to turn the other cheek or demands that they do so to become sympathetic figures.

What it does do, however, is to suggest—at least to some extent—that Robert is particularly sympathetic because he is not wholly black, his "mixed" racial heritage and somewhat self-imposed alienation from both races functioning from beginning to end as a crucial aspect of Nurse Dane's sympathy for him (par. 13, 28). And I would suggest that this aspect of the story might be a fitting place to end discussion, along with questions about the quite complex symbolism of Robert's divided face, "a fine medal" that is "suddenly reversed" at quite interesting moments in the story (par. 14).

Finally, you might spark student interest in the story by letting them in on the fact that Robert serves in the Union Army unit depicted in the movie *Glory*, receiving his mortal wound in the battle on which the movie centers. Given world enough and time, you might even consider showing the movie to students and having them compare the two texts, particularly in terms of their depictions of race and relations between the races during the Civil War era.

QUESTIONS FOR DISCUSSION

1. How does Alcott characterize the two brothers in the story? What is the significance of the fact that Ned and Robert are brothers? Though

Robert is clearly described sympathetically in the story, Alcott explicitly contrasts him to "the saintly 'Uncle Tom.' " Who exactly was or
is Uncle Tom, and why and how does this contrast contribute to
Alcott's characterization of Robert and to the overall effect or meaning
of the story?

2. How might Robert's scarred face function as a symbol in the story?
What might it symbolize? Note the places where Robert's face is mentioned and described in the story. What is the significance of the timing of those descriptions? Since it is Nurse Dane who mediates our
view of Robert's face, what might the timing and specific character of
these descriptions tell us about her and her (changing) attitudes
toward Robert?

3. How does Alcott characterize Nurse Dane? When, why, and in what
particular ways is she drawn to "her contraband"? One critic has suggested that Nurse Dane is herself a contraband of sorts, whose situation as a woman to some extent parallels that of blacks such as Robert.
What evidence in the story supports this view? What evidence might
complicate or undermine this view? How might this interpretation of
Nurse Dane and her relationship to Robert potentially change or complicate your interpretation of the story as a whole?

4. How exactly might this story be different if it were not narrated from
the first-person point of view of Nurse Dane?

5. Though Alcott's story clearly speaks out against the institution of slavery and the oppression of black people, she chooses to make her hero
at least half-white and to characterize Nurse Dane as attracted to Robert, at least in part, because of his "mixed" heritage. How do these
facts complicate the story? Is this explicitly antiracist story also in its
own way racist? How so? How not?

HENRY JAMES

The Real Thing

If "The Cask of Amontillado" is a story about plot or plotting, "The Real
Thing" is a story about character and characterization, and that, plus its
quality, is why it is here. I read the story as suggesting that real ladies and
gentlemen are useless as models for, or representation of, ladies and gentlemen precisely because they are real, and reality is made up of stereotypes. Major and Mrs. Monarch are only useful as models for stereotyped
stories. You might want to point out that this paradox is prepared for in
the first paragraph by the "paradoxical law" that people who looked
famous were never famous and vice versa. Both these paradoxes are debatable, and sooner or later—though perhaps later, toward the end of your
discussion of the story—you may want to raise the issue of the truth of

the story, whether it is the real thing, but by that time you may also have laid the groundwork for discussing the reliability of the narrator.

Something you may have to clear up first is the whole conception of class. I find that my students have great trouble with this concept, particularly as it appears in James or Trollope or any late nineteenth- or early twentieth-century English work (the American-born James being in many ways more English than the English). Many know better, but they insist on using *rich* and *upper-class* as synonyms. They have to be reminded about "the vulgar rich" and the "impoverished genteel," and it is news to many of them that anyone who works for a living, no matter how rich—or mannerly—is, at best, middle-class. It is possible that without some discussion of class the full poignancy of the story (as, in the final paragraph, "it was dreadful to see them emptying my slops") will not fully come across. Not that this poignancy will go unchallenged—someone may ask, "Why shouldn't they empty slops? Somebody's got to do it. Why are they better than anyone else? If they have to make a buck and they have no other skills, then they just have to do the best they can." Can an egalitarian read with sympathy this apparently elitist story? (We are back to whether a 1990s feminist or civil libertarian can read "A Rose for Emily" with sympathy.) How one deals with different, especially unacceptable, political, social, and moral values in reading and appreciating literature is an issue that must be confronted in any course treating literature, especially that of other times or cultures. On the one hand, I want my students to take values and literature seriously, as I am sure most of you do as well, so too latitudinarian a position may subvert our purposes. On the other hand, I do not want to reinforce what I find is an already entrenched bias against appreciating or applauding anything that fails to confirm our own vision and views, for this clearly works against the understanding and sympathy that the study of the humanities and especially the study of literature are meant to encourage. This is a very shadowy area, but the issues are real and important, and, if we are not to sterilize our discipline, I believe we must get it out in the open, in front of the class, with all our prejudices and uncertainties hanging out. What do you think?

When I feel I've sufficiently discussed character and characterization, stereotypes and class distinctions, art and reality, and perhaps literature and values, and life, I like to turn to the very end of the story: "my friend Hawley repeats that Major and Mrs. Monarch did me a permanent harm, got me into false ways. If it be true I'm content to have paid the price—for the memory." That the story is a "memory" of the somewhat distant past is suggested in the very first sentence of the story—"in those days." I am not sure what the value of the memory is that has made it worth so much to the narrator. The memory surely is not pleasant—he hated seeing them empty slops, he had to turn them away after about a week, he does not know whether he did them any good, what their fates were. He does not seem to mean that the memory was in the "lesson"—that art is the illusion of reality and not the representation of it—for the price he has paid apparently is a lessening of his artistic ability ("permanent harm," "false ways"). I'd like to think that James, being James, is turning the screw of the paradox once again, so that if the real thing is not a good model for art, then perhaps what is good for art is not good for our real lives, our humanity. That experience which weakened his art made him a better human being (or "real person"). As I say elsewhere in this text, I do not mind parading my uncertainties before the class when they are real and earned—that is, when I have at least worked at resolving them.

Part of the "earning" here may be trying to come to terms with the character of the narrator himself. He is not successful enough not to want or need paying "sitters" and commercial work doing book illustrations, yet he is quick enough to point out that his professional judgment is not that of a barber or tailor (that he is not merely commercial, a tradesman). His mind is subtle enough to see things paradoxically, shrewd enough to recognize that since Claude Rivet only painted landscapes he would sacrifice nothing in recommending the Monarchs to him for their portraits, and tactful enough not to say so. After you have done so to your own satisfaction, you might want your students to go through the story carefully and thoroughly, searching for details that characterize the narrator. They can then report their results in a paper or discuss them in class.

One question that you may want to raise yourself is what, precisely, is the narrator's attitude toward the country-house class—or toward the Monarchs, for that matter. Why can't the artist—who, if he is not a successful portrait artist, seems to be a skilled illustrator—use his imagination to alter the Monarchs? Why do they always appear so large in his drawings? Could it be that the artist is less confident, less sure of the value of his work and his position in society than he realizes? His distress at seeing the Monarchs down on their luck and emptying slops notwithstanding (or is distress his full feeling?), isn't there a kind of contempt, even hostility in his attitude? Perhaps a kinder way of getting at this is to ask the students to try to deduce from the story exactly what the narrator believes is the value of art and the role of the artist in society. You might also ask them if our narrator seems comfortable with this role and sure of his ability to fulfill it.

CHARLOTTE PERKINS GILMAN

The Yellow Wallpaper

Gilman's tale of one woman's struggle to escape the confines of her ascribed role is a classic story that provokes wonderful discussions and equally wonderful student writing, precisely because it tends to draw fairly passionate responses of one kind or another. Uniquely rich with dense and complex symbolism, the story might be an especially apt text to read, discuss, and/or have students write about in the context of the anthology's "Symbols" chapter, but it is also a particularly fitting text for exercising the kind of reading strategies outlined in the "Culture as Context" and/or "Critical Contexts" chapters, as well as the strategies involved in biographical approaches. Teachers who want to use either of these three latter approaches will find background or primary source material, as well as literary criticism on the story that uses such approaches, in *The Captive Imagination: A Casebook on "The Yellow Wallpaper,"* edited by Catherine Golden (New York: The Feminist Press, 1992), and Diane Price-Herndl's *Invalid Women: Figuring Feminine Illness in American Fiction and Culture, 1840–1940* (Chapel Hill: University of North Carolina Press, 1993).

What's extraordinary about the story, however, is that while it readily lends itself to any or all of these approaches, it also works very well when read all on its own; and every time I read and teach the story I fondly remember how reading and writing about it sparked a keen interest in literature and literary analysis in my very nonacademically minded older sister. As a result, I have found that the trick to a successful discussion of this story isn't getting students started, but keeping them focused, channeling their passions, and convincing them to stick with it after they think they've gotten it.

Since the central conflict in this story is fairly obvious and students do, indeed, think they've gotten it, I always find it best to begin discussion here (rather than fighting it) and then take students deeper into the distinctly less obvious complexities of the story. That obvious conflict is, of course, that between the narrator (and the community of women she comes to represent) and the patronizing attitudes toward women embodied in the other characters in the story. But what is that attitude, and why is it represented as quite literally maddening for this narrator? The conflict comes across most clearly, perhaps, in the very beginning of the story. Here, the narrator makes clear to us that the men in her life—her brother and husband—represent a sort of united front against her and that, being "physician[s] of high standing" (par. 10), their opinions aren't opinions at all but carry all the weight and authority of science. Faced with that, the narrator's opinions are ignored or simply "laugh[ed]" away (par. 5), consigned to oblivion along "with faith," "superstition," and "any talk of things not to be felt and seen and put down in figures" (par. 6). The "practical in the extreme" point of view of the physicians is (par. 6), of course, that "there is really nothing the matter" with the narrator, that her condition is (fittingly enough) imaginary (par. 10). And, in effect, her condition allows her husband to force her into the passive role that he seems to believe all women should play: she is "absolutely forbidden to 'work,' " to write, to think, or to imagine at all (par. 12). All of this despite the fact that it is, as the wife herself knows, her passivity that has caused her illness, knowing "that congenial work, with excitement and change, would do me good" (par. 14). Ironically, the wife thus becomes "exhaust[ed]" and "tired" by the very effort to "be so sly," "to control myself—before him, at least," to pretend that she is the passive, obedient woman that her husband wants her to be (par. 16, 26), a pretense that eventually drives her mad as she becomes obsessed with the only "society and stimulus" available to her (par. 17), the figures in the wallpaper that come to symbolize her own imprisonment.

Once we've gotten the basic conflict out on the table and students have had their say about it (or at least most of their say), I usually begin trying to push them deeper into the texture of the story (and the conflict) by focusing them first on exactly how the wallpaper operates as a symbol for the narrator's situation; what significance particular, highly detailed descriptions of the wallpaper have; and how the narrator's changing attitudes toward the wallpaper reflect changes in her perception of her situation.

Once you've exhausted the wallpaper, you might want to draw students' attention to the symbolic resonance of other aspects of the setting—the fact that the room to which she is confined is a nursery, that it has bars on the windows, that the only furniture is a bed chained to the floor, etc. The first of these facts obviously suggests the childlike status accorded the narrator by her husband, the bars the imprisoning character of that status, and the bed? Well, at least one critic, Loralee MacPike in "Environment as Psychopathological Symbolism in 'The Yellow Wallpaper' " (*Captive Imagination*), suggests that it is

a representation of her sexuality, [which] is nailed to the floor. . . . As the nursery imprisons her in a state of childhood, so the bedstead prevents her from moving "off center" sensually—not merely sexually—in any sort of physical contact with another human being. Her inability to care for her own child is but another fixity in her life, and the immovable bedstead symbolizes the static nature of both the expression and the product of her sexuality, thus denying her this outlet for her energies just as the bars deny her physical movement and the nursery her adult abilities. (p. 138)

Whatever students come up with, once I feel that we've begun to exhaust these other symbols, I then turn to the conclusion of the story. In what sense is the narrator mad and in what sense isn't she? To what extent does the conclusion suggest the ultimate defeat of the narrator and to what extent might it suggest that she enjoys (an admittedly Pyrrhic) victory?

And, finally, I try to conclude discussion of "The Yellow Wallpaper" by discussing the ways in which it is and is not a "dated" story, a sort of nineteenth-century period piece. What aspects of the conflict portrayed here still seem relevant, even if they might look different? What aspects of the conflict seem to be of purely historical interest? Here's where things could, if you're lucky, get interestingly heated.

QUESTIONS FOR DISCUSSION

1. If the basic conflict of this story is that between the attitudes of men toward women and women's needs and desires, then how exactly does the story define those attitudes, needs, and desires?
2. The wallpaper is, as the title suggests, the chief symbol in this story. What exactly does it symbolize and how exactly does it work as a symbol? What details about the wallpaper seem significant? How does the narrator's attitude toward, and vision of, the wallpaper change, and what is the significance of those changes?
3. Clearly the wallpaper here is one of the facets of the setting that carries great symbolic weight. What other aspects of the setting seem to be symbols and what exactly do they symbolize? How do these symbols contribute to the intensification and/or resolution of the central conflict?
4. What do you make of the ending of the story? Does the narrator seem to have been utterly defeated or is there any way of seeing her as triumphant?
5. In what ways does the conflict explored in this story seem dated to you? In what ways does it seem relevant to today's world?

EDITH WHARTON

Souls Belated

This story works well in the classroom because it deals with a subject dear to the hearts of students and does so in a way that requires them to complicate their vision of that subject.

That subject, of course, is the conflict between the need or desire to conform to accepted social conventions and the desire to assert oneself as a free, autonomous individual. Wharton's story begins at a point when that conflict has, presumably, been resolved. After all, as we learn quite early on, Lydia has already abandoned her husband and her home, along with her position as a respectable wife, not (or so she hopes) simply because of her love for Gannett but because of her utter disgust with the "same small circle of prejudices" that defined her wifely life (par. 13). For that very reason, Lydia scorns the idea of marriage to her lover, thinking it a "vulgar fraud upon," and concession to, the "conventional morality" of "a society we've despised and laughed at" (par. 54). Yet as Gannett's proposal and the very stridency of Lydia's response to it suggest, the conflict has been reopened rather than closed by the very divorce papers that signify her escape from the "circle": ironically, that very freedom becomes "the *thing*" "symbolically suspended over her head and his" (par. 11).

By insisting that they stay at the Hotel Bellosguardo, Lydia seeks to embrace her choice and her freedom, vowing that the other residents of the hotel "may think what they please" about her (par. 80). As a result, when Wharton's narrative point of view switches to that of Miss Pinsent (par. 86), we expect—I think—to see Lydia paying the price for her abandonment of the "conventional morality" that Miss Pinsent clearly represents. Ironically, of course, this is not what happens, for by the end of this section of the story it is clear that Lydia has once more become part of a "small circle" that is exactly the same as the one she abandoned, even "mentally agree[ing]" with Miss Pinsent's prejudiced condemnation of the "new people" about whom "nothing is known" (par. 97, 88, 95). Yet the irony of Lydia's position doesn't really become clear to her until she is forced to acknowledge her kinship with the divorcée Mrs. Linton/ Mrs. Cope, who mercilessly points out that "the first day I laid eyes on you I saw that you and I were both in the same box" (par. 159). Lydia's fear of this kinship with Mrs. Cope makes clear to her for the first time how much her yearning to be a part of the kind of small circle she now realizes is also, in Miss Pinsent's words, "a little family" has dictated her actions (par. 86): "These people—the very prototypes of the bores you took me away from, with the same fenced-in view of life, . . . the same little cautious virtues and the same little frightened vices—well, I've clung to them, I've delighted in them, I've done my best to please them" (par. 247).

As a result, as Mrs. Cope's words suggest, Wharton's story ultimately suggests that the freedom-seeking individualist bent on escaping the "fences" of society merely lands himself or herself in another kind of "box," and the denouement of the story clearly suggests that total escape from social conventions is neither possible nor, ultimately, necessarily desirable, even as it also mourns that tragic reality. After all, as Gannett, Lydia, and the reader are forced to ask, "Where would she go?," "[W]here would you go . . . ?" (par. 304, 282). It is a wonderful question with which to end discussion.

QUESTIONS FOR DISCUSSION

1. Why has Lydia left her old life? What exactly does Lydia desire that this old life couldn't give her?
2. What is the effect of Wharton's opening the story *after* Lydia's escape from her old life rather than before? What seeds of conflict are planted in the story's opening? When Lydia, for example, refers to her divorce papers as a *"thing"* "symbolically suspended over her head and his" (par. 11), what does she mean? What symbols do you see here and what do they symbolize?
3. The point of view of the story shifts rather dramatically around paragraph 86. What is the effect of this shift? What did you expect to

happen here and how, if at all, does Wharton's story defy those expectations?

4. What is Miss Pinsent's role in, or contribution to, the story?

5. One could argue that the climax of this story's rising action lies in the conversation between Mrs. Cope and Lydia (especially par. 159). If you agree, why do you think it is the climax? What, for example, is the significance of Mrs. Cope's remark that she and Lydia are "in the same box"? If you disagree, what other moments seem to you more climactic?

6. What do you make of the end of the story? How exactly is the main conflict resolved? What is the significance of the phrase "Where would she go?" What is the effect of the shift to Gannett's point of view?

RUDYARD KIPLING

Without Benefit of Clergy

Though Kipling's "Without Benefit" may prove at first difficult for students, to whom it will no doubt seem foreign in several different ways, it is a wonderfully complex and much-debated story that can be the subject of both insightful discussions and delightful essays.

One way to begin discussion might be to focus tightly on the first few paragraphs of the story, asking students what this section tells us about Holden and Ameera and the two worlds that meet through them. One thing that you might try to bring out here is the complex, even contradictory, nature of both Ameera and the Indian culture that she in some ways represents. On the one hand, both are, through the mention of Ameera's prayers and gifts to a shrine in the second paragraph, associated with ritual, religion, and magic, all of which represent attempts to control one's fate by bargaining with the fates or the gods for whatever one wants and by interpreting every event as a portent of the future. (And this notion of bargaining comes through most clearly when Pir Khan avows, "Never life came into the world but life was paid for it" [par. 44].) In the opening it is Holden who seems to represent the more realistic viewpoint, insisting that the baby might, after all, just as likely "be a girl" as the boy Ameera prays for (par. 1). On the other hand, this view of the conflict in the story as one between Holden's British reason and realism and the irrational, magical worldview of the Indian Ameera is almost immediately undercut when Holden refers to the money with which he purchased Ameera as "the dowry" and Ameera refuses to accept that euphemism, realistically insisting that "I was bought as though I had been a Lucknow dancing-girl" (par. 5–6). And you might at this point want to ask students to continue examining this notion of "reason" or "realism" versus "mysticism" or "ritualism" throughout the rest of the story.

Alternatively, you might want to pause at the beginning of the story just a little longer to address the question of how exactly the prospect of a child destabilizes the situation between Ameera and Holden and/or plants the seeds of conflict, especially in terms of the different attitudes that Ameera and Holden each initially displays toward that prospect. One possible answer has to do with the way in which two seemingly different responses again turn out to be somewhat the same: for while Holden fears the change and disruption that the baby represents—"It interfered with his perfect happiness. It disarranged the orderly peace of the house that was his own"—Ameera sees the baby as her chance to insure herself against the change that she accepts as inevitable, knowing that "The love of a man . . . was at the best an inconstant affair," but one that "might . . . be held fast by a baby's hands" (par. 14). What the baby's imminent arrival brings to the fore, in other words, is the way in which both characters (indeed, all characters) in the story grapple with the inevitability of change and the uncertainty of a future that can be neither predicted nor controlled. The birth of a child forces these characters, as it perhaps does all of us, to confront the future and to worry about the changes it will bring.

As a result, it is possible to see the contrast between the two worlds in the story as ultimately a matter only of the particular means that each employs in this struggle for control or order. For Indians such as Ameera and Pir Khan those means include obeisance to any and every form of magical or religious ritual that seems to promise a measure of control over, or at least knowledge of, future events, an idea emphasized when Ameera prays to both "the Prophet and to Beebee Miriam [the Virgin Mary]" (par. 80). For the British those means focus on self-control; stoicism; "concentrated attention and hard work" (par. 112); obedience to orders distributed through a carefully defined hierarchy; and the employment of rational, scientific methods for "famine-relief, cholera-sheds, medicine-distribution," and "sanitation," all of which "went forward because it was so ordered" (par. 155). The British also constantly use the sort of euphemisms that we see Holden employing from the beginning, as if they believed they could control the most awful events by containing them in what the Deputy Commissioner refers to as rational, "decen[t]" phrases such as "local scarcity and an unusual prevalence of seasonal sickness" (par. 134, 138). Yet the differences between these means begins to break down when, for example, we see the underlying likeness between the British officials' stoicism and the emotional concealment that Ameera insists that she and Holden should adopt after the death of their child, "mak[ing] no protestations of delight, but go[ing] softly underneath the stars, lest God find us out," "saying 'It is naught, it is naught': and hoping that all the Powers heard" (par. 128–129).

For Holden, this British way of life has an obvious, if also incomplete, appeal, the club and his work representing a "mercy" and a "kindness of the gods" that "steadied" him and allowed him to "pull [him]self together" when life-altering events such as the birth and death of his child take place (par. 112, 54, 46). Yet the appeal of this way of life is also incomplete for Holden because he at some level agrees with Ameera that it means that "The white men have hearts of stone and souls of iron" (par. 118). And after the birth of his child, if not before, Holden seems to be just as willing as Ameera to use whatever means are at his command to stave off evil, an idea underscored when Holden participates in the birth-sacrifice initiated by Pir Khan, "speak[ing] in earnest" the ritualistic words he "had learned" but "little thought" he would ever seriously use (par. 43).

The Powers, however, prove deaf to British and Indian alike in this story, both birth-sacrifices and sanitation measures proving to be of absolutely no use whatsoever against the ravages of nature that strike both Holden's home and the country at large, an impotency emphasized when the narrator reports to us that the cholera "struck a pilgrim-gathering of half a million at a sacred shrine. Many died at the feet of their god" (par. 141). As a result, the story seems to suggest that nature or the universe or whatever one chooses to call it, like "the black cholera," "does its work" "without explanation" (par. 159). And one possible interpretation of the story involves seeing both Holden and Ameera as over the course of it discovering and accepting the futility of such feeble human efforts at control, a reading perhaps supported by the fact that they ultimately stop making any such efforts, choosing instead to "s[i]t together and laug[h], calling each other openly by every pet name that could move the wrath of the gods" (par. 154), and by the fact that Ameera's dying words deny that there are any such gods (par. 160).

As a result, as Elliot Gilbert argues in *The Good Kipling: Studies in the Short Story* (Oberlin: Ohio University Press, 1970), Ameera's words might be seen to affirm what Kipling's story as a whole does: that everyone in the world is "without benefit of clergy" in the metaphorical sense that no one is immune from, or in control of, the irrational forces of the universe. In Gilbert's words, "in the universe which Kipling depicts in the story, there are no 'clergy,' no one is privileged, no one, British or Indian, gets a second chance" (p. 40, n. 19).

And, according to this interpretation, Ameera's refusal to escape to the hills along with the *mem-logs* is, in Gilbert's words, "a courageous and honest" decision:

> Why, [Ameera] wonders, should a woman want to live long and be beautiful except for the love of her husband and children? And if this is so, what madness possesses her to give up both husband and children in order to prolong that life and beauty? What end can she hope to achieve by postponing the experience of life from today until tomorrow, especially in a random and irrational universe in which the chance is always great that there will be no tomorrow? . . . Ameera's . . . refusal to withdraw to the hills may seem foolishly willful. But . . . it represents her passionate com-

mitment to an idea, to the idea that life—infinitely precious and, from all she has seen of it, extremely tenuous—is meaningful only when it is being lived. (p. 33)

And it is a decision that embodies the sort of *carpe diem* philosophy that Kipling's story as a whole ultimately embraces. In Gilbert's words, "It is a man's business . . . to live as fully as he can, postponing nothing, recognizing in advance that the more he has, the more he is likely to lose, but not sacrificing any part of experience in the hope of being able to find a happiness he will not have to pay for" (p. 35).

QUESTIONS FOR DISCUSSION

1. How does Kipling characterize each of the two worlds in which Holden lives? What exactly does Holden seem to get from each of these worlds? In what ways are the two worlds (and the people in them) different and in what ways are they alike? When and how does the story begin to suggest the likeness between them?
2. How do Holden and Ameera change over the course of the story or what, if anything, do you think they learn?
3. Critics disagree somewhat about the character of Ameera, some arguing that she is a naive character essentially undone by her envy of the white *mem-log* and her willing servitude to Holden, others that she is the most astute character in the story and most definitely Holden's equal. Much of that debate centers on different interpretations of two events—Ameera's refusal to take to the hills to avoid the cholera and her dying affirmation that Holden is her only God. What is the significance of these events? Which of these interpretations of Ameera's character seem most justified to you? Is there a way to reconcile the two interpretations? Is there another possibility?
4. As Elliot Gilbert explains, "Benefit of clergy, so-called, was technically a privilege allowed to members of the clergy under common law when they were charged with a crime. It meant that they were responsible only to their bishops or the church courts and that ordinary courts had no power over them" (p. 40, n.). Given that "technical" definition of the phrase, what are the metaphorical or symbolic meanings of the title? Who in the story is "without benefit of clergy"?
5. What does the final scene add to the story? Why and how is it a fitting conclusion?

RAYMOND CARVER

Cathedral

Carver's "Cathedral" is a perfect text for the discussion of character and characterization and of the concept of "epiphany." Like most literary terms, this one certainly has its dangers, particularly if it results in students' going epiphany-hunting in every work of fiction. But "epiphany" nonetheless seems like a helpful tool for students in relation to this particular story, especially since the story so clearly plays with conventional associations between epiphany and vision.

As a result, discussion may well work best if students are made to concentrate first on the beginning of the story (up to the final section) and to address questions about the character of the narrator and about the way he characterizes himself through both what he says and how he says it. Ironically or not, we perhaps get most insight into this character through his obvious discomfort with the idea of meeting a blind man. Having encountered the blind only in "the movies" and through "having read" about them "somewhere" (par. 1, 43), the narrator's vision is limited to a series of stereotypes ("the blind didn't smoke," "dark glasses were a must for the blind," etc. [par. 43, 31]). That the narrator tends to see not just blind people but the world in general in terms of such stereotypes is emphasized by his statement that "Beulah" is always and necessarily "a name for a colored woman" (par. 11). More important, perhaps, the narrator seems perfectly content with this limited vision, perfectly happy never to learn any more about the blind, the "colored," or anyone or anything else, a man to whom even a new sofa seems vaguely threatening. And this picture of the narrator as a self-indulgent and self-enclosed man is further reinforced by his reliance on alcohol and drugs (a facet of this story students always want to talk about).

At first glance, then, the narrator seems a fairly unsympathetic character, and it's not very surprising that, as his wife points out, the narrator doesn't "have *any* friends" (par. 10). But is he really so irredeemably unsympathetic? To my mind, he isn't, and what makes the narrator a complex and sympathetic character (rather than a simple and simplistic bigot) is the extent to which he seems himself aware of, and unhappy with, his own limitations, however incapable he is of articulating that unhappiness. When he says, "Maybe I just don't understand poetry" (par. 3), the fact of the admission seems as revealing as its content, and however self-consciously and relentlessly narrow and prosaic this character and his life seem to be, there is more than a touch of poetry in his imaginative reverie—he says, "I'm imagining now"—about the pathos of the blind man's loss of a woman he loved but never saw (par. 16). Thus the fact that the narrator ends that reverie by dismissing as "Pathetic" the blind man's romantically poetic gesture of keeping "half of a twenty-peso Mexican coin" and putting the "other half of the coin" in his wife's coffin, seems as much a commentary on himself and his own latent romantic tendencies as on the blind man (par. 16). The visit of the blind man may thus represent more than one kind of threat to this narrator: merely by being blind he threatens the preconceptions of the narrator, and as the wife's friend and the audience for her poetry, he also clearly possesses a kind of poetic sensibility and a capacity for intimacy that the narrator feels he doesn't and can't offer. Is the narrator, then, rather than Robert the character truly doomed never to "read the expression" on his own wife's face? Never to really know "what she looked like" (par. 16)?

By the end of the story it is clear that Carver suggests that no man is necessarily doomed to that fate, that—in the words of Robert—it is possible to "always [be] learning something," that "[l]earning never ends" (par. 87). At the same time, as the narrator draws with Robert, his "learning" comes with all the suddenness of a revelation, an epiphany not unlike those in Joyce's short fiction and a moment of grace not unlike those in O'Connor's. And, indeed, Carver's "epiphany" depends on an ironic play on the idea of vision that recalls to my mind both the song "Amazing Grace"—this narrator "was blind but now [he] sees"—and Wordsworth's "Tintern Abbey"—this narrator is "laid asleep" in order to "see into the life of things." By closing his eyes, by simply imagining rather than trying to see in terms of what he already knows, by letting himself loose into intimacy with another human being, the narrator, indeed, learns at least for a moment what it means not to be caged "inside anything," including himself (par. 135). As a result, he seems to come closer to God and to poetry than any of the cathedral builders whose simple faith he envies.

As I indicated in the note to Lawrence's "The Blind Man," I very much like to have students read and discuss these two stories together, and I have also found that they are wonderful fodder for comparative essays. That's why I conclude the following list of questions with a question that might help jump-start that comparison.

QUESTIONS FOR DISCUSSION

1. Concentrating on the first few sections of the story, what do the narrator's remarks about the visit of the blind man, about his wife's history, and about himself suggest about what kind of person he is? How would you characterize this narrator's worldview? His values? How is our vision of the narrator influenced by *how* he speaks, by Carver's relentlessly simple sentences, by the fact that the narrator attributes a word such as *inseparable* to his wife, for example? Is the narrator a sympathetic character? If so, why? What makes him sympathetic?

2. What is the narrator's attitude toward the visit of the blind man? Why is he so threatened by the idea of that visit? How might the blind man threaten his worldview and/or values? What do you make of the fact that the blind man and his wife are ultimately the only characters in the story that have names?

3. What is the significance of the fact that the narrator reacts so strongly and so imaginatively to the idea of the death of the blind man's wife? What does this reaction suggest about him? How and why might it change our view of the narrator?

4. What literally happens in the final section of the story? What happens symbolically? Does the narrator seem to be changed? How and why?

What does he mean when he says he feels as if he is not "inside any-thing"?

5. Carver's title suggests that it is significant that Robert and the narrator draw a cathedral together. Why and how is this so significant? What other references to religion appear in the story? How might they help you to understand the significance of the cathedral?

6. What does "blindness" symbolize in our culture? How does Carver's story reinforce or undermine that symbolism?

7. How is Carver's story like and unlike Lawrence's "The Blind Man," which also deals with the visit of a blind man to a married couple? How is Carver's narrator like and unlike Bertie Reid? Isabel Pervin like and unlike the wife in Carver's story? How is the encounter between Bertie, Maurice, and Isabel like and unlike that between the narrator, Robert, and the narrator's wife? How are the endings of the two stories alike and different, particularly in terms of the effects of the one-on-one encounter between the blind and sighted men? What is the effect of the different uses of point of view in the two stories? How else does Lawrence's story differ stylistically and/or formally from Carver's? What are the effects of those differences?

BOBBIE ANN MASON

Shiloh

The problem I have when teaching "Shiloh" is that it lends itself all too easily to the kind of pop psychology with which my students tend to feel very comfortable and with which I tend to feel distinctly uncomfortable: "Norma Jean and Leroy have just never gotten over the death of their little boy," I can hear them say, "they just don't *communicate*." Er, um, yes, but what does that *mean*?

Once my students resort to pop psychology I find it extremely difficult to get them to attend to the story in any meaningful way. Because I'm a chicken who prefers to avoid such problems altogether, I prefer the fron-tal assault, focusing students on the text and on particular questions about it from the outset.

One place to start might be with the hobbies that Norma Jean and Leroy take up after the accident and questions about just what these activ-ities reveal about each of the characters and about the conflict between them. On the one hand, Norma Jean's hobbies seem to be focused relent-lessly on self-improvement, and the aggressively exclusionary character of this improvement is emphasized from the very outset when Leroy has to "dodg[e]" her barbells to talk to her (par. 3). On the other hand, Leroy's obsession with building things from kits seems to indicate a number of different and to some extent contradictory things. Interestingly enough, aside from the log cabin, Leroy's projects all involve building moving objects, "sailing ships," "a macramé owl," a "B-17 Flying Fortress," and "a model truck," which seem to symbolize his yearning for the life "on the road" that he has been forced to give up (par. 6). Yet the log cabin represents, or at least seems to represent, the opposite yearning, to "finally settl[e] down with the woman he loves" and make "a real home" rather than a house (par. 16, 48). Thus one might say that where Norma Jean is focused solely on building her own body and mind, Leroy, however tentatively, wants to build a home for the two of them, to finally stop "flying past" the "scenery" of his own life and focus on "how things are put together" (par. 6).

But why the particular obsession with a log cabin and with building one from a kit? One might say that these particular obsessions reveal a yearning for two different, but related, kinds of simplicity. The first kind, of course, refers to the "simpler" and more primitive way of life suggested to us by log cabins. In this way, Leroy's desire to build a log cabin seems to relate to his desire to return to "the early days of their marriage," to simply "start all over again" "Right back at the beginning," ignoring everything that has happened to the two of them in the interim (par. 9, 146). In the process, of course, Leroy attempts to deny their "history": "They both know that he doesn't know any history" (par. 135). And this is where simplicity in the first sense fudges into the kind of simplicity suggested by the building kits—the desire to be able to build fairly simple things from plans provided by somebody else, avoiding the need to think about the kind of house one wants to build or how to go about building it. And I think it's both kinds of simplicity that come to mind when Leroy says at the end of the story that "building a house out of logs is . . . empty—too simple," "the dumbest idea he could have had" (par. 156).

QUESTIONS FOR DISCUSSION

1. What do Leroy's hobbies tell us about him? What does his obsession with the idea of building a log cabin suggest about him? What does the project and/or the cabin seem to symbolize to him? Why exactly do you think he ends up thinking it was "the dumbest idea he could have had"?

2. What do Norma Jean's hobbies tell us about her? About her attitude toward her husband and/or her marriage and/or the world in general? How is the conflict between Norma Jean and Leroy symbolized in their respective interests and hobbies?

3. Why is Mabel so obsessed with Shiloh? What does it seem to symbolize to her? What might it symbolize to us and how does that symbolism contribute to the story?

4. What do you make of the references to history here (and to Leroy's lack of knowledge about it)? What do you think this story suggests

about personal history? About history per se? About the relationship between them?
5. In what sense might "Shiloh" be an initiation story? What do you think Leroy learns?
6. How do you interpret the very end of the story? Is Norma Jean beckoning to Leroy or not? What's the effect of the fact that we don't know for sure?

PAUL RUFFIN

Lamar Loper's First Case

From the very first paragraph, Ruffin's dark but hilarious story works to create the impression that it will be an initiation story focusing on the disillusionment of the naive Lamar Loper, the tale of his literal and symbolic journey into what the older and more experienced Hammond calls "East Texas *reality*" (par. 7). (As a result, you might consider using this story to supplement those included in the "Literary Kind as Context" chapter of the anthology.) His name recalling images of slowness ("loping") and of foreignness ("interloper"), Lamar is presented from the outset as a naively idealistic young man for whom the well-seasoned and thoroughly disillusioned Hammond acts as an apt contrast and/or foil. Lamar simply can't believe that people of any kind actually *"live"* under the conditions in which Simmie Hawkins lives (par. 2); is only capable of interpreting Hawkins's trailer as the kind of vacation home that someone like him, with a "lovely young wife" and "cuddly son," might own (par. 4, 24); and naively wonders why Hawkins doesn't simply "do something else, something that pays better" (par. 6). Catching Hammond's reference to "the Uvalde Gorge" as a mistake (par. 10), Loper also comes to represent a cultured individual ("Mr. Law" [par. 83]) who believes that it is both possible and necessary to solve problems "like gentleman" through talk, "reason," and legal papers (par. 80) but who is confronted with what Hammond represents as "prehuman peoples," "[a]nimals" living in what amounts to a state of nature in which a "shotgun" is the best or only solution to every problem (par. 11). As Loper says of himself, "I may be young and naive, but I just believe that these people can be dealt with, and I wouldn't be here if I didn't believe it" (par. 70). Suggesting that the problems of east Texas might be solved by killing or castrating "all the male children" "at birth" (par. 23), Hammond has succumbed to the brutal might-equals-right logic of the simian-like Simmie Hawkins and the world he represents; he has, indeed, "stayed too long, too long among people like this" (par. 21).

But the story utterly reverses those expectations, as well as the contrast set up between Hammond and Loper and between "Mr. Law" and the simian, when Lamar Loper threatens Simmie with the shotgun Jeanne Ann ridiculed him for not bringing and with the wrath of an uncle named Jesus and when Simmie Hawkins himself unsuccessfully invokes "the law" to protect himself.

At the same time, the real irony of the story comes in the aftermath of that confrontation. For now it is Hammond who seems the more naive and innocent of the two, and it is Loper who protects that innocence, ironically by allowing Hammond to believe both that Loper himself is still the innocent one and that there is an absolute difference between men of the law like himself and men of violence like Simmie Hawkins. That situational irony is underscored by the dramatic irony entailed in the fact that the reader knows that Hammond is right when he says that Loper got through to Simmie by using "religion, family, money, something more than just reason and flattery and begging" (par. 132), but that he is at the same time absolutely wrong about exactly how Loper used "religion, family," and "money." Oddly enough, then, Hammond continues to read Loper and his actions in precisely the same terms that the beginning of the story encouraged the reader to interpret them, yet the reader now knows just how inadequate and, in a sense, naive that interpretation is. In the end, then, if there is an initiation and loss of innocence and illusion here, it might very well be the reader's.

QUESTIONS FOR DISCUSSION

1. How are the two main characters in this story characterized at the beginning? What kind of worldviews and values does each character represent? How are their characters established through their statements about their client's family and lifestyle? How do the names of the characters reinforce those impressions?
2. What kinds of expectations are created by the first few paragraphs of the story? What do you expect to happen to Lamar Loper? What kind of story do you expect this will be?
3. Does the rest of the story fulfill those expectations? How so and how not? How do our impressions of Loper and Hammond change during and after the encounter between Loper and Hawkins?
4. How and why are the final sections of the story ironic? What kinds of irony are at work here?
5. What is the significance of the many religious references in the final sections of the story? What do you think Ruffin's story is ultimately saying about religion? About the law and/or justice? To what extent is this story ultimately about lawyers and to what extent is it about "us"?

Teaching Poetry

How to begin teaching poetry? The arrangement of the poetry in *The Norton Introduction to Literature* suggests one way; in fact, it suggests a beginning, middle, and end for a course in poetry—moving from some of the simpler issues of interpretation to more complicated ones. Still, you have a lot of choices to make, for few courses offer enough time to raise all of the questions and problems that are built into the textbook. And probably no course offers enough time to discuss adequately all of the poems in the text. The introductory section, "Poetry: Reading, Responding, Writing," addresses some of the issues on students' minds when they begin a course in poetry, and I hope that the discussion there will defuse for you some of the objections that students sometimes raise when they first face the serious study of poetry. For many students, the experience with poetry that you provide them will be the first serious exposure that they will have had, and choosing the right poems for them to study in detail is crucial.

I like to wing it a little in the early class meetings, trying out three or four poems with students before committing myself completely to a syllabus (although that flexibility may not be possible in large, multisection courses with a preset syllabus). But if you have flexibility, use it. Ask your students to talk the first day about poems they have already read and liked, and have them fill out a card indicating how much formal training they've had and what their nonliterary interests are. With such information and with the experience of three or four class meetings, you will be in a better position to choose poems that will interest your students, as each chapter offers a variety of good poems, some dealing with fairly sophisticated issues, and to keep interested those students who may be ahead of the average in your class.

The poems at the ends of chapters give you a chance to do two things in class: (1) read individual poems closely to see what they say, what they do, and how they work; and (2) compare poems that have things, such as subject matter, in common so that individual differences begin to show up very early, even before your students have terminology adequate to describe them fully. Each group of poems, those that are discussed and those that aren't, contains a variety of modern and traditional poems, a sufficient variety to raise many kinds of questions for class discussion, and there are enough poems in each that you can skip any poems you don't like or would rather not discuss. I myself usually do fewer than half the poems in each group, changing the selection every time I teach the course. I raise some technical questions early (it's hard to get far without mentioning, for example, questions of speaker or word choice), but I raise them as the issues come up in particular poems, saving systematic discussion for later.

The chapters in "Understanding the Text" systematically introduce technical problems—tone, speaker, situation and setting, words and word order, figurative language, structure, sound and sight, and stanzas and verse forms. Not every teacher will want to take up all these issues; and in the chapters themselves I have tried to say the most basic and elementary things so that, if you like and if you have time, you can take up some more difficult problems in class, using either the examples I discuss in the chapter or those in the selection of poems at the end of each chapter. You may find, too, that you would rather choose some of your examples from elsewhere in the text (I often do that myself; I don't like to use the same examples every time I teach the course, and besides it is good for students to recognize that any poem can be used as an example of a lot of different things). You may also prefer to teach these chapters in a different order; I like to bring up the issues in this order because it works for me, but I've tried to make it possible for you to move the chapters around to suit yourself. Even when one of my comments looks back at another poem, it could just as easily look ahead.

"Exploring Contexts" remains, as in earlier editions of this book, the most innovative section. The five chapters here introduce more complex issues of context: questions of time, place, and authorship, and issues that go beyond the work on the page and into the cultural milieu from which it comes. The issues here are of several different kinds, and you will want to choose which ones best fit the aims of your course. Many courses, I know, start running out of time at just the moment they arrive at this section, but I hope you will find time to tackle some of these contextual problems. Your best students will especially appreciate it, and often the reluctant poetry readers discover there what poetry is for. Besides, this section is often the most challenging and rewarding one to teach, or so it seems to me.

I have put quite a number of poems in the "Reading More Poetry" section at the back, taking them out of groups and categories altogether. I hope that here you will find some poems you want to teach in one unit or another early in the course; the "open" grouping is intended to suggest more flexibility and invite you to shop for poems you want to teach in a particular way. But there's another reason for the large open group, too: many of these poems are particularly challenging and could well be appropriate at the end of the course when your students will have acquired a variety of skills. It's not a bad idea to see if they can do "everything" with a few of these poems at the end of the course as a kind of review. It is a good confidence builder.

Whether you make up your own syllabus or conform to one already set, one of the toughest decisions involves how to distribute class time. Basically, the decision comes down to the question of intensiveness versus extensiveness; you simply cannot discuss as many poems in class if you do each one thoroughly. Compromises are, of course, possible: you can vary the pace depending on the difficulty of individual poems, you can assign study questions on poems you don't have time to discuss, you can assign four or five poems for a given class meeting and pick only one for discussion, or you can have exceptional days in which, if you usually discuss one poem intensely, you instead teach briefly seven or eight poems (or vice versa). It seems to me helpful to retain some flexibility, perhaps even putting open or catch-up days in your syllabus or occasionally scrapping a planned assignment in favor of something that has become crucial to the class. I usually spend the better part of a class on one poem, especially early on, but I almost never (except for the first two or three class meetings, when I am emphasizing how much there is in every poem and how closely one must read) assign only one poem. Asking students to read one poem five or six separate times probably involves noble intent, but an assignment that consists of only one poem (a few pages of reading at most) doesn't look like much to any student and probably sets a bad class expectation. Often I choose three or four short poems for a day's assignment, discuss the most difficult one in class, and either point to one or two specific problems in the others or (more profitably if there is time) ask students to raise questions that troubled them. Clearly, the key to good class discussion is good preparation (theirs as well as yours), and anything you can do to stimulate sensible preparation is a real help. Getting the whole class involved in discussions seems to me crucial, but sometimes it is difficult, partly because some students seem to be shy of poetry and partly because others get excessively enthusiastic and sometimes want to dominate the discussion. It may take your whole bag of tricks to keep balance and order in the classroom, but you can help yourself somewhat by insisting on the kind of careful and precise preparation that has everyone think deeply about certain problems before class. Sometimes this is best done by a last-minute, looking-ahead comment at the end of a class, sometimes by study questions handed out ahead of time, sometimes by quizzes, and sometimes by assigning brief minireports to individual students for a future class meeting. (See the "Planning Ideas" at the beginning of each chapter. Which ones you try will depend on the makeup of individual classes and on particular opportunities and problems that arise, and I don't know any general rule to use except to keep a close watch on the class dynamics, especially in the beginning.)

One thing that does practically guarantee—at least in the long run—close attention to class discussion is the assignment of challenging and frequent papers (see the "Writing Suggestions" and "Reading/Writing Ideas" at the end of the chapters in the text and this Guide). What you can do in this area—as distinguished from what you'd like to do—will, of course, depend on the size of your class and the number of weeks you have to devote to poetry. The very nature of writing gets students to think deeply and formulate their thoughts and feelings articulately. Papers on one specific aspect of a poem—papers that can be done in four to five hundred words—still almost inevitably ask students to confront the whole poem, and I find that classes become more lively after each paper—at least as soon as the initial disappointments wear off.

Wherever you begin and at whatever pace you proceed, it is almost always a good idea occasionally to sum up and occasionally to set up something for future use. If you begin as I do by holding back as much as possible on technical problems, you may nevertheless want to mention some terms as an issue emerges in a particular poem and perhaps sometimes assign (or point toward) the Glossary or part of a later chapter. I like to give a sort of impression of disorder at first (so much to learn, so little time), and then do some summarizing when we formally consider a particular technical issue, often asking my students to look again briefly at poems we have already discussed. This tends to provide a cumulative feeling about learning, with the added benefit of showing students that they've made real progress in learning to approach poetry analytically and experientially. If you can do it unobtrusively (without playing "What do I have hidden in my hand?" too crudely and obviously), it gives the class a relaxed flow and a quiet sense of direction. A number of the suggestions that follow will (I hope) point you toward other strategies of putting things together; I have made quite a number of suggestions about ways of teaching specific problems, and you may wish to skim through the Guide before looking in more detail at the comments, suggestions, and questions on individual groups and individual poems.

As you begin to read through and use this section of the Guide, you'll notice that it handles the material in a somewhat different manner than does the fiction section. First, I haven't tried to cover all of the poems in the anthology. I've taken this approach both because there are simply too many poems included for me to do them all justice and because these chapters of the anthology do such a good job of suggesting starting points for discussion for many of these poems. For that reason, the notes here focus most often on poems not discussed in the anthology. Second, when and where appropriate, I've also chosen to provide notes and discussion questions for related groups of poems rather than individual ones, assuming that this approach might prove more helpful in certain cases.

Poetry: Reading, Responding, Writing

In talking about the relations of readers and poetry, the introductory chapter of the text stresses the interconnections between the reader's personal emotions and experiences and the reader's response to a poet's words. It may be useful to emphasize and clarify the nature of this complicity among poet, poem, and reader to avoid a problem I sometimes encounter in my classes: the tendency of some students to let their experiences control their readings of some works. (For example, a student who found her volunteer stint in a hospital repulsive may focus on the disgusting images in Olds's "The Glass," recall similar scenes from her time as a candy striper, and seem unable to recognize how Olds transforms the image into a symbol of love and affirmation.) I try to caution students that, while their experiences and feelings will inevitably enter into their responses to poetry (the poet's voice may sometimes seem to speak to them in a very personal way), the poet's experience rarely duplicates the reader's exactly. Readers must take care to study the details of each poem closely, attempting to understand the emotions and experiences the poet strives to convey—whether similar to, or different from, their own.

PLANNING IDEAS

- I like to begin the study of poetry by showing Part II of the six-part PBS video series *The Power of the Word*, moderated by Bill Moyers. In the series, Moyers interviews practicing American poets who also read from their works. Part II of the series explores the poetry of James Autry, a white business executive whose inspiration and subject matter come from the business world and his southern boyhood, and Quincy Troupe, an African-American poet who teaches nontraditional students and writes about his native St. Louis. This segment also explores how the language and subject matter of poetry grow out of the personal experiences of the poets. (Galway Kinnell and Sharon Olds are among those featured in Part I; Li-Young Lee is one of the poets featured in Part IV.)
  a. Before classtime, I ask five students to practice acting out Wayman's "Wayman in Love" as though all of the characters who appear in the poem really existed. (One student serves as narrator.) Then I have them "perform" the poem for the class—in costume (or at least

with Marx and Freud appropriately bearded). I find this is a good way to establish that poetry can be amusing and fun but also to initiate discussion about the strategies various poets employ to convey states of consciousness—thought, memory, dream states—and to discuss Wayman's skill in addressing serious topics in a humorous way.

b. Another entertaining way to introduce Wayman's poem is to show the brief scene from the Woody Allen film *Annie Hall* in which the two main characters think about how dissatisfied they are with their sex life. Those who know the movie will remember Allen's technique of having the female lead seem to rise from their shared bed and talk to the audience, followed by the male character doing the same. After showing the film clip—easily obtainable on video tape—I like to ask students if they see any parallels between Allen's technique for conveying his characters' thoughts and Wayman's.

• I sometimes ask students to choose among the poems in this chapter the work that evoked the strongest response in them. Then I have them bring to class a paragraph describing their responses and explaining what details in the poem contributed to them. In class I ask for a few students to read their paragraphs and use these as a starting point for discussing the poems the students have found most striking. (If you have followed the strategy of keeping your syllabus flexible early in the term, as suggested in the "Teaching Poetry" chapter, this exercise may help you determine what poems should make up the rest of the syllabus.)

• Because I so often find my students to be much more divided in their attitude toward, and experience of, poetry than of fiction, I often begin our discussion of poetry by having students simply discuss their experiences with reading and writing about poetry: what do they already know or assume about poetry and about how to read and write about it? What have they liked about reading and writing about poetry in the past? What have they found most challenging? I find that getting all of these fears, concerns, insecurities, etc. onto the table early on can actually help ensure that the class doesn't become so dramatically divided between the poetic "haves" or "lovers" and the poetic "have-nots" or "haters," while it also gives me a sense of just what we may need to work on most in future classes.

• When I find myself working with a group of students who are unusually inexperienced with or unenthused by poetry, sharply divided among experts and novices, or simply less than lively in general, I always try to find ways to incorporate popular music of various kinds into our study of poetry. In the case of the materials and topics covered in this chapter, I've found that one effective exercise involves having students bring in the lyrics to love songs or bringing in a few myself so that we can analyze them alongside the love poems in this chapter, identifying and discussing common themes, elements, and figurative strategies.

RITA DOVE

Fifth Grade Autobiography

The title of this poem tells us that the speaker is a fifth grader, but the photograph she describes was taken when she was just four years old. Sometimes I ask the students to imagine under what circumstances the speaker would construct such an autobiography—while completing a school writing assignment? During show-and-tell? I also try to get them talking about what kind of people usually write autobiographies—and why the writer/speaker of this particular autobiography is different from the usual, the expected. Certain details—the brother's Davy Crockett cap, his sailor suit—suggest the time period when the photograph was shot. If my students are too young to remember the fads and styles of the late 1950s and early 1960s, I provide the footnotes. I also like to ask them what sense—taste, smell, hearing, sight, touch—evokes the strongest memories for them as a prelude to discussing how sensation helps provoke the speaker's memory in the poem.

QUESTIONS FOR DISCUSSION

1. What devices does the poet use in the poem itself to suggest the age of the speaker?
2. The speaker is describing a photograph, not constructing a linear narrative. How does the description of the visual images in the photograph tell us more about the speaker than simply looking at the picture would?
3. How do the memories triggered in the speaker by the photo make the photo itself clearer to us?
4. Is it difficult to distinguish between description and memory?
5. What makes this an autobiography?

ANNE SEXTON

The Fury of Overshoes

If you've already covered fiction in your course and done some work with initiation stories in particular, you might want to remind students of that and of some of the issues about childhood and adulthood, expectations/

ideals and actuality/reality, you raised there as a way to open discussion of this poem. For the poem is obviously, at least in part, about an adult's confrontation with how wrong our childish conceptions of adulthood are; with how we become "big people" only to discover that we aren't the all-powerful, all-knowing beings we expected or assumed big people to be when we were the little people; with how life does not turn out to be the series of steps to the top we might once have imagined it would be, but a series of "giant steps" that go both everywhere and nowhere (line 42), regardless of the kinds of shoes we wear or how we get them on our feet.

Or is it? Is this all true or the only truth in the poem? Are all of our expectations really so wrong? The power of big people really so insignificant? Certainly that's where the poem seems to end up; but are the feelings and conflicts articulated earlier in the poem utterly erased by this ending? What about the fact that little people really can't tie their shoes by themselves and sink like stones rather than swimming? Isn't it true that big people have a great deal of power, if only by virtue of the fact that they can make little people do things that little people don't want to do, like giving up teddy bears and thumb sucking? Might the phrases *big people/big fish* and *little people* refer to something different from or more than *adult* and *child* (how about *rich people* and *poor people, famous people* and *ordinary people,* for example)? And how might our interpretations of the poem be expanded or changed by considering these other possibilities?

To me the point of asking these questions is, in part, to give more emphasis and meaning to the way the poem so deftly manages to bring out both the falsity of our expectations about the power of big people and the truths that underlie those expectations or beliefs, the ways in which "the little people" are, in fact, powerless compared to the big and in which the world isn't, in fact, theirs. To introduce these possibilities, you might even want to introduce the poem in this way, opening up discussion by not telling students initially which poem you're doing, instead simply writing these phrases or a relevant line from the poem on the board and having students discuss them in isolation before moving into the poem itself. (I assure you that the words *big fish,* taken in isolation, are not immediately going to make students think about adults in general, though this is clearly the words' most direct referent in the poem.)

QUESTIONS FOR DISCUSSION

1. What do you make of the title, particularly the word *fury?* How many different ways can you interpret the phrase *fury of overshoes?* Whose or what's "fury" is expressed or explored in the poem?
2. How does the visual form of the poem, particularly the way the lines are divided, contribute to the meanings of the poem?

SUGGESTION FOR WRITING

Write an essay comparing the attitudes toward childhood and adulthood in "The Fury of Overshoes" to those in Dove's "Fifth Grade Autobiography" and in Lorde's "Hanging Fire."

PRACTICING READING: SOME POEMS ON LOVE

ANNE BRADSTREET

To My Dear and Loving Husband

Bradstreet's poem can provide a good opportunity to open up discussion about just how common it is for poets writing about love to figure that love by measuring it against other things (an idea that may be foregrounded in a way by the poem "The Tally Stick," though that poem clearly "tallies" in a very different way from poems such as Barrett Browning's "How Do I Love Thee?" or Bradstreet's "To My Dear and Loving Husband").

One of the more interesting aspects of Bradstreet's poetic tallying in this poem, and one that my students always want to talk about, is the recurrence of monetary metaphors or images (rather than, or—given line 7—in addition to, the more traditional nature images): "prize" and "mines of gold" (line 5), "riches" (line 6), "recompense" (line 8), "repay" (line 9), "reward" (line 10). To what extent does Bradstreet's use of such words and images to figure the greatness and value of the speaker's love subvert materialistic notions of value by insisting that love can be of greater value than money and to what extent does it actually reinforce such notions by using monetary value as a standard against which everything, including emotions, can be judged and by making emotional debt so central to the relationship between husband and wife?

QUESTIONS FOR DISCUSSION

1. How does Bradstreet's tactic of characterizing her love through a series of metaphors compare with that of Barrett Browning in "How Do I Love Thee?"
2. What do you make of all the monetary or materialistic metaphors here? What is their cumulative effect?
3. How does alliteration help Bradstreet to get the speaker's ideas and feelings across?

WILLIAM SHAKESPEARE

[*Shall I compare thee to a summer's day?*]

Obviously Shakespeare's answer to the question he poses in the first line is yes, and the comparison between his lover and "a summer's day" thereby becomes a prime example of an extended or controlling metaphor (a concept you might want to save for later discussions of language or preview here by juxtaposing this poem with poems earlier in the chapter that use series of metaphors). One good way to begin discussion of the poem is to have students unpack that metaphor by listing on the blackboard the qualities the speaker imputes to "a summer's day" and those he imputes to his lover: why, in other words, is he or she ultimately "more lovely" (line 2)? At first glance, the answer to this question seems all too easy: he or she is more "temperate" (line 2), more consistent than anything in nature, which is all too changeable and given to extremes ("too hot," "too short" [lines 5–4]). Ultimately, however, what's "temperate" here is thus less the lover himself or herself than love and what is being compared to a summer's day is not only the person of the lover but also the emotion of love, which immortalizes and beautifies what it touches, rendering it unchangeable.

What, however, happens in the final lines of the poem? What exactly is "this" that "long lives" and "gives life to thee" (line 14)? As the phrase "eternal lines" (line 12) suggests, "this" is the very poem we are reading, which is "given life" by love and, in turn, "gives [eternal] life to thee," the lover, and to love. In this way, the poem becomes not just about the immortality of love and its power to immortalize but also about the immortal and immortalizing power of poetry itself, an idea underscored by the way the stresses and alliteration of the last lines draw our attention to the "long" "life" conferred and enjoyed by "lines." (If you've discussed Bradstreet's poem, then you may want to return for a moment to its final lines, comparing Bradstreet's use of similar words and alliterative patterns.)

QUESTIONS FOR DISCUSSION

1. What qualities does this poem associate with a "summer's day"? What are the effects of the speaker's choice of a summer day over a spring or autumn day? Why and how exactly is the speaker's lover better than such a day?

2. What do you make of the final lines of the poem? How would you describe the movement or development of the poem from beginning to end? Might you say that the speaker or the reader in a sense learns something by the end or sees things in a different way?

LEIGH HUNT

Rondeau

If you want to preview formal issues at this stage, Hunt's "Rondeau" provides a good chance to do so since the poem's very title announces the fact that Hunt's poem follows a quite strict traditional form. For those of you who (like me) know very little about the "rondeau," here's one dictionary definition:

> . . . a fixed form of verse based on two rhyme sounds and consisting usually of 13 lines in three stanzas with the opening words of the first line of the first stanza used as an independent refrain after the second and third stanzas . . .
> From *Merriam-Webster's Collegiate® Dictionary,* Tenth Edition.
> © 1996 by Merriam-Webster, Incorporated. By permission.

Obviously, Hunt's poem doesn't meet these strict requirements because it's so short, but it does end with the envoi described here.

When I teach the poem, I actually begin not by spouting this definition but by merely pointing out that the rondeau is a traditional poetic form, asking students to define that form by merely describing the form of this particular poem and putting their individual observations on the blackboard until they accumulate into a fairly complete description. In doing so, the point I most want to get to and stress is the circularity of the structure, the way the poem returns to its beginning, which in this case entails returning to the event—the kiss—that initiated the poem in the first place. Once students get to this point, I ask them why and how Hunt's use of the circular rondeau form contributes to the meaning of the poem, guiding them to see—among other things—the way this circularity of form underscores the idea that the "insides" of the poem communicate about the importance and value of a single, perfect, isolated moment and/or event, forever protected from time's thievery by both memory and poetry.

QUESTIONS FOR DISCUSSION

1. A rondeau is a very particular and traditional poetic form. What can you tell about that form by analyzing the form of Hunt's poem? How does Hunt's use of the rondeau form reinforce the ideas expressed in the poem?
2. How does the poet's use of the name of this type of poem as the title affect your interpretation of the poem, your sense of what it's about? Might it make the poem as much about poetry as about love? If so, how does it compare to Shakespeare's "[Shall I compare thee . . .]," a poem that is also simultaneously about love and about poetry?

3. Even if this poem was written about an actual woman named "Jenny," what are the effects of Hunt's choice to use this name? (What would you make, for example, of a similar poem about a man named "John" kissing the speaker?) How might these effects work together with those achieved by the use of the rondeau form?
4. How is time characterized here and what role does it play in the poem? How does this characterization of time and time's role compare to those in the other love poems that you've read so far?

SUGGESTION FOR WRITING

Write an essay comparing "Rondeau" and Shakespeare's "[Shall I compare thee . . .]" or Lorde's "Recreation" in terms of how each figures the relationship between love and poetry.

_____

DENISE LEVERTOV

Love Poem

My students tend to have a relatively hard time with this wonderful, but enigmatic poem, though they also tend to get very excited once they've gotten into it, a reaction that both makes this a great poem to focus on in class early in your discussions of poetry and makes the trick of teaching the poem more about getting discussion started than about keeping it going. Since I often find comparative questions that allow students to build on work they've already done especially useful for difficult poems, I start discussion of "Love Poem" by focusing first on comparisons between the main topic or focus of this poem and those of the other love poems we've already read and discussed, using Levertov's epigraph as a starting place. For as the epigraph suggests, the poem's central focus isn't so much on characterizing the speaker's own feelings about, or emotional gifts or payment to, his or her lover (as in Bradstreet) or the lover himself or herself (as in Shakespeare), but on characterizing the feelings and "gifts" the speaker receives from the lover, the ways and reasons why they are "good for each other." (Sometimes, if we've recently discussed Bradstreet's poem and its focus on emotional "debts," students want to talk at this stage about how the notion or metaphor of the "gift" is similar to, and different from, that of debt. If not, it's still a great question, and one you might want to take up now or later.)

Once we've established the basic focus of the poem, I begin asking questions about the similar qualities shared by all of the particular gifts or images of love here—sunlight, a swaying branch, etc. With any luck, it doesn't take students long to articulate the idea that these gifts are all intangible or nonsensual, things one can't touch or (it's time to go to line

9) "taste." Sometimes students want to say that you can touch a branch, but almost as soon as that comment is out of their mouths, they realize that once you touch the branch, it isn't swaying anymore, and it's the swaying rather than the branch that's the focus here.

At this point, the conversation almost invariably and quite naturally turns to the fifth stanza (if these can really be called stanzas) and the contrasting "other joys" it describes: what's the difference between these "joys" and those associated with love? How does the mention of these other joys reinforce the picture of love Levertov's creating here? (Sometimes I find it useful to reintroduce the term *conflict* that we used throughout our discussions of fiction—what two kinds of joy are being portrayed as in conflict or at least in contrast here?) As words such as "taste" and "roots" (lines 9, 12) suggest, these joys are, of course, figured as more bodily, sensual, and earthly and, as a result, as short-lived, followed quickly by disappointment, bitterness, etc. (Remember those berries earlier in the poem? Remember that the earlier images reach skyward?). With any luck, students are off and running straight into the final stanza at this point and into questions about the way it beautifully and paradoxically captures the spiritual aspects of the most sensual/sexual aspects and acts of love.

QUESTIONS FOR DISCUSSION

1. How is the focus or central question of this poem similar to, and different from, those of love poems you've read earlier? What does the epigraph suggest about what the poem is about?
2. The words *give* and *gift* are repeated several times in the poem. What is the effect of that repeated emphasis on gift-giving and on love as a gift (or a lot of gifts)? How is the gift as a metaphor for love similar to, and different from, that of "debt" (as in Bradstreet's "To My Dear and Loving Husband")?
3. What qualities do all of Levertov's "gifts" share? What overall characterization of the "joys" of love emerges from these various images? What qualities are associated with "other joys" here? What's the overall characterization of these "other joys"? How does this characterization serve to reinforce Levertov's characterization of the joys unique to love?
4. How does the layout or form of the poem contribute to the portrait of the joys of love offered within the poem?
5. To what extent or in what way does the rather generic title of Levertov's poem detract from the poem? Add to the poem?

[*Stop all the clocks, cut off the telephone*]

Oddly enough, there's a quite moving reading of this poem during the funeral scene that comes toward the end of the film *Four Weddings and a Funeral.*

QUESTIONS FOR DISCUSSION

1. To whom or what do you imagine the speaker of this poem is speaking? What's the significance or effect of the poet's use of the language of command or entreaty (do this . . . , do that . . .)?
2. What's the significance or effect of the way the poet mixes references to telephones, airplanes, and traffic policemen with references to stars, the moon, and the ocean? Of the way the poet moves from more concrete images from everyday life to more abstract and traditionally poetic ones? Or is the movement that direct and straightforward?
3. What's the significance or effect of the regular rhyme scheme?

Recreation

If you are teaching this poem early in the course, your students may not hear the pun in the title, and you may need to point them to the theme of creation (lines 12, 17–18, 22) and re-creation; you may also want to remind them that the original meaning of recreation is a renewal or remaking of oneself.

QUESTIONS FOR DISCUSSION

1. What is the "leash" referred to in line 11? Why does it need to be cut?
2. Lorde creates a comparison between writing and making love. In what senses are the act of writing and the act of love similar?

To Have without Holding

QUESTIONS FOR DISCUSSION

1. As the first line's reference to loving "differently" suggests, this poem seems to contrast two types of love or ways of loving someone. What

does the poem seem to suggest about the essential characteristics of each type or way? What do you imagine about the speaker's situation, the nature of his or her relationship to the "you" addressed in the poem? What evidence in the poem would you use to support your interpretation of the situation? How does the poem relate the situation to the conflict or contrast between types of love?

2. Like many love poems, this poem uses very concrete images to describe or capture very abstract concepts or feelings, in this case having to do with types or ways of loving. What's the significance and effect of the particular images in this poem? How does each image contribute to the poem's tone?

3. How does alliteration—as in "candle," "cave," "consciously," "conscientiously, concretely constructively" (lines 19–21)—contribute to the poem?

LIZ ROSENBERG

Married Love

QUESTIONS FOR DISCUSSION

1. What sacrifice does the speaker make to marriage? What does she gain from being married? Why does she address her husband as "Oh, husband," rather than calling him by his name?

2. How does the poem create the sense of the woman's isolation?

3. How do the "As ifs" function in the last stanza?

4. How does this poem compare to Rich's "Living in Sin"?

JOHN DRYDEN

[Why should a foolish marriage vow]

QUESTIONS FOR DISCUSSION

1. Obviously, this poem is in a sense an argument explaining why "a foolish marriage vow" should not "oblige" a husband and wife who no longer love each other (lines 1, 3). How does the poem define such obligations? What arguments does the speaker use to explain why the marriage vow shouldn't entail these obligations?

2. As the footnote indicates, this poem is part of a play about marriage. Drawing on the details of the poem, what do you imagine about the speaker? About the situation? About the attitude toward the speaker that the poem (and/or play) as a whole encourages us to adopt?

3. What's the significance or effect of the repetition of the word "love"

and "loved" in lines 5 and 6? Of "pleasure" and "pleasures" in lines 7 through 9? Of the poet's use of rhyme?
4. The first lines of the second stanza are quite confusing. What exactly is the speaker saying here, and how does this question serve to further the argument about marriage?

MARY, LADY CHUDLEIGH

To the Ladies

Students rarely have trouble understanding the message of this poem, but they may need help in appreciating the skill with which the poet expresses her—or the speaker's—feelings about a wife's place in the world early in the eighteenth century. One way to start is by asking students to locate the many absolutes sprinkled throughout the poem: "nothing," "all," "never." These not only emphasize the speaker's complaint that women who marry are utterly imprisoned but also help create the speaker's desperate and angry tone. Aspects of form also contribute to the poem's sense of constriction: the exact end rhyme, the tight precision of the iambic tetrameter.

QUESTIONS FOR DISCUSSION

1. Given that in 1703, married women had almost no legal rights, might you still take issue with the speaker's pronouncements about the status of wives in her time? What statements might you dispute?
2. If the speaker overstates her case to a degree, why might she do so? What possible purpose(s) might she have?
3. Could this poem have been written in the 1990s? What details would you need to alter to update the speaker's complaint and advice?

SUGGESTION FOR WRITING

Do some library research on the circumstances of Mary, Lady Chudleigh's life, and write an essay in which you theorize about the experiences that might have led to the composition of "To the Ladies."

RICHARD LOVELACE

To Althea, from Prison

A wealthy and well-born courtier, Lovelace purportedly composed this poem during his (political) imprisonment in the Gatehouse prison in

1642. After serving Charles I in 1645 and the French king in 1646, Lovelace was again imprisoned in 1648; and it was in prison that he prepared his first volume of poetry, *Lucasta; Epides, Odeas, Sonnets, Songs etc.*, for publication. Lovelace died impoverished in 1657 or 1658, his remaining poems being published after his death in *Lucasta: Posthume Poems*.

QUESTIONS FOR DISCUSSION

1. What do Lovelace's title and the details within the poem itself suggest to you about the situation of the speaker? If he is in prison, what do you imagine he has been imprisoned for?
2. How specifically does the poem redefine the meaning of imprisonment and freedom? If "Stone walls do not a prison make" (line 25), what does? What might be the significance or effect of the very fact that the speaker is "singing" here about his love for his king, his lover, etc.? What does this suggest about whether and how the speaker is free?
3. What different kinds of love are described in this poem and how are they interrelated? What does the poem suggest, for example, about the relationship between the speaker's love for his lover (as in the first stanza) and the love he feels for his king (as in the third stanza)? And/or about the general relationship between the personal and the political?

EDNA ST. VINCENT MILLAY

[*What lips my lips have kissed, and where, and why*]

QUESTIONS FOR DISCUSSION

1. What does this poem suggest about the nature of what is remembered and what forgotten?
2. What is the significance of the metaphor that the speaker uses to describe herself in lines 9 through 11? What does the use of metaphor allow the poet to express that the more direct statements that come before and after the metaphor don't?
3. What exactly does the speaker mean when he or she says that "summer sang in me"? How specifically does this line, as well as the metaphor in the preceding lines, draw on our notions of what various seasons of the year symbolize? What are all the different things that "winter" and "summer" seem to symbolize here?

THEODORE ROETHKE

She

QUESTIONS FOR DISCUSSION

1. How specifically is this poem about "what is" (line 2)? "what was" (line 16)? "what would be" (line 16)? What does the poem suggest about the speaker's situation in the past and the present? What is suggested by the fact that the poet refers to "what would be" rather than to "what will be"?
2. In line 14 the poet refers to "that slow dark that widens every eye," a statement that literally refers to the fact that our pupils widen in the dark. But how exactly does this image function symbolically or metaphorically in this context?
3. How do all of the various water images in the poem (the references to "sea-chambers" [line 6], "a river flowing south" [line 8], and the way "[s]he moves as water moves" [line 15]) work together? What exactly does the poet convey through them? How might these images, which are themselves about movement, relate to the movement of the poem as a whole, as well as the rhythm of particular lines, such as "She makes space lonely with a lovely song. / She lilts a low soft language" (lines 4–5)?

KAREN CHASE

Venison

QUESTIONS FOR DISCUSSION

1. What seems to be happening in the final stanza of the poem? What aspects of this stanza seem to, or might, refer to a dream? What aspects seem "real"? If some or all of the stanza refers to things that happen in a dream, what's the significance of the dream and how does it relate to what happens when the speaker is awake?
2. What's the significance of the fact that the speaker asks *"Where are you"* while she is "grubb[ing] through the cupboards" for something to eat (lines 7–8)? That the venison arrives immediately after she poses this question?
3. How specifically does this poem interrelate loving, having sex, hunting, and eating? What does the poem seem to suggest about why and how these various acts are alike?

APHRA BEHN

On Her Loving Two Equally

QUESTIONS FOR DISCUSSION

1. Does it surprise you that a seventeenth-century woman would write a poem about loving two men equally? If so, what might your own surprise reveal about our conceptions of history and/or of love and/or of women?
2. In what way is the representation of love in this poem conventional or traditional? In what way does it challenge or play on conventional representations of, or assumptions about, love?
3. How does the poem characterize the experience of "loving two equally"? What does it suggest about why and how one's love is stronger when "divided" (line 2)?

WILLIAM SHAKESPEARE

[Let me not to the marriage of true minds]

QUESTIONS FOR DISCUSSION

1. How is Shakespeare's representation of the relationship between love, time, and poetry here similar to, and different from, that in his "[Shall I compare thee . . .]"?
2. Unlike "[Shall I compare thee . . .]," which focuses primarily on a single, controlling metaphor, this poem uses several metaphors. What are they? How do they work together to characterize true love? To characterize false love? (Might this poem be said to contrast two types of love or ways of loving much as Piercy's "To Have without Holding" does?)
3. What might the speaker mean when he says that love doesn't "ben[d] with the remover to remove" (line 4)?
4. How would you describe or characterize the way the speaker's picture of true love develops over the course of the poem?
5. What exactly is the poet saying in the last two lines of the poem? How do these two lines relate to the rest of the poem, or what exactly do they contribute to it? How would the poem's meaning and tone change if these last two lines were removed?

SUGGESTION FOR WRITING

Write a paragraph or a whole essay exploring the meaning and importance of one significant line or sentence from a poem in this chapter.

Examples:
(1) "[T]he wonder to me is that it did not disgust me" ("The Glass").
(2) "Who the hell did my cousin marry" ("Thirteen Years").

READING/WRITING IDEAS FOR POETRY: READING, RESPONDING, WRITING

Though I've made it a policy not to offer reading and writing ideas for the various "Reading, Responding, Writing" chapters of the anthology, I'm violating that policy in this case because this seems the most appropriate place to share with you the exercise assignment that has become most central to my work with students on poetry. I first encountered the exercise many, many years ago when I was myself a student in an introduction to literature course (taught by none other than Jerome Beaty), a fact I share with you because I think that it speaks volumes about how useful the exercise can prove to be for at least some students. The exercise is essentially a more extended version of the first of the writing suggestions offered at the end of this chapter of the anthology in which students write what I call "translations" (rather than paraphrases) of poems whose diction and syntax might prove especially challenging. The specific wording of that exercise goes something like this:

Translate this poem sentence by sentence (rather than line by line) by reordering each sentence so that it conforms as closely as possible to normal English word order—subject, verb, direct object, with modifying phrases and clauses at the beginning or end. Add words that you think the sentence needs to include to make sense in this order, but put those words in brackets to distinguish them from the words actually present in the poem. As you reorganize the sentences, translate words that are unfamiliar to you, using a dictionary to find out the denotative and connotative meanings of the words and putting these into parentheses in your translation. Do the same thing with words and whole phrases that are awkward or that seem to have multiple meanings. When you're finished, your translation should look something like the following translation of Jonson's "On My First Son."

> [I wish] Farewell and joy [to you], (you) child of my right hand; loved boy, My sin was (having too much hope for or feeling too hopeful about or having too many hopes for) (you and your future).
> You (were) lent to me [for] seven years, and on the (exact or right) day I pay [the price] (your) fate exacted [for you].
> O[if only] I could now lose all [that part of me that is a] father!
> for why (does) [every] man lament the state [of death], [which] he should envy [because it allows one] to so soon (escape) [the] rage [of the] world and [the] flesh [and to escape the misery of] (aging, getting old, being an old person), if no[t] other [kinds of] misery [as well]?
> [You, my son, should] Rest in soft peace and [when you are] asked, [you should say to whomever asks the question], "Here lie[s] Ben Jonson's best piece of poetry."
> For [the] sake (of that poem and dead son), All (Ben Jonson's) vows [will] (from now on) be (the kinds of vows that) may never [be] like[d] too much [by] what (Ben Jonson) loves.

Sometimes early on in the course I don't include the part of the assignment about finding multiple meanings, or at least I don't emphasize it very much, wanting to wait to really emphasize these issues until the class gets to language.

The great thing about the exercise is that it always proves helpful both to those students who are intimidated or put off by poetry, as I was as a student (and sometimes am now!) and to quite advanced students, who I find are often tempted to jump into interpretation before they've paused long enough to fully understand the literal meaning of the poem. And, quite frankly, I've become more and more devoted to the exercise and begun to use it more and more in other courses because I find that it otherwise often proves extraordinarily difficult for my students (even "good" ones) to simply understand the literal meaning of the convoluted sentences so common to poetry. What's great, too, is that even students who think they are above this exercise (and there's always one, sometimes two) almost always come to admit its usefulness at some point (perhaps because I help them to by pointing out in class when we're "translating," or when we need to translate, or when we've corrected an outright misinterpretation by going back and translating, etc.) It's also one of the exercises I assign that students seem to truly and completely internalize (as I did as a student), to make a natural part of the process they always use when first tackling a new poem, or at least poems whose language is especially off-putting or confusing.

Finally, comparing translations of whole poems or of particular words and phrases can be a terrific way to spark discussion or to move it forward, these comparisons inevitably turning up differences and disagreements among translations that can often open up big interpretive questions and issues about the text.

Understanding the Text

13

TONE

"Don't use that tone with me!" "What tone?" my teenage son replies, feigning innocence. He knows, of course, that I'm objecting not to *what* he says but to *how* he says it. Tone is that elusive quality that allows us to make subtle alterations in the gap between what we say and what we mean. In short, tone makes irony possible. It also provides a way of making poetry seem alive and human to students whose previous experiences with poems have left them cold. Since we have all felt anger, fear, elation, sadness, desire, and frustration, students can learn to experience poetry fruitfully by learning to recognize that a poet has felt the same things— and has found just the right tone to make the experience come alive for the reader.

But while tone is the main focus of the chapter, the chapter also introduces and discusses the concepts of subject and theme, concepts with which students may well be familiar. And by considering how these three elements work together within texts, the chapter provides yet another way to ease students into the analysis of poetry by potentially opening up to view the similarities, as well as the differences, between poetry and the prose fiction that they are often more comfortable analyzing.

PLANNING IDEAS

- A good way of helping students recognize varieties of tone is to save a few of the poems in the section to be read during class. Before having the students read them, I list on the blackboard isolated phrases or lines that could carry a variety of tones, depending on the context. Examples: "Doesn't she look pretty?" ("Barbie Doll," line 23); "That's all." ("Leaving the Motel," line 25); "He had been our Destroyer" ("Hard Rock Returns," line 34). I divide the class into small groups and assign one of the lines to each, asking each group to construct several imaginary contexts in which the line might appear. Each context should imply a different tone. I then ask a student from each group to explain to the whole class how the line might be delivered in at least one of the more interesting contexts. The class then plays "Name That Tone," generating a series of nouns or adjectives to identify the tone. Next, the students read the poem from which the line has been taken. In clarifying the differences between the tone of the line in the poem and in its imaginary context, the ensuing discussion gets students not only looking closely at an isolated passage but also thinking about how the part fits into the whole.

• Another option: at the end of the class preceding the one on tone, have each student draw an adjective from a hat (examples: *gentle, worried, eager, frustrated, cynical, joyful*). The student writes a four-line epigram that conveys the tone. The epigrams can be turned in or discussed in class.

MARGE PIERCY

Barbie Doll

Certain word choices in this poem readily lend themselves to a discussion of tone. Examples: *"as usual"* (line 1), *"magic of puberty"* (line 5), *"wore out / like a fan belt"* (lines 15-16). This last image also works to introduce not only the concept of the simile but also the relation of rhythm to meter. Rhythm is the actual pattern of stressed and unstressed syllables in a line; meter is the prevailing pattern of stressed and unstressed syllables. Rhythm, then, is variable; a line in a Shakespearean sonnet may well depart rhythmically from the poem's meter. Needless to say, good poets provide rhythmic variations for good reasons. Lines 15-16 of "Barbie Doll" do not sound "poetic" in part because of the simile (how poetic are fan belts?) but also in part because of the rhythm. As imagery affects tone, so does rhythm.

QUESTIONS FOR DISCUSSION

1. Why is it that "Everyone" sees "a fat nose on thick legs" (line 11) only after the speaker's image of herself has changed?
2. What does the title add?

MANY TONES: POEMS ABOUT FAMILY RELATIONSHIPS

GALWAY KINNELL

After Making Love We Hear Footsteps

One way to begin discussion of Kinnell's funny and moving poem is to start with the title, considering it both on its own terms and in terms of the way it might be interpreted as both title and first line simultaneously (. . . we hear footsteps, for . . .). In doing so, I try to get students to pay particular attention to the word *footsteps,* asking what different things the word calls to mind in this context. If you're lucky, good, and/or as pushy as I am, you will end up with several possibilities, but I always try to elicit or mention at least two that seem particularly relevant, the phrase "the pitter-patter of little feet," which often serves as a way of talking about children-to-be, and the phrase "following in someone's footsteps." How and when and why might the poem render the idea of the "pitter-patter of little feet" funny or ironic? At what point and in what ways does the poet manage to convert a comic tone into something else?

QUESTIONS FOR DISCUSSION

1. Why do you think Kinnell includes such a vivid description of Fergus's pajamas? Of the thoughts Fergus may later have about baseball players? What specifically does this add to the poem?
2. What does Kinnell mean when he refers to Fergus as the "sleeper only the mortal sounds can sing awake"? What exactly are "mortal sounds"?

SEAMUS HEANEY

Mid-Term Break

One thing to draw attention to in this poem is the last line, in part because it calls attention to itself. What's the significance of that isolated last line? Though there are many possible answers, including the idea that the line enacts the "knock[ing] clear" described in the preceding line (line 21), one might suggest that the line implicitly correlates the coffin containing the dead boy's body with the poem that memorializes it. In a sense, in other words, the poem might be seen as a verbal "box" that contains that death and that is itself, of course, composed of "feet" (line 22).

The notion of emotional containment seems especially relevant in light of the way the speaker of the poem so carefully, almost detachedly, depicts the emotional reactions of others, while saying almost nothing about his own, a fact all the more surprising given the first-person point of view.

Also interesting and perhaps relevant in this regard is Heaney's use of enjambment and caesura, features that you may not want to name for students at this point in their study of poetry, but that you can still draw attention to by asking simple questions about punctuation. Though enjambment and caesura together clearly contribute to the sense of a struggle in the poem between contained formality (medial caesura and end-stopped lines) and uncontained informality and/or emotion (variable caesurae and enjambment), it still remains a question to me whether the poem resolves that struggle in favor of one or the other.

QUESTIONS FOR DISCUSSION

1. How would you describe the tone of "Mid-Term Break" and/or the way the poem characterizes the speaker's response to his brother's death? (How does this speaker's response compare, for example, to that recorded in other poems about the death of a loved one, such as Auden's "[Stop all the clocks . . .]"?)
2. How does the form of the poem contribute to this characterization, particularly the way that lines and even stanzas run into each other (as with " . . . my mother held my hand / In hers . . ." [lines 12–13]) and the way that commas and periods often force us to pause in the midst of a line (as with "No gaudy scars, the bumper knocked him clear" [line 21])?
3. What do you make of that isolated last line? What's the effect of setting the line off in this way? How does the isolation of the line contribute to the image depicted in the line? How does it relate to the rest of the poem?

PAT MORA

Elena

Students will undoubtedly be quick to articulate the idea that the basic subject and theme of this poem have to do with the estrangement between family members that can occur when a family immigrates to a new place and when some of its members assimilate more easily and readily than others. But what you may have to push students to see are the particular nuances of the poem, the specific ways it expresses this theme and conveys the emotions associated with such estrangement. What is the significance of the poet's use of words and concepts such as "deaf" (line 21) and "dumb" (line 11)? How do those words take on new meaning in this context?

You might want to make students probe deeper by asking them whether or how the poem might be about more "universal" issues as well and/or whether and how the poem might suggest that the cultural and linguistic divisions between family members might reveal other divisions rather than only or simply being the cause of such division. Might even a mother who spoke the same language as her children feel some of these feelings anyway? Why might the husband "frow[n]" when he sees Elena with her English book (line 13), or what is revealed by the fact that he does? Might the oldest child be right when he says that the husband "doesn't want [Elena] to be smarter than he is" (lines 14–15)? What's the significance of that reaction? Of the very fact that the child says such a thing at all?

Clearly one of the more poignant aspects of the very common situation described in the poem, an aspect revealed in part by the speaker's continual references to "embarrassment," is the way in which the linguistic and cultural differences within the family upset traditional family dynamics, children becoming more powerful than their parents in certain ways, forty-year-old adults suddenly having to study schoolbooks like children, wives who learn English becoming "smarter" than the Spanish-speaking husbands who are supposed to be their equals. As a result this poem may suggest that the situation of this family and of families like it reveals, by upsetting, kinds of intrafamilial division or difference that are generally unseen, because so expected and so acceptable.

As a result, the poem might also lead us to pose certain questions that otherwise might not seem like questions at all: (why) should someone in Elena's situation be embarrassed for not knowing how to speak English and/or for wanting to know how? (How) does knowing a particular language or more than one language make someone smarter than others who don't? Does learning a second language inevitably change your relationship to the first language and/or to the people who speak only that language?

QUESTIONS FOR DISCUSSION

1. What are the primary emotions expressed by the speaker in the poem? What does and doesn't the poem explain about the origin of those feelings? Why, for example, is Elena "embarrassed" (a word repeated twice in the poem)?

2. To what extent or in what ways is this poem about the particular situation of families who immigrate to a place where the dominant lan-

guage is different from their own first language? To what extent or in what ways are the situation and emotions described in the poem more "universal"? In what ways are the divisions within this family peculiar to a family of immigrants and to what extent aren't they? Is language the only thing that divides and differentiates the family's members? How so? How not?

SUGGESTION FOR WRITING

Rewrite "Elena" (in the form of a poem or as a short prose piece) from the point of view of the oldest child or the husband. What is lost and gained by envisioning this situation from a different point of view or through the eyes and voice of a different speaker? How might the tone, in particular, differ?

SHARON OLDS

I Go Back to May 1937

One way to begin discussion of Olds's "I Go Back" is to focus, first, on the double entendre of its title, in which "going back" seems to mean both something like "remembering" and something like "dating or tracing my own origin." That double entendre wonderfully captures the two views of the past and of the meeting of the speaker's parents in conflict within the poem, one that sees that meeting or any past event as necessarily completed and over, as something that can only be remembered and/or regretted; and one that sees or wishes to see that meeting or any event as an interruptable beginning to a chain of unintended, yet somehow inevitable, events (including one's birth). (In this way Olds's poem ironically echoes a poem that it otherwise differs from dramatically—Kinnell's "After Making Love We Hear Footsteps.") These two conflicting views compete from the very outset of the poem, particularly in the way in the first 12 lines the poet renders seemingly mundane details of setting—"the / red tiles glinting like bent / plates of blood" (lines 4–6), the "wrought-iron gates" looking like "black" "sword-tips" (lines 9–10)—into vivid, grim, foreboding specters of all the "bad things" that will ultimately come of this "innocent" meeting (lines 18, 13). Having vividly rendered the scene, the poet moves in lines 14 through 25 to convey her desire to intervene, while lines 26 to 31 convey her acceptance of the inevitability of what has already happened.

In terms of tone, what you might want to emphasize is how deftly Olds manages to convey tremendous anger and bitterness toward her parents even as she also, I think, expresses sympathy for them or at least for the innocent young people they used to be.

QUESTIONS FOR DISCUSSION

1. How many different ways can you interpret Olds's title? What significance do those various meanings have in relation to the poem as a whole?
2. What questions do you think this speaker is asking about families, life, etc. by "going back to" this scene in May 1937, or what issues is she raising and exploring in the process? How might you articulate the theme or themes of the poem?
3. How would you describe the tone of this poem? Obviously, the speaker is quite angry about the "bad things" that her parents have done to her, but is that the only emotion conveyed here? What techniques does Olds use to convey these various emotions?

SUGGESTION FOR WRITING

Write an essay analyzing the different views of the past (or of the relationship between past and present) that the speaker of "I Go Back" expresses. Does the poem as a whole ultimately embrace or advocate one of these views? If so, how and where and why?

LI-YOUNG LEE

Persimmons

This poem is in one sense about the imprecision of language as contrasted to the precision of images, yet particular words connect the events in the speaker's life and the parts of the poem. It is also a poem about ignorance and intolerance—and the way that the meaning of words or signs varies from person to person, based on their perspectives and experience. Stanzas four and five address these issues in ways students often find quite moving, and so I tend to start discussion there. In stanza four, we discover why different-sounding words have close associations in the speaker's mind because of his personal experiences, and in stanza five we discover that the teacher's experience and knowledge are not in all ways superior to her student's (a development my students tend to relish).

QUESTIONS FOR DISCUSSION

1. How does translation work as a theme in the poem?
2. How does the ability to paint while blind compare to the poet's ability to express himself in a language other than his own?

SUGGESTION FOR WRITING

Write an essay comparing "Persimmons" and Mora's "Elena" in terms of what each poem seems to say about the role of language in familial relationships (or in relationships more generally).

ELIZABETH ALEXANDER

West Indian Primer

QUESTIONS FOR DISCUSSION

1. What is a "primer"? What is the significance of the fact that the poet refers to this poem as a "West Indian Primer" (both in the title and in the last line of the poem)?
2. What's the significance of the poet or speaker's remark that he or she "know[s] more about Toussaint / and Hispaniola than my own / Jamaica" (lines 17–19)?
3. What kinds of things does the speaker know about her family and what do the stories told to the speaker reveal to us about the family and its various members? What might the poem suggest about what the speaker has gotten from her various family members?
4. What does the poem tell us about the culture(s) of the West Indies?

EAMON GRENNAN

Pause

Grennan's "Pause" portrays exactly what its title indicates—that moment of "pure / waiting, anticipation" when "everything" is "about to happen" but hasn't happened yet, that time of "infinite possibility" (lines 3–6, 18). While in such moments time itself comes to a "pause," a "stillness" (line 1), the poem suggests that "your mind" refuses that stillness, jumping ahead to imagine what is about to happen (line 6). And that is precisely what happens as the speaker vividly imagines his daughter's homecoming, an event that, in fact, never literally occurs in the poem. Yet the real or most significant pause here might well be that moment in the second sentence when the speaker himself pauses in the act of imagining, stepping out of the moment to ponder what this moment tells him "about the shape of the life [he's] chosen to live" (line 17). In the process, the speaker contemplates, I think, the significance of everyday "moments," the way in which "those vast unanswerable" abstractions like "love and disaster" in fact reside in the seeming chaos of the most mundane, everyday happenings, even in "the casual scatter of your child's winter clothes" (lines 19–21).

QUESTIONS FOR DISCUSSION

1. What, if anything, actually happens in this poem? Does it have a plot? If so, how so?
2. How does Grennan characterize the "pause" that is the subject of this poem? Is there more than one pause or type of pause in the poem? What does the speaker mean when he says that in this moment "everything seems just, seems *justified*" (line 5)? Is there more than one way to interpret the term *just* here?
3. How would you articulate the theme of "Pause," what the poem as a whole says about the kind of pauses it describes?
4. How does the form of the poem, particularly the fact that it is composed of only two sentences, contribute to the characterization of "pauses" and/or to the theme?

SUGGESTION FOR WRITING

Write a paragraph describing a perfectly ordinary moment of a perfectly ordinary day in your life. In another paragraph or two try to sum up what this moment might tell you or someone else about "the shape of the life you've chosen to live."

JIMMY SANTIAGO BACA

Green Chile

One effective way to begin discussion of Baca's poem is to ask students to list and discuss the different characteristics associated with red and green chiles in the poem. Notice that red chiles are portrayed in the poem not as food, but as mere decoration. After all, even when eaten, the red chile simply seems to decorate the speaker's eggs and potatoes. Lending "historical grandeur" to "vegetable stands" (lines 6, 5), such chiles seem like "haggard" "old men," yellowing" relics of something that is dead or lost (lines 9–10). Green chiles, on the other hand, come alive in the poem through both the author's words and the "caressing" touch of the grand-mother (line 22). Unlike the "old" red chiles, the green chile seems like "[a] well-dressed gentleman" with "an air of authority and youth" (lines 19, 16). Its seductive, phallic qualities emphasized by Baca's reference to it as an "oily rubbery serpent" that brings "mouth-watering fulfillment" (lines 22–23), the green chile represents a vibrant, all-encompassing sensuality that is at once sexual and gastronomic, both very much alive and live giving.

One might then want to ask students what precisely Baca seems to be saying about the speaker and his grandmother by associating the former with the red chile and the latter with the green. Might he thereby suggest that the young man is ironically dead to something that his grandmother remains sensuously alive to? Since the speaker describes himself as eating a rather traditional "American" breakfast of "eggs and potatoes" (lines 1–2), might that "something" be his Hispanic heritage, which has—as it were—merely become a kind of decoration, something laid "over" his American self rather than something truly integral and essential?

One might then ask students how the final stanza of the poem contributes to and/or complicates this reading. To what extent might the speaker and the grandmother stand for two different generations and to what extent does the speaker's description of numbers of "sunburned men and women" from all over New Mexico "reliv[ing] this old, beautiful ritual again and again" suggest that the speaker isn't representative of a generation, but is instead an individual "I" cut off from a culture that is still thriving around him (lines 39, 45)? And does the poem really ultimately suggest that he or his generation are cut off or is something different made possible by both the poem itself and the "old, beautiful ritual" it describes?

QUESTIONS FOR DISCUSSION

1. Though the title announces that Baca's main concern here is "Green Chile," there are—in fact—two kinds of chiles described in the poem. How are red and green chiles each described and characterized in the poem? How exactly does the initial description of red chiles help the poet convey the particular character, meaning, and significance of green chiles?
2. How do descriptions of the two kinds of chiles help to characterize the actual characters in the poem—the speaker and his grandmother? The "sunburned men and women" who gather and roast the green chiles? The ways of life and/or worldviews associated with each? How does the introduction of these other characters and the reference to multiple New Mexico towns at the end of the poem broaden or change your sense of the subject and/or theme of the poem?
3. What is the speaker's attitude toward his grandmother and to the men and women described at the end of the poem? Do you think there's a conflict here? If so, what and where is that conflict? Is the conflict resolved at the end of the poem? If so, how?

SUGGESTIONS FOR WRITING

1. Write an essay that suggests what the speaker in "Green Chile" might learn or come to see about himself, life, family, and/or culture by contemplating his grandmother's preparation of green chiles.
2. Write an essay that explores the question of whether or not Baca's speaker ultimately depicts himself as irrevocably cut off or estranged from the way of life represented by his grandmother and the "sunburned men and women" in the poem.

ROBERT HAYDEN

Those Winter Sundays

Like many poems and stories about childhood, Hayden's "Those Winter Sundays" hinges on an implied contrast between the view of his situation and his father that the speaker had as a child and that which he has now, as an adult. Though students often don't recognize them right away, there are many obvious cues in the poem that point to the unhappiness of the speaker's childhood and suggest that he has only recently come to appreciate some of the things his father did for him rather than to blame him for all that he didn't do. One way to get to that is to call to students' attention line 9 where the speaker refers to his fear of "the chronic angers of that house." What might this line suggest about what the relationship between father and son was like? What's the significance of the fact that the speaker talks about "angers" in the plural and without reference to any particular person (including himself)? Might words such as "blueblack" (line 2) take on added significance in light of these references to anger and fear? How about the setting overall, especially the fact that the speaker remembers winter in particular?

You might want to consider having students read and write about "Those Winter Sundays" in conjunction with Roethke's "My Papa's Waltz," a poem that my students tend to respond to enthusiastically and to write about very effectively and that deals with similar issues in a very, very different way. (And, if your course covers poetry and fiction, you might even have students also read or reread Joyce's short story "Counterparts," which describes a father's abuse of his son, but does so from the father's rather than the son's perspective and with more emphasis on the causes rather than the aftereffects of abuse.)

QUESTIONS FOR DISCUSSION

1. Why do you think the poem begins "Sundays too" (rather than "On Sundays")? What does that *too* tell us, and how might it set the stage for the rest of the poem?

2. What does the poet's use of alliteration, as in "clothes" "cold" "cracked" (lines 2–3) and "blueblack" "banked" "blaze" (lines 2, 5), contribute to the poem?
3. What is the significance of the speaker's reference to his fear of "the chronic angers of that house" (line 9)?
4. What are the "austere and lonely offices" of love in the poem (line 14)? Why and how exactly are they "austere"? "Lonely"? "Offices"?
5. What does the poem suggest about how the speaker felt as a child about his father? As an adult? What's the significance and/or effect of the repetition of the phrase "what did I know" in line 13?

JAMES MASAO MITSUI

Because of My Father's Job

QUESTIONS FOR DISCUSSION

1. Who do you think the "us" in the first line of the poem might refer to? How can you tell?
2. What's the significance of the fact that the speaker "explain[ed] away" his father's crock of vegetables by referring to Popeye (lines 2, 6)? What does this tell us about the speaker's relationship as a child to his father? To his Japanese heritage?
3. What's the significance of the fact that Jimmy Osler "didn't change his friendship in '41" (line 27)?
4. How is the speaker's attitude toward his father and toward his Japanese heritage different in the present, as an adult? What's the significance of the fact that the speaker sees his father's "thick biceps" in the mirror (line 38), and how might this contribute to the speaker's attitude toward his father?
5. What's the significance or effect of the way the speaker dwells here on what he doesn't remember? The way the poem ends by discussing what "doesn't matter" (line 40)? What do you think does matter?
6. What do you make of the title? What does the poet seem to attribute to his father's job? How does the speaker's job as a poet figure in the poem?

SIMON J. ORTIZ

My Father's Song

On a first reading, this poem seems to recount the speaker's memory of a moment shared with his father. If students read it this way, then you can focus discussion, first, on what exact "things" the father "says" (line 1) to the son through stopping his work to "gently" "scoo[p]" up helpless mice (line 18) and what "things," in turn, the speaker "says" about his father by recounting the episode in the way that he does, especially in terms of the "softness" of the rhythm and diction (line 24).

But once students have discussed that, draw their attention to the way the form of the poem in fact suggests that it recounts not the speaker's memory of a moment shared with his father, but instead an account of the speaker's memory of his father's account of a moment shared with the speaker's grandfather. The poem literally embodies, in other words, one of the "things" his father "said" to him; it is his "father's song." Thus the first stanza serves as a frame for the subsequent narrative, which in fact becomes a memory within a memory connecting not two but three generations. How does that fact change the emphasis and meaning of the poem?

One answer is that the poem thereby becomes not just about one man "saying things" to his son through his actions but also about the importance and the interconnectedness of remembering and of "saying" themselves, about the way memories become stories and stories themselves become memories (and poems) by being "planted several times" (line 9), and about how memories (and relationships) as potentially fragile as any "tiny pink animals" are thereby preserved alive in the present (which is, in fact, the tense in which the poem ends) (line 18). One way to get at the latter connections would be to ask students what connects the things said within the narrative to the description of the father's "saying" that precedes it. How does one echo and reinforce the other?

QUESTIONS FOR DISCUSSION

1. What exactly does the man in the poem communicate to his son by stopping his work to scoop up the mice? What would the subject and/ or theme of the poem be if it described only this scene? How does the specific way the father's actions are described (diction, etc.) contribute to our sense of the meaning and significance of those actions?
2. How is your notion of the subject or theme of the poem changed by taking the frame narrative into consideration? What is the relationship between the descriptions of the father's song with which the poem opens and the scene depicted later in the poem?
3. What do you make of the fact that the poem doesn't return to the frame narrative at the end?

SUGGESTIONS FOR WRITING

1. Write a paragraph or a whole essay analyzing the significance of the fact that "My Father's Song" ends in the present tense, that the poem

never returns to the frame narrative or the particular time and place with or in which it opens.

2. Write an essay analyzing what exactly "My Father's Song" suggests or asks about one of the following subjects:
   (a) What a man, or a person, or a father should be like.
   (b) What the relationship between and/or role of memory, story, and song or poetry is or should be.
   (c) What the relationship between generations is or should be like.

3. Write an essay exploring whether and how the facts that Ortiz was born in the Acoma Pueblo in New Mexico and/or that he is a Navajo affect your interpretation of "My Father's Song."

SUSAN MUSGRAVE

You Didn't Fit

QUESTIONS FOR DISCUSSION

1. How many different definitions of the word *fit* seem to be at work in this poem? How does the meaning of the word change over the course of the poem?

2. In what sense or in what way didn't the speaker's father "fit" in the past? How exactly is the father characterized in the poem? In what way didn't or doesn't the speaker herself "fit"? How exactly does she characterize herself? Does the poem ultimately suggest that the speaker and her father did or do "fit" somewhere or somehow? If so, in what way or where and how?

3. What do you make of the last two lines of the poem? What idiomatic expressions does the speaker play with here and what does she convey in doing so?

ERIN MOURÉ

Thirteen Years

QUESTIONS FOR DISCUSSION

1. What exactly do you think happened at the wedding described in the poem? How exactly does the poem's account of events differ from yours? What's the significance or effect of the way the poem describes the events, particularly the way the speaker revises her own account as she goes along?

2. How might you speak the final line of the poem? What tone of voice

would you adopt and why? How might the different tones make the line and the poem as a whole mean differently?

3. How does the form of the poem—particularly the way lines are broken up and run together, the use of the ampersand (&) (line 8), the italicized phrase *"[t]he friend of the family"* (line 14)—contribute to the meaning of the poem?

READING/WRITING IDEAS FOR CHAPTER 13

ESSAYS ABOUT TONE AND THEME

Because this chapter discusses both tone and theme, it suggests essay assignments that might focus on either or both of these elements.

More tone-focused assignments might simply ask students to analyze the tone(s) of a given poem, analyzing the ways in which tone is conveyed and the ways that tone contributes to the meaning (or theme) of the poem and/or to the attitude the poem as a whole encourages us to adopt toward a particular subject, character, or situation *or* the ways in which shifts in tone over the course of a poem reveal changes in the speaker's attitude toward, or view of, a subject, person, or situation. Obviously, however, one could make even primarily tone-focused assignments also focus on theme by simply wording the assignment so that students are guided toward essays that considered how tone contributes to theme. (And, as I suggest below in "Troubleshooting," I have found that assignments about tone tend to produce better essays when they include attention to theme.)

If you're considering more theme-focused assignments, you might want to look back at the discussion of such assignments in "Reading/Writing Ideas for Chapter 8" and/or to use some of the exercises described there to get students started thinking and writing about theme.

That discussion focuses mainly, however, on assignments that ask students to analyze the theme of a single text (largely because I find it most helpful to have students first write about poetry and about theme in particular by focusing tightly on a single text). You might, however, want to have students write essays that analyze more than one poem in the chapter, comparing what two or more poems say or ask about a given topic or subject and/or what tones they convey. Possible comparative essay assignments of this type are included in "Suggestions for Writing" that follow the note on "Persimmons" and in the note to "Those Winter Sundays," but there are also obviously plenty of other possibilities, including the following sample prompts:

• How do poems about family relationships compare to more traditional "love poems," such as those contained in the last chapter? How are poems about marriage like other family relationship poems you've read and how are they like love poems?

- Compare two or more poems that take the death of a loved one as their subject. To what extent are the poem's about the speaker's particular relationship to the loved one and to what extent are they about grief, death, or some other more general subject?
- Compare Hayden's "Those Winter Sundays," Mitsui's "Because of My Father's Job," and Ortiz's "My Father's Song." How do these poems represent the role of fathers? The relationship between fathers and sons? The way in which that relationship changes over time?
- Compare any two or more of these poems in terms of what they ask and say about the relationship between the past and present and/or about memory and the way adults grapple with childhood experiences.

If you do choose to assign a comparative essay along these lines, you may want to take a look at the discussion of comparative essays in "Reading/Writing Ideas" for Chapters 9 and 23, perhaps even using some of the exercises described there to get students started.

TROUBLESHOOTING

When students are writing essays about tone, especially in relation to a single text, I find that it's pretty essential that I guide them to consider theme or something like it as well; otherwise students' may be encouraged to produce rather bland essays that describe more than analyze the tone of a poem, characterizing the tone without really saying much about why tone matters (or why it matters that we agree with their interpretation of the tone). Another way to avoid this problem, however, involves having students develop theses that focus on how different, even competing tones coexist in a single poem.

With poetry, as with fiction, I find that "theme" can become problematic in various ways for student writers (see "Reading/Writing Ideas for Chapter 8"). Thus with poetry, as with fiction, I find that it's helpful to steer students toward using words such as *conflict* to describe what's at issue in particular texts, and I do so precisely to focus students on the idea that something is at issue in texts rather than being decided and simple in the way that "theme" can often seem to be. One might, for example, argue that "Those Winter Sundays" explores the conflict between the speaker's two different views of his father and his childhood or that "Thirteen Years" explores the conflict between the speaker and her family's different views of, or attitudes toward, what happened to her at thirteen, etc. The task of papers focusing on such conflicts would be to name and fully characterize these two competing views, to explore how and why they are at conflict within the text, and to suggest how, or if, the conflict is eventually resolved. Obviously, "conflict" may mean something different or work differently in poetic texts than it does in fiction, but it still seems like a helpful and viable way to talk about "theme" (and to connect the analysis of theme in poetry and fiction).

The "conflict" approach has the added advantage of helping students structure their essays effectively, encouraging them to organize their arguments not according to the structure of the poem itself (thus producing a kind of stanza-by-stanza exposition) but according to the logic of their own ideas about the character of the different views expressed in the poem, the way those views conflict, and the way the poem does or does not resolve the conflict.

14

SPEAKER

The speaker of a poem might be thought of as the voice of the poem. Students (and some critics), following what we might call the biographical impulse, often confuse the voice of a poem with the poet's voice, and sometimes, of course, this identification is justified. Living in an age of confessional talk shows and made-for-TV self-exploitation, we are constantly bombarded with the sounds and images of public self-exposure. In this atmosphere, it is good to remind our students that while a poem may in part be an exercise in self-revelation—and certainly confessional poetry of one sort or another has been a dominant form since at least the arrival of the Romantics—it is just as likely to speak through an imaginary person or thing as through the voice of the poet. (Indeed, even the most avowedly personal poem is conveyed in a voice modulated by artifice, one never precisely equivalent to the poet's voice.) In discussion, students will slip and use the poet's name instead of "the speaker" (as on occasion I do), but it is well to maintain the distinction as much as possible so that students do not go astray when they move on to analytical writing assignments. If you also cover fiction in your class, you might find it helpful to have students revisit "point of view" and "characterization," discussing how the concept of "speaker" relates to these concepts or elements.

PLANNING IDEAS

- You might want to open your discussion of the "speaker" by assigning one of the poems in which the speaker clearly is not the poet—"In a Prominent Bar in Secaucus One Day," perhaps, or "In Westminster Abbey." Then turn to some poems that could be autobiographical— "Hanging Fire," "The Lifting," "She Dwelt among the Untrodden Ways." If you include Atwood's "Death of a Young Son by Drowning" in your discussion of apparently personal poems, you can help the students see how complicated this issue can be (see the note in Guide).

- If you plan to discuss the biblical allusions in the conclusion to Olds's "The Lifting," have students look up two biblical passages—Hebrews 9 and Acts 9:1–22—in a King James Bible and bring brief synopses of both passages to class. Since students often have trouble with the seventeenth-century English of the King James Bible, exposing them to the verses that Olds alludes to and asking them to work out what the passages mean can make discussion more fruitful, even if you still must provide some help in translating the biblical passages into modern English.

- Have students read or reread Olds's "The Glass" and "I Go Back to May 1937" in conjunction with "The Lifting," comparing the various feelings Olds's speakers display toward their parents.

SHARON OLDS

The Lifting

This is a poem about a single, fleeting experience. In the first line, the poet recreates her own surprise and brings the reader, without introduction, into a particular situation: "Suddenly my father lifted up his nightie." How does the speaker surprise herself by her own response? Notice how Olds moves from the specific to the general in the course of the poem. You might ask students to compare this to the progression of her poem "The Glass." Ask them to define the various feelings the speaker has toward her father in these two poems. How effective is the poet's use of shocking images in this poem and disgusting images in "The Glass"? Do these images become less shocking and disgusting by the end of each poem? Why?

It may be useful to explore the allusions embedded in the concluding lines of Olds's poem. The ending of the poem metaphorically conflates the raising of the father's nightgown and several biblical images. The nightgown is compared to a "veil" that will rise after one dies (see Hebrews 9 in the King James Version of the Bible). Hebrews describes the veil that covers the "Holy of Holies"—the sacred place in the temple beyond which the ark of the covenant lies, where only the high priest may venture. In this New Testament passage, Christ metaphorically becomes the high priest, the one privy to the truths behind the veil. To move beyond the veil is to gain access to the revelations that Christ will give to those who accept him and thereby receive the promise of eternal life.

Veils do not actually fall from anyone's eyes in the Bible—despite Olds's statement—but in Acts 9:1–22, "scales"—or something like them—

fall from the apostle-to-be Paul's eyes after he has been struck blind on the road to Damascus. Paul's archetypal conversion experience transforms him from a persecutor of Christians into a missionary, a martyr and, eventually, a saint. In biblical terms, he is portrayed as being blind to the truth of Christianity until the scales fall from his eyes.

Olds's use of biblical allusion is complicated and by no means clearcut. She doesn't say the veil *will* rise; she says "we were promised" it "would" rise. You might want to ask students why they think Olds alludes to these biblical images. You might also want to ask how and why the speaker equivocates in her evocation of them.

QUESTIONS FOR DISCUSSION

1. Can we assume that Olds is a Christian because she alludes to passages in the New Testament in her poem?
2. Is the speaker making fun of Christianity by comparing her father's self-exposure to Christ's revelation?
3. What is Olds's purpose in employing these allusions at the end of this particular poem? Does the speaker have mixed feelings about the promises to which she refers? Why might these promises seem appealing, whether or not the speaker believes they will be fulfilled?

SUGGESTION FOR WRITING

Read two or three of Olds's other poems in conjunction with "The Lifting." Write an essay analyzing the character of the speaker in each of the poems and discussing whether or to what extent the same speaker seems to be speaking in all of the selections.

AUDRE LORDE

Hanging Fire

Lorde's poem can potentially open up for discussion a number of interesting questions, some of which can be framed in terms of the relationship between speaker and author. For at first glance, this poem seems to be about the pains of all adolescents, the first few lines of the poem—for example—capturing the pain and confusion of those years when our bodies begin to "betra[y]" us in a number of different ways (line 2). And you may, in fact, want to ask students to pause over this line and the word *betrayed* in particular, asking students to dwell on the word's various meanings, which include something like "turned against me" and something like "revealed the truth about me" (cf. the reference to how people will "tell the truth about me" in line 18). In what sense or in what ways are both meanings of the word appropriate and revealing in the context of the poem and of our experiences of adolescence? The most obvious truth our bodies reveal about us in adolescence is our gender, an idea that resonates with other details in the poem, particularly the reference in the last stanza to the boy picked for the Math Team despite having bad marks. Might he have been picked because he was a boy? Might the poem be about girls in particular as well as, or instead of, adolescents in general? Or do we doubt the veracity of this speaker?

As these questions suggest, I think this single line can open up a whole series of questions about the extent to which the experiences and feelings recorded in this poem refer to those of any fourteen year old and the extent to which they are gender and even race specific. After all, the particular feature of this speaker's body that is figured as betraying her is "my skin," and she later worries about her "ashy" knees, not, for example, about acne, the more universal adolescent skin problem we might expect to be at issue here (line 7). How exactly does our interpretation of the poem change if we read it as "universal"? As particular to female experience? As particular to the experience of people of color? Might we see the poem as working in all of these ways at once?

How might our interpretation be affected by the fact that Lorde herself was both female and African-American? How, if at all, might or should these facts affect our interpretation of this poem, especially given the fact that the speaker of the poem is clearly not (the adult) poet herself?

QUESTIONS FOR DISCUSSION

1. What does the phrase *hanging fire* mean? How does Lorde's use of this phrase as a title affect your interpretation of the poem?
2. What do you make of the references to death that recur in each stanza of the poem? What's the significance or effect of the timing of such references? What about the references to the mother's closed door?
3. What exactly do you think the speaker might mean when she says "my skin has betrayed me" (line 2)? Might there be several possible interpretations? If so, what are those interpretations and how do they each work in the context of the poem as a whole?
4. What is the speaker's gender and race? What details in the poem support your answers? To what extent and in what ways is this a poem about any fourteen-year-old person? To what extent and in what ways is this a poem about race- and/or gender-specific experiences? Would knowing the race and gender of the author affect your interpretation? If so, how and why? If not, why not?

SUGGESTION FOR WRITING

After reading Lorde's "Hanging Fire," write a personal essay describing in some detail the frustrations of being a fourteen-year-old girl or boy. Or write an essay comparing the frustrations that you felt at fourteen and those you imagine might be experienced by a fourteen year old of a different race or gender or cultural background. What's the same? What's different?

JOHN BETJEMAN

In Westminster Abbey

The gender of the speaker is indicated here by the end of the first stanza, and the "lady" is characterized very quickly, mostly through her own words and attitudes. Having students detail how she is characterized and what precisely is implied by each of her self-righteous, self-centered, and bigoted statements can be the basis for a good discussion of how characters reveal themselves through language. A thorough discussion of characterization here almost makes a discussion of "speaker" as such superfluous, for everyone will recognize that poetry sometimes dramatizes a character as in a play instead of presenting an authorial voice speaking directly.

QUESTIONS FOR DISCUSSION

1. Where is Westminster Abbey? How does the setting of the poem contribute to the characterization of the speaker?
2. Do you agree with the speaker that, although she is a sinner, she has "done no major crime" (lines 25–26)?

HENRY REED

Lessons of the War: Judging Distances

My students often argue with each other about whether there really are two speakers as such in the poem or whether, instead, the poem is a reverie in someone's mind, a reverie in which two voices re-create a kind of scene. The lack of quotation marks may contribute to the latter view, but either way of reading comes to much the same thing. (All dramatic dialogues are, in one sense, similarly reveries in a poet's mind.) In any case, it's important to emphasize the extreme differences of language between the two voices: the jargon-spouting, thoroughly "army" drill instructor who dogmatically, ungrammatically, nonsensically (see especially lines 10–11), and rudely badgers his pupils in lines 1–22 and 31–36, versus the recruit who rejects the army way for a highly metaphoric (and perhaps too dreamy and "poetic") mode of speech that, however, leads him to common-sense conclusions in lines 25–30 and 37–42.

QUESTIONS FOR DISCUSSION

1. What is accomplished by describing distance as time in the last line? How does it relate to the poem's title? Where else in the poem is space regarded as time?
2. What passages would you emphasize if you were considering the poem as (a) an antiwar statement? (b) an account of military mentality? (c) an analysis of ways of perceiving natural landscape? (d) a dialogue between stereotyped articulation and instinctive feeling? (e) a description of man's relationship to nature? (f) a contrast between things that endure and temporal or temporary things? What passages would you have to omit or de-emphasize to regard the poem in each of these ways? Does having to ignore part of the poem invalidate the thesis?

GWENDOLYN BROOKS

We Real Cool

The speaker in this poem purports to speak for a group. I try to get my students to notice how the collective nature of the poem's statement is emphasized through the form Brooks imposes on it. The word *We* dangles unexpectedly at the end of each line except the last. The speaker is never identified as an individual. While the collective character of the speaker's group is partially revealed through the group's actions, the form and meter of the poem also contribute to its characterization. The "We" of the poem share certain behaviors and expect to share an early death. The title suggests that "coolness" involves doing what others do—being part of the crowd or of a particular crowd. The conclusion of the poem suggests where such behavior can lead.

QUESTIONS FOR DISCUSSION

1. How does the rhythm of the poem contribute to the characterization of the speaker(s)?
2. What does it mean to "Strike straight"? To "Thin gin"? To "Jazz June"? How do these phrases help to characterize the speaker(s)?
3. Is the speaker's idea of what is "cool" and the poet's idea of what is "cool" the same? (Are the poet's perspective and the speaker's perspective the same?)

SIR THOMAS WYATT

They Flee from Me

This poem seems to me deceptively difficult, and often I assign it early in the course, do little with it in class, and then return to it later in the course when students have more fully developed their analytical skills. On a first reading, its themes of loneliness and betrayal are quite evident, and it fits well with the poems about speaker because it provides a revealing self-portrait. What seem to me interesting about the poem's complexity are two things: (1) the delicate tonal control, the move from the boasting of the first stanza to the dreamy nostalgia of the second to the anger and self-exposure of the third; and (2) the portrayal of a speaker who comes to seem more and more bitter and out of control.

Class time on both of these issues can be well spent, especially since the poem is an older poem, and students often have trouble with poems not in a modern idiom. But here even the unfamiliar words (*newfangleness* for example) are emotionally loaded; working with the OED (this can be a good early library exercise) can become part of the analysis of tone and feeling. Very good discussion can be generated about just what words and structural strategies in the poem create the abrupt mood and tonal shifts that contribute to the portrayal of the speaker. Ask your class exactly what was "special" about the experience of stanza two, and get them to articulate exactly what the speaker objects to in the behavior of this woman. Then get them to analyze the speaker's own behavior and attitudes and compare the two "characters" in the poem.

(*Note:* Students of Wyatt sometimes argue that the speaker in the poem is someone very much like Wyatt himself, and there may be a question here as to how self-conscious the portrait of the speaker is. It takes a very sophisticated group of readers to get into the question of intention here, but you can get at the character of the speaker well enough through the text of the poem without having to get into historical or biographical issues. Save those for later, perhaps returning to this poem when you do consider them.)

QUESTIONS FOR DISCUSSION

1. What is the implied metaphor in lines 3–7? What does the metaphor suggest about the speaker's attitude toward the women he has known?
2. In what tense(s) is the poem written? Trace the changes in tense from line to line.
3. Characterize the speaker. Do you think he has a right to be bitter? Why or why not?

[*I celebrate myself, and sing myself*]

In the preface to *Leaves of Grass* (1855), Whitman makes clear that he considers the work a personal, poetic manifesto defining what American literature should be if it is to embody the national character as he perceives it. I sometimes like to introduce this first section of that longer work by telling my students Whitman's stated aim (without adding much biographical or literary-historical detail). Then I ask them what sort of speaker Whitman invents to convey this new, quintessentially American poetry. The egotism of the speaker is readily evident to them from the outset, but some students will notice that the overweening self-confidence of lines 1 and 2 is complicated and softened by the easy egalitarianism of line 3: "For every atom belonging to me as good belongs to you." At this point, I try to draw them into a brief discussion of how notions of ego and equality combine in our perceptions of our American heritage.

Once we've established that, in celebrating himself, the speaker also means to celebrate the uniqueness and complexity of all things American, I ask the class to look for details in the poem that suggest what Whitman's vision of America might be.

QUESTIONS FOR DISCUSSION

1. The speaker is portrayed as leaning, loafing at his "ease," and observing "a spear of summer grass." If the speaker is the author of a new American poetry, what "American" qualities are suggested in this description?
2. What does the speaker mean when he says he "now thirty-seven years old in perfect health [begins]"? What is he beginning?
3. What characteristics—of the speaker, his poetry, and things American—are revealed in the final stanza?

SUGGESTION FOR WRITING

Go to the library and look up Henry David Thoreau's letter to H. G. O. Blake, dated November 19, 1856, in which he talks about Walt Whitman and his poetry. Write an essay analyzing Whitman's poem in light of Thoreau's comments.

PAT MORA

La Migra

Though this poem undoubtedly has a particular resonance and meaning for students like mine who have all had encounters of one sort of another with the Border Patrol, I love teaching this poem because it speaks about such border-specific issues in terms of a situation and a speaker that are familiar to all of us. For the speaker of this poem seems to be that kid in everyone's neighborhood who is both bossy and imaginative enough to always get to choose the game and to decide which role everyone gets to play, which invariably means choosing the best role for himself or herself. In this way the poem manages to suggest the parallels between such neighborhood power dynamics and those within and between the neighborhoods we call nation-states. For, like most children's games, the one this speaker invents speaks volumes about the adult world it mimics. Yet like many such games it does so not only or simply by mimicking that world but also by providing a way for children to question how that world works, which is exactly what this speaker seems to do by thinking and rethinking the question of just which role in this game is best and why.

QUESTIONS FOR DISCUSSION

1. What do you know and what do you imagine about who this speaker is? About whom he's speaking to?
2. How exactly is the relationship between *La Migra* and Mexicans characterized in the first stanza of the poem? What exactly makes one person or group more powerful than the other? To what extent or in what ways is gender, as well as ethnicity or citizenship, figured as a factor in determining the shape of this relationship?
3. What answers to these questions are suggested in stanza two? How precisely is the characterization of the relationship between *La Migra* and the Mexican maid revised or reconceived in this stanza?
4. What do we discover over the course of the poem about the character of this speaker and of the speaker's relationship to whomever he is speaking to? What's the significance of the roles he ascribes to himself in their game?
5. How specifically might this poem be about this speaker and the type of person the speaker represents? How specifically might this poem be about the relationship between *La Migra* and Mexicans? How would you articulate the theme of the poem in each case? How do these two facets or layers of the poem and/or these two themes work together?

SUGGESTION FOR WRITING

Write an essay describing a game that you played with others as a child and analyzing the game in terms of what the game and the roles of various participants might reveal about the larger, adult world and about your perceptions of that world in childhood.

SYLVIA PLATH

Mirror

QUESTIONS FOR DISCUSSION

1. This poem opens with the speaker—the mirror—characterizing itself in large part by saying what it is not—it has "no preconceptions" (line 1), it sees everything "as it is, unmisted by love or dislike" (line 3), it is "not cruel" (line 4). Such negative constructions suggest that the mirror is either implicitly contrasting itself with something or someone else or defending itself against someone's possible "preconceptions" about its character (or, perhaps, both). If the former, who or what do you think that someone or something else is that has preconceptions, sees things misted by love and dislike, is cruel? What might those preconceptions be or have to do with? If the latter, why might we (or someone) tend to envision a mirror as all the things this mirror claims not to be and/or what might such preconceptions about the mirror tell us about ourselves (or this someone)?
2. What does Plath achieve by making the mirror and the lake the speakers here rather than the people who look into them?
3. What is the significance or effect of the fact that the person who looks into the lake is a woman?
4. What's the significance or effect of the fact that the woman who appears in the lake is likened to "a terrible fish" (line 18)?

SUGGESTION FOR WRITING

Write a poem or a short prose piece in which you adopt the point of view and voice of an inanimate object that you use on a daily basis. How do you think that object would see you? What do you think the inanimate object might be able to see about you that you might not see?

SEAMUS HEANEY

The Outlaw

QUESTIONS FOR DISCUSSION

1. How does the poet use metaphors to characterize the bull and the act of sex here?
2. Who or what are "outlaws" in this poem? In what ways does the bull seem like an outlaw? In what ways doesn't he? How might and/or might not the title be ironic?
3. What is the speaker's attitude toward Old Kelly? The bull? The cow? The events within the poem? How is the speaker's attitude like and unlike those of the other characters in the poem, including not only Old Kelly but also the bull and the cow? Does the speaker's attitude change at all over the course of the poem? If so, how and when and why?
4. What might this poem be about besides a bull "servicing" a cow?

MARGARET ATWOOD

Death of a Young Son by Drowning

I've had very good luck with students' writing on this poem. It is difficult but clear, and the final image of staking out new territory by planting a flag (in this case psychological territory for the recovering speaker) brings the events and images of the poem together very nicely. Close analysis really pays off here, and the "character" of the speaker reliving the child's death and her experience in coming to terms with it becomes clear when the poem is read and reread several times.

Students usually assume, I find, that the "speaker" here is Atwood herself and that she is writing about a personal tragedy. Some of that assumption is probably generic—whatever we say about speaker, many readers believe that writing is narrowly autobiographical, in any case—and some stems from the sheer vividness of the poem, from the repetition of the child's birth journey in his death journey to the "claims" made on new land by the speaker at the end. There is so much precise detail, such a powerful sense of loss. It is, therefore, very useful to put the poem in its proper context, a context that makes clear why it is important to distinguish poet from speaker. This poem is from Atwood's book *The Journals of Susanna Moodie* (1970); all the poems in the book are written as if spoken by Susanna Moodie, a real person (1805–1885) who emigrated from England to upper Canada and wrote several books about her experiences.

In these poems, Atwood fictionalizes the life considerably but bases many of the poems on actual incidents recounted by Moodie. "Death of a Young Son by Drowning" is from Section II of the book, which recounts incidents in Moodie's life between 1840 and 1871.

QUESTIONS FOR DISCUSSION

1. Does Atwood's poem provide any internal evidence to suggest it is not a personal, confessional poem? How might one discover that Atwood based the poem on another's experience?
2. Does the knowledge that Atwood based her poem on incidents in the life of Susanna Moodie change your reaction to the work?

READING/WRITING IDEAS FOR CHAPTER 14

ESSAYS ABOUT SPEAKERS

Because the speaker in a particular poem is quite often simultaneously the central character and the central consciousness from whose point of view the poem is written (to use language employed in the fiction section of the anthology), essays about speaker can fairly closely follow certain of the essay types described in "Reading/Writing Ideas" for Chapters 2 and 3. To take the more character-focused types first, students might, for example, be asked to write essays:

- Showing that and how a speaker embodies a particular worldview or way of looking at something, perhaps by showing how the speaker's view contrasts with other views articulated directly or indirectly within the poem.
- Showing how and why a speaker experiences a conflict between particular ways of looking or being.
- Showing how the speaker's attitude toward, or thoughts about, something or how our vision of the speaker's character changes over the course of a poem.

Sample Thesis Paragraph

Maxine Kumin masterfully uses the humorous anecdote of woodchucks invading a garden to put the reader at ease; then with the same recognition the world had as German's small invasions became WWII, the reader sees through the poet's clever guise in the last lines: "If only they'd all consented to die unseen / gassed underground the quiet Nazi way." Reading these lines, one cannot help believing that something dark and dangerous lies within the "sub-sub-basement" (line 6) of the seemingly light-hearted "Woodchucks." Not only do these last lines suggest that this poem could be viewed as an allegory in which woodchucks become persecuted Jews and the speaker a Nazi, but they also emphasize the enormous changes that have come over the speaker over the course of the poem. The speaker's own personality and ideas clearly change as she moves from being a "pacifist" (line 15) to an obsessive "murderer" (line 23) who dreams of killing her final victim. "Woodchucks" explores the speaker's own inner struggle, yet horrifies the reader by showing how willing people can be to sacrifice their morals to hatred.

From Sebastian Fuhrer, "Derr Woodchuckenfoffer," unpublished student essay.

- Showing how different characters in more dramatic poems (such as Hardy's "The Ruined Maid" or Heaney's "The Outlaw") represent or embody conflicting worldviews.

Sample Thesis Paragraph

Robert Frost, in the poem "Home Burial," explores some of the difficulties and emotions that couples can experience when dealing with the loss of a child. In the poem, a man and woman deal with the death of their son. Frost brings the reader in amidst an on-gong conflict between the two. Frost, through the character's conflict, explores two different ways of handling grief and expressing emotion. . . . Frost explores, in the man, an inexpressive, move-on-with-life approach to grief and, in the woman, an openly expressive, cling-to-grief approach.

From Scott Cundy, " 'Home Burial': Where Does the Sympathy Lie?," unpublished student essay.

More point-of-view-focused essay assignments might ask students to show precisely how the poet's choice of this particular speaker contributes to the poem's overall meaning, perhaps by considering how the poem would differ if written in the voice and through the eyes of a different speaker.

But because, as the headnote to this chapter indicates, students invariably seem to have more trouble separating poetic speakers from poets than they have separating fictional narrators from fiction writers, this chapter also suggests another, very different kind of essay assignment that would ask students to somehow consider the relationship between poet and speaker. And many of the suggestions for writing within this chapter and Chapter 13 of the Guide are of precisely this type, asking students to write about how knowledge of certain facts about an author might affect their interpretation of the theme(s) of a particular poem (such as Lorde's "Hanging Fire") or about the likeness between speakers of different poems by a single poet (such as Sharon Olds).

TROUBLESHOOTING

Whenever I have my students write the latter poet-and-speaker type of essay, I always have to work to make sure that students understand that biographical information about an author can only supplement rather than substitute for evidence from within the poem itself—to appreciate, for example, that Audre Lorde's race would have absolutely no relevance to our interpretation of "Hanging Fire" if the poem itself made no references whatsoever to skin color. Information about an author, in other words, might help to draw our attention to particular details within a poem that might open up a different interpretation, but such information can't in any way substitute for the poem or make the poem be about something that it isn't.

Note, too, that if such an approach seems to you too author and biography oriented, you might want to have students focus on the issues of race, ethnicity, and/or culture so that the biographical approach takes on a more cultural focus—i.e., finding out that Audre Lorde was a woman and an African American may make us attend to cultural issues explored in her poetry that are by no means purely "personal" or "autobiographical." Or you might simply want to emphasize to your students precisely what the essay assignment and the exercise below themselves imply: that one kind of interpretation or approach to a text doesn't exclude others; two such interpretations can even be part of a single, coherent essay of precisely the kind these assignments will help them to produce.

SPEAKER-FOCUSED WRITING EXERCISES

If assigning the kinds of character-focused or point-of-view-focused essays described above, you could easily adapt the exercise described in conjunction with those essay assignments (in "Reading/Writing Ideas" Chapters 2 and 3 of the Guide) as a way to get students started.

If asking students to write the third, poet-and-speaker-focused essay assignment, however, you might want to instead or also ask students to begin writing about their poem by ignoring any information they might have about the author, essentially drafting the essay that they would write about this text in the absence of such information. You might want to follow this up by having the students talk about their drafts in class, generating questions or ideas about what kinds of information about their author they think might be relevant. Then you can either provide them with very brief biographical sketches or have them look up information in the library. (Resources such as *Contemporary Authors* are especially good for this.) Then have them return to their drafts, adding a second section to their essays in which they flesh out the other interpretation(s) opened up to them by this information and suggest how these various interpretations might complement (or contradict) each other.

15

SITUATION AND SETTING

This chapter asks students to focus on three questions: What is going on in the poem (what is the situation)? Where does the situation occur? When does it occur (what is the setting?)? Some discussion about how these issues intertwine may be helpful. For instance, a couple arguing loudly about money troubles will evoke one reaction if they are portrayed arguing in their own kitchen—another perhaps if they are in bed—a different reaction still if they are in a grocery store or just outside the office of the husband's or wife's boss. We view a spot of blood in one light if it appears at the tip of a hunting knife held by a hunter, in another light if it appears on the same knife held by an abused spouse. The spot of blood may take on entirely different associations if it appears on bedclothes following a wedding night.

As in the case of Dickey's "Cherrylog Road," the time of day and the time of year may also contribute significantly to the situation. In Dickey's poem, the heat of high noon in summer suggests the passionate heat of the coupling that took place between the speaker and Doris Holbrook and intensifies the sense of lustful excitement the poem conveys.

PLANNING IDEAS

- Bring in pictures or show slides of several very different settings. Spend a few minutes discussing each, asking students to determine the location, the time of day, and the season represented. Then ask them to choose a scene and write a couplet describing as much about the setting and situation as possible. Have volunteers share these with the class, and then discuss the variety of responses evoked by each scene.
- To convey the idea that setting and situation are often inextricably linked, ask students to describe in a paragraph a setting that they ordinarily associate with peacefulness and calm. After they have written the description, ask them to write another paragraph describing a sit-

uation in which they would no longer feel relaxed in that same place.
- If you use novels in your course, you might assign students to read Emily Brontë's *Wuthering Heights*, creating a teaching unit on situation and setting using Brontë's poetry and prose and some biographical detail about the moors on which she grew up (see "Suggestions for Writing" following the note on "The Night-Wind"). Hardy's *Return of the Native* and selections from his poetry would also work well.
- If you plan to teach Musgrave's "I Am Not a Conspiracy . . . ," you might show a brief clip from David Lean's 1946 film of *Great Expectations* (available on video)—the scene in which Pip, who has stolen food for the escaped convict, encounters a herd of cattle and imagines them looking accusingly at him. Pip's paranoia has amusing similarities to the speaker's in Musgrave's poem.

SITUATIONS

MARGARET ATWOOD

Siren Song

Much of the comedy, ingeniousness, and point of Atwood's poem will be lost on students who don't have a clear and rather vivid sense of traditional depictions of the Sirens and their wicked ways. For that reason, you might consider sharing some or all of the following information with your students, perhaps distributing a handout when you first assign the poem or having students themselves do a little research:

> The Seirenes were in form not unlike the Harpies, but without their loathsomeness and their powers of snatching their prey. Generally (but not in Homer) represented as birds with the heads of women, it is not at all impossible that they were originally soul-birds, with the usual dangerous power of the dead to draw others to them. But their method was to sing enchantingly to all who passed their island, inviting them to land; those who tried to do so, were wrecked on the rocks and drowned. Odysseus stopped the ears of his men with wax and had himself bound to the mast, giving strict orders to tie him faster if he tried to get loose. He thus heard the song, which filled him with intense desire to join the singers, and at the same time neither he nor his crew was harmed. (H. J. Rose, *A Handbook of Greek Mythology*, New York: Dutton, 1959, p. 245)

As the more colloquial contemporary usage of the term *sirens* suggests, however, the myth has been altered somewhat over time; students will probably think of sirens as physically beautiful and alluring women, and it's entirely in keeping with Atwood's poem, if not Homer's epic, that they should.

For Atwood's poem is obviously all about complicating our vision of the sirens by telling the story from their point of view rather than from that of the (male) hero who succumbs to, or eludes, them. And you might want to start the discussion by asking students at what point in the poem their own expectations were thwarted, how exactly the poem manages first to draw us in just as the sirens did sailors only to then turn our expectations on their heads, probably for almost everyone in lines 11–12. What's amazing and amazingly funny about the poem to me is that it nonetheless manages to do something very similar once again before the poem is done and, in the process, to make a very pointed commentary on the egotism of those taken in by the siren's song.

Because Atwood's "Siren Song" is such a wonderful rewriting of one portion of *The Odyssey*, you might consider saving it to read in conjunction with the other poems about Odysseus/Ulysses in the "Cultural Belief and Tradition" section of Chapter 23 or having students reread the poem at that point, discussing how its meaning is different on its own and in the context of these other poems.

QUESTIONS FOR DISCUSSION

1. Who or what were the sirens in classical mythology? How were they characterized? How is Atwood's depiction of the sirens and this mythological situation and setting like that in classical mythology?
2. At what point did the poem begin to upset the expectations you brought to the poem about situation, setting, and the character of the sirens? Why and how precisely were they upset? What do you think Atwood accomplishes by raising and then upsetting our expectations in this way?
3. What does the poem ultimately suggest about the reason why the sirens were so successful at luring sailors to their deaths? What new view does Atwood offer us here of the sirens and of the situation associated with them?
4. Why write or read a poem about sirens in the late twentieth century? Does Atwood manage to make sirens seem relevant? If so, how and why? How might this poem be about more than sirens and sailors? What might that "more" be?

ANDREW MARVELL

To His Coy Mistress

See "A Sample Analysis," p. 468. Note, too, that "To His Coy Mistress" is imitated in poems contained in Chapter 23 of the anthology.

MARY OLIVER

Singapore

QUESTIONS FOR DISCUSSION

1. How would you describe the situation and setting of "Singapore"? Might the poem in fact have two situations and settings? If so, how and why does the poet interrelate them?
2. How does the speaker in Oliver's poem define the traditional expectations for, or definitions of, poetry? What does she suggest we usually want a poem to be and do? What does she suggest about whether and how this poem does or does not fulfill those desires and expectations? Do her ideas about this change over the course of the poem? If so, why and how? What does she mean when she says that "this poem is filled with trees, and birds" (line 38)?
3. Why and how does the speaker's attitude toward, or conception of, the woman in the airport bathroom change over the course of the poem? How do you think she and/or the poem as a whole define "the light that can shine out of a life" (line 35)?
4. What's the significance of the fact that the poem (or part of the poem) is set in an airport? In Singapore? How do these two details of setting contribute to the meaning of the poem?

LOUISE GLÜCK

Labor Day

QUESTIONS FOR DISCUSSION

1. What do you imagine about the exact nature of the situation depicted in "Labor Day"? Of the relationship between the speaker and "Johnston-baby"? Do you think he's literally or only figuratively a "pimp" (line 11)? How might you read the poem as a whole differently in each case?
2. What's the significance of Glück's title? What do we typically associate with the phrase "Labor Day," and how does the poem invoke and play on those associations?
3. What's the significance or effect of the way the speaker omits the subject (presumably Johnston) from the first lines of the poem? Of the way the speaker is positioned as a direct and indirect object to or with whom things are done until she becomes an "I" in line 9?
4. What's the significance of the detailed description of the "Pastures"

in lines 10–11? What do you associate with the word *pasture,* and how might this poem invoke and play on such associations?

JOHN DONNE

The Sun Rising

QUESTIONS FOR DISCUSSION

1. How would you describe the situation and setting of the poem? Where and when is the poem set?
2. What other characters are described in the poem? How exactly is the sun characterized?
3. How would you describe the tone of the poem and/or the speaker's attitude toward the sun? Does this change over the course of the poem? If so, when and how?
4. What do you make of the many references to government and/or royalty in the poem? How exactly do these help Donne to characterize his love and to shape his "argument" with the sun?
5. How is Donne's characterization of love here like and unlike that within other love poems you've read, particularly in terms of his use of metaphor? (See, for example, Bradstreet's "To My Dear and Loving Husband," Levertov's "Love Poem," and Auden's "[As I walked out . . .]," as well as the notes to these poems.)

HART CRANE

Episode of Hands

QUESTIONS FOR DISCUSSION

1. What is the situation and setting of the poem? What do you imagine has happened just before this "Episode of Hands"?
2. How does the poem characterize the two characters it features? What do the descriptions of their hands tell us about each?
3. What's the significance or effect of the fact that the poet describes the thoughts of the "factory owner's son" (line 8) but not those of the wounded man?
4. What's the significance of the fact that the "knots and notches" on the wounded man's hand are compared to "the marks of wild ponies' play,— / Bunches of new green breaking a hard turf" (lines 16–19)? Do you think this simile represents the thought of the owner's son?

Why or why not? How might the image serve to characterize him as well as the hand itself?
5. What do you think the phrase "factory thoughts" refers to (line 20) and why and how do you think they are "banished" (line 21)? What do you make of the ending? What do you think has symbolically or figuratively happened over the course of the poem?

EMILY BRONTË

The Night-Wind

Setting and situation merge in this poem as the speaker imagines a part of the natural world, the wind, beckoning her outside into the night. The poem takes the form of a dialogue or discussion between the narrator/speaker and the wind. Although the speaker asks to be left alone, the poet gives the wind the last word; and the speaker, for all her protest, seems complicit in her own seduction. Students who have learned something about Brontë's love of the outdoors may note the special care with which the dialogue is crafted to suggest how compelling she finds the countryside at night.

QUESTIONS FOR DISCUSSION

1. What is the speaker's relationship with nature? Where do you find evidence about this relationship?
2. "The Night-Wind" ends inconclusively with the wind still making its appeal. Do you think the wind succeeds in tempting the speaker out into the dark night? Explain your answer.

SUGGESTION FOR WRITING

Research the setting in which Brontë grew up and skim entries from Brontë's journals for references to Haworth and the moors. Write an essay exploring her relationship to the landscape surrounding her home.

TIMES

WILLIAM SHAKESPEARE

[*Full many a glorious morning have I seen*]

QUESTIONS FOR DISCUSSION

1. This sonnet takes several turns marked by the words "Anon," "Even so," "But," and "Yet." In this sense, the poem itself imitates what it describes—clouds passing in front of the sun and blocking its light, then moving by and letting the light shine again. How is this inconsistency accentuated by the poet's choice of words such as "Flatter," "Gilding," and "mask'd"? By the reference to alchemy?
2. What is the importance of the final distinction between "Suns of the world" and "heaven's sun"?

JOHN DONNE

The Good-Morrow

QUESTIONS FOR DISCUSSION

1. This is a poem about waking and discovery. How many different kinds of discoveries does the speaker describe? What is the parallel between exploration of "new worlds" and the way the speaker feels about his new love?
2. What does the speaker mean by "got" in line 7? What does he mean by "possess" in line 14?
3. What might the fear in line 9 refer to?
4. What is the ideal of love expressed in the poem? To what is it contrasted?

SYLVIA PLATH

Morning Song

Morning in this poem has both a metaphorical and a literal meaning. A child is born and thus enters the morning of its life. Mornings have changed for the mother who must rise to care for her crying child. How does the birth of the child fit into the mother's conception of nature? Of her own life? Why doesn't she feel responsible for the birth of the child (lines 7–9)?

A Description of the Morning

Unlike the last three morning poems, this poem is not concerned with private feelings but with creating a sense of place. Although the poem is called "A Description of the Morning," it describes only people, not nature. What do the brief descriptions of morning routines tell us about the individual people? The neighborhood?

Meridian

QUESTIONS FOR DISCUSSION

1. How does the speaker characterize our view of the world at "First daylight" (line 1) in the first stanza of the poem? What does the image of "the hired man's shadow" contribute to that characterization (line 5)? What's the effect of the fact that the speaker depicts a morning in "high summer" (line 2)?
2. How does the speaker characterize our view of the world at "noon" in the second stanza of the poem? How does each image contribute to that characterization? How specifically does noon differ from "First daylight"?
3. How is our sense of the conflict between these two views of the world affected by the way the stanzas run together? In hindsight, is there any hint in the first stanza of the conflict to come?
4. How does the speaker's characterization of "thunderheads" in the third stanza contribute to our sense of the conflict in the poem? What's the significance or effect of the way the last line is split in two?

As I Walked Out One Evening

This poem is in many ways perfect for exemplifying the notion that poems, like fictional texts, often represent a conflict between two different worldviews, and it's also a perfect text for showing how form can operate as part of the thematization of conflict.

The poem ultimately presents two contrasting views of the relation between love and the confines of time and space. Stanzas two through five embody the first and in some ways most traditional view. The words of the lover's song insist that "[l]ove has no ending" (line 8), that love is bigger, more powerful, and longer lasting than even "the ocean" and "the seven stars" (line 13, 15), that it knows no geographical boundaries (like those that separate China and Africa [line 10]), and that it will last until all of the world's rules are overturned (when "salmon sing in the street" [line 12]). As a result, the poem enacts the traditional view of love espoused in classic love poems such as Donne's "The Sun Rising," a point reinforced by Auden's use of the traditional ballad stanza.

Stanzas six through fourteen, however, represent the opposing or contrary view, which is put into the mouth of "the clocks in the city" (line 21). Here Time is personified as someone who "will have his fancy" (line 31), triumphing over all sooner or later ("To-morrow or to-day" [line 32]). You might want to ask students to think and talk about exactly how Auden characterizes Time and its effects, especially in terms of the emphasis on the slowness and even comic aspects of Time's "triumph." How does Auden's characterization of time differ from what we might expect?

You probably want to draw attention, too, to the way that the tone and emphasis of the poem changes in stanza ten, even as the voice remains that of the clocks. How exactly does the tone and emphasis change? What are the clocks telling the reader to do? Do their words represent a possible resolution to the conflict between the two views of time represented in the poem? Or are their imperatives still simply a part of their "slanted" view of the issue?

One way to answer the latter question is to look at the first and last stanza of the poem, which essentially set up a kind of "frame narrative" for the conflict between the views of the lover and the clocks. How does the first stanza serve to set the scene for the conflict by, for example, referring to the people on the street as "fields of harvest wheat" (line 4)? Does this image of people as wheat ready for harvest suggest that the poem as a whole is on the side of the clocks, as it were? How does the last stanza—particularly its emphasis on the disappearance of the lovers, the silencing of the clocks, and the running of the river—comment on the conflict? In what ways does this last stanza underscore and/or undermine the view of the clocks? What's the significance of the fact that the poem is set in the "evening"? In a city street rather than, say, a field of wheat?

QUESTIONS FOR DISCUSSION

1. How is love characterized in the lover's song described in stanzas two through five of the poem? What is the lover's argument about the

character and power of love? How is this argument like those expressed in other love poems you've read?

2. How is that argument countered by the whirring and chiming of the clocks described in stanzas six through twelve? What happens in stanza thirteen? How does the clocks' song change here?

3. Which of these two views or arguments do you think the poem as a whole embraces? Or is there another possibility?

4. How does the frame narrative contribute to the articulation and/or resolution of this conflict?

5. What's the significance or effect of the fact that the poem is set in the evening? In the city?

SUGGESTIONS FOR WRITING

1. Writing an essay comparing Donne's "The Sun Rising" and Auden's "As I Walked Out One Evening" in terms of both the way each poet represents the relationship between time and love and the way the settings of the two poems contribute to these representations.

2. Write an essay comparing Auden's and Volkman's characterizations of evening in the poems "As I Walked Out One Evening" and "Evening." What's similar and different about the way evening is characterized in each poem? What might this time of day symbolize in each poem and/or what issues does each poet raise through his or her depiction of evening?

WILLIAM SHAKESPEARE

Spring

"Spring" is one of two poems (the other is "Winter," in "Reading More Poetry") that close *Love's Labour's Lost*, one half of "the dialogue . . . in praise of the owl and the cuckoo" (V.ii). By invoking (if not really "praising"), the cuckoo and the cuckoldry it traditionally symbolized, the poem both builds on and complicates our notion of spring by poking fun at the potential negative side effects of the budding sensuality associated with the season. And various appeals to the senses are a key part of the poem, which moves from descriptions of the vivid colors of the season to the sounds and from flora to the fauna whose behavior becomes the real subject of the poem.

If your students are anything like mine, however, they may have no clear sense of why and how exactly the cuckoo's song "Mocks married men" (lines 6, 15), so you may have to help them understand the symbolism of the cuckoo, which is associated with spring because it is (like the robin) a migratory bird that returns to England in the spring and with cuckoldry because it lays its eggs in the nests of other birds, leaving its young to be raised by these unwitting foster parents. Thus the chief "fear" of a cuckold is presumably that he will be unwittingly saddled with another man's child, and spring may evoke such fears because we associate the season not only with "treading" itself but also with birth.

SUGGESTION FOR WRITING

Read *Love's Labour's Lost*, the play of which "Spring" is a part. Write an essay comparing the different ways the poem works or means on its own and in the context of Shakespeare's comedy.

ARCHIBALD LAMPMAN

In November

QUESTIONS FOR DISCUSSION

1. What is the tone of the poem and how do specific images contribute to it? What, for example, is suggested by the speaker's description of the fields as "sowed softly through with snow" (line 6)?
2. What qualities and activities do we tend to associate with the month of November? With evening? How exactly does Lampman's poem reinforce and build on those associations?
3. What does the speaker convey about himself in the poem? Is his self-characterization in any way ambiguous or contradictory? If so, how so?
4. Might the poem be about a particular time in life as well as a particular time of year and day? If so, how so?

PLACES

APRIL BERNARD

Praise Psalm of the City-Dweller

QUESTIONS FOR DISCUSSION

1. A psalm is a song used in worship, and we are probably most familiar with psalms from the Bible, such as Psalm 23 (included in the anthology). What expectations about this poem are created by Bernard's use

of the word *psalm* in the title? To what extent does the poem fulfill those expectations and to what extent does it defy or re-route those expectations? How does the poem's situation and setting, in particular, differ from those of a traditional psalm? In what sense is the poem a song of praise or worship? What is being praised or worshipped here?

2. How might the poem also play on our traditional conceptions of "the city" and of "the city-dweller"?

SUGGESTION FOR WRITING

Using Psalm 23 as an example of a traditional psalm, write an essay analyzing the similarities and differences between Bernard's "Praise Psalm of the City-Dweller" and traditional psalms. What precisely does Bernard accomplish by using the psalm form in this new way?

ANTHONY HECHT

A Hill

QUESTIONS FOR DISCUSSION

1. What do you think the speaker means when he says that Italy is a place "where this sort of thing can occur" (line 1)? When he tells us all the things his vision was not? What's the significance or effect of the poem opening in this way? How exactly does it set the stage for the rest of the poem? What does it suggest to us about the speaker? What expectations or attitudes might it encourage us to adopt about or toward what follows?

2. What emotions and qualities does the speaker associate with Italy? How exactly is Italy in general and the piazza in particular characterized here? What emotions and qualities does the speaker associate with "the hill" in his vision? How exactly is this setting characterized? How do the two scenes or settings interrelate? Why and how does the poem render these two scenes part of a single moment, experience, and poem?

3. What do you make of the last stanza? Why and how exactly is the speaker "scared" by his vision (line 35)? What's the significance or effect of the revelation that "All this happened about ten years ago" (line 36)? That the speaker has just "remembered that hill" (line 38)?

4. What does the poem ultimately seem to suggest or ask about memory and/or about the relationship between past and present? About the relationship between the two scenes or settings the poem describes?

SUSAN MUSGRAVE

I Am Not a Conspiracy . . .

The speaker in Musgrave's humorous poem appears to be a poet who is undergoing an "image makeover" at the hands of someone named Paul, a photographer with whom she may or may not have an intimate relationship. Whatever her relation to Paul, it is clear that the speaker is uncomfortable to the point of hysteria with the new image Paul has in mind for her—understandably, since it involves her being photographed standing naked in high heels in a cornfield! Her discomfort with Paul's vision of her is evident when she says, "What Paul sees is something different from / me."

I like to ask my students to find where evidence of the speaker's hysteria first appears and to talk about the meaning of lines 5 and 6. There may be disagreement about the significance of the references to the corn god whispering about whiskey and cocaine (lines 14 and 15). Perhaps whiskey and cocaine seem appropriate accoutrements for the wild, new image Paul wants the speaker to project. Perhaps the speaker is tempted to escape from her discomfort with the new image through alcohol or drugs. Perhaps the speaker actually uses drugs recreationally and, under the strain of the "makeover," becomes paranoid about the chance that she will get caught.

There is likely to be more agreement about another aspect of the speaker's situation—her discomfort at being naked under these circumstances. I like to ask students where in the poem they find evidence of this discomfort. Generally they are quick to note, in line 29, the echo of the word "shuddering" from line 13 and to make the connection between her horror at the notion of purses being made from the skins of unborn calves and her horror at standing before a camera naked in a cornfield.

Paul is trying to make the speaker into a salable image, into a consumer product. The last verse of the poem suggests the degree to which his effort causes the speaker to feel disassociated from herself. In her paranoid fantasy, her very work, one source of her identity, becomes suspect.

QUESTIONS FOR DISCUSSION

1. Why does the speaker imagine the cows interrogating her? What state(s) of mind does this fantasy suggest?
2. Why might the speaker associate her poems with illegal drugs?
3. Is this a poem about image making and advertising, or a poem about men's and women's roles, or a poem about the nature of poetry, or all of these?

THOMAS GRAY

Elegy Written in a Country Churchyard

In addition to affording a chance to introduce the word *lugubrious* into students' vocabularies, this poem lends itself to a discussion of the relation between sound and sense. From the long vowels of the first quatrain to the strategy of delayed negation in the fifth and the sixteenth (we are given images of vitality before we learn that "No more" can the inhabitants of the churchyard partake in them, that "Their lot forbade" fame and glory), the poet impresses on the reader a profound sense of loss, of unfulfilled potential (lines 20, 65). The speaker's tone is understandably sorrowful as he contemplates the departed villagers' common lot.

QUESTIONS FOR DISCUSSION

1. What might be the message of the "uncouth rhymes" and the scriptural passages mentioned in lines 79 and 83?
2. Some say the poem would be better unified and more effective if it ended after line 92. Do you agree?
3. Who is the "thee" of line 93? Why does the poet employ this strategy?

COMPARING PLACES AND TIMES: THE SENSE OF CULTURAL OTHERNESS

AGHA SHAHID ALI

Postcard from Kashmir

Ali's "Postcard" wonderfully captures the ironies involved in our idealizations of the past and of home. Moving seamlessly from present ("Kashmir shrinks into my mailbox" [line 1], to past ("I always loved neatness" [line 3], to future ("When I return" [line 6]), the poem dramatizes those familiar moments when all of the moments of our lives seem to come together, even as it also dramatizes just how irrecoverable are moments and places from our past. For, as the speaker recognizes in lines 5 and 6, this postcard is "the closest / I'll ever be to home"; despite the fact that he imagines "return[ing]" to Kashmir in the very next line, the speaker recognizes that this real place can never match the picture of "home" captured on the postcard and in his own nostalgic memories: "the colors won't be so brilliant, the Jhelum's waters so clean, so ultramarine" (lines 7–9). At the same time, the descriptions of how the postcard "shrinks" Kashmir into a single, "neat," "half-inch" image suggests the way in which nostalgia and memory, like photography, ironically simplify and reduce, even as they also idealize and magnify, reality (lines 1, 2, 4). For that reason, the language of photography provides the speaker with apt metaphors for this process, and I usually conclude discussion by asking students to unpack those metaphors, to ponder why, in the future, the speakers "love" won't be "so overexposed" (line 10)? What he means when he says his memory will be "a little out of focus," "undeveloped" like a "giant" "black and white" "negative" (lines 11–14)?

QUESTIONS FOR DISCUSSION

1. What's the significance or effect of the speaker's use of words such as *shrinks* and *neat* to describe the representation of Kashmir on the post-card (lines 1, 2)? Of the precise details about how many inches long and wide it is? Of the fact that Kashmir itself rather than the postcard is the subject of this first sentence of the poem?
2. If, as the speaker imagines in line 6, he will one day "return" to Kash-mir, then why and how exactly is the postcard "the closest [he]'ll ever be to home" (lines 5–6)?
3. What does the poet mean when he says his memory will be "a little out of focus," "undeveloped" like a "giant" "black and white" "nega-tive"? What does the poet say about himself and his relationship to his "home" through the use of these photography-related images?
4. How would you describe the conflict experienced by the speaker in this poem? What does the poem ultimately seem to say or ask about memory, home, etc.? How specifically is this poem about the partic-ular situation of immigrants? About the the situation of anyone who has left home. About relationships between East and West?

CATHY SONG

Heaven

Because this poem moves so seamlessly between present and past, it may be best to begin by having students talk about what's literally going on in the poem, establishing who the main characters are and where and when they are. The poem begins in the present, with the speaker con-trasting her son's vision of "a Chinese heaven" with their life "on the pancake plains / just east of the Rockies" (lines 2, 16–17). The past is first introduced at the end of stanza two, with the speaker's question about the "dream" of the "boy in Guangzhou" who was her grandfather (line

24), and it is to him that the speaker turns in stanza four, before returning to the present in the last stanza. The history of the family gleaned from the poem thus begins in the nineteenth century, when the speaker's grandfather came to the United States from China to work on the railway, and concludes in the twentieth century, with the speaker herself partnered with a Caucasian man with "blond hair" and now living with her two children (line 3), a son ("the dreamer" [line 33]) and a daughter "who is too young to walk" (line 34), in the American Midwest.

After establishing those facts and that narrative, however, one can then ask students how our vision of the family and its history is affected by the fact that the poem moves back and forth between past and present rather than straightforwardly from past to present as does the narrative we've just constructed. What kind of relationship between past and present is implied by our linear narrative and what kind of relationship is implied by the back-and-forth movement of the poem? One answer may be that whereas a linear narrative implies that the movement from past to present and, in this case, from China to the United States is straightforward, direct, and logical, one in which there is no "go[ing] back" (line 42), Song's back-and-forth narrative implies a more complex and confused relationship between past and present and between China and the United States, one in which the past and China continue to be a part of life in the present and in the United States and in which the relationship between events, decisions, and moments isn't at all clear or logical. It is possible, after all, to see the speaker and her own parents as having adopted the linear notion of history, these "two generations" burying the past in an "unmarked grave" (lines 52–53), letting it "lay fallow" (line 52), seeing "each mile of track" as leading one "further away" from the past and from their Chinese heritage (line 44). Her son's dream of "a Chinese heaven" (line 2), however, forces the speaker to see the past, her grandfather, and her Chinese heritage as alive and significant, even as it also forces her to confront the senselessness of her own and all history, the way in which acts and intentions and/or dreams differ: though she is "here," in part because this was her grandfather's "last stop" (line 25), her grandfather "always meant to go back" (line 42), never "dream[ed] of this / as his last stop" (lines 24–25).

QUESTIONS FOR DISCUSSION

1. What exactly is the speaker's current situation? What sense of the speaker's family history can you glean from the poem? How would you tell the story of this family?
2. What's the significance or effect of the fact that the poem itself doesn't tell this story straightforwardly but moves back and forth between past and present, between various times and characters?
3. In what sense might the son's dream of a Chinese heaven create a conflict for the speaker, and how would you describe that conflict?

Might different characters in this poem—the speaker, her son, her parents, and her grandfather—represent different worldviews? If so, how would you characterize them and how or why might they be in conflict? Is the conflict resolved in the poem? If so, how so?

MARILYN CHIN

We Are Americans Now, We Live in the Tundra

QUESTIONS FOR DISCUSSION

1. How is China characterized in the poem? How do particular images— the comparison of China to "a giant begonia" (line 2), the references to "Bengal tigers" and "giant Pandas" (line 8), "Bamboo, sassafras, coconut palms" (line 14), "Hirsute Taoists, failed scholars" (line 20)— contribute to that characterization? What about the reference to extinction and impotence (lines 7, 11)?
2. How is the United States characterized in the poem? What does the speaker mean when she speaks of "the tundra / Of the logical, a sea of cities, a wood of cars" (lines 17–18)? What's the significance or effect of her use of natural metaphors (tundra, sea, wood) to describe things that aren't natural (cities, cars)?
3. What do you make of the end of the poem? What do the wetnurse and her comments contribute to the depiction of the conflict between life in China and in the United States?

CHITRA BANERJEE DIVAKARUNI

Indian Movie, New Jersey

"Indian Movie" contrasts the safe homeliness of the world experienced by Indians inside an Indian movie theater and the threatening, everyday world outside. Inside, as the speaker says, "It is safe" and "cool" (lines 11–12); everyone is part of a single unified "we" who "know the words already" and can "sing along" together (lines 9–10). Outside, there is disunity and discord both within the immigrant community—in the shape of "sons / who want mohawks and refuse to run / the family store, [and] daughters who date / on the sly" (lines 21–24)—and between the immigrants and the rest of the community, as is made abundantly clear through references to "motel raids, canceled permits, stones / thrown through glass windows, daughters and son / raped by Dotbusters" (lines 34–36). The fact that the safe environment is a movie theater renders the poem distinctly ironic, since it is inarguably movies that teach us the "movie truths" about America that so seldom prove true (line 50), that create the image of "the America that was supposed to be" (line 51), the America in which "sacrifice," "love and luck" are supposed to mean "success" (line 50).

QUESTIONS FOR DISCUSSION

1. How is the world within the Indian movie theater characterized in the poem? How and why exactly is it "safe here" (line 11)? How is the world outside the theater characterized? How and why is it not safe?
2. What is the significance of the movie theater setting?
3. What do you think the poem ultimately asks or says about the "movie truths" referred to in the final lines?

SUGGESTION FOR WRITING

Write an essay comparing two of the poems in this section. What does each poem ask or say about the relationship between past and present, the nature and meanings of home, the nature of life in America, or the sense of cultural otherness? What's alike and different about the poems' treatment of this subject or issue? How does the particular situation and setting of each poem contribute to its vision of the issue?

READING/WRITING IDEAS FOR CHAPTER 15

ESSAYS ABOUT SITUATION AND SETTING

Though attention to situation and setting are obviously crucial to effectively reading and writing about poetry, I find that it's both rare and difficult for students to write effective essays that focus solely on the situation and setting of a single poem. The exceptions to this rule, however, are essays focusing on poems, such as Hecht's "A Hill" and Song's "Heaven," that themselves hinge on the comparison of two different situations/settings.

In general, however, essay assignments that ask students to compare multiple poems that focus on similar situations and/or settings are more workable than those focusing on the situation and setting of a particular poem. If you want to go this route, you might, for example, ask students to

• compare the way morning is described and exploited for poetic effect in two or more of the following poems: Shakespeare's "[Full many a glorious morning . . .]," Donne's "The Sun Rising" and "The Good-Morrow," Plath's "Morning Song," Swift's "A Description of the Morning," Oliver's "Morning," Mora's "Sonrisas," Rosenberg's "Break of Day in the Trenches," and Stevens's "Sunday Morning";

- compare the way a particular season is described and exploited for poetic effect in two or more of the following poems: Shakespeare's "[Shall I compare thee to a summer's day?]," "Spring," and "[That time of year . . .]," Hayden's "Those Winter Sundays," Lampman's "In November" and "Winter Evening," Oliver's "Roses, Late Summer," Hopkins's "Spring and Fall," Keats's "To Autumn," and Parker's "Indian Summer";
- compare the way in which a particular place is exploited as a setting by different poets, such as airports in Oliver's "Singapore" and Winters's "At the San Francisco Airport" or beaches in Plath's "Point Shirley" and Arnold's "Dover Beach," etc.;
- compare two poems that look at a similar situation from different angles. Obvious candidates for such treatment are poems that deal with exactly the same situation, such as Atwood's "Siren's Song" and the relevant sections of *The Odyssey* or the poems in the "Imitating and Answering" and "Cultural Belief and Tradition" sections of Chapter 23 (if you don't mind students' skipping ahead). But less obvious and equally workable are poems such as Pastan's "To a Daughter Leaving Home" and Winters's "At the San Francisco Airport," both of which deal with the situation indicated by the very title of Pastan's poem.

TROUBLESHOOTING

Almost all of these assignments essentially demand that students consider the symbolic resonance of particular situations and settings: to compare the way in which spring functions in Shakespeare's "Spring" and Hopkins's "Spring and Fall," for example, almost necessarily entails considering both the traditional symbolic meanings of *spring* and the way each particular poem exploits and/or revises those traditional meanings. As a result, you may want to save these assignments until after you've done the section of Chapter 16 that deals explicitly with symbolism. Since students are rarely utterly unfamiliar with the concept of symbolism, however, and since it's also possible to get at the same issues in different terms if necessary, the assignments can—with effort—work quite well even if the class hasn't yet explicitly tackled "the symbol."

Part of that effort, for me, entails wording the assignment so that it includes questions that point students toward these more thematic or symbolic considerations, precisely as does the second writing exercise that follows the note to Auden's "As I Walked Out One Evening." And I also find the following exercise helpful in this regard.

SITUATION- AND SETTING-FOCUSED WRITING EXERCISES

Identifying Differences and Similarities in Situations and Settings

Whether students are comparing situations and settings within or across poems, I find that it's useful to get them started by having them do an exercise that requires them to tackle a series of questions to generate ideas about similarities and differences. Obviously, those questions will look different, depending on exactly which assignment you're having them tackle; but here are two sample wordings of the exercise, one pertaining to the single-text assignment (on Hecht's "A Hill") and one to a comparative assignment (Auden's "As I Walked Out . . ." and Volkman's "Evening").

Read over Hecht's poem carefully with the following questions in mind. As you do so, work not only to generate answers to the questions but also to take note of details in the poem that support those answers.

- What emotions and qualities does the speaker associate with Italy? How exactly is Italy in general and the piazza in particular characterized?
- What emotions and qualities does the speaker associate with the hill? How exactly is this setting characterized?
- What are the speaker's attitudes toward each setting? What do each of these settings seem to signify or symbolize to the speaker (and/or to tell us about the speaker)?
- In what way do the depictions of the two settings here depend or draw or play upon your preconceptions, as a reader, of Italy? Of winter? Etc.
- What relationship do the two settings have to each other within the poem? Why and how are both settings part of a single experience and/or poem? Might they, for example, together symbolize or create some kind of conflict within the speaker? If so, what might that conflict be? Is the conflict resolved within the poem? If so, how so?

Carefully read over Auden's and Volkman's poems with the following questions in mind. As you do so, work not only to generate answers to the questions but also to take note of details in the poem that support those answers.

- What qualities or characteristics are associated with evening in these two poems?
- What attitude does the speaker of each poem adopt toward evening and/or what effect does he or she suggest evening has on him or her?
- What qualities or meanings do we typically associate with evening? How does each of these poems draw on those associations? Does it reinforce them? Revise them in some way?
- How would you describe the theme of each poem? What role does the setting play in the articulation of the theme? How are the themes alike? Different?

16

LANGUAGE

If in earlier classes you have been emphasizing—from time to time, at least—the significance of individual words, shifting the focus to language in this section will be natural and easy for the class. In my own classes, I usually teach the poems at the end of this chapter by asking the students to isolate some key words in the poems, and we discuss each of these in detail—for precision of word choice, for the connotations of each word, for the multiple suggestions (or "ambiguities") that some words usefully provide, for allusions to other literature or traditional ideas, for references to specific facts and events, and for the placement of the word in relation to the larger emphases of the poem. Written exercises can be especially useful in this group; they can be focused on a single word in a poem or on a group of related word choices.

PLANNING IDEAS

- Before class, give students a series of sentences to complete by supplying an extended simile. Encourage them to use their imaginations and to employ vivid language. (Sample sentences: My first date was like ____; When I get angry, I am as ____ as a ____; The building this class meets in is like ____.) Ask them to share these in class.
- Ask each student to come up with a word to describe how one might enter a room (*dash, saunter, sneak,* etc.); then discuss the connotations of the words supplied. What is suggested about a character if she is portrayed "skipping" into a room? "Racing"? "Slinking"?
- Bring to class several small objects, and pass a different object down each row of desks. Have the students in each row list as many possible symbolic associations for their object as they can. (Good objects include keys, light bulbs or candles, a single flower, an apple, a white piece of cloth, an object bearing the school insignia.) Have students share their lists with the class. Then focus on one of the objects and

discuss how it might be used in a poem as a personal symbol, suggesting a concept (or concepts) with which the object is not usually associated.

PRECISION AND AMBIGUITY

SHARON OLDS

Sex without Love

Students tend to fall roughly into two camps in their responses to this poem. One group views the speaker's portrayal of those who have sex without love as sneakily judgmental but accepts that, in some cases, her judgment might be correct. The other finds in the speaker's metaphors evidence of a shrillness, almost a hysteria, that suggests the speaker's approach to sexuality may be considerably more skewed than that of those who have sex without love. It seems to me that both views can be supported, and since the commentary and questions in the text tend to bolster the latter interpretation, I offer here some notes exploring the former.

Students quickly recognize that the metaphors and images the speaker uses to describe those who have sex without love become increasingly disturbing as she piles them one on one. The graceful image of dancers gives way to the chilly reference to ice skaters and ice, which gives way to a grossly physical description of lovers "fingers hooked / inside each other's bodies, faces / red as steak, wine" (lines 4–6). Sometimes a student will note that the traditional elements of a romantic dinner (for nonvegetarians, at least) here become the basis of a distinctly unromantic and off-putting picture, one that concludes with a simile involving mothers who plan to give their children away. Students who believe that the speaker is unbalanced will point to this harsh and shocking comparison as evidence. Those who believe the speaker is making a valid point will sometimes interpret the metaphor as implying the unnaturalness and sterility of sex without love.

Some students will be reluctant to discuss lines 8–16, where the speaker develops her ideas using religious imagery—but in an unexpected way—suggesting through repetition and spacing (lines 8 and 9) the experience of sexual climax. If you have the nerve, and a little dramatic talent, this is a good passage to read aloud, even though it sometimes provokes embarrassed laughter. Some students have no trouble understanding the speaker's use of "God," "Messiah," and "priest" as metaphors. Others will be so conditioned to respond to these words in specific ways that they will need some nudging to recognize that the "God" for those who have sex without love is pleasure or orgasm (according to the speaker), and the "false Messiah" or "priest," who is not to be mistaken for the god, is the sexual partner.

Usually the extended runner/athlete metaphor developed in lines 18–24 of the poem is more easily decipherable, although there may be some controversy about whether the last three lines actually delineate a "truth" for the person who embraces sex without love or for the speaker of the poem.

QUESTIONS FOR DISCUSSION

1. What do you make of the phrase "light / rising slowly as steam off their joined / skin"? Why does the speaker include this description? In what way does it contribute to the comparisons developed in the middle section of the poem?
2. What is the ambiguity in the phrase "its own best time"? How do the dual meanings of the phrase enrich the poem?

GERARD MANLEY HOPKINS

Pied Beauty

This poem is a celebration of beauty, but of imperfect beauty. Rather than searching for wholeness or perfection, Hopkins calls attention to those things in nature and in the human world that are unusual and unexpected. More than likely, students will need considerable help with the vocabulary of this poem. It may be well to guide them through a line-by-line paraphrase, giving special attention to the words Hopkins coins and the archaic words he resurrects. This is also a superb poem to study when you deal with sound effects.

QUESTIONS FOR DISCUSSION

1. How does the poem itself fit the speaker's description of something "counter, original, spare, strange"? How do alliteration, assonance, and word choice make this into a strange and surprising poem?
2. What is the effect of the final "Praise him"? Does the poem lead you to expect such an ending?

The Red Wheelbarrow

This is one of the most admired short poems of the twentieth century, and much of its force derives from its careful and precise choice of words and the way those words are deftly set into place. Your students may appreciate its art more fully if you ask them to try to rewrite the poem, keeping exactly the same visual objects (wheelbarrow, rainwater, and chickens) but presenting them differently. You can either set specific rules (change the opening phrase; keep the objects in the same order, etc.) or give them a free hand to try to create another poem with only the same basic materials.

QUESTIONS FOR DISCUSSION

1. What are the advantages of a visual scene?
2. What is the function of the first four words? Why does the poem begin with a vague term like "so much"?
3. Does the poem's major effect depend on an agreement between different readers on exactly what those words mean? Do the objects in the poem stand for anything? That is, are they "symbolic"?

E. E. CUMMINGS

[in Just-]

Cummings is famous for his unconventional manipulations of words and space on the page. I like to begin talking about this poem by asking students to explain the logic and effect of "eddieandbill" (line 6) and "bettyandisbel" (line 14). Then I ask them to explain the effect and force of "mud-luscious" (lines 2–3) and "puddle-wonderful" (line 10).

QUESTIONS FOR DISCUSSION

1. How does the interaction of the children and the old man relate to the tension between newness and tradition?
2. What are the implications of the allusion to Pan?

RITA DOVE
_____

Parsley

Dove's "Parsley" is a good poem to teach during any discussion of language precisely because the poem is all about the power of words. The
poem draws our attention to that power in a rather obvious way by focusing on an historical moment in which the life and death of thousands
depended on their pronunciation of a particular word—*perejil*, the Spanish word for "parsley." But it also does so in a less obvious way by presenting an almost exact reversal of the biblical story of creation. Being
"all the world there is" (lines 5–6), El General appears to those in the cane
fields very like the God of the Old Testament, yet this God's words bring
not life, but death, not creation, but destruction.

By dividing the poem into two parts—one representing the point of
view of the workers in the fields and the other that of the general in his
palace—Dove manages to render this incident all the more poignant by
juxtaposing the godlike power of the general and the sweeping effects of
his every word and action with the all too human reactions to a particular, personal situation that inspire those words and actions. As a result,
the poem also becomes bitterly ironic, suggesting that the general's callous destruction of thousands of people comes out of his mourning over
the death of one person.

Dove manages to make that juxtaposition all the more meaningful
through her own deft use of language, particularly the recurring words,
images, and metaphors that cut across, and connect, the two sections:
the cane that rises "out of the swamp" to be "cut down" as the workers
themselves will be in the first section and the walking cane that is buried
and then blooms in the second section; the teeth of the children, the
general, and the mother; and, of course, the parrot "imitating spring"
and the green parsley itself. Students who have learned through their
readings of the poems in the last chapter to be attentive to the poetic
uses and meanings of the seasons will also undoubtedly notice and want
to discuss the way in which Dove plays with those meanings throughout
this poem.

QUESTIONS FOR DISCUSSION

1. Taking both the footnote and the text of the poem itself into consideration, how would you narrate the events recorded in the poem?
   What exactly happens? What does the poem suggest about why it
   happens?
2. What's the significance or effect of the twofold division of the poem
   and the two points of view offered in each? How would you characterize the point of view of the first section? How would you charac-

terize the point of view of the second section? How do the two sections work together? What does each section contribute to the poem?

3. What recurring words and images can you identify here? How do those images and/or their meaning or significance change over the course of the poem?

4. What might this poem say or ask about language? How does the poet's own use of language contribute to the poem's messages about language?

SUGGESTION FOR WRITING

Write an essay comparing Dove's "Parsley" to Li's "Persimmons" in terms of what each poem seems to say about the power of words and of pronunciation (the precise sounds of words when spoken). How does each poet's use of language in the poem contribute to that poem's messages about language?

SUSAN MUSGRAVE

Hidden Meaning

Musgrave's "Hidden Meaning" is, to use her own word, a "terribly" funny poem that poses some at least potentially serious and interesting questions about just what poetry is and just what poetry does for, and/or to, its readers. When I teach the poem, I ask students to go through it stanza by stanza, describing the view of poets and of poetry that seem to be offered in each, while also drawing their attention to how complex and even self-contradictory each of those views potentially is.

By associating poets with taxi drivers Musgrave creates comedy by calling attention, I think, to the way we tend to put both poets and poetry on a pedestal, seeing them as occupying a world or plane of existence very different from that occupied by cabbies. Yet a cab ride itself seems to become more fantastical when one imagines asking a taxi driver to take one to Costa Rica, as the speaker does in the first stanza. What, then, does this stanza suggest about how a poem is like a taxi ride? About what kind of taxi ride a poem is like? About how the relationship between poet and reader is akin to that between taxi driver and rider?

How is that vision of poetry, poet, and reader complicated by the reference to "a *real* poet" in the second stanza? In what sense is the poet/ taxi driver in the first stanza not "a *real* poet"? What does this stanza suggest about the difference between "real" poets/poetry and "fake" poets/poetry? About the exact character of each kind of poet/poetry? What's the significance or effect of the reference to the line from Robert Penn Warren here? In what sense is this question relevant to the rest of the poem?

What's the significance of the "snowy Saskatchewan" setting of the third stanza? How exactly does this image complicate the vision of poetry? What about the reference to the fact that "the poet has not made a dollar"? (Notice that money is key to the relationship between drivers and riders and, by extension, poets and poetry readers, but it hasn't been mentioned up until this point in the poem.) What might the poet mean when she says that "poetry / gets you nowhere faster than anything"? How might this statement complicate the comparison between poetry and taxi rides?

Who is the "one another" mentioned in the last stanza? Why might the discovery of "two poets frozen together" lend "the world" an altogether new "meaning" (lines 18–20)? What does the poem suggest about what that meaning is or might be?

QUESTIONS FOR DISCUSSION

1. What view of poets and of poetry is conveyed in each stanza of Musgrave's poem? How does each view/stanza build on and/or complicate the last? How would you describe the overall movement of the poem from beginning to end?
2. What meanings does the phrase "hidden meaning" take on in this poem (lines 20–21)?
3. What are the denotative and connotative meanings of the word *terrible*? Of *occasion*? What's the significance or effect of Musgrave's use of these words in the final line of the poem?
4. What is the significance or effect of the poet's use of imperative language or, in other words, of sentences that are commands ("imagine this")? How might this contribute to, or complicate, the vision of poets, of poetry, and of the relationship between poet and reader offered within the poem?

SUGGESTION FOR WRITING

Write a poem or an essay comparing poetry or poetry writing or poetry reading to some other thing or activity. What different views of poetry emerge when you explore that comparison from different angles as Musgrave does in "Hidden Meaning"?

EMILY DICKINSON

[*I dwell in Possibility*—]

Dickinson's "[I dwell in possibility—]" works well in this unit for many reasons, but one is the fact that the poem itself is, in some ways, an elaborate definition of the words *possibility* and *poetry* (the latter word, interestingly enough, is never mentioned in the poem). Dickinson here defines both terms through the explicit and implicit contrast to prose and through the extended metaphor comparing both poetry and prose to houses. For that reason, I often start discussion by writing *poetry/possibility* and *prose/?* on the board. Then I have students walk through the poem together stanza by stanza, listing on the board both the adjectives and nouns associated with poetry/possibility and the students' ideas about what each word suggests about the qualities of poetry/possibility and, by extension, of prose/?. By grouping the words/ideas list by stanzas, I can lead students to see, among other things, the way the poem moves from references to small, man-made things to more natural, grandiose, and ultimately supernatural ones; the way religious allusions first enter the poem through the words "Cedars," "Eye," "Everlasting," and "Sky" in the second stanza; the way the poem moves from images of openness and breadth to images of strength and durability before finally bringing these various paradoxical qualities together in the final image of "narrow Hands" "spreading wide" "To gather Paradise" (lines 11–12). Once we've finished with the list, I ask students to throw out ideas about the word that the poem suggests best defines prose (as possibility defines poetry). And, after we argue about that for a while, I always end discussion by having them return to the metaphor of the house itself, asking them why and how it works in the poem and, if they don't bring it up themselves, whether and how the poem builds on traditional associations between houses and bodies (as in "the eyes are windows to the soul," etc.).

QUESTIONS FOR DISCUSSION

1. What adjectives and nouns are associated with poetry and possibility in the poem? What do each of these words and/or images suggest about the character of poetry? Of prose?
2. How would you describe the movement of the words images in the poem? How do those in the second stanza relate to, and differ from, those in the first? How do those in the third stanza relate to, and differ from, those in the second?
3. If the poem suggests poetry is possibility, then what word does it suggest best describes prose?
4. What's the significance or effect of Dickinson's choice of a house as a metaphor for poetry? Why and how does the house work as a metaphor here?
5. What's the significance or effect of the fact that the word *poetry* never appears in the poem?
6. Like E. E. Cummings, Dickinson uses conventional syntax but substitutes unexpected words, giving the poem an element of surprise and ambiguity. How does the unconventional use of prepositions in this poem compare to that in other Dickinson poems you have read?

SUGGESTION FOR WRITING

Because it implicitly compares poetry to "dwelling in possibility," Dickinson's "[I dwell . . .]" might be said to be just as much about poetry as Musgrave's "Hidden Meaning" is. Write an essay comparing the two poems in terms of the views of poetry offered in each. Which view(s) seem most like, or compatible with, your own?

JOHN MILTON

from *Paradise Lost*

QUESTIONS FOR DISCUSSION

1. How does the poem generate the directional effect of lines 44–49? How much of the gravity portrayed depends on word order? How, exactly?
2. Compare the tone and pace in Wordsworth's "Tintern Abbey." What factors account for the very different tonal effects achieved in blank verse here?

METAPHOR AND SIMILE

Metaphor can be very hard to teach if one tries to teach individual metaphors in isolation. To many students, individual metaphors often seem mere decoration (sometimes, of course, they are) and therefore rather precious and effete. Good basic metaphors are, of course, more vigorous and functional than that, and I think it is best first to emphasize poems that depend on metaphor, usually a single extended metaphor or at least a series of related ones. "[That time of year thou mayst in me behold]" works well as an introduction because of its three closely related metaphors for aging and coming death. The first metaphor is expansive and rather general and doesn't give much of a sense of urgency; its focus on a whole season of the year makes the aging process seem long and drawn out. But the other two metaphors are progressively more limited in time, and they project an increasing sense of urgency, as if, by the twelfth line, death were imminent. Because the poem is so carefully structured on the basis of the metaphors (four lines being devoted to each), it is easy for the students to work out and discuss, and with a little prompting from you they will be able to see the progress of the metaphors and their relation to the tone of the poem. Another poem that seems to me to work especially well in a discussion of metaphor is "The Death of the Ball Turret Gunner," which has the advantage of being very short and based on a single metaphor. Its birth metaphor (or rather prebirth metaphor—the gunner is hunched into a fetal position), although not altogether easy to see at first, makes for an especially lively discussion because of the irony of its use in the context of death; the metaphor takes the discussion quickly to the center of the poem. Other poems in the group use equally crucial and interesting metaphors, and it is probably a good idea to offer at least some variety in your selection of poems to discuss in class—choosing some poems that use more submerged metaphors and some that use multiple metaphors, as well as those that work from one central one. It may be useful, too, to go back to some poems you have discussed earlier, looking at the function of particular metaphors in the poet's conception of an individual poem.

RANDALL JARRELL

The Death of the Ball Turret Gunner

The introduction to this section (above) suggests some aspects of the poem to emphasize. Here is another line of questioning: What have "sleep" (line 1), "dream" (line 3), and "nightmare" (line 4) to do with the basic action of the poem?

DOROTHY LIVESAY

Other

When teaching Livesay's "Other," I often have students read and discuss the poem together in class stanza by stanza precisely because of the way the poem's initial statement accretes meaning as the poem develops. On a first reading, many of my students tend to read the poem's initial statement that "Men prefer an island" in universal terms, taking "men" to refer to something like "humankind," and they also read the statement as more literal than metaphorical. All that changes, however, in the third stanza, which introduces gender into the poem and suggests that the earlier images of islands and roads can also be read as metaphors for the "woman" that "Men prefer" (line 9), a point underscored by the repetition of the initial line at the end of the first section. From here, the rest of the poem uses a variety of landscape images to create a vivid picture of the contrast between two ways of being and/or of loving another, one associated with men, the "Other" with a speaker that the poem implies is female. As a result, I find it useful at some point to have students characterize those two ways, making two lists of ideas on the board and walking through the poem to see how individual images contribute to and/or complicate those characterizations. (You might also or instead try making word lists of the type suggested in the discussion of "The Dacca Gauzes," below.)

QUESTIONS FOR DISCUSSION

1. Read the first stanza of Livesay's "Other" aloud. What does the poet convey about men in this stanza? Read the second stanza aloud. What does the poet convey about men in this stanza? How does it work together with the first? How are the images alike?
2. Read the third stanza aloud. What does the poet convey about men in this stanza? What is suggested by the comparison of the woman men prefer to "a shell / On a sheltering island" (lines 11–12)? How does this stanza alter your sense of what and whom the poem is about? How might this stanza encourage you to revise your sense of the first two stanzas and the images therein?
3. How and why does the speaker characterize herself in the next section of the poem? How exactly does she differ from the men whom she characterizes in the poem? From the woman men prefer? How would you characterize the two ways of being and/or of loving someone that are contrasted in the poem? How do each of the landscape images contribute to the poet's characterization of each?
4. What is the significance or effect of the repetition of the statement that "Men prefer an island"? How does the line's meaning shift over the course of the poem? What is the significance or effect of the fact that the poem ends with the same line it begins with (in a fashion that recalls the characterization of the island in line 2 of the poem)?
5. What do you make of the title?

HART CRANE

Forgetfulness

This highly suggestive poem is crafted almost entirely of similes and metaphors and appears to end with a paradox. I often start by asking students if they notice any difference between the comparisons drawn in the first stanza and the comparisons created in the second. If responses are slow in coming, I call attention to the words "song," "freed," "reconciled," and "unwearyingly" in the first stanza, which seem to have positive connotations, even to celebrate the liberating effects of forgetfulness. In the second stanza, the comparisons are more difficult to categorize. Is "rain at night" bad or good? Does it make one gloomy or lull one to sleep, for example? What are the connotations of comparing forgetfulness to "an old house in a forest"? Is the house peacefully secluded or woefully neglected? How is forgetfulness a "child"—in the sense that we associate a child with purity? With irresponsibility? The second stanza ends by suggesting that forgetfulness can have far-reaching effects for good or evil, an observation that helps resolve the seeming paradox of the final line. You might ask students when in their own lives forgetfulness has been a good thing and when a bad.

QUESTIONS FOR DISCUSSION

1. What do you make of the references to "white" in line 8? What connotations does the color white have, conventionally? Does the second mention of "white" in the line carry the same connotations as the first?
2. Explain how forgetfulness might "stun the sybil into prophecy." How might it "bury the Gods"?
3. What does the last line of the poem mean?

CAROLYN FORCHÉ

Taking Off My Clothes

I find that Forché's "Taking Off My Clothes" presents a good opportunity to bring the issue of tone back into my classes' discussions of poetic language because the poem's metaphors contribute a great deal to the poem's dramatic oscillation between anger and a kind of "quiet" softness (line 10), violence and sensuality. The anger and sense of violence comes through quite clearly in the first stanza of the poem, especially in the vivid description of shaving as "scrap[ing] off the hair" "with a knife" (lines 3–4), and, as a result, the stanza and the poem as a whole clearly play with our assumptions about what it means to "show" one's body to a lover or to prepare oneself for such an intimate encounter. The series of metaphors through which the speaker characterizes her various features in the following two stanzas—"chopped maples," "cooked" "beans," "Coal fields" on "torn-up hills," a cracked and aged "Ming bowl"—further that sense of odd and surprising juxtapositions not only because the vehicles are (with the exception of the Ming bowl) unexpected, untraditional, and potentially unlovely but also because each metaphor insists somehow on damage.

The poem works even better in class if read and discussed in conjunction with the more traditional love poems whose conventions this poem clearly plays with, especially poems (such as Constable's "[My lady's presence makes the roses red]" or Roethke's "I Knew a Woman") in which a male speaker uses metaphors to characterize his female beloved's body part by part. Also relevant here might be Shakespeare's "[My mistress's eyes . . .]," which highlights—by defying—such poetic traditions.

QUESTIONS FOR DISCUSSION

1. How does the poet's use of language in the first stanza set the tone of the poem? How and why precisely is that language unexpected?
2. How would you characterize the metaphors in the second and third stanzas? What does the speaker communicate about herself and/or about her attitude toward her own body and/or her lover through those metaphors? In what way are her metaphors surprising and/or untraditional?
3. What does the metaphorical reference to "a wall of a man" in line 12 suggest about the speaker's lover, her attitude toward him, and/or her relationship with him?
4. What might the speaker mean when she says that her lover only "think[s]" he "lived through destruction"? That he "can't explain this night, my face, your memory" (lines 14–15)?
5. What might the speaker mean when she says that "Your own hands are lying" (line 17)?
6. What's the significance or effect of the way the poem addresses the lover (and the reader) as "you" throughout the poem? Puts "you," the reader, in the position of the male lover?

SUGGESTION FOR WRITING

Write an essay comparing Forché's "Taking Off My Clothes" to a more conventional love poem such as Shakespeare's "[Shall I compare thee . . .]" or Clare's "Love's Emblem." Analyze the similarities and differences between the character and function of metaphors in the two poems.

EMILY DICKINSON

[*Wild Nights–Wild Nights!*]

This poem is by far my favorite Dickinson poem to teach, in large part because it is a great text for illustrating what I call "yes-and" rather than "either/or" interpretations. For while the poem ostensibly suggests that the speaker envisions her love as a kind of safe harbor or refuge from the storm outside, there is also a great deal of emphasis on the storm itself throughout the poem, suggesting that love is—in some ways—the very opposite of a safe harbor, instead being more like an adventure on storm-tossed emotional (and even sexual) high seas. For that reason, I tend to begin discussion with the kind of broad, thematic question that I usually save for late in our discussions of particular texts, asking students simply, "What does the poem, especially its sailing metaphors, suggest about the character of the speaker's feelings for her lover?," "To what exactly is she comparing her love?" Sometimes these questions immediately spark debate, some students avowing one interpretation, some another; in this case, my job initially is to help ensure that each side fully articulates and defends its argument with reference to the text. Often, however, the whole group pushes for one interpretation or the other because they either can't get beyond the orgiastic images conjured up by the phrase "wild nights" or can't accept that the reclusive Emily Dickinson could write such a sexually charged poem. In this case, my role becomes more that of devil's advocate, drawing students' attention to the abundant counterevidence in the poem. In either case, however, my ultimate task and goal is to lead students to see that both interpretations are valid and far from mutually exclusive, each equally crucial to the experience of the poem—after all, isn't love more than a little like this?

QUESTIONS FOR DISCUSSION

1. To what exactly does the speaker in this poem compare her love? How exactly is the speaker's love characterized through metaphor?
2. What are the different possible meanings or connotations of the phrases "Wild Nights should be / Our luxury" (lines 3–4)? "Done with the Compass— / Done with the Chart!" (lines 7–8)? What characterization of love emerges from each interpretation? How might these two characterizations or interpretations work together in the poem?
3. To what extent does the phrase "Rowing in Eden" constitute a kind of mixed metaphor (line 9)? Does the mixing of metaphors work here? If so, why and how?

AGHA SHAHID ALI

The Dacca Gauzes

At the risk of vivisecting this lovely poem, I sometimes begin discussion by asking students to help me list on the blackboard the words and phrases associated with the Dacca gauzes. We begin with the descriptive names: "woven air, running / water, evening dew" (lines 2–3) and add "dead art," "heirloom," and "lost." If no one brings it up, I mention that the grandmother's comment at the end of the poem reemphasizes the notion that touching Dacca gauze was like touching air—in her comparison, the wonderfully fresh, "dew-starched" air of an autumn morning.

Against these associations, we set a list of phrases referring to the actions of the British imperialists, who diverted the cotton once woven into Dacca gauze to England for use in English cotton mills. That list includes references to amputation and silencing and shares with our other list references to death and loss. Placing the lists side by side throws into sharp relief the contrast between the loveliness, softness, and delicacy of the fabric the Bengali weavers once made and the coarse muslin that remains as a legacy of British usurpation. If, as most historians now attest, the story of the amputations is apocryphal, it nevertheless serves its purpose in the poem. The amputation of the weavers' hands symbolizes the amputation of a form of indigenous artistic expression and the brutal and wanton destruction of a culture for economic gain. The Dacca gauzes—and the remnants of the old culture—remain alive only in the memories of the old, who will soon perish as well.

QUESTIONS FOR DISCUSSION

1. What do you make of the epigraph? What relationship does it have to the poem and its message?
2. Does it matter that the story of the amputations is not true? What is true about it? Why might the author have been taught this story in history class? Have you ever been taught something about your history that later proved not to be true?

SUGGESTION FOR WRITING

Do some library research on the history of British rule in what is now Bangladesh. Write an essay discussing the aspects of Bengali culture that were altered or lost when the British seized control. Did British rule have any positive effects?

JOHN DONNE

[Batter my heart, three-personed God . . .]

QUESTIONS FOR DISCUSSION

1. How is the God in this poem characterized? What position does the speaker want to occupy with respect to his God?
2. Do you find the sexual imagery shocking?

3. What is the impact of the paradoxes in the last three lines?
4. The poem suggests comparisons with different types of poems. Compare its language of conquest to Donne's "The Good-Morrow," its violence to Angelou's "Africa," and its religious fervor and structure to Hopkins's "God's Grandeur."

ANONYMOUS

The Twenty-third Psalm

The organization of Psalm 23, like other Hebrew psalms, depends not on meter or rhyme but on a structure of half-lines that repeat words, phrases, and cadences. This way of structuring a poem, called parallelism, is not common in poetry written in English (Walt Whitman's poetry is one exception). You may want to bring in some other psalms to read in class so that students can get a sense of how this structure works.

QUESTIONS FOR DISCUSSION

1. What is the effect of the repetition of such phrasing as "He maketh," "he leadeth," "he restoreth," "thou preparest," "thou anointest"?
2. How is this structure appropriate to the themes of protection, safety, and peace in the psalm?

SUGGESTION FOR WRITING

Contrast the God in Psalm 23 to the God in Donne's "[Batter my heart . . .]." The speaker in Donne's poem is driven by passionate desires, but the speaker in the psalm says that his God takes care of his needs: "I shall not want" (line 1). Contrast the forms of the two poems. How does the sonnet form make "[Batter my heart . . .]" seem more urgent and harsh?

SYMBOL

"Symbols 'ray out,' " a teacher of mine used to say while flamboyantly striking off long rays or arrows in chalk on the blackboard. What she meant by the statement was that symbols and their meanings are rarely simple equations of object and idea. Good symbols tend to be richly suggestive, to have multiple "rays" of meaning. You may need to press your students a bit to make them move beyond the easiest or most readily evident symbolic associations. Nine poems mentioning roses are included in this section (five in the Shorter Edition) and one, Burns's "A Red, Red Rose," is placed earlier in the chapter to help students explore the many ways that a single symbol can be used.

EDMUND WALLER

Song

Because of its antiquated diction and syntax and its rather confusing use of pronouns, Waller's "Song" is a good candidate for the kind of translation exercise suggested in "Reading/Writing Ideas for Poetry: Reading, Responding, Writing." Because it uses a symbol to make a seductive argument, the poem also works well when read and discussed in conjunction with poems such as Donne's "The Flea."

By literally asking the rose to be his messenger at the outset, Waller cleverly foregrounds the messenger-like role of all symbols and of the rose in particular (both in poetry and in everyday life). Here the symbolic messages are fairly conventional: "sweet and fair" (line 5), the rose symbolizes the beauty of the woman, yet—as the speaker insists—it is a beauty that must be seen to be appreciated and that must be appreciated now because, like all mortal things, the rose, the woman, and their beauty will inevitably die. Despite its conventionality, however, Waller's poem manages to surprise, especially—I think—with the directness of the command "Then die!" in line 16, which brings to the fore the surprisingly harsh and threatening tone of the whole poem.

JOHN GAY

[Virgins are like the fair flower in its lustre]

Like Waller's "Song," Gay's "[Virgins . . .]" brings to the fore the harsher aspects of the traditional symbolic equation between the rose and a beautiful woman. In this case, however, the threat is not death itself but the loss or death or virginity. What I often have to help students to see is how cleverly the poem makes that symbolic "argument" through the reference to Convent Garden, a place where women did sell both flowers and their own bodies. What I also like to point out, however, is that the poem thereby equates a woman's loss of virginity (by any means) with prostitution.

[Go not too near a House of Rose—]

QUESTIONS FOR DISCUSSION

1. How is a "House of Rose" like a "House of Possibility" in Dickinson's "[I Dwell in Possibility]"?
2. What is the relationship between the first and second stanzas?
3. What is "Joy's insuring quality?"

WILLIAM CARLOS WILLIAMS

Poem [The rose fades]

Whereas Dickinson celebrates the fragile, ephemeral quality of the rose in nature, Williams celebrates the representation of the rose in poetry because a poem preserves its splendor. What does the poet mean by "naturally"? What is the poem's attitude toward nature? Toward poetry?

MARY OLIVER

Roses, Late Summer

"Roses, Late Summer" is a wonderful poem to have students read and discuss in the context of the other rose poems here because of the way it uses the traditional association between roses and mortal transience to draw attention to the ways in which the very act of symbol making is, like the fixation on transience itself, part and parcel of the consciousness that distinguishes human beings from roses and animals. While roses, foxes, and tree branches can simply be and thereby enjoy "unstinting happiness" (line 28), human beings "reason" (line 34) and ask "foolish question[s]" (line 36) (like those that open the poem) about the nature and end of being and, as a result, experience "fear" and "ambition" (line 33) even in the midst of happiness.

Because "Roses, Late Summer" uses roses to symbolize the unconscious joy experienced by natural things much as Keats's "Ode to a Nightingale" uses the nightingale, the poems work well together; because Oliver's poem draws attention to the way in which symbol making operates as part of the consciousness that differentiates humans, it also works well in conjunction with another Romantic poem, Coleridge's "Frost at Midnight" (not included in the anthology).

DOROTHY PARKER

One Perfect Rose

The speaker is drawing on two romantic conventions—the rose as a symbol of love in poetry and the social custom of sending flowers to a woman. What does the speaker mean by "I know the language of the floweret"? How does she debunk both of these traditions in the poem?

QUESTIONS ON THE ROSE POEMS

1. In which poems is the figurative language used structurally, to build or unite a particular section or sections of the poem? When figurative language is used structurally, how is the transition made from one section to another? Which poems are based almost completely on one metaphor?
2. Which uses of figurative language in this group are purely ornamental? In what different ways does figurative language contribute to meaning? What other figures besides metaphor are illustrated in the group?
3. Make a list of the different things and/or qualities that roses are used to symbolize in these poems. What items on the list seem most surprising and/or unconventional? Why? Which poems strike you as most surprising and/or unconventional on the whole? Why? Which poems do you find the most compelling? Why? Are the most compelling poems also the most surprising? If so, how so? If not, then why and how exactly are poems that aren't surprising still so compelling to you?
4. Which poems might be said not only to use the rose as symbol but also to comment on that (traditional) symbolism in some way or to ask questions about it? How exactly do they do so? What exactly are those comments and questions?

KATHA POLLITT

Two Fish

QUESTIONS FOR DISCUSSION

1. This poem sets up one image of love and then turns it into an image of death. The speaker is clearly responding to another person's attitude toward such images. What is the difference in attitudes toward love of the speaker and the person she addresses?
2. In symbolic terms, who are the two fish in the title?

ROO BORSON

After a Death

I like to start discussion of Borson's poem by asking why the speaker symbolically replaces the person who has died with a chair. I try to lead students to brainstorm about possible reasons: the person who has died has literally left a chair empty—at the dinner table, in the living room; in addition, one can sit on a chair or curl up in it, as the speaker might have sat on the lap of the deceased; a chair is also a place to "rest," as the speaker suggests in line 8; the chair, in a sense, provides support. The poem also implies that—except when the speaker goes "out into the world" (perhaps to work, to buy groceries, etc.)—she sits and thinks about the one she has lost. For this activity, the chair is perfect.

QUESTIONS FOR DISCUSSION

1. Given the evidence of the poem, what kind of relationship do you think the speaker had with the person who has died? What evidence might you use to support your ideas?
2. What does the speaker mean when she says, "I can do what I do best"? What does she do best?
3. Why does the speaker need the chair? How might you interpret the last three lines of the poem?

READING/WRITING IDEAS FOR CHAPTER 16

ESSAYS ABOUT LANGUAGE

Precision and Ambiguity

I and many of my colleagues have had very good luck with the first essay assignment described at the end of Chapter 16 of the anthology, the assignment that asks students to write an essay focusing on the function of a single word within a poem. On occasion, I've broadened the assignment, allowing students to focus on a phrase (such as "hidden meaning") or even on a line rather than on a single word, but the single-word version of the assignment has always worked best. The assignment works well for many reasons, not least because it requires students to focus tightly on the text rather than to wander into generalities; because it ironically tends to encourage them to produce a truly coherent, idea-focused essay that analyzes the poem as a whole rather than a kind of stanza-by-stanza "exposition"; and because my students always seem to find this assignment peculiarly rewarding, surprising themselves by how very much they can ultimately say about a single word. I also find that the assignment tends to work best when I follow the suggestion embedded in the anthology's wording of the assignment, encouraging students *not* to focus on a word that is the explicit focus of a particular poem, but on a word that might at first not seem that important to the poem. (The assignment also, by the way, can work just as well for prose as it does for poetry.)

Metaphor and Simile

My students also tend to write quite interesting essays by focusing on metaphor or simile, either analyzing the way in which a particular figure changes over the course of a poem (such as Waller's "Song") or the way in which different figures work together in a poem (such as Shakespeare's "[That time of year . . .]"). In both cases, however, I find that I sometimes have to work to get students to truly analyze the way in which different figures and/or different turns on the same figure contribute to the development (of intensity, complication, conflict and resolution, etc.) that takes place over the course of the poem. Otherwise, again, their essays can devolve into lists of figures or of versions of a figure that don't really add up to a single, coherent argument about the text as a whole.

Symbol

A version of the metaphor and simile assignment works well if you want to have students write about a symbol or symbols in a particular text. If so, the discussion of symbol-focused essays and exercises in "Reading/Writing Ideas for Chapter 6" might also be helpful.

That discussion, however, focuses entirely on essay assignments that ask students to focus on a single text, whereas this chapter of the anthology can provide a good opportunity for instead having students write about multiple texts and the way in which different poets handle a particular traditional symbol. While you might want to have students concentrate, as the chapter does, on rose poems, you could also have students first work together on these in class, and then have students read through the anthology, identifying other recurring symbols to generate their own ideas about other possible texts and topics for comparative essays. Among the many possibilities are birds (as in Keats's "Ode to a Nightingale," Dunbar's "Sympathy," and Hopkins's "The Windhover"), houses and/or apartments (as in Dickinson's "[I dwell . . .]" and Rich's "Living in Sin"), times of day and/or seasons (as in the various poems in Chapter 15, which students might enjoy now reconsidering in different terms), and dances or dancing (as in Merrill's "Watching the Dance" and Williams's "The Dance"), etc. Much of the excitement of this assignment for students, however, involves the sense of discovery that comes of identifying recurring symbols for themselves, so I tend not to offer examples at all, or at least not to do so until after they've had a chance to look and think about this for themselves.

LANGUAGE-FOCUSED WRITING EXERCISES

1. Translating a Poem with a Dictionary

Whether or not I'm having students write essays about diction, I always include at some point in our study of poetry an assignment that asks students to do the kind of translation exercise outlined in "Reading/Writing Ideas for Poetry: Reading, Responding, Writing," this time using a dictionary. I ask them to use the dictionary to look up the denotative and connotative meanings of particular words and to put these various meanings into parentheses within their "translation." Sometimes I insist that students use the *Oxford English Dictionary* for this exercise if only because I want students to get a sense of how useful the OED can be to them in their study of literature. In addition to the simple translation, however, (and especially if they're using the OED) I insist that they conclude the exercise with a sort of mini-essay that describes exactly how the multiple meanings of particular words work or what they signify within the poem. (Since this chapter also draws students' attention to syntax, I sometimes also ask them to consider in this mini-essay how syntax contributes to the poem. What do they notice about syntax when they compare their syntactically rearranged version to the original? What are the effects of particular syntactical arrangements?)

Though, as I've said, I always include this exercise—regardless of the essay assignment students are working on—the exercise works particularly well, with modifications, as a first step for students tackling the essay on a single word assignment described above.

2. Identifying Symbolic Patterns

If you're having students write the kind of comparative assignment described above, then you might want to get them started by having them tackle an exercise or exercises modeled on "Questions on the Rose Poems," above. Or if you're letting students venture out on their own (identifying symbols and poems to write about, etc.), you might use your discussion of the rose poems in class to essentially have students develop their own exercise, coming up with a list of questions and/or reading/writing processes that might help any writer tackling this kind of comparative essay to begin generating ideas about similarities and differences, etc.

3. Generating Theses

Because it can be very difficult for students to organize their ideas about similarities and differences into a truly coherent comparative essay, I always have each student come up with a list of possible thesis statements and then devote a day of class to collectively discussing some of them. The goal of that discussion is not only to help particular writers refine particular theses but also to help the class as a whole develop a clear sense of the qualities that make for a truly workable thesis for this type of essay.

17

THE SOUNDS OF POETRY

Occasionally a student turns up in my office worried about the sheer amount of reading required for the course. The student is willing to put in lots of time but reads slowly. "Others can zip right through these assignments," I hear, "and they seem to do fine. But it takes me forever." More often than not I find that these students learned to read by sub-vocalizing rather than by visually processing the printing on the page. They may not move their lips when they read, but they might as well; since they hear each word in their heads, they can't read much faster than they can speak.

I try to encourage these students by explaining that while reading takes them a long time, there are advantages to subvocalizing: mentally hearing every word gives one, over the years, a fine feel for the language. I tell such students that they have the rhythms of English in their bones. Often, in fact, these students do better than their faster friends at reading aloud and at scansion. I tell them to look forward to this chapter; it should appeal to them.

PLANNING IDEAS

- It always pays to have students practice reading poems aloud, but that is especially the case in this chapter. One way of getting students to respond to the nuances of oral performance is to bring in recordings of poets reading their own work. The class may decide that a student's rendition of a poem by, say, T. S. Eliot or E. E. Cummings is better than the poet's reading. Note: Norton makes available a videotape of Agha Shahid Ali, Judith Ortiz Cofer, amd Alberto Ríos reading from their work.
- Harper's "Dear John, Dear Coltrane" works better if the class has heard a recording of Coltrane's "A Love Supreme" and perhaps "Naima."
- Make sure early on that students understand about enjambment; many

of them automatically pause at the ends of even unpunctuated lines. It can be useful to mark on the board both the placement and the length of pauses; a written exercise on how pauses are indicated and controlled by a poet can also be helpful.

- Kinnell's "Blackberry Eating" might well have been included in this chapter; the poem's sounds are clearly inseparable from its sense.
- For students frightened (as I am!) of scansion, pop music is again a good way to ease into it.
- I also find that students seem to be helped by reading and hearing different explanations of meter and scansion. For that reason, I often have students read this chapter in conjunction with Paul Fussell's *Poetic Meter and Poetic Form*, a text that is surprisingly appealing and helpful to my students.

JOHN DRYDEN

To the Memory of Mr. Oldham

I find the questions that conclude the discussion of Dryden's "To the Memory" within the anthology very useful for helping students appreciate the different functions of metrical variations (or rhythm) not only in this poem but also in most others (which is why, as the "Reading/ Writing Ideas" section of this chapter suggests, I use them as the basis for exercises on all kinds of poems). Such questions are key precisely because my students sometimes become so obsessed with scansion itself that they can easily forget the whole point of scansion, which is to recognize not only the "sound effects" of a poem but also the contribution of particular sound effects to the sense of the poem.

The rhythm of this poem most obviously echoes sense in lines 13–16, which both discuss and enact "the harsh cadence of a rugged line." But, like so many iambic poems, "To the Memory" also uses variations (especially trochees) for emphasis and for marking structural breaks or shifts in the poem (as in "O early ripe! [line 11] and "Once more, hail and farewell" [line 22]).

QUESTIONS FOR DISCUSSION

1. What exactly does the poem state and imply about the nature of the relationship between the speaker and Mr. Oldham?
2. What is the speaker's attitude toward Oldham? Toward Oldham's poetry? At what points in the poem does that attitude seem to change?
3. How exactly does the speaker characterize Oldham's poetry? What does he suggest about its strengths and weaknesses?

4. How does the speaker characterize himself and his own poetry in the poem, especially through his allusions to Vergil?
5. How would you characterize this speaker's definition of a good poem? Does his own poem qualify? How so? How not?

WILLIAM SHAKESPEARE

[*Like as the waves make towards the pebbled shore*]

Lines 368–69 of Pope's "Sound and Sense" read, "But when loud surges lash the sounding shore, / The hoarse, rough verse should like the torrent roar." What devices for imitating the sound of waves do Pope and Shakespeare share? How do their strategies differ?

ALFRED, LORD TENNYSON

Break, Break, Break

QUESTIONS FOR DISCUSSION

1. What metrical units does the poem use most frequently? How does the effect of line 13 differ from that of line 1? To what extent does the force of each of the two lines depend on broken expectations? On repetition? Pause?
2. Compare Shakespeare's "[Like as the waves make towards the pebbled shore]" and the passage from Pope's "Sound and Sense" quoted just above. How do the different poetic purposes lead to different uses of sound and pause? Compare Arnold's "Dover Beach" to Tennyson's poem. To what extent is each poem's tone dependent on its rhythm and pace?

THOMAS NASHE

A Litany in Time of Plague

I like to begin discussing this poem by playing the devil's advocate. In my most sincere voice, I say, "Now, here is a poem that doesn't have much to say to us today; modern medicine has done away with things like the plague." It doesn't take long for students to think about HIV and

AIDS. Perhaps someone points out that we may enjoy the benefits of first-rate medical technology, but most of the world doesn't. In any case, the discussion leads to the question of whether the poem would have anything to say to a society that had wiped out all diseases. Technology has changed, but has our basic human condition? Is the line "Earth's but a player's stage" less applicable today than it was in 1600?

QUESTIONS FOR DISCUSSION

1. What is a litany? Why is it an appropriate form for embodying the speaker's concern with both his own impending death and that of all created things?
2. The poem's basic metrical pattern is iambic. How does the rhythmic variation from iambics in the repeated line "I am sick, I must die" make the line effective?
3. A book reviewer recently quoted Nashe's line, "Brightness falls from the air" (line 17) as if it described a world bathed in light. Is that what Nashe means?

EDGAR ALLAN POE

The Raven

The basic meter of "The Raven" is five lines of trochaic octameter followed by a sixth line of trochaic tetrameter, though there are obvious variations. As or more important, perhaps, is the regular and repetitive *abcbbb* rhyme scheme in which the *b* words all rhyme with "nevermore." As Poe himself commented on this single-word refrain in "The Philosophy of Composition" (*The American Tradition in Literature*, 5th ed., New York: Random House, 1981):

> Having made up my mind to [have] a refrain, the division of the poem into stanzas was, of course, a corollary: the refrain forming the close of each stanza. That such a close, to have force, must be sonorous and susceptible of protracted emphasis, admitted no doubt; and these considerations inevitably led me to the long *o* as the most sonorous vowel, in connection with *r* as the most producible consonant.
>
> The sound of the refrain being thus determined, it became necessary to select a word embodying this sound, and at the same time in the fullest possible keeping with that melancholy which I had predetermined as the tone of the poem. In such a search it would have been absolutely impossible to overlook the word "Nevermore." In fact, it was the very first which presented itself.
>
> The next *desideratum* was a pretext for the continuous use of the one word "Nevermore." . . . [T] the difficulty lay in the reconciliation of this monotony with the exercise of reason on the part of the creature repeating the word. Here, then, immediately arose the idea of a *non-reasoning* creature capable of speech; and, very naturally, a parrot, in the first instance, suggested itself, but was superseded forthwith

by a Raven, as equally capable of speech, and infinitely more in keeping with the intended *tone*.

I had now gone so far as the conception of a Raven—the bird of ill omen—monotonously repeating the one word, "Nevermore" at the conclusion of each stanza, in a poem of melancholy tone, and in length about one hundred lines. Now, . . . I asked myself—Of all melancholy topics, what, according to the *universal* understanding of mankind, is the *most* melancholy?" "Death"—was the obvious reply. "And when," I said, "is this most melancholy of topics most poetical?" From what I have already explained at some length, the answer, here also, is obvious—"When it most closely allies itself to *Beauty*." The death, then, of a beautiful woman, is, unquestionably, the most poetical topic in the world. (pp. 458–459)

GERARD MANLEY HOPKINS

Spring and Fall

The speaker's vocabulary and syntax are anything but normal; little attempt is made here to capture the rhythms of ordinary speech. Words like *wanwood* and *leafmeal* are Hopkins's coinages, and a construction like "Leaves, like the things of man, you / With your fresh thoughts care for, can you?" takes some sorting out to yield a paraphrase like, "Are you able, in your youth, to care as much about the falling of the leaves as you do for humanity?" Why does the poet delay the "can you?" For most readers, Hopkins's suggestions for stressed syllables seem especially odd. What difference in meaning does stressing a word like *will* (line 9) make?

(See also the note to Hopkins's "The Windhover" for a brief discussion of the rationale behind his use of "vocabulary and syntax" that "are anything but normal.")

QUESTIONS FOR DISCUSSION

1. Can you paraphrase the message of the speaker to Margaret?
2. Does the alliteration serve any special purpose?
3. How does the use of language in this poem compare to that in Hopkins's "Pied Beauty"?

EMILY DICKINSON

[*A narrow Fellow in the Grass*]

QUESTIONS FOR DISCUSSION

1. How does the structure of the poem itself re-create for the reader the growing uncertainty and the element of surprise experienced by the speaker?

2. What leaves the speaker frightened at the end of the poem? Is it fear of harm or fear of uncertainty?

ROBERT HERRICK

To the Virgins, to Make Much of Time

Several things indicate that Herrick does not intend this to be a straightforward *carpe diem* poem. For one thing, there are several echoes of the New Testament parable of the Wise and Foolish Virgins (Matthew 25:1–13), which places the advice to "seize the day" in a specifically religious context. That the title addresses not virgins in general but *the* virgins would perhaps not indicate an allusion to the parable if Herrick did not also include terms like "lamp of heaven," "prime," and "tarry." Besides, the speaker's advice to virgins is hardly typical *carpe diem* strategy: the virgins are invited not to enjoy a tryst but to "go marry."

QUESTIONS FOR DISCUSSION

1. Can the poem be enjoyed without picking up on the New Testament echoes? How does the poem change once the allusions are pointed out?
2. Does *coy* (line 13) seem to mean *coquettish* here or simply *shy* (its usual meaning in the seventeenth century)?

READING/WRITING IDEAS FOR CHAPTER 17

ESSAYS ON SOUND (AND SENSE); TROUBLESHOOTING

Precisely because my students have a great deal of trouble both with scanning poems and with writing about the significance of what they discover through scansion, I find it essential to have them write at least one essay during the semester in which they must say something about the meter and rhythm of a particular poem. As this phrasing suggests, however, I find it works best—because of their nervousness—when I frame the assignment so that it asks them to consider meter as one piece of evidence within an essay whose primary focus is elsewhere, usually on one of the elements we've already covered (such as theme, speaker, or language). In this way, they get the practice they need in thinking and writing about the contribution of sound to sense, while they get to do so by building on skills and strategies with which they are already much more familiar and comfortable. And, indeed, such an assignment ensures that they will focus on the relationship between sound and sense rather than compiling a list of random observations about a poem's rhythm and meter. Sometimes, in fact, I have students tackle this assignment by returning to an essay that they have already written during our work with poetry, revising that essay so that it includes a discussion of the poem's meter and other "sound effects." Doing so, however, will prove difficult for students who have written on a poem without a distinctive rhythmic pattern, so you will need to consider what students have already been writing when deciding whether to use this version of the assignment or whether to ask students to write an entirely new essay.

I also find it helpful to have students read essays that include analysis of meter and that thus illustrate the techniques essay writers use to incorporate such formal evidence into their arguments. While several of the literary critical essays included in Chapter 25 might work well for this, I tend to use less-intimidating student essays, including an essay that I wrote in an introduction to literature course. (In writing courses that include a lot of peer critique, students get a kick out of having the opportunity to critique a piece of the instructor's writing.) The following excerpts represent the opening and form-focused paragraphs of that essay. (Notice, by the way, the awkwardness of words such as *comparison, structure,* and *verse paragraph,* which reveal a great deal, I think, about what I lacked—and what other students might lack—in terms of a conceptual vocabulary with which to talk about poetry.)

Within "On a Drop of Dew," Andrew Marvell uses a single comparison to examine the nature of the soul and the possibility of its salvation. Marvell uses a drop of dew and the natural cycle of which it is a part to illustrate the nature of the soul and its relation both to the heaven which creates it and to the earthly body in which it lives. His vision of the soul is one of a pure and complete entity which embodies, at birth, the Heaven which created it. Yet, as a drop of dew is threatened with contamination from its contact with the earth, so, he implies, is the soul threatened by the potentially corruptible elements of an earthly form. He ends by suggesting that salvation comes not only from the natural state of the soul, which tends toward the goodness of its creator, but also from the active grace of God and, perhaps, from the actions of man himself. Marvell expresses this idea through this overriding comparison with the dew in addition to other underlying images and finally through the structure of the poem itself.

Through these [overlapping] images, Marvell has moved the reader from a basic description of a dew drop, to an active comparison between it and the soul, and finally, to his conclusion of both the comparison and of his vision of the soul. The structure clearly follows and aids the movement of Marvell's ideas by its three verse-paragraph form. Within these paragraphs too, Marvell's structuring mirrors and supports his ideas. As the drop of dew exists in a "restless," "unsecure," and "trembling" state, so the poem begins with an erratic meter and rhyme scheme. As the drop becomes "inclosed" and assumes its "coy figure," so does the poem tighten in form. Within lines 27–32, Marvell increases the regularity of the length and meter of his lines as well as the rhyme scheme so that they, too, move toward harmony and balance with the soul's movement. This regularity also emphasizes the culmination of his active comparison, which occurs within this section. In the third verse paragraph, the same rhyme scheme is retained so that regularity is still apparent, but Marvell uses, too, the somewhat looser, flowing and yet highly regulated iambic lines to emphasize the contrasting description of the soul as being "loose" yet "girt." At the last, the poem again seems to largely lose its regularity, perhaps reflecting the dissolution of the soul; yet, there are also many heavy stresses, caesuras, and strong couple, rhyme, which emphasize the summation of his poem, the powerful of the almighty, and the salvation of the soul itself.

From Kelly J. Mays, "An Analysis of Images and Structure within Andrew Marvell's 'On a Drop of Dew,' " *Student Writers at Work and in the Company of Other Writers*, 2nd series, Boston: Bedford, 1986, pp. 180–181, 183.

SOUND-FOCUSED WRITING EXERCISE

Identifying and Analyzing Metrical Patterns and Variations

I find it very helpful to have students do at least one exercise that allows them to practice scanning poems on their own, typing a poem out and marking its stressed and unstressed syllables. The exercise proves most helpful, however, when students are also asked to conclude the exercise by writing a paragraph or two about the significance of the discoveries they made in scanning the poem. To help them generate ideas for those paragraphs, I give them a list of questions something like the following:

- How would you describe the basic meter of the poem?
- How does this basic metrical pattern contribute to the overall "sense" of the poem by, for example, helping to create a certain tone or mood?
- Where and how exactly does the poem's rhythm vary from its basic, underlying metrical pattern?
- Where and how do those variations
    complement or enact the sense of a given line?
    seem to work against or complicate the sense of a given line?
    indicate emphasis?
    mark a structural break in the poem, a shifting of gears, as it were?
- Where and how does the poem's meter work with or against the other "sound effects" of the poem—such as alliteration, (internal and external) rhyme, etc.?

18

INTERNAL STRUCTURE

As human beings we seem to be able to absorb experience only if we organize it in some way that conforms to previous knowledge. For poets, whatever they want to show us or tell us, a major problem is to formulate their perceptions in sequences to which readers can readily respond. Like other artists, poets have to depend not only on how their own minds organize experience but also on how their audiences relate to that organization of experience. In one sense every element of a poem is part of its organization; every decision about craftsmanship leads to other decisions—and also proscribes other possibilities—so that considerations of word choice and word order, patterns of metaphor, and choices of speaker, situation, and setting are inevitably factors that go into the organization of a poem. But broader conceptions of aim and intention are involved too: often poets have some kind of structural model in mind as they construct their work—an accepted and familiar mode of perception (perhaps one adapted from another work or art), a structure that will provide the reader a flash of recognition and something to hang on to.

Teaching form and structure is always difficult, and it is easy for the discussions to become abstract, often slipping into arguments about definition and leaving individual poems behind completely. The crucial issue, most effectively addressed with specific examples before the class, is how the structures of one mind can be shared with another. For example, how do the details in the first and last lines of "Sir Patrick Spens" imply an organizational strategy? How about the stanzaic structure of "Sonrisas"? The choice of images in "Auto Wreck"? It seems to me important that the issue of structure be raised at several points in the course, not just in this unit. What I do with this group is raise the whole issue of how our minds sort things so that they can be grasped and shared. Then I try to note in other units the organizational implications of whatever artistic strategies are used.

PLANNING IDEAS

- Like other medieval ballads, "Sir Patrick Spens" has come down to us in a variety of forms. Have students find in the library some variants and explain why a particular variant is more or less effective than the version in our text. A more ambitious project, one that could be done as a writing assignment, involves checking in a good dictionary to see whether the roots of the variants in several versions of a ballad are Latinate or Germanic and drawing conclusions about the poetic suitability of each version.
- Before having students read Williams's "The Dance," show a slide of Brueghel's *The Kermess* (sometimes spelled *Kermis*). Ask the class to describe what the artist seems to want the viewer to notice in the drawing. If the question has not come up after some discussion, ask, "Is Brueghel celebrating with the peasants or making fun of them?" Then read "The Dance," and compare Williams's emphases to Brueghel's.
- A similar exercise can be done with a slide of *The Kermess* or any other work of visual art, especially one that does not depict a familiar scene. Divide the class into groups, and ask each group to discuss a particular organizing principle of the work: one group might answer the question, "How does the artist lead the viewer's eye from one spot to the next?"; another, "What patterns of lighter and darker areas can you find?"; another, "What contrasts other than light and dark can you find?"; another, "What emotional response does the work invite?"; another, "What story does the work tell?"; and another, "What is the point or message of the work?" The exercise should help students discover that organizing principles are various, that asking questions about structure helps one see things that one didn't see before—that one does not at first glance get a work of visual art any more than one gets a whole poem on a first reading.

ANONYMOUS

Sir Patrick Spens

The situation calls to mind Shakespeare's *The Tempest*, written over three hundred years after this ballad. The first scene of Shakespeare's play stages the storm referred to in the title. As in "Sir Patrick Spens," part of the point is that when it comes to powerful natural events like a storm at sea, political rank means nothing—less than nothing, in fact, if the nobles allow their assumption that rank makes them invulnerable to cloud their judgments about practical matters.

There are, of course, differences between the play and the poem. The Boatswain in *The Tempest* takes command during the storm, ordering the noblemen to obey him. If a similar situation arises in "Sir Patrick Spens," the reader (or hearer: students need reminding that medieval ballads made the rounds orally before being circulated in writing) isn't told so explicitly. Spens and his sailors know that the journey will very likely end in disaster, but there is no talk of disobeying the king's orders.

A second difference is that Shakespeare typically puts a twist on the inversion of social roles during a time of natural disturbance. While the Scottish lords in "Sir Patrick Spens" learn (too late) that they, like the commoners, are subject to the elements, the elements are not really in control in *The Tempest*: the play's second scene reveals that the magician Prospero (who is not only a magician but the *rightful* ruler) is actually in command of the storm. A useful question for discussion is how "Sir Patrick Spens" would be changed if it were revealed that the rightful king of Scotland were a magician who had arranged the storm.

Perhaps the crucial difference between the poem and the play is that the central event on which both turn—the storm—is never depicted in the poem. The key structural device in "Sir Patrick Spens" is a sort of dramatic elision: the reader is presented with scenes before and after the storm but not the storm itself. How is it that the poem's haunting effect arises from the strategy of leaving something out?

QUESTIONS FOR DISCUSSION

1. In what ways does the king's "Drinking the blude-reid wine" help set the tone of the ballad?
2. Like the sailors, the Scots lords are reluctant to set sail—but for different reasons. What does the difference reveal?
3. What is the significance of the last line?

SUGGESTION FOR WRITING

Some might argue that a ballad like "Sir Patrick Spens" is politically subversive, exposing as it does the folly of the ruling class. Others could point out that the hierarchical structure of medieval Scottish society is never called into question—that Sir Patrick Spens and his sailors dutifully follow orders. Which view, if either, does the poem support?

T. S. ELIOT

Journey of the Magi

QUESTIONS FOR DISCUSSION

1. Many of the thoughts and images in this poem are connected by the words *and* and *but*. What does this tell us about how the speaker's

mind is working? Is this a carefully constructed account of the journey or a spontaneous one?

2. What happens to the narrative in lines 32–35? What does the speaker mean by "set down?"

3. The first two stanzas describe an event in the past, and the last stanza interprets it. How has the speaker's state of mind been changed by the journey? Why are the magi "no longer at ease"?

KARL SHAPIRO

Auto Wreck

QUESTIONS FOR DISCUSSION

1. At what points does the poem violate strict chronology? For what purpose?

2. What is the speaker's relationship to the main action?

3. What kind of expectation is created by the short, terse title? Why does the poem not contain the usual word for such an event, *accident*? Which words, phrases, and images seem especially intended to shock or create revulsion? What evidence is there in the poem that the poet is consciously working against the common assumption that only certain subjects are poetic?

4. Describe and compare the psychological effects of the similes in lines 3 ("artery"), 22 ("tourniquets"), and 35 ("flower"), and the metaphors in lines 4 ("floating"), 6 ("wings"), 21 ("husks"), and 29 ("wound").

5. How many details are given about the wreck itself? List all of the details given about the scene. What do the details emphasize? Why does the poem begin after the fact, with the coming of the ambulance instead of with the crash itself? Why are we told so little about the victims?

6. What is the poem "about"? What philosophical question does it ask? How does the poem make its shift from the details of the scene to issues of cause, responsibility, fate, and the selection of victims? How are we prepared for the terms "expedient" and "wicked" in the last line?

RICHARD WILBUR

The Pardon

Though there are many ways of describing the structure of Wilbur's "The Pardon," one obvious one has to do with the poem's division into two parts, the first of which (lines 1–13) describes the ten-year-old boy's discovery of, and reaction to, the body of his dead dog, the second (lines 13–24) the adult man's dream of the dog's return and "the pardon" itself. The actual turn from one event to the other, however, takes place in the middle of line 13, with the words "And buried him" bridging the two halves. This enjambment helps convey the extent to which the literal burial of the dog and the more symbolic burial involved in the boy's refusal to face death prompt the dream: neither the dog, the reality of death, nor the past itself stay buried.

Also interesting are the way that the two sections of the poem draw on different sensory images, the initial description of the dog in stanza two focusing on the sounds and smells associated with the dead body (which is, fittingly enough, never described), while the dream presents a quite vividly visual picture of the dog that the speaker only now, as an adult and in a dream, can look at.

QUESTIONS FOR DISCUSSION

1. How would you describe the structure of "The Pardon"? In what way does the imagery of the poem help to reinforce its structure?
2. What's the significance of the phrase "kept alive" (line 4)? What does the speaker seem to mean when he says that his "world" in boyhood was "kind" (line 10)? What else might this phrase suggest?
3. What do you make of the diction in the penultimate stanza, especially the reference to "the carnal sun," the "hymn of flies," and the "lively eyes" (lines 18–19)? Are there metaphors or similes here? If so, what are they and what do they contribute to the poem?
4. One normally asks pardon for a sin. What's the speaker's sin in this poem? What is the significance of the fact that he begs "death's pardon" for that sin rather than, say, the dog's or God's (line 24)?

ROO BORSON

Save Us From

At first glance Borson's poem is structured like a simple list of things that the speaker wants to be saved from, or—as the periods and repetition of the phrase "Save us from" indicate—three such lists, one focusing on "night" (lines 1–24), the second on "insomnia" (lines 25–36), the last on "nightmares" (line 37 to the end of the poem). (One might also see the first "list" as itself divided in two by the "save us from them" of line 16.) Once students have recognized these basic structural divisions, I turn their attention to questions both about the internal logic or structure of each of these lists and to the relation between the lists and the structure or developmental logic of the poem as a whole. (If students have trouble with such questions, I find it helpful to list on the board the objects described in the poem in the order that they are described, i.e., "highways," "gas stations," "engines," "cafés," "slices of pie," etc.)

As students are fairly quick to see the first "list" is structured in an almost narrative or dramatic fashion, as if the poem follows someone as he or she moves from the "open highways" (line 2) into the interior of a particular "all-night café" (line 8) and then into its "bathroom" (line 17), finally focusing tightly on the face and internal feelings of someone looking in the mirror of that bathroom. When the second list begins in line 25, its reference to "insomnia" almost comes to us as an explanation for the situation and setting of the previous scene; and here, too, the section seems to move from the general to the specific, the external to the internal, even though its structure doesn't seem so neatly narrative or dramatic as that of the first. The third section, with its reference to "nightmares," again seems to explain the first and second sections—as if we've finally moved "inside" enough to get to the heart of the problem from which the speaker wishes to be saved—nightmares that reveal the "horror" "concealed" in everyday things (line 36), even "the mute, immobile contours / of dressers and shoes" (lines 40–41), the lack of sleep making days "measureless" (line 42), "time" "meaning[less]" (line 7).

WILLIAM CARLOS WILLIAMS

The Dance

QUESTIONS FOR DISCUSSION

1. Does your understanding of this poem depend on your having seen Brueghel's painting? Is this just a description of a painting?
2. How is the poem like a song? Like a dance? How would you describe the structure of the poem?

SUGGESTION FOR WRITING

Write a poem based on a work of visual art you find appealing or evocative. What techniques might you use to make the poem similarly evocative to your readers?

PERCY BYSSHE SHELLEY

Ode to the West Wind

Just as Williams's "The Dance" creates the music and movement of the dance, this poem creates within itself the sound and movement of the wind. It is written in *terza rima*, a form that links each three-line stanza with end rhymes (*aba, bcb, cdc*, etc.). This creates a sense of connectedness that is then interrupted by the section break. The effect is something like that of a wind blowing, dying down, and blowing again.

SUGGESTION FOR WRITING

Trace the imagery of dead leaves through "Ode to the West Wind." How many different ways is this image used and with what figurative devices? How does this one image unify the poem?

READING/WRITING IDEAS FOR CHAPTER 18

ESSAYS ABOUT INTERNAL STRUCTURE

Because structure can, in practice, prove a quite difficult concept for students and because my students, at least, tend to get confused at times about the distinction the anthology makes between "internal structure" and "external form," I quite often choose to teach Chapters 18 and 19 together, having students write a single essay in which they consider the interrelation of structure and form in a particular poem and/or questions about how the structure of a particular poem works with and against that imposed or at least suggested by the form.

If you choose to have students write solely about structure, however, I've also had good luck with the first, fairly open-ended essay assignment suggested at the end of this chapter of the anthology. That assignment works well because it focuses students on "structural principles" in general, allowing them to talk about structure in the particular way suggested by their particular poem rather than encouraging or requiring them to simply identify the structure in terms of some rigid formula or framework. Another way to say this is that I've discovered that my students seem to analyze structure more effectively when I encourage them to focus primarily on identifying and thinking about the significance of a particular poem's key divisions, turning points, or what I sometimes call "hot spots" than when I steer them toward asking questions about whether the poem's structure is primarily "narrative" or "meditative," etc.

That's so, in part, because the former kind of assignment, as the student essay in the anthology suggests, encourages them to see that such structural hot spots are "hot" precisely because they relate to some other element of the text, particularly (but not exclusively) speaker and theme or conflict. A hot spot, in other words, often signals or overlaps with a development in the poem's or speaker's view of the situation and/or the theme. Only by considering structure in relation to one or both of these other elements can my students effectively go beyond mere observations about structure into an effective analysis of the *significance* of structure.

TROUBLESHOOTING

As the latter comments begin to suggest, I've found that the chief problem students face in tackling essays on structure is the temptation to describe rather than to truly analyze the structure and/or structural principles of a particular poem. Another, sometimes related, problem is the tendency to substitute for a real holistic analysis of structure a kind of exposition in which the essay itself essentially mimics or takes its own structure from the structure of the poem, being organized not in terms of the student writer's ideas about the poem as a whole, but in terms of the order of the poem itself. For example, in the first two stanzas of the poem . . . , in the second two stanzas . . . , etc. What they need to be encouraged to focus on, in other words, are not the parts in and of themselves, but how and why the parts fit and work together, something that they can do much more easily if they write about the poem in more holistic terms and/or think in terms of "principles," as the assignment suggests. Although there are several ways to get students to focus on how parts fit together, one way is to encourage them to generate claims (and/or actual theses) that characterize the overall movement or development within a poem. For example, the speaker initially thinks X but by the end of the poem has come to see Y; or the reader is initially encouraged to think X about the situation but is ultimately encouraged to think Y instead.

STRUCTURE-FOCUSED WRITING EXERCISE

Identifying and Analyzing Structural Breaks and/or Hot Spots

As the interpretations of the structure of particular poems offered in this chapter of the anthology suggest, a reader can often most effectively begin to analyze structure by first identifying the major breaks or shifts or turns in a poem, the points at which the speaker or the poem as a whole seem to shift focus logically or emotionally or temporally. Thus I often have students begin working toward essays about structure by having them do an exercise in which they identify such moments in the poem they're working on and generate claims about the number of "parts" the poem has. For example, " 'Save us From' is divided into three parts" and " 'The Pardon' is divided into two parts." Once they've generated that basic claim, however, the real work begins, for they now have to brainstorm about the significance and meaning of the division(s), considering some or all of the following questions:

- How would you characterize each of the parts you've identified? What makes this part distinctive (in terms of tone, imagery, etc.)?
- How and why exactly does each part follow from, and develop on, the last? Even if the poem's structure is descriptive or chronological, there

is probably a deeper or more speaker- or theme-related "development" here. How would you characterize it?

- How do these structural breaks work with or against more formal breaks (such as stanza and line divisions, shifts in rhyme scheme, etc.)?
- How and why exactly do all of the parts comprise a whole and how exactly would you characterize the overall movement or development of the poem (across all of its parts)?

19

EXTERNAL FORM

While this chapter contains specimens of several poetic forms—the villanelle, the sestina, and the concrete poem, for example—the editor has chosen to illustrate in detail one form—the sonnet—so that students can get to know it well and see not only its basic form but also the variations that can be played on it. This way, too, students can begin to see what the form is good for: what can be done within its limits and challenges, and why poets are attracted to a particular form for particular tasks and ideas.

PLANNING IDEAS

• Years ago I decided that the best way to teach the sonnet was to have students write their own. Some of the early results were so charmingly innocent of poetic convention that I combined a few of the more egregious qualities in a parody that I now use in an exercise called "How to Write a Lousy Sonnet." I hand out copies of the following compilation, which I gladly bequeath to you:

> My loneliness is lonesome. Woe is me!
> My heart is full of feelings that I feel.
> These feelings come from one that I'll call "Thee."
> Thou closed thy heart, and over I did keel.
> At first thou gave me hopefulness to hope,
> Then stripped my heart as one would peel an orange.
> Thou made me feel the feelings of a dope;
> My heart is opened as is door on door hinge.
> And only sorriness is left to me,
> The sorriness of sorrow without end:
> Thou left me as a beached whale leaves the sea,
> And landed in the arms of my best friend.
>> Now all that's left is chewed-up orange rind,
>> Unless immortal verse can change thy mind.

Since I tell the class that this is a student-written piece, it gives even first-time sonneteers great confidence: "Nothing I write," each one thinks, "can be *that* bad." And it actually works, helping students avoid some common problems: lack of enjambment, reliance on abstraction (all those "feelings") rather than concrete imagery, padding ("hopefulness to hope"), cliché ("Woe is me!"), stretched metaphor or simile (that "whale"), mixed diction ("Thou" and "dope" in the same poem—even the same line), too-easy rhyme ("me" / "thee"), and strained rhyme ("orange" / "door hinge").

- If the above exercise doesn't do the trick, try the passage in *The Adventures of Huckleberry Finn* in which Huck is stricken by the beauty of the fourteen-year-old Emmeline Grangerford's elegy for Stephen Dowling Bots, who drowned in a well. Representative lines:

> They got him out and emptied him;
>   Alas it was too late;
> His spirit was gone for to sport aloft
>   In the realms of the good and great.

- The following pairs of poems play off each other well: Constable's "[My lady's presence makes the roses red]" and Shakespeare's "[My mistress' eyes are nothing like the sun]"; Wordsworth's "Nuns Fret Not" and Keats's "On the Sonnet"; Johnson's "Sonnet to a Negro in Harlem" and McKay's "The Harlem Dancer"; Milton's "[When I consider how my light is spent]" and Thomas's "Do Not Go Gentle into That Good Night"; Lampman's "Winter Evening" and Roberts's "The Potato Harvest"; Cullen's "Yet Do I Marvel" and Jordan's "Something Like a Sonnet for Phillis Miracle Wheatley."
- Wordsworth's mention of "altar, sword, and pen, / Fireside . . ." in "London, 1802" provides a good way of introducing *metonymy*.

THE SONNET

JOHN KEATS

On the Sonnet

The speaker's implicit claim here is that while formal constraints may be necessary for poetry, the form should be adapted to embody in an appropriate way the individual poem's content. Because we all tend to be Romantics or post-Romantics without knowing it when it comes to our conceptions of poetry, students may have trouble seeing Keats's "argument" as anything other than simply natural or commonsensical. One way to begin defamiliarizing that argument is to simply ask them to think and talk about why Keats might need to make it, what other possible "arguments" or views the poem itself suggests he is responding to or countering.

QUESTIONS FOR DISCUSSION

1. The speaker seems frustrated that the sonnet "must" be fettered by "dull rhymes" despite its "painéd loveliness" (lines 1, 3). If the speaker really thinks the sonnet has no need of rhyme, why doesn't the sonnet employ blank verse?
2. What are the "dead leaves" (line 12)? Does Pope's "Sound and Sense" offer examples of such dead leaves? Does Constable's "[My lady's presence . . .]," unlike Keats's sonnet, contain an example of one of Pope's "expletives" ("Sound and Sense," line 346)?

DANTE GABRIEL ROSSETTI

A Sonnet Is a Moment's Monument

Rossetti's "A Sonnet . . ." is a perfect example of the English or Shakespearean sonnet structured around a series (in this case, composed of but two) distinct but related images, one building on the other. Here that sense of relation and building is created in part through the single word *orient,* which does—as the footnote suggests—mean "sparkling," but does so precisely because this adjective form of the word relates to the verb meaning to face or point something, especially a church, to the East (toward the rising sun). Thus this single word both resonates with and completes the image of the sacred "monument" and sets up the turn to the reversible "coin" of the next stanza. (Which also, by the way, suggests that one might want to make the task of looking up this and other words part of the reading assignment. And, since the poem's language and syntax will undoubtedly prove challenging to students, you might want to have them also do a version of the translation exercises described in the "Reading/Writing Ideas" sections of both "Poetry: Reading, Responding, Writing" and Chapter 16.)

"Orient" also is merely one of many examples—"lustral rite or dire portent" (line 4), "ivory" or "ebony" (line 6), "Day or Night" (line 7)—of the poem's emphasis on opposition or duality, its association of the sonnet both with light and dark, life and death. But what exactly is the point of that emphasis? One possibility is the suggestion that the sonnet can or must encompass and/or express the most dire extremes of human existence and nonexistence. That possibility is underscored by *this* poem's role as the opening to *The House of Life* (1870, 1881), a sonnet sequence in which Rossetti does use the sonnet to examine the extremes of life and death, earth and heaven, body and soul, as well as the relationship of "Love's high retinue" to all of the above (line 12).

Regardless of the possibilities you and your students come up with, however, the metaphors of the monument and the coin help make this sonnet a great foil to Keats's because they suggest a very different "argument" about the character of the sonnet than do the images of Poesy and her naked feet.

QUESTIONS FOR DISCUSSION

1. The anthology suggests that the English or Shakespearean form of the sonnet tends to work "well for constructing a poem that wants to make a three-step argument (with a quick summary at the end), or for setting up brief, cumulative images" that build up a picture of the thing or state that is the subject of the poem" (see discussion under "The Sonnet"). Often, however, the final couplet serves less as a vehicle for summary than for a "turn" or reversal. Which, if any, of these characterizations suits this English sonnet?
2. What are some of the implications of the phrase "moment's monument" (line 1)? How exactly is the monument metaphor developed in the first stanza? What exactly does Rossetti suggest about the character of the sonnet through this metaphor?
3. How is that characterization furthered and/or complicated by the metaphor of the coin? How is this metaphor like and unlike the first? What about the final, isolated couplet?
4. The reference to "ivory and ebony" in line 6 is only one of many examples of duality or opposition in the poem. What others do you see? How do they work together? What exactly do they ultimately suggest about the character of the sonnet?
5. How exactly does Rossetti's image of the sonnet compare to Keats's in "On the Sonnet"?

COUNTEE CULLEN

Yet Do I Marvel

Cullen's "Yet Do I Marvel" offers a wonderful play on the last-minute "turn" characteristic of the Shakespearean or English sonnet, since only in the final couplet does the speaker reveal to us how crucial race is and has been all along to his questioning of God's goodness. Up until that point in the poem, that questioning is, as it were, universally valid, and, indeed, Cullen seems to go out of his way to make it seem so through his allusions to figures from classical myth. The first of these is Tantalus who, according to H. J. Rose's *Handbook of Greek Mythology* (New York: Dutton, 1959, p. 81), "is everlastingly hungry and thirsty. He stands in a pool of water which plashes against his chin, but always vanishes when he tries to drink it; overhead hang all manner of fruit-trees, which are always tossed out of his reach by a wind when he tries to gather their fruit." The second is the better-known Sisyphus, "condemned eternally to roll a great stone up a hill; every time he reached the top with his burden, it slipped from him and rolled down again" (p. 81). Thus if Tantalus is a figure for human needs, desires, and aspirations that can never be met or fulfilled, Sisyphus stands in for the futility of human labor and struggle. And since, according to legend, both of these figures were doomed to their fates by gods angered by their transgressions, the second quatrain that contains these allusions serves to intensify and deepen the doubts expressed in the first quatrain about whether God is truly "good, well-meaning, kind" (line 1), thus creating the kind of "building" across quatrains typical of the form. As a result, this quatrain paves the way for the emphasis on the "awfulness" of God in the penultimate couplet, "awful" meaning both "inspiring awe" and "terrible or horrific" (line 12).

When the speaker then begins the final couplet with "Yet do I marvel," what we expect—I think—is a dismissal of all the questions through an affirmation of the speaker's continuing adoration of God's "marvels." What we get, however, is the exact opposite, an intensification and reformulation of the questions themselves. For in this final couplet, the speaker implicitly compares his own labors as a black poet to the futile, never-ending labors of Sisyphus, his desires for song and poetry to the "fickle fruit" that continually tempts and evades Tantalus (line 6). And, as the poet insists, this particular, racial dilemma is not less but even more "marvelous" and inexplicably "curious" than all of these other situations that make us doubt God's beneficence (line 13). What, then, is the speaker's ultimate attitude toward God? And how does Cullen's use of the most traditional, regular, and revered poetic form in the English tradition contribute to and/or complicate his vision of the dilemma of the black poet?

QUESTIONS FOR DISCUSSION

1. How would you describe the structure and movement of "Yet Do I Marvel"? How exactly do the internal structure and the external (sonnet) form work together here? Does the last couplet come as a surprise? Why or how so? Why or how not? How exactly does Cullen's use of the sonnet form contribute to the poem, particularly in terms of the poem's exploration of the situation of the black poet?

2. What is the significance and effect of the allusions to classical literature/myth (in general)? To these myths in particular? How exactly do

they individually and collectively help characterize the speaker's situation?

3. What do you make of the diction of Cullen's sonnet? His use of (alliterative) adjectives in particular? (Notice what happens to the poem when all of the adjectives are removed.)

4. Does the speaker's attitude toward God or our sense of that attitude shift or change over the course of the poem? If so, how so? Where does he and/or do we end up?

GWEN HARWOOD

In the Park

Harwood's "In the Park" uses a version of the Italian or Petrarchan sonnet to do something similar to what Wordsworth does with the sonnet form in "Nuns Fret Not." For this poem, like that one, both formally and thematically explores a particular kind of specifically female confinement—in this case, that induced by the role of mother. Reinforcing that exploration is the irony entailed in the woman's statements about how her children "grow and thrive" (line 11), their "names and birthdays" celebrated (line 10), while she remains nameless, uncelebrated, and, as her clothes and her former lover's imagined response to her indicate, the very opposite of growing and thriving. The ultimate irony of the poem, however, is reserved for its conclusion, which reverses the fear of parental cannibalism or of eating one's own children.

QUESTIONS FOR DISCUSSION

1. Unlike the last two poems, Harwood's is a version of the Italian or Petrarchan sonnet rather than the English. What difference, if any, does that make here?

2. How exactly is the woman in the poem and her situation characterized? How do the descriptions of the other characters and her interactions with them contribute to that characterization? What contribution is made by the sonnet form itself?

3. What are the implications of the final line of the poem?

EMMA LAZARUS

The New Colossus

Though none of my students will admit that he or she doesn't know the final lines of this poem by heart, and though most know that the words are associated with the Statue of Liberty, very few of them can claim to know that it is part of a poem, much less a sonnet by Emma Lazarus titled "The New Colossus." And my students, at least, get a real kick out of looking at these lines as "poetry." Perhaps the most surprising and revealing thing to them about the poem is the way the "Mother of Exiles" is characterized through the opposition with the (male) colossus, the huge statue that graced the harbor of Rhodes in ancient Greece. Unlike the "storied pomp" (line 9) of that "brazen giant" with his "conquering limbs" (lines 1–2), this "new colossus" is a "welcom[ing]" mother with "mild eyes" (line 7).

EDWIN MORGAN

Opening the Cage

Though students tend to see this poem at least at first as a simple gimmick and though I don't know (to answer the question posed by the anthology) whether the poem qualifies as a sonnet, I do think it's a great poem. Morgan's play on Cage's remark is certainly in some sense a gimmick, but it's also a smart and pointed form of linguistic play. To help students get the intelligence and point of that play, I generally have a particularly good reader read the poem aloud to everyone slowly, asking him or her to turn the words of the poem into sentences as he or she reads. As the student reads, the rest of us listen for the pauses, putting in appropriate punctuation marks at the places suggested by the way the reader reads the poem. (I also make sure to tell them up front not to interrupt, that we'll do other readings later.) Once the reader has finished, and we've got a fully punctuated version of the poem, I usually give them some time to read the poem over silently, thinking about what the poem seems to be "about" when punctuated in this way. Then, if they seem to have lots of ideas about other possibilities, I let one or two more readers have a go at it and talk about their versions. At some point, however, I always have to simply say "Stop," so that we can talk about the significance of the fact that the poem itself isn't punctuated. Then and only then do we get to the question of how and why the poem is and is not a sonnet.

Another way to do this without using up so much valuable class time is to tell students, when assigning them the poem, to read the poem aloud to themselves and insert punctuation. Then they come into class with versions ready to go so that the first part of this in-class work moves more quickly.

JOHN MILTON

[*When I consider how my light is spent*]

"[When I consider . . .]" is a classic Italian or Petrarchan sonnet. The poem's one variation on that form involves the disjunction between the formal and structural breaks caused by the fact that Patience's reply begins in line 8 rather than in 9, the beginning of the final sestet. Is it too much of a stretch, my students would ask, to say that Patience is thus not displaying patience in the poem, leaping into the poem before his or her time? (You be the judge.)

What you may also need to judge or at least think about is whether or to what extent the poem is about the speaker's blindness—as the reference to "light denied" in line 7 might, according to some, suggest—and whether or to what extent it is about his peculiar "talent" (perhaps poetic creativity)—as the reference to "hid[ing]" his own light suggests (line 3). The former interpretation almost certainly requires that we bring to bear the knowledge that the poet himself did, indeed, go blind, knowledge that my students—at least—often don't possess. Whatever you and/or your students decide, it's interesting that this very debate brings to light, as it were, a related, but different, question, which has to do with the degree to which the speaker takes responsibility for the way his talent is "spent."

QUESTIONS FOR DISCUSSION

1. What exactly do the first eight lines suggest about the speaker's situation? About his attitude toward, or feelings about, that situation? What exactly is the speaker asking in lines 7–8?
2. What might "light" and "talent" (lines 1, 3) refer to, or be metaphors for, in this poem?
3. What is the meaning and significance of Patience's reply? What different view of the speaker's situation is offered here? Does the poem seem to resolve the conflict between these different views? How so? How not?
4. What variations from the regular Italian sonnet form, if any, do you see here? What is the significance and effect of those variations? Of Milton's use of the Italian form itself?

CLAUDE McKAY

The Harlem Dancer

McKay's "Harlem Dancer" is an absolutely regular version of the English or Shakespearean sonnet, both structure and sense absolutely coinciding, and the final couplet embodying the classic "turn." As a result, the movement of the poem might be said to be as "perfect" (line 2), "gracefu[l] and calm" (line 5) as the dancer herself is described as being. If one argues for that parallel between poem and dancer, however, then that suggests that the audience for the poem and our approach to the poem are being aligned somehow with the audience within the poem, an audience divided between the speaker, "to whom she seemed" "lovelier for passing through a storm," and the youths, prostitutes, boys, and girls who either "laughed" or "devoured" her. What exactly does that suggest about our reading? And what do the final two lines say about the poem itself: is its (and/or the poet's) soul or "self" also somehow somewhere else? somehow inaccessible to our "eager passionate gaze"? Is the poet depicting himself as merely playing for coins while thinking and caring about something else?

QUESTIONS FOR DISCUSSION

1. How exactly does McKay characterize the dancer and her dance? What attitude does the speaker adopt toward her?
2. What is the relationship between the speaker's attitude toward the dancer and those suggested by the reactions of the "youths" and "prostitutes" at the beginning of the poem (line 1)? The "boys" and "girls" later in the poem (lines 10–12)? How would you characterize the various reactions here and the differences between them?
3. What do you make of the final two lines of the poem? What do these lines suggest about the dancer's attitude toward those we've been seeing responding to her throughout the poem?
4. How exactly might form relate to content in this poem? How might McKay's particular use of the sonnet form contribute to his characterization of "The Harlem Dancer"? Toward his exploration of the different responses to her?
5. Might the poem implicitly suggest a parallel between itself and the dancer? If so, how so? What might be the ramifications of that parallel, especially in terms of the poem's characterization of the different responses of different audience members (audiences for the dancer and the poem) and in terms of the meaning and significance of the final couplet?

HELENE JOHNSON

Sonnet to a Negro in Harlem

"Sonnet to a Negro in Harlem" works well in conjunction not only with the other sonnets in this chapter but also with the poems by African

Americans in the "Cultural Belief and Tradition" section of Chapter 23. That's so not because the sonnet is about an African American (a pretty reductive way of looking at things) but because it focuses on the tension between the two halves of the phrase *African American* in a way that is interestingly similar to, and different from, the poems in that section, especially Jordan's "Something Like a Sonnet for Phillis Miracle Wheatley." Especially interesting, in those terms, are Johnson's use of references to "rich, barbaric song, / Palm trees and mangoes" (lines 7–8) to characterize the pride in Africanness that contributes to the Harlem Negro's "disdainful" "magnificen[ce]" (line 1).

QUESTIONS FOR DISCUSSION

1. Make a list of the adjectives associated with the man in the poem. What exactly do these adjectives cumulatively suggest about his character? His worldview and values? How exactly do lines 7–8 contribute to that characterization? What attitude does the speaker adopt, and encourage us to adopt, toward the man and the worldview and values he might be said to represent?
2. How does the poem characterize the worldview and values of the "others" mentioned in lines 9–10 of the poem? Why and how are these "others" important to the poem?
3. How and why exactly is the man "too splendid for this city street" (line 14)?
4. How is "Sonnet to a Negro in Harlem" like and unlike McKay's "Harlem Dancer"?

WILLIAM WORDSWORTH

The world is too much with us

It has been said that Wordsworth longed to see Proteus and hear Triton only because he was secure in the knowledge that he never would. Nevertheless, lines like "Great God! I'd rather be / A Pagan suckled in a creed outworn" were calculated to seem shocking in nineteenth-century England—and can still seem bold. Part of the reason is a function of form. The poem follows a standard rhyme scheme for the Italian sonnet, but Wordsworth deviates from the standard shift in content between the octave and the sestet. Instead, the octave "invades" the sestet; the first part of line 9 concludes the sentiment expressed in the first eight lines— as though the world really *were* too much with us. (Compare this to Milton's "[When I consider . . .]" and the note to that poem.) On the heels of "It moves us not," then, "Great God!" seems to explode with all the force of repressed desire.

QUESTIONS FOR DISCUSSION

1. Since part of the speaker's complaint is that we *aren't* moved by the world around us, in what sense is the world "too much with us"?
2. Does the poem's tight structure complement or conflict with the poet's desire for the wildness of pagan belief?

PERCY BYSSHE SHELLEY

Ozymandias

QUESTIONS FOR DISCUSSION

1. This poem is structured by three levels of address: that of the speaker, the traveler, and the statue itself. How does this narrative structure fit with the image of the ruins?
2. What qualities are attributed to the sculptor? Is there an implied parallel between sculptor and poet? If so, how might the writing of the sonnet compare to the sculpting of statue? What implications for the historical place of art do the words on the statue have?

SIR CHARLES G. D. ROBERTS

The Potato Harvest

"The Potato Harvest" makes interesting use of the Italian sonnet form, the octave being rendered a coherent unit not only by virtue of the regular, repetitive rhyme scheme (*abba abba*) but also by the fact that it concentrates wholly on describing a series of objects that are neither directly connected to each other nor made part of sentences in a way that would lend coherence or depth to the scene. Those objects are, moreover, in a sense static or inanimate, the poem focusing attention, for example, on "a clamor of crows" rather than the crows themselves. All of that beings to change, however, as we move into the sestet, following the poem as it moves not only to human beings but also into complete sentences that forge connections between people, things, and actions.

QUESTIONS FOR DISCUSSION

1. How would you describe or characterize the internal structure and movement of "The Potato Harvest"? How exactly does Roberts use the (external) sonnet form to enhance that (internal) movement?

2. How would you describe the tone of the poem? How do Roberts's images individually and collectively help to create that tone? How, in particular, does he use color? How do the poem's aural, as well as visual, images work together with the poem's own sounds?

ROBERT FROST

Once by the Pacific

In this sonnet, Frost portrays the ocean as a powerful, dangerous, implacable force whose threat to the shore, as the last line makes clear, becomes symbolic of more general, pervasive, unnamed threats to humanity and civilization. Thus the poem, like the scene, serves to warn humanity of the impending arrival of an age-long "night of dark intent" (line 10). Though the year of the poem's publication might indicate that the threat here is that of war, the poem in fact is all the more ominous both for its refusal to name that threat—its insistence on how "misty" the "din" is and how impossible it is for the speaker or anyone else to "tell" what exactly is happening or what kind of "rage" is about to be unleashed on mankind (lines 1, 7, 12)—and its repeated use of a particularly colloquial (and, perhaps, "Frostian") type of understatement (as in *"Someone* had better be prepared" [line 12]).

Two questions seem especially ripe for discussion. First, how is God portrayed here and what role is ascribed to him in the poem? With its obvious allusion to the biblical portrayal of God creating the world by first commanding "Let there be light," the poem ends with the threat that God will destroy his own creation with the reverse command, yet that terrible action is rendered all the more terrible by being imagined in such human, colloquial terms, likened to someone simply snuffing out a candle. Second, how does Frost's use of the sonnet form and of an even more than usually regular rhyme scheme (all couplets) contribute to the poem? Does it undermine or enhance the sense of threat and doom here?

WILLIAM WORDSWORTH

London, 1802

QUESTIONS FOR DISCUSSION

1. What aspects of English life and institutions are portrayed as stagnant? What evidence does the poem offer? What strategies does the poem use to persuade us that England needs renewal?
2. Why is a poet called on for the solution? Why Milton?

GWENDOLYN BROOKS

First Fight. Then Fiddle

What is the major opposition at work in the poem? Does the poem really believe that fighting and fiddling can live in two separate spaces? Describe the tone of the poem.

CLAUDE McKAY

The White House

This and McKay's "Harlem Dancer" are my two favorite poems in this chapter, and I'm almost tempted to say that comparing the two of them closely can teach students as much about the range of the sonnet as they can learn from reading all of the others in the chapter. For where the full implications of "Harlem Dancer" in a sense sneaks up on you to get you where you live, as it were, this poem gets you by being so powerfully relentless and forthright even in its use of ambiguity. The best example of that, perhaps, is the title itself, which obviously refers to the house where the president lives, but pulls no punches in drawing our attention to the fact that it is as white on the inside as it is on the outside and that, in this sense, many of the houses of power are white. As in "Harlem Dancer," too, part of the poem's effect is its use of, and implicit commentary on, the relationship between poem and reader and, in a sense, between poet and poem. For in this poem the use of the "you" essentially forces the reader to be that person who both shuts the door "against [the speaker's] tightened face" (line 1) and must, as a result, bear the brunt of the "passion [that] rends [his] vitals" (line 6). At the same time, McKay's use of the regular sonnet form to express so much energy and rage enacts the process whereby the speaker must constantly exert his every power "To hold [himself] to the letter of your law" (line 12).

QUESTIONS FOR DISCUSSION

1. What are some of the implications of McKay's title? How does reading the poem change your sense of the meanings of the title?
2. Who exactly is the "you" of the poem? What is the significance and effect of McKay's use of the "you" here?
3. How does the speaker characterize himself? His situation?
4. The anthology suggests that "confinement" is a recurring theme or motif of sonnets. In what sense might this poem be about "confine-

ment"? What different kinds of confinement are portrayed in the poem? How specifically does McKay use the sonnet form to portray that confinement and/or, more generally, to convey or embody the speaker's situation?

5. How does "The White House" compare to McKay's other sonnet, "The Harlem Dancer"? What might these two poems together suggest about the sonnet form and the ways poet can adapt, play with, and use the form to convey meaning? In what sense, if any, might both poems he said to be about poetry and/or about the particular situation of the African-American poet?

WILLIAM SHAKESPEARE

[*My mistress' eyes are nothing like the sun*]

QUESTIONS FOR DISCUSSION

1. Is Shakespeare's speaker ultimately as critical of his mistress as remarks such as "black wires grow on her head" (line 4) suggest? What sense, if any, does the poem give you of what she looks like? If Shakespeare isn't criticizing her, then what is he trying to say about her by describing her features in this way?
2. What, in the process, is Shakespeare saying or asking about beauty (both physical and poetic)? What, in particular, do you make of his reference in the final line to "false compare" and the way it "belie[s]"? What exactly does it "belie"?
3. What kind of "argument" might Shakespeare be seen to make here about poetry? About the sonnet and/or particular kinds of sonnets? How does this argument relate to those implied in Rossetti's "A Sonnet Is a Moment's Monument" and Keats's "On the Sonnet"?

DIANE ACKERMAN

Sweep Me through Your Many-Chambered Heart

QUESTIONS FOR DISCUSSION

1. What techniques does the poet use to make the poem seem off balance? How is this appropriate to the speaker's state of mind?
2. Compare this poem to another sonnet, Donne's "[Batter my heart, three-personed God . . .]." Do you see any thematic or formal similarities between the two?

MORE SONNETS: A LIST

Other sonnets in the anthology that might be used to supplement this unit include

Browning	How Do I love Thee
Donne	[Batter my heart, three-personed God . . .]
	[Death be not proud, though some have calléd thee]
Frost	Design
	Range-Finding
Gilbert	Sonnet: The Ladies' Home Journal
Keats	Bright Star
	On First Looking into Chapman's Homer
	On the Grasshopper and the Cricket
	When I Have Fears
McKay	America
Millay	[I, being born a woman and distressed]
	[What lips my lips have kissed, and where, and why]
Yeats	Leda and the Swan

STANZA FORMS

DYLAN THOMAS

Do Not Go Gentle into That Good Night

At first it might seem strange that Thomas chose as exacting a form as the villanelle for a poem that seems an outburst of passion. But the passion is highly constrained, presumably by the speaker's sense of frustration that his relationship with his father has somehow remained unfulfilled. Just as the wise, good, wild, and grave men rage against the dying of the light not because they are fearful but because somehow all their wisdom, goodness, wildness, and gravity have not been enough in this world, the speaker asks his father to "Curse, bless" him as an appropriate response to human vulnerability—as though it wouldn't matter whether his father cursed or blessed him, as long as the tears were fierce. The villanelle lends itself to this kind of sentiment: for one thing, the repetition of the first and third lines lends the poem a sense of urgency. For another, the four-line sixth stanza, with its inclusion of the two catch lines at the end, both provides a sense of closure and strains against clo-sure: the final line could as well be the beginning of a new tercet as the end of a quatrain (or it could be the *last* line of a new tercet—that's where the ear expects the repetition of "Rage, rage . . . ," and so the first two lines of that tercet seem to have been left out).

Note that students might find Thomas's words familiar and meaning-ful in surprising ways because of their appearance in the theme songs for the film *Dangerous Minds* and/or for the television series based on the film.

QUESTIONS FOR DISCUSSION

1. What do the wise, good, wild, and grave men have in common? What do they have to do with the speaker's father?
2. Who are the wild men?
3. Trace the variations on imagery of light and darkness in the poem. How do we know that light represents life and darkness death (rather than, say, sight and blindness)?

MARIANNE MOORE

Poetry

Is the speaker more concerned with reading or writing poetry? What is her idea of "the genuine" (line 3)? What does she dislike about poetry?

ELIZABETH BISHOP

Sestina

It generally takes my students quite a while to derive a definition of the sestina from their reading of Bishop's poem, but having them do so makes for an interesting in-class exercise. (And breaking the class up into small groups helps to ensure that they *all* contribute to the process). As the anthology suggests, doing so proves difficult because we expect such def-initions to be about rhyme, whereas this form is instead all about the placement of words and is characterized by the absence of rhyme. As a result, when students return from their groups, I try to get them to talk about the very difficulty of the process and what it suggests about the way we read poetry, about what it means that the kind of aural and visual repetition entailed in rhyme leaps out at us in a way that the actual rep-etition of words doesn't.

At any rate, my students do always eventually come up with the definition: six stanzas of six lines each, the words that come at the end of
the lines in the first stanza—in this case, "house," "grandmother,"
"child," "Stove," "almanac," "tears"—being the concluding words in the
lines of each subsequent stanza, though they are ordered differently each
time. The poem then concludes with a three-line stanza in which those
words reappear again within, as well as the ends of, the lines.

ARCHIBALD MacLEISH

Ars Poetica

QUESTIONS FOR DISCUSSION

1. How is this poem structured?
2. What is the effect of juxtaposing statements about poetry with poetic
   images?
3. Can you summarize the poem's ideas about what poetry should be?

THE WAY A POEM LOOKS

E. E. CUMMINGS

[Buffalo Bill's]

QUESTIONS FOR DISCUSSION

1. What accounts for the sense of time's having passed? What evidence
   is there of contrast between present and past? How is each viewed by
   the speaker? How is the speaker characterized?
2. Does the poem seem to be mostly about Buffalo Bill as a person? Buffalo Bill as a performer? Buffalo Bill as an act? About death? About
   youth and vitality? About memory? What parts of the poem would
   you emphasize to defend your answer? Are there parts you would have
   to ignore?
3. How does the personification of "Mister Death" (line 11) differ from
   the personification in Donne's "[Death, be not proud, though some
   have callèd thee]"? How much of the difference depends on Cummings's withholding of it until the last line?

GEORGE HERBERT

Easter Wings

QUESTIONS FOR DISCUSSION

1. What's the relationship in "Easter Wings" between the size or shape and the sense of particular lines?
2. What are the implications of the claim that "the fall" shall "further the flight in me" (line 10) and that "Affliction shall advance the flight in me" (line 20)? What does "flight" signify or symbolize in the poem? How does the poem's layout reinforce these ideas and associations?
3. Though the poem looks like wings when upright on the page, what does it look like when you turn the page over and begin to read the poem? (Some readers have suggested it then resembles a baptismal font.) How do these two different visual images work together with each other and with the content of the poem?

ROBERT HERRICK

The Pillar of Fame

QUESTIONS FOR DISCUSSION

1. What the significance or effect of the fact that the poem is titled "The Pillar of Fame" rather than "The Pillar of Poetry"?
2. Is "The Pillar of Fame" a sonnet? If so, what's the effect of combining the sonnet and shaped verse forms here?
3. What do you notice about, and make of, Herrick's use of rhyme?
4. How does this poem compare to Shakespeare's "[Not marble, nor the gilded monuments]"?

E. E. CUMMINGS

[l(a]

This poem has more than once sparked debate in my classroom about exactly what a (good) poem is and about when and how the visual and aural play with words so central to poetry becomes alienating and/or gimmicky. What often happens in those discussions is that many students end up discovering along the way how much they missed or "didn't get" about this poem on a first reading, particularly the way it uses typography—capitalizing on the exchangeability of the letter *l* and the number *1*; drawing our attention to the way the word *loneliness* incorporates the word and letter/number *1*; becoming itself an example of "shaped verse" of a particular kind, its shape visualizing not an object so much as the action and feeling it describes, etc.

EARLE BIRNEY

Anglosaxon Street

To fully appreciate the way in which form and content work together in this poem, students will undoubtedly need more than a little help and information. For Birney's poem adapts the form of Old English (or early Anglo-Saxon) poetry to modern English to create a poem that contemplates the continuation (in the modern world) of Anglo-Saxon racial and cultural domination. The formal qualities of the poem that echo Old English include the division into half-lines; the emphasis on a particular pattern of alliteration, consonance, and assonance; the compound nouns (such as "catcorpse" [line 8] and "hatedeeds" [line 26]); and, more generally, the emphasis on concrete nouns and objects.

As a result, you might find it useful to share some or all of the following material with your students—either putting together a handout for them to read alongside the poem or waiting until after they've discussed the poem as fully as they can on their own terms and then summarizing some of it for them. First, a couple of lines of "The Seafarer" in the original (from John C. Pope's *Seven Old English Poems*, New York: Norton, 1981):

> Hwīlum ielfete sang
> dyde iċ mē to gamene, ganotes hlēoðor
> and hwilpan swēġ fore hleahtor wera,
> mǣw singende fore medu-drince. (pp. 33–34)

Second, a translation of those lines from Burton Raffel's *Poems from the Old English* (Lincoln: University of Nebraska Press, 1964):

> The song of the swan
> Might serve for pleasure, the cry of the sea-fowl,
> The croaking of birds instead of laughter,
> The mewing of gulls instead of mead. (p. 31)

Third, two passages describing some of the key features of Old English poetry:

Partly because it was chanted, or even sung, partly because the [Old English] language is rich in words beginning with the same sound, the verse pattern is a four-beat alliteration, the second and third beats almost always alliterating, the first frequently, the fourth rarely. The resultant cramping of normal syntax, as the poet maneuvers to put the right sounds in the right places, encourages metaphor to run wild: epigrammatic concision is a cardinal and essential virtue in the required tight-knit webbing. . . . A ship will be a "sea-horse," the sea will be "the whale's road," and so on. (Raffel, p. 7)

Nouns, adjectives, infinitives, and participles generally take precedence over finite verbs and adverbs, and these in turn tend to be stronger than personal pronouns, prepositions, conjunctions, and the unemphatic demonstrative or definite article. (Pope, p. 106)

SUGGESTION FOR WRITING

Poetry was originally oral, and poets and critics since the seventeenth century have complained that the printing press is destroying poetry as an art. In recent years worries have become especially intense and articulate; some critics insist that linear form radically distorts sequential experience by forcing the eyes to translate through a sign language that is more artificial and less natural than the aural symbols. Pick one or more poems from this chapter that seem(s) to respond to that criticism, and write an essay addressing the relation between the visual and the aural in the poem(s).

READING/WRITING IDEAS FOR CHAPTER 19

ESSAYS ABOUT EXTERNAL FORM

This chapter could easily be used as part of a unit culminating in a comparative essay assignment of any of the types described and discussed in "Reading/Writing Ideas for Chapter 23," and many of the writing suggestions in this chapter of the anthology and the guide would work quite well for this, while many of the questions for discussion might be the basis for several more.

I have postponed the in-depth discussion of such assignments until Chapter 23, however, because I actually find it more productive to have students write at least one essay that closely analyzes the form of a particular text before having them tackle comparison, and this chapter seems to provide wonderful grist for that mill. As the word *closely* is meant to suggest, I think that writing an entire essay that takes a detailed look at the form of a single poem teaches them valuable skills that they need to master and that it's helpful if they do so before venturing into larger, more broadly focused comparative projects (projects that can easily become too general and/or unfocused if students haven't already mastered the art of focusing).

As with other assignments, I go back and forth on the question of how restrictive or directive to be with this one, how rigid to be about the role external form must play in the essay, etc. The most directive approach, illustrated both by the following sample assignments and by some of the chapter's writing suggestions, has the obvious advantage of allowing you to make sure that students focus tightly not only on form but also on the formal issues and questions that you decide are most important.

Sample Assignments

- Write an essay in which, through a close analysis of both the form and content of "Yet Do I Marvel," you consider the ways in which Cullen's particular use of the (English) sonnet form contributes to his portrayal of the situation of the African-American poet.
- Write an essay in which you consider the question of whether and how Chasin's "Joy Sonnet in a Random Universe" or Morgan's "Opening the Cage" is and is not a sonnet and how that question relates to the poem's theme(s). What are the central questions or themes explored in each poem? How exactly does the use of an ambiguously sonnet-like form contribute to that exploration?
- Write an essay in which you closely analyze both the form and content of Thomas's "Do Not Go Gentle into That Good Night." Why might Thomas have chosen to use (or what are the ramifications of Thomas's choice to use) the rigid villanelle form for a poem that seems to be an outburst of passion? How and why does this form work in this case?

The less directive approach has the benefit of allowing students to choose the text that most appeals to them and of requiring them to formulate (and/or learn how to formulate) questions about form for themselves. As the following sample assignments are meant to suggest, however, there are obviously varying degrees of open-endedness.

- Choose any sonnet in the anthology and write an essay in which you analyze how the sonnet form contributes to the author's portrayal of a particular situation, theme, and/or conflict. Does this poem come closest to being an Italian or English sonnet? How exactly does the poem conform to, and vary from, the traditional form? How does the poem's particular form, including its variations on the classical form, contribute to its meaning and effects? What are the significance and effect of the very use of a version of this most traditional and revered of forms?
- Choose any poem in this chapter (or in the anthology as a whole) that employs a traditional stanzaic form (sonnet, villanelle, ballad, etc.). Write an essay in which you analyze how the use of this form contributes to the author's portrayal of a particular situation, theme, and/or conflict. In what specific ways does the poem conform to, and vary from, the traditional form? How does the poem's particular form, including its variations, contribute to its meaning and effects? What are the significance and effect of the very use of a version of a traditional form? Is this traditional form typically associated with particular themes and/or structures? How, if at all, does this poem use those traditional associations (whether to conform to, or violate, them)?
- Choose any poem in this chapter (or in the anthology as a whole) and write an essay analyzing the significance and effect of the poem's external form—its particular pattern of rhythm and rhyme, its stanzaic form, the way it looks and/or is organized on the page. How exactly does the form contribute to meaning in this particular poem?

If the poem uses a traditional form of one sort or another—such as the villanelle, the sonnet, or shaped verse—what's the significance or effect of the use of this traditional form? How exactly does the poem conform to, and vary from, the traditional form of which it is a version? How does the poem's particular form, including these variations, contribute to its effects? Is this traditional form typically associated with particular themes and/or structures, believed to create certain expectations about content? In what sense might this poem be said to use those expectations (whether to defy or fulfill them)?

20

THE WHOLE TEXT

This chapter includes several very short poems, poems brief enough to discuss fairly exhaustively in terms of all the poetic elements we have explored thus far in the text. When you take up this chapter, it may be helpful to provide students with a list of these elements to serve as a reminder and checklist for future analyses of poems. Of course, no poetry analysis should be a mere exploration of one isolated element after another, and this is a point well worth emphasizing and reemphasizing. Like the Dacca gauzes described in Ali's poem, any work of literature is made up of interwoven parts. The real task is to understand how the parts combine and interrelate to create the whole.

PLANNING IDEAS

- In preparing your syllabus, you might consider using this unit as an opportunity to revisit poems explored more narrowly in previous chapters and to study some favorite selections from the "Reading More Poetry" section at the end of the text.
- Ask students to choose a poem discussed earlier in the term principally in regard to one element. Before class, have each write a paragraph describing the other aspects of the poem that contribute to the work as a whole and their interrelations. Spend one class period discussing the poems the students have chosen to write about.
- Bring to class a short poem (sonnet length or briefer) that the class has not studied before, making the poem available through use of photocopies or an overhead projector. Give the class several minutes to come up privately with as many critical observations about various elements of the poem as it can. When you discuss the poem as a whole, supplement student observations as necessary, encouraging students to see the interrelatedness of the various elements they observe.

W. H. AUDEN

Musée des Beaux Arts

This poem offers a layered perspective on the Greek myth of Icarus. The myth of Icarus can be read as a moral tale about excessive ambition and its consequences. Brueghel, an "Old Master," interpreted the myth in painting by changing the setting to a sixteenth-century Dutch peasant society. The speaker in the poem, looking at the painting, gives his own gloss on the painting and myth.

QUESTIONS FOR DISCUSSION

1. Describe the speaker's views about suffering.
2. Does your understanding of the poem depend on seeing the Brueghel painting?

SUGGESTION FOR WRITING

Look up Ovid's story of Icarus and his father, Daedalus, and read it carefully. Then study a reproduction of Brueghel's *Icarus*, giving attention to the details Auden "borrows" for his poem. Write an essay discussing Auden's use of story and picture in "Musée des Beaux Arts." Are story and poem equally important to the poem's message(s) and effects?

GEORGE HERBERT

The Collar

"The Collar" seems to capture Herbert's own ambivalent feelings about the rigors and restrictions of the religious life or, in the words he used to describe all of his poetry, "a picture of the many spiritual conflicts that have passed betwixt God and my soul, before I could subject mine to the will of Jesus my Master." Though Herbert was elected public orator at Cambridge in 1620, a post that required him to take orders within seven years, for much of his tenure he seems to have had more secular ambitions, leaving most of his university duties to underlings and serving in Parliament in 1624 and 1625. He was ordained deacon around 1624 and in 1626 became a canon of Lincoln cathedral. In 1629, two years after his mother's death, Herbert married and became rector of Bemerton, near Salisbury, being ordained as a priest in the fall of 1630. When he came down with consumption three years later, Herbert reportedly sent his poems to a friend with the request that they be published only if they would "turn to the advantage of any dejected soul."

QUESTIONS FOR DISCUSSION

1. To what might the title "The Collar" literally and figuratively refer? (Might *choler* be one of the many possibilities?) What are some of its implications? What might it suggest about the situation of the poem's speaker? What cues do you get from the final four lines of the poem?
2. Make a list of the many metaphors the speaker uses. How do they individually and collectively help characterize both his situation and his attitude toward it?
3. The poem may be seen to depend heavily on the ambiguity of certain words, including "lines" (line 4) and "suit" (lines 6, 31). What are the various meanings of these words, and how does each meaning work in the poem?
4. Overall, how would you characterize the two attitudes toward his situation that the speaker articulates in lines 1–32 and lines 33–36 of the poem? Might more than two attitudes be suggested here?

EMILY DICKINSON

[*My Life had stood—a Loaded Gun—*]

For an interesting interpretation of the poem, see the comments of poet Adrienne Rich in the note to her "Snapshots of a Daughter-in-Law" in Chapter 22 of the Guide. Because of its focus on the ambiguity of power, Dickinson's poem also works well in conjunction with Rich's "Power."

What are the implications of describing one's life as a loaded gun? As a gun, the speaker is owned, possessed, and carried away; but she is also powerful, lethal. How is this contradiction summed up in the last stanza? Analyze the use and meaning of *power* in this stanza and in the poem as a whole.

ROBERT FROST

Design

Since Frost's poem confounds our usual associations for "whiteness," I like to open discussion by asking students to list the conventional asso-

ciations of the color white on the board. After we have a list—probably
including notions of purity, innocence, goodness, absence (of color),
marriage—I turn our attention to the poem and to Frost's creepy tableau
of albino spider, moth, and flower. Frost's choice of words in the poem
forces us to see this whiteness as unsettling, with his references to
"witches' broth" and "death and blight" in the descriptive octave of the
sonnet. In the sestet, he proffers the questions such an eery confluence
of elements prompts.

QUESTIONS FOR DISCUSSION

1. What parallels do you see between the existence of this scene in nature
   and its crafting as an image in the poem? How appropriate to his
   theme is Frost's choice of the sonnet form?
2. What philosophical questions are raised in the final couplet of the
   poem? In what sense might the "design of darkness" be appalled by
   the scene Frost describes?

SUGGESTION FOR WRITING

Compare the form and content of "Design" to that of "Pied Beauty" by
Hopkins. Both poems consider the design, or the lack of design, in nature.
How do their conclusions differ?

ANNE SEXTON

With Mercy for the Greedy

To open discussion of this thought-provoking poem, I like to ask students
to look closely at the way the speaker describes the cross her friend has
sent her. Some of the description is quite conventional: "no larger than
a thumb, / small and wooden." Other aspects of her description are jolt-
ingly *un*conventional: "He [Jesus] is frozen to his bones like a chunk of
beef." Exploration of such lines will quickly reveal how subtly and powerfully the speaker's relationship to Christianity and the problems of
belief are conveyed in her reactions to the gift.

Some attention to the first and last stanzas may also prove fruitful. The
friend's request in the first stanza (that the speaker attend confession as
well as wear the cross) and the speaker's response to this request in the
last stanza reveal that the speaker thinks her life work has been one long
confession. Her poetry holds the catalog of sins she has to confess. (Note
the biblical echo from Genesis 25:29ff, in the reference to "pottage.")

QUESTIONS FOR DISCUSSION

1. What is the speaker's reaction to her friend's request and gift? Is she offended? Pleased? Touched?
2. Why does the speaker suggest that poems offer "mercy for the greedy"?
3. What sense do you make of the metaphors for her poetry that the speaker offers in the last two lines of the poem?

SUGGESTION FOR WRITING

Read several of Sexton's poems from the volume *The Awful Rowing Toward God*. Write an analysis of "With Mercy for the Greedy," based on your understanding of Sexton's response to Christianity.

READING/WRITING IDEAS FOR CHAPTER 20

ESSAYS ON THE WHOLE TEXT

Whereas Chapters 13–19 provide great opportunities to focus student writers on element-specific types of essays and to thereby expand their repertoire of readerly and writerly techniques and strategies, I find that this chapter is very useful for helping my students develop strategies for dealing with open-ended essay assignments of the type often assigned in upper-division courses. As a result, my whole text essay assignment often asks students to choose the text that they want to write about (from this chapter or from the anthology as a whole) and to develop their own topic from scratch. I use writing exercises to help them develop strategies for developing the kinds of questions that lead to effective topics and theses and to help the class as a whole focus on general writing issues that aren't dealt with in the kind of element-specific exercises described in earlier chapters. (For obvious reasons, however, there is some overlap between the exercise assignments for this essay and those described in earlier chapters.)

Often, I word the assignment so that it explicitly requires that somewhere and somehow in his or her essay each student should address at least three of the elements that we've covered and preferably address all of them: an essay on Marvell's "On a Drop of Dew," for example, might focus primarily on Marvell's use of the dew as *metaphor* or *symbol* for the soul but would also undoubtedly need to consider the *theme* or *conflict* that Marvell explores through that metaphor or symbol, as well as the significance and effect of both the poem's *internal structure* and its use of *sound* and/or *external form*.

TROUBLESHOOTING

Some of my students are intimidated by open-ended assignments, but frankly it's because they're intimidated and because such assignments are so common that I feel students need to learn strategies for coping with them. And many of my students have the opposite response, reveling in the freedom to write about exactly what they want.

On occasion, I find that whether intimidated or not students have a tendency to return to what is most familiar in tackling such assignments, half-forgetting everything we've done since they came into the class and writing the kinds of essays they came into the course writing. On the one hand, that tendency is natural for all of us, and many students produce good writing when they write from their strengths and from within their comfort zones, as it were, while doing so in the context of a composition-focused class allows them to build on those areas of strength. On the other hand, returning to the kind of essay they wrote when they came into the course can be a problematic choice for many students. That's why I organize the exercises for this assignment so that they both help students to cope with the open-ended assignment and require that they do so by at least considering the full range of options available to them.

WHOLE TEXT–FOCUSED WRITING EXERCISES

When giving students an open-ended assignment, I usually kick things off by describing the assignment and then encouraging questions and discussion about it. If the question of how to pick a poem to work with doesn't come up, then I introduce it. Invariably my students will argue that you should write about a poem you like, and I try to push them to explain exactly what this means, why and in what way "liking" the poem makes for a more effective essay and why not liking a poem might itself be a productive starting place; often at this stage, I can do so by referring back to a particular in-class discussion in which some or all of them ended up getting a great deal from, and even liking, a poem that at first seemed impenetrable and alienating to them. Though I encourage students to seriously consider writing about poems that puzzle or challenge them in some way rather than poems that they get right away, my main goal here is to simply get students thinking about the costs and benefits involved in such choices: if you choose a poem you immediately like and get, what might your challenges be in trying to write effectively about it? If you choose a poem you don't like or get immediately, what might your writerly challenges be?

After that, I simply let them have at it and (depending on the class) either have them begin working on the exercises outlined below or start off with one or two of the more basic exercises described in earlier chapters (such as the translation exercise described in "Reading/Writing Ideas for Poetry: Reading, Responding, Writing"). In the case of several of these exercises, I reproduce here the actual text of my assignments rather than descriptions of them. As some of the assignments make clear, I devote class time to each exercise after the students have completed it, having the whole class discuss thesis types with reference to particular students' theses the day after they've done Exercise 1, having the class break up into small groups to discuss counterarguments, etc.

1. Formulating Theses

Below, I describe three types of theses common to literary critical or analytical essays, and I give you one or two examples of each type. Your assignment is to craft at least two theses of type A, one type B thesis, and one type C thesis, any of which you might use as the basis for your essay.

A. As we've seen, one kind of literary critical essay focuses primarily on a **particular element** of a poem—such as its tone, theme, speaker, situation and setting, or its use of language (especially metaphor and simile or symbol).

Examples:

Over the course of Maxine Kumin's "Woodchucks," we see the **speaker** slowly change from a committed pacifist to an almost joyful murderer. Thus, as the poem's own references to Nazism suggest, "Woodchucks" explores the process whereby even the most peace-loving individual or society can become bent on the destruction of a whole group or species.

Emily Dickinson's "My Life had Stood—a Loaded Gun" explores the **conflict** between the desire for power and the fear that power is necessarily destructive.

In "The New Colossus," Emma Lazarus uses the "Mother of Liberty" as a **symbol** for America, characterizing both the statue and the country it stands for by juxtaposing this symbol with that of the "old" colossus at Rhodes.

B. Another kind of literary critical essay focuses on posing and exploring possible answers to **a difficult question** about a literary text or a question, puzzle, or contradiction within the text. Such a question can focus on a particular action (why does character X do such and such?), on theme (is the author saying this or this?), on form (why the sonnet?), or on a particular moment (why does the speaker say this?), etc. As the second example below demonstrates, a question essay can offer an answer or answers to the question, and/or it can explore the effect of ambiguity itself, the significance of the fact that the question *isn't* really answerable. Just remember that even if your essay will ultimately answer your question, you can argue effectively that this answer is right only if you explore other potential answers along the way.

Examples:

Throughout "A Sonnet is a Moment's Monument," Dante Gabriel Rossetti characterizes the sonnet as a creature of extremes—light and dark, day and night, life and death, etc. But what exactly are the ramifications of that characterization—is Rossetti suggesting that the sonnet itself can be a living or dead form depending on the use that is made of it, or is he suggesting that the sonnet necessarily focuses on, and encompasses, the range of human experiences?

In the first line of Alfred, Lord Tennyson's "Ulysses," Ulysses refers to himself as an "idle king," yet in the very next line he describes the duties that he does and must take on as king of Ithaca. What, then, is the truth about Ulysses's situation and about

Ulysses himself? To what extent does the poem ask us to see Ulysses as dishonest with himself and others and even as wrong to leave Ithaca, and to what extent does it portray him as right about the choice he faces and ultimately makes?

C. Among the many, many other types of essays about literature and one that is sometimes very like the last type is one in which one argues that and why some **detail in or about a text that seems insignificant** is, in fact, of crucial importance. One might, for example, focus on a particular, seemingly minor character or object or image, a particular word or phrase, a particular action or moment in the text, a detail of setting, a particular facet of the form, etc.

Example:

At first glance, it may not seem very important that the speaker in Audre Lorde's "Hanging Fire" describes not her body in general but her "skin" in particular as betraying her and that she later worries about her "ashy" knees (not, for example, about acne, the adolescent skin problem we might expect to be at issue in a poem that is about adolescence). A second glance, then, suggests these two phrases are, in fact, of crucial importance, helping to make "Hanging Fire" not just about the confusion faced by any child in adolescence, or even by any girl child, but also about the particular experiences of people of color.

2. Gathering Evidence

Once you've developed a thesis, the next step is to gather the facts you will use to support and develop that thesis in the body of the essay.

In class, we will talk about the various kinds of facts in and about a literary text that one can use as evidence. To prepare for that discussion, you should reread the student essays on poetry in your anthology. As you do so, highlight or underline the facts that the writers refer to, whether those facts are taken from the text or are about the text or the author. Which facts are used as evidence? What *kinds* of facts are used as evidence here? What other kinds of facts might one use as evidence in a literary critical essay? What specific techniques do these writers use to gracefully incorporate facts into the essay?

Facts alone are simply facts; they aren't evidence for anything. To turn a fact into evidence, then, you have to both present the fact itself to the reader and tell the reader what you infer from the fact to show him or her how and why it is evidence for your idea. Usually, every paragraph in the body of an essay should begin by articulating a particular subidea, and everything inside the paragraph should be either an inference or a fact that contributes directly to supporting and developing that idea. Look at the student essay again; this time, mark the ideas and the inferences. What specific techniques does the writer use to turn facts into evidence for particular ideas, to link facts directly to inferences? Are there moments in the essay when the use of evidence seems weak? Is it because there aren't enough facts? Because there aren't enough inferences? Because the two aren't linked clearly?

Now that you've closely examined the way another student writer presents facts and turns them into evidence, it's time to begin the work of gathering facts for your own essay. Doing so will require that you decide on your thesis. Remembering what we discussed about the function of literary critical essays (for authors and for readers), which of the theses you formulated in the last class or came up with since then seems to you to promise the most interesting and effective essay both for you and for your readers?

Type that thesis out; then look back over your poem with that thesis in mind. Underneath your thesis, make a list of the facts from and about the text that you think will be most necessary to supporting and developing that thesis. That list should include at least one fact about the form of the poem (its rhyme, meter, etc.). Beside each fact (including the facts about form), brainstorm about the implications of that fact and about the ways you might use it in your essay. What idea might this fact be good evidence for? What are the inferences that make it evidence?

I find it useful when possible to spread this exercise across two days, first having students concentrate on the use of evidence in general and then on the use of evidence in this particular essay. Sometimes I've found it useful to handle the former discussion by breaking the class up into groups, each group being assigned a particular student essay to concentrate on; being asked to generate lists of kinds of evidence, of techniques for using evidence effectively, and of problems with the use of evidence; and being asked to illustrate their points with examples from their essay. At the end of class, we discuss what they've come up with; and I collect their lists and examples, compiling them to make up a handout on the use of evidence that they can all use in crafting this and future essays.

3. Identifying Counterevidence and Imagining Counterarguments

Since you don't want to oversimplify the literary text to make your argument persuasive, to make your argument overly simplistic, or to undermine your credibility with your reader, you always want to consider possible objections to your argument, counterarguments, alternative interpretations, etc.

One way to do that is to look for evidence that seems to contradict or at least complicate your initial thesis. So come up with one or two facts from or about your poem that might seem to contradict your thesis, that suggest a different answer to your question, etc. Comment briefly on how you might use the fact or facts as evidence in your essay: how might you interpret this fact in a way that shows that it does not, ultimately, contradict your thesis? Conversely, how might you use this fact to build on and complicate your argument?

Another way to accomplish the same goal is to imagine that you are a defense attorney preparing for an upcoming trial in which you will have to persuade a jury to accept your interpretation of your poem. To prepare your case effectively, you're going to have to imagine the counterarguments that the prosecutor might come up with to undermine your argument. What's the prosecutor's most powerful argument? How will you defend your argument against that possible counterargument in your essay? If the counterargument is more persuasive than your own argument, how does your argument need to change?

4. Critiquing Body Paragraphs

I've found that a terrific way to follow up on the evidence/inference discussion generated by Exercise 2 (and to make draft day productive) is to have each student exchange drafts with a colleague. I then ask the students to turn to page 3 of the draft and carefully read the first full paragraph on that page, identifying the main idea or topic sentence, each fact, and each inference. I then ask them to look over their markings to evaluate the paragraph, discussing their evaluation with the writer. Do all the facts and inferences here relate to, and help support, the main idea? Are there enough facts to support the main idea? Are the inferences ample and clear enough to show exactly how particular facts support the idea?

As with other small-group work, I conclude class by bringing everyone back together to discuss what they've learned, and I frankly never cease to be amazed at how productive this exercise always turns out to be. Sometimes, students discover that they really don't understand the concepts well enough to distinguish ideas, facts, and inferences, giving us the opportunity to discuss and clarify. More often, students discover that they can identify them just fine, and what surprises them are the problems they discover in their writing by doing so: paragraphs that don't have clear main ideas or stray from them, paragraphs that consist almost entirely of facts or of inferences, etc.

Exploring Contexts

Poems treated in isolation, as if art belonged to a separate world having nothing to do with the real world, can very quickly come to seem irrelevant, effete, and boring; this section explores the various ways in which we, as readers, can relate the concerns of poems to ordinary reality. The connections are not always easy, but they are rewarding and exciting. Even if your course does not allow you time to consider fully all of the issues raised in this section, you can point outward from the poems by assigning the poems in at least one or two chapters and thus at least suggesting to your students that poetry is vitally connected to the world at large, not an insulated and purely academic exercise. I have found the kind of issues suggested here to provide the most exciting teaching experiences of any I have had; among other things, attention to these groups of poems can minister to the students' need to connect things, rather than seeing them in neat little course-size blocks, and to see their subject matter in an interdisciplinary way.

Success in these chapters can be pretty much guaranteed by proper preparation during the earlier class meetings. If, for example, you have at least tentatively or suggestively raised questions along the way about what poems by the same author have in common, or whether knowing about the historical context affects one's interpretation of a poem, you will find students ready for the greater depth such questions can take on here. Along the way in this Guide, I have tried to raise such issues fairly often; and if you have broached such questions at all, you are well set up to investigate them in more detail through the groups here.

21

THE AUTHOR'S WORK AS CONTEXT: JOHN KEATS

Studying Keats's poetry works well in part because of its sensuous appeal and in part because the poems included here were written over a relatively short period of time and thus are fairly homogeneous (although one can certainly see an increasing confidence and an acceptance of the world's pain). The poems Keats wrote after "To Autumn"—none of which are included in the anthology—are generally thought vastly inferior to, say, the ones written during the great creative outburst of May 1819. An interesting exercise, especially for advanced students, is to compare the poems written after September 1819 to the ones written earlier (see "Reading/Writing Ideas for Chapter 21," below).

PLANNING IDEAS

- If you are going to spend three or four days on Keats, I suggest using the letters near the beginning—on the first or second day—so that the poet's own ideas about his work can become an integral part of the continuing discussion. Poems especially illuminated by the prose include "Ode to a Nightingale," "Ode on a Grecian Urn," "Ode on Melancholy," and "To Autumn." Excerpts from two relevant letters not included in the anthology can be found in the note on Keats's letters, below.
- It is useful to review Keats's "On the Sonnet" before reading the sonnets in this chapter.
- A slide of Albrecht Dürer's *Melencolia I* works well with Keats's "Ode on Melancholy."
- As the index indicates, quite a number of poets are represented by several poems, and you may want to teach in a unit groups of poems by one or more additional authors. Or you may want to vary which authors you teach intensively, sometimes teaching someone other

than Keats and Rich. Emily Dickinson and Sharon Olds, generously represented in the anthology, are other authors whose poems teach especially well as a group, and in this edition the editor has included quite a number of poems that are seldom anthologized. The ranges of tone and subject are more varied in Dickinson than teachers working from standard anthologies may have been led to expect, and the Olds poems play very subtle variations on recurrent situations and relationships. John Donne is another good poet to teach in such a unit.

- It works well to have the students work in groups of four to seek out information for in-class presentations. Each student is responsible for one of the following: (1) relevant biographical details, (2) relevant cultural context, (3) typical poetic techniques, or (4) poetic development.
- If you're having students study Keats's poetry closely and if you can spare the time, you might well want to consider supplementing the Keats poems in the anthology with at least one of Keats's longer poems (or encourage students writing on Keats to do so). Especially useful, I think, is Keats's *Endymion*, which deals extensively with many of the themes dealt with in the shorter poems, including the relationship between the ideal/immortal and the actual/mortal worlds and between dreams and creativity. Conversely, you might want to have students read some or all of Keats's "supernatural" Romance poems—*Lamia*, "The Eve of St. Agnes," *"La Belle Dame Sans Merci,"* etc.—precisely because they at first seem to reveal such a different "Keats" from that suggested by the more naturalistic poems on offer here.

On First Looking into Chapman's Homer

The Italian sonnet offers a variety of options for the rhyme scheme of the sestet. Here Keats chooses to follow the *abbaabba* of the octave with *cdcdcd*. This is an open-ended pattern; the ear half-expects another line, one with a *c* rhyme, after the fourteenth. This openness, combined with the lack of a full stop in the exotic-sounding *"Darien"* (compare the "gold"/"hold"/"told"/"bold" of lines 1,4,5, and 8), partly accounts for the tone of awed discovery of something mysteriously grand that is also created by the metaphorical comparison of reading Chapman to discovering a new planet or seeing the Pacific for the first time from the New World.

Its also worthwhile to ask students what they make of the glaring "mistake" in the poem—Keats's reference to "stout Cortez" rather than Balboa in line 11. What students unfamiliar with Keats's biography and with nineteenth-century culture may miss is how very revealing and (arguably) crucial to the poem that mistake is. Keats's contemporaries and fellow poets, Byron and Shelley, might never have made such a mistake for precisely the same reason that they might never have been excited enough about reading Chapman's translation of Homer to write such a poem: both of these poets, unlike Keats, received the extensive, classical education that was the preserve of well-born gentleman in the nineteenth century (as well as a marker of such status); as a result, they didn't need, as Keats did, to read a translation of Homer but could and did read him in the original Greek. The son of an ostler, Keats did not belong to the elite as these poets did, nor did he receive the same education (though he did learn Latin). (As the headnote on Keats in the *Norton Anthology of English Literature*, Vol. 2, 6th ed., p. 766 states, "No major poet has had a less propitious origin.") At the age of fifteen, and in the same year Shelley was expelled from Cambridge, Keats left school to undertake what we would think of as "vocational training" when he was apprenticed to an apothecary-surgeon. I find analogies helpful in conveying all of this to students, likening the position of ostler to that of auto mechanic, apothecary-surgeon to something like pharmacist, the social position of Byron and Shelley to that of the Kennedys or Rockefellers.

And while all of this may seem extraneous at first, I find that it actually helps draw students to Keats who might otherwise find little to identify with in his poetry.

QUESTIONS FOR DISCUSSION

1. What is the significance or effect of the way the speaker likens his experience of reading a book to looking at the night sky and the Pacific Ocean? To the "discovery" of the New World by Europeans?
2. What do you make of the reference to the "wild surmise" of Cortez's men in line 13? What might this mean or refer to? What does it contribute to the poem?
3. Would a poet writing today be as likely to refer to Cortez's (or Balboa's) "discovery" in the way Keats does? What might the poet's depiction of this scene tell us about cultural assumptions in early nineteenth-century England?
4. What's the significance or effect of the fact that Keats mistakenly refers to Cortez rather than Balboa here? Does this mistake detract from, or add to, the power of the poem?
5. Does this sonnet fall prey to the problems with the sonnet form that Keats's describes in "On the Sonnet"? Or does Keats here manage to "find" "Sandals more interwoven and complete / To fit the naked foot of Poesy" ("On the Sonnet," lines 4–6) and to bind "the Muse" "with garlands of her own" ("On the Sonnet," lines 13–14)? If so, how so?

On the Grasshopper and the Cricket

"On the Grasshopper and the Cricket" may not be based directly on Aesop's "The Ant and the Grasshopper," which concludes with the ant telling the grasshopper that "If we sang and danced and drank all summer we would starve in the winter and it looks as though that is what you are going to do" and the moral "Save while you are young or you'll have nothing when you are old" (*Aesop's Fables: A New Version Written by Munro Leaf*, New York: Heritage Reprints, 1941, p. 48). But both the poem's title and the poem itself do recall this and other fables that derive morals from juxtaposing the behavior of one animal with that of another. And certainly Keats's grasshopper looks more than a little like Aesop's, both "tak[ing] the lead / In summer luxury," "never done / With [their] delights" (lines 5–7), though Keats's poem ultimately celebrates this "poe[t] of earth" in a way that Aesop never would (line 9).

QUESTIONS FOR DISCUSSION

1. What qualities and values are associated with drowsiness?
2. In what sense is the grasshopper's song "poetry of earth" (line 9)? In what different sense is the term appropriate for the cricket's song? For Keats's own song? What might the poem say or ask about poetry in general?
3. What role is played by the birds in the poem?
4. What is the significance or effect of the fact that line 9 contains eleven syllables (the technical term is *hendecasyllabic*) instead of ten?

On Seeing the Elgin Marbles

My students are sometimes so obsessed with the vision of the young, dying Keats that they read foreshadowings of his early death even into poems like this one, written well before Keats became seriously ill. But while Keats's poetry is undoubtedly obsessed with death and while it is undoubtedly true that illness and death were an essential part of Keats's personal experience, what too-simplistic autobiographical readings of the poetry can occlude are the more philosophical (as opposed to purely personal) dimensions of that obsession, so it's these that I try to get my students to focus on, asking them how this and other poems figure the fear of, and desire for, death and what death seems to symbolize or signify for Keats.

In the case of this poem, one might ask why the Elgin marbles call up visions of mortality. For Keats, mortality and pain (as well as the consciousness of both) define the human condition, differentiating human beings from the eternal things of nature—the "sky" (line 5) and "sun" (line 14)—and the things of art, yet, ironically or not, being an essential part of the human experience of both (cf. both "Ode to a Nightingale" and the excerpt from the letter to George and Georgiana Keats, below). And it is for that reason, I think, that the speaker's vision of timeless "Grecian grandeur" necessarily also calls up visions of "the rude Wasting of old Time" (lines 12–13) and of himself as "a sick eagle looking at the sky" (line 5), much as the "high requiem" of the nightingale in "Ode to a Nightingale" makes the speaker of that poem envision himself as becoming an earthly "sod" (line 60).

QUESTIONS FOR DISCUSSION

1. As the title of the poem and footnote 6 suggest, the subject of this poem is the poet's or speaker's first experience of the Elgin marbles. When and how does the poem mention or allude directly to that experience or to the marbles?
2. Much of the poem is not about the marbles, but about thoughts of "mortality" (line 1). What does the poem suggest about why this is so? Why might "seeing the Elgin marbles" lead to thoughts of mortality?
3. What similes and metaphors does the speaker employ to describe his feelings in the first five lines of the poem? What does he convey through them?
4. Line 6 begins with a "Yet," suggesting that the speaker is now qualifying or countering what he said in the first five lines. How exactly does he do so in lines 6–8?
5. What are the "dim-conceived glories of the brain" in line 9? The "indescribable feud" they "Bring round the heart" (line 10)?
6. How does this poem compare to "On First Looking into Chapman's Homer"? The experience of seeing the marbles to the experience of reading Chapman's Homer?

When I Have Fears

QUESTIONS FOR DISCUSSION

1. What does the metaphor of lines 1–4 imply about the nature of poetic creation? The imagery of lines 5–8?
2. How do the ideas about poetry and creativity expressed in this poem compare to those expressed in Keats's letters?

Ode to a Nightingale

When I have students who have difficulty grasping the nature and significance of structure, I find that this poem can sometimes bring home to them in a way that others don't a sense of the movement and development within a poem. Perhaps that's so because this high Romantic poem is actually structured almost like an "argument" in the sense that it articulates and probes a problem—the conflict between the human world of consciousness, pain, and mortality and the immortal, unconscious, joyous being of the things of nature and art—and posits a series of solutions, only to ultimately move toward a kind of acceptance of the necessity and power of the problem itself. Perhaps, instead, it's because the form of the poem so subtly and yet so powerfully enacts the very problems and solutions it articulates, form being an obviously necessary part of content in the case of this poem. But regardless of the reason, I do find that the poem's structure is key in a way that students can readily grasp and appreciate, and I thus tend to lead discussion (as the following questions suggest) by walking students through the poem, asking pertinent questions along the way.

QUESTIONS FOR DISCUSSION

1. How exactly is the "lot" of the nightingale characterized in the poem? What feeling does the speaker express toward the nightingale's lot? How is the song or the singing of the nightingale characterized?
2. How exactly does the poem characterize the "lot" of the speaker (and of all human beings)? How exactly does the human condition differ from that enjoyed by the nightingale? What are the attractions of "numbness" (line 1) and "easeful Death" (line 52)?
3. What different ways of joining (and/or of approaching a state more like that of) the nightingale does the speaker propose in stanzas I–III? In stanza IV?
4. What exactly does the speaker mean when he says "Still wouldst thou sing, and I have ears in vain— / To thy high requiem become a sod" (lines 59–60)?
5. What does stanza VII contribute to the poem? How exactly does it build on earlier descriptions of the bird's song?
6. What exactly seems to happen to the speaker at the beginning of stanza VIII? How does this stanza modify the solutions of the early stanzas?
7. What do you make of the very end of the poem, of the fact that the poem ends with questions and with these particular questions?
8. How might this ending relate to Keats's discussion of dreaming in the "Letter to Benjamin Bailey"? How might the poem as a whole relate to Keats's discussion in the same letter of the "Life of Sensations" and the life "of Thoughts"?

Ode on a Grecian Urn

While this poem both structurally and thematically mirrors Keats's "Ode to a Nightingale," juxtaposing the ideal/immortal (in this case, the world of art) and the real/mortal world in which all actions are completed, all pleasures paid for with pain, the speaker's attitude toward the ideal is even more debatable here than in "Nightingale," particularly in terms of whether, when, how, and why that attitude changes over the course of the poem. To get students thinking about this question and about those vexed final lines, you might begin or conclude discussion by giving students a taste of the following interpretation, which insists that the speaker's attitude does change and which essentially dismisses as irrelevant the "special problem" posed by the final lines of the poem:

> The seesaw opposition of earthly and urnly values gets under way immediately [in the poem] with the implications of unnaturalness in "unravish'd bride" and "foster-child," and it continues with increasing intensity through the first three stanzas. In the fourth stanza the speaker takes a fresh look at the urn, worries more onesidedly about the perpetual immobility of the sacrificial procession and the permanent emptiness of the unseen town whence the people have come, and with "desolate" in 40 (cf. "forlorn" in *Nightingale*) arrives at a final acceptance of the real world of time and mortality. The closing lines present a special problem of interpretation, but it seems clear that, while the urn is not entirely rejected at the end, its value lies in its character as a work of art and not in its being a desirable alternative to life in the real world.
>
> Jack Stillinger, *John Keats: Complete Poems*, Boston: Belknap, 1982, p. 469.

QUESTIONS FOR DISCUSSION

1. How exactly does the poet characterize the urn in the first few lines of the poem? What does each of the speaker's three metaphors for the urn suggest about it? What's similar about the metaphors?
2. What details does the poem provide about the "tale" told by the urn? Why can the urn as "sylvan historian" (line 3) express the tale "more sweetly" than a poem (or human poet) can?
3. Why does the poem place so much emphasis on uncompleted actions? On "melodies" "unheard" (line 11)? What explanation seems to be offered in the third stanza?
4. In the final stanza of the poem, the speaker returns to a description of the urn itself, rather than the pictures on the urn. How does the speaker characterize the urn here? How is this characterization and the speaker's attitude toward the urn here like and unlike that of the poem's opening stanza? If you see the speaker's attitude toward the urn as changed here, is that change predicted and/or explained earlier in the poem? If so, where and how?
5. What is the tone of the final two lines? How heavily does a tonal description of these lines depend on whether all, or just part, of the lines are presumed to be "said" by the urn (see footnote 6)? As Jack Stillinger insists, "With or without the quotes there is considerable uncertainty about who speaks the last thirteen words of the poem, and to whom. The four most frequently mentioned possibilities are (1) poet to reader, (2) poet to urn, (3) poet to figures on the urn, and (4) urn to reader" (p. 470). What evidence would you use to make a case for each of these possibilities? How might your reading of the

poem as a whole differ in each case? What's the significance or effect of the very ambiguity? How does this ending compare to those of other Keats poems you've read?
6. What's the significance or effect of all of the questions in the poem? What might such questions reveal about the speaker and the human world he represents?
7. What's the significance of the preposition *on* in the title? How, for example, does the phrase "Ode *on* a Grecian Urn" differ from the phrase "Ode *to* a Grecian Urn"? In what different senses is the ode *on* the urn?
8. In what sense might this poem enact or consider what Keats calls in the "Letter to George and Thomas Keats" "negative capability"?

Ode on Melancholy

Although the opening stanza ostensibly tells the reader to *avoid* the sources of melancholy, the long vowels establish a melancholic tone, qualifying the *kind* of melancholy the speaker wishes to consider: the kind whose onset is "Sudden" (line 12; note the effectiveness of the trochee in this position). The speaker's claim is that only an elite company characterized by the one "whose strenuous tongue / Can burst Joy's grape upon his palate fine" (lines 27–28) can experience melancholy. If the poem in effect invites the reader to become a part of that company by participating in the speaker's sorrow (if we didn't do that, we couldn't appreciate the poem), the speaker also claims that such participation has a cost: consorting with Melancholy leaves one's soul "among her cloudy trophies hung" (line 30).

At some point, this "Ode" actually began with the following stanza, which was later removed from the poem and which has sometimes inspired interesting, and even heated, discussions in my classes (about whether and how exactly its inclusion might change the poem):

> Though you should build a bark of dead men's bones,
>   And rear a phantom gibbet for a mast,
> Stitch creeds together for a sail, with groans
>   To fill it out, bloodstained and aghast;
> Although your rudder be a Dragon's tail,
>   Long sever'd, yet still hard with agony,
>   Your cordage large uprootings from the skull
> Of bald Medusa; certes you would fail
>   To find the Melancholy, whether she
>   Dreameth in any isle of Lethe dull.

QUESTIONS FOR DISCUSSION

1. What do lines 9 and 10 mean?
2. Is the mistress of line 18 a human being or the "She" of line 21—that

is, Melancholy personified? What difference does it make?

3. Why does the speaker claim that Melancholy lives with Beauty, Joy, Pleasure, and Delight? What explanation is offered by the precise way in which the speaker describes "Beauty," "Joy," etc.?

4. How exactly does the speaker characterize the "him" who somewhat suddenly appears in line 27? What's "him's" role in the poem?

5. Does the poet distinguish here between different kinds of melancholy or between different attitudes toward melancholy? If so, how is each defined?

6. What similarities do you see—in terms of form and content—between this ode and the Keats poems you've read earlier?

7. How might this poem consider the issues raised in Keats's 1819 letter to George and Georgiana Keats (quoted below in the discussion of Keats's letters)?

To Autumn

In part because it was definitely the last written of Keats's odes and in part because of its own form and content, "To Autumn" is often seen by critics as offering Keats's final, conclusive look at the issues and questions raised throughout the odes. Particularly relevant in this regard is the way the poem raises, only to quickly dismiss, what Jack Stillinger calls a "yearning for the otherworlds of the nightingale and the urn" in lines 23–24, while the rest of the poem wholeheartedly affirms and "celebrates" the actual "world of process" that is embraced only with a kind of resignation toward the end of "Ode to a Nightingale" and "Ode on a Grecian Urn" (Stillinger, p. 477). One might, however, see this poem as offering less a conclusion than an alternative view, or even a view that—because of the poem's reference to the equal "music" of spring and autumn (line 24)—isn't necessarily all that different from, or at odds with, those offered in earlier odes. It is interesting, nonetheless, to note that this poem, like "Ode on Melancholy," creates a sense of conclusiveness, in part, by its minimal use of the questions that are so crucial to the earlier odes, embodying—as they do—the very restlessness of human consciousness, the difficulty of simply being, that the poems themselves consider.

QUESTIONS FOR DISCUSSION

1. What stage of autumn is described in each stanza of "To Autumn"? What images are associated with each stage?

2. What qualities described here are associated in other Keats poems with the world of imagination?

3. Compare this poem with the four preceding odes. How would you describe the tone of each? What similarities and differences do you see in terms of imagery and theme? In terms of form?

Passages from Letters

I have had more than one student leave my class at the end of a semester avowing that Keats's letters were among their favorite reading, a reaction that has taught me not to treat these letters as mere containers for Keats's ideas about poetry (as I am wont to do), but instead as texts as rich and delightful in their own way as Keats's poems. To that end, I try to make sure that my classes at some point discuss the style, as well as the content, of Keats's letters, comparing Keats's prose style to that of his poetry and considering how the prose stylistically embodies some of the ideas about creativity, imagination, thought, sensation, etc. conveyed in the poems. (More advanced students might even benefit from reading some or all of Clifford Siskins's remarks on these issues in his *The Historicity of Romantic Discourse.*)

Because of their content, rather than their form, the following two excerpts (from letters not included in the anthology) have proven very helpful and illuminating to my students when grappling with Keats. (And though I've taken these quotations directly from Gittings's edition of Keats's letters, both are included in the more readily accessible second volume of the *Norton Anthology of English Literature*, 6th ed.) The first excerpt, from a letter to Richard Woodhouse (October 27, 1818), contains Keats's famous description of the "camelion Poet":

> As to the poetical Character itself, (I mean that sort of which, if I am any thing, I am a Member; that sort distinguished from the wordsworthian or egoistical sublime; which is a thing per se and stands alone) it is not itself—it has not self—it is every thing and nothing—it has no character—it enjoys light and shade; it lives in gusto, be it foul or fair, high or low, rich or poor, mean or elevated. . . . What shocks the virtuous philosop[h]er, delights the camelion Poet. It does no harm from its relish of the dark side of things any more than from its taste for the bright one; because they both end in speculation. A Poet is the most unpoetical of any thing in existence; because he has no Identity—he is continually in for—and filling some other Body—The Sun, the Moon, the Sea and Men and Women who are creatures of impulse are poetical and have about them an unchangeable attribute—the poet has none; no identity—he is certainly the most unpoetical of all God's Creatures.

Robert Gittings, ed., *Letters of John Keats*, New York: Oxford University Press, 1986, p. 157.

In the second excerpt, from a letter written to George and Georgiana Keats from February 14 to May 3, 1819, Keats expresses his convictions about the necessity of human suffering and articulates his vision of the world as a "Vale of Soul-Making":

> The most interesting question that can come before us is, How far by the persevering endeavours of a seldom appearing Socrates Mankind may be made happy—I can imagine such happiness carried to an extreme—but what must it end in?—Death—and who could in such a case bear with death—the whole troubles of life which are

now frittered away in a series of years, would the[n] be accumulated for the last days of a being who instead of hailing its approach, would leave this world as Eve left Paradise—But in truth I do not at all believe in this sort of perfectibility—the nature of the world will not admit of it—the inhabitants of the world will correspond to itself—Let the fish philosophise the ice away from the Rivers in winter time and they shall be at continual play in the tepid delight of summer. Look at the Poles and at the sands of Africa, Whirlpools and volcanoes—Let men exterminate them and I will say that they may arrive at earthly Happiness—The point at which Man may arrive is as far as the paralel [sic] state in inanimate nature and no further—For instance suppose a rose to have sensation, it blooms on a beautiful morning it enjoys itself—but there comes a cold wind, a hot sun—it cannot escape it, it cannot destroy its annoyances—they are as native to the world as itself: no more can man be happy in spite, the world[l]y elements will prey upon his nature— The common cognomen of this world among the misguided and superstitious is "a vale of tears" from which we are redeemed by a certain arbitrary interposition of God and taken to Heaven—What a little circumscribe[d] straightened notion! Call the world if you Please "The vale of Soul-making" Then you will find out the use of the world . . . I say *"Soul Making"* Soul as distinguished from an Intelligence— There may be intelligences or sparks of the divinity in millions—but they are not Souls the till they acquire identities, till each one is personally itself. I[n]telligences are atoms of perception—they know and they see and they are pure, in short they are God—how then are Souls to be made? How then are these sparks which are God to have identity given them—so as ever to possess a bliss peculiar to each ones individual existence? How, but by the medium of a world like this? (Gittings, pp. 249–250)

QUESTIONS ON THE POETRY AND PROSE OF KEATS

1. Bowers recur often in Keats. How are they characterized? What kind of emotional reactions do they generate? What other images does Keats associate with them?

2. How frequently is Keats concerned with the external world of pain and fretfulness? What alternative escapes from the external world or solutions to its problems does he suggest or portray? How do the alternatives vary from the early poetry to the late? Is there any pattern of tonal differences from the early to the late poetry?

3. What themes recur most often in the poems here? What images? What kinds of images? What metrical pattern does Keats seem most fond of? What stanza forms? Does Keats seem more successful in exploiting the potential of the sonnet or the ode? What tendencies of each form seem to attract him? What changes in Keats help to explain his preference for the ode in later poems?

4. Which poems are most illuminated by knowledge of Keats's life? By familiarity with his letters? What kind of contribution to a poem's effect is made by biographical information? Are any of the poems completely inaccessible without biographical knowledge?

READING/WRITING IDEAS FOR CHAPTER 21

ESSAYS ON THE AUTHOR'S WORK AS CONTEXT

Among my favorite assignments, one that I have found both very useful and very enjoyable for students, is the assignment that asks them to write about "the author's work as context" or to produce what I call multiple-text, single-author essays. Students find this assignment both instructive and gratifying for a number of reasons, not least the sense of accomplishment they get from feeling that they have become experts on something. Requiring students to make some use of the excerpts from Keats's prose included in the anthology adds even greater depth to the assignment because it allows students to begin to use primary source material in a relatively painless way, allowing them (and you) to focus on questions about why and how writers use such material to make arguments before getting caught up in questions about how researchers locate it.

The multiple-text, single-author essay presents a series of useful challenges for student writers, especially when it comes to theses and structure. For that very reason, I always begin this assignment sequence by having students read multiple sample student essays to address questions about why one writes such essays, about what kinds of theses and structures tend to work, and about how writers decide which structures fit their arguments.

I have discovered over the years three types of workable structures for such essays, and I generally try to provide students with sample essays that represent each of these types. Though I have yet to come up with satisfying names for these three structures, I can offer the following rough characterizations:

1. The "side-by-side" or "simultaneous" structure in which a writer discusses all of the works by his or her author simultaneously. Within the body of the essay, topic sentences tend to be claims about the author and his or her work in general and paragraphs include evidence from all or most of the texts under discussion. Obviously, this structure tends to work best when the writer has one overarching interpretation that fits all of the texts under discussion, when the poems all seem to fall into a single, basic pattern.

Sample Thesis I

Paradoxically, Whitman considers himself simultaneously a god and a man. He embraces the contradiction by proclaiming himself a divine human: mortal but immortal, flawed but perfect, creator although created.

Sample Body Paragraph Beginnings I

Whitman is not always such a forward teacher. In one poem he refers to himself as "A man who . . . turns a casual look upon you and then averts his face, / Leaving you to prove and define it, / Expecting the main things from you" ("Poets to Come"). Whitman feels that the willingness of each individual reader will determine who reaps the benefits of his wisdom. In his poem "On the Beach at Night," Whitman sums up his role as writer. He describes a scene on a seashore in which a little girl, grasping her father's hand, watches clouds swallow the night sky. The girl begins to cry at the sight of the stars disappearing under the blackness. Her father comforts her, saying:

> Something there is
> (With my lips soothing thee, adding I whisper,
> I give thee the first suggestion, the problem and indirection)
> Something there is more immortal even than the stars

Whitman is to us as the father is to the child: mortal also, and therefore equal, but figuratively older and therefore wiser. . . .

What, according to Whitman, makes all humans divine? Whitman turns to the notions of immortality and overlapping souls to help explain this. He claims that all life stems from a great timeless and universal spirituality. As a result, life and death are intertwined. "The living are the dead," he writes ("Pensive and Faltering"). Death is even a form of blessing, and serves as an escape from an "excrementitious" body ("To One Shortly to Die").

> From Janet S. McIntosh, "These Incredible Gods We Are: Walt Whitman's Vision of a Religious Democracy." In *Exposé: Essays from the Expository Writing Program Harvard University 1987–1988*, Cambridge, Mass.: Harvard Expository Writing Program, 1988, pp. 38–41.

2. The "serial" or "one-text-at-a-time" structure. Here, the body of the essay is divided into text-specific sections, the challenge being to craft very clear and careful transition paragraphs. This structure tends to work best (or only) when students can show that and how one text somehow complicates the view of an author's work that might be suggested by another text. It works especially well for essays that make arguments about the development of an author's work over time, exploring—for example—the way that Keats's odes move from a desire to escape the human, mortal world to a celebration of it.

Sample Thesis II

If there is to be a common imaginative vision for the [West Indian] islands, it must find its way between an attitude of bitterness and rejecting all connection with the colonial past, and an attitude of merely mimicking the nations that controlled that past. Creating this vision is the work of the poet, and [Derek] Walcott's work can be seen as a struggle toward it.

Sample Body Paragraph Beginnings II

In his long autobiographical poem "Another Life" (1973), Walcott describes his friend Harry, a man who is bitter and obsessed with rejecting everything European, anything connected to the oppression and destruction caused by colonial powers. Harry wants to "black out" the millennium, the future and the past, to embrace a nativist idea of his country, "telling himself that although it stank this was the vegetable excrement of natural life." . . .

Walcott suggests the need for a more complicated attitude toward the past than Harry's as early as "Ruins of a Great House" (1962). The poem tells of his wanderings around the remnants of an old colonial mansion. . . . He is unable to erase the bad and the good effects of the colonial era on him, and he is perplexed by the different types of influences colonial rule has had on him. "Hawkins, Walter Raleigh, Drake" were all "ancestral murderers" and criminals, yet they were also poets, poets whom Walcott had studied and enjoyed. . . .

[Walcott] believes that poetry has the power to pull the past into the present in such a way that the past becomes a history, a true, constructive, and self-defined history that allows the present to have a foundation upon which culture can develop.

> Poetry, which is perfection's sweat but which must seem as fresh as raindrops on a statue's brow, combines the natural and the marmoreal; it conjugates both tenses simultaneously: the past and the present, if the past is the sculpture and the present the beads of dew or rain on the forehead of the past. ["The Sigh of History," *New York Times* 8 Dec. 1992: A25.]

Walcott is often successful in creating this poetry. "The Schooner Flight" in particular provides a poetic discussion, in a West Indian voice, of history and race in a context of contemporary Caribbean life.

"The Schooner Flight" is the story of a sailor, Shabine, who journeys throughout the Caribbean sea. The sea is pivotal in Walcott's attempt to reformulate a history of the islands, for it contains a memory of the fragments of the past.

From Mary Rose Kwaan, "Poetry Mends History: Derek Walcott and the West Indian Past." In *Exposé: Essays from the Expository Writing Program, Harvard University, 1992–1993*, Cambridge, Mass.: Harvard Expository Writing Program, 1993, pp. 9–14.

Sample Thesis III

Through her verse, Dickinson shows her readers how her contemplative, secluded life helped her achieve personal happiness. Reading her hundreds of poems, one realizes that her isolated introspection not only helped purify her perceptions, but was a crucial part of her self-identity and both a source of pleasure and a preparation for personal fulfillment.

Sample Paragraph Beginnings III

In her poetry, Dickinson divides her existence into two distinct spheres—one of happiness and another of unhappiness. As she indicates in "I can wade grief," she sees her earthly existence as the sphere of unhappiness and happiness itself as a strange experience. . . . In this poem, as in many of her poems on the topic of fulfillment, Dickinson describes unhappiness and happiness in physical, tangible terms. She describes grief as a heavy body of water, and happiness as a "push" that trips her up, that brings her to a psychological inebriation. . . .

This sharp division between happiness and unhappiness reflects the nature of desire and fulfillment in Dickinson's poetry. In order for a need to be fulfilled, for a desire to be satiated, for an unhappiness to be transformed into a happiness that is recognized as happiness, a marked contrast must exist between the present state in which one exists and the ideal state towards which one aspires. Dickinson explains this idea concisely and elegantly in "Water is taught by thirst." . . . One who has not lived in deprivation (and thus has not longed for a particular ideal state) cannot fully appreciate happiness at its highest potential value.

In "Success is counted sweetest," Dickinson again suggests that only through the experience of failure does one develop true appreciation of an ideal.

> From Lauren Marie Kim, " 'Come Slowly, Eden!': Desire and Fulfillment in Dickinson."
> In *Exposé: Essays from the Expository Writing Program, Harvard University, 1994–1995*,
> Cambridge, Mass.: Harvard Expository Writing Program, 1995, pp. 34–37.

3. The "lens" structure in which a writer focuses primarily on one text, using it as a "lens" through which to look closely at the entire canon of the author's work, using references to other texts merely to support or amplify points about the focal text. This structure tends to work best when students see one text as particularly typical and/or revealing of an author's work.

As the "Planning Ideas" for this chapter suggest, you could easily have students write such essays about poets other than Keats, and the exercises below should prove usable (perhaps, with modifications) for any of these poets.

As with other kinds of assignments, you'll undoubtedly also confront questions about how specific to be with the assignment, whether to specify the texts and topics that students must consider in their essays or whether to allow them to identify their own. The exercises described below will probably work best in the latter case, but you could also use an in-class discussion of Exercise 1 to generate a list of possible topics from which students can then choose (thus imposing at least some limits). If, on the other hand, you want to give students more direction and guidance from the beginning, you might consider using one or more of the following prompts (all of which, in fact, still leave student writers a great deal of room to maneuver).

- Reread the passages from Keats's letters of November 22 and December 21, 1817, especially the description of "Negative Capability" and the analogy of the flower. (In the latter passage Keats puts a new twist on the old argument about whether it is better to be a spider [to spin out one's own creations] or a bee [to transform what has been gathered from others into something new].) Then reread the poems. Write an essay that explores the question of whether and how Keats's poetry is consistent with the ideas expressed in these letters.
- Suppose Keats were the only poet identified with the Romantic sensibility. Basing your ideas solely on Keats's poetry and prose, write an essay that uses examples drawn from this material to outline the main characteristics of Romanticism.
- Find, in a complete edition of Keats's poetry, the poems he wrote during the last seventeen months of his life. Write an essay that analyzes the differences between these late poems and those included in the anthology.
- Locate and read the other odes that are considered part of the group that includes "Ode to a Nightingale," "Ode on a Grecian Urn," "Ode on Melancholy," and "To Autumn." Write an essay that considers how these poems work together as a group. What kind of formal and thematic progression, if any, do you see occurring across

these poems? *Or* write an essay that considers how our interpretation of any one of these poems might differ if we read it on its own and as part of the group. What is lost and gained in taking each approach?

- Write an essay in which you consider what Jack Stillinger calls the "special problem" of interpretation posed by the final lines of Keats's "Ode on a Grecian Urn," concentrating on how one might better understand and/or resolve those problems by considering this poem in relation to all of Keats's other poems and prose.

Note that this last prompt would most likely steer students toward the third, lens-type essay described above.

TROUBLESHOOTING

Careful, thoughtful discussion of structure is key to helping student writers to write truly successful multiple-text, single-author essays because the real danger is that such essays prove to be either incredibly repetitive (again in this text we see . . .) or incredibly incoherent, rambling through a series of similarities without really making connections between them or indicating their overall significance.

AUTHOR'S WORK AS CONTEXT–WRITING EXERCISES

1. Identifying and Describing Patterns in the Author's Work

The following is an exercise that has proved very helpful to my students as a way to generate ideas for essays about multiple texts by a single author.

Read through your author's poems at least once, underlining words and passages that seem significant to you. As you read, work not only to understand the individual poems but also to look for patterns across these poems, similarities that link them together into a coherent whole, make them part of a unified canon. Once you have finished, think more about these similarities, working to answer the following questions as if you were trying to capture for someone who hadn't read your author the essence of that author's work. You may well also want to make notes about which of the words and passages you underlined in reading the poems might serve to illustrate or support the claims you make.

- How would you describe your author's typical **speaker?** What makes them alike? What (internal and external) characteristics do they tend to share?
- Which speaker seems most typical in light of your description? The least typical? Why?
- How would you describe and/or categorize the **other characters or objects** whom the speakers encounter, or interact with, in the poems? Are there similar types?
- Which character(s) or objects seem the most typical? the least typical? Why?
- How do the poems tend to characterize the relationship between the speaker and the object or character you've just described—do they operate as foils to the speaker, clear antagonists? What attitudes do the speakers tend to adopt toward the things and/ or persons they interact with and/or describe in the poems? What similarities and differences do you see here?
- How would you describe the **situation and setting** of these poems? The significance

and role of the setting in the poems? In light of situation and setting, which poems seem most typical? Least typical?

- How would you describe the **problems or conflicts** that the speakers of these poems typically face or that the poems tend to explore?
- In terms of conflict, etc., what's the most typical poem? The least typical? Why?
- How would you describe the **internal structure** of the poems?
- In light of this description of structure, which poem is the most typical? The least typical? Why?
- How would you characterize the author's use of **language and imagery**?
- Are there recurring images or types of images? How are individual poems similar to, and different from, each other in terms of their treatment of these images?
- How would you describe the **sound qualities** of these poems, the author's use of rhyme, alliteration, meter, etc.?
- What else do you notice about the **form** of these poems? (How) does the author use traditional forms?
- What's the overall **tone** or **mood** of these poems—the feelings they tend to evoke? How do they do so? In terms of tone, which poems seem most typical? Least typical? Why?
- What do you think are the **themes**, concerns, problems, or issues articulated or tackled in these poems? How are individual poems similar to, and different from, each other in terms of their treatment of these themes?
- In terms of any or all of these elements, what claims might you make about how the poet's poetry changes over time? For example, do later poems treat or view certain subjects, themes, and/or conflicts differently from earlier ones?

Taking all of these factors into account and without referring to any particular poem, use this sheet of paper to narrate, outline, script out, or draw a map or flowchart that captures the basic features, action, elements, etc. of your author's poetry.

If appropriate do the same thing again, this time working to illustrate how that poetry changes over time, how later poems differ from earlier ones.

2. Generating Theses and Describing Structures

See "Reading/Writing Ideas for Chapter 8."

3. Crafting Titles with Quotations in Them

One way to get students thinking about their own titles and about strategies for making them both compelling and informative involves having students do an exercise during the planning or drafting of their essays in which they identify lines or just single words from the author's work that might be incorporated into their titles in some way. Though the easiest way involves following up a quotation with a colon and the "real" title, I also like to have students experiment with other possibilities. I find that doing this exercise not only tends to improve their titles (if only by making them think about what titles do), and turns out to be quite fun for them, but also can help them refine their ideas about just what their essay is all about and, sometimes, just which poem really carries the crux of the argument. (Note that the first and last student essays cited above have precisely this kind of title.)

22

THE AUTHOR'S WORK IN CONTEXT: ADRIENNE RICH

While Keats's poetic career lasted only a few years, Adrienne Rich's poetry has developed over several decades, changing remarkably in the process. Despite these changes, and despite the complexity of her work, the poems remain fairly accessible. And what W. H. Auden said of her first volume of poetry (*A Change of World*, 1951, published when Rich was twenty-one) remains true of her most recent work: "[T]he poems a reader will encounter in this book are neatly and modestly dressed, speak quietly but do not mumble, respect the elders but are not cowed by them, and do not tell fibs: that, for a first volume, is a good deal." While retaining the "good deal" of understatement, deference, and polish of her early poetry, Rich's more recent work speaks in a voice very much her own. Rich talks openly about the development of her poetry in "Talking with Adrienne Rich" and in excerpts from other essays that are included in the notes below.

PLANNING IDEAS

- As with Keats, it makes sense to introduce Rich's prose before discussing much of the poetry.
- Poems by Rich that are not included in this chapter are listed in the author index. "Letters in the Family" pairs usefully with "For the Record."
- The Norton Critical Editions of *Adrienne Rich's Poetry* (1975) and *Adrienne Rich's Poetry and Prose* (1993), both edited by Barbara Charlesworth Gelpi and Albert Gelpi, contain much material by and about Rich that might prove very illuminating and helpful to students working on the poet. For that reason, I've included a great many quotations and excerpts from the latter of these volumes (cited as Gelpi and Gelpi) in the notes below, leaving it up to you to decide which, if any, such

excerpts you want to share with your students and which of the essays I've excerpted you might want to have students read in their entirety.
- Other poets, especially Donne, Dickinson, and Olds, can be studied intensively. See the last of the planning ideas in the previous chapter for details.

At a Bach Concert

With its emphasis on "This antique discipline" (line 4) and "Form" as "the ultimate gift that love can offer" (line 7) and with its own carefully disciplined use of language and rhyme, "At a Bach Concert" perfectly expresses and embodies the formalist approach to, and ideal of, poetry that Rich attributed in 1964 to the young poet she once was:

> In the period in which my first two books [including *A Change of World* (1951), from which "At a Bach Concert" is taken] were written I had a much more absolutist approach to the universe than I now have. I also felt—as many people still feel—that a poem was an arrangement of ideas and feelings, pre-determined, and it said what I had already decided it should say. There were occasional surprises, occasions of happy discovery that an unexpected turn could be taken, but control, technical mastery and intellectual clarity were the real goals, and for many reasons it was satisfying to be able to create this kind of formal order in poems.
>
> Only gradually, within the last five or six years, did I begin to feel that these poems, even the ones I liked best and in which I felt I'd said most, were queerly limited; that in many cases I had suppressed, omitted, falsified even, certain disturbing elements, to gain the perfection of order. ("Poetry and Experience: Statement at a Poetry Reading," Gelpi and Gelpi, p. 165)

As Judith McDaniel observes, the poem suggests—through both form and content—that "[o]nly through controlled, restraining forms can . . . emotion be communicated safely. The danger is twofold. Too great a compassion is sentiment, not art; and the artist may reveal more of herself than is safe for her, or than her critical audience would wish to read" (" 'Reconstituting the World': The Poetry and Vision of Adrienne Rich," Gelpi and Gelpi, p. 312).

As Rich's own comments on this early work suggest, not only in "When We Dead Awaken," but also in "Talking with Adrienne Rich," she would later come to see this emphasis on form and on the careful containment of emotion as itself a revealing symptom of her oppression and repression, describing the "formalism" of these years in the essay "When We Dead Awaken" as "part of the strategy [that]—like asbestos gloves, . . . allowed me to handle materials I couldn't pick up barehanded" (Gelpi and Gelpi, p. 171). As a result, one could easily describe her own early poetic voice in the same terms she herself uses (in the same essay) to describe that of Virginia Woolf, "trying to sound as cool as Jane Austen, as Olympian as Shakespeare, because that is the way the men of the culture thought a writer should sound" (p. 169).

QUESTIONS FOR DISCUSSION

1. Where is the "here" of line 3?
2. What is "this antique discipline" (line 4)?
3. What claims is the poem making about art? How do the structure and form of the poem reinforce these claims?
4. What exactly are the dangers, according to this poem, of emotion—in art and in life?

Storm Warnings

This poem develops a complex metaphor of changing weather to describe human emotions and psychology and to explore a conflict between emotional "storms" and their containment that is very similar to that in "At a Bach Concert." In this poem, however, the conflict is much more explicit and visceral, the sense of control much more cautious and fragile. Thus, as Rich has recently said of it, " 'Storm Warnings' is a poem about powerlessness—about a force so much greater than our human powers that while it can be measured and even predicted, it is beyond human control. All 'we' can do is create an interior space against the storm, an enclave of self-protection, though the winds of change still penetrate the keyholes and 'unsealed apertures.' "

As in "At a Bach Concert," poetic form itself becomes part and parcel of such efforts at containment and control, itself a kind of "defense against the season" (line 26). In the words of Judith McDaniel, "The controlled iambic rhythm, broken appropriately in the first, fourth, and sixth lines by an anapest as the wind strains against the glass, contains the threat of violent weather, just as the imagined room protects the poet. The form of the poem is a device, used exactly as the drawn curtains and the hurricane lanterns [are]" (" 'Reconstituting the World': The Poetry and Vision of Adrienne Rich" [1978], Gelpi and Gelpi, p. 311).

QUESTIONS FOR DISCUSSION

1. What is the speaker's relationship to her internal weather, especially in lines 15–21 and lines 26–28?
2. How would you describe the form of "Storm Warnings"? How does the form of the poem relate to its content?
3. This poem was written in the same year as "At a Bach Concert" and "Aunt Jennifer's Tigers." What similarities of form and theme can you identify in these two poems? How might the metaphor of an internal storm apply to the other poem?

Living in Sin

Published in Rich's second volume of poetry, *The Diamond Cutters and Other Poems* (1955), "Living in Sin" technically belongs to her earliest, "formalist" phase. Nonetheless, it often and I think rightly strikes my students as somewhat less rigidly formal than the preceding poems, as well as more speculative and emotional—to use Rich's own words, more a poem that is an experience than one that is *"about* experiences" ("Poetry and Experience: Statement at a Poetry Reading," Gelpi and Gelpi, p. 165). "Rightly," in part, because the poem itself is so very much about the disorder of our physical and emotional lives, about the distance between the order we imagine or hope for and the "relentless" "grime" and grind of reality (lines 26, 4).

The structure of the poem works to highlight this conflict and the differences between the man's and woman's experience of it. Lines 1–7 seem to articulate the woman's early romantic vision of what "love" should look and feel like—her belief that love, like the "studio," "would keep itself" perfectly neat and orderly and beautiful without any effort at all. Lines 8–14 describe the messy, unkempt reality of the studio and the love it both symbolizes and houses; while lines 15–22 describe the different reactions of the woman and her lover to this reality, describing the work she undertakes to "keep" a studio and a relationship that doesn't, after all, "keep itself," to fight back "the minor demons," along with the dirt (lines 1, 19). And, finally, lines 23–26 indicate both the success and the ultimate failure of that work, the extent to which the woman manages to work herself "back in love again," even if she cannot "wholly" or permanently chase away the dust or the demons (lines 23–24).

With its focus on a woman's dissatisfaction with heterosexual love, its use of words such as "heresy" (line 3) to describe that dissatisfaction, and its emphasis on man as (ineffectual) music maker and woman as caretaker, the poem also may be seen to embark—however tentatively—on the kind of feminist critique of gender roles, family, romance, and "compulsory heterosexuality" to which Rich would later devote herself and much of her poetry. Yet part of its tentativeness resides, as Rich herself suggests of other early poems, in the way the poem refuses to personalize the emotions it depicts, instead creating "an imaginary woman," "a person as distinct from myself as possible—distanced by the formalism of the poem, by its objective, observant tone" ("When We Dead Awaken," Gelpi and Gelpi, p. 171; see also the excerpt from this essay following "Snapshots of a Daughter-in-Law" in the anthology).

As Rich would later remark of the decade in which these early poems were written and of her own experiences as writer and mother,

[T]hese were the fifties, and in reaction to the earlier wave of feminism, middle-class women were making careers of domestic perfection, working to send their husbands through professional schools, then retiring to raise large families. People were moving out to the suburbs . . . ; the family was in its glory. Life was extremely private; women were isolated from each other by the loyalties of marriage. I have a sense that women didn't talk to each other much in the fifties—not about their secret emptinesses, their frustrations. I went on trying to write; my second book and first child appeared in the same month. ("When We Dead Awaken," Gelpi and Gelpi, p. 173)

Looking back at poems I wrote before I was twenty-one, I'm startled because beneath the conscious craft are glimpses of the split I even then experienced between the girl who wrote poems, who defined herself in writing poems, and the girl who was to define herself by her relationships with men. ("When We Dead Awaken," Gelpi and Gelpi, p. 171)

But at the middle of the fifties I had no very clear idea of my positioning in the world or even that such an idea was an important resource for a writer to have. I knew that marriage and motherhood, experiences which were supposed to be truly womanly, often left me feeling unfit, disempowered, adrift. ("Blood, Bread, and Poetry: The Location of the Poet," Gelpi and Gelpi, p. 244)

QUESTIONS FOR DISCUSSION

1. How would you describe the structure of "Living in Sin"? What vision of the studio and of love is offered in the first seven lines of the poem? What are the various meanings of the statement that "She had thought the studio would keep itself" (line 1)? How does this vision or thought relate to the vision that follows in lines 8–14?
2. What do the actions of the man and woman described in lines 15–22 suggest about their individual attitudes toward, and roles in, the relationship? What does the poem suggest about the nature or causes of "the minor demons" that "jeered" at the woman (line 19)? What's the significance of the coffee pot boiling over in line 22?
3. What do you make of the final lines of the poem? What kind of resolution, if any, does it offer to the problems or conflicts depicted in the poem? In what way is it a "happy" ending? In what way isn't it?
4. What do you think the milkman means or symbolizes (to us and/or to the woman within the poem)?
5. What do you make of the title?
6. What similarities and differences do you see between this poem and those that preceded it, both in terms of form and in terms of content or themes?

Snapshots of a Daughter-in-Law

Both Rich and her critics and reviewers insist that "Snapshots of a Daughter-in-Law," written as the 1950s turned into the 1960s, marks her first major movement away from the poetic, emotive, and psychological formalism and restraint of her early work and toward a kind of risk taking that includes a greatly intensified and increasingly articulate feminist consciousness. Both that new experimentalism and the remnants of the dedication to restraint are, as Rich's own discussion of this poem in "When We Dead Awaken" suggests, embodied in the way "Snapshots" oscillates between the deeply personal and autobiographical even as it insistently makes use of *she* rather than *I* to refer to the main character and speaker.

It seems important, however, that the poem begins not with that speaker, but with a mother modeled after Rich's own—a Southern "lady" and accomplished pianist whom Rich describes in "Split at the Root: An Essay on Jewish Identity" (1982) as a "frustrated artis[t] and intellectua[l]," "a lost composer" (Gelpi and Gelpi, p. 225). The mother initiates the poem by serving as a symbol of the choice of conventional femaleness and femininity over creativity and art or "materna[l]," altruistic love over artistic "ego[ism]," as Rich's puts it in the section of "When We Dead Awaken" included in the anthology. As a result, the question that drives the poem is whether the daughter-in-law has or must make the same choice and the same sacrifice, whether eating "wedding-cake" necessarily entails the "mouldering" of the female "mind" (line 7), along with its supposedly selfish desires and ambitions, or whether the daughter truly can "gro[w] another way" (line 13).

A related issue raised fairly early on in the poem is the relationship between women, an issue that in later years becomes increasingly vital to Rich's poetry and prose. In this poem, women are seen as destructive enemies to, rather than supports for, one another precisely because they "Kno[w] themselves too well in one another" (p. 40). The poem thus seems to suggest that women can deal with the choices and limitations imposed on them as individual women only by insistently and even violently imposing them on other women as well—"the old knives / that have rusted in my back, I drive into yours, / *ma semblable, ma soeur!*" (lines 37–39).

The woman in the poem does find "sisterhood" and supportive female peers and role models of a sort, however, in the women writers who have come before her, including Emily Dickinson (line 45), Mary Wollstonecraft (lines 69–75), and even, indirectly, Simone de Beauvoir (lines 76ff. and n. 3). And because Dickinson and Wollstonecraft are so crucial to the poem, I often have students read either "[My Life had stood—a Loaded Gun]" and excerpts from *A Vindication of the Rights of Woman* in conjunction with this poem or excerpts from Rich's own remarks about these two writers. The most directly relevant of those remarks can be found in the essays "Blood, Bread, and Poetry: The Location of the Poet" (1984) and "Vesuvius at Home: The Power of Emily Dickinson" (1975). Both of these essays are in Gelpi and Gelpi, but the following excerpts also stand perfectly well on their own:

It was in the pain and confusion of that inward wrenching of the self, which I experienced directly as a young woman in the fifties, that I started to feel my way backward. . . . And I began searching for some clue or key to life, not only in poetry but in political writers. The writers I found were Mary Wollstonecraft, Simone de Beauvoir, and James Baldwin. Each of them helped me to realize that what had seemed simply "the way things are" could actually be a social construct, advantageous to some people and detrimental to others, and that these constructs could be criticized and changed. The myths and obsessions of gender, the myths and obsessions of race, the violence of exercise of power in these relationships could be identified, their territories could be mapped. They were not simply part of my private turmoil, a secret misery, an individual failure. I did not yet know what I, a white woman, might have to say about the racial obsessions of white consciousness. But I did begin to resist the apparent splitting of poet from woman, thinker from woman, and to write what I feared was political poetry. ("Blood," Gelpi and Gelpi, p. 245)

There is one poem ["My Life had stood—a Loaded Gun"] which is the real "onlie begetter" of my thoughts here about Dickinson; a poem I have mused over, repeated to myself, taken into myself over many years. I think it is a poem about possession by the daemon [of artistic creativity], about the dangers and risks of such possession if you are a woman, about the knowledge that power in a woman can seem destructive, and that you cannot live without the daemon once it has possessed you. The archetype of the daemon as masculine is beginning to change, but it has been real for women up until now. But this woman poet also perceives herself as a lethal weapon. . . . Here the poet sees herself as split, not between anything so simple as "masculine" and "feminine" identity but between the hunter, admittedly masculine, but also a human persona, an active, willing being, and the gun—an object, condemned to remain inactive until the hunter—the *owner*—takes possession of it. The gun contains an energy capable of rousing echoes in the mountains and lighting up the valleys; it is also deadly, "Vesuvian"; it is also its owner's defender against the "foe." It is the gun, furthermore, who *speaks for him*. If there is a female consciousness in this poem it is buried deeper than the images: it exists in the ambivalence toward power, which is extreme. Active willing and creation in women are forms of aggression, and aggression is both "the power to kill" and punishable by death. The union of gun with hunter embodies the danger of identifying and taking hold of her forces, not least that in so doing she risks defining herself—and being defined—as aggressive, as unwomanly ("and now we hunt the Doe"), and as potentially lethal. That which she experiences in herself as energy and potency can also be experienced as pure destruction. . . . The poet experiences herself as loaded gun, imperious energy; yet without the Owner, the possessor, she is merely lethal. Should that possession abandon her—but the thought is unthinkable: "He longer *must* than I." The pronoun is masculine; the antecedent is what Keats called "The Genius of Poetry." ("Vesuvius," Gelpi and Gelpi, pp. 189–191)

QUESTIONS FOR DISCUSSION

1. The poem opens with the main character/speaker's description of her mother. How exactly is the mother and the "way" she has "grow[n]" or lived characterized here (line 13)? What do the various similes here contribute to that characterization, especially the reference to her

"mind" "mouldering like wedding-cake" (line 7)? What's the significance of the fact that the mother is envisioned "play[ing] a Chopin prelude" (line 4)? What is the significance or effect of the fact the poem starts in this way, with the mother rather than the daughter?

2. What's the significance of the messages conveyed to the woman by the "angles" in the second section of the poem? Of her confusion about whether they really are angels (line 23)?

3. What do you think the speaker means when she says that "A thinking woman sleeps with monsters" (line 26)? How does this statement relate to the depiction of relationships between women in this section and the beginning of the next?

4. In section four, the speaker refers to an Emily Dickinson poem that you may have read, "[My Life had stood—a Loaded Gun]." How is that poem relevant to the situation in this poem? How does the poet Emily Dickinson figure for the woman in this poem? How might this reference to Dickinson follow from or qualify the depictions of the relationships between women that precedes it?

5. What other female authors and/or works by women are mentioned in the poem? What role do they play, separately and together? What about male authors and/or works by men? As the excerpt from "When We Dead Awaken" suggests, Rich later came to see this poem as "too literary, too dependent on allusion," but what (positive) role do such allusions play in the poem, especially in terms of characterizing the speaker and the various conflicts she experiences? Later in the essay Rich goes on to say that she used so many allusions because "I hadn't found the courage yet to do without authorities," but might you see that battle with authorities as an important part of the poem itself? If so, how so? If not, how not?

6. What do you make of the end of the poem? What kind of resolutions, if any, does it offer to the problems or conflicts explored in the poem? One critic, Albert Gelpi, sees this ending as providing an "image of fulfillment," an "archetypical" "self-image" "at once individual and collective: a signal of forces which would become a national movement [for women's liberation] within the decade" ("Adrienne Rich: The Poetics of Change," Gelpi and Gelpi, p. 286). What do you think Gelpi means? Do you agree with him? Even if you do, what other interpretations of the ending might you offer?

7. Both Rich and other readers of her work tend to see this poem as a dramatic departure from her earlier work, both in terms of style and in terms of content. How would you describe the character of that departure? What evidence from this and earlier poems might you use to support your argument about those differences? Even if you agree that the poem differs greatly from Rich's earlier work, how would you describe the similarities between this poem and earlier ones? What evidence from this and earlier poems might you use to support your argument about those similarities?

Planetarium

In "When We Dead Awaken," Rich describes "Planetarium" (written at the end of the sixties and during the time that Rich began to identify herself with the civil rights and women's liberation movements) as heralding the beginning of a new stage in her poetic development, because "at last the woman in the poem and the woman writing the poem become the same person" (Gelpi and Gelpi, p. 175). By the same token, the speaker's bombardment by signals and pulsations in "Planetarium" (lines 35–45) presents a very different image from that of the speaker in "Storm Warnings," who closes the shutters against the elements. This woman is more active than those in the preceding Rich poems; the speaker here sees herself as not only the passive receiver of signals but also the translator of them.

Rich's comment in "When We Dead Awaken" that the woman in the poem and the woman writing the poem become the same help us understand the role of Caroline Herschel as an inspiration for the poem. As Rich herself insists in that essay, the poem "was written after a visit to a real planetarium, where I read an account of the work of Caroline Herschel, the astronomer, who worked with her brother William, but whose name remained obscure, as his did not" (Gelpi and Gelpi, p. 175). As this comment and the poem itself suggest, Herschel was a woman who did more than gaze at the stars, using her intelligence and imagination to make a contribution, although she went unrecognized for it. In turn, Rich renders her own poem a similar kind of contribution, using her own imagination and intelligence to bring Herschel and her work out of obscurity and into the light, embedding her own writing (as in poems such as "Snapshots of a Daughter-in-Law") in a continuous, female tradition that includes not only Herschel but also, in the words of the dedication, many more nameless "others."

Uncovering that tradition allows us, the poem suggests, to learn to see women past and present as themselves observers and creators, not merely as the "Galaxies" and "monster[s]" observed and imagined by others (line 13, 1; cf. the monsters in line 26 of "Snapshots . . ."); as scientists able to study the moon instead of merely being "ruled" by it (line 9), an image that obviously refers to menstruation and the myth that, for women, "anatomy is destiny." Such "learning" is, after all, one crucial form of the process of "translation" that the end of the poem both describes and insists is necessary "for the relief of the body and the reconstruction of the mind" (lines 44–45). As depicted here, such translation seems to be very like the process that Rich will in "When We Dead Awaken" call "re-vision":

> Re-vision—the act of looking back, of seeing with fresh eyes, of entertaining an old text [and history itself] from a new critical direction—is for women more than a chapter in cultural history: it is an act of survival. Until we can understand the

assumptions in which we are drenched we cannot know ourselves. And this drive to self-knowledge, for women, is more than a search for identity: it is part of our refusal of the self-destructiveness of male-dominated society. A radical critique of literature [and of history], feminist in its impulse, would take the work [or the past] first of all as a clue to how we live, how we have been living, how we have been led to imagine ourselves, how our language has trapped as well as liberated us, how the very act of naming has been till now a male prerogative, and how we can begin to see and name—and therefore live—afresh. A change in the concept of sexual identity is essential if we are not going to see the old political order reassert itself in every new revolution. We need to know the writing [and history] of the past, and know it differently than we have ever known it; not to pass on a tradition but to break its hold over us. (Gelpi and Gelpi, pp. 167–168)

It is also not altogether unlike the process Rich would later poetically label "diving into the wreck."

QUESTIONS FOR DISCUSSION

1. Despite the fact that the poem's speaker receives the "most / untranslatable language in the universe," she is "trying to translate pulsations into images" (lines 37–38, 43–44). What figurative resources does the poet employ to translate the (nearly) untranslatable? Can you generalize about why poetry must always use figurative devices rather than more immediately transparent language?

2. In what other ways might one see this poem as itself a "translation" or as what Rich elsewhere calls a "revision" of history, particularly in terms of the role and contribution of women? What conventional and/or stereotypical views of women does the poem articulate? How exactly does the poem challenge such views?

3. Why is it important for Rich to write to and about historical women? How is this different from writing about mythic or imaginary women? About a famous contemporary or a relative? About herself?

4. Might this poem challenge the dichotomy of maternal love versus egotism that Rich describes in "When We Dead Awaken?" If so, how so?

5. Rich describes this poem as marking a crucial stage in her development as a poet because here for the first time, "the woman in the poem and the woman writing the poem become the same person." Why do you think this use of the "I" is so important and significant to Rich? What exactly does the use of first-person contribute to the poem, and how does it make this poem different from earlier Rich poems? In what ways does the poem seem similar to earlier poems?

Dialogue

Though written only four years after "Planetarium," "Dialogue" appeared in Rich's first collection of the seventies, *Diving into the Wreck: Poems*

1971–1972, published in 1973, just three years after the death of her husband, Alfred Conrad, and the end of her seventeen-year marriage, just at
the beginning of her identification not only with feminism but also with
lesbian feminism.

This particular poem can prove quite difficult for students because it
is so very enigmatic. As a result, I try to start by having students use the
cues in the poem to generate ideas about the situation and setting, the
speaker and other character, etc. Insisting all the while that we allow for
the way that the poem itself is quite self-consciously and relentlessly
ambiguous, allowing for many different possible interpretations, I try to
push the conversation forward by talking about how the statements with
which the poem ends mean or signify something different according to
these different interpretations of the situation, setting, speaker, and other
character. Then, I try to move toward a consideration of what stays the
same, the typically "Richean" issues in the poem, such as the necessity
and difficulty of knowing or speaking the truth or recognizing and overcoming "illusion" (line 10); the impossibility of separating one's true self
from external messages about who and what we are or should be (cf. the
"pulsations" of "Planetarium" and the "book of myths" in "Diving into
the Wreck"); the illusionary quality of sexuality, in particular; the joy and
terror of personal (and social) growth and change so radical that it disturbs any easy asssurance of continuity or stability; and the joy and terror
of discovering that, to quote Rich herself, "the way things are" is a
changeable "social construct" rather than a necessary fact.

QUESTIONS FOR DISCUSSION

1. Building on the cues provided in the poem itself, what do you imagine
   about the situation and setting of "Dialogue"? About the character of
   the speaker and the person with whom he or she converses in the
   poem?
2. How do the meaning and significance of this person's statements to
   the speaker differ depending on how you interpret the nature of the
   situation, setting, and the characters?
3. How do the meaning and significance of this person's statements
   remain the same regardless of what one assumes about the situation,
   setting, and characters? What issues or questions remain central
   regardless? What's the significance or effect of the very ambiguity, that
   fact that the poem doesn't tell you much about who the "She" or the
   "I" is (or even what gender "I" is)?
4. What thematic and formal similarities do you see between this poem
   and other Rich poems that you have read? What differences do you
   see?

Diving into the Wreck

Of the questions for discussion that follow, the fifth is clearly the most important and the most difficult to answer. If you would like to spark discussion or keep it moving by having students consider the answer of another reader, here is the very lyrical, but itself rather enigmatic, answer of novelist and poet Margaret Atwood:

> [*Diving into the Wreck*] is . . . a book of explorations, of travels. The wreck she is diving into, in the very strong title poem, is the wreck of obsolete myths, particularly myths about men and women. She is journeying to something that is already in the past, in order to discover for herself the reality behind the myth. . . . What she finds is part treasure and part corpse, and she also finds that she herself is part of it, a "half-destroyed instrument." As explorer she is detached; she carries a knife to cut her way in, cut structures apart; a camera to record; and the book of myths itself, a book which has hitherto had no place for explorers like herself. . . .
>
> The truth, it seems, is not just what you find when you open a door: it is itself a door, which the poet is always on the verge of going through. ("Review of *Diving in the Wreck*," Gelpi and Gelpi, pp. 280–281)

QUESTIONS FOR DISCUSSION

1. The diver in this poem says that she came for "the wreck and not the story of the wreck / the thing itself and not the myth" (lines 62–63). Why isn't Rich's diver interested in the story of the wreck? What exactly is she interested in and why? If Rich's diver isn't interested in stories, then why does she talk so much about language in lines 53ff.?
2. What's the significance of the specific activities through which Rich's diver prepares for her dive and of the equipment she takes with her? What about the descriptions of the difficulties she experiences at the beginning of the dive (stanza three)?
3. What is the diver's relationship to the sea (lines 39–40)?
4. What is the significance of the diver's description of herself as both "mermaid" and "merman," "she" and "he" in lines 72–73 and 77? Has she been changed in some way by her arrival at "the place" or is there another explanation for why this description comes here in the poem (line 71)?
5. What different things might the wreck and the dive symbolize? What evidence from the poem would you use to support each of your interpretations?
6. What do you make of the ending of the poem, particular the switch from "I" to "We" in line 87? Of the fact that the poem ultimately ends with the statement that "our names do not appear" in the "book of myths" (lines 92–94)?
3. How does this wreck compare to the ruins in Shelley's "Ozymandias"?

Is Shelley's speaker, unlike Rich's, more interested in the story than the ruins themselves? Why?

Power

"Power" is the first poem in Rich's 1978 collection *The Dream of a Common Language,* a collection that centers on the series of lesbian love poems previously published in 1976 as *Twenty-One Love Poems.*

In "Power," Rich uses the story of Marie Curie's radiation sickness as a kind of metaphor through which to pose a number of probing and disturbing questions about the relationship between the "wounds" and the "power" women have historically suffered and enjoyed under patriarchy, or between what she calls in "Diving into the Wreck" the "damage that was done / and the treasures that prevail" (lines 55–56). Unlike "Diving into the Wreck," which merely juxtaposes "damage" and "treasures" without commenting on their relationship to one another, however, "Power" very clearly insists that the two emerge "from the same source" (line 17).

Despite the clarity of that statement, however, the strength of the poem as a whole ultimately lies in the fact that it offers more questions than answers: Is the condition exemplified by the story of Marie Curie a thing of the past or of the present? Is all power or discovery (including poetry writing) as dangerous as uranium, or only traditional forms of creativity or power? In what sense are the "wounds" that are co-extensive with power inflicted only or with peculiar severity on (creative) women and to what extent are they inflicted on any (creative) person? Is the problem with the source of power itself or with ignorance and denial, as it seems to be in the poem's presentation of Marie Curie?

What's the relationship between the "real" power discovered by Curie and the "cure" that is discovered "in the earth-deposits of our history" at the beginning of the poem? Does the poem treat the promise of that "cure" straightforwardly or, as one critic suggests, ironically? Is the revelation of the common source of "wounds" and "power" via the story of Marie Curie itself the "cure"?

QUESTIONS FOR DISCUSSION

1. What "lesson" does Rich seem to draw from the story of Marie Curie's radiation sickness? What exactly do you think the poet means when she says that Marie Curie "died" "denying" "her wounds came from the same source as her power" (lines 14–17)?
2. What's the relationship between the discovery of a "cure" in the beginning of the poem and the story of Curie? Do you think the poem wants us to believe in the "cure" or to view it ironically? What's the

relationship between the cure and the first line of the poem?

3. What do you think Rich's poem ultimately asks or says about "power"?

4. What's the significance or effect of the spacing of words in the poem? The way lines are divided?

5. How is Rich's treatment of Marie Curie in "Power" similar to her treatment of Caroline Herschel in "Planetarium"? How is it different?

6. How is Rich's treatment of "power" in this poem like and unlike that in her reading of Emily Dickinson's "[My Life had stood—a Loaded Gun]" (see excerpt in discussion of "Snapshots of a Daughter-in-Law" above)?

For the Record

QUESTIONS FOR DISCUSSION

1. What war or wars does the speaker seem to refer to here? How might your answer to that question change over the course of the poem? What's the significance or effect of the ambiguity?

2. Compare this poem with Rich's "Letters in the Family." To what extent or in what precise way are each of these poems about literal warfare and to what extent or in what precise way does each, as one critic puts it, use war "as a metaphor"? A metaphor for what?

[My mouth hovers across your breasts]

Juxtaposing this love poem with "At a Bach Concert" and "Storm Warnings" is a terrific way to open up to view the tremendous changes in Rich's conceptions both of love and poetry between the 1950s and the 1980s. For where those two earlier poems insist in both form and content on "discipline" and restraint and use the imagery of weather and changing seasons to describe the external and internal threats to that poetic and emotional containment, this poem dives directly into, and celebrates, the "hot" "joy" of unleashed emotion and desire (line 4) and "the pleasures of" both internal and external weather (line 10), rejecting the need for "defense against the season" so crucial to the speaker of "Storm Warnings."

QUESTIONS FOR DISCUSSION

1. How would you describe the tone of this poem?

2. How does the poem use its winter setting? How do the descriptions of weather contribute to the characterization of sex or love in this poem?

3. To what extent or in what precise way is this a lesbian love poem?

What's the significance or effect of the fact that the poem itself does not ever announce itself to be such, never indicates whether the speaker is, like her lover, a woman?
4. Compare this poem to "At a Bach Concert" and "Storm Warnings." What similarities and differences do you see here, particularly in terms of Rich's portrayal of love and her use of weather imagery?

Walking down the Road

Published in 1989, five years after Rich's relocation from the East Coast to the West, "Walking down the Road" explores the ways in which the northern California landscape, like any landscape, both disguises and reveals the history of human struggle that has shaped it. As in other poems that deal with the ways in which that history shapes human beings and their relationships with one another, Rich envisions here history in terms of struggle between the powerless and the powerful, in this case between "whitemen," Mexicans, Indians, and gringoes.

Students might better or at least differently appreciate some of the rich ironies or paradoxes of the poem if they are asked to pause for a moment to consider what they know about, or associate with, Carmel (line 21). A village set on one of the most beautiful stretches of the California coast, whose "downtown" features many an exclusive boutique, art gallery, and restaurant, Carmel now ranks with Marin as one of the wealthiest communities in northern California, facts students may be aware of, in part, because the actor Clint Eastwood was Carmel's mayor for some time in the 1980s.

QUESTIONS FOR DISCUSSION

1. How would you describe the tone of "Walking down the Road"? When and how does the tone of the poem, as well (perhaps) as your sense of what the poem is about, change over the course of the poem?
2. What exactly is "Manifest Destiny" (line 17) and how does this phrase function or what does it mean in this context?
3. What do you make of the series of images (associated with Carmel) that close the poem?
4. How is this poem like and unlike other Rich poems that you have read, particularly in terms of its portrayal of the nature and significance of history?

Delta

"Delta," like "History," is a wonderful poem to read in the context of a chapter on the author's work in context precisely because it so directly and rather elegantly challenges our temptation to adopt a too-simplistic view of personal and public history, insisting that both kinds of "stor[ies] flo[w] in more than one direction" (line 6) and that they keep "mov[ing] on" (line 3).

QUESTIONS FOR DISCUSSION

1. Whom might "you" in this poem refer to? How does the poem characterize "your" interest in the speaker's past and the reasons or motives behind that interest?
2. How does the image of "rubble" in this poem compare to that of the wreck in "Diving into the Wreck"? To what extent does this poem constitute a revision of the views about history and the task of "diving into the wreck" of the past suggested by earlier poems? To what extent is this vision similar to, or compatible with, that of earlier poems?

History

One reason that Adrienne Rich makes such a wonderful subject for the study of the writer's work in context is that so very much of her own prose and poetry has been devoted to studying her own life and work in precisely that way, and "History" is a good case in point.

While the poem speaks for itself on these points, some of it might also speak more clearly or at least differently to students if read alongside the following excerpts from Rich's "Blood, Bread, and Poetry: The Location of the Poet" (1984), precisely because this essay not only tells us more about Rich's view of the significance of the events portrayed in the poem (including the suicide of "the socialist queer Christian teacher" in line 27) but also details the process whereby Rich herself slowly came to reject the idea of poetry and sexuality as ahistorical and apolitical and to embrace the necessarily historical and political character of both poetry and the most "personal" aspects of our lives:

> I was born at the brink of the Great Depression; I reached sixteen the year of Nagasaki and Hiroshima. The daughter of a Jewish father and a Protestant mother, I learned about the Holocaust first from newsreels of the liberation of death camps. . . . The process through which nuclear annihilation was to become a part of all human calculation had already begun, but we did not live with that knowledge during the first sixteen years of my life. And a recurrent theme in much poetry I read was the indestructibility of poetry, the poem as a vehicle for personal immortality. (Gelpi and Gelpi, pp. 239–240)

> Because of the attitudes surrounding me, the aesthetic ideology with which I grew up, I came into my twenties believing in poetry, in all art, as the expression of a higher world view, what the critic Edward Said has termed "a quasi-religious wonder, instead of a human sign to be understood in secular and social terms" ["Literature as Values," *New York Times Book Review*, Sept. 4, 1983, p. 9]. The poet

achieved "universality" and authority through tapping his, or occasionally her, own dreams, longings, fears, desires, and, out of this, "speaking as a man to men," as Wordsworth phrased it. But my personal world view at sixteen, as at twenty-six, was itself being created by political conditions. I was not a man; I was white in a white-supremacist society; I was being educated from the perspective of a particular class; my father was an "assimilated" Jew in an anti-Semitic world, my mother a white southern Protestant; there were particular historical currents on which my consciousness would come together, piece by piece. . . . My personal world view, which like so many young people I carried as a conviction of my own uniqueness, was not original with me, but was, rather, my untutored and half-conscious rendering of the facts of blood and bread, the social and political forces of my time and place.

I was in college during the late 1940s and early 1950s. The thirties, a decade of economic desperation, social unrest, war, and also of affirmed political art, was receding behind the fogs of the Cold War, the selling of the nuclear family with the mother at home as its core, heightened activity by the FBI and CIA, a retreat by many artists from so-called "protest" art, witch-hunting among artists and intellectuals as well as in the State Department, anti-Semitism, scapegoating of homosexual men and lesbians, and with a symbolic victory for the Cold War crusade in the 1953 electrocution of Ethel and Julius Rosenberg.

Francis Otto Matthiessen, a socialist and a homosexual, was teaching literature at Harvard when I came there. One semester he lectured on five poets: Blake, Keats, Byron, Yeats, and Stevens. That class perhaps affected my life as a poet more than anything else that happened to me in college. Matthiessen had a passion for language, and he read aloud, made us memorize poems and recite them to him as part of the course. He also actually alluded to events in the outside word, the hope that eastern Europe could survive as an independent socialist force between the United States and the Soviet Union; he spoke of the current European youth movements as if they should matter to us. Poetry, in his classroom, never remained in the realm of pure textual criticism. Remember that this was in 1947 or 1948, that it was a rare teacher of literature at Harvard who referred to a world beyond the text, even though the classrooms were full of World War II veterans studying on the G.I. Bill of Rights—men who might otherwise never have gone to college, let alone Harvard, at all. Matthiessen committed suicide in the spring of my sophomore year. (Gelpi and Gelpi, pp. 241–242)

By 1956, I had begun dating each of my poems by year. I did this because I was finished with the idea of a poem as a single, encapsulated event, a work of art complete in itself; I knew my life was changing, my work was changing, and I needed to indicate to readers my sense of being engaged in a long, continuous process. It seems to me now that this was an oblique political statement—a rejection of the dominant critical idea that the poem's text should be read as separate from the poet's everyday life in the world. It was a declaration that placed poetry in a historical continuity, not above or outside history. (Gelpi and Gelpi, p. 247)

QUESTIONS FOR DISCUSSION

1. How does the poem characterize American life and the changes therein in the 1940s and 1950s? What does the poem suggest about the factors that helped to determine what that life was like?

2. What is the significance and effect of the repeated references to dreams and dreaming (lines 8, 10, 16)? What different dreams might the speaker refer to?

3. What do you think the speaker's "scribbling" in line 20—"this map stops where it all begins"—means? What's the significance of this line in the context of the poem as a whole? (How might this line resonate with references to maps in other Rich poems, such as the statement "words are maps" in "Diving into the Wreck" [line 54], and/or mean in the context of Rich's canon as a whole?)

4. What does the poem suggest about the meaning or significance of the atomic bomb explosions referred to in line 26? Of the execution of Julius and Ethel Rosenberg (lines 31–32)?

5. How exactly does Rich here connect sexuality and/or personal history ("my life" [line 1]) with history in the more general or public sense? What might the poem suggest, despite the speaker's denials, about "how I began to love men" and "how I began to love women" (lines 2–3)?

6. How does the portrayal of the nature and significance of "history" in this poem compare to that in other poems that you have read?

QUESTIONS ON THE POETRY AND PROSE OF RICH

1. Among the many recurring images in Rich's poetry are the images of the "wreck" ("Diving into the Wreck") and "rubble" ("Delta"), of maps ("Diving into the Wreck" and "History"), of weather ("Storm Warnings" and "[My mouth hovers . . .]"), of monsters ("Planetarium" and "Snapshots of a Daughter-in-Law"), and of coffee pots ("Living in Sin," "Snapshots of a Daughter-in-Law," and "History"). How would you characterize the meaning and significance of each of these images within and across particular poems? What other recurring images do you see here?

2. History (as both reality and myth) is obviously a crucial and continuing concern of Rich's poetry and prose. How do the various poems and prose pieces that you've read characterize the nature and significance of history? What do they say or ask about what our view of, or relationship to, history (both reality and myth) should be? How does Rich characterize the nature and significance of the process that she variously calls "translation" ("Planetarium"), "revision" ("When We Dead Awaken"), and "diving into the wreck" ("Diving into the Wreck")? What's alike and different about each description or characterization of this process? How would you answer the same questions with regard to the notion of "power" (rather than history)? What other thematic concerns seem to recur in Rich's work?

3. In her comment on the poem "Orion" in "When We Dead Awaken," Rich says that "the word 'love' is itself in need of revision." How exactly is love treated and redefined in Rich's poetry and prose?

4. In the two interviews included in the anthology (and in many of the excerpts included in the notes to poems above), Rich makes several statements (or arguments) about the changes in her poetry and her conceptions of poetry after the 1950s, placing particular emphasis on the way her poetry became increasingly informal and exploratory, as well as more overtly "political." What evidence from the poetry itself would you use to support Rich's arguments about her poetic development? What other arguments might you make about exactly how Rich's poetry has evolved both formally and thematically?

5. Rich's own comments (as well as the very term *evolution*, perhaps) suggest that Rich's poetry has qualitatively improved over time, that the early poetry (particularly that written in the 1950s) is weaker than the later poetry. In what particular ways do you think Rich's poetry has improved? How might you counter Rich's assessments, particularly of her early poetry?

READING/WRITING IDEAS FOR CHAPTER 22

ESSAYS ON THE AUTHOR'S WORK IN CONTEXT

While this chapter can easily be used in exactly the same fashion as the last chapter, as part of a unit culminating in an essay that explores the world of a given poet from a particular angle, it also provides the materials and opportunity for at least two other kinds of essay assignments. The first of these would ask students to make some kind of argument about the development of a poet's work over time, exploring the way that the poetry changes in terms of its treatment of a particular theme, its use of particular imagery (such as "wrecks" and "rubble," in the case of Rich) or other devices (such as allusions to historical figures), and/or in terms of form. That assignment might either allow students themselves to identify the particular theme, formal qualities, or image they want to explore in their essays or specify for students the terms or focus of the argument, as the following sample assignment does:

Rich recently said of her college days in the late 1940s, "I had no political ideas of my own, only the era's vague and hallucinatory anti-Communism and the encroaching privatism of the 1950s. Drenched in invisible assumptions of my class and race, unable to fathom the pervasive ideology of gender, I felt 'politics' as distant, vaguely sinister, the province of powerful older men or of people I saw as fanatics. It was in poetry that I sought a grasp on the world and on interior events, 'ideas of order,' even power." Using the poems collected in the text, as well as other poems by Rich, write an essay that charts the development of the poet's political consciousness. Address the question of what is gained and what is lost in the movement from the early, ostensibly apolitical poems to the more overtly political ones of Rich's later years.

The second kind of assignment would ask students to consider, instead, the ways in which history (or "cultural context" and changes therein) might be said to inform either a particular poem (or our interpretation of it) or the changes in a poet's work over time. And, again, such assignments would work quite well whether one made them fairly open ended or specified the poem or poems and/or the events or issues about which students should write. The following sample assignment represents a more restrictive version of such an assignment:

Adrienne Rich wrote "Snapshots of a Daughter-in-Law," a poem that she and many of her readers see as marking a major departure from her earlier poetry, just as the 1950s gave way to the 1960s. How might we see both the form and content of this poem, and the change in Rich's poetry it represents, as being informed by, articulating, or grappling with the changes occurring during this time period not only in Rich's life but also in American society at large? What might Rich's later critical comments on the poem in turn suggest about subsequent changes in Rich's attitudes and in those of at least certain segments of American society?

In both cases, there is also always the middle ground, which is where I usually tend to stand—wording the assignment so that it includes an example or examples like the ones above and then concludes by telling students that they can create their own specific assignment or question.

Though any of these assignments could easily be pursued in relation to any number of poets in the anthology, Rich herself is an especially good candidate, not only because of the materials on offer in this chapter and readily available elsewhere (see "Planning Ideas") but also because much of that material deals specifically with her development as a poet and with the relationship between that poetry and the events that dramatically reshaped both Rich's life and, in different ways, the lives of all North Americans between the 1940s and the 1990s.

TROUBLESHOOTING

The very abundance of statements by and about Rich that can serve to make any of the above assignments particularly rich and rewarding for students could also quite easily become a handicap to them if they ever begin to see those statements as gospel truth (as we are all sometimes wont to do, especially with the statements of authors) rather than as themselves being particular and potentially faulty and inconclusive interpretations and arguments. As a result, I find it crucial to find ways to encourage students to take the latter view of these materials from the outset and to actually model that approach for and with them. One such modeling technique involves doing the kind of thing suggested in the fifth question for discussion that follows the note to "Snapshots of a Daughter-in-Law," a question that is in fact a series of questions that involve, among other things, treating Rich's own later comments on this poem as an interpretation that can be seen as, in a sense, "wrong" or at least faultily partial (in insisting that the allusiveness of the poem is only or necessarily a mistake rather than a crucial and revealing aspect of the poem). Another technique would involve both assigning essays about Rich by critics other than Rich herself and highlighting in discussion what those arguments leave out or ignore (and thus leave available for students to write about); how much the critics disagree with each other (thus identifying the kind of problem areas that make for good essay topics); and how particular pieces include and handle disagreements with Rich's own arguments about her poetry (a good example of this being the "Postscript" to Albert Gelpi's "Adrienne Rich: The Poetics of Change," Gelpi and Gelpi, pp. 297–299).

It also seems important to note here the potential problem that might be created less by any of these writing assignments than by the very study of Rich's poetry, which will undoubtedly disturb at least some students either because of its overtly political tone, the nature of its (feminist) politics, and/or its treatment of lesbianism. Though I have, for good or ill, been known to respond to student discomfort in this particular case by simply implicitly or explicitly saying "tough," I wouldn't advocate that strategy, but I would suggest that you'll probably need to give some thought to what your strategy will be if (or more likely, when) students respond in this way to Rich's poetry. I find that it helps, in this regard, if my class has already at some point discussed questions about what literature is and does because that discussion has almost certainly included talk about how important it is that literature allows us to occupy or consider different points of view (even about the nature of literature itself); if so, I can easily refer back to that "talk" when students begin to demur in a specific case. It also helps that Rich herself has had a great deal to say about why political poetry, feminism, and lesbianism tend to "disturb" us, making it even easier to use the "turn the problem into an advantage" strategy, which in this case means having students use and analyze their discomfort in their discussions and writing about Rich's poetry and insisting that, in doing so, they take account of what Rich herself has had to say about such discomfort (in essays such as, depending on the problem, "Blood, Bread, and Poetry" and "Compulsory Heterosexuality and Lesbian Existence").

The second, cultural context assignment suggested above might itself inspire a different, but often related, kind of problem—the student who believes in the ahistorical and apolitical character of (good) literature and of (good) literary criticism and who thus disagrees with the whole project of reading a text in terms of its historical and cultural context. Again, I think it helps if you can have such a student read Rich's "Of Blood, Bread, and Poetry," the essay in which she most directly takes on that view (which she herself once had). It also helps that students who hold such views tend to favor very author-centric or even intentionalist approaches to texts, in which case—again—it helps that Rich has in this essay and elsewhere expressed the intention or demand that her work be read in terms of historical and cultural context. Again, there's always a version of the "turn the problem into an advantage" strategy described above.

And if worse comes to absolute worst, I (and maybe you) can always fall back on what I think of as the utilitarian (or "eat your spinach") argument (which I also happen to believe in), an argument that goes something like this: "developing the skills and mastering the strategies involved in this kind of assignment will help you to develop as a reader and writer and will even come in handy in other classes. And, even if you don't necessarily believe in this approach right now, who knows? You might, like Rich, change your mind later and, if nothing else, be glad you had the opportunity to try it out."

AUTHOR'S WORK IN CONTEXT–FOCUSED WRITING EXERCISES

You might get students started on any or all of the essay assignments described above by having them tackle a version of the first exercise described in "Reading/Writing Ideas for Chapter 21" and/or (if Rich is their focus) by having them consider some or all of the questions posed in "Questions on the Poetry and Prose of Rich," perhaps even doing an exercise in which they use these questions as a guide in formulating a question or two for themselves. And, depending on the exact nature of your essay assignment, you might also find some or all of the following exercises helpful to students along the way (all of which assume that Rich is the focus of the assignment, but which could easily be modified for students focusing on other writers).

1. Identifying Terms and Argumentative Claims

Since any of the essay assignments described above will almost necessarily demand that students somehow interrelate Rich's poetry and prose, you might want to get them started on this by having them do an exercise in which they concentrate primarily on the prose, going through that material to identify terms they might use to make their own arguments about Rich's poetry and/or argumentative statements that they will need to consider in their own arguments. Obviously, however, the exact nature of the exercise will depend on the kind of essay assignment students are tackling and what exercises, if any, they've already done.

If, for example, students are being asked to write an essay on some aspect of the evolution of Rich's poetry and to define for themselves the aspect they will focus on, you could use this exercise to get students started, having them read through the prose to generate a possible list of aspects or topics, taking note of what are to them the most interesting aspects or topics identified by Rich herself and then adding to this list things that seem important to them but that are ignored by Rich. You might even consider wording the essay assignment itself so that it demands that students use a phrase or whole passage from Rich's prose as the starting point for the essay, having students use this prose-focused exercise to identify and brainstorm about what to them seem the two or three most promising such phrases or passages. Or you could instead have students start with the first exercise described in "Reading/Writing Ideas for Chapter 21" and then have them do a prose-focused exercise comparing Rich's statements about the patterns or a particular pattern in her work to their own exercise to figure out which of these might interest them most as an essay topic (in terms of what Rich does or does not say about it).

If, on the other hand, you've given students a specific topic, you might have them read through the prose to identify passages that are relevant to that topic and then ask them to brainstorm about how exactly those passages address the topic at hand, about what passages or ideas they might use to turn your question into their thesis, and about what other uses they might make of passages from the prose in their essays.

2. Identifying and Locating Primary and Secondary Source Material

Especially if you're having students tackle the cultural contest essay assignment described above, you might want to consider devoting some class time to generating ideas about the kinds of primary and secondary sources that might be helpful to them in writing their essays and/or about particular contextual questions for which they need answers (or at least need to know how to go about answering for themselves). Then you might break students into groups, assigning each one a particular kind of information or source material or a particular question that they will then research, ultimately somehow presenting their findings to the class as a whole. (When I assign such presentations, I find it helpful to require that they include both an oral presentation by the group and a handout or handouts that individual students can refer to later.) Depending on the kind of topics and assignments students are pursuing, the questions or materials assigned to groups might end up being as general as "biographical information" or "relevant information about cultural context" or as specific as "Rich's parents" or "Rich's statements on lesbianism" or "family life in the 1950s" or "the history of women's studies programs."

23

LITERARY TRADITION AS CONTEXT

J. V. Cunningham's two-line poem "History of Ideas" not only provides a well-turned example of the epigram, one that admirably fulfills Coleridge's criteria in "What Is an Epigram?" but also strings together the first section of this chapter ("Echo and Allusion") and the last ("Cultural Belief and Tradition"). The nod to the New Testament claim that "God is love" (1 John 4:8) is abruptly inverted: in the modern world, "Love is God." As the poem's title hints, this idea arguably encapsulates a prevailing myth of the twentieth century. The point is worth making early on; students often assume that myths belong to other cultures and not to their own. Part of the problem is slippage in the usage of the word *myth*. To a good many it means simply "that which is not true." But we are using it to mean something like, "the kind of story or idea that we accept without thinking, the kind that gives us a sense of our place in the world." If your students have already read and discussed in any depth the poetry of Adrienne Rich (particularly "Diving into the Wreck") they will undoubtedly have at least a passing familiarity with this understanding of myth. But even for these students, it might prove worthwhile to spend a little class time generating ideas about the myths of our culture. For example, do the stories we hear and see in movies and on TV (including the commercials) bear out Cunningham's claim about the point we have reached in the history of ideas? By what other myths do we orient ourselves?

Characteristic of poets who take on mythic subjects from ancient cultures is the desire to supply something that the myth is lacking, to claim the myth and make it relevant for readers today. Choosing a character or incident from a mythological tradition places the poet within that tradition, in dialogue with other poets. Hence the concern in this chapter with allusion, traditional poetic genres, and parodies of well-known poems. The authors here frequently draw on and challenge popular conceptions and misconceptions of mythic stories. Some poems take off from a textual source for the myth, others on imprecise recollections reinforced by popular symbolism in our culture. In class, I find it useful to try with students to determine what a poet's point of departure is. I ask them to read a poem and to see if they can identify the myth from memory. Next, we try to find one or several textural sources for the myth; look for other poems that retell the same myth; and finally, discuss how the accumulated information changes our understanding of the poem. I also get students to consider the difference between reworking an important myth in the culture and making up a new story, including the poet's advantages and disadvantages in using a story toward which his or her readers may already have strong feelings or opinions.

PLANNING IDEAS

- As most of our students have inherited their ideas about poetry from the Romantics, they need to be shown that a good poem need not be a spontaneous outpouring of emotion, that it does not necessarily come directly "from the heart." Marlowe's "The Passionate Shepherd to His Love" provides a good starting point. Exposure to even the sketchiest account of Marlowe's life—his generally rebellious spirit, his undercover work for Queen Elizabeth, his reputed atheism and association with the "School of Night," his violent death in a tavern brawl—may make him seem an unlikely author of a poem like "The Passionate Shepherd." Try asking students who know nothing of Marlowe's life to speculate, on the basis of the poem, about what sort of person he must have been. The result can bring home the idea that poets sometimes write as an intellectual exercise—an experiment in creating an interesting specimen of a particular "kind"—not as an expression of their innermost feelings.
- A good companion piece (in addition to Ralegh's "The Nymph's Reply to the Shepherd" and Williams's "Raleigh Was Right") for Marlowe's poem is Marvell's "The Garden," since it comments humorously on the pastoral tradition. As it also touches on the biblical account of Adam and Eve in the Garden of Eden, it can lead nicely to a discussion of "Adam's Task," "Eve Names the Animals," and "Eve."
- Be sure to have your students read the Williams ("This Is Just to Say") and Arnold ("Dover Beach") poems (and the originals for the other parodies and replies) at least a few days before they read the Koch and Hecht parodies so that they will get the full effect from a first reading. Looking at a parody first and then an original makes for an artificial reconstruction of effect.
- My students seem to better understand and appreciate the significance of the different uses of the literary tradition covered in this chapter when I begin our discussion of a particular kind either by having them look back at poems that we've already read that illustrate that use or by simply referring briefly to a few such examples. I begin "Echo and

Allusion," for example, by referring back to Rich's "Snapshots of a Daughter-in-Law" (with its allusion to Dickinson, etc.), "Cultural Belief and Tradition" by referring back to Atwood's "Siren Song," etc.

- A good way of broadening your discussion of the epigram is to have students read Wilde's *The Importance of Being Earnest,* which not only is chock-full of epigrams but also can potentially open up for discussion how the epigram and the particular brand of humor associated with it have a particular meaning in a particular sociohistorical context.
- I sometimes expand the "Cultural Belief and Tradition" section of this chapter into an entire unit that I tend to call "Re-Visions." For one such unit, for example, I had students read and write about the Ulysses poems in the chapter, as well as H. D.'s "Helen" and Atwood's "Siren Song," in conjunction with excerpts from Homer's *Odyssey* and Dante's *Divine Comedy.* Another time, I did an even longer version in which students read and wrote about the poems in the chapter that allude to Africa in conjunction with Conrad's *Heart of Darkness,* Achebe's *Things Fall Apart,* more Walcott poetry, and essays by Ngugi wa Thiong'o and Chinua Achebe.

ECHO AND ALLUSION

WILLIAM BLAKE

The Lamb

Because my students have an infinitely easier time with "The Lamb" when it's paired with its companion piece, "The Tyger," I always try to teach the two poems together even when I want to focus primarily on one or the other. And doing so, in this context, can make even more apparent the ways in which both poems allude to and explore the traditional, biblical images of God.

QUESTIONS FOR DISCUSSION

1. What do you notice about the form of "The Lamb"? What is the significance and effect of the poem's various formal qualities, especially its rhyme, meter, diction, and use of questions and repetition? How might the poem's form, as well as its content, be part of its technique of "echo and allusion"?

2. How would you characterize the tone of this poem? Though the poem is overtly quite musical, innocent, and downright "pleasant," are there any hints that something else might be going on?

Boom!

"Boom!" clearly echoes the Bible in terms of form, as well as content, particularly through its language and rhythms (especially from stanza 2 on) and its (ironic) echoing of biblical phrases, such as "my cup runneth over" (which becomes "every modern convenience runneth over" in line 32). What's wonderful to me (and to many of my students) about the poem, however, is the way it manages to become not a parody of the Bible in its own right but a scathing, if also painfully funny, indictment of the way contemporary society itself parodies and trivializes the religious impulse enshrined in ancient religions. One way I think Nemerov accomplishes this is by incorporating into the poem the language of the newspaper clipping that serves as epigraph, thus allowing the Reverend Edward L. R. Elson's words to condemn both him and those he represents.

Among the many aspects of contemporary American life brought to view (and ridicule) in the poem are our irrational collective faith in science and technology ("nobody disbelieves / for a second" in "airplanes" [lines 4–5]); our tendency to treat religion like any other kind of leisure activity or form of consumption ("The churches are full, / the beaches are full, and the filling stations" [lines 8–9]; "prayers and praises / from belfry and phonebooth" [lines 16–17]); "people of the stop'n'shop / 'n'pray as you go" [lines 40–41]); our tendency to see and treat natural wonders not as miraculous gifts of a creator (and/or our means of access to him or her), but as things to use, abuse, and throw away ("God's great ocean is full / of paid vacationers" [lines 10–11]); our tendency to honor and desire the things of this world rather than aspiring to any other (so that "Chris Craft" and "Miss Universe" are infinitely more important than, for example, Christ [lines 37,45]); our worship of money, in particular; and, to paraphrase Wallace Stevens, our "rage" not for order but for ease.

QUESTIONS FOR DISCUSSION

1. What echoes and allusions do you see at work in "Boom!"? What do they individually and collectively contribute to the poem? How might you see the poem's form as alluding or echoing?
2. What attitude does the poem take toward the texts to which it alludes?

Is this poem in any sense a parody? If so, how and of what? If not, why not?

3. In addition to well-known texts such as the Bible and Dante's *Divine Comedy*, this poem also might be said to allude to and/or echo the text that Nemerov uses as an epigraph here. Where and how does the poem do so, and what do such echoes and allusions contribute to the poem? How might you read the poem differently if the epigraph weren't printed at the head of it (and if you couldn't recognize certain parts of the poem as echoes of this epigraph)? How does the information about the quotation—"Atlantic City, June 23, 1957 (AP)"—affect its meaning or significance?

4. Why or how might it be significant or telling that the poem itself was published in 1960? In what ways might or might not its portrait of American life and religion mean something different in its original context and in the context of the 1990s?

5. To what extent might the meaning or significance of the poem differ according to the reader's religious background or beliefs? How might the poem mean something different, for example, to a practicing Christian and to someone from a Judeo-Christian background who is agnostic or atheist? To a Buddhist or Muslim who also happens to be American?

MARIANNE MOORE

Love in America?

In teaching this poem, I always put especially heavy emphasis on the footnotes, guiding students first to think about the mere fact of the footnotes and the extent to which they are and are not a part of the text; then to think about how the information within the footnotes can guide our interpretation of the text or help us to understand it in a particular way; and—finally—to think about just how selective and enigmatic the footnotes themselves are and how the poem's meanings change when we bring to bear information about Midas or the Minotaur that isn't mentioned in the poem or the footnotes. Moore's footnote on the minotaur, for example, doesn't really tell us anything about the minotaur or about the situation and setting with which he is associated, while her footnote on Midas wittily doesn't say as much as it does say about why and how Midas (and those he touched) "was inconvenienced when eating or picking things up." Students will also undoubtedly know as little as I do about the Spanish philosopher Unamuno to whom Moore attributes the phrase "Nobility that is action," a fact that one might turn to advantage by sending a student to the library and/or by using it to spark discussion about the significance or effect of obscure allusions (which, of course, also entails questions about what constitutes obscurity, what is obscure to whom, etc.).

QUESTIONS FOR DISCUSSION

1. How does the title, including the question mark, set the stage for the poem?
2. What might the speaker mean by "the opposite of the way / in which the Minotaur was fed" (lines 4–5)?
3. The footnotes here are Moore's own and, as such, a part of her poem. What is the significance and effect of the mere presence of such footnotes? What about the specific content of those footnotes?
4. Moore's footnotes are very selective in what they do and do not tell us about the people and quotations in question. What do you know about the story of the Minotaur and Midas? How exactly does the poem draw and reflect on those stories to characterize "Love in America"? What do you know about Unamuno and Churchill? How exactly does the poem draw on our knowledge of these two historical figures?

ROBERT HOLLANDER

You Too? Me Too—Why Not? Soda Pop

QUESTIONS FOR DISCUSSION

1. Who or what is "Hippocrene," and how does the reference to Hippocrene in the poem contribute to the poem's characterization both of Coca-Cola and of Coca-Cola's status or role in American life?
2. How does Hollander use color in the poem? Why might the "brown shade mak[e]" the speaker "long to watch them harvesting the crop / which makes the deep-aged / rich brown wine of America"? What is that crop and what is its significance?
3. How does Hollander play on the word *pop* in the poem? What other wordplay do you see at work here?

POETIC "KINDS"

As with stanza forms, we have chosen to exemplify two kinds in detail rather than give single examples of many different kinds; this intensive method can provide your students with a full sense not only of what an epigram or a haiku is but also of what the notion of poetic kinds is good for.

I prefer to assign a large number of poems of a given kind before even suggesting any definition; that way students can put together a kind of empirical definition of their own, helped perhaps by poems that explicitly ("What Is an Epigram?") or implicitly ("Epitaph on Elizabeth, L. H.") describe characteristics of the kind.

Originally, epigrams were poems inscribed on something: a temple, grave marker, shrine, monument, or triumphal arch. But very early poets developed imitative poems that, like such inscriptions, pretended to be designed to attract the attention of "passers-by." The origin suggests the reason for the tendency toward brevity (and demonstrates how conventions develop in a poetic kind), although some poems that have passed as epigrams are pretty long. The epitaph, although not so popular as it once was as an actual inscription for tombstones, is probably the most common modern variety of epigram that still bears a recognizable relationship to its origins.

Most English epigrams are more or less based on the model of Martial, the witty and sophisticated poet of first-century Rome who brought the kind to its most accomplished level in Latin. In Martial's hand the epigram was usually short, pointed, and often satiric. But some English poems draw from an alternate (and earlier) version of the tradition exemplified and preserved in the *Greek Anthology*, a collection of poems written over many centuries, some of them dating from as early as the sixth century B.C. Some of these Greek epigrams fit the description of Martial's epigrams, but some lack the "turn" at the end, and many are neither comic in tone nor satirical in intention. Some poems have plaintive or sensuous or even sublime tones and some have substantial philosophical intentions, despite their brevity.

Epigrams were especially popular in the early seventeenth century, and they have had several vogues since, most notably in the nineteenth century. Eighteenth-century poets wrote surprisingly few epigrams, perhaps because preference for the couplet did not mean the absolute independence of each couplet. Pope, for example, made most of his couplets seem complete in themselves, and their witty turns would allow many of them to pass as epigrams, but their full effect usually depends upon connections, imagistic or otherwise, with the surrounding context. An interesting exercise might be made of comparing some two-line epigrams with Pope's couplets in "Sound and Sense."

The anthology includes a fairly extensive discussion of the origin and nature of haiku.

SAMUEL TAYLOR COLERIDGE

What Is an Epigram?

In conjunction with this poem or as part of general discussions about the rise and fall of the popularity of the epigram, students might be interested in the following excerpts from *Biographia Literaria (Norton Anthology of English Literature*, Vol. 2, 6th ed.) in which Coleridge discusses his early reactions to the "epigrammatic" poetry of the eighteenth century:

> I was not blind to the merits of this school ["Pope and his followers"], yet as from inexperience of the world and consequent want of sympathy with the general subjects of these poems they gave me little pleasure, I doubtless undervalued the *kind*, and with the presumption of youth withheld from its masters the legitimate name of poets. I saw that the excellence of this kind consisted in just and acute observations on men and manners in an artificial state of society as its matter and subjects, and in the logic of wit conveyed in smooth and strong epigrammatic couplets as its *form*. . . . [A] *point* was looked for at the end of each second line, and the whole was as it were a sorites or, if I may exchange a logical for a grammatical metaphor, a *conjunction disjunctive*, of epigrams. Meantime the matter and diction seemed to me characterized not so much by poetic thoughts as by thoughts *translated* into the language of poetry. (p. 381)

> [T]his style of poetry which I have characterized above as translations of prose thoughts into poetic language had been kept up by, if it did not wholly arise from, the custom of writing Latin verses and the great importance attached to these exercises in our public schools. Whatever might have been the case in the fifteenth century, when the use of the Latin tongue was so general among learned men that Erasmus is said to have forgotten his native language; yet in the present day it is not to be supposed that a youth can think in Latin, or that he can have any reliance on the force or fitness of his phrases but the authority of the author from whence he had adopted them. Consequently he must first prepare his thoughts, and then pick out from Virgil, Horace, Ovid, or perhaps more compendiously, from his *Gradus*, halves and quarters of lines in which to embody them. (p. 382)

> I excluded from the list of worthy feelings [excited by poetry] the pleasure derived from mere novelty in the reader, and the desire of exciting wonderment at his powers in the author. (p. 383)

> Our faulty elder poets sacrificed the passion and passionate flow of poetry to the subtleties of intellect and to the starts of wit; the moderns to the glare and glitter of a perpetual yet broken and heterogeneous imagery, or rather than an amphibious something, made of half of image and half of abstract meaning. The one sacrificed the heart to the head, the other both heart and head to point and drapery. (p. 383)

BEN JONSON

Epitaph on Elizabeth, L. H.

It was customary to abbreviate titles and last names on tombstones in Jonson's time, and it has been suggested that Elizabeth was titled (L = lady), a small child, and the last in her family line (see line 10). In any case, Jonson uses the epitaph as a metaphor for talking about poetry and the demands of the epigram in particular.

QUESTIONS FOR DISCUSSION

1. What details suggest the poem's self-consciousness about the tradition of the epigram? What dramatic situation and relation between author or speaker and audience is implied by "Reader, stay" (line 2) and "Farewell" (line 12)? What different meanings are implied in "a little" (line 2)?
2. Is line 4 simply a courtly compliment or does it make a serious philosophical statement? Line 6? How can you tell in each case? What attitudes does the poem take toward death? Toward the ongoing world? Toward the life of *noblesse oblige?*
3. Is the poem witty? Is it funny? Does it contain a "sting"? Describe the poem's tone.

MARTIAL

[You've told me, Maro, whilst you live]

QUESTIONS FOR DISCUSSION

1. How would you characterize the "turn" that occurs in the poem? What exactly is the speaker doing in the final two lines with or to the statement described in the first four lines of the poem?
2. How exactly does meter and rhyme contribute to the poem?

RICHARD CRASHAW

An Epitaph upon a Young Married Couple, Dead and Buried Together

QUESTIONS FOR DISCUSSION

1. What traditional conceptions of, and metaphors for, marriage are mentioned or alluded to within the poem? How exactly does the poem play on those conceptions and metaphors?

2. How does this poem envision or embody the relationship between speaker, subject, and audience? In what way is this vision and/or the poet's use of direct readerly address like and unlike that in Jonson's "Epitaph on Elizabeth, L. H."?
3. What are the significance and effect of the rhythmic variations in the poem? Of the use of rhyme?
4. How might this poem change or broaden your conception or definition of the epigram? How specifically is it like the other epigrams that you've read and how exactly does it differ?

X. J. KENNEDY

Epitaph for a Postal Clerk

QUESTIONS FOR DISCUSSION

1. What devices help to make this poem witty? How do those devices, the movement within the poem, and/or the quality of the humor here compare to those of the other epigrams you've read, especially Martial's "[You've told me, Maro . . .]"?
2. In what way is your response to this poem similar to, and different from, your response to poems written in more distant times and places?

COUNTEE CULLEN

For a Lady I Know

QUESTIONS FOR DISCUSSION

1. How does Cullen characterize the "lady" of the poem? What is suggested by his very use of the term *lady*? How does the poem's speaker implicitly characterize himself? What is the tone of the poem?
2. What's the significance of the word "even" in line 1?
3. Is this poem humorous? If so, how is its humor (and the devices through which Cullen achieves it) similar to that of other epigrams you've read?

MARY BARBER

To Novella, *on her saying deridingly, that a Lady of great Merit, and fine Address, was bred in the* Old Way

QUESTIONS FOR DISCUSSION

1. How does the title set the stage for this epigram? What attitude does the title encourage you to adopt toward the speaker, the lady, and Novella? What is the significance of the name *Novella*?
2. How is the "turn" in this poem like that in Martial?
3. How is the attitude of speaker to subject and audience or the relationship implied between the three here like and unlike that in the other epigrams you've read?

PETER PINDAR

Epigram

QUESTIONS FOR DISCUSSION

1. How does Pindar's characterization of Midas differ from that of Marianne Moore in "Love in America?"
2. What or who exactly does "This" (line 3) and "them" (line 4) refer to?
3. As the poem itself suggests, the humor of "Epigram" depends on its "revers[al]" of a traditional statement or story. How is this process of reversal like and unlike the "turns" of other epigrams you've read?

QUESTIONS ON THE EPIGRAMS

1. Based on the evidence of the epigrams that you've read, how would you define the chief (formal and thematic) characteristics of the epigram? In light of your definition, which epigram seems least typical? Most typical?
2. What kind of relationship between speaker, audience, and subject do epigrams tend to imply or embody? In these terms, which epigram seems least typical? Most typical?
3. How would you describe the kinds of humor or wit found in these epigrams? The devices that the poets use to achieve that humor? What poem would you use to exemplify each kind? Which epigrams seem to depend on irony?

4. Do you see any important differences between the older epigrams and the later ones?

5. The anthology suggests that it is possible to see the epigram "as a kind of summary of Western poetic values (involving reason, certainty, intellection, egotism, closure, and cleverness)" (see the introduction to "The Epigram"). Another value might be the emphasis on the ability to effectively manipulate language, to engage in a particular kind of wordplay. Which of these poems do you see as embodying or endorsing these values? Are there any that seem to you to endorse other, even contrary, values?

QUESTIONS ON HAIKU

1. What seasons are explicitly or implicitly called to mind in each haiku? What patterns, if any, do you see in the way each of the seasons is characterized in the haiku (plural) and/or in the emotions associated with each season?

2. Though, as the anthology states, haiku traditionally describe objects from nature and associate these with, or use these to suggest, human emotional and/or mental states, many of these poems also or instead describe man-made objects, such as villages and bells, roads, bridges, etc. What human emotional and/or mental states are associated with such objects? How exactly, if at all, do these haiku connect nature and humans?

3. What do you make of the poems, such as "[Another year gone—]" and "[As I grow older]," that directly allude to the individual speaker; how, if at all, do these poems differ from those in which the speaker is less present or less individualized in the poem? What might these poems help you see about the character and role of the speaker in the other poems?

4. How would you describe the range of tones of haiku? In terms of tone, which haiku seem most typical? Most surprising?

5. Make a list of the objects described in the various Japanese haiku. Based on your reading of these haiku, what conclusions, if any, might you draw about the conventional symbolic resonance of each of these objects?

6. Compare the various translations of Basho's "old pond" haiku. How exactly does each of the interpretations of the poem differ—in terms of omissions, additions, and emphasis? What exactly seems to remain constant? Based on these comparisons, what might we see as the major interpretive problems or questions central to Basho's poem?

7. What patterns do you see in the haiku written in English in terms of subject, tone, etc.? How would you characterize the differences between these haiku and those translated from the Japanese?

8. The anthology suggests that it is possible to see "the haiku as embody-

ing Eastern values (openness, emotion, intuition, and associational or extralogical connections)" (see the introduction to "Haiku"). Another value might be the emphasis on the visual (as opposed to the verbal), on the ability to see (as well as say) effectively. Which of these poems do you see as embodying or endorsing these values? Are there any that seem to you to endorse other, even contrary, values? The emphasis on "Eastern," as opposed to "Western" values, suggests that there may be certain tensions in haiku written by Western poets that aren't present in haiku by writers who are themselves Eastern. Is there any evidence in these haiku to suggest that this is true?

IMITATING AND ANSWERING

SIR WALTER RALEGH

The Nymph's Reply to the Shepherd

WILLIAM CARLOS WILLIAMS

Raleigh Was Right

QUESTIONS FOR DISCUSSION

1. What (besides *if*) are the key words in Ralegh's answer?
2. According to Ralegh, what does the pastoral vision ignore?
3. Though Williams's poem, as its title implies, agrees with Ralegh's criticisms of the pastoral vision, it also suggests many other reasons why (or ways in which) the pastoral vision is "wrong." What are those reasons and ways? Which of them might you attribute to the differences between life in seventeenth-century England and in twentieth-century United States/America and which might you not? What does the poem itself suggest about this question (especially in lines 9–13)?
4. After you have read Ralegh's parody of "The Passionate Shepherd" and Williams's response to both poems, do you find Marlowe's poem less effective? More effective? Does Marlowe seem conscious of the kinds of questions that the later poets raise? What indications are there in the poem that he ignores the questions on purpose? Does such a refusal to raise questions make the poem more simple? More complex? Might simplicity of some kinds or in some cases be a virtue? What about complexity?

[(ponder,darling,these busted statues]

QUESTIONS FOR DISCUSSION

1. In what ways is this poem easier to read after you have analyzed "To His Coy Mistress"? What specific evidence can you find that "[(ponder, darling . . .]" is a response to Marvell's poem?
2. Why are the first and last parts of the poem in parentheses? In what way does the nonparenthesized section differ from the parenthesized sections? What other devices of contrast do you find?
3. Why are such formal and archaic words as *ponder* and *yon* juxtaposed with slang such as *busted* and *motheaten*?
4. How do the ravages of time in this poem differ from those in "To His Coy Mistress"?
5. How does this poem vary from the basic *carpe diem* pattern? Could you tell, from the language of the poem itself, that it was not written in the seventeenth century, when the *carpe diem* motif flourished?
6. What is the setting of the poem? How is the setting important? How does the aqueduct unite the setting with the theme of the poem? Try to explain the speaker's habit of associating what he looks at with the argument he is trying to construct.
7. How do you explain the stanza divisions?

PETER DE VRIES

To His Importunate Mistress

QUESTIONS FOR DISCUSSION

1. Look again at the definition of *parody* in the "Imitating and Answering" section of the anthology. How would you defend the claim that "To His Importunate Mistress" is a parody in this strict sense? That it isn't?
2. In addition to parodying or imitating, how exactly does De Vries's poem "answer" Marvell's? Is there a serious point here?
3. One of the things that makes the poem funny is the juxtaposition of grand and now-antiquated Marvellian language and references to "Bag lunches" (line 8) and "bloke[s]" (line 26). What other techniques does De Vries use to achieve a similar effect? What do you make, for example, of the play on the term "mistress" in lines 17–20?

KENNETH KOCH

Variations on a Theme by William Carlos Williams

ANTHONY HECHT

The Dover Bitch

QUESTIONS FOR DISCUSSION

1. How closely is each poem based on its model? (See Arnold's "Dover Beach" and Williams's "This Is Just to Say.")
2. How much knowledge of the original does each depend on?
3. Is the relationship between model and parody strictly structural?
4. In what way does the original help the imitation toward a particular organization?
5. Does the problem of organization seem easier when there is "a poem behind the poem"?

WENDY COPE

[Not only marble, but the plastic toys]

QUESTIONS FOR DISCUSSION

1. What characterization of contemporary British life is suggested by Cope's various images? In what sense does the poem criticize that way of life? How does your sense of that characterization and/or criticism change or grow when you compare these images directly with those in Shakespeare's "[Not marble, nor the gilded monuments]"? What, for example, do you make of the difference between the way Shakespeare refers to government and politics and the way Cope does?
2. Notice the way in lines 11–12 Cope uses alliteration ("Tulse" and "trendy," "Upper Norwood" and "underground") to reinforce the image of almost unimaginable social reversals. What other formal devices seem especially effective here?

SUGGESTION FOR WRITING

Write an essay considering the accuracy and inaccuracy of the speaker's claim that "all my verse is rotten" (line 14). It might be helpful, in doing so, to consider the poem's model, Shakespeare's "[Not marble, nor the gilded monuments]." How and why specifically might one see Cope's poem as falling short of Shakespeare's? How and why specifically might one see Cope's poem as an effective reply to, or update of, Shakespeare's? Use your analysis of Cope's poem to consider, at least briefly, how one might or should evaluate the effectiveness of poems that "imitate and answer."

CULTURAL BELIEF AND TRADITION

JOHN HOLLANDER

Adam's Task

SUSAN DONNELLY

Eve Names the Animals

Both of these poems expand on the role of naming in the biblical creation myth from Genesis 2–3, and so it is not surprising that both focus on language. But the two are quite different in tone. Which poem revels more in the sounds of words? Which more clearly makes a point? What might be the point of revelling in the sounds of words?

CHRISTINA ROSSETTI

Eve

QUESTIONS FOR DISCUSSION

1. This poem tells the story of Genesis from Eve's perspective. According to the poem, who is to blame for the expulsion from the garden? What was Adam's role? The serpent's?
2. What does this poem take from the biblical account and what does it add?

3. Is there a difference between Eve's account of herself and the account of the narrator?
4. How is Rossetti's portrayal of Eve and Eve's perspective like and unlike Donnelly's?

QUESTIONS ON THE ADAM AND EVE POEMS

1. How many of the poems in the group are "religious"—that is, how many of them have specific doctrinal aims? Chart the themes and rhetorical aims of the poems in the group. What patterns do you find?
2. Which poems draw on highly detailed biblical information? How much knowledge of the Bible do different poets assume? Are there any patterns in this assumption (for instance, do twentieth-century poems seem to assume less specific knowledge)?
3. Which poems draw specifically on a sense of appropriateness associated with certain events, seasons, or traditions? Are the poems in the group more solemn than average? Less solemn? What generalizations can be made about the tones of poems that draw heavily on knowledge of the Judeo-Christian tradition? Sample some poems elsewhere in the anthology in which footnotes point you to biblical allusions. How many different kinds of purposes can you find for the allusions? Poems worth considering include Plath's "Lady Lazarus," Betjeman's "In Westminster Abbey," Stevens's "Sunday Morning," Donne's "[Batter my heart, three-personed God . . .]", Larkin's "Church Going," Herbert's "Easter Wings," Yeats's "The Second Coming," the passage from Milton's *Paradise Lost*, and Nemerov's "Boom!"
4. Do you notice any pattern to your expectations as you approach a poem on a specific religious topic? Are you more than usually dependent on footnotes here? Describe the difference between your emotional response to allusions you immediately recognize and those that you understand only after you have read a footnote or done research. Is your response even more complex after doing research or reading a biblical passage alluded to in a poem?

SUGGESTION FOR WRITING

Write an essay comparing the role of woe in "Eve Names the Animals" and "Eve." (See especially line 22 in Donnelly's poem.)

ALFRED, LORD TENNYSON

Ulysses

Since I often teach "Ulysses" in the context of English literature survey courses and classes on Victorian literature, as well as in writing about literature courses, I find it very interesting to compare the ways the poem speaks to students in these different contexts. In the courses in which students read more poetry by Tennyson and his contemporaries, discussion of this poem tends to turn almost immediately to ideas about (the mythic conceptions of) imperialism as a process of discovery and exploration versus imperialism as the process of civilizing "savage" peoples and about the nature of heroism and the Victorian need to search for heroes in the literature and legends of the past (out of a sense that they are unavailable in the present). In this context, students also tend to read the emphasis on Ulysses's age, on how "Little remains" (line 26), and on the almost desperate need to "seek a newer world" (line 57) as having a wider, cultural significance, resonating as that does with Arnold's depiction of his age as "Wandering between two worlds, one dead / The other powerless to be born" (*Stanzas from the Grande Chartreuse*, lines 85–86). On the other hand, students who read the work isolated from that context tend to see the poem, not surprisingly, as being more about Ulysses himself, as depicting and exploring this mythic character's worldview, values, and even psyche (though, as the word *mythic* is meant to suggest, they often do end up concluding that this exploration has a certain meaning because Ulysses ranks as a prototypical "hero" in the Western tradition).

While all of these can be apt and insightful ways into the poem, I find that students reading "Ulysses" in the particular context that the anthology creates for it sometimes tend to adopt a version of the latter view that can lead them to ignore much of the poem: because "Ulysses" seems so much more "pro-Ulysses," as it were, than the poems of Waddington and Millay, students can easily miss this poem's more subtle, but nonetheless crucial, ambivalence about, and even criticism of, Ulysses, as well as the way the poem questions what it means for a man to become a myth ("I am become a name" [line 11]). As a result, I tend to let students express and develop their "pro-Ulysses" interpretation of the poem (if that's where they seem to want to go), and then I begin pointing out facets of the poem that potentially call that interpretation into question. In the first stanza, for example, Ulysses refers to himself as "an idle king" in line 1, but then almost immediately describes the activities that he does and must undertake as king ("I mete and dole" [line 3]): what are we to make of this seeming contradiction, especially when we consider all of the ramifications of stanza 3 and the fact that some of Tennyson's most significant alterations of Dante's account occur here? (Tennyson's primary source, Canto XXVI of Dante's *Inferno*, barely mentions Telemachus, Ulysses here referring only to the fact that his "fondness for my son" wasn't "able to defeat in me the longing / I had to gain experience of the world and of the vices and the worth of men" (*The Divine Comedy of Dante Alighieri. Inferno*, trans. Allen Mandelbaum. New York: Bantam, 1980, p. 243). (I am myself, happily enough, indebted to the following student essay for this insight—Elaine Yeung's "Poet and Personae in Tennyson's 'Ulysses.'" In *Exposé: Essays from the Expository Writing Program Harvard University 1994–1995*. Cambridge, Mass: Harvard Expository Writing Program, 1995.)

QUESTIONS FOR DISCUSSION

1. How does the poem characterize its situation and setting? Since the poem is a dramatic monologue by Ulysses, the poem allows us only his point of view. How, then, might his characterization of the situation help to characterize him? Is there any evidence in the poem that might suggest that his characterization is in any way faulty or one sided?

2. How does Ulysses explain and justify his choice to leave home? How, in the process, does he characterize the two ways of life associated with staying and leaving? What are the costs and benefits associated with each? Again, is there any evidence in the poem that his characterization and evaluation of those ways of life might be in any way faulty or one sided, that there is another possible way to understand or evaluate the choices Ulysses faces?

3. How are Telemachus and Penelope characterized here? What role does each character play in the poem? What might Ulysses's mode of referring to these characters tell us about him? What is the significance, for example, of the fact that Ulysses simply and only refers to Penelope as "an agéd wife" (line 3)?

4. What might Ulysses mean when he says "I am become a name" (line 11)? In what way is that a bad thing? A good thing? Does any other portion of the poem seem to bring up the question of what it means to "become a name"?

5. What do you make of the poem's emphasis on the age of Ulysses and his mariners and on endings (rather than beginnings)?

6. What do you make of the way in which Ulysses begins to speak of himself as part of a "we" rather than as an "I" toward the end of the poem?

7. On the whole, in what ways might the poem be said to celebrate Ulysses, his choice to leave Ithaca, and the kind of heroism he and that choice represent? In what ways might the poem be said to be ambivalent about, or critical of, Ulysses, his choices, and this particular brand of heroism?

MIRIAM WADDINGTON

Ulysses Embroidered

Like Millay's "An Ancient Gesture," "Ulysses Embroidered" revises the myth of Ulysses by telling part of that myth from the point of view of Penelope, here envisioned as both blind and old. In the process, both poems offer interesting insights into the gender politics of that myth. And since something similar might be said of both Atwood's "Siren Song" and H.D.'s "Helen," which look at different parts of the stories of the Trojan War and Ulysses's journeys, I like to have students read or reread these two poems alongside Waddington's and Millay's.

Though Waddington's poem obviously draws on the story of the ruse whereby Penelope succeeds in deflecting her many suitors during her long wait for Ulysses, I often find that this poem (and even Millay's, which refers to it more directly) still says more to students when I give them a bit more information. Basically, all they need to know is that Penelope did, indeed, wait many, many years for Ulysses, so long that he was assumed dead and Penelope was pressured by her son and others to remarry. To avoid that fate, Penelope successfully convinced everyone that she could not marry until she finished her weaving, and she ensured that this end would never come by unweaving every night all that she wove during the day. In Homer's account, this "ruse" is significant, in part, because it makes Penelope appear like, and arguably in some ways equal to, her husband, whose heroism is often attributed in the text to his status as the wily "master of invention." If your students (as mine sometimes do) want more, you might consider sharing with them the following excerpt from Robert Fitzgerald's translation of Homer's *Odyssey* (New York: Anchor, 1963), in which Penelope explains her "Ruses" to a disguised Ulysses:

> Ruses served my turn
> to draw the time out—first a close-grained web
> I had the happy thought to set up weaving
> on my big loom in the hall. I said, that day:
> "Young men—my suitors, now my lord is dead,
> let me finish my weaving before I marry,
> or else my thread will have been spun in vain.
> It is a shroud I weave for Lord Laërtês
> when cold Death comes to lay him on his bier.
> The country wives would hold me in dishonor
> if he, with all his fortune, lay unshrouded."
> I reached their hearts that way, and they agreed.
> So, every day I wove on the great loom,
> but every night by torchlight I unwove it;
> and so for three years I deceived the Akhaians,

But when the seasons brought a fourth year on,
as long months waned, and the long days were spent,
through impudent folly in the slinking maids
they caught me—clamored up to me at night;
I had no choice then but to finish it.
And now, as matters stand at last,
I have no strength left to evade a marriage,
cannot find any further way; my parents
urge it upon me, and my son
will not stand by while they eat up his property.
He comprehends it, being a man full grown,
able to oversee the kind of house
Zeus would endow with honor. (Book XIX, p. 358)

QUESTIONS FOR DISCUSSION

1. How are Penelope and her relationship with and to Ulysses depicted in "Ulysses Embroidered"? How is this depiction like and unlike that in Tennyson's "Ulysses"?

2. How does the poem use and elaborate on the story of Penelope's weaving? What are some of the implications of the title "Ulysses Embroidered"? Of the poem's depiction of Ulysses "taking shape," "gr[owing]" "from the blind hands of Penelope" (lines 26, 32–34)? Of the final two lines of the poem? What different kinds of "journeys" are suggested and compared in the poem? In what sense might each kind of journey imply a different kind of heroi(ni)sm?

3. How exactly does Waddington change the Ulysses story by narrating it from Penelope's point of view, or what does she encourage you to notice about the story by doing so? What, in particular, might doing so allow Waddington to ask or say here about the way gender roles are depicted in the story?

EDNA ST. VINCENT MILLAY

An Ancient Gesture

1. What are the implications of the way the speaker characterizes the gesture of wiping her tears away with her apron by calling it "authentic, antique / In the very best tradition, classic, Greek" (lines 11–12)? In what sense might these lines and the poem as a whole play upon the word "classic"? Upon the word "gesture"?

2. How are Penelope and her relationship to and with Ulysses characterized in this poem? How is that characterization like and unlike that in Waddington's "Ulysses Embroidered"?

3. How is Millay's representation and use of the story of Penelope's weaving like and unlike Waddington's?

QUESTIONS ON THE ULYSSES POEMS

1. What patterns do you see in terms of what all three of these poems do to and with the story of Ulysses? In what ways might all of them be said to criticize certain aspects of that story? Is there any pattern in terms of what aspects are criticized or at least viewed in a different way? What might the three poems together say or ask about the character of heroes and of heroism (or the myths about heroism that pervade Western culture)?
2. What about the poems of Waddington and Millay in particular? What's alike and different about the two views they offer of the woman's side of the story? Might either or both of these poems be labeled "feminist"? How might that label be a helpful one? An unhelpful one?
3. What patterns do you see across all of the poems in this section that narrate a "classic" story from a woman's point of view, including not only Waddington's and Millay's poems but also Donnelly's "Eve Names the Animals" and Rossetti's "Eve" (and, if appropriate, Atwood's "Siren Song" and H. D.'s "Helen")? What, if any, patterns do you see in the way the poems depict the nature of a specifically female point of view? The traditional conceptions of (or myths about) women's and men's characters and roles? What do they collectively suggest about the problems with such traditional conceptions or myths? What alternative conceptions or myths do they offer?
4. Why do you think writers feel the need to write poems based on ancient myths? What do you think they hope to accomplish in doing so? How might such needs and hopes relate to the author's gender and/or race (even or especially in the case of Tennyson, for example)? The specific cultural context within which he or she writes? How, for example, are poems in which writers look again at an ancient myth similar to, and different from, poems—such as Hayden's "Those Winter Sundays" or Mouré's "Thirteen Years"—in which writers look again at moments from their own past?

LANGSTON HUGHES

The Negro Speaks of Rivers

QUESTIONS FOR DISCUSSION

1. This poem and three of the four poems that follow (the exception being Walcott's "A Far Cry from Africa") all deal in some way with

what it means to be an African American, having at least two different heritages, at least two different systems of myth informing who one is and how one sees oneself. How does the speaker in this poem depict the relationship between the various myths he inherits as both an American and a person of African descent? How exactly are Africa and America each characterized in the poem? What does the speaker seem to gain or suggest about himself through the images of Africa (lines 4–6)? Through the images of America (lines 7–8)?

2. How does the poem use the river as both metaphor and symbol? How exactly does the meaning and significance of the phrase "I've known rivers" shift and grow over the course of the poem?

3. How does Hughes's use of images of Africa and references to "Abe Lincoln" in this poem compare to the invocation of historical figures in the poetry of Adrienne Rich, especially "Planetarium," "Snapshots of a Daughter-in-Law," and "Power"?

JUNE JORDAN

Something Like a Sonnet for Phillis Miracle Wheatley

QUESTIONS FOR DISCUSSION

1. In what ways is and isn't Jordan's poem "something like a sonnet"? What is the meaning and significance of that qualification ("something like")? How might the sonnet form and Jordan's remarks about it in the title contribute to the poem's vision of the relationship between the African and American aspects of Wheatley's heritage (and that of most African Americans, including Jordan)?

2. How specifically are Africa and America characterized here? What is each imagined as giving to Wheatley/African Americans?

3. How are reading and writing characterized and opposed to each other in the poem? Why and how is it important to the poem that Wheatley herself was a poet?

4. How does "Something Like a Sonnet" compare to other poems—such as Cope's "Emily Dickinson," Dryden's "To the Memory of Mr. Old-ham," Auden's "In Memory of W. B. Yeats," and Crane's "To Emily Dickinson"—in which one poet writes to, for, and/or about another? How are such poems like and unlike those earlier in the chapter that allude to, or echo, a particular poem?

Africa

QUESTIONS FOR DISCUSSION

1. How is Africa characterized in this poem? How is this characterization of Africa like and unlike that in "The Negro Speaks of Rivers" and "Something Like a Sonnet"?
2. What are the implications of the image of Africa as a woman? How does the image of Africa as a woman work in concert with the image of violence in this poem?
3. What is the significance and effect of the use of direct, imperative phrasing in the final stanza of the poem? What kinds of relationships among speaker, subject, and reader might Angelou thereby build into the poem?
4. What are the effects of Angelou's use of verbs in the poem, particularly in terms of the way the poem differentiates between kinds of action and attributes agency and responsibility for certain actions?

DEREK WALCOTT

A Far Cry from Africa

To appreciate "A Far Cry from Africa," especially in this context, students may need to know that Walcott is not—as Hughes, Jordan, Angelou, and Reed are or were—an African American, but instead a native of the British West Indies (St. Lucia, to be specific). Nonetheless, he does envision the situation of the African West Indies in much the same terms that these African-American poets do, as being—in the words of this poem—"poisoned with the blood of both" the European colonizers and the African "savages" (line 10), "divided to the vein" (line 27) not only by virtue of birth but also by virtue of an education that has made him own and love "the English tongue" and much of the English cultural tradition (line 30). That situation is captured even in the eloquently ambiguous title of the poem: the speaker is both responsible to the cries that reach out to him from the far shores of Africa and "a far cry" from being a native African.

In emphasizing this aspect of the speaker's situation, however, Walcott's poem might be seen as more self-critical or self-conscious about the appeal to, and of, (a mythic) Africa than are "The Negro Speaks . . ." or "Africa," even though the poem obviously also insists, as those poems do, on the crucial importance of Africa, both real and mythic, to people (and especially writers) of African descent. (The poem, after all, ends with the question, "How can I turn from Africa and live?" [line 33].) One can see another version of the difference in the way that Walcott's poem contemplates not only the kind of abstract "Africa" of the other poems but also at least one specific, actual, and fairly recent moment in African history (or, more specifically, the history of the "wrestling" between Europe and Africa): the Mau-Mau war that rocked Kenya in the 1950s. (If you or your students want a bit more information on the colonization of Africa and on literary explorations thereof, see the note to Laurence's "The Rain Child" in Chapter 11 of this guide, as well as "Planning Ideas" for that chapter.)

QUESTIONS FOR DISCUSSION

1. What do phrases such as "natural law" (line 16) and "brutish necessity" (line 22), and the image of "The gorilla wrestl[ing] with the superman" (line 25) suggest about the nature of, or causes behind, the struggle between Europeans and Africans? What related phrases and images do you see in the poem? What is the speaker's attitude toward these phrases and images? Does the poem offer alternative characterizations and explanations?
2. How do lines 9 and 10 reflect the larger dilemma of the poem?
3. What does the speaker mean by the claim that "upright man / Seeks his divinity by inflicting pain" (lines 16–17)?
4. What are the various implications of the title "A Far Cry from Africa"? How is each of those implications followed up on within the poem itself, particularly—perhaps—in its final stanza?
5. How would you characterize the structure of this poem? What do you make of the way the poem becomes more personal toward the end? In what senses does and does not it become "personal"?
6. How is Africa and the relationship between Africa and Europe characterized in this poem? How is that characterization like and unlike that in the other poems that you've read? How, for example, does Walcott's image of Africa as an animal with a "tawny pelt" (line 1) compare to Angelou's depiction of Africa as a woman? What might the very presence of footnotes to this poem in the anthology, as well as the content of those footnotes, suggest to you about the similarities and differences between this poem and those of Hughes, Jordan, and Angelou?

ISHMAEL REED

I Am a Cowboy in the Boat of Ra

QUESTIONS FOR DISCUSSION

1. What are the various implications of the title "I Am a Cowboy in the Boat of Ra"? How might the title itself be said to suggest and explore

the question of what it means to be African American? What specific myths are being put together in the title? How does the rest of the poem continue that process of juxtaposing and intertwining American and African mythology (including, or as well as, references to American popular culture)?

2. How does Reed's poem ultimately characterize the relationship between the African and American facets of the speaker's heritage? How is his treatment of that dual heritage similar to, and different from, that of the other poems that you've read? How, for example, does this poem differ in terms of tone? Does the tone of Reed's poem ultimately make it any less pointed or serious than those of Hughes, Jordan, Angelou, and Walcott or does it just make its points a different way?

3. What is the significance of the poem's play with the meaning, sound, and look of particular words (especially in its final stanza)? Do you see any relationship between this poem's linguistic play and Walcott's reference to the conflict "Between this Africa and the English tongue I love" (line 30)?

QUESTIONS ON THE POEMS ABOUT AFRICA

1. What patterns do you see here in the way that these poets characterize Africa? Europe and/or America? The relationship between actual Africans and Europeans and between the African and European strands of culture (or mythology) that inform who they are? What patterns do you see in the role that Africa or African mythology plays or in the significance that the poems grant to Africa?

2. In what different ways do these poems use references to the past and/or to history? What difference, if any, is there between poems that allude to specific historical events and figures and those that refer to the past in a more general or abstract way?

3. Which poem most effectively makes you feel what it's like to be an American or West Indian of African descent? Which poem seems to offer the most intellectually complex picture of the problems and possibilities entailed in being an American or West Indian of African descent? Which poem comes closest to offering both?

SUGGESTIONS FOR WRITING

1. In a book of essays titled *Homecoming: Essays on African and Caribbean Literature, Culture and Politics* (Westport, Conn.: Lawrence Hill, 1983, p. xviii), Kenyan novelist, literary critic, and postcolonial theorist Ngugi wa Thiong'o describes his interest in West Indian literature and culture as being

> buttressed by my belief in the basic unity of the black experience and the necessity of unity in the black world. We have the same biological and geographic

origins; we have suffered the same colonial fate (slavery, colonialism, neo-colonialism). . . . Yet it is another sad truth that the forces which have militated against continental and even national unity are the same ones that have kept black peoples disunited, for they want to remain arbiters between African peoples. Africans abroad have been fed on the myth of Tarzan's Africa, and we too have been fed on the myth of "negroes," who have lost all links and interest in Africa.

Reconsidering the poems in this section in light of Ngugi's comments, write an essay in which you consider the extent to which these poets seem to agree with Ngugi's statements about the reality of, or need for, "unity in the black world" and about the necessity of dismantling the negative myths about Africa held by "Africans abroad" in order to achieve that sense of unity. In what sense might one see some or all of these poems as engaging in this process of dismantling and/or as trying to create the sense of "unity" Ngugi describes? In what sense might one see some or all of these poems as challenging or questioning the possibility of such "unity"?

2. Regardless of your ethnic heritage, you know something of the universal human dilemma of divided allegiances: various groups make their claims on you, and sometimes those claims conflict. Using Walcott's "A Far Cry from Africa" as a reference point, write an essay describing your experience of being pulled in two directions. Use the library to find out something about Walcott, and read as many of his poems as you can. How is your experience of self-division like and unlike Walcott's? To what extent does Walcott represent his sense of being "divided at the vein" as representative of the experience of all West Indians, all African West Indians, and/or all of those belonging to what some call the African diaspora?

JUDITH ORTIZ COFER

How to Get a Baby

Obviously there are few Western scientists who would buy the Trobiand Islanders recipe for "getting a baby," though there are undoubtedly not a few anthropologists who would love to dissect it and would do so with utter, scientific detachment. Like the first kind of scientists, my students often don't really know what to make of, or do with, this poem. As a result, I tend to focus discussion on the epigraph and the way it embeds within the poem the latter of these "scientific" reactions to, or treatments of, the myths of "others," a treatment very different from that within the text itself, which gets inside the myth and the way this (and, I think, other myths) are—in terms of content and in terms of the process of telling—as much about ways to understand relationships as they are about "how to" do anything. Approaching the poem in this way not only gives students the framework or vocabulary they need to really work with the poem but also allows me to open up for discussion larger issues about the tendency to treat the stories and beliefs of others as quaint myths and to see our own as more solid. If the myths of other cultures are interesting because they give us insight into their worldviews and values, then how can we begin to recognize our own myths as myths and to understand the insights about ourselves they offer? How can we learn to put on that detached "Malinowskian" outsider's perspective in relation to our own cultural myths and artifacts?

QUESTIONS FOR DISCUSSION

1. How would you describe the tone of the epigraph? What sense do you get of Malinowski's relationship to the process he describes? To his reader? How would you describe the tone of the poem itself?
2. How would you describe the speaker here? His or her relationship to the process he or she describes? To his or her reader?
3. What is the effect of this juxtaposition of texts, tones, and speakers?

ALBERTO ALVARO RÍOS

Advice to a First Cousin

QUESTIONS FOR DISCUSSION

1. How are each of the characters in the poem (including the speaker) characterized here? The relationship between the characters? How does the grandmother characterize the different kinds of scorpions? In what way does the poem suggest that her advice is really about relationships between people? What, then, is the real advice here? Who is the "they" in line 30? What is their role in the poem?
2. What do the grandmother and the poem as a whole suggest about why she gives the advice? About the significance of the fact that the advice is given to one grandchild but related to us by another? How does the process of telling itself become part of the tale within the poem?

SUGGESTION FOR WRITING

It would be easy to "explode" the myth described in Cofer's "How to Get a Baby": the system for receiving a *waiwaia* involves frequent sex, which of course would increase the woman's chance of becoming pregnant. Or the myth of the scorpions in Ríos's "Advice to a First Cousin": scorpions do not really reason, as the speaker's grandmother claims they do. Write an essay on either or both of these poems, explaining what would be lost by exploding the myth and exploring what kinds of truths might be conveyed in the telling of such myths.

LOUISE ERDRICH

Jacklight

Though my students tend to presume that "Jacklight" describes (and essentially deplores) hunting of any and all kinds, I think the details of the poem, as well as its very title, make much more sense and mean something quite different when one recognizes that the poem depicts the particular practice of hunting at night with a "jacklight." In the southern United States, where I grew up, the practice is sometimes called "fire hunting" and typically involves driving along a road at the edge of the woods, shining high-powered lights into the trees. Deer are so mesmerized by the light that they will simply stand frozen in place, essentially waiting to be shot down; and that's at least part of the reason why the practice is illegal. In Georgia, for example, it's legally considered a form of poaching, involving what the law calls "harassment" of animals (a wonderfully poetic form of understatement in its own right). As such laws suggest, fire hunting is regarded even by most hunters as a peculiarly cruel and unfair practice that gives all the advantages to the human hunter, facts and feelings that give a distinctly different cast to Erdrich's use of this practice in "Jacklight" as a metaphor for relations between the sexes and particularly to her vision in the final stanza of the deer nonetheless outwitting the hunters. "Jacklight" pairs usefully with Karen Chase's "Venison."

QUESTIONS FOR DISCUSSION

1. How does Erdrich's strategy of looking at fire hunting from the point of view of the hunted rather than the hunter compare to the use of the female point of view in the poems earlier in this chapter about Adam and Eve and Ulysses and Penelope?

2. To what extent is and is not this poem about Chippewa myths in particular? Erdrich's epigraph draws our attention to the ways in which myths are embedded in language itself, the very vocabulary we use everyday. What are some of the words and idiomatic expressions you use or have heard others use to describe "flirting" or "intercourse"? What myths are embedded in those expressions and the metaphors they often imply?

READING/WRITING IDEAS FOR CHAPTER 23

LITERARY-TRADITION-AS-CONTEXT ESSAYS

This chapter is so rich and paves the way for so many types of essay assignments that I almost don't know where to begin. But certainly, from a readerly/writerly technique point of view (rather than the poetic technique point of view of the chapter), the common denominator here has to be the task of (intertextual) comparison of one sort or another, however widely those "sorts" may vary. Below, I've tried to describe some of those different sorts by breaking them up into three broad categories and by illustrating each category with sample assignments and, in one case, with an excerpt from an actual student essay. Because the sample assignments are intended to illustrate how assignments can be worded to encourage students to look at and write about texts in a particular way, I've offered multiple rewordings or versions of the "same" assignment rather than a lot of different assignments.

1. The comparison in which the writer focuses primarily on a single text but uses another text or texts in the service of that analysis, exploring the meaning of the primary text by examining how it *differs from, alludes to, answers,* or *imitates* the other text(s).

Sample of a "Differing From" Assignment

Write an essay in which you analyze Tennyson's *Ulysses* by focusing on the specific ways in which Tennyson here alters Dante's account in Book XXVI of the *Inferno*. To craft a coherent essay, you may well want to pick out one alteration or one kind of alteration that seems especially significant rather than tackling them all.

Sample of a "Differing From" Thesis

> Perhaps the most startling departure from the [Ulysses] myth, which also creates the greatest ambiguity in interpreting the poem, is Tennyson's inclusion of a speech which Ulysses delivers about his son Telemachus[, a speech that is not present in Dante's account]. . . . The contrast between Telemachus and Ulysses, absent in Dante's version, suggests that the inclusion of Telemachus reinforces important themes unique to Tennyson's version of the myth.
>
> Elaine Yeung, "Poet and Personae in Tennyson's 'Ulysses.' " In Exposé:
Essays from the Expository Writing Program Harvard University 1994–1995,
Cambridge, Mass.: Harvard Expository Writing Program, 1995, pp. 50–54.

Sample of an "Alluding To" Assignment

In section four of Rich's "Snapshots of a Daughter-in-Law," the speaker refers to an Emily Dickinson poem that you may have read, "[My Life had stood—a Loaded Gun]." Write an essay in which you explore the significance of that reference or allusion. How is Dickinson's poem relevant to the situation in this poem? How does the poet Emily Dickinson and/or the speaker in "[My Life had stood . . .]" figure for the woman in this poem? How does this single allusion fit within, and contribute to, the poem as a whole?

Sample of an "Answering" Assignment

Write an essay analyzing Williams's "answer" to Marlowe's "The Passionate Shepherd to His Love" and the way in which Williams's answer builds on that of Ralegh in "The Nymph's Reply to the Shepherd." Though Williams's "Raleigh Was Right," as its title implies, agrees with Ralegh's criticisms of the pastoral vision, it also suggests many other reasons why (or ways in which) the pastoral vision is "wrong." What are those reasons and ways? To what extent is Williams updating, as well as building upon, Ralegh's critique?

Sample of an "Imitating" Assignment

Write an essay in which you analyze the serious theme or themes that De Vries considers in "To His Importunate Mistress" by poking fun at Marvell's "To His Coy Mistress."

2. The comparison in which the writer focuses equally on several texts, directly comparing the different "versions" those texts offer of some thing (such as a particular event, character, myth, or story) or of some poetic kind, the point being primarily to understand and appreciate the unique qualities of each particular text. This type of comparison undoubtedly comes closest to the traditional "comparison and contrast" (a term I never use, however, because it implies that contrast isn't essential to comparison, an implication that doesn't make sense to me).

Sample Assignments

Write an essay comparing Tennyson's "Ulysses" with Dante's treatment of the same situation and character in Book XXVI of Dante's *Inferno*. How is Ulysses and his situation characterized in each poem? What attitude does each poem take toward Ulysses? To what extent is he portrayed as an admirable "hero" in either or both poems? To what extent is he criticized? What is unique about each poem and its treatment of Ulysses?

According to Rich's interpretation of Dickinson's "[My Life had stood—a Loaded Gun]" in "Vesuvius at Home," Dickinson's poem explores women's ambivalence about their own power to create, an ambivalence arising out of the sense of a conflict between power and creativity, on the one hand, and femininity, on the other. Using Rich's comment as a starting point, write an essay comparing Rich's "Snapshots of a Daughter-in-Law" or "Power" with Dickinson's "[My Life had stood . . .]" in terms of what each poem seems to say or ask about these issues.

Write an essay comparing Marlowe's "The Passionate Shepherd to His Love," Ralegh's "The Nymph's Reply to the Shepherd," and Williams's "Raleigh Was Right" *or* De Vries's "To His Importunate Mistress" and Marvell's "To His Coy Mistress." What does each poem seem to suggest about what life and/or love is or should be like?

Write an essay comparing two or more haiku or two or more epigrams. How does each poem differently meet the requirements of its poetic kind? How does each poet manipulate the form to communicate his or her own particular vision?

3. The comparison in which, as in type B, one directly compares several texts, but in which the point of the comparison is more about *thematic or formal* similarities or patterns than about differences, the point being primarily to understand and appreciate how these texts work together as

part of a single, ongoing dialogue about whatever the "thing" in question is or as part of a single poetic kind. This essay type differs dramatically from the others in that its focus is less on the texts themselves than on using the texts to contemplate some more general (literary, philosophical, social, or political) issue or question.

Sample Assignments

Write an essay comparing Tennyson's "Ulysses," Dante's treatment of the same situation and character in Book XXVI of the *Inferno*, Waddington's "Ulysses Embroidered," and Millay's "An Ancient Gesture." By analyzing all four poems, consider the question of what Ulysses has meant and does seem to mean to Western writers. Why do you think so many writers have been tempted to look and relook at the story of Ulysses? How exactly has the myth of Ulysses evolved over time?

Write an essay comparing Waddington's "Ulysses Embroidered," Millay's "An Ancient Gesture," Donnelly's "Eve Names the Animals," Rossetti's "Eve," Atwood's "Siren Song," and H. D.'s "Helen." What patterns do you see in the way the poems depict the nature of a specifically female point of view? The traditional conceptions of (or myths about) women's and men's characters and roles? What do they collectively suggest about the problems with such traditional conceptions or myths? What alternative conceptions or myths do they offer? Why does it seem to be so important to women writers to revise ancient myths in this way?

Write an essay comparing Marlowe's "The Passionate Shepherd to His Love," Ralegh's "The Nymph's Reply to the Shepherd," and Williams's "Raleigh Was Right." How do the poems work together as part of an ongoing dialogue about the pastoral and/or about the symbolic resonance of "country" and "city" in Western culture? How might you connect changes in writers' views of the pastoral to changes within Western culture and society itself?

Drawing on all of the haiku and epigrams that you have read, write an essay in which you explore what's right and what's wrong about the anthology's (admittedly tentative) claim that haiku reflects or embodies values associated with Eastern culture, the epigram values associated with Western culture. *Or* write an essay that focuses only on one kind and one claim, analyzing how the epigram does and does not valorize "reason, certainty, intellection, egotism, closure, and cleverness," or how the haiku does and does not valorize "openness, emotion, intuition, and associational or extralogical connections."

TROUBLESHOOTING

I have found that comparative essays pose challenges to student writers that are very similar to those posed by the multiple-text, single-author essays described in earlier chapters, the key challenges in both cases being crafting effective theses and effective argumentative structures, which is precisely why I've emphasized structural differences in the above descriptions of the different types of comparison essays. What I've also tried to emphasize there is the way that structures and goals tend to interrelate (as they do in poems themselves)—type B essays that compare in order to differentiate tend to "need" structures that move from likeness to difference and, often, from the kind of "simultaneous" to "one text at a time" structures described in "Reading/Writing Ideas for Chapter 21," while type C essays that compare in order to make claims about likeness of one kind or another tend to "need" some version of the "simultaneous" structure, and type C essays that compare in order to make claims about development over time tend to "need" "one text at a time" structures. I find that whatever I can do to help students think about essays in terms of that interrelationship between goals and structure improves not only their writing but also their ability to think and talk about their writing in strategic and helpful ways.

For these reasons, you might well want to consider *not* using the kind of writing assignments I've sampled above, but instead sketching out the assignment for students by doing something along the lines of what I've just done here, giving them a sense of the range of possible options and letting them pick and choose, essentially formulating their own assignment or project and then strategizing about how best to write their way into it.

LITERARY TRADITION–FOCUSED WRITING EXERCISES

As I've just suggested, I find that the challenges entailed in writing comparative essays are best tackled by focusing students first on questions about *why* one writes comparative essays of all or a particular type and then on questions about *how* one writes effective ones. Though I have been successful in having discussions about such issues in the abstract, I find it much more effective when possible to have students discuss such abstract issues in the light of specific examples, sample essays (by students or scholars) of the type they are being asked to produce or sample assignments of the type I've offered above. (The essay by A. Alvarez in Chapter 25 or the final sections might serve as one such sample, since it concludes with a discussion of the different myths about the family conveyed and reflected on in poems by Plath, Roethke, and others.) Again, the point of such discussion is to generate ideas about the purpose of comparative essays first and then about the form such essays need to take to fulfill those purposes (which also means discussing what form specific elements of the essay, such as the thesis, need to take). As this description is meant to suggest, such discussions are productive whether they focus on the particular kind of comparative essay that your particular assignment asks them to produce or is designed to sketch out the range of options, strategies, and types available to them and thus prepare them to essentially craft their own assignment or project.

24

HISTORICAL AND CULTURAL CONTEXTS

This chapter offers the opportunity to read and analyze poetry within the specific historical and cultural contexts of each poem. While you will want to make students sensitive to their lack of knowledge about some contexts (so that they will seek out the knowledge they need instead of blithely analyzing poetry with no sense of the background), it can be counterproductive to make them feel ignorant. That is why I like to begin with a poem for which many students will understand the contexts immediately. Ai's "Riot Act, April 29, 1992" works well for my purposes, since most students will know about the series of trials associated with the Rodney King beating and the riots in South Central Los Angeles that were the aftermath of the acquittal of the officers involved. Once students realize how their special knowledge of the L.A. riot gives them useful expertise as readers and critics of this poem, they move more readily and enthusiastically toward *becoming* experts on the contexts of other poems that treat subjects remote from their experience. Williams's "Thinking about Bill, Dead of AIDS" can also prove helpful in this way, particularly since it focuses not—as Ai's "Riot Act . . ." does—on a single event but on a more general cultural milieu.

PLANNING IDEAS

- Before the first class day on this chapter, give the students a photocopy of Ai's "Riot Act, April 29, 1992," without footnotes and Williams's "Thinking about Bill, Dead of AIDS." Ask them to supply the footnotes they believe future generations might find helpful in understanding the poems and to bring these to class.
- Well before class, assign several groups of students to do background research on a number of the poems in this chapter and to share their findings at the appropriate time (e.g., research methods of warfare used in World War I as background to Owen's "Dulce et Decorum Est").
- Create a unit to study and discuss issues of African-American identity

and racial equality using such poems as McKay's "America," Hughes's "Harlem (A Dream Deferred)," Hayden's "Frederick Douglass," and Ai's "Riot Act, April 29, 1992." Ask different students to research the context of each poem before class, paying particular attention to the social and legal situation of African Americans at the time each poem was written. You might also or instead create a unit on war generally or World War I specifically (see note to Owen's "Dulce et Decorum Est").
- If you assign the poem "Sonnet: The Ladies' Home Journal," ask each student to choose and bring to class a magazine article that portrays what he or she considers a false picture of some aspect of American life. Use these as the basis for a discussion of the poem's message and its continued relevance.

TIMES, PLACES, AND EVENTS

MILLER WILLIAMS

Thinking about Bill, Dead of AIDS

Because most of our students have grown up in an era in which the AIDS epidemic has become a taken-for-granted fact of life and are, therefore, quite knowledgeable about the facts and feelings surrounding that epidemic, this poem (like Ai's "Riot Act . . .") provides a great opportunity to highlight the way in which all of the taken-for-granted facts and feelings they can bring to bear on this poem constitute "knowledge" of precisely the kind they may or may not possess about the more remote times, places, and events referred to in other poems. One of the chief, yet subtle, ways this poem depends on our knowledge is the way it refers to a time before "we" "kn[e]w" "about" the nature and causes of AIDS and before we knew how to emotionally handle the deaths of young and previously healthy people. The poem thus assumes that we know about how mysterious the disease was at first to both scientists and laypeople, about how shocking it was when young friends and loved ones began to die, and about how a whole society has had to become slowly but surely "knowing" about both the disease and the process of death itself.

QUESTIONS FOR DISCUSSION

1. What metaphor for AIDS is suggested by the language of the first two stanzas of the poem? What is the significance of this metaphor in the context of the poem as a whole?

2. Who is the "we" who speaks the poem? What is the significance and effect of Williams's use of "we"?
3. What is the situation and setting of the poem, especially in terms of time? What knowledge do we need to have to fully appreciate the setting and themes of the poem?
4. What do you make of the poem's repeated reference to knowledge? In what sense is the poem a poem about knowledge (and the knowledge "we" have at different times), as well as a poem that draws on our knowledge of a particular time, place, and event?

IRVING LAYTON

From Colony to Nation

QUESTIONS FOR DISCUSSION

1. What cues do you get from the poem and the poem's title about the time, place, or event the poem considers? What, for example, is the significance of the word "From" in the title?
2. Though you may not know what colony or nation Layton has in mind, you undoubtedly do know something about colonies and nations and about the historical transition from one to the other. Based on that knowledge and the text of the poem itself, how would you interpret the poem? Who, for example, might the "dull people" be who are referred to repeatedly throughout the poem?

MARY JO SALTER

Welcome to Hiroshima

QUESTIONS FOR DISCUSSION

1. How precisely does the poem draw on our knowledge that Hiroshima was the site of one of the two atomic bomb explosions that ended World War II? How exactly do the specific images of present-day Hiroshima in the first five stanzas of the poem call that event to mind?
2. What exactly does the speaker emphasize through her descriptions of the Hiroshima memorial museum in the second half of the poem?
3. What different views of the relationship between past and present are suggested in stanzas 5, 7–8, 11–12? Which view, if any, does the poem as a whole seem to ultimately embrace? To what extent is the poem about Hiroshima in particular and to what extent does it use Hiroshima—past and present—to pose more general questions?
4. What does the poem suggest about the symbolic significance of the

Hiroshima explosion? Of the specific ways it has been remembered and memorialized (or not remembered)?

DWIGHT OKITA

Notes for a Poem on Being Asian American

QUESTIONS FOR DISCUSSION

1. What does the speaker suggest in the first two stanzas about how the image of the egg does and does not work as a metaphor for the experience of being Asian American?
2. How exactly are each of the two moments described in the last two stanzas "uniquely Asian American" (line 14)? What do they individually and collectively suggest about what it is like to be Asian American? About the attitudes some Americans have about Asian Americans? What is the significance of Hiroshima here? The image of Marimekko sheets?
3. How exactly is this poem's use of references to Hiroshima similar to and different from that in Salter's "Welcome to Hiroshima"? What might the Hiroshima explosion be said to symbolize in each poem?

DONALD JUSTICE

Children Walking Home from School through Good Neighborhood

QUESTIONS FOR DISCUSSION

1. What historical or cultural knowledge does "Children Walking Home . . ." draw on?
2. What are the "two worlds" mentioned in line 5?
3. What exactly is the "glass ball" referred to in line 1? What are the implications of this simile?

CLAUDE McKAY

America

QUESTIONS FOR DISCUSSION

1. How does the poem manipulate the opposing forces of energy and stability into qualities both positive and negative for the speaker?

2. Could you prove, from the poem itself, that the poet was an African American? Which details in the poem take on a new dimension when you keep this fact in mind?

SUGGESTION FOR WRITING

Write an essay comparing McKay's "America" to Shelley's "Ozymandias." Which poem is the more specific? Which do you find the most effective in conveying its message?

LANGSTON HUGHES

Harlem (A Dream Deferred)

This poem was written in 1951, before the explosion of the civil rights movement in the 1960s. The dream in the poem may refer to the aspirations of African Americans to move out of the poverty-stricken conditions of the urban ghetto in Harlem and elsewhere and to participate in the "American Dream." More generally, it refers to any frustrated plan of self-fulfillment. None of the alternative similes describing what happens to a dream deferred is hopeful. How does the bleakness of this poem compare with the poems written by Adrienne Rich in 1951?

ROBERT HAYDEN

Frederick Douglass

This poem has something to say about what it means for a person or a group of people to remember and claim a hero, what it means to pursue the dream of a great leader. You might use discussion of this poem as an opportunity to explore the issues of leadership and hero worship in contemporary terms. For whom is Bill Clinton a hero? O. J. Simpson? For whom is Hillary Clinton a leader? Anita Hill?

QUESTIONS FOR DISCUSSION

1. Which lines of the poem do *not* deal with remembering?
2. In what repute or esteem is Frederick Douglass held today? To what degree does the answer to that question depend on whom you consult, according to age, race, political affiliation, etc.?

SUGGESTION FOR WRITING

Read the article on the candidacy of Marion Barry for mayor of Washington, D.C., in the September 5, 1994, issue of *The New Yorker* magazine. Write a sonnet similar to Robert Hayden's *or* a campaign song in which you either praise Barry and support him as a mayoral candidate or judge him and assert that he could not serve his city well.

MBUYISENI OSWALD MTSHALI

Boy on a Swing

Because this poem offers almost no clues about historical and cultural context, yet is written by a poet who considers that context vitally important, this poem presents a great opportunity to discuss the ways in which our interpretations of a poem differ before and after we have information about historical and cultural context. As a result, I tend to have students read and discuss the poem on its own terms first, including in that discussion questions about what the poem itself suggests about its situation and setting and/or historical and cultural context and about what questions they might want answered that aren't answered by the poem. Then and only then do I offer them the following short biography, asking how exactly the information it contains might change or broaden their interpretation of the poem.

Zulu poet Mbuyiseni Oswald Mtshali was born Oswald Joseph Mtshali in Natal, South Africa, in 1940. (Like many African writers, Mtshali thus chose to exchange his Christian given name for an African one.) Though his first poetry collection, *Sounds of a Cowhide Drum* (1972) received much praise, his second book *Fireflames* (1980), dedicated "to the . . . brave schoolchildren of Soweto," was banned by the white government because of its radical anti-Apartheid politics. Mtshali describes his writing as motivated by the effort "to share my experiences by commenting to all my readers who want to know [how] I feel about living in an apartheid society where the white minority is oppressing the black majority" (*Contemporary Authors*, Vol. 142, Detroit: Gale Research, 1994, p. 313).

THOMAS HARDY

The Convergence of the Twain

Though, with some vigorous prodding, even students utterly unfamiliar with Hardy can get from the poem itself a fairly accurate sense of what phrases such as "The Immanent Will" and the "Spinner of the Years" mean, you may want to consider sharing with them some or all of the following helpful descriptions of Hardy's poetic technique and beliefs (from Walter E. Houghton and G. Robert Stange's *Victorian Poetry and Poetics*, 2nd ed., New York: Houghton Mifflin, 1968):

> Hardy's reaction to an episode "has behind it and within it a reaction to the universe." Sometimes an incident is placed in a vast setting where it is seen as a meeting-point of past and future, or as part of the great network of cause and effect which links the farthest stars and far corners of the earth with every human action. What Hardy says of Winterborne and Marty in *The Woodlanders* is expressive of his poetic conception:
>
> > Hardly anything could be more isolated or more self-contained than the lives of these two walking here in the lonely hour before day. . . . And yet their lonely courses formed no detached design at all, but were part of the pattern in the great web of human doings then weaving in both hemispheres from the White Sea to Cape Horn. (p. 812)
>
> In the universe as Hardy saw it there was no deity; men were part of a great network of cause and effect, impotent prey to the chance ordering of things. . . . Borrowing the terminology of the Germans, he sometimes referred to the unconscious force behind the universe as the Immanent Will, sometimes as the Spinner of the Years, Fate, Doom, or even God; whatever its name it determines all things— and not often for good. Though not consciously cruel or malignant, Fate is an automaton, blindly pulling the strings of the human puppets, a "sleep-worker" who may someday awake—perhaps to destroy the universe, perhaps to "adjust, amend, and heal." (p. 813)

QUESTIONS FOR DISCUSSION

1. What do you think the speaker means by "Pride of Life" (line 3)?
2. The first five stanzas describe the sunken *Titanic*. What do the images of the *Titanic* in these stanzas individually and collectively suggest about the meaning and significance of the sunken *Titanic?*
3. Stanzas 6–11 offer an answer to the question posed at the end of stanza 5—"What does this vaingloriousness down here?" What is that answer? What, for example, might the speaker mean by "The Immanent Will" (line 18)? "[T]he Spinner of the Years" (line 31)? How and why exactly are the *Titanic* and the iceberg "twin halves of one august event" (line 30)?
4. On the whole, what does the poem suggest about the meaning and significance of this "august event"?

WILFRED OWEN

Dulce et Decorum Est

Horace's poem on which the title is based can make an interesting comparison; it is the second ode in his third book of *Odes*. The poem also works well in conjunction with the other poems about war in the "Constructing Identity, Exploring Gender" section of this chapter, particularly the other World War I poems—Rosenberg's "Break of Day in the Trenches," Guest's "The Things That Make a Soldier Great," and Owen's own "Disabled."

(*Note*: Owen was killed in November 1918, barely a week before the Armistice. Only four of his poems had been published at the time of his death.)

QUESTIONS FOR DISCUSSION

1. Which physical details in the first stanza are the most dramatic?
2. What is implied by the comparison to "beggars" (line 1)? To "hags" (line 2)?
3. Why are the shells said to "hoot" (line 7)? To be "disappointed" (line 8)? What is accomplished by giving human attributes to inanimate objects?

DUDLEY RANDALL

Ballad of Birmingham

Like "Harlem," this poem offers a despairing picture of the lives of African Americans, this time at the height of the racial violence of the 1960s. Rather than similes, however, this poem uses realistic details. Describing an historical event, it focuses on a particular story to show that no one, no matter how innocent, can escape the violence of the struggle. The irony is that a child is killed as a result of her mother's attempts to protect her from harm.

QUESTIONS FOR DISCUSSION

1. What devices make this account more than a detached description of an event?
2. How do the dialogue, repetition, and symbolism contribute to the poem's power to go beyond the specificity of the particular incident?

AI
_____

Riot Act, April 29, 1992

Either through student reports (see "Planning Ideas" above) or through general discussion, review the events preceding the April 29 riots: the repeated TV screenings of the Rodney King beating, the much-publicized venue change for the police officers' trial to mostly white Sonoma County, and the trial verdict. Students will readily see how important knowledge of this background is to understanding Ai's poem. After establishing the trial context, I like to ask students what additional elements of the poem they believe should be annotated to help future generations understand Ai's work (see "Planning Ideas"). Their list will probably include the brand names Reebok and Nike and references to sports and entertainment personalities Michael Jordan, Magic Johnson, and Spike Lee. It might also include the street slang appellation *homey,* references to movies (*The Night of the Living Dead, Mo' Money*), and the "trickle down" theory of economics current during the Reagan and Bush administrations. A century from now, readers might also need to know something about the social and economic situation of African Americans living in South Central Los Angeles at this time.

QUESTIONS FOR DISCUSSION

1. Characterize the speaker. How does he view his day-to-day life?
2. What is the speaker's view of what's "out there" (line 4)—the things that are *not* part of his daily existence?
3. Who are the "zombies" the speaker refers to in line 26? What is the speaker's view of white America? How does the speaker imagine that white America views him?
4. How, in the course of the poem, does the speaker justify his actions? What do you make of his references to self-destruction?
5. Does it matter whether the poet is African American, Asian, or white?

SUGGESTIONS FOR WRITING

1. Research the aftermath of the Rodney King trial in the library, consulting at least three magazine and three newspaper articles from *different* magazines and newspapers. Write an assessment of the accuracy of Ai's poem, based on your research.
2. Taking Ai's "Riot Act, April 29, 1992" as a model, write your own poem on the riot, describing it from the point of view of an Asian shopkeeper in South Central Los Angeles or from the perspective of a white member of the trial jury.

CONSTRUCTING IDENTITY, EXPLORING GENDER

Focusing on poems that draw on and reflect what the anthology calls "information about ideas and consciousness" rather than about "time and event," this section of the chapter offers an opportunity to explore "historical and cultural context" in a way very different from that suggested by the first section. For by encouraging students to read a poem such as Lovelace's "Song: To Lucasta, Going to the Wars" in terms of the assumptions about gender that it encodes, even though the poem is not explicitly "about" gender in the way that Hardy's "The Convergence of the Twain" is about the sinking of the *Titanic* or even in the way Gilbert's "Sonnet: The Ladies' Home Journal" is about gender, the section will likely also raise questions among students about reading methods and strategies. For even if they don't or won't say so explicitly, students often see such an approach as strange and/or "unfair," to use a term I often hear. One of the assumptions that often seems to underlie that reaction is the idea that reading a poem such as Lovelace's in this way inevitably entails judging the poem against contemporary, politically correct standards. As a result, I find it useful to get that assumption onto the table as early as possible (along with all the other questions about methodology that might be raised here) and to encourage students to discuss whether and how it might be possible to analyze, without evaluating, such messages (a discussion that you may want to revisit once you do get to "Evaluating Poetry"). Discussing or rediscussing Gilbert's "Sonnet: The Ladies' Home Journal" can also be useful in this regard, since the poem can be seen as itself embodying this approach to texts. It also helps, I think, that the section encourages students *not* to see gender as a "women's issue," instead offering poems that are about both men's and women's roles and that are written from the perspective of both men and women.

ROBERT BROWNING

My Last Duchess

In this poem there is no commentary at all and no obvious reflection; this poem is an almost pure example of a straight dramatic situation. Because it is spoken by a single character, this kind of poem is often called a dramatic monologue (see "Glossary"). Characteristic of the dramatic monologue is a gradual revelation of the situation and the speaker's character. The speaker gradually gives himself away, creating in the reader a stronger and stronger sense of horror at the duke's past actions, his present intentions, and his character. Some students will decipher the syntax of this poem with relative ease, but don't be surprised if some need help.

QUESTIONS FOR DISCUSSION

1. Describe the dramatic situation. Characterize the speaker in detail. How is each aspect of his character suggested? What do his descriptions of the painting and statue tell you about him? When do you begin to sense his role in the earlier events he alludes to?
2. Characterize the duke's "last duchess."
3. What is the auditor like? How can you tell?
4. What information is withheld for dramatic effect? Describe the effects of timing in disclosing the information. How important is the precise time of disclosure? Evaluate the structure here against traditional descriptions of dramatic structure.
5. What does the poem suggest about the nature of men's and women's roles through its characterization of the duke and his characterization of his "last duchess"?

RICHARD LOVELACE

Song: To Lucasta, Going to the Wars

QUESTIONS FOR DISCUSSION

1. What does this poem suggest about the nature and causes of war? What is suggested, for example, by the image of war as "a new mistress" (line 5)? By the references to "faith" (line 7) and "honor" (line 12)?
2. What does the poem imply about men's and women's different attitudes toward war? Toward love? About men's and women's roles in general?
3. Based on the evidence of "Dulce et Decorum Est," what might Wilfred Owen think of Lovelace's representation of war?

ISAAC ROSENBERG

Break of Day in the Trenches

QUESTIONS FOR DISCUSSION

1. What do you make of the speaker's description of the rat as "queer," "sardonic" (line 4), and "droll" (line 7)? How and why precisely are

the rat's "sympathies" "cosmopolitan" (line 8)? What does Rosenberg
suggest about the war through his portrayal of the rat?

2. What is the meaning and significance of the images of poppies? How,
   if at all, might Rosenberg's poem rework the traditional symbolism of
   the poppy (see footnote 7)?
3. How is Rosenberg's portrayal of war and of men's roles like and unlike
   that in Lovelace's "Song: To Lucasta . . . "? Owen's "Dulce et Decorum
   Est"?

EDGAR A. GUEST

The Things That Make a Soldier Great

QUESTIONS FOR DISCUSSION

1. What does this poem suggest about the nature and causes of war?
   About why particular soldiers fight in war? What does stanza 2, for
   example, suggest about what *doesn't* inspire soldiers to fight?
2. What does the poem's emphasis on the idea that soldiers fight for their
   children, etc., imply about what men's roles more generally are and
   should be? What do you make of the absence of references to women
   in the poem?
3. How would you describe the structure and form of the poem? What
   is the significance and effect of the poem's form?
4. How exactly is this poem's portrayal of war like and unlike Lovelace's?
   Rosenberg's? Owen's?

WILFRED OWEN

Disabled

QUESTIONS FOR DISCUSSION

1. Like Owen's "Dulce et Decorum Est," "Disabled" explores the conflict
   between the idealistic vision of war and its reality, but in this case
   Owen does so by focusing on war's aftermath and effects rather than
   on the actual experience of warfare. How exactly does this poem
   describe the idealistic vision of war, especially through its depiction
   in stanzas 4 and 5 of this soldier's reasons for joining the army?
2. What's the significance of the memories of football matches? To what
   extent does and does not football become a metaphor for war in the
   poem?
3. What does the poem suggest about what exactly the soldier has lost

in losing his legs, particularly through its emphasis on his encounters with women before and after his injury? What do you make of the speaker's comment that the soldier "threw away his knees" (line 10)?

4. How does the vision of war, of male roles, and/or (male) heroism in "Disabled" compare to that in "Dulce et Decorum Est"? In the poems by Lovelace, Rosenberg, and Guest?

PAULETTE JILES

Paper Matches

QUESTIONS FOR DISCUSSION

1. How exactly do the activities of "wash[ing] dishes" and "squirt[ing] each other on the lawn with / garden hoses" differ from each other (lines 1–3)? What exactly does the juxtaposition of these activities suggest about the nature of men's and women's roles?
2. What exactly is Aunt Hetty's role in, and contribution to, the poem? Is there an implied contrast here between her attitudes and those of the speaker (in lines 5–8)? If so, how would you characterize those two attitudes?
3. What are the implications of the phrase "We come bearing supper" (line 13)? What expression or text might be echoed and/or alluded to here? What are the some of the implications of the "paper matches" simile? Of the final line of the poem?
4. How precisely is Jiles's vision of gender roles in this poem like and unlike those in the poems earlier in this section?

MARGE PIERCY

What's That Smell in the Kitchen?

QUESTIONS FOR DISCUSSION

1. What's the significance of the fact that the poem begins with, and then repeats, the phrase "All over America women are burning" (lines 1, 6)? With descriptions of the different kinds of food women are burning in "Peoria," "Providence," "Chicago," "Big Sur," and "Dallas" (lines 2–5)?
2. What different things does cooking become a symbol of, and/or metaphor for, in this poem?
3. What exactly does the speaker mean when she says that "Burning dinner is not incompetence but war" (line 22)?

ELIZABETH

When I Was Fair and Young

This poem is a response to the spirit of *carpe diem*, but this time from the woman's perspective. The speaker clearly sees her refusals of male advances as a kind of power, but that power is bound to her youth and beauty. When the youth and beauty have faded, the speaker no longer feels the power of refusal. If you read this poem in conjunction with Herrick's "To the Virgins, to Make Much of Time," Lovelace's "To Amarantha, That She Would Dishevel Her Hair," and Marvell's "To His Coy Mistress," you might use the questions below as prompts for discussion.

QUESTIONS FOR DISCUSSION

1. What kind of power do the women in these poems possess?
2. What are the grounds for the arguments of the men?
3. What fears do the men play on, and how is that fear borne out in this poem?

KAY SMITH

Annunciation

I always have to start discussion of this poem by asking students exactly what they know about the annunciation and about paintings of this subject. When I'm being good, I actually bring a picture of one in for us to look at and talk about in conjunction with the poem, as well as the relevant passages from the Bible. But I find that the poem works well even when I don't do this, as long as we get out the basic fact that the annunciation refers to the moment when the angel visits Mary to announce that she has been chosen by God to bear Jesus. If I have a willing group of students, I actually like to pause at this point to talk about this biblical story and about what it in and of itself might suggest about the roles ascribed to women within the Bible. Otherwise, I move straight into the poem, asking what interpretation of the annunciation it suggests, particularly in emphasizing the contrast between the book and the angel. What do each of these seem to symbolize or to suggest about the nature of Mary's situation? What does the speaker mean when she says that she and her companion "Believ[ed] [they] could ignore / All messages," that they were "Unobliged to wings or words," that they lived "in the vibrant space" (lines 21–24)? What might those messages be? What exactly does the final stanza suggest about how the speaker's attitude toward these messages has changed? What does she mean when she suggests that she lives in "the space between" the angel and the book (line 36)?

Though there are many possible answers to this question, I think that one interpretation involves seeing the poem as exploring two over-lapping conflicts. The first has to do with the extent to which we (in this case, the we referring to women in particular) are subject to the "messages" about who we are and should be that are conveyed in paintings, literature, etc.; in the poem, the speaker seems to see herself as once upon a time feeling that she "could ignore" such messages and be whatever and whomever she chose to be and as now experiencing the latent power of those messages, finding it difficult to simply "laugh" them away. The second has to do less with the question of how much power such messages have over us than with the question of their content. In this regard the poem might be said to explore, through the symbolism of the book and the angel, something very like what Adrienne Rich describes as the conflict, for women, between "materna[l]," altruistic love and artistic "egoism" (see the excerpt from Rich's "When We Dead Awaken" in the anthology). For at the moment of the annunciation Mary is being called to give up the life she has known and her own ambitions and desires to serve as Christ's mother and, in turn, as a kind of mother to the world at large, a vessel for the hopes, dreams, and salvation of all humankind. By associating the life that Mary is called to give up with an open book, the poem may also be seen as envisioning this conflict between egotism and altruism as also being a conflict between mind and body. What the end of the poem seems to concentrate on is how difficult it ultimately is to ignore or avoid such conflicts and how much easier it might be simply to choose one role or another.

EDNA ST. VINCENT MILLAY

[*Women have loved before as I love now*]

Taking up this poem for discussion provides a good occasion to talk about how context can affect tone. Millay here chooses two grand stories of illicit love—two among the most dramatic and tragic in the annals of literature—to serve as the bases of her speaker's comparison. Provided with a little information about the place of Tristan and Isolde and Helen and Paris in the literary history of lovers, students will quickly recognize the *hubris* of the speaker's claims.

QUESTIONS FOR DISCUSSION

1. How do the allusions to Tristan and Isolde and Helen and Paris help characterize the speaker's style of loving? By implication, how does

the speaker characterize the love affairs in which she is likely to be involved? How would *you* characterize them?

2. Would you like to be the speaker's roommate? Have you ever been tempted to describe one of your own romantic relationships in dramatic and absolute terms?

3. How, by implication, does the speaker view modern romance?

APHRA BEHN

To the Fair Clarinda, Who Made Love to Me, Imagined More Than Woman

Like Donne's "The Flea" and other metaphysical poems, Behn's "Clarinda" is a poem dominated by a single metaphor or conceit that becomes a justification for love between the speaker and the object of the poem. That conceit involves imagining "the Fair Clarinda" as a kind of hermaphrodite who is at once both male and female. By imagining Clarinda as a "lovely charming youth" (line 4), the female speaker "justif[ies]" her passion (line 5), while by imagining Clarinda as a "Fair lovely maid" she manages to "lessen" the "constraint" and "blushes" she would experience if she were speaking to a man (lines 1, 6, 7): thus the speaker may "love and yet be innocent," preserving both her virginity and her modesty (line 13). And, indeed, as a comparison to the love poems of Donne or Herrick or Marvell will suggest, this poem is modest in a way that those seduction poems are not, focusing more on the speaker's "struggle" with her own passionate feelings than with a "struggle" to seduce a resistant lover (line 9). It is Clarinda, rather than the speaker, who is most often imagined as the active party or seducer here, "the bright nymph betray[ing] us to the swain" (line 11), "the manly part" "plead[ing]" and "the image of the maid" "tempt[ing]" (lines 20–21).

LIZ ROSENBERG

The Silence of Women

QUESTIONS FOR DISCUSSION

1. What does this poem suggest about why women "get angrier" as they grow older, while men "grow softer, sweeter" (lines 1–2)?

2. What is the literal and figurative meaning of the claim that "even their bones will turn / against them, once the fruitful years are gone" (lines 8–9)?

3. What is the meaning and significance of the images of "houselights,"

"cells," and "chicken" and "egg" in lines 10–12? Of the musical images that conclude the poem?

SHARON OLDS

The Elder Sister

This poem describes the relationship between women's bodies. The speaker describes her attitude toward her sister in physical terms. She uses metaphors to describe her sister's body and her own. Are the relationships between women's bodies in this poem metaphors for the emotional and psychological relationships between them? What are the implications of the final metaphor of the hostage?

ELIZABETH BISHOP

Exchanging Hats

QUESTIONS FOR DISCUSSION

1. What do hats and the "trying on" of hats seem to symbolize in the poem (line 2)? What explanation might be suggested in the second stanza? Does the poem suggest that there is a difference in the meaning and significance of the uncle's and the aunt's "experiment[s]" (line 8)? If so, how exactly are they different?
2. Who do you imagine the "we" of the poem is? How might you interpret the poem differently depending on how you identify the "we"? What does Bishop's use of "we" (rather than "I" or "they") contribute to the poem? Who exactly are "they" in the final stanza of the poem?
3. What exactly does "Anandrous" mean (line 9)? What cues does the poem offer? What's the significance or effect of Bishop's use of this kind of term?

JUDITH ORTIZ COFER

The Changeling

QUESTIONS FOR DISCUSSION

1. Like Bishop's "Exchanging Hats," Cofer's poem describes an "experiment" in trying on the roles and clothing of the other sex. What does the young girl's "game" suggest about her conception of men's roles?

About her attraction to the game of transforming herself into "boy shape" (line 8)? What answers to these questions are suggested by the description of her "brother's closet" as a "dark cubicle / that smelled of adventure" (lines 6, 24–25)? How is your sense of the meaning of the game and the conception of roles it embodies affected by the fact that the speaker describes it as an attempt to vie "for [her] father's attention" (line 2)?

2. What is the significance of the fact that her father "would listen with a smile" (line 18)? That her mother "was not amused" (line 21)? What does the poem suggest about why the mother might be more upset by the girl's antics than her father is?

3. What does the description of the game and the final stanza suggest about women's roles? What are the implications of the speaker's reference to the kitchen as "the real world" (line 29)?

4. Keeping in mind that *Webster's* defines a changeling as "a child secretly exchanged for another in infancy," what are the different implications of the title "The Changeling"?

AMY LOWELL

The Lonely Wife

QUESTIONS FOR DISCUSSION

1. What do the wife's descriptions of landscape and weather in the first and last stanzas suggest about her situation and feelings? How do the images at the beginning and end of the poem differ? What might those differences suggest about her situation and feelings?

2. In the second stanza of the poem, the speaker implicitly compares herself to a dripping candle and a fading flower. What does each image suggest about her situation? About how she thinks of herself?

3. What image of the roles of wife and husband is suggested by the speaker's reference to "that divine dream which is my Lord" (line 8) and to "your so Unworthy One" (line 12)? To what extent does and does not the wife portray herself as subservient to her husband? As contented or discontented with her situation?

ELIZABETH SPIRES

The Bodies

QUESTIONS FOR DISCUSSION

1. How would you describe the tone of "The Bodies"? What details contribute to that tone?

2. What might the speaker mean when she says that the bodies "give up their pose" (line 11)?
3. What is the significance and effect of the way the speaker describes "The Bodies" in the sauna? What might the speaker's descriptions imply about her conception of female beauty? What conceptions of female beauty might the poem implicitly counter?
4. What does the fourth stanza suggest about the nature of relationships between women?
5. How exactly are men characterized in stanza 5? What exactly does this stanza, in concert with the rest of the poem, suggest about the similarities and differences between men and women?
6. What is the significance of the speaker's various uses of the word *body* in stanza 6?
7. What happens in the final two stanzas of the poem? How exactly do the thoughts expressed in these two stanzas relate to the rest of the poem?

MARILYN HACKER

[*Who would divorce her lover . . .*]

QUESTIONS FOR DISCUSSION

1. How does the speaker characterize the difference between her lovers' attitudes toward their relationship and her own?
2. What is suggested by the image of the parenthesis in line 15?

HA JIN

The Past

QUESTIONS FOR DISCUSSION

1. How would you characterize each of the attitudes toward the past described metaphorically in each of the first four stanzas of the poem? How exactly does each one differ from the others?
2. Though the speaker begins by characterizing his or her relationship to the past by comparing it to that between body and shadow, he or she uses a very different metaphor at the end of the poem. How exactly does the shroud metaphor differ from the shadow metaphor? What is suggested by the image of turning a shroud into shoes?

DIANE WAKOSKI

The Ring of Irony

QUESTIONS FOR DISCUSSION

1. Why might the speaker see her wedding ring as symbolizing her "love" of "irony" and her penchant for "understatement / and paradox" (lines 13–16)?
2. In what sense would an ounce of gold carried in a velvet bag be "Worth so much more" than the wedding ring (line 36)? What does the rest of the poem suggest about why it wouldn't be?
3. What does the speaker mean when she says that "gifts / freely given" can "appease destiny" (lines 46–48)? How does this relate to the allusions to Iphigenia and Isaac? To the descriptions in lines 52–57 of all that she has given? How exactly are these gifts like the sacrifices of Iphigenia and Isaac? Is it significant that neither Iphigenia nor Isaac was ever actually sacrificed?
4. What do lines 62–82 suggest about what's wrong with the idea that "gifts / freely given" can "appease destiny"?
5. What is the significance of the question that the speaker's "innocent students" ask her (line 72)? Why does the question bug her, and what do the question and her response have to do with the bargain with fate she's contemplating here? In what sense is her reply an understatement? Ironic? Why and how does "the past swallo[w] up everything" after this answer (line 79)?
6. What is the meaning and significance of her decision to give up the ring? Her ultimate statement about why she's giving up the ring?
7. What does the poem suggest about irony, "the obvious," and the relationship between the two?
8. What are some of the implications of the title "The Ring of Irony"?

EDNA ST. VINCENT MILLAY

[I, being born a woman and distressed]

In this poem the speaker is concerned with what she perceives as a conflict within herself between passion and reason. Millay skillfully employs the Italian sonnet form to set up the situation in the octave (the proximity of the man she addresses stirs her senses and confounds her brain) and to respond to the situation in the sestet (whatever her bodily response to the man, her heart and brain reject him). Students are sometimes reluctant to discuss their own experiences in handling tensions between passion and reason when the focus is sexuality, but I can often get them to talk about their mixed responses in some other area of their lives, e.g., the tongue says "eat more of this German chocolate cake" while the brain says, "you are going to feel bloated and overweight if you indulge."

QUESTIONS FOR DISCUSSION

1. What does the speaker feel is the relationship between being a woman and being "undone, possessed" (line 8)?
2. What do "stout blood" and "staggering brain" suggest in the context of the poem, and how does the former commit "treason" against the latter (lines 9–10)?
3. What are the assumptions the speaker is challenging in the person she addresses? Do these assumptions differ by gender?

READING/WRITING IDEAS FOR CHAPTER 24

ESSAYS ABOUT CULTURAL CONTEXT

Because Chapter 24 focuses primarily on the strategies involved in analyzing fictional texts as artifacts informed by their particular sociohistorical contexts, it could very easily be used as part of a unit culminating with one of three slightly different types of essay assignments.

The first would ask students to write essays that interpret a text by using information about its historical and/or cultural context. Students might, for example, write about why and how Hughes's "Harlem (A Dream Deferred)" is shaped by the fact that it was written in the 1950s, Randall's "Ballad of Birmingham" by the fact that it was written in the 1960s, or Owen's "Dulce et Decorum Est" during World War I. And as this phrasing suggests, information about historical and/or cultural context might involve very broad topics—such as the state of race relations in 1951 or changes in attitudes toward the war between 1914 and 1918—or quite specific ones—such as the events surrounding the Birmingham bombing or the techniques of warfare that made World War I different from previous wars. This assignment, then, would ask students to bring facts from outside sources to bear in their analysis of a particular poem.

My students often tend to be both very excited and engaged by assignments like this one that ask them to incorporate source materials of various kinds and to read a text in terms of them, but they are also often uncertain about how to go about doing so effectively. One of the biggest challenges they face in tackling assignments that involve analyzing a text in terms of information about cultural context in this way is the temptation to let their essays turn into reports on that information or on that context, rather than crafting essays that use such information in the service of analysis. Thus from the beginning of our work on such an assignment, I simply try to emphasize the similarities between this kind of essay and the kinds of analytical essays they've been writing all semester, to insist that analysis and the poetry should remain the focus.

The second type of assignment might help you to avoid such problems altogether by encouraging a very different readerly and writerly strategy that involves not simply bringing facts to bear in analyzing a poem but instead analyzing "factual" and "poetic" accounts in a similar, if not identical, way, asking what different writers (in whatever genre) do with the same (or at least similar) facts. Such as assignment would, in other words, ask students either to compare different poetic accounts or uses of a particular time, place, or event or to compare a poetic account or accounts of a given time, place, or event to journalistic and/or fictional accounts of it. Students might, for example, compare the different ways that Hiroshima figures as a symbol in Salter's "Welcome to Hiroshima," Okita's "Notes for a Poem on Being Asian American," and, perhaps, Rich's "History," or they might compare Hardy's "The Convergence of the Twain" with newspaper accounts of the *Titanic*'s sinking and/or with historians' accounts.

The virtue of this assignment, as opposed to the first, is that it emphasizes the comparison of different accounts in a way that encourages students to see journalists' and historians' accounts as texts to be analyzed in the same way that the poetry itself is. Instead of treating sources as containers for facts, in other words, students must ask of all of their texts questions like the following: Which facts about the time, place, or event does each author choose to give particular emphasis? To ignore or de-emphasize? What does this emphasis and de-emphasis suggest about how this particular author understands the significance or meaning of this particular time, place, or event? What other elements of the text (such as language, structure, etc.) contribute to suggesting this interpretation of the event and its meaning or significance? How would you characterize the overall interpretation of the time, place, or event offered in each particular text? How might one interpretation respond to, or "answer," another? What seems most in debate in these texts about this time, place, or event and its significance? (Such questions could, by the way, serve as the basis for a getting started writing exercise.)

Since such assignments somewhat resemble the symbol essay assignment discussed in "Reading/Writing Ideas for Chapter 6" and the author's work in context assignment discussed in "Reading/Writing Ideas for Chapter 22," they have the added advantage of at least potentially allowing students to use previously acquired skills and strategies in somewhat new ways.

If you choose to go with either the first or second type of assignment, you will likely have to require students to identify and locate both primary and secondary materials relevant to their text and/or topic. Since doing so may require that students locate and employ secondary sources, you might want to consider either saving this chapter and assignment until after students tackle the use of secondary sources in the "Critical Contexts" chapter or using versions of the exercises described in "Reading/Writing Ideas for Chapter 11" to get students started.

The third assignment would ask students to think about cultural context in yet another way, analyzing how a particular text or texts draw on, contribute to, or call into question our culture's beliefs about some issue, such as the nature of men's and women's roles, the nature of relationships between men and women, the nature and causes of war, etc. Especially if one uses the word *myths* rather than *beliefs*, this assignment can, with work and with attention to the potential problems discussed in the headnote to "Constructing Identity, Exploring Gender," flow quite smoothly out of the kind of work students were doing in Chapter 23. For while that chapter essentially focused students on questions about how particular poems engaged with *literary* traditions and myths, this assignment would instead ask them to think and write about how particular poems engage with *cultural* traditions and myths. Nonetheless, I would suggest that the above-mentioned headnote describes pretty accurately the potential problems with this assignment.

A version of assignment three that might help in this regard would involve turning those problems into the very substance of the assignment by asking students to consider the ramifications of this kind of analytical approach, showing what is lost and gained by reading a particular poem on its own terms and by reading it in terms of the beliefs about some issue it conveys, however unwittingly. One might, for example, have students analyze Lovelace's "Song: To Lucasta, Going to the Wars" to consider questions about what is lost and gained by reading the poem solely in terms of the themes and issues—love and war—that are its explicit focus and by reading it in terms of the myths about gender it implicitly conveys.

25

CRITICAL CONTEXTS: A POETRY CASEBOOK

Offering students an opportunity to read, discuss, and write about a particularly powerful poem and to engage with equally powerful arguments about that poem, this chapter allows students a chance to hone their analytical skills by actively participating in a lively, ongoing conversation about a wonderfully enigmatic text. Students can, at least at first, feel intimidated when confronted with the polish and sophistication of scholarly essays and with the prospect of having to find something to say that the critics haven't. But I find that such feelings can prove to be extremely short-lived if I encourage students to open their eyes to just how diverse the criticism is and yet how incomplete and if I help them see for themselves that scholarship is, indeed, a kind of never-ending conversation in which there is always more to say, always another angle to take or another question to ask or another detail to take into account. In figuring out how best to help students make those discoveries, one of the big questions I face is just how late in the reading and writing process to have students read and write about the critical essays. Should I have students read and talk about the poem only briefly at first and then jump straight into the criticism, allowing students to tackle writing topics suggested by the criticism? Or should I have my students begin to craft their own arguments about the poem first and only then have them try to place that argument within the critical conversation or context? These questions remain questions for me, however, precisely because either approach can and does work, and in "Reading/Writing Ideas for Chapter 25," I've tried to discuss the different ways these two approaches can work, as well as the costs and benefits of each.

PLANNING IDEAS

- Students may approach "Daddy" and the criticism on it with more confidence if you have them also read and discuss the other Plath poems in the anthology, allowing them to use the skills they developed in Chapters 21 and 22.

- If you want to broaden the discussion of Plath still further, you might consider assigning some or all of the autobiographical *The Bell Jar*, perhaps also or instead showing students the film based on the book (which is widely available on videotape). Such materials might prove especially helpful to students given that the literary criticism itself draws to some extent on information (and implied arguments) about the relationship between the poetry and Plath's own life.

- Since students will undoubtedly have trouble with some of the terminology and allusions within the critical essays that aren't footnoted in the anthology, you might want to offer them some additional information before assigning particular essays, perhaps creating a handout with your own footnotes. (To help with this, I've provided some footnotes of this type for each of the essays.) Conversely, you might simply warn students that they may encounter such difficulties and ask them both to make a list of questions as they read and to bring those lists to class on the day you discuss the essay(s).

- Since one such allusion involves Steiner and Howe's comparison of "Daddy" to Picasso's "Guernica," you might want to bring in a slide or picture of this painting when you discuss these essays.

- If you're not having students keep a reading journal throughout the term, you might want to have them start something of the sort now to record their responses to the critical essays in this chapter, encouraging them to use their journal as a place to pose questions about the essays as they read them, to talk about what bugs them about particular essays and/or what points they agree and disagree with, to make notes about aspects or elements or moments of and in the poem that aren't discussed in the essays or that they interpret in a different way than a particular author does, and even about writing techniques used by these writers that they might want to try out in their own writing. I personally find that doing so is a way to help students feel that, even as readers, they are active participants in, rather than passive witnesses to, scholarship.

SYLVIA PLATH

Daddy

This poem alternates between the particular and the general experiences of oppression. The person speaking in the poem is a particular woman, remembering her childhood and her father. She feels sympathetic toward others who have suffered, but beyond that, she begins to lose her own identity: "I began to talk like a Jew. / I think I may well be a Jew" (lines

34–35). She sees her pain as the pain of every woman: "Every woman adores a Fascist, / The boot in the face, the brute, / Brute heart of a brute like you" (lines 48–50). What she perceives as a woman's love of pain accounts for her trying to get back to (or get back *at*) her dead father.

As the scholarly essays in this chapter of the anthology suggest, critics disagree rather vehemently about the exact character of the relationship between the "particular" and "general" experience of oppression within the poem and about the extent to which Plath's blending of the two is successful. (Irving Howe's argument represents the most negative view.) Among the many other issues debated in the criticism that you might want to preview in your initial discussion of the poem is the relationship between the poem's form and content. Many critics note that the poem resembles a nursery rhyme (and/or "ritualistic incantation"), its language even recalling the particular rhyme about the old woman who lived in a shoe, yet they disagree about the significance or implications of that resemblance. (See, for example, the essay by Kroll and the essay by Annas.) You might also want to introduce the question of the relationship between speaker and poet here, perhaps by asking students to consider Plath's own characterization of the speaker (in an interview quoted by Alvarez; see also the note to the Alvarez essay below).

QUESTIONS FOR DISCUSSION

1. To what is the speaker referring in line 58? In line 67?
2. Why does the speaker say, "Daddy, I have had to kill you" (line 6)?

Rather than notes of the type accompanying the poetry in the anthology, the following include brief footnote-like explanations for some of the terminology or references within the essays that might give students trouble.

GEORGE STEINER

Dying Is an Art

- Par. 5: *the tracts of Simone de Beauvoir*—de Beauvoir's most influential "tract" was *The Second Sex* (published in 1949 as *Le Deuxième Sex*), a book in which de Beauvoir explores and explodes traditional myths about women, particularly those embodied within biological and psychoanalytical theory.
- Par. 5: *the novels of Edna O'Brien and Brigid Brophy*—Irish-born novelist Edna O'Brien's work include *The Country Girls* (1960), *The Lonely Girl* (1962), and *Girls in Their Married Bliss* (1963), which follow two women

from their girlhood in the country and their convent education to their adult experiences in Dublin and London. As Margaret Drabble suggests in the *Oxford Companion to English Literature* (1995), the "themes" of O'Brien's "lyrical" and uninhibited novels "are female sensuality, male treachery, Irish nostalgia, and celebration of the intermittent 'good times' which even her much abused and self-abusing heroines enjoy" (p. 719). The novels of Oxford-educated Brigid Brophy include *Hackenfeller's Ape* (1953), *Flesh* (1962), *In Transit* (1969), and *Palace Without Chairs* (1978).

QUESTIONS FOR DISCUSSION

1. What does Steiner mean when he says that Plath's poems "are too honest, they have cost too much, to be yielded to myth"? What kind of reading strategy does he seem to be advocating in this statement? What kind of reading strategy does he seem to be criticizing?
2. What claims does Steiner make about the peculiarly feminine qualities and/or woman-centered focus of Plath's poetry? About the significance of both, particularly in terms of historical and cultural context?
3. What does Steiner mean when he says that, unlike Dickinson, Plath "fully assumed her own condition"? How exactly is he characterizing the poem in this statement?
4. What does Steiner suggest about why Plath was so attracted to images of the Holocaust? About why she could write about it so effectively? About the potential problems with Plath's use of such images?
5. What does Steiner mean when he says that "Daddy" "achieves the classic act of generalization"? What does he suggest about the poem by comparing it to the "Guernica"?

IRVING HOWE

The Plath Celebration: A Partial Dissent

- Par. 2: *hysteria*—"[fr. *hystera* womb; fr. the former notion that hysteric women were suffering from disturbances of the womb] **1:** a psychoneurosis marked by emotional excitability and disturbances of the psychic, sensory, vasomotor, and visceral functions **2:** unmanageable fear or emotional excess" (from *Webster's New Collegiate Dictionary*).
- Par. 5: *"The more perfect the artist . . ."*—quotation from the essay "Tradition and the Individual Talent" (1919, 1920) in which Eliot expounds what he calls his "Impersonal theory" of poetic creativity, a theory that counters the Romantic view of poetry as, to quote Wordsworth, "the spontaneous overflow" of the poet's own "powerful feelings." Howe here uses the quotation from Eliot to suggest that Plath's

poetry does not live up to Eliot's definition of good poetry (a definition with which he obviously agrees).

QUESTIONS FOR DISCUSSION

1. Howe suggests that the speaker of Plath's poem is persuaded that her father "has betrayed her by dying." What might this characterization of the speaker's attitude toward her father ignore or leave out?
2. What does Howe mean when he says that neither the poem nor Plath's life "offers any warrant" for the "assaults" made on the father in "Daddy"? What do these remarks suggest about the criteria Howe is bringing to bear in criticizing the poem?
3. In what ways is Howe's view of the relationship between the personal and the general in "Daddy" like and unlike that of Steiner? What does he suggest about this by comparing "Daddy" to Picasso's "Guernica"? What do Howe's remarks about this issue suggest about his definition of what a good poem is like? What are the implications of the quotation from T. S. Eliot with which Howe closes his essay?
4. Like Steiner, Howe uses the term *hysteria* to describe "Daddy," though he refers to the speaker rather than the poem itself as hysterical and also clearly views that hysteria in more negative terms than Steiner does. How would you characterize the disagreement between Steiner and Howe on this point? Look up the word *hysteria* in the *Oxford English Dictionary*. What are some of the implications of critics' use of this term to describe "Daddy" and its female speaker?

A. ALVAREZ

Sylvia Plath

• Par. 3: *Electra complex*—a term, originating with Freud, to describe the condition of the girl who does not successfully overcome her incestuous sexual attraction to her father. Freud named the complex after the Greek playwright Sophocles's *Electra*, whose eponymous heroine he saw as perfectly demonstrating this condition. (In similar fashion, Freud labeled the male version of this condition the Oedipus complex after the hero of Sophocles's *Oedipus Rex*.) In the following excerpt from "The Transformation of Puberty" (*The Basic Writings of Sigmund Freud*, New York: Random House, 1938, pp. 617–618), Freud describes this dysfunction without explicitly naming it the Electra complex:

> [Sexual] object selection is first accomplished in the imagination, for the sexual life of the maturing youth hardly finds any escape except through an indulgence

in phantasies; that is, in ideas which are not destined to be brought to execution. In the phantasies of all persons, the infantile tendencies, now reënforced by somatic emphasis, reappear, and among them one finds in regular frequency and in the first place, the sexual feeling of the child for the parents. Usually, this has already been differentiated by sexual attraction, namely, the attraction of the son for the mother [what Freud elsewhere calls the Oedipus complex], and of the daughter for the father. Simultaneously with the overcoming and rejection of these distinctly incestuous phantasies, there occurs one of the most important as well as one of the most painful psychic accomplishments of puberty; it is the breaking away from the parental authority, through which alone is formed that opposition between the new and old generations, which is so important for cultural progress. Many persons are detained at each of the stations in the course of development through which the individual must pass; and accordingly, there are persons who never overcome the parental authority and never, or very imperfectly, withdraw their affection from their parents. They are mostly girls, who, to the delight of their parents, retain their full infantile love far beyond puberty, and it is instructive to find that in their married life these girls are incapable of fulfilling their duties to their husbands. They make cold wives and remain sexually anesthetic. This shows that the apparently non-sexual love for parents and sexual love are nourished from the same source, *i.e.*, that the first merely corresponds to an infantile fixation of the libido.

QUESTIONS FOR DISCUSSION

1. In what sense might Alvarez's statement that Plath is "always in intelligent control of her feelings" offer a counterargument to Howe? In what sense does this statement nonetheless suggest that Alvarez agrees with Howe about the character of a good poem?
2. Why and how does Alvarez use the quotation from Plath at the beginning of his essay? What is he, in a sense, trying to prove by quoting Plath?
3. What do you make of the quotation itself? What does it suggest about how Plath herself sees some of the issues discussed by Steiner, Howe, and Alvarez?
4. What might Alvarez mean when he says that "it is the very closeness of her pain which gives it a general meaning"? What might Steiner or Howe say in response to this statement?
5. What does Alvarez's discussion of the "anonymity of pain" in contemporary life suggest about the symbolic significance of the Holocaust? What might it imply about why Plath was particularly attracted to that symbolism?
6. How is Alvarez's characterization of Plath's attitude toward her father similar to, and different from, Howe's? His characterization of the tone(s) of "Daddy"? His claim that "Despite everything, 'Daddy' is a love poem"?
7. How do Plath's comments about the speaker of "Daddy" compare to those of Steiner, Howe, and Alvarez? What is an Electra complex?
8. What might Alvarez mean when he says that "When suffering is there whatever you do, by inflicting it upon yourself you achieve your iden-

tity, you set yourself free"? What evidence would you use to suggest that this is or is not a valid interpretation of what happens in "Daddy"?

JUDITH KROLL

Rituals of Exorcism: "Daddy"

• Par. 3: *The Bell Jar*—a heavily autobiographical novel published by Plath (under the pseudonym Victoria Lucas) in 1963, just one month before her suicide. Beginning in 1953, the year of the execution of Ethel and Julius Rosenberg, the novel follows its heroine/narrator Esther Greenwood through her stint as a college-student intern on a woman's magazine, her relationship with Yale medical student Buddy Willard, her nervous breakdown, and the suicide attempt that leads to institutionalization and electroshock therapy. It concludes with Esther's preparing to leave the asylum and return to college after the suicide of a friend and fellow inmate and a successful sexual encounter with a math professor.

QUESTIONS FOR DISCUSSION

1. How does Kroll's statement that " 'Daddy' ends in a ritual intended to cancel the earlier 'sacred marriage' which has suffocated her" compare to Alvarez's and Steiner's claims that the poem formally resembles a nursery rhyme? What does Kroll suggest about the poem by pointing out that it echoes the particular nursery rhyme about the old woman who lived in a shoe? That the ritual of exorcism within the poem is like the rituals described by Sir James Frazer in *The Golden Bough*?
2. What is the significance or effect of the fact that Kroll suggests that "Daddy" refers not only to the speaker's and/or Plath's father but also to her husband? What does Kroll here and elsewhere imply about why and how the plight of the speaker in "Daddy" is general rather than personal?
3. How exactly does Kroll use and build on Alvarez's claim that "Daddy" is a love poem?

MARY LYNN BROE

from *Protean Poetic*

• Par. 2: *Thanatos's libido*—in Greek mythology, Thanatos is a death-demon figure and/or minor god. The term *Thanatos's libido* is essentially another term for the death drive. As the term *libido* suggests, the sex and death drives are linked in Freudian theory.

QUESTIONS FOR DISCUSSION

How exactly does Broe's argument build on, yet disagree with, Kroll's? What does she suggest about why and how the speaker's attempt at exorcism fails? Where and how does Broe support her counterclaim by using evidence that Kroll does not use? By interpreting the same evidence differently? How, in particular, does Broe differently interpret the nursery rhyme–like qualities of the poem?

MARGARET HOMANS

from *A Feminine Tradition*

- Par. 2: *the tradition of woman as medium of exchange with that of woman as object*—Homans here refers to two well-known and interrelated theories about women's status and social role, one suggesting that women are "objectified" and/or placed in the position of object (to be looked at, desired, spoken or written about, even owned) while men occupy the position of subject (to look, desire, speak, write, own), the second suggesting that, as a result, women are essentially objects that men exchange with each other, which means that women are essentially just a "medium" through which men conduct their relationships with each other. Elsewhere in the essay Homans associates "objectification" with what she calls "literalization." Simply speaking, Homans is here drawing on the distinction between the literal and figurative or symbolic meanings and uses of language, suggesting that women are associated with the literal and men with the symbolic or figurative. Though Homans relates "objectification" and "literalization" in a number of different ways, one is the way in which both suggest that women are more often seen and tend to see themselves as objects of the speech and writing of men rather than as speakers and writers in their own right, as not having the same automatic right to, and power over, language as men do and thus as both silent and silenced.

QUESTIONS FOR DISCUSSION

1. What do you think Homans means by "identify[ing] the self as literal"? By the claim that doing so is equivalent to "ratify[ing] women's age-old and disadvantageous position as the other and the object"? How might your readings of poetry by men and about women help you understand Homans's remarks? How do her remarks on the

equation between Plath and her speakers help to explain what she means? What does she mean when she says that any reading that makes such an equation "is unfair to the woman" and "obscures her poetry's real power"? In what way does this statement agree and disagree with the statements of Steiner, Howe, and Alvarez?

2. In footnote 1, Homans suggests that she is "indebted" to Kroll for her "persuasively positive readings of Plath." What exactly has Homans taken from Kroll's argument? How exactly does she build on, or go beyond, Kroll's argument?

3. How does Homans's claim that at the end of "Daddy" the speaker "returns herself to the silence that the poem came into being to protest" compare to Broe's claim that "[i]nstead of successfully binding the spirits, commanding them to remain silent and cease doing harm, and then ordering them to an appointed place, the speaker herself is stricken dumb"?

PAMELA J. ANNAS

from *A Disturbance in Mirrors*

- Par. 2: *Emma and Mr. Knightley*—the heroine and hero of Jane Austen's novel *Pride and Prejudice* (1814). Though Mr. Knightley is not literally Emma's teacher in the novel, he does figuratively engage in the process of educating her over the course of the book, which culminates in the marriage of "teacher" and "student."
- Par. 2: *Lucy Snowe and the professor*—the heroine and hero of Charlotte Brontë's novel *Villette*, another nineteenth-century novel in which the heroine and hero, (male) teacher and (female) pupil, fall in love. This novel, however, ends more ambiguously than Austen's, with the reader uncertain whether the professor has been killed in a shipwreck or returns to marry Lucy.

QUESTIONS FOR DISCUSSION

1. How does Annas's claim that in "Daddy" sadomasochism "stands for the authority structure of a patriarchal and war-making society" compare to the implicit and explicit claims made by Kroll, Broe, and Homans? How, in particular, does Annas's interpretation of lines 8–13 of "Daddy" compare to that of other critics?

2. How specifically might Annas's claim that "Daddy" "suggests that the victim has some control in a brutalized association—at least to the extent she chooses to be there"—differentiate her interpretation of the poem from others you've read?

3. How does Annas's use and interpretation of Plath's comments about the speaker of "Daddy" compare to that of Alvarez?
4. How are Annas's arguments about the ritual of exorcism within "Daddy" like and unlike those of Kroll, Broe, and Homans?

STEVEN GOULD AXELROD

Jealous Gods

- Par. 3: *not as an expanding universe of beneficial influence (as depicted in Eliot's "Tradition and the Individual Talent")*—a reference to the 1919 essay of poet and literary critic T. S. Eliot, which argues that "[t]he existing monuments [of literature] from an ideal order among themselves, which is modified by the introduction of the new (the really new) work of art among them." Axelrod here suggests that Plath's view of the literary tradition is quite different from Eliot's, that where he saw the literary tradition as happily incorporating new works and the poet as becoming a part of, and yet changing, that tradition with every poem, Plath saw the literary tradition as less easily changeable and the poet as having to in a sense fight for her place by displacing others.
- Par. 16: *superego*—a Freudian term for one of the three essential elements and/or developmental phases of the individual psyche, each of whose nature and function is described in the following excerpts from Dr. A. A. Brill's "Introduction" to *The Basic Writings of Sigmund Freud* (New York: Random House, 1938):

> According to Freud's formation the child brings into the world an unorganized chaotic mentality called the *id*, the sole aim of which is the gratification of all needs, the alleviation of hunger, self-preservation, and love, the preservation of the species. However, as the child grows older, that part of the id which comes in contact with the environment through the senses learns to know the inexorable reality of the outer world and becomes modified into what Freud calls the ego. This ego, possessing awareness of the environment, henceforth strives to curb the lawless id tendencies whenever they attempt to assert themselves incompatibly. (p. 12)
>
> [J]ust as the ego is a modified portion of the id as a result of contact with the outer world, the super-ego represents a modified part of the ego, formed through experiences absorbed from the parents, especially from the father. The super-ego is the highest mental evolution attainable by man, and consists of a precipitate of all prohibitions and inhibitions, all the rules of conduct which are impressed on the child by his parents and by parental substitutes. The feeling of *conscience* depends altogether on the development of the super-ego. (pp. 12–13)

QUESTIONS FOR DISCUSSION

1. How does Axelrod's use and interpretation of Plath's comments about the speaker of "Daddy" compare to those of Alvarez and Annas?

2. How is Axelrod's claim that "Daddy" "evokes the female poet's anxiety of authorship and specifically Plath's strategy of delivering herself from that anxiety" (par. 1) and that " 'Daddy' tells a tale of the daughter's effort to speak" (par. 5) like and unlike the claims of the other critics? Compatible with those arguments?

3. How and to what ends does Axelrod use facts about Plath's life and quotations from her letters and journal entries?

4. What does Axelrod mean when he says that Plath regarded the literary tradition as "a Spencerian agon in which only the fittest survived" (par. 3)? How is Axelrod's allusion to T. S. Eliot like and unlike Howe's?

5. How does Axelrod use references to Otto Rank's *Beyond Psychology* to explain why and how Plath used references to the Holocaust? How are his arguments about this like and unlike those of other critics?

6. How does Axelrod's interpretation of the nursery rhyme–like form of "Daddy" compare to the interpretations of other critics?

7. How does Axelrod's discussion of the ironic qualities of "Daddy" differentiate his interpretation from those of other critics?

8. Using Axelrod's descriptions of the various generic categories into which Plath's "Daddy" might fit, what claims might you make about what genre the other critics here implicitly take "Daddy" to be?

9. What does Axelrod's discussion of the popularity of the domestic poem in the 1950s suggest about how "Daddy" is informed by its historical and cultural context? What does he suggest about the relation between text and context when he says that "The 'domestic poem' became a system of signs in which each individual text's adherence to the system and deviations within the system produced its particular literary meaning" (par. 13)? What does Axelrod's discussion of the domestic poem allow him to see and say about "Daddy" that other critics don't? How exactly does this discussion relate to, and build on, his earlier arguments about "Daddy"? What answer to the latter question is suggested by Axelrod's claim that "[in] addition to killing the father in its fictional plot, the poem seeks to discredit the forefathers through its status as poetic act" (par. 15)? What exactly does Axelrod argue about how "Daddy" succeeds in "discrediting the forefathers"?

GENERAL QUESTIONS ON THE LITERARY CRITICISM

1. What is the thesis and basic argument of each of these essays?

2. In addition to, or in the process of, forwarding his or her own argument about "Daddy," each of these authors mentions other possible arguments or interpretations, whether to agree or disagree with them. While arguing that "Daddy" is a "domestic poem," for example, Axelrod mentions that the poem also has been or might be read as a "confessional poem." What other implied thesis statements do you see in these essays?

3. On what specific points do the critics agree with each other and with the other implied theses they note in passing? On what points do they

disagree? To what extent are these interpretations or arguments compatible with each other, and to what extent are they incompatible or mutually exclusive?

4. What moments within, or aspects of, the poem do each of these authors see as central to it? What questions about those moments or aspects does each take to be central to interpreting the poem? To what extent do some or all of these critics agree about which moments, facets, and/or questions are important, even if they interpret or answer them differently?

5. What aspects of the poem or what questions about the poem do these critics ignore or consider only briefly?

READING/WRITING IDEAS FOR CHAPTER 25

ESSAYS ABOUT CRITICAL CONTEXT

In my experience, both literature-based composition courses and composition-focused literature courses tend to require students over the course of a term to write at least one essay that incorporates secondary sources, usually literary criticism of one sort or another. Such assignments have proved both beneficial and enjoyable to my students for a host of reasons, not least the fact that "research essays" are so commonly assigned in all types of courses, yet my students often feel very uncertain about their skills in this area. But such an assignment can also be truly rewarding to students because it helps them see their essays not just as responses to assignments that have value only in the context of a particular classroom but as real contributions to real scholarly debates, their chance to be part of a conversation that includes, but extends well beyond, a particular classroom.

I personally have begun to require my students to write two research essays, providing them with the secondary source material for the first assignment and requiring them to identify and locate some or all of their source material for the second. This arrangement works well for me because it allows me to focus separately on the very different issues of research per se and of writing with sources, focusing first solely on the techniques and strategies involved in actually incorporating source material into one's writing, as well as questions about why one bothers to do so, and then and only then on actual research strategies and techniques. Thus for my purposes and for those of you who—like me—aren't blessed with an extensive university library, the "Critical Contexts" chapter of the anthology works well for the first kind of essay assignment, saving me the time and labor that I usually put into assembling packets of secondary source material.

With this essay assignment, as the headnote indicates, I find that a central question I face is when and how exactly to introduce the critical essays, and this question for me raises all kinds of methodological issues, some of which I tackle here and some of which I discuss below in describing the "Drafting without Sources" exercise. Ironically, I find that one way that I can sometimes begin to answer this question is by first asking and answering another question, which is just how specific I want the assignment to be: do I want to give students a very specific topic to write about or to simply require that they make an argument about the text that somehow incorporates material from the provided literary criticism? These questions are to some extent related to the ones about when to introduce the criticism because I find that while the open-ended assignment works well regardless of when and how the critical readings are introduced, the specific topic assignment tends to work best when the topic or topics come directly out of the critical readings. In the case of the materials provided in the "Critical Contexts" chapter of the anthology, for example, a specific topic assignment might ask students to tackle one of the following topics or questions (or to choose one from a list).

- Several of the critics here, including Steiner, Howe, and Alvarez, make implicit and explicit claims about the degree of control and craft Plath exercises over, and in, "Daddy," and in these three arguments the issue of control becomes linked with questions about the relation between intellect and emotion and between Plath and the poem's speaker. Using these essays (and any others that seem relevant) as a springboard, write an essay in which you explore one or more of these issues. In doing so, you should consider both the strengths and weaknesses of these critics' arguments in order to formulate your own. Doing so will require that you yourself closely analyze the text of "Daddy."
- Several of the critics here make competing claims about the meaning and significance of the form of "Daddy," particularly its nursery rhyme–like qualities. Using those claims as a springboard, write an essay in which you make your own argument about the relationship between form and content in "Daddy."
- Broe, Kroll, Homans, Annas, and Axelrod all claim that "Daddy" portrays the speaker's attempt to successfully "exorcise" one demon or another, though they disagree rather dramatically both about what exactly that demon is and about the whether and how that exorcism (not the poem) is successful or unsuccessful. Using their arguments as a springboard, offer your own interpretation of the process of exorcism enacted in the poem, considering the question of what demons the speaker is trying to exorcise and whether she is successful.
- More than one of these essays considers Plath's claim that the speaker in "Daddy" suffers from an Electra complex. With the help of a reference librarian, find out a little more about this term, which originated with Sigmund Freud. Use your findings to write an essay exploring how and why this term might or might not be a useful way to understand the speaker and the poem as a whole. In what way does your argument about this disagree and agree with the interpretations offered by other critics? If we agree with Plath in seeing the speaker as suffering from an Electra complex, does that necessarily mean that the poem is only about one dysfunctional individual's illness, as Howe seems to suggest?
- Write an essay comparing Plath's "Daddy" to one or more of the "domestic poems" by Plath's contemporaries mentioned by Axelrod. To what extent do you agree and disagree with Axelrod's interpretation of the similarities and differences between "Daddy" and this other poem (or these other poems)? You might also use want to use

the poet Adrienne Rich's comments on the nature and status of the family in the 1950s to consider questions about the significance of such "domestic poems."

Instructors: these comments can be found in the prose excerpts in Chapter 22 of the anthology and in the notes to the Rich poems included in this Guide.

I myself, after much trial and a lot of error, have pretty much settled on the loosest form of assignment for this kind of essay, one that simply asks students to make some argument about the text in question and, in so doing, to incorporate material from the secondary sources. I do so because, as I've said, one of the real benefits that my students derive from the "Critical Contexts" essay assignment is a feeling of being genuine participants in an ongoing scholarly conversation about a text, and I have found that being allowed to formulate their own topics and questions, while making the assignment more difficult in certain ways, makes it easier in other ways by encouraging that feeling. I find that this more open-ended assignment, unlike the specific topic assignment, tends to leave open for me the question of when and how to introduce the critical readings. Sometimes I have students do the sourceless draft exercise described below before reading any of the critical essays, and sometimes I have them jump straight from the poem into the critical essays, using our discussion of those essays and the source-related exercises described below to help students to generate their own essay topics and questions from their reading of the secondary material.

Thus your decision about how specific you want the assignment to be—as well as other factors that I've tried to describe below—will necessarily affect decisions both about which, if any, of the following writing exercises to assign, which order to assign them in, and how exactly to phrase them. Whichever option you choose, however, you might well want to also assign a version of the thesis-generating exercise described in "Reading/Writing Ideas for Chapter 20" at some point in the process.

TROUBLESHOOTING

One of the main challenges that my students face in writing "Critical Contexts" essays (or "research essays" of any sort, for that matter) is the tendency to let sources dominate the essay and drown the students' ideas out. I've found that this problem tends to take one of two forms in my students' essays: first, is the essay that simply reiterates the argument of a source; second, the essay that spends all of its time arguing with a source or sources, yet "forgets," in a sense, that the only way to make such an argument is to provide an alternative interpretation of the text. Such problems are precisely what has led me so often to assign the sourceless draft exercise described below, despite my reservations about it, because it at the very least ensures that students have their own argument to make about the text and that sources come second, contributing to that argument rather than overtaking it. But regardless of whether I assign that exercise, the main thing I try to do is insist from the beginning that (and how and why) the text itself has to be the focus, that even arguments with sources can only be substantiated by interpretation of evidence from the text. Though it doesn't always serve to head off such problems, the function and use of sources exercise described below and the discussion I build out of it helps me a great deal in terms of at least getting such issues on the table and giving students the kind of vocabulary they need to diagnose and cure such problems when they do come up.

CRITICAL CONTEXT–FOCUSED WRITING EXERCISES

Because using sources effectively in their own writing requires that students have an understanding of the uses of sources, have an accurate understanding of the sources they plan to use, and have their own independent argument about the text in question, I've found it helpful to require my students to do exercises that ensure that they master each of these steps one at a time, though I vary the exercise assignments and the order in which I assign them to fit specific essay assignments.

1. Identifying the Functions and Uses of Sources

To prepare students to write essays that the use secondary sources, I almost always begin by having them read one or two essays that do so. Though I often use student essays from past courses, it seems to me that the essays on "Daddy" in the anthology would themselves make for fruitful discussions of this type (and some of the "Questions for Discussion" are designed to get students thinking about such issues). My goal in having students read and then discuss such essays is to have them begin to ask questions not only about *how* writers use secondary sources but also about *why* they do so, the idea being that one can't do something effectively unless or until one knows what the purpose of doing so is. In preparation for discussion, then, I ask students to read the essays very carefully and to pay particular attention to the use of sources, asking them to formulate answers to the following basic questions as they read.

- Mark the places where each writer refers to secondary sources. How does the writer introduce source material? What does the writer tell you about each source? Are there any places where you feel the writer doesn't give you enough or gives you too much information about a source?
- What function does each reference to a source seem to serve in the essay? Why does the writer refer to each source? What precise contribution does it make? Are there any places where you feel the purpose of source material isn't clear? Where source material doesn't seem to make much of a contribution?

In discussion, I allow students a fairly free rein, while making sure that we focus at some point on the three issues that I see as key to using sources effectively:

- Specific techniques for incorporating source material effectively (use of signal phrases to introduce source material, for example).

- Specific functions that secondary sources serve.
- Specific ways in which writers manage to use secondary sources without having them take over their argument.

2. Summarizing Critical Conversations

Because using source material requires that students can understand and effectively describe not only individual arguments but also the relationships between different arguments and because I've discovered—much to my chagrin—that these tasks often prove difficult for students, I always have my students write short summaries of source material. I usually ask them to first write very short summaries (say, three sentences long) of the argument of each source and then to write what I call a "synthetic summary" that brings those arguments together in two or so paragraphs, showing how they all fit together as parts of one argumentative "conversation." Doing so requires that they define the main questions that are at issue in the conversation and that they essentially define a spectrum of possible stands on those issues, indicating what place each source occupies on that spectrum. Sometimes I also have students conclude their summary with a paragraph or two in which they evaluate the sources, pointing out weaknesses in the arguments, identifying questions or details ignored by critics, etc. The "Questions for Discussion" earlier in this chapter are designed to help students begin approaching the essays in this way, and you might use some of them in crafting the wording of the assignment for this exercise.

3. Drafting without Sources

As the anthology points out, all of us, but especially student writers, often have a hard time figuring out what we think or want to write about a text once we've read other arguments about it. For this reason, I quite often have students write notes toward, or even an actual draft of, an essay on a text before I have them read or begin to discuss and work with sources. Only after that do I have them do Exercise 2, substituting the generic evaluation paragraph(s) with paragraph(s) in which they begin to articulate the relationship between the argument they've been sketching out and the arguments of the sources and to articulate their plans for incorporating material from specific sources into their essays.

The obvious advantage of this approach is that it ensures that students have their own independent arguments and don't allow their essays to devolve into reportage on the arguments of sources. The disadvantage is that it tends to convey the message that our initial close readings of a text are in some sense "pure" until we "contaminate" ourselves by reading secondary sources and that conversations about a text are ancillary to our individual experience of it rather than a potentially productive part of the experience of reading, thinking, and writing about literature. Even though I find myself conveying that message in subtle ways all the time, I am also troubled by it, finding it a rather odd and even contradictory message to convey in courses that are all about teaching students how to participate effectively in both written and oral conversations about literature. Such courses by their very nature seem to assume that such conversations are an integral part of the experience of literature and that literature itself is an integral part of a host of ongoing conversations, an assumption or message somewhat undermined by this kind of exercise, even thought it also—quite frankly—works.

26

THE PROCESS OF CREATION

Some of your students will be closet poets, and among them will be a few who not only write poems but also actually labor at and revise their work. These amateur poets will have some sense of the effort behind the vision and revision of a poem. Most students, however, have thought little about the process of poetic creation and may think of poems (when they think of poems at all) as literary artifacts that fall complete from poets' minds onto paper. This chapter offers examples suggesting the process by which the pretty good poems of excellent poets become much better, even great poems. Some of the "Planning Ideas" offer a way to let students experiment themselves with the same process.

There are actually two slightly different ways to approach discussions about poetic revision. The first is the approach implied in the last paragraph, which entails thinking of a particular version of a poem as the best and truest version and of revision as a process of getting closer and closer to that best version in which the poem becomes most truly itself. The second approach instead involves treating each version of a poem as, in a sense, a complete poem in and of itself, comparison between versions serving to highlight the uniqueness of each. In a sense, the latter approach treats the versions of a particular poem in much the same way that Chapter 23 encourages students to read different poetic versions of a particular myth or story. In theory, each of these approaches is based on very different assumptions and sends very different messages to students, but in practice I find myself switching back and forth between the two, tending—for example—to approach the Keats's poems in the first way, the three versions of Pope's "Ode on Solitude" in the second. For this reason, I like to raise with students questions about these two approaches and the assumptions underlying each and to make such questions an integral part of our discussions about "The Process of Creation." In this and other ways, this chapter can also usefully serve to connect discussions of poetry with discussions of students' own writing/revising process.

PLANNING IDEAS

- Supply students with a draft of a short, amateur poem. (I have provided one sample below.) Using an overhead projector, revise the poem as a class, sharpening images, polishing language, and strengthening the overall effect of the work. (When there is disagreement about a revision that cannot be worked out through discussion, resolve the disagreement with a class vote.)

  Sample Poem

  A Missing Table Leg

  How can you say that?
  Feelings and emotions can't be spoken
  like the 7 o'clock weather report.
  Gentle hands and soft, wet lips
  are the only way to talk with someone
  that you loved.
  It only takes a little of that once
  abundant love
  to stop a person from turning into
  a crushed tomato soup can that lies next to
  the egg shells and coffee grounds.

- Divide students into groups of three or four. Give each group the same early version of a poem by a major poet—a poem *not* represented in this text. Ask each group to revise the poem, improving it in as many ways as possible. Have a spokesperson from each group share the results with the class, briefly explaining their choices. Then supply the final version of the poem—the poet's ultimate revision—so that the groups can compare their efforts with the poet's.
- Photocopy the "final" versions of the poems you assign, and provide copies for each student so that it will be easier for them to place the versions side by side and make comparisons.

JOHN KEATS

[*Bright Star! would I were steadfast as thou art!*]

To begin, you might ask two students to compile a list of "variants" on the blackboard so that the class can focus easily on the specific changes Keats made between the earlier and later versions of his poem. Remind the class that even changes in punctuation and spacing can make a difference in the poem's effect. For example, in the later version of this sonnet, Keats changes the emphatic exclamation point at the end of line 1 to a dash. In the earlier version, the exclamation point brings the first line to a full stop. The dash that replaces it in the later version helps create continuity between the first line and those that follow, but it also sets off lines 2–8, which clarify what the speaker does *not* want to imitate about the star's situation: *"Not* in lone splendor" (my emphasis). This bracketing also helps to clarify the contrast between lines 2–8 and lines 9–14, in which the poet describes the aspects of the star's situation that he *would* like to share.

The first revision of wording that occurs in the later version is the substitution of "aloft" for "amid" (line 2). This, for me, is an example of revision toward greater clarity and away from the expected. The word *aloft* not only conveys a sharper visual picture of the star high in the sky but also is the more original, less-expected word choice. (One might suggest, too, that including "loftiness" among the qualities the speaker does *not* want to share with the star reinforces the contrast with the image in line 10.) The second word substitution—"patient" for "devout"—seems in some ways a more significant revision, since a lover would *want* to portray himself as being devout, but in the earlier version the word "devout" appears in the section listing the things the poet does *not* want to imitate. Other kinds of revisions include (1) revision to create ambiguity, (2) revision for greater metrical regularity, (3) revision toward greater euphony, (4) revision to create or reinforce image patterns, and (5) revision to alter the poem's meaning.

QUESTIONS FOR DISCUSSION

1. Why do you think "morning" waters become "moving" waters in the later version? What is gained through this change?
2. How is the rhythm or meter of line 8 altered by the addition of the word "the"? Line 13 by the addition of "still, still" and the omission of "to feel"?
3. Why do you think Keats gets rid of the construction "Cheek-pillowed" (line 10)? Why does he substitute "to feel" for "to touch" (line 11)?
4. How do the changes in the final couplet of the poem alter its meaning and effect?

JOHN KEATS

To Autumn

Though Keats's most significant revisions to "To Autumn" obviously come in the second stanza, there are interesting changes even in the first.

One that can be especially pertinent to students in writing classes is the substitution in line 4 of "With fruit the vines" for "The Vines with fruit" because the change makes the line more grammatically correct and clear (in the first version, isn't the fruit rather than the vines running round the thatch eaves?). Also interesting here is the substitution of the more visual adjective "ripeness" for the "sweetness" in line 6 and the reverse kind of substitution of "sweet" for "white" to describe the "kernel" in line 8, such changes ensuring that all of the senses are appealed to here. The hyphenation in this stanza of words such as "bosom-friend" also contributes not a little to the rhythm of the poem.

The revisions to the second stanza have many different aims and effects, one of which is to get and keep the focus on autumn herself by cutting out the reference to the sun (in the original version of line 16) and by getting the emphasis onto autumn's sleep and off of the field (the emphasis falling on the latter in the version of line 17 that ends with "the half reaped field"). (Another potential tip for student writers: readers tend to focus on whatever comes last in a prose sentence just as they do in a line of poetry.) But in addition to getting and keeping the focus on autumn, Keats also works toward more consistency in portraying the physicality of autumn both by getting rid of the word "haunt" in line 12 (which suggests a much more ghostly autumn than is elsewhere depicted in the poem) and by instead mentioning the "store" so crucial to her association with nature's bounty. Finally, the substitution of "Drowsed" for "Dos'd" in line 17 obviously allows Keats to much more vividly reinforce the image of autumn's sleep, that twilight, dream state that Keats always associates with creativity and imagination. Both "Dos'd" and references to the "red" poppies themselves rather than their fumes also would seem to suggest an image of autumn actually dosing herself with opium, whereas the revised version is much more dreamy and suggestive.

ALEXANDER POPE

Ode on Solitude

For various reasons I tend to approach Pope's "Ode on Solitude" in the second of the two ways discussed in the headnote, finding it more productive in this case to frame discussion around questions about the differences between the versions rather than about the way the poem gets better or more itself (as both of the Keats poems seem to do). In the first two versions of the first stanza, Pope figures solitude—the rural, gentlemanly life—by way of contrast with the way of life and the values associated with "towns" and, in the second version, with "courts," making explicit the idea that the praise of solitude within the poem constitutes a kind of counterargument to the idea that towns and courts are the real center of things. The original version of line 10, with its image of years passing "silently," implicitly underscores that contrast. In the third version, however, that explicit contrast and/or conflict disappears utterly from the poem, which in a sense now refuses—like the "happy" "man" it depicts—to even concern itself with towns and courts. Interestingly enough, the first stanza here, with its reference to "paternal acres" makes even more explicit that man's gentlemanly status, while also associating solitude with familial and historical continuity. Interesting in a slightly different way is Pope's substitution of "unheard" for "unseen" in the second version of line 17, which seems to make the poem potentially more about himself, as poet.

EMILY DICKINSON

[Safe in their Alabaster Chambers—]

Dickinson's 1861 version of her 1859 poem, with its completely different second stanza, shows us poetic genius at work. The earlier version is a neat, fairly conventional poem about the great divide between life and death and the uselessness of human wisdom in the face of mortality. In the later version, the theme alters slightly: the later version is perhaps more about the insignificance of human activity from the perspective of death. Yet the change in theme is not Dickinson's triumph. The triumph is that she took an undistinguished poem treating a common poetic theme and revised it to make it something wholly original.

The revised stanza forces us to share the perspective of the coffin's inhabitants. Instead of standing outside the picture, as we do in the 1859 version, in the 1861 version, we *feel* the world rotate above those who are buried and sense movement from their perspective. Almost simultaneously, we are brought to realize that these same great movements have no noise, no effect, for the inhabitants of the alabaster chambers themselves.

QUESTIONS FOR DISCUSSION

1. The words and images of the revised second stanza have a grandeur and a sweep of which the original version has not the slightest hint or whisper. Where does the power of the second stanza come from?
2. What is the effect of the greater number of dashes in the later version of the second stanza?
3. What sense do you make of the last line of the 1861 version?

READING/WRITING IDEAS FOR CHAPTER 26

ESSAYS ABOUT THE PROCESS OF CREATION

As the headnote to this chapter suggests, there are actually two slightly different ways of approaching revision: one that involves treating earlier versions as "drafts" and the process of revision as the process of improving a poem until it becomes better and better by becoming, in a sense, more and more the poem it "really" is or should be and one that involves treating each version of a poem as a poem in its own right. Though in in-class discussions, as I've said, I actually tend to use these two different approaches almost interchangeably, the differences become more important, I think, when deciding how to frame essay assignments about the process of creation because each approach suggests, I think, a very different kind of argumentative strategy and/or structure. In assigning essays on this topic, then, I try to word the assignment either so that it steers students toward the exact approach that I want them to take or so that it gives students a framework for understanding the differences between the two approaches and requires them to essentially choose which they want to take in their essays. Assignments of the first, "here's the approach you should take" type, might look something like this:

Write an essay in which you closely compare the three versions of Pope's "Ode on Solitude," showing exactly how the particular changes Pope makes to the poem help to improve it by, for example, making the poem's tone, theme, situation, etc. more consistent and powerful or making sound contribute more effectively to sense.

Write an essay in which you closely compare the three versions of Pope's "Ode on Solitude," showing exactly why and how the distinct features of each version make it mean something different than the others. If it helps, generate ideas by first pretending that the poems are by three different authors, each of whom writes about the subject of solitude in his own particular, distinctive way.

The "describe the approaches and let students choose" version might, instead, look something like this:

One could write about the process through which Pope created "Ode on Solitude" in two very different ways. The first way would involve seeing the most recent version as the "real" and best version of the poem, the one that represents the author's final, most considered approach to the subject of solitude. Taking this approach, then, would entail discussing how the specific changes Pope makes serve to improve the poem by, for example, making the poem's tone, theme, situation, etc. more consistent and powerful or making sound contribute more effectively to sense. The second way would instead involve seeing each of the versions as a perfectly good poem in its own right (after all, Pope thought them good enough to publish), each representing a distinctive and equally valuable piece of poetic craftsmanship. Taking this approach, then, would entail discussing how the specific choices Pope makes in each version give that version a meaning different than the others. Choose the approach that to your mind best suits the poems and your views of them and write an essay that makes an argument about the various versions of "Ode on Solitude."

TROUBLESHOOTING

The problem students will probably face, regardless of which version of the assignment you choose to use, will be the tendency to produce not a single, coherent, idea-driven essay but a series of unrelated or only loosely related observations about specific changes (basically a glorified list). One way to help students avoid this problem is to discuss it with them to help them strategize about ways to organize this essay just as they have other kinds of essays over the course of the semester. Especially important will be encouraging students to see how this problem might crop up if they try to hang entire essays on claims or theses that are too general or vague, such as "Keats changes this poem a lot in revision" or even "Keats improved this poem a lot in revision."

Depending on your goals for the course, you might also consider avoiding the "glorified list" problem in one of two other ways. The first would be to have students write essays more like those they've already written for the course and have them simply use facts about how an author revised a poem as part of the evidence they consider in their analysis. A student might, for example, write a thematic essay focusing on Keats's treatment of the relationship between earth and heaven in "[Bright Star!]" that shows how that issue is treated differently in the various versions of the poem and/or how that treatment becomes more consistent and powerful as Keats moves from draft to final version. The second would instead involve simply having students write something other than essays (so that they wouldn't have to worry so much about argumentative organization and coherence). One might, for example, ask students to imagine that Keats has sent them the various versions of "To Autumn" and asked them to help him figure out whether and why the final version is better than the others. Their job is thus to respond to Keats with a letter that tells him why and how exactly they think he did or did not improve his poem in revision. (Some part of me is particularly pleased by the idea of having students write a letter to someone as famous for his letters as Keats is.)

Finally, because all of the "how does this poem get better" assignments implicitly or explicitly involve (or assume) evaluation, as well as analysis, you might want to consider either saving this assignment until students have tackled the "Evaluating Poetry" section of the anthology, combining these chapters and assignments, or simply having them take the evaluation part of the assignment for granted for now (assuming that the author himself has evaluated the various versions and decided that the last is best) and revisit this aspect of the assignment when you begin discussing evaluation, using it as an example of the way evaluation and analysis can at times work together.

Evaluating Poetry

One of the most vexed questions in literary-critical circles is whether our judgments about literature are so implicated in a limited, even oppressive worldview that it would be better to abandon the whole enterprise of literary evaluation. Even the term *evaluation* can be seen as unduly emphasizing a poem's *value*, which in Western industrialized culture has a primarily monetary connotation—as if a poem would need to sell well in order to be good.

But while there is certainly some danger of being overly proscriptive about literature, particularly in an increasingly pluralistic society, one can just as easily (perhaps even more easily in the current climate) err on the other side by assuming that all literature is equally good. Our students know better. In my experience the great majority are uneasy with shilly-shallying about the quality of a poem: they want to know whether it is good and how they can tell. One course is to be as clear as possible about criteria for evaluation, all the while trying to remain aware of the cultural limitations that make us see the world the way we do. Another, very different approach is discussed in "Reading/Writing Ideas for Evaluating Poetry."

PLANNING IDEAS

- The chapters above include planning ideas or writing topics that ask students to write their own poems. While I tend not to have students evaluate their peers' poetry (not only because many of the students are fledgling poets who regard their creations as personal but also because some of the evaluators are fledgling critics), having students evaluate their own poems can be fruitful. Such evaluation can be done in an analytical essay or fairly informally in a journal. Either way, it helps to get students thinking about why some things worked well and some didn't, especially if they can find examples of similar moments of success and failure in the poems in the text.
- Layton's "Street Funeral" pairs well with Shakespeare's "[Th' expense of spirit in a waste of shame]." Both poems depict sensory pleasures as ultimately illusory, but of course both make their cases by employing imagery that strongly appeals to the senses.
- Have students read all the short Emily Dickinson poems in the "Read-

ing More Poetry" section along with "[The Brain—is wider than the Sky—]." Many of these poems are not usually anthologized, and they suggest a poet more playful, more comic, more fanciful, and more flirtatious than the somewhat somber Emily Dickinson that emerges from some of the more familiar lyrics. Dickinson—as represented in this book—is a good poet to study in combination with Adrienne Rich, not only because Rich remembers and consciously departs from her mode of seeing and telling (see "Snapshots of a Daughter-in-law," lines 43–46) but also because Dickinson's quiet but resolute bursting of formal bonds resembles so closely that of Rich in an early poem like "Aunt Jennifer's Tigers."

• See the "How to Write a Lousy Sonnet" exercise, detailed in the first of "Planning Ideas" in Chapter 7.
• To spark in-class discussion (or debate) about evaluation, have students read or reread Irving Howe's essay on Plath's "Daddy." Have them note the places where Howe makes explicit or implicit evaluative claims and the places where the assumptions and values that underwrite those claims come closest to the surface. How exactly does Howe define a good poem and what does he suggest about why "Daddy" isn't one? What poem in the anthology might Howe admire more? In class, you might not only discuss Howe's claims and assumptions but also use these to help students begin to formulate their own. (See also Exercise 2 in "Reading/Writing Ideas for Evaluating Poetry.")

IRVING LAYTON

Street Funeral

Ostensibly this poem makes a fairly straightforward statement: "We're better off dead." Several things, though, call that idea into question. First, the speaker doesn't really state that the unnamed subject of the poem is glad to be turning slowly into grass instead of putting up with life's troubles; the last sentence is a *question*. Not only does the speaker's use of a question instead of a statement imply that one might disagree with the dead man's opinion, it would of course be impossible for a dead man to have an opinion if consciousness had really ended with his biological life. The only ones who can conceivably be glad—about anything—are those who are alive on earth now and those whose consciousness extends beyond earthly life. The poem, then, centers on a paradox: the suggestion of an unthinking being's thoughts. Perhaps the real focus is on the *speaker's* thoughts as those of the dead man are contemplated.

The phrase *"long adultery / with illusion"* might seem despairing, but the metaphor of adultery implies that the possibility exists for a *legitimate* relationship with the world—a relationship that would not be illusory.

Note that while the speaker seems fully aware of the degrading, deluded, unfulfilling life we ordinarily live, the speaker is quite clearly capable of appreciating beauty; degradation isn't the *whole* picture.

The glimpses of beauty in the poem are all confined to the areas traditionally thought to be not only subrational but also subanimal: the vegetable world and the weather. It is the "frosty morning" that makes the "coffin wood" burst into "brilliant flowers." It is the "clean grass" that will provide a preferable alternative to our animalistic existence.

QUESTIONS FOR DISCUSSION

1. Why is it significant that the dead man has no name?
2. What does the phrase "other animals" imply about the speaker's view of the human condition?
3. The poem's first three lines make eating meat seem disgusting. How, though, does the poem differ from a simple vegetarian manifesto?
4. Are the "child" and the "sly man" whose conscience bothers him different people? The same person? Which reading makes more sense?
5. How is it that the speaker manages, in the last three lines of the first stanza, to make erotic love seem like a disease?

SUGGESTION FOR WRITING

"Street Funeral," like Marvell's "To His Coy Mistress," incorporates all three of the "souls" that the psychology of Marvell's day attributed to human beings: the vegetable, the animal, and the rational. Whereas the speaker in "Coy Mistress" ostensibly opts for the animal soul over the vegetable, that situation is reversed in "Street Funeral." In both poems, though, the rational part of us plays a much greater role than a first reading might imply. Using details from both poems, write a four- or five-page essay developing this idea. Devote the last page or so to an explanation of which poem is more effective in its handling of our complex makeup.

GALWAY KINNELL

Blackberry Eating

This poem bears some resemblance to Marvell's "The Garden," especially to passages like, "The luscious clusters of the vine / Upon my mouth do crush their wine." Like Marvell, Kinnell uses onomatopoetic words to give the reader the sensory impression of actually eating fruit. Note that fruit-to-mouth exchange is immediate; the speaker's hands do not touch the berries directly: "as I stand among them / lifting the stalks to my mouth, the ripest berries / fall almost unbidden to my tongue, / as words sometimes do." The connection between the sensory experience of eating and the choice of words is explicit. Kinnell provides a clue about what it is about words like *"strengths," "squinched," "squeeze,"* and *"splurge"* that makes them appropriate: they are "many-lettered, one-syllable lumps"— and so they resemble blackberries, with their clustered surfaces, more than they would, say, blueberries or cherries.

QUESTIONS FOR DISCUSSION

1. How does the sound echo the sense in a line like, "among the fat, overripe, icy, black blackberries"? In a passage like, "the stalks very prickly, a penalty / they earn"?
2. Why does the speaker claim that blackberry making is a "black art" and blackberry eating a "black language"?

EMILY DICKINSON

[*The Brain—is wider than the Sky—*]

QUESTIONS FOR DISCUSSION

1. In this poem, as in "[I Reckon—when I count at all—]," the speaker values the brain—and, implicitly, at least, the poet—above all else. What other similarities do you see between these two poems, which were probably written around the same time? How do they differ from other Dickinson poems you have read?
2. In "[The Brain . . .]," what is the implication of the *"and You"* of line 4? How do *"Syllable"* and *"Sound"* differ? What does the difference imply about the relation between the brain and God?

READING/WRITING IDEAS FOR EVALUATING POETRY

EVALUATIVE ESSAYS

As the headnote to this chapter of the Guide suggests, evaluation has become a rather vexed issue among contemporary literary critics and theorists. And the headnote also suggests one quite viable way of steering through those rough waters, while still teaching evaluation in the terms suggested by the anthology. If you choose to use this approach, the following assignment would work very well as a supplement to, or substitute for, the writing suggestions in the anthology:

Imagine that you are the poetry editor of a good periodical, one that appeals to a broad spectrum of well-educated readers (*The New Yorker*, say, or *The Atlantic*). You have space in the upcoming issue for only one poem, and you have narrowed the choices from a field of several dozen to two, both of which should be included in the anthology.

Write a three-page rejection letter to the author of the runner-up. Explain in precise terms why you ultimately decided on the other poem. If you wish, spend a paragraph or two on the chosen poem's strengths, but the bulk of your letter should describe the weaknesses of the second-place finisher, while saying enough about its strengths so that poet isn't discouraged from trying again. Be careful here not to short-circuit your argument by deciding ahead of time which sorts of poems are appropriate and which are not. Don't say, for example, "Our readers like uplifting poems, and yours is depressing" or "Your poem is unrhymed, and our readers prefer rhyme." Are *all* depressing poems artistically inferior to uplifting ones? Should *all* poems be rhymed? Assume that your readers would answer no to both questions; they enjoy all sorts of poetry, as long as it is carefully crafted and somehow compelling. Your rejection letter, then, should point out in as much detail as possible why the poem is not quite successful in fulfilling its goal, in doing its job.

For various reasons that I will now try to explain, I tend to adopt an approach that's quite different from this one. That approach begins with my discomfort with teaching students to "evaluate" poetry in the sense of asking whether it's good or bad poetry, real art or junk, a discomfort arising, in part, from the fact that evaluating texts is not something I do very often or feel good about doing. However, as a feminist, a materialist, a historicist, a sometime postcolonialist, and all other sorts of "ists," I evaluate poetry all the time in the sense that I consider the messages particular texts send about race, gender, class, and other issues and/or communities, and I constantly make value judgments about those messages.

For this reason, I am more comfortable being as honest about this with my students as I have just been with you, approaching evaluation in this more comprehensive sense by opening up for discussion the different issues and criteria one might consider in evaluating poetry. Though I was worried the first time I tried this, the whole problem has in fact turned out to be a blessing in disguise, since it's essential that anyone writing an evaluation of anything first clearly define the criteria of evaluation and articulate a fairly clear sense of the ideal against which they are measuring that thing and also that they make those standards somehow relevant and palatable to their readers. Thus having different definitions, standards, and criteria present in the classroom and drawing them out can give students a very real and vivid sense of audience in this sense and of the need to argue for evaluations, while it also can produce exactly the kind of environment necessary to becoming truly articulate about one's own definitions, learning how to argue effectively for them. And teaching evaluation in this way, where various kinds of evaluations are themselves being evaluated, as it were, makes our work with evaluation flow much more smoothly out of our earlier conversations about literary tradition and cultural context than it otherwise would.

As a result, the essay assignment for this unit that works best for me asks students to carefully establish criteria, define their terms, etc., while allowing them to choose whether to write about one text or multiple texts, parts or elements of texts or whole texts, and whether to focus on more issue-related or more form-related kinds of evaluation, whether— that is—to shoot for theses that make claims about a poem or poems being "good or bad poems" or for theses that make claims about a poem or poems "conveying positive or negative messages about X."

I also tend to encourage students to think and write in less absolute terms, concentrating more on showing what's negative *and* what's positive about the messages here or what's good *and* what's bad about the craftsmanship, etc. Doing so is important for me because I feel it is a great deal more consistent with the model of writing I've been advocating throughout the course, a model that emphasizes the exploration of an issue, problem, or question from various angles (as I believe literature itself does) rather than the "position paper" type of argument that insists on a single, ironclad view, solution, or answer (if only because airtight answers can only be argued for effectively if a writer shows he or she has considered others).

For the same reason, I try to frame both the assignment and our discussions of evaluation so that students are required to consider potential criticisms of, and questions about, both form- and issue-related forms of evaluation. For example, if one determines that Donne's "The Sun Rising" is sexist, does that mean it is bad? Should we dismiss or not read or teach "The Sun Rising" because it conveys negative messages about or to women? "Daddy" because it isn't emotionally restrained and impersonal or objective? Or is there a way to acknowledge both the negative aspects of these poems, while still seeing their merits? If one of the virtues of literature is, in a sense, to disturb us by challenging our assumptions and making us inhabit different points of view, then at what point does issue-related evaluation begin to undermine that virtue? If one of the virtues of literature is, in a sense, even to disturb our notions of what literature is and should be, then at what point does form-related evaluation begin to undermine that virtue?

Finally, one option that works well here regardless of the particular approach you're taking is to have students write an evaluative essay by reworking an essay that they wrote earlier in the semester. If a student wrote an essay on the messages about gender in Guest's "The Things That Make a Soldier Great," for example, he or she could now rewrite that essay so that it not only analyzed but also evaluated those messages. Or, if a student wrote an essay on the symbolism of "When Lilacs Last in the Dooryard Bloomed," he or she could now rewrite that essay so that it not only analyzed but also evaluated Whitman's use of symbolism. Or students could go back and evaluate the work of Keats or Rich.

TROUBLESHOOTING

Inviting disagreement into the classroom in this way, particularly about issues that will undoubtedly hit close to home for different students in

different ways, obviously poses certain risks—that students will feel reluctant or unable to admit that their standards differ from their instructor's
or colleagues'; that students will disagree so vehemently that the conversation will get too heated, too personal, etc.; or that students will feel
discombobulated or attacked at having their own standards revealed not
to be universally accepted truth. For those reasons, I tackle these questions in this way only when we are well into the course, have worked
together closely for a while, and have proven that we can do so peaceably
even in the face of disagreement (though I plant the seeds for it early in
the semester when we talk about all of our definitions of what literature
and especially poetry does and is). If we hadn't proven that we could work
together peaceably, I suppose I would abandon this unit or handle it in
a different way, but I haven't ever encountered these problems. (Perhaps
other factors come into play here, as well. Being relatively young and
female, and looking younger than I am, I haven't had trouble with students being afraid to disagree with me when invited. And perhaps more
important, my students tend to be first-generation college students, many
of whom are from working-class families and from a wide array of ethnic,
racial, and cultural backgrounds. As a result, many are as attuned to the
politics of evaluation as I am and infinitely less or at least very differently
invested in the idea of universal standards than students I've taught elsewhere who come from white, upper-middle-class backgrounds.)

Finally, inviting discussion of this kind and in this way can, I think,
actually head off the other potential problem students have with writing
evaluative essays, the problem of *not* feeling the need or having the skills
to define and defend the criteria of evaluation.

EVALUATION-FOCUSED WRITING EXERCISES

1. Developing Definitions and Criteria

To get students started on this assignment, I generally have them do
a version of an exercise that my class as a whole usually does together in
the very first few days of the class. That exercise entails giving students a
chart something like the following to fill out and/or asking them to make
such a chart themselves. My basic chart looks like this (only it takes up a
whole sheet of paper, turned sideways):

Purposes or Functions of a "Good" Poem

For Writers: For Readers:

Formal Elements or Features That a "Good" Poem Needs to Have to Fulfill Those
Functions:

In the case of this particular version of the exercise, I often put this
model of the chart on the board and then encourage each student to

adapt it as he or she does the exercise in order to fit the exact approach to evaluation he or she is going to take. Thus students who want to focus on a particular element or aspect of a poem or poems, such as symbolism or meter, might want to substitute words referring to those elements for the word *poem* (though I also point out to them how much their evaluation of a particular element may depend on their evaluation of others); and students who want to focus on more thematic or issue-oriented kinds of evaluation might substitute for *poem* the words *poem about X* (*X* being "women" or "men" or "whites," etc.).

Once students have completed this exercise, I then have them work with each other in small groups to compare and critique charts, giving each other feedback about potential problems, areas of disagreement and/or possible counterarguments, etc.

2. "Charting" Other Writers' Definitions and Criteria

Another option here is to have the students do Exercise 1 only *after* they've done a version of that exercise that asks them to read sample student and/or scholarly essays that evaluate a text and to make a chart that lists the definitions and criteria stated and implied in those essays. While student essays are good for this, I also find the Howe and Alvarez essays included in Chapter 25 especially apt and useful because they both implicitly and explicitly evaluate "Daddy," disagreeing in their evaluations yet often employing very similar, if not identical, criteria. (Reading a primarily analytical essay such as Alvarez's in this way can also be especially helpful in facilitating discussion about the similarities and differences between analysis and evaluation and about just where, and when, and how one kind of argument slides into, and/or implies, the other.)

A SAMPLE ANALYSIS

ANDREW MARVELL

To His Coy Mistress

The title suggests the situation—a man is speaking to his beloved—and before we are far into the poem we recognize his familiar argument: let's not wait, let's make love now. But much more is going on in the poem than this simple "message."

Seduction is a promising subject, but it is nearly as easy to be dull on this subject as on less fascinating ones, and the subject has inspired some very dreary poetry. The interest and power of this poem depend on more than the choice of subject, however useful that subject is in whetting a reader's expectations. No reader is likely to use the poem as a guide for his or her own life, and few readers are likely to read it at a moment when their own lives precisely parallel the poem's situation. Its relevance is of a larger kind: it portrays vividly and forcefully a recognizable situation, saying something about that situation and, more important, making us react to the situation and feel something about it. Experiencing a poem involves not only knowing what it says but also feeling the pleasures provided by its clever management of our own ideas and emotions. All poems have a design on us—they try to make us feel certain things—and the full experience of a poem requires full recognition of the complexities of design so that we can feel specific emotions and pleasures—not only the general ones of contemplating seduction.

Let's begin at the beginning. What do you expect of a poem about a would-be seduction? One thing you can be almost certain of is that it will contain attractive images of physical enjoyment. The first verse-paragraph (lines 1–20) contains such images, and so does the third (especially lines 33–38). The first set of images suggests the languorous, lazy appeal of a timeless world where physical enjoyment seems to fill all time and all space. First are images of rich sensuousness; the leisurely contemplation of enjoyment, the timeless walks in exotic lands, the finding of precious stones, the luxury of delaying the supreme moment. Gradually sensuousness becomes sensuality, and the speaker imagines himself praising various parts of the young woman's body. In line 33, the poem returns to sexual contemplation but with much more intensity. Now the young woman seems to be not a passive object of admiration but a live, breathing, perspiring, passionate respondent. And a moment later, the speaker projects the beauty and energy of the love act itself. He suggests something of his anticipation of supreme ecstasy by the vividness and intensity of the images and language he uses: from the languid, flowing, floating suggestions of the early lines through the breathless anticipation of lines 33–37 to the violence of lines 41–44 with their explicit visualization of the union, the rolling into one, of "strength" and "sweetness."

But not all the poem portrays glorious pleasure. The second verse-paragraph (lines 21–32) contains some pretty grim stuff. Instead of the endless languor of unhurried walks and exotic places in the early lines, we have anxiety and consciousness of time—a hurrying chariot moving up fast from behind. And instead of the centuries of body worship, eternity consists of vast deserts. Grimmest of all is the image of a different kind of fall than the one the speaker desires—the carefully preserved virginity of the young woman, the speaker imagines, will be tested and destroyed in the grave by worms. The speaker summarizes with gross understatement and macabre humor in lines 31–32:

> The grave's a fine and private place,
> But none, I think, do there embrace.

The contrast with all that grimness of future dryness and death emphasizes both the unreal romanticism of the timeless world—which, according to the speaker, the young woman seems to want—and the vividly portrayed sensual pleasures of a potential moment right now. Such contrasts work for us as well as for the young woman; in fact, they are part of a carefully contrived argument that organizes the poem. We might well have expected, just from the title and the opening lines, that the poem would be organized as a formal argument. The first words of each paragraph clearly show the outlines: (1) "Had we" (If we had no limits of time or space); (2) "But" (But we do have such limits); (3) "Now, therefore." The poem is cast as a long, detailed hypothetical syllogism; it uses the form of a standard argument, with vivid examples and carefully contrived rhetoric, to suggest the urgency of enjoying the moment. It is a specious argument, of course, but real people have fallen for worse ones. But this isn't real life; the story doesn't even end. As in most other poems (and unlike most drama and fiction), the "plot" and its resolution have little to do with the final effect. Part of the point here is to notice the flaw in the argument. A good logician could show you that the speaker commits the fallacy of the "denied antecedent," that is, he proves what cannot happen but fails to prove what can. Of course seduction seldom gets worked out in purely logical terms, and so in one sense the logic of the argument doesn't matter—any more than whether the speaker finally seduces the young woman. But in another sense it matters a great deal and contributes to our complex experience of the poem. For if we spot the illogic and find it amusing (since the argument is obviously an effective one, logical or not), we not only feel the accuracy of the poem's observation about seduction but also experience something important about the way words work. Often their effect is more far-reaching than what they say on a literal level, just as this poem reaches much further than any literal statement of its "message" or "meaning." Poetry often exploits the fact that words work in such mysterious ways; in fact, most poems, in one way or another, are concerned with the fact that words may be used suggestively to open out on horizons beyond logical and syntactical categories.

Reading a poem about seduction is hardly the same thing as being seduced, and only a very peculiar poet or reader would expect it to be, though some of the censorship controversies over the teaching of poems like this may sometimes imply that life and art are the same thing. Anyone who thinks they are is bound to be disappointed by a poem about seduction, or about anything else. One does not read a poem instead of being seduced, or as a sublimation, or as a guide. A poem about anything does not intend to be the thing itself, or even to re-create it precisely. Poetry, like other literature, is an ordered imitation of perceived reality expressed in words. By definition, by intention, and by practice, poetry modifies life to its own artistic ends, "ordering"—that is, making meaningful—what is only a version in any case. What poetry offers us is not life itself, naked and available, but a perspective (perceived reality) on some recognizable situation or ideas; not Truth with a capital T, but interpretations and stances; not passion itself, but words that evoke associations and memories and feelings. A poem can provide an angle of vision that in "real life" is often blurred through our closeness to experience.

And just as the poet fictionalizes—whether he begins with a real event or not—we as readers end with his version, which exists in tension with other things we know, about words, about poetry, about arguments, about seduction, about everything. That tension tests not the "truth" of the poet's vision but the effects produced by the poem; the more we know, the richer these effects are likely to be.

Anyone with developed sensitivities and a modest amount of knowledge of the suggestiveness of words can find the crucial words that express and evoke the sensual appeal. The devices of contrast (the flowing Ganges flanked by rubies versus vast deserts; spacious wandering versus the confinement of a marble vault; eternal adoration versus those traditional symbols of mortality, ashes and dust) may be readily seen by anyone willing to look at the poem carefully. In short, much of the poem is readily available to almost any reader who looks carefully; much of its power is right there on the page, and a reader need make only a minimal effort to experience it.

But a number of things in the poem require a special skill or knowledge. The poem's parody of a hypothetical syllogism is only available to those who can recognize a hypothetical syllogism and see the distortion in this one. Of course, not recognizing the syllogism is not too serious, as long as the reader "senses" the falsity of the argument and finds the incongruity in its effectiveness; he simply misses a joke which is part of the poem's complexity. But some other matters in the poem are more crucial, for lack of knowledge about them not only would drain the poem of some of its richness but might even force a misunderstanding of what the poem says on its most literal level.

Look, for instance, at the following words: "coy" (title) and "coyness" (line 2); "mistress" (title); "complain" (line 7); "vegetable" (line 11); "adore" (line 15). All of these words are common enough, but each offers a problem in interpretation because of changes in meaning. The poem was written more than three hundred years ago, in the mid-seventeenth century, and many words used then in a specific way have changed over the years. Words are, in a sense, alive and ever-changing; change is a part of the excitement of language as well as a potential frustration, and if we construe each of these words exactly as it is construed now we will be badly misled. The most obvious change in meaning is in the word *mistress,* for to us it implies a specific sexual relationship, one that would make the elaborate seduction plea here seem a little late. The most common seventeenth-century meaning of *mistress* was simply "a woman who has command over a man's heart; a woman who is loved and courted by a man; a sweetheart, lady-love." This definition comes from the *Oxford English Dictionary,* a valuable reference guide that lists historical as well as modern meanings, with detailed examples of usages. The *OED* can also show us that the new meaning of *mistress* was coming into use when this poem was written, and perhaps the meanings are played off against each other, as a kind of false lead; such false leads are common in poetry, for poets often like to toy with our expectations and surprise us.

Coy and *coyness* offer a similar problem; in modern usage they usually suggest playful teasing, affectation, coquettishness. But originally they suggested shyness, modesty, reluctance, reserve, not simply the affectation of those things. Of course, we find out very little about the young woman herself in this poem (except what we can infer from the things the speaker says to her and the way he says them), but we are not led to think of her as sly and affected in her hesitancy to receive her lover's advances.

Complain and *adore* are more technical. The former indicates a lover going through the ritual of composing a "complaint"—a poem that bewails his misery because of a lady's disdain. Thus the speaker here self-deprecatingly (but comically) imagines himself (in the unreal, timeless world of the first verse-paragraph) as a pining swain, while his love is luxuriating halfway across the earth, oblivious to his pain. Obviously, the speaker wants no part of such sadomasochistic romantic nonsense; he prefers sexual pleasure to poetic posing. *Adore* technically means "to worship as a deity"; there is a certain irony in regarding the young woman's body as an object of religious worship; but this speaker carries through his version of the young woman's fantasy, modestly refusing to name those parts he wishes to devote thirty thousand years to, and regarding her "heart" (usually synonymous with soul in the Renaissance) as the ultimate conquest for the last age.

The term *vegetable* is even more complex, for it depends on a whole set of physiological/psychological doctrines in the Renaissance. According to those doctrines, the human soul was made up of three souls that corresponded to the different levels of living matter. The Vegetable Soul man possessed in common with plants and animals; the Sensible Soul he possessed in common with animals; the Rational Soul was possessed by man alone. The Vegetable Soul was the lowest and had only the powers of reproduction, nourishment, and growth. The senses, the passions, and the imagination were under the power of the Sensible Soul. A "vegetable love" would be without feeling or passion, appropriate to the lowest form of life. The speaker thus reduces the notion of timeless, romantic, non-physical love to what he considers its proper level—a subhuman, absurd one. He pictures love without physical involvement not as a higher spiritual attraction but rather as a lower, nonsentient one.

Several other parts of the poem similarly require historical knowledge. Lines 33–36 depend on Renaissance love psychology, which considered physiological reactions (the rosy skin, perspiration) to be stimulated by the release of "animal spirits" in the blood. This release happened when the emotions were heightened by sight of the beloved; phantasms from the eye descended to the soul and released the animal spirits. The soul was thus "present" in the physiological response (the animal spirits), and the speaker pictures it here as involved in the very moment of desire, trying to unite—through the body—with the soul of the beloved. This love psychology may seem somewhat naive, but it is a humbling experience to try to explain our modern notions of how eyes and emotions relate to bodily processes.

The final two lines of the poem depend heavily on specific knowledge. First there is an allusion to Greek mythology—an allusion that actually began several lines before the end with the reference to Time's slow-chapped (i.e., slow-jawed) power. According to the myth, Chronos (Time) ate all his children except Zeus (who had been hidden by Rhea), and Zeus afterward seized Chronos' power as chief of the gods. Zeus later made the sun stand still to lengthen his night of love with Alcmene. We cannot, the speaker says, make time stand still as Zeus did, but we can speed it up. His argument assumes the seventeenth-century belief that each sex act made a person's life one day shorter. The speaker keeps insisting that the coming of death—time's end—is easier to cope with if you have something interesting to do while you wait.

Up to now we have not even mentioned the man who wrote the poem, Andrew Marvell. Whether Marvell ever had such a coy friend as this poem implies is not very important to us (though it may have been very important to him). For us, the relevant point is the fiction of the poem—regardless of whether that fiction is based on actual fact. But some facts about authorship may be very useful to us as readers of the poem, as long as we use them to help us with the poem and do not simply engage in biographical speculation. In many cases, knowledge about the poet is likely to help us recognize his or her distinctive strategies, and reading other poems by the same poet often reveals his or her attitudes or devices so that we can read any one poem with more clarity, security, and depth; the index can guide you to other poems by Marvell. A reader may experience a poem in a satisfactory way without all of the special knowledge I have been describing, but additional knowledge and developed skill can heighten the experience of almost any poem. Poems do not "hide" their meaning, and good poets usually communicate rather quickly in some basic way. Rereadings, reconsiderations, and the application of additional knowledge allow us to hear resonances built into the poem, qualities that make it enjoyable to experience again and again. We have really only begun to look closely at this particular poem, and if you were to continue to reread it carefully, you would very likely discover riches that this brief discussion has not even suggested. The route to meaning is often clear on first reading a poem, but the full possibilities of experience may require more time, energy, and knowledge of the right questions to ask.

Reading More Poetry

W. H. AUDEN

In Memory of W. B. Yeats

QUESTIONS FOR DISCUSSION

1. What is the significance of the specific images of winter in the first stanza?
2. What does the entire first section of the poem (particularly in lines 11–12 and 17–23) suggest about what happens to a poet and to his or her poetry when he or she dies?
3. What might the speaker mean when he says "You were silly like us" (line 32)? What answers are suggested by the lines that follow this one?
4. How is the vision of the nature and significance of poetry in the second section of the poem like and unlike that in the first? In the third?
5. What is implied by the images of imprisonment and freedom in lines 27–28 and 64–65?
6. What does the poem suggest about the relationship between poetry and politics? Business? Nature?

HART CRANE

To Emily Dickinson

QUESTIONS FOR DISCUSSION

1. How exactly does the speaker characterize Emily Dickinson in the first five lines of the poem? What might "the labor" and "the quest" (line 3) refer to?
2. Whom or what does "sweet, dead Silencer" (line 6) refer to? What is "that Eternity possessed" "in every breast" (lines 7–8)? What does this second stanza suggest about the nature of Dickinson's poetry?

3. What might be meant by "Some reconcilement of remotest mind" (line 12)?
4. What's the significance of the "Else" in line 14?
5. How does the poem's form contribute to its characterization of, and meditation on, Dickinson?

H. D. (HILDA DOOLITTLE)

Helen

H. D.'s "Helen" offers readers the opportunity to compare two contrasting views of Helen of Troy, the traditional condemnatory view originating with Homer and a more positive, modern, perhaps feminist, reinterpretation. According to the traditional view, Helen—daughter of Zeus and wife of the Greek king Menelaos—caused the Trojan War when she allowed herself to be carried off by Paris, a Trojan "enchant[ed]" by her extraordinary beauty (line 10). As a result, "God's daughter" was (line 13), as the poem suggests, "hate[d]" and "revile[d]" by "All Greece" for the very beauty that sent so many men to their doom (lines 1, 6); and H. D. emphasizes the extreme, unrelenting nature of that hatred through devices such as repetition, which also underscores for the reader just how long this view of Helen has endured. At the same time, however, H. D. implies another, more sympathetic view of Helen throughout the poem, especially through the constant emphasis on Helen's "white[ness]" and "maid[enly]" purity (lines 5, 9, 16); through the general emphasis on the irony whereby one, "wan" "maid" becomes the object of the virulent hatred of an entire country (as well as centuries of commentators who adopt their view) (lines 9, 16); and through the presentation of Helen as a passive and even sorrowful figure who "grows" even more "wan and white" at the memory of "past enchantments / and past ills" (lines 9–11).

JOHN DONNE

The Canonization

The central metaphor or conceit of "The Canonization" is the comparison of the speaker and his lover to saints. As a result, as Cleanth Brooks suggests in "The Language of Paradox" (*John Donne's Poetry*, New York: Norton, 1966, p. 179), Donne "daringly treats profane love as if it were divine love," a daring comparison that becomes, in a sense, doubly paradoxical: for "[t]he canonization is not that of a pair of holy anchorites who have renounced the world and the flesh. The hermitage of each is the other's body; but they do renounce the world, and so their title to sainthood is cunningly argued." According to this interpretation, the speaker's disapproving interlocutor comes to represent the world that the speaker and his lover renounce, a point cunningly made through the reference to his reverence for "the king's real or his stampéd face" (line 7)—that is, the world and values associated with the court (the real king) and with business (the coin with the king's picture on it). In the second stanza Donne furthers his argument about the distance between the everyday, practical world of the speaker and the world of the lovers by asking a series of questions that emphasize how little their love really affects that practical world and thus how little right or interest his interlocutor should have in "chid[ing]" the speaker (line 2): "What merchant's ships have my sighs drowned?" (line 11), he asks, as if to say, "Why do you care? Who are we hurting?" In the third stanza, the tone and the focus of the poem shift rather dramatically, as if the speaker were no longer concerned with arguing with his interlocutor's world at all or with that world's devaluation of his love, but instead with a serious consideration of the lovers' own sense of the character and value of their love. Obviously, however, this consideration still involves explicit and implicit contrasts between the practical world and the world of the lovers, especially—for example—in the contrast between the practical world's public monuments and "chronicle[s]" (line 31), on the one hand, and "sonnets" and "well-wrought urn[s]," on the other (lines 32–33). As Brooks suggests,

> The lovers are willing to forego the ponderous and stately chronicle and to accept the trifling and insubstantial "sonnet" instead; but then if the urn be well wrought, it provides a finer memorial for one's ashes than does the pompous and grotesque monument. . . . But the figure works further; the pretty sonnets will not merely hold their ashes as a decent earthly memorial. Their legend, their story, will gain them canonization; and approved as love's saints, other lovers will invoke them.
>
> In this last stanza, the theme receives a final complication. The lovers in rejecting life actually win to the most intense life. This paradox has been hinted at earlier in the phoenix metaphor. Here it receives a powerful dramatization. The lovers in becoming hermits, find that they have not lost the world, but have gained the world in each other, now a more intense, more meaningful world. Donne is not content to treat the lovers' discovery as something which comes to them passively, but rather as something which they actively achieve. They are like the saint, God's athlete. . . . The image [in the final lines of the poem] is that of a violent squeezing as of a powerful hand. And what do the lovers "drive" into each other's eyes? The "Countries, Townes," and "Courtes," which they renounced in the first stanza of the poem. The unworldly lovers thus become the most "worldly" of all. (pp. 181–182)

QUESTIONS FOR DISCUSSION

1. What are the various implications of the title "The Canonization"? How does the poem itself build on and use those implications?

2. What hints do you get here about whom the speaker might be speaking to in the poem? How exactly is that person characterized? What is the tone of the poem at the outset?

3. What is the significance of the questions in stanza 2? What is the speaker saying to his interlocutor by asking these questions?

4. How does the speaker characterize his love through each of the metaphors of stanza 3? What is the significance or effect of the mere fact that he invokes a series of metaphors to describe his love? Might the tone of the poem be said to shift here? If so, how so?

5. What is the significance or effect of the contrasts suggested in stanza 4 between "tombs," "Hearse," "chronicle," and "half-acre tombs," on the one hand, and, on the other, "verse," "sonnets," "a well-wrought urn," and "hymns"? What does the speaker mean when he says "all shall approve / Us canonized for love" (lines 35–36)?

6. Who speaks the words with which the poem ends? What is suggested by the image with which the poem concludes? How does this image resonate with others in the poem? Why and how might you see this as a fitting conclusion?

7. What does the poem suggest about the nature and significance of poetry? How might the poem be seen to enact the messages it conveys about love and poetry?

8. Literary critic Cleanth Brooks argues that the images and themes of "The Canonization" involve several overlapping paradoxes. What do you think he means? What paradoxes do you see at work within the poem?

JOHN DONNE

[Death be not proud, though some have calléd thee]

QUESTIONS FOR DISCUSSION

1. Why exactly does the poem suggest that death should not be proud? What different reasons does the poem give?

2. Why exactly can't death kill the speaker (line 4)? What are the various implications of Donne's comparison of death to sleep?

3. How does Donne's use of the sonnet form contribute to the poem's meditation on death?

A Valediction: Forbidding Mourning

You might want to consider beginning or ending your discussion of this or other Donne poems by having students consider the various charges and countercharges made about Donne's poetry over the years. Purportedly it was Samuel Johnson who first used the label "metaphysical poets" to describe the school founded by Donne, calling them a " 'race of writers' who display their learning, use far-fetched comparisons, and lack feeling" (*Oxford Companion to English Literature*, 1995, p. 653). As a result of such charges, the metaphysical poets remained largely unread and unappreciated until the critical intervention of T. S. Eliot in the 1920s. Whereas Johnson and his contemporaries saw Donne and his ilk as "lacking feeling," Eliot argued that their work embodied an integration of thought and feeling that was historically unique, the reflection of an era in which thought and feeling were not seen as antithetical to one another as they tended to be seen to be in the modern era.

QUESTIONS FOR DISCUSSION

1. What is the situation and setting here? To whom does the speaker speak?
2. In stanza 1, the speaker describes another situation, using it as an analogy for the way he and his lover might behave (as the "So let us" that opens stanza 2 suggests). What are some of the implications of that analogy? What are the implications of Donne's use of words such as "profanation" and "laity" (lines 7, 8)?
3. In stanzas 3–6 the speaker contrasts two kinds of love. How are each of these kinds characterized, particularly through metaphor? What are the implications of the word "elemented" (line 16)? "refined" (line 17)? How exactly do stanzas 3–5 build on the first two stanzas? How exactly does stanza 6 build on stanzas 4–5?
4. What are the implications of the metaphor of stanzas 7–9?
5. Eighteenth-century critics charged the poetry of Donne and his contemporaries with "lacking feeling" and being overly intellectual and affected. Twentieth-century critics, however, have championed Donne's poetry, suggesting that it reflects a unique and powerful integration of intellect and feeling. What do you think?

Sympathy

Students who know that Paul Dunbar is an African-American poet (born to parents who were themselves slaves) and/or who glimpse the connection between Dunbar's poem and Maya Angelou's *I Know Why the Caged Bird Sings*, will, perhaps, immediately see the experience of the caged bird as a metaphor for the experience of African Americans. And the poem certainly takes on an added poignancy and intensity if read in these terms, particularly if one reads the descriptions of "a pain" that "still throbs in the old, old scars" as referring both specifically to the scars left by the beatings endured by slaves and more generally to the impossibility of simply forgetting a long, painful history of racial oppression (line 12). In this light, too, references to the caged bird's song connect Dunbar's own "song" to African-American spirituals, songs that were—indeed— often "a prayer" sent "upward to Heaven" by slaves who had no other outlet for expressing the depth of their sorrow or the injustice of their situation (lines 19–20).

If students do not immediately glimpse the racial dimensions of the poem, then I generally encourage them to first discuss the poem in more general and/or universal terms, and then I introduce the idea that it is about the African-American experience, asking them how the poem works differently if read in these terms and what is lost or gained by reading the poem in these two very different ways. In the process, I try to lead students to see, on the one hand, how ironically limiting the humanistic or universalizing interpretation is and, on the other, how Dunbar himself encourages such a reading by not directly addressing the issue of race in the poem.

The Road Not Taken

I find that students have a hard time with this poem, not because it's difficult for them, but precisely because it seems all too clear and easy, a simple endorsement of individualism and self-reliance over conformity. As a result, I generally allow students to flesh out this interpretation and its implications first. Then I begin drawing their attention to evidence within the poem that suggests a more complicated view of the poem and of the speaker's situation. Much of that evidence comes in the second stanza's emphasis on the sameness of the two roads (each of which is "just as fair" [line 6] and "worn" "really about the same" [line 10]) and on the uncertainty about "the better claim" of the chosen road indicated by the word "perhaps" (line 7).

THOMAS HARDY

The Darkling Thrush

QUESTIONS FOR DISCUSSION

1. Notice the date on which Hardy composed the poem. How might that dating affect your interpretation of the poem? What does it suggest about the symbolic significance of the winter evening setting of the poem?
2. What are the implications of the speaker's description in lines 5–6 of how "The tangled bine-stems scored the sky / Like strings of broken lyres"?
3. What are the various implications of the word "pulse" (line 13)?
4. What do these first two stanzas together suggest about the speaker's vision of the state of the world at the turn of the century? How does this differ from what you might expect someone to feel at the beginning of a new century?
5. How does Hardy characterize the thrush and his song? What do both seem to represent or symbolize to the speaker?
6. What various things might "blessed Hope" refer to (line 31)?
7. Hardy once commented that his "poetry was revolutionary in the sense that I meant to avoid the jewelled line in poetry," the implication being that "bejeweled" poetry wasn't an apt vehicle for modern poetry and the modern situation. How does Hardy avoid "the jewelled line" in this poem? Why and how might particular aspects of his "unpretty" style contribute to the poem's meaning?
8. How is this poem like and unlike Keats's "Ode to a Nightingale"?

GERARD MANLEY HOPKINS

God's Grandeur

QUESTIONS FOR DISCUSSION

1. What do the similes in lines 2–4 have in common? What exactly do the two together suggest about the nature of "God's Grandeur"? About how we can experience that grandeur?
2. What does the speaker mean when he says that "all is seared with trade" (line 6)? "bleared, smeared with toil" (line 6)? How does sound

contribute to sense here and elsewhere in the poem?

3. What does the speaker mean when he says that "foot" can't "feel, being shod" (line 8)? What is the significance or effect of syntax here and elsewhere in the poem?

4. What is the significance and effect of the compression in line 10 (the omission of connecting words or prepositions such as *in*)? How does the image of "freshness deep down things" resonate with the images with which the poem opens?

5. What is the significance of the final image? To what is the Holy Ghost implicitly compared here?

6. What's the significance and effect of Hopkins's use of the sonnet form? Of the poem's meter or rhythm?

GERARD MANLEY HOPKINS

The Windhover

"The Windhover" is, perhaps, the most difficult poem of a self-consciously difficult poet, yet despite or because of that my students tend to love this poem and to have trouble tearing themselves away from their debates about it. As a result, I often let them struggle with it on its own terms, despite the fact that "The Windhover" and much of Hopkins's poetry makes a great deal more sense when you know a little about his ideas about "inscape"—the distinctive, individual qualities unique to each person, thing, or emotion—and "instress"—the experience one has when suddenly awakened to a full apprehension and appreciation of the inscape of a person or thing, as well as his conviction that poetry should be less a record of the poet's experience (of inscape and/or instress) than itself an embodiment of that experience. For sounds and words were or should be, Hopkins believed, as charged with (holy) significance as the things they described. The latter beliefs are key to Hopkins's stylistic pyrotechnics, particularly the reliance on multiple meanings or linguistic ambiguity and on compression and ellipsis "either to suggest the immediacy of actual speech, or to express the swift movement of the mind in the act of thought, flashing from image to image, or in the act of perception seizing in a single unity various facets of observation" (Walter E. Houghton and G. Robert Stange, *Victorian Poetry and Poetics*, 2nd ed., New York: Houghton Mifflin, 1968, p. 692).

QUESTIONS FOR DISCUSSION

1. In the first stanza, the speaker describes a hawk that he saw this morning. How exactly does the speaker characterize the falcon? What does his description suggest about why and how exactly the "bird" "Stirred"

his "heart" (lines 7–8)? What is suggested by Hopkins's use of words such as "minion" and "dauphin" (lines 1–2)? What's the significance and effect of the reference to "the achieve of" (rather than "the achievement of") in line 8?

2. What do lines 9–11 suggest about why and how exactly the "bird" "Stirred" the speaker's "heart"? Why and how does "fire" break "from thee then" (line 10)?

3. To whom or what does "O my chevalier!" (line 11) refer? Is it the hawk? Christ? Both?

4. What is meant by "No wonder of it" (line 12)? What exactly do the two final images (of plowed fields and falling embers) have to do with what has come before? What do these two images have in common with each other (and with the images at the beginning of "God's Grandeur")? What different things might these images serve as metaphors for?

5. How exactly does the epigraph affect your interpretation of the poem?

ANDREW MARVELL

On a Drop of Dew

An excerpt from an essay on this poem is included in "Reading/Writing Ideas for Chapter 7."

JOHN MILTON

Lycidas

As its epigraph suggests, "Lycidas" is a pastoral elegy occasioned by the death of the young clergyman Edward King, yet because King's religious and poetic vocation and aspirations parallel Milton's own (as the poem suggests, "we were nursed upon the self-same hill / Fed the same flock" [lines 23–24]), the poem is often taken to be as much or more about Milton as or than it is about King. But whether the subject is King or Milton or both, the poem deftly draws on both pastoral and biblical conventions to render poetic and religious vocations and aspirations inseparable from each other and to mourn the world's lack of consideration for both. For, as the speaker asks in lines 64–66, "What boots it with uncessant care / To tend the homely slighted shepherd's trade, / And strictly meditate the thankless Muse?" Why not give up such a "laborious" life to enjoy the "delights" of the flesh that come so much more easily (line 72), especially when—like King—one's life or powers can all too easily be cut off before one achieves the worldly "Fame" that "is the spur" to such labors (line 70)? More central to the poem than the fear of mortality, however, is the speaker's anger at the fact that unqualified priests and poets—"Blind mouths! that scarce themselves know how to hold / A sheep-hook, or have learned aught else the least / That to the faithful herdman's art belongs!" (lines 119–121)—rule the day and frustrate the efforts of the true aspirants to these high and holy offices, leaving "The hungry sheep" among their flocks not only "not fed" (line 125) but also "inwardly" "Rot[ting]" (line 127). "Lycidas," whoever one takes him to be, thus comes to represent the true "herdman," whose "large [heavenly] recompense" promises eventual "good / To all that [continue to] wander in that perilous flood" (lines 184–185), thus allowing the speaker to conclude the poem with a hopeful spirit and images of beginnings rather than endings.

SYLVIA PLATH

Lady Lazarus

"Lady Lazarus" quite vividly embodies what George Steiner, in an excerpt from "Dying is an Art" not included in Chapter 25, calls the "essential theme" of Plath's poetry—"the infirm or rent body, and the imperfect, painful resurrection of the psyche, pulled back, unwilling, to the hypocrisies of health." The cyclical quality of such resurrections suggested in the poem's opening stanza ("I have done it again. / One year in every ten / I manage it—"), along with its references to the Holocaust, clearly depersonalize, even mythologize them, even as, in the words of A. Alvarez, the poem is rendered "far more intimately" personal than earlier poems by the correspondences between "The deaths of Lady Lazarus" and Plath's "Own crises"—"the first just after her father died [in 1931 when Plath was nine], the second when she had her nervous breakdown [at age nineteen], the third perhaps a presentiment of the death that was shortly to come" with her suicide in February 1963 (see Alvarez's essay in the anthology).

What's particularly jarring about the poem to me, however, is the way in which Plath manages not only to intertwine suicide and genocide and thus to figure the speaker's personal self-destruction as both the culmination and only possible answer to others' efforts to destroy her but also to envision both as a particularly feminine performance—"The big striptease" (line 29). What the use of this image in conjunction with those drawn from the Holocaust does, in effect, is to lay bear the violence at the root of what Margaret Homans calls the process of women's reification, literalization, and/or objectification. In Homans's words, " 'Lady Lazarus' borrows the most appalling of Nazi imagery to accuse a generalized figure of male power of the ultimate reification. Not only is the dead victim of 'Herr Doktor' and 'Herr Enemy' an object in being dead [and a stripper] but she is also reduced to the actual physical objects from which the Nazis profited by destroying human bodies" (see Homans's essay in the anthology).

As a result, critics tend to see the poem as, like "Daddy," enacting a kind of ritual exorcism in which the speaker attempts to overcome not only the "generalized figure of male power," but also the versions of herself that remain enthralled to, and helpless before, that power. Thus the poem concludes with an at least somewhat positive image of both rebirth and retribution, the speaker rising like a phoenix "Out of the ash" and threatening to "eat men" (lines 82–84), cannibalizing them as the poem suggests they have previously cannibalized (by objectifying and consuming) her.

EZRA POUND

The Garden

Like Marvell's "The Garden," though in a much more ironic fashion, Pound here draws on our associations of gardens with Edenic innocence. In Pound's poem, however, Kensington Gardens becomes the site of humankind's fall into two distinct classes, neither of which has much to offer. On the one hand, as the epigraph suggests, is the upper class represented by the woman "dying piece-meal / of a sort of emotional anæmia" (lines 3–4), her "exquisite and excessive" "boredom" signaling the enervation and lifelessness (line 9) that lies beneath her beauty. As the statement, "In her is the end of breeding" (line 8) suggests, the poem implies that she represents humanity essentially refined to the point of inhumanity, embodying a kind of living death so fragile that any human contact represents a much-feared "indiscretion" (line 12). On the other hand is the nameless "rabble" who represent everything that she is not—unlovely, yet distinctly alive and still "breeding" (line 8). "Filthy," yet "unkillable" (line 6), these human cockroaches are—the poem suggests with heavy irony—the meek who "shall inherit the earth" (line 7).

WALLACE STEVENS

The Emperor of Ice-Cream

Like all Stevens's poetry, "The Emperor of Ice-Cream" proves extremely difficult, yet ultimately rewarding, for most of my students. Part of the difficulty here undoubtedly lies with the fuzziness of the situation and setting, so I tend to open discussion with questions about that, focusing particularly on the cues offered in the second stanza's references to "cover[ing] her face" with a sheet (line 12). The dead woman whose funeral is described here has been labeled by some critics as a prostitute, "the wenches" of the first stanza being her former cohorts (line 4), but whether or not one wants to go that far, it is certainly true that she is associated with the life of physical sensations and satisfactions ruled by, and embodied in, "the emperor of ice-cream." But while lines 8 and 16 suggest that this life and the emperor himself are sovereign, the poem in fact ends up suggesting that death and the actuality of being and non-being are the ultimate rulers: whatever her seeming pleasures in life, the woman now lies "cold" "and dumb" (line 14) beneath the very sheet on which she once enacted her "concupiscence," being becomes the "finale of seem" (line 7).

WALLACE STEVENS

Sunday Morning

"Sunday Morning" explores the conflict between the Christian view that the earthly life is a mere preparation for the real life to come in heaven and the pagan view that sees the earthly life as itself the focus and point of being. Though a fit topic for a "Sunday Morning" reverie, it's both surprising and significant that the poem attributes that reverie not to a priest in a church, but to a modern woman whose dress and surroundings indicate from the outset her leaning toward the more pagan view. Thus the first section sets up the conflict with wonderful economy and eloquence; the first few lines depict her as luxuriating in the earthy pleasures of every sense—taste ("Coffee and oranges"), touch ("peignoir" and "sunny chair"), sight ("the green freedom of a cockatoo / Upon a rug"), and even hearing ("The holy hush")—while the lines that follow invoke both the threat of mortality that necessarily mingles with such pleasures ("The pungent oranges and bright, green wings / Seem things in some process of the dead") and the Christian view of such pleasures suggested by the story of Christ's crucifixion. As the image of "her dreaming feet" moving toward Palestine suggests (lines 13–14), there is more than a hint here that, however much she luxuriates in her pagan pleasures, the woman also yearns for the something beyond earth that is (or was once) offered by Christianity.

Each section of the rest of the poem represents a particular point of view on, or way of thinking about, this conflict. In section II, the woman dismisses (or tries to dismiss) the yearnings and/or sense of dissatisfaction that arise at the end of section I, vowing to "find in comforts of the sun," "In any balm or beauty of the earth, / Things to be cherished like the thought of heaven" (lines 19, 21–22) and thus avowing that "Divinity must live" not in heaven, the after-life, God, or any other "silent shadows" or "dreams," but "within herself" and in the things of this world (lines 23, 18). In section III, the woman turns to a particular pagan creed represented by the Greek god Jove, finding in that creed the possibility of a view that reconciles and/or equates earth and heaven; accepting that view, she thinks, would make "The sky" "much friendlier then than now, / A part of [earthly] labor and a part of [earthly] pain" (lines 42–43) rather than representing a heaven opposed to such labor and pain. In section IV, mortality again enters the picture, for how, she seems to ask, can earthly things be our heaven when they don't last, "when the birds are gone, and their warm fields / Return no more" (lines 49–50)? Such questions and worries intensify and yet begin to be resolved in sections V and VI as the woman contemplates her continuing need for "some imperishable bliss" (line 62), only to decide that death and transitoriness themselves produce both beauty and bliss (lines 63–65, 88–90). Section VII seems to envision the triumph of this pagan view that embraces death and transitoriness, the "insipid lutes" of the last section (line 87) now giving way to an orgiastic and "boisterous" "chant" of "devotion" to a "savage" human God (lines 92–95). Finally, in section VIII, the conflict is resolved both through the final dismissal of the Christian view ("The tomb in Palestine" is only a "grave" [lines 107, 109]) and through a series of images that seem to serve as analogies for the ideal view of earth as the site of the life, beauty, and bliss born of mortality.

WALT WHITMAN

When Lilacs Last in the Dooryard Bloomed

Whitman's elegy on the death of Abraham Lincoln is a very good text to use to supplement the poems included in the "Symbols" chapter of the anthology, for it entirely hinges on three central symbols—the "sprig of lilac," which the poet "give[s]" to the "coffin that slowly passes" (lines 44–45) (and which thus becomes identified in a sense with the "gift" of the poem itself, so much more homely, informal, and personal an offering than "the pomp of the inlooped flags," "the show of the States" [lines 35–36]); the "powerful western fallen star" (line 7), which rather unambiguously stands for Lincoln himself; and the "shy and hidden bird . . . warbling a song" (line 19) that becomes an affirmation of life in the face of death, an affirmation that the poet himself can't embrace so long as he is "detained" by thoughts of death itself, "The star my departing comrade" (lines 69–70) and the "mastering odor" of "the lilac" (line 107). In the end, however, that affirmation of life comes, ironically, through the speaker's vision of the "myriad" "battle-corpses" of the Civil War dead (line 177) and his recognition that they, like Lincoln himself, are not mournful and discontented as he had imagined, but instead "fully at rest" (line 181), a state that the speaker himself seems to achieve as the poem concludes with an image of wholeness and integration: "Lilac and star and bird twined with the chant of my soul, / There in the fragrant pines and the cedars dusk and dim" (lines 205–206).

WILLIAM WORDSWORTH

Lines Composed a Few Miles above Tintern Abbey . . .

Students unfamiliar with Romanticism and with Wordsworth can get a wonderful introduction to both through "Tintern Abbey," which describes the poet's return to the Wye Valley after a five-year absence. Among the many typically Wordsworthian and Romantic themes explored in the poem is the valorization of nature over culture and poetic solitude over society, a valorization based on the idea that nature is the source of "tranquil restoration" and the "sensations" and "pleasure" that, ironically or not, make a person capable of "good[ness]," "kindness" and "love" toward others (lines 27, 30, 33, 35; see, too, lines 109–111 and 125–134). But communion with nature is also valorized because it makes possible that suspension of "corporeal" life in which one momentarily "become[s] a living soul" in harmony with nature and able to truly "see into the life" or (heavenly) soul that lies deep within the "things" of this world (lines 44–49), that "motion" and "spirit" that "rolls through all things" (lines 100, 102). (If students have read some or all of Keats's odes, you might want to have them compare his vision of the poetic dream state to Wordsworth's "blessèd mood" [line 37].) Equally key is Wordsworth's association of childhood with this state of oneness with nature, an association based on the vision of the child as a mere "animal" to whom nature is "all in all" (lines 74–75) because experienced solely through emotion rather than the "thought" or reason and "interest" that an adult brings to it (line 82).

What students may have more trouble appreciating are the anxieties that lie beneath the surface of the poem, propelling and energizing the speaker's thoughts on these topics from beginning to end. Among them is the fear that the poet's (natural supernatural) vision of nature as animated, as he is, by a soul—that vision so necessary both to his "cheerful faith that all which we behold / Is full of blessings" (lines 133–134) and his sense of nature as both "anchor" and "nurse" (line 109)—is only, after all, a "vain belief" (line 50), wholly a creature of his fancy rather than only "half create[d]" and half perceived (lines 106–107). And related to that fear is the poet's concern that he, like every other individual, is each utterly isolated, trapped within his own thoughts and perceptions, creating the universe all by himself. Only by attending to the presence of such fears can students appreciate, I think, the appearance of the sisterly auditor toward the end of the poem and the crucial role she plays.

Finally, I always like to end by having students think about the significance both of the seeming formlessness of "Tintern Abbey"—the way it doesn't conform to any traditional poetic form and seems to "wander" in exactly the (organic) way the speaker describes the Wye as doing—and of the title, the way it not only encourages the reader to equate poet and speaker but also insists on specifying the exact occasion that gave rise to the poem. If students have read Adrienne Rich's comments about why and how she began to date her poems, you might use those comments as a way to open up a discussion about the meaning and significance of Wordsworth's title: how and why might Wordsworth's rationale for specifying his poem's occasion differ from Rich's?

W. B. YEATS

Easter 1916

"Easter 1916" wonderfully captures a complex duality at the heart of Yeats's poetry which, on the one hand, cannot help but be shaped by the tremendous political energy of turn-of-the-century Anglo-Irish politics, particularly the Irish nationalism to which so much of his own poetry and drama contributed so much and, on the other, encodes an almost desperate yearning to escape, to become an art imagined to transcend time and timebound (political) concerns. As the poet Adrienne Rich remarks of her own experiences with Yeats (in the essay "Blood, Bread, and Poetry: The Location of the Poet" (1984), *Adrienne Rich's Poetry and Prose*, New York: Norton, 1993, p. 243),

> I know I learned two things from his poetry, and those two things were at war with each other. One was that poetry can be "about," can root itself in, politics. Even if it is a defense of privilege, even if it deplores political rebellion and revolution, it can, may have to, account for itself politically, consciously situate itself amid political conditions, without sacrificing intensity of language. The other, that politics leads to "bitterness" and "abstractness of mind, makes women shrill and hysterical, and is finally a waste of beauty and talent: "Too long a sacrifice / can make a stone of the heart."

These two contradictory messages about the relationship between art and politics are perhaps most clearly expressed in the poem's second stanza, with its reference to the poetic activities and aspirations of Patrick Pearse and Thomas MacDonagh and the "fame" they might have "won" if their political activities and aspirations hadn't intervened (line 28). Yet, as the recurring refrain "A terrible beauty is born" suggests, all of these men and women have managed to gain fame and to create a kind of beauty, however "terrible."

Teaching Drama

Many teachers find plays harder to teach than either stories or poems, perhaps because they are usually longer, and sometimes more complex structurally, and because some teachers consider plays out of place on a page instead of on the stage. But these difficulties can be turned into virtues, for the features they represent all need to be discussed openly in class, especially the page/stage distinction. In the text we have tried to distinguish *drama* (that is, the play as literature, the work written down in letters) from *play* (the work performed on stage). We have, in deference to the function of the anthology as an introduction to literature, treated the plays as "drama," though we realize that it is difficult to make that distinction stick and that this may not suit every teacher or every class. Many students have seen many plays or even acted in, directed, or otherwise assisted in play production. Not all students in an introductory literature course are literature majors, and some may even be theater majors or at least have a serious interest in the theater. So we have tried to redress the balance somewhat by emphasizing here, for you, the "play" and to lend some assistance to those who want to teach plays as works to be performed on stage (though we have not entirely abandoned those who want to teach drama as literature).

Your students will almost certainly need guidance and attention on issues of production and staging, and many may get involved rather more quickly in this kind of discussion than in the more literary discussions. Even students with no experience in play production or even in seeing plays often become fascinated with questions of how words on the page are fleshed out in speech and action.

The age-old custom of reading aloud in class, if not done too often (boredom, predictability, embarrassment) or with unrealistic expectations of how students will do at first (fear of failure, lack of confidence) can be especially effective in teaching plays. Usually it's best to do short scenes only, interrupting to ask questions about movement, or gesture, or intonation and (later) of interpretation. It is advisable to change parts often so that everyone gets involved. Diagrams on the board can help chart space and movement. Walk-throughs may be discouraging at first (students will unconsciously, or perhaps consciously, compare each other and themselves to actors on film or TV), but many will notice more readily than in reading how little things—a slight shift in tone, a small movement—make all the difference. The fact that your students have grown up on television and with movies is an immediate asset in teaching drama, though you may have to call attention to how the conventions of a stage are quite different from the "realism" of a camera. Participation can be a great asset in the drama part of your course, despite the well-known curse of the class ham. You may have to alter your strategy if there is a too-experienced actor who knows it all, or a class clown, or a born disrupter who takes advantage of the temptations of theatricality.

Several of the dramas in the text have been produced in excellent film versions. Although class time may be too precious to spend watching complete films, showing brief scenes on video works well to initiate discussion. And of course students can be assigned to watch videos outside of class. Written responses generally work well when they address some aspect of the differing demands of film and stage. Showing different film versions of a play or of particular scenes from a given play also works very well in initiating discussion and as the basis for essay assignments that ask students to compare various versions or interpretations.

The discussions that follow suggest, in most cases, some things to emphasize that do not come up for much attention in the chapters themselves. We hope that the discussion will suggest to you some ways of varying, and complicating, the main emphases in the chapters.

Drama: Reading, Responding, Writing

SUSAN GLASPELL

Trifles

PLANNING IDEAS

- The first several hundred lines of this play belong almost exclusively to the male characters, even though most of the play is devoted to the conversation and activities of the two women. I often start class by asking what effect this opening might have on the reader or audience. In practical terms, why do the men speak first? Glaspell provides a fair amount of stage direction at the beginning of the scene but little throughout the opening conversation between the men. You may want to ask the class to spend a few minutes blocking the movements of each character and suggesting appropriate gestures, expressions, etc. Should the men move, stand, or gesture differently from the women? The sheriff is described as taking off his overcoat and marking the beginning of "official business." Perhaps the class will want the men to move more expansively and authoritatively than do the women. If so, what gestures might convey their sense of authority? What gestures, posture, etc., seem appropriate for the women? Does it seem more important to create actions that distinguish one male character from the others or to distinguish between the two female characters?
- You might ask several pairs of "actors" from your class to enact one of the play's moments of discovery—perhaps the scene in which Mrs. Hale notices that the table is half-clean and that the "newly" baked bread has been left outside the breadbox. Include enough of Mrs. Peters's dialogue so that she is an integral part of the action. You might have three or four pairs of actors take a stab at performing this portion of the play, one right after the other. Ask those in the "audience" to take careful note of the differences in interpretation from pair to pair. After each pair has performed, ask the class for a critique of each performance, emphasizing the directorial choices over the acting abilities of the students, and the ultimate indeterminacy of the written words.

COMMENTARY

As the play unfolds and the two women begin to uncover the evidence that would provide a motive for the murder, the tension between their different perspectives is heightened. The women's gradual discovery of the "trifles" that could seal the case against Mrs. Wright offers several dramatic challenges. Because the clues are trifles, they need to receive enough dramatic emphasis so that the audience will register them, yet they must seem trivial enough to be missed by those trained to investigate crimes.

Gradually over the course of the play, the conflict between the women meliorates until, at the end, they are one in their determination to hide the evidence from the men. The class will readily observe that the men's condescending comments help to draw the women together, and you might lead them to note the many instances in which stage directions or whispered dialogue makes that happen—as though they are unconsciously driven to huddle near each other. Someone in the class may note that the women are also drawn together by their secret, shared discoveries about the murder and about the apparent desolation of Mrs. Wright's life. You may want to ask at what point the class believes Mrs. Peters begins to shift her loyalties from her husband and the law to Mrs. Wright. It seems to me that the real change begins when Mrs. Peters recalls the murder of her kitten and remembers the vehemence of her anger toward the boy who killed it. Mrs. Hale's implicit comparison between Mrs. Wright and the caged bird completes the sympathetic portrait. When the men return and renew their jokes about "the ladies," the decision is made.

QUESTIONS FOR DISCUSSION

1. If we were watching a production of *Trifles*, we would gradually piece together the information that Mrs. Peters is the Sheriff's wife. What are the earliest lines of dialogue that would allow an audience to derive this information?

2. Unsurprisingly, Mrs. Peters is more concerned than Mrs. Hale with the legalities of the case, and—at least in the first part of the play—she defends the men from Mrs. Hale's criticism by observing that what they are doing is "no more than their duty." Mrs. Hale, the Wrights' neighbor, appears more sympathetic to Mrs. Wright's situation and more aggressive in criticizing the men's behavior. Why might Glaspell make the women different in these ways? How do their differences contribute to the conflict of the play? To its resolution?

3. How broadly should Mrs. Hale mark her discovery in terms of vocal expression, gesture, facial expression? What should Mrs. Peters be doing at the time of the discovery? Should she be still? Should she be upstage? Downstage? How distracting would it be to the audience if Mrs. Peters were moving busily downstage during Mrs. Hale's discov-

ery? That is, how do you make sure the audience has its eyes on Mrs. Hale when she registers the significance of the half-dirty table and the misplaced bread? (Would this be a good point at which to introduce what lighting can do?)

4. In this play it is notable that all the villains are male: the patronizing trio that investigates the murder, the lately murdered Mr. Wright, and the kitten-killing boy. Has Glaspell stacked the deck in her play? Does it make any difference that the play was published in 1920? When were women granted the right to vote?

5. To what degree are the characters in the play "round" or well-developed? To what degree are they stereotypes?

SUGGESTIONS FOR WRITING

1. Write a three- to five-page essay in which you explain exactly how and why Mrs. Peters's character seems to change or develop over the course of Glaspell's play.

2. Write a three- to five-page essay in which you explore the various meanings of, and attitudes toward, "trifles" in Glaspell's play.

3. I have had very good success with a writing format that can be applied to any of the plays in the anthology. The "staging paper" asks students to isolate twenty-five to thirty lines of dialogue and to think through a range of ways in which a director might handle the exchange. The student discusses these interpretive options in a two-page introduction that ultimately defends one option as particularly appropriate. The rest of the paper divides the text into what actors call "beats"— units of dialogue during which a character's motive for speaking (or remaining silent, or gesturing, or turning, or moving . . .) remains constant. When the character changes tack, even slightly (and the reason for the change might well be unconscious), a new beat begins. A beat is seldom more than a sentence long, and it can be as short as a word. The bulk of the staging paper consists of the student's comments after each beat. Each comment is written as though the director were explaining to the actor what caused the character to say what he or she said and move as he or she moved. In getting students to look closely at a short passage, the exercise gives them firsthand experience of drama's complexity—of the play's interpretive range and its collaborative requirements.

DAVID IVES

Sure Thing

PLANNING IDEAS

- Since so much of the point of Ives's play has to do with throwing into question the idea of any outcome being a "sure thing," it might be easy for students to focus either too much or not enough on the particularity of the situation, setting, and characters. To get students thinking and talking about such elements, you might try putting them into groups of two or three and having them invent and then act out alternative scenarios—two women meeting in a grocery store, two men at a football game, a man and woman on the first day of class, etc. How exactly are each of their "plays" dramatically and thematically like and unlike Ives's? What exactly is lost and gained in changing the situation and setting, as well as the genders of the characters involved?
- An exercise that helps students think and talk in slightly different terms about the gender dynamics of the play (and that takes a good deal less time) involves asking students to act out the first few "scenes" of the play, having the actor playing Bill speak Betty's lines and vice versa. Are certain stereotyped visions of gender roles the one truly "sure thing" in this play?

COMMENTARY

Sure Thing is a funny and infinitely teachable play that can work very well in the classroom: the characters and the situation are familiar to all of us and particularly to students who are quite close in age to the characters themselves. The one potential problem, I've found, is some students' tendency to dismiss the play too quickly, either because it is so familiar and accessible (isn't great drama less accessible?) and/or because they find it gimmicky. (For these reasons the play might also work well as part of your discussion of "Evaluating Drama.") In my class, then, I try to get the gimmick problem on the table fairly early in discussion so that I can insist that we first discuss the thematic point behind the gimmick and only then move to critique.

Students will undoubtedly find it easiest to see the point of the play as involving a commentary on the ways in which people, and particularly men and women, create identities for themselves that will be attractive to other people. Each time the bell tolls, the characters essentially revise their words and themselves to elicit different responses from each other, thus creating different outcomes. As a result, the play also essentially gives Bill and Betty endless opportunities to do the kind of thing we're implicitly wishing we could do every time we say something like, "Gee,

I just wish I'd said . . ." In this case, however, the characters are revising more than what they say, for they are also in the process continuously inventing new images of who they are and who they've been, as Bill does, for example, when he describes himself as an alumnus of Oral Roberts University, then as a man who "never really went to college" at all because he "just like[s] to party," and then as a graduate of Harvard. Through portraying this process of invention, then, the play suggests that the outcome of every romantic encounter is anything but a "sure thing," because it depends in large part on how successful we are at creating a romantically interesting and appealing self. In the process the play also draws our attention to how important our every statement is in that process of self-creation or why, as Bill himself puts it, "It's all in the timing."

As a result, it might be easy to see the play in fairly traditional terms, as depicting two characters making up stories about themselves to interest someone of the other sex. And the play has certainly been read in this way. But is the play necessarily that traditional or that simplistic? To my mind it isn't, in large part because such a reading suggests that we can assume that some of the things these characters say about themselves are true and that others aren't, even though the text of the play really doesn't ever suggest anything of the sort.

Instead, might the point of the play and its gimmick, then, have much broader implications, exploring and enacting the idea that every moment in life might contain a multitude of options, our every action unleash a number of possible reactions and outcomes? If so, the play might also almost be seen as a kind of *metadrama* that subtly comments on the assumptions about life embedded in traditional drama and in our own reading of dramatic texts. For doesn't the traditional plot structure of drama (and of fiction) assume a much more linear and straightforward and logical relationship between cause and effect? A notion of characters (and people) as consistent and unified individuals whose every word and action is not only, in a sense, predictable but also predictable precisely because it is assumed to be a statement of their unique selfhood (if only because we, the audience, work to reconcile one particular with another to get a picture of a greater, unified whole called "personality")? Certainly, the latter is precisely the kind of work we're engaging in when we try to make Bill and Betty into characters who are "falsely" representing their personalities and histories.

QUESTIONS FOR DISCUSSION

1. If you were staging a production of *Sure Thing*, which depends so much on the fluidity of the characters' identities, how might you costume the main actors? How would you handle the scenery? (How, for example, would you convey the idea that the café is busy, as Bill's interest in Betty's chair and his inability to flag down a waiter seem to suggest it is?)

2. How would you describe the structure of *Sure Thing*? How is its structure like and unlike that of traditional plays, such as Glaspell's *Trifles*?
3. What's the role or significance of the bell ringing throughout the play?
4. What are some of the implications of the play's title?
5. What's the significance of the allusion to Faulkner's *The Sound and the Fury*? Why do you think Ives's might have picked this novel for the characters to refer to?
6. What's the significance of the discussion of time in the play?

SUGGESTION FOR WRITING

Write an essay in which you compare *Trifles* and *Sure Thing*, showing how the notions of plot and character are similar and different in the two plays. If you would like, you may treat *Trifles* as an embodiment of "traditional" drama to show why, how, and to what ends *Sure Thing* plays with and/or questions the conventions of traditional drama.

Understanding the Text

This section of the anthology offers students a chance to read and discuss four quite different plays—Hellman's *The Little Foxes,* Shaw's *Pygmalion,* Ibsen's *Hedda Gabler,* and Shakespeare's *Hamlet*—and invites them to do so by considering four primary dramatic elements—character; structure; stages, sets, and setting; tone and theme—and the way these work together in particular plays. Rather than having students consider all of these elements as they read and discuss each of the plays in this chapter, you might want to consider focusing primarily on one element in each particular play, having students read, for example, *Hedda Gabler* to foreground questions about character; *Pygmalion* for structure; *Hamlet* for stages, sets, and setting (especially since this would allow you to foreground questions about the similarities and differences between theatrical conventions in Shakespeare's day and in our own); and *The Little Foxes* for tone and theme.

<hr>

LILLIAN HELLMAN

The Little Foxes

PLANNING IDEAS

- A good lead-in to this play is *A Streetcar Named Desire.* Even if you're not having your students read Williams's play, Elia Kazan's fine film version offers an effective point of comparison between Blanche DuBois in *Streetcar* and Birdie in *The Little Foxes.*
- As the "Commentary" (below) suggests, Hellman's play also works well when read and discussed alongside *Hamlet* and/or *The Cherry Orchard.*
- Have a group of students do some research on Lillian Hellman. What were her political convictions? She wrote this play in 1939. Does the play reflect in any way the social or political circumstances of that time?

COMMENTARY

While much less complex than *Hamlet, The Little Foxes* is in some ways structurally and thematically similar. The Old South/New South dichotomy in Hellman's play roughly mirrors the Medieval/Modern tension informing Shakespeare's; both reflect the passing of an agrarian, paternalist society and the uneasy emergence of a more individualist culture. Moreover, in both cases a protagonist—the title character in *Hamlet* and Regina in *The Little Foxes*—has been denied something that is arguably his or hers by right (in Hamlet's case the kingship and in Regina's—whose name, interestingly, means *queen*—a share in the family fortune). Both protagonists assert will and imagination to do battle with powerful antagonists. In doing so, Regina and Hamlet both do things that are at best morally dubious and at worst despicable.

In Hellman's play, the modern, or New South, mentality is, of course, represented by Ben, Oscar, Regina, and Leo Hubbard, characters who each take materialistic individualism to new heights in his or her scheme to secure to the largest share of the fortune to be made in the deal with William Marshall. Fittingly enough, of course, that deal centers on importing northern industry, substituting the qualities associated with Chicago, which Regina calls "the noisiest, dirtiest city in the world," for the "horses" and "azaleas" of the agrarian Old South. Such a mentality involves valuing the bottom line above all else, including beauty and art. As Marshall says of himself, "I've never heard of anything but brick houses on a lake, and cotton mills." Northern industry, then, the play insists, is inseparable from "northern" values, including both materialism and the ruthless individualism embodied in the competition among the Hubbard family and in the family's impeding dissolution at the end of the play and expressed in Marshall's comments on the difference between the Hubbard family and his own: "That is very pleasant. Keeping your family together to share each other's lives. My family moves around too much. My children seem never to come home." In Hellman's play, such individualism and materialism combine to render the people of the "New South" incapable of seeing other human beings as anything more than tools to be used or obstacles to be gotten around, whether they be the "poor ignorant niggers" whom the Hubbards "chea[t]" in order to earn their fortune, the daughter whom most of the family is willing to marry off to her amoral cousin, or the husband whom Regina happily watches die.

Through the character of Birdie, most obviously, Hellman portrays the Old South mentality as instead focusing on family and on tradition—or, as Marshall puts it "keep[ing] together"—and on the kind of concern for the well-being of others that is reflected in Birdie's desire that her husband stop shooting the animals that might provide food for the poor, in her wish to save Alexandra from the machinations of the rest of the family, and in her genuine joy at Horace's return. Fittingly enough, Birdie herself makes clear that these values are themselves an "old-fashioned" product of family tradition when she describes her own mother's anger at, and contempt for, people like the Hubbards, "who killed animals they couldn't use, and who made their money charging awful interest to poor, ignorant niggers and cheating them on what they bought," and her father's refusal to "let anybody" at Lionnet "be nasty-spoken or mean." But Lionnet also represents more than the kindness and concern for others that Hellman via Birdie associates with the Old South; for Birdie the plantation—with its "smooth" lawn, "zinnias and red-feather plush," its organ, and the "nice coat of paint" her father insisted it get every year— also embodies a lost emphasis on the importance and value of beauty for its own sake reflected in the fact that her parents went "all the way to Europe just to listen to music." And, as Birdie's memories of playing music with Horace and the contents of his safety box suggest, both the love of beauty and of family and tradition are values that he once shared and that he has rediscovered through his illness (fittingly enough, heart disease); as Horace himself puts it, "My 'thinking' has made a difference."

Obviously, however, in this battle between old and new mentalities, the old is as doomed as Horace himself is; for "After all," as Ben explains, "this is just the beginning. There are hundreds of Hubbards sitting in rooms like this throughout the country. All their names aren't Hubbard, but they are all Hubbards and they will own this country some day. We'll get along." And, as his remarks also suggest, this conflict and the triumph of the Hubbards is a national, rather than regional, phenomenon, the Old South in Hellman's play merely representing the last bastion of the values and way of life that Hellman seems to suggest were once shared by all: as Marshall puts it, "you Southerners occupy a unique position in America." That idea is reinforced in the play by the way in which Hellman depicts the defeat of the Old South way of life not as the result of the importation of northern values, but as a result of internal tensions and conflicts. After all, as the Hubbards themselves make clear, the business deal with Marshall is merely the culmination of a "long story," a story of the triumph of "Hubbardian" values over those of the southern aristocracy. As Ben says to Marshall, "To make a long story short, Lionnet now belongs to *us*. . . . Twenty years ago we took over their land, their cotton, and their daughter."

Clearly, the play's sympathy lies with the way of life represented by Birdie and her memories of Lionnet, however doomed; but the play also suggests the seeds of that doom lie in the southern aristocracy itself, whether because, as Ben puts it, their love of tradition and pride in their own values made them "Too high-tone to try" to "adapt" to a world changing before their eyes or because they weren't able and willing to fight to preserve their own way of life in the face of that change, an idea eloquently expressed by Addie: "Well, there are people who eat the earth and eat all the people on it like in the Bible with the locusts. Then there are people who stand around and watch them eat it. . . . Sometimes I think it ain't right to stand and watch them do it." As if enacting that very problem, Birdie responds to Addie by wishing once again that "we could only go back to Lionnet" and then reaching for a drink.

QUESTIONS FOR DISCUSSION

CHARACTER

1. Many different alliances are formed among the characters in this play. One central alliance is that between Birdie, a mistreated, childish woman; Addie, a black woman; Horace, an invalid; and Alexandra, a young woman. What do these characters have in common? Why is their support of each other threatening to Oscar, Ben, and Regina? What constitutes the bonds among these last three characters? Is it family loyalty? Greed? What kinds of loyalty do they have for each other?

2. How do parents treat their children in the play? Can we see the reproduction of women like Birdie and men like Oscar and Ben in the characters of Alexandra and Leo? How would you direct Alexandra's character? Does she show any independence? Why is Leo so ineffectual? Contrast Birdie with Regina. Both women are the products of southern culture. How do the men in the play treat the women? What is Birdie's relationship to the past? What myths and dreams does she rely on? In what ways does the play examine the past lives of the family members?

STRUCTURE

1. As the anthology suggests, plays (like other literary texts) often center on a dramatic conflict between the values represented by different characters and/or groups of characters, each of which must "at one point or another see[m] to have a chance to triumph." How, then, might you describe the central conflict in *The Little Foxes*? How does Hellman convince you that each side has "a chance to triumph"? At what points in the play does the energy shift from one side to the other? How is the conflict resolved at the end of the play? Does one side win or is the conclusion more complex than that? Why does Hellman suggest things end the way they do?

2. What's the effect and significance of the play's division into three acts?

STAGES, SETS, AND SETTING

1. What's the effect and significance of the fact that *The Little Foxes* takes place entirely within Regina Hubbard's home?

2. Hellman gives very precise descriptions of the setting, even specifying that the action of the play opens in the spring of 1900 (a fact that Ben makes much of later). What is the significance of that specificity, particularly when it comes to time? How would you stage the play to bring Hellman's setting to life for the audience?

3. What economic and social changes were taking place in the American

South in 1900? How does the play reflect these changes? What aspects of the prewar South do the various characters want to preserve? Which are they anxious to discard?

TONE

The anthology points to one moment in the play's second act when tone becomes especially important to "alter[ing] the meaning of the [characters'] words," and then goes on to illustrate how tone instead underscores the meaning of the characters' words in a specific moment in *Pygmalion*. At what other points in Hellman's play does tone seem especially important, whether because it reinforces or alters the meaning of the characters' words? Why might it be important, for example, that Hellman insists that Addie speak "softly" when she remarks, "Sometimes I think it ain't right to stand and watch them do it"?

THEME

1. Think again about the way in which you described the central conflict of *The Little Foxes*. Does this description seem an effective statement of the play's theme? If not, how might you re-word it so that it does?
2. To what extent does the theme of Hellman's play seem specific to the South and/or to the early twentieth century? To what extent doesn't it?

SUGGESTION FOR WRITING

At least two characters in Hellman's play—Ben and Addie—suggest that the southern aristocracy itself was responsible for its own defeat at the hands of people like the Hubbards, whether because—as in Ben's view—aristocrats like Birdie were "too high-toned" to "adapt" or because—as in Addie's view—they simply "stood and watched" as things went downhill. Write an essay in which you explain whether and how the play as a whole supports either or both of these views.

BERNARD SHAW

Pygmalion

PLANNING IDEAS

- Before assigning the play, have all the students read a good translation (such as the Loeb edition) of Ovid's brief Latin account of the Greek myth of Pygmalion in his *Metamorphoses*, and divide the class into groups to report on Renaissance retellings of Ovid's version. Two groups will simply compare the Loeb translation to sixteenth- or seventeenth-century ones (Arthur Golding's *Metamorphoses* [1567] or George Sandys's *Ovid's Metamorphoses* [1626]); the others will compare the Loeb translation to a Renaissance commentary on the story (the one from William Caxton's *Ovid, His Book of Metamorphose* [1480], or *Tottle's Miscellany* [1557], or John Marston's *The Metamorphosis of Pygmalion's Image* [1598], or Carel van Mander's *Painter's Manual* [1604], or the one following Sandys's translation). In each case the idea is to see what is changed or emphasized in the Renaissance version, to comment on how the emphases reflect the culture in which they were written, and to speculate on how the Pygmalion myth might be told today. After discussing the play return to the exercise, concentrating on how Shaw's version differs from any of the others. The goal is to give students some sense of five layers of artistic tradition: that of an Ancient Greek myth, a Latin interpretation of that myth, a Renaissance interpretation, an early twentieth-century one, and a late twentieth-century one.

- Have students watch the 1941 film version starring Wendy Hiller and Leslie Howard (whom students might know as Ashley in *Gone With the Wind*). Have each student write a one-paragraph response explaining one thing he or she would have done differently if acting in or directing the play. An alternative is to show in class the scenes that are exclusive to the movie, the ones marked off in our text with asterisks, and to discuss what the scenes add to or detract from the artistic integrity of the stage version. Or have students compare Shaw's *Pygmalion* to Lerner and Loewe's *My Fair Lady* (which is available on videotape and in a 1975 Signet paperback, where it is published alongside *Pygmalion*).

- After the students have read the drama itself but not the narrative epilogue, spend some time in class speculating about what happens next. Then, as a lead-in to the first writing suggestion in the textbook, have the class read and discuss Shaw's epilogue. In this case the question of whether to trust the tale or the teller is a fascinating one.

- To give the class a better sense of phonetics, pair students, each student with someone from a different geographic background, and have each transcribe at least a hundred-word paragraph of the other's speech. It works to use the phonetic alphabet at the bottoms of dictionary pages, but if one of Shaw's pet projects is to be fully appreciated, it is even more fruitful for students to develop their own phonetic spellings: for example, AH-ee for a midwestern I, and just AH for a southern one. An alternative is to have the class phonetically transcribe the lyrics of a popular song (country and rap work well.)

- To fill in a few of the details of the Victorian/Edwardian scene, have students provide brief reports on the following: Pre-Raphaelitism, William Morris, Edward Burne-Jones (these first three all associated with Mrs. Higgins), the fin-de-siècle Decadent Movement, Oscar Wilde (especially his witty aphorisms; see *The Importance of Being Earnest*), and the Bloomsbury Group. And while footnotes are not necessary to appreciate the play, here are a few terms with which Shaw expected his audience to be familiar but that may no longer be well known or that have changed their meaning: in Shaw's England a *slut* was a filthy (and perhaps impudent) girl—not necessarily a sexually promiscuous one; a *dustman* was a garbage man; a *navvy* did heavy manual labor, especially digging; *bloody* was a much more scurrilous curse word than it is today (hence the severity of Mrs. Eynsford Hill's response to Clara's outburst); *shew* meant (and was pronounced) the same as *show*; when Higgins says, "It dont matter, anyhow," he is not being ungrammatical, purposely or otherwise; the usage was acceptable. And it is of course *Scylla and Charybdis* that Doolittle butchers as "the Skilly of the workhouse and the Char Bydis of the middle class."

COMMENTARY

Part of the reason Bernard Shaw's *Pygmalion* provides an ideal chance to discuss "the whole text" is that the play presents such an artful blending of received tradition, character exposition, plot development, and social commentary. Since it begins with a myth and provides a compellingly ironic modern theatrical version of that myth, which in turn has been made into a popular movie (not to mention the musical-comedy spinoff *My Fair Lady*), and since our text includes not only the scenes exclusive to the movie but also the narrative epilogue, sorting through all the generic layers demonstrates not only what is peculiar to the stage but also how drama can shade into myth, into cinema, and into narrative prose.

Shaw claims in the preface that his *Pygmalion* is "intensely and deliberately didactic." And so it is—but not always as transparently as he implies. The clear target of the play is the class system, and the clearest statement of the ideal comes from Higgins: "The great secret, Eliza, is not having bad manners or good manners or any other particular sort of manners, but having the same manner for all human souls: in short, behaving as if you were in Heaven, where there are no third-class carriages, and one soul is as good as another." Fair enough, most American students are likely to think. But ask them to think about whether Higgins really lives up to the ideal he claims for himself. Does he really treat Eliza as well as he treats, say, Pickering? His mother? While he can be refreshingly blunt with anyone, Higgins would hardly hurl at the Colonel the kind of abuse to which he subjects Eliza. And can you imagine hearing him call Mrs. Higgins a "presumptuous insect"? The fact is that Higgins treats Eliza as an animal or an object most of the time, and his treatment of her is a function of her socioeconomic background. He *says* to her, "Remember that you are a human being with a soul and the divine gift of articulate speech," but he himself seldom remembers the fact. (Ask the class whether the speech serves Eliza or Higgins himself.) There may not be a touch of irony in Higgins's reply to Eliza's insistence that she is a "good girl": "Very well, then, what on earth is all this fuss about? The girl doesn't belong to anybody—is no use to anybody but me." Not only does he assume that a girl can be a belonging; he implies that her proper destiny is to be used.

The women, though, are on to him. Mrs. Pearce, Mrs. Higgins, and Eliza herself all object to his treatment of her; all three actually *behave* as though a Cockney flower girl should be accorded the dignity proper to all human souls. When Mrs. Higgins suggests that Doolittle financially support his daughter (he has recently been "delivered . . . into the hands of middle class morality" by the Wannafeller Moral Reform World League), Higgins flies into a rage—not that Eliza can be bought, but that he has already bought her: "She doesn't belong to him. I paid him five pounds for her. . . . Either youre an honest man or a rogue." Doolittle's reply should be disarming: "A little of both, Henry, like the rest of us: a little of both." But Higgins is too self-righteous to acknowledge his own fallibility. He again insists that he bought Eliza, fair and square, and upon learning that she is upstairs says that he will "fetch" her down.

Even Pickering shares something of Higgins's obtuseness, his refusal to think of Eliza as fully human. While Pickering is aware that "the girl has some feelings," he is just as surprised as Higgins to learn that Eliza is upset at being used as a guinea pig and then, after the experiment, simply discarded. When he hears that she has thrown Higgins's slippers at him, Pickering is without clue as to the reason: "But why? What did we do to her?" He does end up treating Eliza kindly, but even this genial character helps the play dramatize the depth of the divisions among the classes and between the sexes.

In part through a witty exchange centering on the five-pound blackmail, "middle class morality" comes in for some rough treatment in this play. When Higgins offers ten pounds instead of the five requested, Doolittle turns down the greater sum on the ground that "Ten pounds is a lot of money: it makes a man feel prudent like; and then good-bye to happiness." With witty inversion worthy of Oscar Wilde, Shaw has Doolittle assure Pickering that the five pounds will be put to good use: "Dont you be afraid that I'll save it and spare it and live idle on it. There wont be a penny of it left by Monday. . . . Just one good spree for myself and the missus, giving pleasure to ourselves and employment to others, and satisfaction to you to think it's not been throwed away. You couldnt spend it better." Doolittle also turns down Higgins's half-serious offer to remake him into a successful politician or preacher, saying that politics, religion, social reform, and "all the other amusements" are not for him.

Pygmalion takes occasional swipes at the upper class as well as the middle—most obviously in the central plot device of Eliza's successfully passing herself off as a duchess. At the embassy party Higgins's ex-client Nepommuck proudly asserts his royal lineage and claims that Eliza too must be of royal Hungarian descent. When Higgins asks how he knows, Nepommuck replies, "Instinct, maestro, instinct. Only the Magyar races can produce that air of divine right, those resolute eyes. She is a princess." The fun comes in knowing what to make not only of Nepommuck but also of the aristocratic Host and Hostess, who immediately swallow the whole story.

The play's attack on class is relentless, but on reaching the somewhat troubling conclusion, students are likely to be more interested in matters of structure than of theme. Why does Shaw not provide the match between Higgins and Eliza that he has set us up to expect? After all, we expect verbal banter between two such healthy, attractive adults to signal sexual attraction just beneath the surface of the dialogue—as it does in the case of, say, Beatrice and Benedick in Shakespeare's *Much Ado about Nothing*. And Shaw provides signals in the text that this is exactly the game he is playing: after the embassy party Higgins says to Eliza, "Most men are the marrying sort (poor devils!); and you're not bad-looking: it's quite a pleasure to look at you sometimes." Given the conventions of the comedy of manners, in which witty verbal exchanges go hand in hand with sexual exploits, and given what we know about Higgins, it doesn't take a psychoanalyst to deduce that Higgins is masking his sexual attraction for Eliza with the disclaimer that the "marrying sort" are "poor devils" and the backhanded compliment that Eliza is "not bad-looking." This, with the admission that "sometimes" Eliza is "quite a pleasure to look at," seems to tip Higgins's hand. We know what he does not want to admit to her and perhaps not even to himself: he is in love with her. Why else would the thought of Freddy drive him into such derision? And why would Eliza fall so precipitously into Freddy's arms unless she were pushed there by her true love's rebuffs? Doesn't the play *demand* that Higgins and Eliza get together in the end?

But Act V ends with the somewhat hollow sound of Higgins's laughter as he contemplates Eliza's marriage to Freddy. A little light may be shed on the situation by biographical detail. It seems that Shaw had a crush on an actress who had become Mrs. Patrick Campbell by the time she starred as Eliza in the first production of *Pygmalion*. The two had had a somewhat tempestuous relationship, as do Higgins and Eliza, and she had led him on for a while. In the end, though, she had married a much younger man. The playwright's depiction of Freddy as a bumbling weakling, coupled with Higgins's derisive laughter at the end of the play, may thus be read as Shaw's revenge on his rival. If Shaw's epilogue is right, though—if the pairing of Higgins and Eliza should appeal only to those whose imaginations are "enfeebled by their lazy dependence on the ready-mades and reach-me-downs of the ragshop in which Romance keeps its stock of 'happy endings' to misfit all stories," then the details from the playwright's life may be moot. Regardless of any personal motive on Shaw's part, one could argue, the playwright is in control of his material. We may *want* to see Higgins and Eliza paired up, but the artistic integrity of the play demands otherwise.

Since part of the play's artistry involves reversals of expectation, Shaw's flouting the requirements of Romance and the Comedy of Manners may be part and parcel of his artistic project. If the genre insists that witty wordplay is really foreplay, then Shaw will craft a new genre. If, in our post-Freudian age, we are likely to read *all* human intercourse as ultimately sexual (can we even hear the word *intercourse* and not think *sex?*), then Shaw will teach us otherwise. If, as heirs to the sexual permissiveness of the 1960s and 1970s, which has been somewhat tempered of late (or has it?) by the spread of AIDS, we are likely to conclude that two healthy, consenting adults jolly well ought to hop into the sack (perhaps taking proper precautions), then Shaw will tell us that our destiny is something higher than that. In short, we may not like the ending, but that is precisely the point: the playwright does not want us to.

Yet for many readers Shaw's epilogue seems disingenuous; given the psychological complexity of both Higgins and Eliza, there seems to be something perverse in Shaw's insistence that Higgins means exactly what he says: that he is a confirmed old bachelor who has no time for romance. And it seems naive to take at face value Higgins's statement to his mother, "Oh, I cant be bothered with young women. My idea of a lovable woman is somebody as like you as possible." Is there *nothing* Oedipal going on here? True, Higgins may be trying to butter up his mother; he has, after all, come to ask a favor. But Shaw's epilogue takes the statement seriously—as though any sensible man in Higgins's position, and with a mother like his, would find young, attractive women simply bothersome.

One possibility for helping make sense of the play remains to be mentioned: that in Shaw's view *Pygmalion* centers not on the love interest (or the absence thereof) but on phonetics. True, the rather arcane discipline of phonetics has implications about class division: part of the point of the play is that how we talk determines the way we are treated. And, of course, how we talk is largely determined by social class. But for a great many readers in the 1990s, Higgins's passion for phonetics seems an interesting aspect of his odd, passionate personality: an incidental element in the play rather than its focus. Shaw may be serious, though, when he says in the preface that the play's "subject" is phonetics. After all, his passion for the science was as strong as Higgins's. In the early years of the twentieth century, to those who shared this passion (and there were more than a few) it really seemed possible that an army of trained phoneticians could virtually wipe out social injustice: that normalized speech (supported by phonetically correct spelling) would play no small part in ushering in a utopian age. Hence Shaw's boast in the preface that although phonetics "is esteemed so dry," *Pygmalion* "has been an extremely successful play, both on stage and screen, all over Europe and North America as well as at home." Surely, though, in his more lucid moments a playwright as astute as Shaw knew that what people were flocking to see was not a play about phonetics but one about two fascinating characters whose lives intersect in a way that makes for good theater.

QUESTIONS FOR DISCUSSION
CHARACTER

1. When Doolittle's presence is announced, Higgins says, "Send the blackguard up." Pickering replies, "He may not be a blackguard." Higgins answers, "Nonsense. Of course he's a blackguard." Why does Higgins assume so? Is he right?
2. What is Shaw up to in having Doolittle call politics, religion, and social reform "amusements"?
3. When Higgins wants to make sure Doolittle will not return after the initial five-pound payment, he orders Doolittle not to stay away but to return often: "Stop. Youll come regularly to see your daughter. It's your duty, you know. My brother is a clergyman; and he could help you in your talks with her." Why does Higgins say what he says? Do you suppose he really has a brother in the clergy?
4. Higgins says to his mother, "I know I have no small talk; but people dont mind." A little later, when the Eynsford Hills have stopped by, Clara says, "*I* havnt any small talk. If people would only be frank and say what they really think!" Higgins replies, "Lord forbid!" Why does Higgins say this? Is he being inconsistent with his own beliefs? What is the force of the italicized *I* in Clara's line?

STRUCTURE

Certainly it strains credulity that Higgins and Pickering run into each other at the portico of St. Paul's Church just as the former is about to leave for India to meet the latter, who in turn has come to London to meet the former. Would Shaw know that believing such a chance encounter is a stretch? If so, what is he up to here?

STAGES, SETS, AND SETTING

Are Shaw's stage directions more for the reader or the actor? For example, can an actor make as much as a reader out the statement, *"Eliza's beauty becomes murderous"?* What about the fact that Mrs. Higgins is *"long past taking the trouble to dress out of the fashion"?*

THEME

Can you make sense of Shaw's usage of apostrophes? Why do some contractions get them while others do not? Higgins says, for example, "Youre her father, arnt you? You dont suppose anyone else wants her, do you? I'm glad to see you have some spark of family feeling left. She's upstairs." The reason is clear enough in a case like *its* versus *it's*; one is a possessive pronoun and the other a contraction for *it is*. The apostrophe needs to be there for clarity. But why *I'm* and *She's*? (Hint: leaving the apostrophe out of a contraction like *don't*, as Shaw does, can't lead to a misreading.

I'd, though, gets an apostrophe in Shaw's system. What is the difference between *don't* and *I'd?*)

SUGGESTIONS FOR WRITING

1. In Act II Higgins says to Eliza, "Well, dont you want to be clean and sweet and decent, like a lady? You know you cant be a nice girl inside if youre a dirty slut outside." Is Higgins right? Can Eliza not be a "nice girl inside" without his help? Is she better off in the end having met Higgins than she otherwise would have been? (Note the exchange in Act IV when Eliza says that before she met Higgins, "I sold flowers. I didn't sell myself. Now youve made a lady of me I'm not fit to sell anything else. I wish youd left me where you found me.") How does the idea of clean or dirty insides and outsides relate to the larger concerns of *Pygmalion?* Write a four-page essay that addresses these questions.
2. When Pickering asks Doolittle, "Have you no morals, man?" Doolittle replies, "Cant afford them, Governor." Write an essay of three to five pages that explains how the play comments on this exchange.
3. Near the end of the play Higgins delivers a speech that makes Eliza call him a "cruel tyrant." Higgins says, "If youre going to be a lady, youll have to give up feeling neglected if the men you know dont spend half their time snivelling over you and the other half giving you black eyes." Reread the whole exchange, and take either Higgins's side or Eliza's. Using the tone and diction that your character would employ after having calmed down, write a two-page letter to the other character explaining your position more fully.

HENRIK IBSEN

Hedda Gabler

PLANNING IDEAS

- To help students appreciate the difference between the stereotype and the fully developed character, I spend the last few minutes of the session before the first one on *Hedda Gabler* with the class divided into four groups. Each generates a list of as many attributes as possible for one of the following types: the Absentminded Professor, the Lady's Man, the Ice Queen, and the Lecher. Each group is assigned one character to report on after reading the drama. Group 1, "How is Tesman more than an Absentminded Professor?"; 2, "How is Loevborg more than a Lady's Man?"; 3, "How is Hedda more than an Ice Queen?"; and 4, "How is Brack more than a Lecher?"
- Ibsen uses set design, movement, and gesture in highly symbolic ways

to define and reinforce the impressions of Hedda's character and situation that we derive from the dialogue. I like to tackle the function of set design first. I divide the class into four groups and assign the members of each group to prepare, before class, a written analysis of setting and stage direction for one of the four acts. I also ask them to provide a simple sketch of the set Ibsen describes at the beginning of the play, altered appropriately for the act they've been assigned to discuss. Because the setting of *Hedda Gabler* remains virtually the same throughout the four acts, you don't have to ask the class to cope with several different set descriptions and sketches. I've sometimes found students don't want to take the time to visualize settings properly when they're reading drama, but the setting of *Hedda Gabler* demonstrates for most of them that understanding setting and the characters' movements within it can provide a key to unlocking mysteries of character and theme.

When I make this assignment, if I have not already done so in earlier classes, I give a brief explanation of staging terms such as center stage, stage right, upstage, etc. I remind students to pay close attention to the use of props, lighting, color, and Ibsen's instructions about the appearance and movements of the characters. They should also note the degree to which the setting changes from the beginning of one act to its end. I suggest, too, that they review the act immediately before theirs (unless, of course, they are assigned to analyze the first act) to see how the setting and the characters' positions in it may have altered from one act to the next. From a description of these elements, they should derive an explanation of their significance—especially in relation to Hedda. You might explain the procedure by drawing attention to the details outlined in "Commentary," below.

COMMENTARY

When the curtain rises on Act I, flowers are everywhere—in vases, bowls, lying on furniture. We soon discover that Aunt Juju is responsible for the profusion, although Mrs. Elvsted has sent one of the bouquets. At the beginning of Act II, Mrs. Elvsted's flowers appear in a vase downstage, close to the audience, but many of the other flowers are gone. (It may be well to ask why Mrs. Elvsted's flowers should be so prominently displayed.) The room seems less colorful, less full of life. It is clear that Hedda, with her concern for taste, propriety, and control, has banished the flowers from the rooms. You may want to ask your students what this suggests about her.

Between the close of Act I and the opening of Act II Hedda's piano has also been removed from the front room and placed (as we find out later) in the back room where her father's portrait hangs. An "elegant" writing table, a bookcase, and a small table have been added to the furnishings— also, we are certain, on Hedda's orders. You might ask students what the significance of the movement of furniture might be, judging from the information we receive in Act I. It isn't clear whether these additions have been purchased or simply moved from other parts of the house, but we know from Act I that the Tesmans can't afford new furniture, and we suspect Hedda has bought it anyway.

At the beginning of Act II the French windows are again open. (Hedda had drawn the drapes in Act I to shut out the bright morning sun streaming in through the windows.) However, Hedda's posture near the open windows loading a revolver makes them less inviting than they were in the first act(!). As the various student groups report on their scenes, a pattern should begin to emerge. The French windows, the back room, the stove, and General Gabler's portrait will be mentioned more than once. You may want to establish headings on the blackboard for the most important of these scenic elements and chart what parts they play in each act of the work. This will help students realize how closely setting is tied to characterization and meaning.

During class discussion about setting and stage movement, you might encourage each group to plot Hedda's movements in relation to the other characters. Brack enters through the back door, for which Hedda criticizes him, yet she is willing to entertain him alone and to be physically near him. Why is he allowed this freedom and proximity? Hedda also allows Loevborg to be near her—in fact she places herself near him—but she avoids physical contact with Aunt Juju and George (at least while on stage). What are we to make of this? And what are we to make of Hedda's actions toward Mrs. Elvsted—the hair stroking, the frenzied embrace? What difference might it make in the play had Hedda's father been a living presence rather than a portrait? How might his presence change our perception of Hedda?

I try to bring out, sometimes by assigning one act at a time, that we keep framing and reforming our opinions and feelings about Hedda, following a pattern of assessment and reassessment. Another way to talk about *Hedda Gabler* is to examine this pattern, as I have suggested in the text. I sometimes start by asking the class what we find out about Hedda before she appears on stage. Then I ask to what degree the impression they receive by secondhand report—through Aunt Juju, Bertha, and George—is confirmed or altered by Hedda's entrance. For example, Aunt Juju recalls that Hedda was always surrounded by admirers and calls her "The beautiful Hedda Gabler!" However, when Hedda enters, she appears elegant and tastefully attired but cold, self-contained, and merely attractive, not beautiful. I like to ask the class why Aunt Juju might call Hedda beautiful if she really isn't. More than one reason, and more than one acceptable reason, usually emerges.

As the class works through the play, their catalog of impressions might end up something like this: When we first hear about Hedda, we expect someone lovely but difficult. When Hedda appears on stage, the latter impression is borne out; the former is not. Hedda seems haughty and bruises Aunt Juju's feelings by mistaking her new hat—bought "for Hedda's sake"—for the maid's. Later we discover that Hedda knew the hat was Aunt Juju's and insulted the generous older woman on purpose. At this point we probably think Hedda is a pretty nasty piece of work, but when we discover her attraction to Loevborg and her idealistic dreams, we may excuse her to ourselves, imagining that her lost romance with Loevborg is at the source of her frustration and despair. Our sympathy may shift briefly in Hedda's direction. Then Hedda challenges Loevborg to drink, despite his problems with alcohol, and we wonder if she is malevolently destructive. As it turns out, Hedda is hoping to wrest Loevborg from Mrs. Elvsted's influence and vicariously live out her own aspirations of nobility through him. While Hedda never has our full sympathy, Ibsen presents her in such a way that we never feel comfortable condemning her entirely. You may want to ask your students what they would direct an actor playing Hedda to emphasize so as to create the most sympathetic portrait possible. How might an actor convey that Hedda is a victim of society? A tragic heroine? The class might want to consider whether they believe the play can work if the audience has absolutely no sympathy for Hedda.

QUESTIONS FOR DISCUSSION

CHARACTER

1. Hedda admits to Judge Brack that she purposely mistook Miss Tesman's hat for Bertha's. What in Hedda's character accounts for this cruelty? Why does Hedda behave in such an aloof manner to her new relative?
2. In her refusal to call Miss Tesman "Auntie Juju," Hedda is maintaining strict formality much as one would in addressing a friend or relation by *vous* instead of *tu* in French. Examine other occasions when the use of informal names is important, as when Hedda mistakenly remembers Thea's name as Tora, becomes upset when Loevborg calls her Hedda, and finally addresses George by his Christian name.
3. The first act ends with the apparent revelation that Hedda is the woman from Loevborg's past. What does this tell us about Hedda that we did not already know? What new expectation does it arouse?
4. What purpose does the opening scene of Act II serve besides making Judge Brack's intentions perfectly obvious? What new information do we learn? What does it tell us about Hedda's character? Why does the scene open with a pistol shot?
5. Hedda complains to Judge Brack of her honeymoon, on which she went six months "without even meeting a single person who was one of us, and to whom I could talk about the kind of things we talk about." What kind of things do they talk about? Distinguish the layers of Hedda's boredom with the world.

6. Why did Hedda draw out Loevborg and act as his "confessor" when they were young? Why does Loevborg mistake the action for love?
7. Discuss Judge Brack's character and his role in the action of the play. What segment of society does he represent? What segments do Hedda, George, and Loevborg represent? What qualities or abilities does the judge possess that allow him to create the "triangle"?

STRUCTURE

1. The scenes between Hedda and Loevborg, then Hedda, Mrs. Elvsted, and Loevborg in Act II are central to the themes of cowardice and courage. Define the quality of Hedda's cowardice and Mrs. Elvsted's courage and how they find expression in Loevborg.
2. Why is Loevborg upset when Hedda reveals Mrs. Elvsted's concerns for him in the city?
3. Compare and contrast Hedda's envy of Mrs. Elvsted and George's envy of Loevborg. How do they conflate in the identification of the manuscript as Loevborg's and Thea's "child"?
4. Why does Hedda insist that Loevborg end his life "beautifully"?
5. Act IV opens on a note of formal mourning. In the course of the act which characters die, and what responses do their deaths elicit from the others?
6. Hedda protests Brack's hold over her because she is "not free." What freedom does Hedda require, and how does she employ it?
7. Brack's last line is an echo of Hedda's when she tells Mrs. Elvsted that "People don't do such things" regarding Loevborg's mystery woman who shot at him. How is the echo meaningful?
8. Is Hedda's suicide an act of cowardice or courage? What is your reaction to it?

STAGES, SETS, AND SETTING

1. The portrait of Hedda's father, General Gabler, often dominates the set in productions of *Hedda Gabler*. Why is the portrait given such a central position in the set, and how is the general's "presence" important to the play's action?
2. Miss Tesman drops some broad hints about Hedda's pregnancy early in the play. How obvious are they in the text, and how obvious should they be in production?

SUGGESTIONS FOR WRITING

1. Act III of *Hedda Gabler* concludes with the burning of Loevborg's manuscript, and with that action earlier references to "burning" resonate with new meaning. Write an essay that traces the development of this image by examining as many references to burning as possible. Pay particular attention to the moments when Hedda says that Loevborg

will return with a "crown of vine-leaves in his hair. Burning and unshamed" and when George is shocked by Hedda's apparent ardor, surprised that "you're burning with love for me, Hedda."

2. Read the fascinating article by Elinor Fuchs titled "Mythic Structure in *Hedda Gabler*: The Mask behind the Face," in the journal *Comparative Drama*, vol. 19 (fall 1985), pp. 209–21. Then reread the drama, paying particular attention to passages that bear on the relation between the characters and their mythological counterparts. Write a four-page essay that summarizes Fuchs's argument in the first two pages and, in the last two, uses textual evidence that Fuchs does not mention. Point out how this evidence either supports or refutes Fuchs's theory.

WILLIAM SHAKESPEARE

Hamlet

PLANNING IDEAS

- In view of *Hamlet's* complexity, it may be useful to put your students, individually or jointly, in the position not of Polonius but of Hamlet and ask them, at the beginning of the hour, to write out in twenty-five to a hundred words a summary of the play. In *Writing about Literature* we have offered three such summaries of *Hamlet*:

  1. A young man, seeking to avenge the murder of his father by his uncle, kills his uncle, but he himself and others die in the process.
  2. In Denmark, many centuries ago, a young prince avenged the murder of his father, the king, by his uncle, who had usurped the throne, but the prince himself was killed, as were others, and a well-led foreign army had no trouble successfully invading the decayed and troubled state.
  3. From the ghost of his murdered father a young prince learns that his uncle, who had married the prince's mother, much to the young man's shame and disgust, is the father's murderer, and he plots revenge, feigning madness, acting erratically—even to the point of insulting the woman he loves—and, though gaining his revenge, causes the suicide of his beloved and the deaths of others and, finally, of himself.

  The first emphasizes the revenge motif, the second adds a political dimension, and the third introduces the possible Oedipal overtones. If you are lucky, your twelve, twenty, or thirty-five students will offer a variety of readings. They may cover most of the orthodox and unorthodox ways of looking at the play or at the hero—as an intellectual, a man incapable of decisive action, a man troubled by obesity, a homo-sexual, or a man too much in love with his mother. There are bound to be a number of different readings or summaries with differing emphases. It might be profitable to have one read out and ask how many others are similar and group similar ones together, perhaps even asking the students involved to come up with a joint summary. Then you might ask for a summary that seems radically different, have it read and see if that reading has adherents, etc. If there is surprising homogeneity from the beginning, there will still be enough to generate useful class discussion in trying to determine the best wording or add-ing the most essential matters left out.

- If you cannot get enough fruitful controversy going with student sum-maries, you may want to offer a provocative reading of your own, such as the following: "Hamlet is a shrewd, ambitious politician whose actions are morally reprehensible, and Claudius is not much more than another politician who has eliminated his opponent and is in turn eliminated." Since virtually all readers and viewers find Hamlet a com-pelling character (what makes this moping, melancholic figure so attractive, by the way?), the notion that Hamlet is *merely* a shrewd, immoral politician is bound to generate disagreement. As the twenty-five thousand (no kidding) studies of *Hamlet* indicate, in fact, it is reductive to call the title character *merely* anything. With that caveat in mind, I'll explore in more detail below some of the play's political implications.

COMMENTARY

HAMLET: Do you see yonder cloud that's almost in shape of a camel?
POLONIUS: By the mass, and 'tis like a camel, indeed.
HAMLET: Methinks it is like a weasel.
POLONIUS: It is backed like a weasel.
HAMLET: Or like a whale?
POLONIUS: Very like a whale.

Some of our students, I am afraid, feel as if we were playing Hamlet to their Polonius when we offer a reading or interpretation of a piece of literature—particularly when the work is as complex, awe-inspiring, and, for some, hard to follow and comprehend as *Hamlet*. One way of making sense of the great sweep of its structure is to see it as mirroring the tur-bulence surrounding Europe's transition from a medieval to a modern sensibility. In this reading Old Hamlet embodies the passing medieval order. Or perhaps *embodies* is too strong a word: the old king is a mere ghost, straining to maintain authority as he makes his son's feudal obli-gation plain. Young Hamlet quickly promises to exact his revenge, but the old order's reliance on paternal authority and the sacredness of one's vows has lost its hold on the prince. Young Hamlet is, after all, a sort of protoscientist: he will attempt to observe data objectively, test the evidence, and draw his own conclusions. But the world in which he finds himself will not allow him to do so.

Shakespeare is here concerned with questions of succession to power and the virtues appropriate to private and public persons. Because Hamlet is a prince, he has no real choice about his career, about when he is to become king, about whom he is to marry; Shakespeare and his audience shared these and other notions about the meaning of being a prince. We see Hamlet at a difficult juncture in his life. He has been brought up to rule, and we suspect with Fortinbras that he could be very effective. Yet at the height of his maturity (he is thirty), he has been denied his rightful place. Even before he sees the Ghost of his father, Hamlet is behaving in a peculiar manner. He dresses in black and goes about the court with his eyes on the ground, deliberately calling attention to himself and his plight.

In the Shakespearean tragic world, order is the supreme value, and those who sin against it will ultimately be punished. Claudius is the king, Hamlet the subject; therefore, Hamlet's ambition becomes morally ambiguous. He wants to fulfill what he sees as his God-given destiny to become king of Denmark, but to do so he must commit the most disorderly act he can think of, to kill a king. He does not even have the excuse of Bolingbroke in *Richard II* that the king is doing a bad job. Claudius seems to be an effective ruler, however much Hamlet despises him. Hamlet can justify action against him only if he can prove that the king came to the throne in a criminal way. The Ghost appears to offer definitive evidence, but Hamlet is aware that the devil can ensnare an unwary victim with such "proof." And even if the Ghost is telling the truth, the crucial question remains: Does Hamlet have the right to take the law into his own hands and punish the usurper, or should he wait for the power that guides the universe to restore order in its own way? Can order be restored by disorderly acts?

Hamlet is a superlative actor, as I believe Shakespeare thinks that every successful public figure must be. The image that the public has of him is as important to him as it is to Claudius, who is afraid to act against him directly because of his popularity. As Hamlet admits to his mother, the ostentatious acts of public mourning are "actions that a man might play." With evidence provided by the Ghost as his justification, he then proceeds to act out for the people his perception of the situation. Using the analogy of the king as the head of the body that is the state, he makes his madness into the figure of an illegitimate kingship. The disorder in his head represents the disorder in the kingdom. The plan is politically skillful; but Claudius, the play's other consummate politician-actor, sees through it at once.

The appearance of the actors provides Hamlet with a chance for the even more theatrical coup of the play-within-the-play. He proceeds from metaphor to stage representation, but he chooses to make the murderer the nephew of the king as a warning to Claudius. Again Claudius understands and takes the only action he sees as possible, to arrange the death of Hamlet. The situation reverses itself, and Hamlet sees immediately what Claudius has in mind. Throughout the play there is a struggle between two evenly matched politicians—a technique that adds to the power of the play.

In addition to the question of succession, the play engages the problem of the relation between private and public virtues. This is done through a series of foils to Hamlet and through the description of his relation to Ophelia. The primary foil is Fortinbras, who like Hamlet is a prince, the son of a dead king. The contrast between him and Hamlet is a problem even to Hamlet himself, and it is Fortinbras who is ultimately able to restore the order and assume the kingship in a proper manner. Fortinbras is more fortunate than Hamlet in two ways: he can curb his ambition, and he is in the right place at the right time. Therefore, he succeeds where Hamlet fails. The part of Fortinbras is frequently cut in performances of the play, but doing so undermines some of what the play says. At the other extreme from Fortinbras are Rosencrantz and Guildenstern, the epitome of the ordinary subjects:

GUILDENSTERN: On Fortune's cap we are not the very button.
HAMLET: Nor the soles of her shoes?
ROSENCRANTZ: Neither, my lord.

They call attention to Hamlet's inability to accept the role of subject. Between these two extremes is Laertes, the person in the play most like Hamlet. They are the same age, both of noble birth. Both have a preference for living away from home, and both are expert fencers. Both are called on to avenge their fathers' deaths, and both love Ophelia. They finally confront each other at Ophelia's grave. Laertes seems very much what Hamlet would have been if he had not been a prince. Finally there is Horatio, the good private man. Hamlet understands his virtue, but knows that it is not for him.

Hamlet's relation to Ophelia also underlines the contrast between private and public virtue. If Hamlet had been a private individual, the play seems to suggest that he and Ophelia would have married. Yet Hamlet chooses to use her for political ends just as if she meant nothing to him. His cruel treatment of her in Act III, Scene 1 (not to mention his public abuse of her in the play-within-a-play scene) is shocking and effective as a sign of madness, because it is such an incongruous way for a well-bred prince to treat a virgin of the court, and particularly for this prince to treat this virgin. As in the scene with his mother, Hamlet paints himself as unbelievably callous. It is arguable that only a man who puts political necessity above everything else would do such things. But see discussion question 8 under "Character," below.

QUESTIONS FOR DISCUSSION

CHARACTER

1. What does Laertes' warning to Ophelia suggest about the character of Hamlet?
2. Hamlet tells his mother in Act I, Scene 2, that his manner of dress and his deportment are "actions that a man might play." In which scenes does Hamlet seem to be "acting," playing a public role?
3. What issues are presented in Hamlet's soliloquies that can be presented otherwise only with difficulty? Do any of the other characters have soliloquies?
4. Hamlet uses a trick of speech of repeating a word or phrase several times. Do any other characters have individual speech mannerisms? What purpose might such mannerisms serve?
5. From time to time Hamlet makes unfavorable remarks about the king's behavior and appearance. Do the other characters make such remarks? To what extent should Hamlet's remarks influence the choice of an actor to play Claudius?
6. Compare the situation of Hamlet and young Fortinbras at each of the times Fortinbras is mentioned or appears. The character of Fortinbras is frequently omitted in performance. Why is it easy to cut the role? What does such a cut do to the play?
7. As his death approaches, Hamlet asks Horatio, first, to see that his actions and death are properly reported and, second, to use Hamlet's name and posthumous influence to bring about the election of Fortinbras as king. How is the order of the two requests significant?
8. Is it necessarily true that "only a man who puts political necessity above everything else" (see "Commentary," above) would behave the way Hamlet does, especially toward women? Are there other explanations? Is there any explanation that seems complete, or does each leave something out?

STRUCTURE

1. Although the eldest son of the king was customarily chosen to succeed his father, the monarchy of Denmark is depicted in the play as elective. Why was Hamlet passed over in favor of his uncle in the election that preceded the opening of the play?
2. What are the circumstances of Horatio's return to Elsinore from Wittenberg? How does the timing of his arrival contribute to the exposition?
3. Describe Hamlet's behavior, his appearance and actions, before he learns even of the appearance of his father's Ghost. To what action does it prompt Claudius, of which we learn in Act II, Scene 2? Why does the king permit Laertes to return to Paris and at the same time refuse Hamlet's request to return to Wittenberg?

4. Is Hamlet surprised by the revelations of the Ghost?
5. When Rosencrantz and Guildenstern appear, Hamlet correctly interprets the king's strategy in sending for them. Does he see through other moves made by Claudius? What does this suggest about the relation between the two antagonists?
6. Why are the players introduced? Why is the king in the play-within-a-play murdered by his nephew?
7. The climax of the play occurs when the king stops the play-within-a-play. What has Hamlet learned and how does it affect his course of action? How is Claudius affected by events of the scene?
8. What prior actions bring about the death of Polonious? The Madness and death of Ophelia? What later actions result from the death of Polonius?
9. What is the purpose in terms of dramatic structure for the scene between Hamlet and Horatio at the beginning of Act V, Scene 2?
10. What dramatic functions are served by having both Horatio and Fortinbras alive and on stage at the end of the play?

STAGES, SETS, AND SETTING

1. The Shakespearean stage featured a large central acting area, around three sides of which members of the audience sat or stood. In addition, there were, very probably, an elevated area above the main stage, a recessed area upstage, and one or more trap doors. If you were staging *Hamlet* on such a stage, how would you treat the various scenes? What use would you make of the subsidiary acting areas?
2. As a member of the company that performed his plays, Shakespeare seems to have written a part for a particular actor on occasion. What part in *Hamlet* might have been written for a specialist in sententious old men? For a specialist in effeminate young men? For another kind of specialist? Are there scenes in which the actor's part seems to have been lengthened or emphasized to take advantage of his specialty?
3. In several speeches Hamlet talks about the theatrical practices of the period and the purposes of the drama. To what extent, if any, can we assume that Hamlet's comments represent Shakespeare's own ideas? What are some of the particular abuses that Hamlet cites? Have they disappeared from theatrical practice?
4. It was not until after Shakespeare's day that women acted on the public stage in England. In acting companies like his (The Lord Chamberlain's Men, and after 1603 The King's Men) boys who had not reached puberty played the women's parts. Does *Hamlet* refer to this? How would such a practice affect the writing of a play? Of this particular play?
5. When the play ends, what should be the position of Hamlet's body relative to the other actors? How should it compare with his relative

position at his first appearance? How would your staging affect the audience's experience of the play?

THEME

1. A central image in the play is the comparison between the body and the state, the "body politic." Such an image pattern assumes an analogy between two levels of reality, the body and the state. One occurrence of the image is in the Ghost's account to Hamlet of his death by having poison poured in his ear and of the report of his death as an abuse of the ear of Denmark. Can you find others? In terms of the image of the body politic, why does Hamlet choose to feign madness?
2. There are a number of references in the play to warfare and weapons and to hunting, fishing, and trapping. Do these constitute meaningful image patterns that contribute to the internal complexity of the work? Are there other such groups of references?
3. In a number of his plays Shakespeare seems to be commenting on the relation between virtues appropriate to public life and those appropriate to private life. In some cases—for example, Brutus in *Julius Caesar*—they seem so distinct as to be irreconcilable. Laertes touches on this issue in his advice to Ophelia. Are there other places where it is treated? What does the play say about the distinction?

SUGGESTIONS FOR WRITING

1. Some writing about tragedy talks about the concept of *hamartia*, the notion that the central character's fate is brought about by a tragic flaw or failing of character. Hamlet's speech beginning "So oft it chanceth in particular men" suggests something similar. Does Hamlet have such a tragic flaw? If so, name it and write a paper supporting your contention.
2. Another idea common in writing about tragedy is that the hero is guilty of *hubris*, an overstepping of the bounds of his destiny and the destiny of humanity. This suggests some universal moral principles beyond the control of human beings. Write an essay that discusses the play's handling of such principles.
3. In 1600 (the approximate date of *Hamlet*) Queen Elizabeth I was sixty-seven and had no direct heirs. England had been subjected to wars and rebellions over the succession to the throne for the preceding two centuries. Write an essay that shows how these historical circumstances are reflected in *Hamlet*.

READING/WRITING IDEAS FOR UNDERSTANDING THE TEXT

ESSAYS

Since this chapter focuses on several dramatic elements at once and on the way they work together in a particular play, it provides a fine opportunity to discuss with students how one can use these various elements to create different kinds of essays about drama. As a result, an open-ended essay assignment that allows students to approach a particular text from any one of a number of different angles might work well, especially if you help students build up to that essay by assigning exercises aimed at getting students to recognize the different "angles" they might take and the different essay types they might produce as a result. If you choose to go this route, you might want to create a series of exercises modeled on those outlined in the reading and writing ideas for Chapters 7 and 20 of the guide.

Or you might do something similar, while providing students with a bit more direction, if you allow them to choose their topic from a list of prompts, each of which reflects an element-specific approach. The following prompts are examples of two kinds that might work well for this kind of assignment, the first being both text- and element-specific, the second focusing only on element and allowing students to choose the text on which they would like to focus. You might also add to this list by choosing appropriate prompts from the writing suggestions in this chapter of the anthology and the guide. (And, again, it might also be helpful to consult the more in-depth discussion of essays on character in "Reading/Writing Ideas for Chapter 3," on tone in "Reading/Writing Ideas for Chapter 13," and on theme in "Reading/Writing Ideas for Chapter 6" and "Reading/Writing Ideas for Chapter 13.")

Sample Character Assignments

- Though easily overshadowed by his scheming in-laws and the lively, if pathetic, Birdie, Horace clearly plays a key role in *The Little Foxes*. In a short essay, analyze Horace's character, explaining how his character seems to have evolved over time and how and why his character (and its development) are so significant to the play as a whole.
- One might see *Pygmalion* as a play that is about character in the sense that it explores the relationship between characteristics we might call "external," such as dress or speech, and those we might call "internal," such as moral values. Write a short essay in which you explore exactly what the play ultimately seems to say about the nature of "character" and the relative importance of internal and external characteristics.
- *Hedda Gabler*, as its title suggests, is primarily a study of the character of Hedda herself, and a key question the play seems to pose about her is whether Hedda or the social conventions of her time are responsible for her moral depravity. In a short essay, consider both sides of this question to formulate your own argument about which, if either, view the play ultimately advocates.
- Obviously critics have spent a great deal of ink debating the strengths and weaknesses of Hamlet's character and the extent to which he is himself responsible for the tragedy that unfolds in Shakespeare's play. But critics have had a great deal less to say about the character and role of the minor characters, such as Laertes, Horatio, and Ophelia. Write an essay in which you explore the character and role of one of these minor characters. What worldview or values does this character seem to represent? What is this character's significance to the play as a whole?

Sample Structure Assignments

- As the anthology suggests, plays (like other literary texts) often center on a conflict between the values or worldviews represented by different characters or groups of characters, each of which must "at one point or another see[m] to have a chance to triumph." In a short essay, describe and explore the conflict that you see as central to either *The Little Foxes, Pygmalion, Hedda Gabler*, or *Hamlet*. How exactly does the playwright convince you that each side in the conflict has "a chance to triumph"? How is the conflict ultimately resolved and what does the play suggest about the causes behind this outcome?
- Choose any of the four plays in this chapter and write an essay in which you explain the significance of your particular play's formal structure. Why do you think the play is divided into acts and/or scenes in the way that it is? What is the effect or significance of these divisions?
- The ending of Shaw's *Pygmalion* seems to defy all of our expectations, expectations that seem to derive both from the specific nuances of this particular play and from our experience of romantic and comedic drama and fiction in general. In the process, however, Shaw's play brings to the fore more general issues about the structure of plays, particularly the nature and function of endings. Write an essay in which you explore the significance and/or effect of the way any one of the playwrights in this chapter chooses to end his or her play.

Sample Stages, Sets, and Setting Assignments

- Write an essay describing the ways in which you would stage any of the four plays in this chapter if you were going to "update" that play to make it appealing and mean-ingful to a contemporary audience. In doing so, focus primarily on how you would dress the stage and the characters, on explaining the effects and significance of your decisions, and on justifying those decisions with reference to the text of the play. *Or,* if you don't think your play can or should be updated but must be staged so as to be faithful to its original setting, make an argument that explains why and how this is so and how you would dress the stage and the characters in order to realize the author's original vision.
- Write an essay in which you explore and explain the significance of the particular setting of any of the four plays in this chapter. In doing so, remember to focus on both major and minor aspects of setting. Why, for example, is it important that *The Little Foxes* is set in the spring of 1900, as Hellman insists it is, that all of the action of the play takes place within Regina Hubbard's home, and that Hellman emphasizes that the furniture of that home is "expensive" but "reflects no particular taste"?

Sample Tone Assignment

- Choose one line from any of the plays in this chapter that you think is especially crucial to the play and especially interesting in terms of tone. Write an essay in which you explain exactly why and how tone is crucial to the meaning of this line and why and how the line itself is so central to the play as a whole.

Sample Theme Assignments

- One might say that the theme of both *Hamlet* and *The Little Foxes* centers on the conflict between old and new mentalities, whether those be the medieval/modern in Shakespeare's play or the Old South/New South in Hellman's. Write an essay in which you explore this conflict/theme in one of these two plays. What characterizes each mentality? What are the strengths and weaknesses of each? What attitude does the play encourage you to adopt toward each? How is the conflict resolved at the end of the play, and how does the play rationalize or explain that resolution?

- One might say that social class is a key issue in *The Little Foxes, Pygmalion,* and *Hedda Gabler,* however differently the issue is treated in each play. Write an essay in which you explore either Hellman's, Shaw's, or Ibsen's treatment of the issue: what worldviews or values are associated with the various classes in the play? What attitude does the play adopt toward these different worldviews or values? What does the play suggest about the nature and function of class in the society it depicts—in, for example, determining individual character and/or the relations between characters?

Exploring Contexts

27

THE AUTHOR'S WORK AS CONTEXT: ANTON CHEKHOV

In some ways the three Chekhov plays in this chapter could hardly be more different—*The Bear* representing the exuberant young playwright's foray into no-holds-barred farce; *The Cherry Orchard* displaying the mature playwright's full complexity; and *On the Injurious Effects of Tobacco*, published just one year before *The Cherry Orchard*, combining many of the elements of the two longer works into a richly suggestive tragicomic monologue. In other ways, though, one can see Chekhov's characteristic concern with the vanity of human pretense and with what Ivan Nyukhin calls the "nonsense, pettiness and vulgarity" of contemporary Russian life carrying through from one play to the other. Both *The Bear* and *The Cherry Orchard* feature a confrontation between a boorish man (some translators title the shorter play *The Boor* or *The Brute*) and an aristocratic woman whose powerful sexuality lies just beneath the surface, whereas *On the Injurious Effects of Tobacco* might be seen to reverse or complicate this gendered polarity through the characters of Nyukhin and his vulgar, shrewish wife. Exchanges of money figure prominently in all three plays; all three also satirize society's have-nots and the haves, who are nominally their betters.

Chekhov clearly meant the two shorter plays to be farces, but it may come as a surprise that he referred to *The Cherry Orchard* as a farce as well (and sometimes simply as a comedy). But Constantin Stanislavsky, Chekhov's great director at the Moscow Art Theatre, wept when he read the play (as some readers might be tempted to do after finishing *On the Injurious Effects of Tobacco*). Insisting that *The Cherry Orchard* was essentially tragic, Stanislavsky staged it accordingly. In fact both of these later plays resist simple categorization. Although no character comes off as particularly admirable, several, including the ridiculous Nyukhin himself, have the truly compelling moments of epiphany we usually associate with tragedy. Side by side with these moments, though, are dashes of the broad humor that inform *The Bear*.

ANTON CHEKHOV

The Bear

PLANNING IDEAS

- *The Bear* presents good opportunities to discuss various aspects of theatrical production in a relatively short and simplified form. Assigning a brief written analysis of character may be useful for setting up a discussion that moves to visual, aural, and staging effects. Chekhov's descriptions of Mrs. Popov and Smirnov are very brief; have your students describe each character more fully, detailing the way both would present themselves at first appearance. Some questions of definition: how would you have Mrs. Popov display her ritualistic fondness for grief? What clothes, gestures, or facial expressions might provide a contrast to her gloomy words? How subtle does the contrast need to be to make the play work theatrically?
- Assign several groups of students to discuss how they would direct the part of the play in which Mrs. Popov and Smirnov have their first encounter, especially the short passage of dialogue from Mrs. Popov's question, "Can I help it if I've no money today?" to her exit. Does one character speak more loudly than the other? Should both shout? Whisper? Hiss? In a speech of about twelve lines, Smirnov reacts to Mrs. Popov's refusal to give him the money he needs. How should the actor playing Smirnov deliver this speech? Should he speak his lines calmly, but with a hint of suppressed frustration? Force his words through gritted teeth? Scream? Should the tone and volume of his words remain constant or change? If the latter, which specific points in the speech mark changes of approach, even subtle ones? As each group reports their directorial instructions for the meeting between Mrs. Popov and Smirnov, I like to encourage debate over the appropriateness of their decisions and ask them what actor and actress they would like to see cast in their production.
- Dividing the class into groups assigned the same task is one way to proceed, but *The Bear* also lends itself to another sort of division: have one group responsible for stage props, another for costumes, a third for blocking and stage movement, a fourth for the gestures and intonation of actors, and have them work on a short scene together. The discussion can't go far before the students see how intertwined the questions are and how someone will have to provide clear direction based on a certain interpretation of the play.

COMMENTARY

The Bear is hardly what we would call a realistic play. A man pops up without prior warning and demands payment of a debt in cash on the spot. The woman from whom he requests payment has gone into absurdly deep mourning after the death of her cruel and faithless husband. She treats the stranger's desperate plea for payment with infuriating nonchalance. Challenged to a duel, the woman must request that her challenger, the stranger, teach her how to fire a pistol. The two characters hate each other almost on sight but end up in a clutch a few hundred lines later. Much of the play's comedy derives from the absurdity of the characters' responses and actions. You may want to ask your students to suggest other, additional sources of comedy. Answers might include dramatic irony (given the conventions of comic drama, we know Mrs. Popov and Smirnov will get together long before they do), manipulation of sexual stereotypes, the use of stock characters (the timid but interfering servant, the warring lovers-to-be), and physical humor (Smirnov's inadvertent destruction of the furniture, the primping motif).

Comedy—a farce like *The Bear* no less than more subtle comic theater—depends on timing, gesture, and careful modulation of tone and atmosphere. Many actors and directors say comedy is more difficult to produce than is tragedy because these variables are so difficult to master. To get students thinking about how to stage this comedy successfully, I like to ask them about the comic elements in the play. When we read *The Bear* initially, do we realize it is going to be a comedy from the very first line? How far into the play must we read before we know we're in comic territory? You may want to ask how the first scene might be staged to create a humorous effect from the very beginning (as the curtain rises and before Luke speaks). How might the room be lit? Should it be bright, or should it be so dark and shuttered that the footman stumbles over Mrs. Popov's footstool? Chekhov gives no instructions about background music. Should there be music? If we decide there should be, what sort of music would enhance the comic effect of the scene? Someone may suggest, and rightly, that there are advantages to delaying the comic effects— that there might be good reasons to hold back on these effects early in the play, then build to a crescendo at the end. You might want to have the class debate the advantages and disadvantages of a relatively subdued opening. If a student does not bring it up, you might ask what kind of audience your performance is intended for and introduce here the concept of performing comedies in different ways—with broad humor or subtle or both or neither—for different audiences, and perhaps introduce questions on the function of audience and (for the dramatic text) the analogy with reader response.

Any audience will quickly realize the comic possibilities of the meeting between Mrs. Popov and Smirnov—she, young, genteel, attractive, and melodramatically determined to live out her life as though dead; he, crude, passionate, and bursting with life force. She is disillusioned with men; he is disillusioned with women. Since the plot of the play is almost entirely predictable, you may want to ask your students how it maintains our interest. Why do we want to read it through to the end? We all love a happy ending, and traditional comedy offers to fulfill our desire that things end well, but what are the play's other inducements?

QUESTIONS FOR DISCUSSION

1. When Mrs. Popov describes her late husband, what details provide clues that she will find Smirnov attractive? And in Smirnov's long misogynous speech, the one in which he declares, "I can't be fooled any more, I've had enough," how do we know that he's really fooling himself?
2. If you were directing the play, how would you stage the exchange in which Smirnov teaches Mrs. Popov how to use the gun?
3. Chekhov once said that if a playwright introduced a pistol at some point in a play, it had to go off before the final curtain. Why isn't that the case in *The Bear?*

On the Injurious Effects of Tobacco

PLANNING IDEAS

- Though *On the Injurious Effects of Tobacco* is printed second in the anthology in deference to the fact that it chronologically preceded *The Cherry Orchard*, you may want to consider having students read and discuss this play only after they have read the later one, thus allowing them to come into this very brief and enigmatic monologue with a clear sense of typical Chekhovian themes and techniques.
- Though the text of Chekhov's play clearly implies that Madame Nyukhin does not ever actually appear in the play, you might want to have students debate the effects of including her in their production, perhaps having her appear in the audience when Nyukhin first mentions her arrival. What would be the effects, both positive and negative, of such a staging decision? What and how might it contribute to the play? How exactly might it take away from the play? How might Madame Nyukhin's appearance, manner, etc. be staged so as to maximize the benefits and minimize the costs?

COMMENTARY

Though clearly the briefest and most enigmatic of the three Chekhov plays printed in the anthology, *On the Injurious Effects of Tobacco* is nonetheless a quite complex and subtle piece and one that becomes all the more obviously so when read after, and in the light of, *The Bear* and *The Cherry Orchard*. For like *The Cherry Orchard*, *On the Injurious Effects of Tobacco* brilliantly interlaces farce and tragedy, while also—in the process—embodying many typical and quite serious Chekhovian themes and that typically complex Chekhovian mixture of contempt and sympathy for the *dramatis personae*. And, indeed, it is the very economy of the play, the way in which Chekhov manages to embody so much in a single character and a single scene, that makes *On the Injurious Effects of Tobacco* so compelling.

For in this play even more obviously than in *The Bear* and *The Cherry Orchard*, theme is inseparable from character—in this case, the character of Ivan Ivanovich Nyukhin and, by implication, of his wife. And, ironically, it is in some ways the wife's character that comes across most strongly in the play: domineering and "money-grubb[ing]," Madame Nyukhin embodies the "nonsense, pettiness and vulgarity," as well as the materialistic individualism, that seems to characterize the ascendant bourgeoisie in all of Chekhov's plays, an idea also signaled by the fact that she is mistress of a boarding school (or at least a school "not unlike something of that sort") that presumably helps girls from ambitious families (like her own) attain "something" "not unlike" the accomplishments of their social betters. While the triviality and shallowness of such accomplishments is signaled by the fact that Nyukhin himself teaches "mathematics, physics, chemistry, geography, history, solfeggio, literature," "dancing, singing, and drawing," Nyukhin's constant references to things being "not unlike" others—he calls his articles and lectures "not unlike scientific," for example—indicates the extent to which everything in a world ruled by Madame Nyukhin and her ilk simply apes the genuine article. It is only in such a world, after all, that Nyukhin, a self-declared tobacco user, would be called on to lecture "on the injurious effects of tobacco."

The fact that he ultimately cannot do so, of course, indicates the extent to which Nyukhin's entire performance constitutes a kind of protest against the values of his wife and the social order she represents, the lecture itself the only outlet available to a man so isolated and defeated by that order that he has "no one at all to complain to," no one to take his tears seriously. That protest obviously comes to a climax toward the end of the play, as Nyukhin's sense of the tragedy of his own life—"such sorrow that I can't possibly express"—utterly overtakes his wish to dutifully follow out his wife's orders, and he avows his desperate wish "to run away from this rotten, vulgar, cheap life, which has turned me into an old, pitiful fool, an old, pitiful idiot." Not accidentally, the only object or end Nyukhin can envision for himself is a return to nature and a moment of genuine appreciation of the real beauty that Madame and her ilk can never fathom. Thus when he imagines "stop[ping] somewhere far, far away in the field and . . . stand[ing] there like a tree, a post, a garden scarecrow, under the wide sky, and the whole night through, watch[ing] how the silent, bright moon is hanging over you," the conflict between himself and Madame Nyukhin begins to look very like that acted out in *The Cherry Orchard*, a play that pits an appreciation of the beauty of the cherry orchard against a purely economic view of it.

As this suggests, there is, at the heart of both plays, a real sympathy with the traditional worldview embodied here by Nyukhin, which does, indeed, seem "superior," "more clean and pure," and more "human," a sympathy that demands we see Nyukhin's submission to his wife as more tragedy than farce. At the same time, and in typically Chekhovian fashion, however, the play also forces us to see Madame Nyukhin (like Lopahin in *The Cherry Orchard*) as possessing a vitality, energy, and/or power, as well as a kind of sense, that Nyukhin (like Madame Ranevsky) lacks: however beautiful his vision, after all, the fact that Nyukhin can dream *only* of escaping (rather than changing) his world and that his dreams involve either stopping time or going backward into his "memories of . . . youth" renders that vision as "old, poor, [and] dilapidated" as his frockcoat and makes Nyukhin himself seem in some ways and in his own words "a fool, a nonentity."

QUESTIONS FOR DISCUSSION

1. How would you characterize the two worldviews represented by Nyukhin and his wife? What evidence do we have to support Nyukhin's contention that his wife and the worldview she represents is characterized by "nonsense, pettiness and vulgarity"? What is the significance, for example, of the fact that she runs a boarding school (or at least a school "not unlike something of that sort")? That she "doesn't want to give parties" and "never invites anyone to dinners"? What attitude does the play encourage us to adopt toward each of these characters and worldviews? In what sense, for example, is and is not Nyukhin himself "a fool, a nonentity"?

2. How specifically is the conflict between worldviews in this play like and unlike that in *The Bear* and/or *The Cherry Orchard*? How, in particular, does each play treat the subject of nature (which enters this play when Nyukhin describes his vision of escaping and "stop[ping] somewhere far, far away in the field")?

3. What is the significance of the topic of Nyukhin's lecture? Of the way in which he continually digresses from that topic? What's the significance or effect of the fact that Chekhov gives the play the same title as Nyukhin's lecture?

4. What's the significance or effect of Nyukhin's references to his daughters, particularly the fact that he refers to them as "her" (that, is his wife's) daughters? To occurrences of the number thirteen? To things being like or "not unlike" other things—as when he says his scientific articles are "not unlike scientific, as it were"?

5. Chekhov's letters, particularly that to D. V. Grigorovich, indicate that he, to some extent, saw himself early in his career as being much like Nyukhin in certain ways—as writing primarily for money (on behalf of his family), just as Nyukhin lectures for money, and as writing only half-seriously and/or "consciously," just as Nyukhin indicates he does

both through his inability to stick to the topic and through his references to nothing that he says mattering anyway. How might your interpretation of the play change if you see it in these terms, as in some fashion Chekhov's exploration of himself and his own "performance" as a writer? How might the setting of the play—in which the stage really is a stage—and the fact that the title of the play and the lecture are the same reinforce this interpretation?

The Cherry Orchard

PLANNING IDEAS

- Before reading the play, distribute a handout with isolated lines that could be read in a variety of ways, depending on the context. Examples: Trofimov's "A peasant-woman in the train called me a mangy-looking gentleman," Lopahin's "All must be as I wish it." Have the class demonstrate various ways of delivering the line, explaining in each case what context might justify such delivery. Then, after reading the play, ask how the same lines should be spoken. Discuss the question of how the actor ought to decide on the best reading in each instance.
- When Chekhov's *The Seagull* was first staged, the audience, used to melodrama and bombastic acting, hardly knew what to make of the play's subtle treatment of the complexities of ordinary life. So it laughed at what it thought was abysmally bad theater. It wasn't until Stanislavsky staged a production that the audience appreciated the play's nuanced seriousness. Have groups of students choose a brief scene from *The Cherry Orchard* that should be played seriously but that would invite laughter if misunderstood. Have each group stage the scene appropriately, and then discuss the techniques employed to make the staging work.
- Have students provide brief presentations on various cultural movements influencing Russian life in the nineteenth and early twentieth centuries. Examples: czarism, the emancipation of the serfs, Marxism, Darwinism, the Decadent Movement, Bolshevism.

COMMENTARY

Twice in *The Cherry Orchard* something happens that almost pulls the action out of the realm of naturalistic theater altogether: a distant sound like that of a string breaking seems to fill the whole sky. The first time, when Lyubov asks, "What is that?," Lopahin answers, "I don't know. Somewhere far away a bucket fallen and broken in the pits. But somewhere very far away." The exchange is instructive: even though Madame Ranevsky is the one whose fate has been decided, her response is open-ended. She asks a question. Lopahin at first admits his ignorance but then quickly offers a rational explanation. It's as though Lopahin were uneasy with this kind of mystery.

Even if we stick with Lopahin's explanation, the sound is haunting. Nor is the mystery of its origin diminished by the fact that it seems "very far away." Certainly by the time we hear it again, at the very end of the play, it seems far more than something happening in a distant mine. Probably it would be a mistake to go the way of Lopahin, to pin down the mystery to something specific. The sound may suggest the end of something we usually associate with an almost musical beauty, just as it may suggest the release of tension after a long strain. To be more specific than that, though, would be to make the same kind of mistake as pigeon-holing a play like this one in a particular genre.

Just as the snapping string is enormously evocative, Chekhov's language exhibits a wonderful economy, containing volumes in a few phrases. Take the very first comment on the setting: *"A room which has always been called the nursery."* Here Chekhov conveys a sense of tradition: presumably for as long as anyone can remember ("always") the room has been called "the nursery," and it is not just Lyubov or Anya or Gaev who calls it that; it simply *has always been called* by that name. The line, though, may also imply that the name is now somehow inappropriate. Are there no more babies? Has the room changed its function but kept its name? Is there something infantile about the unwillingness to admit that it is no longer a nursery, some hopeless desire to believe in the fertility and security that the name evokes? Or take a line like Madame Ranevsky's oft-repeated remark, "You're just the same as ever." She seems delighted that the nursery and the orchard and the other characters are just as they *always* were. But by this point we know that such things soon *will* change, regardless of her desires. The question is whether *she* will change—whether she will learn to accept the inevitable fate of the estate, and whether she will learn to recognize her version of the past—not to mention the present—as an idyllic dream.

Even in the family's straitened circumstances, Madame Ranevsky cannot abandon the habit of doling out money to strangers. She is fully aware that her habit is hastening the family's destruction, but she cannot seem to stop: "My poor Varya feeds us all on milk soup for the sake of economy; the old folks in the kitchen get nothing but pease pudding, while I waste my money in a senseless way." Why is it that she can't break the habit? Perhaps she provides a clue when she remarks to Lopahin, "I keep expecting something, as though the house were going to fall about our ears. . . . We have been great sinners." She says *we,* but she means *I;* it is really her own sins that bother her, as she says in her next line. She knows that she has done things wrong, but she fails to take full responsibility for making things right. Could her continued extravagance be a way of attempting to compensate for these wrongs? Are her financial and her moral prodigality somehow related? Does she hope, rather desperately, that maintaining the appearance of *noblesse oblige* will make her morally noble?

Such an interpretation would help explain her absolute refusal to do the one thing that might make the family financially solvent: cut down the orchard to make way for summer cottages. As though refusing that option were entirely noble, she says, "Villas and summer visitors—forgive me saying so—it's so vulgar." We may agree (as, very likely, did Chekhov). But Madame Ranevsky seems to think that her refusal is noble in every sense of the word—that her proud assertion of social nobility can somehow escape the charge of irresponsibility. Or consider her gratuitously biting response to Lopahin's innocent comment that he has recently seen a funny play: "And most likely there was nothing funny in it. You shouldn't look at plays, you should look at yourselves a little oftener. How gray your lives are! How much nonsense you talk." If such an outburst from such a generous soul seems surprising, it may seem so because she protests too much.

But Madame Ranevsky is not the only one who is overly sensitive about social position. When Dunyasha says that she feels faint, Lopahin replies, "You're a spoilt soft creature, Dunyasha. And dressed like a lady too, and your hair done up. That's not the thing. One must know one's place." There is no small irony that this comes from a *nouveau riche*, a peasant.

It is Lopahin who comes up with the most practical, but also the ugliest, plan for saving the family estate, a plan that involves destroying all the old buildings, including the ancestral home and the cherry orchard. Not that Lopahin is completely blind to the estate's beauty—only for him its beauty is so wrapped up in his own financial liberation that he is blind to the fact that his financial plans will destroy its beauty: "If my father and my grandfather could rise from their graves and see all that has happened! How their Yermolay, ignorant, beaten Yermolay, who used to run about barefoot in winter, how that very Yermolay has bought the finest estate in the world! I have bought the estate where my father and grandfather were slaves, where they weren't even admitted into the kitchen." Can one read the drama without sharing a sense of Yermolay's triumph?

Ever the practical man, it is Lopahin who tends to glance at his watch, who knows that the train pulls out in precisely forty-seven minutes. He has his flights of romantic fancy, but ultimately his triumph is one of crass practically over beauty. The mark of his crassness is his failure even to think of waiting until the train has pulled out before beginning to cut down the orchard. He agrees to delay the destruction for a few minutes, but he does not really see why.

Given Lopahin's practicality, however, why does he not make the eminently practical move of marrying Varya, of whom he is quite fond? One possibility is that he is smitten by Madame Ranevsky, to whom he says, "I do want you to believe in me as you used to. I do want your wonderful tender eyes to look at me as they used to in the old days. Merciful God! My father was a serf of your father and of your grandfather, but you—you—did so much for me once, that I've forgotten all that; I love you as though you were my kin . . . more than my kin." But surely a man as shrewd as Lopahin doesn't seriously entertain the prospect of a union with Madame Ranevsky. Her adopted daughter, Varya, however, is another matter. Lopahin doesn't seem to think of the choice as between the two women but between Varya and no one at all. He himself is mystified by his inability to act; yet he fails to make the proposal. Is a lingering class consciousness in play here? Does he subconsciously consider himself socially unworthy not only of Madame Ranevsky but also of Varya? In any case, his hesitation despite his intention to act mirrors Madame Ranevsky's inability to refrain from giving money away despite her knowledge of the consequences.

Varya herself also fails to make the connection between stated intent and actual behavior. Given her role as a woman in czarist Russia, she may not have the option of initiating a marriage proposal. But she conceivably could act on her repeatedly stated desire to join a convent—especially in light of Lopahin's failure to suggest marriage. When she tells Anya about her fondest wish, she says, "I would go off to Kiev, to Moscow . . . and so I would spend my life going from one holy place to another. . . . I would go on and on. . . . What bliss!" Even without knowing Varya very well at this point, we know better; anyone who indulges the notion that a monastic vocation is pure bliss is in the realm of fantasy, not thoughtfully planned action.

If Varya occasionally finds refuge in an imaginary world, others have even more active (and more frivolous) fantasy lives. Gaev is mentally playing billiards when he isn't offering an impassioned rhapsody to Nature or a bookcase; Epihodov indulges in histrionics about shooting himself.

Perhaps the most thoroughgoing fantasy is Trofimov's. In light of what we know about twentieth-century Russia and the Soviet Union, Trofimov's ideals take on a force that Chekhov himself could hardly have imagined.

Trofimov is not only fond of saying "Humanity is advancing" but also says "I am in the front ranks." And, apparently true to his advocacy of change, he himself has changed so much that at first Madame Ranevsky doesn't even recognize him. But the change is superficial; he is still a student, still a tireless talker. Trofimov imagines himself a champion of work in an age of the aristocracy's smug exploitation of workers; but as both Madame Ranevsky and Lopahin point out, he himself talks rather than works. He enjoys playing the role of the desperately poor student, but his identification with the truly poor is artificial. As Madame Ranevsky tells him, he hasn't really suffered and so cannot possibly comprehend the human sorrow that transcends class distinctions. Nor does he understand love. More than once he says of his relationship with Anya, "we are above love."

What does she think of that? At one point Anya suggests that Trofimov has destroyed for her the beauty of the orchard: "Somehow, Petya, you've made me so that I don't love the cherry orchard as I used to. I used to love it so dearly. I used to think that there was no spot on earth like our garden." Trofimov's reply is no mere restatement of his antiromantic sentiments; he delivers what is perhaps the play's most moving speech: "All Russia is our garden. The earth is great and beautiful—there are many beautiful places in it. [*A pause.*] Think only, Anya, your grandfather and great-grandfather, and all your ancestors were slave-owners—the owners of living souls—and from every cherry in the orchard, from every leaf, from every trunk, there are human creatures looking at you. Cannot you hear their voices? Oh, it is awful! Your orchard is a fearful thing."

Trofimov's image of the ghosts of former slaves looking out from the cherry orchard and demanding retribution stands in contrast to Firs's insistence that things were better in the old order. That the more conservative sentiment comes from a servant rather than a member of the upper class lends it some plausibility, as does Firs's firsthand recollection of the serfs' reaction to their emancipation: "I remember what rejoicings they made and didn't know themselves what they were rejoicing over." No doubt Firs is right that a good deal was lost, a good many things were forgotten, and plenty of new problems were created by the abolition of serfdom. But it is Lopahin, the successful son of a serf, who wryly puts Firs's wistful nostalgia in perspective: "Those were fine old times. There was flogging anyway."

In the end Firs is still in the house, more or less holding his own at the age of eighty-seven. But just as *The Cherry Orchard* refuses to glorify the changes sweeping across the country, the play offers no glorification of the faithful servant who endures in the midst of change; all his loyalty, as he himself remarks, amounts to nothing.

QUESTIONS FOR DISCUSSION

1. Early in the play Anya says of her mother, "How well I understand her, if only she knew!" Given the immediate context of the line, how is it ironic?
2. Should Firs's line "Now I can die" be played for laughs?
3. When Lopahin offers to get the family a loan so that they can build the summer cottages, he says, "Think of it seriously." Varya angrily replies, "Well, do go, for goodness sake." In light of the fact that Lopahin is trying to be helpful, why is Varya so angry?
4. Reread the exchange beginning with Gaev's "I won't speak. I'll be silent. Only this is about business." Varya responds; and after more explanation from Gaev, Anya does. Then Firs enters and addresses Gaev. In each case, how does the speaker's remark reveal his or her character? Which speaker makes the most sense? Which seems most deluded?
5. Gaev appears at times to be more willing than is his sister to face the painful fact that the family must sell the orchard. What other details suggest that Gaev is a realist? What details suggest that he is in fact *not* good at facing facts?

6. Just after Epihodov calmly remarks that he thinks he might shoot himself, Charlotta remarks, "Always alone, alone, nobody belonging to me . . . and who I am, and why I'm on earth, I don't know." Are these the stereotyped "stock" characters one would expect to find in a farce, or are there real human beings who say such things?

7. What does Gaev mean when he says, "I'm a man of the eighties"?

8. Lopahin offers Trofimov money, saying "I'm offering you a loan because I can afford to. Why turn up your nose? I'm a peasant—I speak bluntly." Trofimov replies, "Your father was a peasant, and mine was a chemist—and that proves absolutely nothing whatever." What is Trofimov's point here? Why does he turn down the money? Does the play as a whole bear out the idea that parentage means "absolutely nothing"?

SUGGESTIONS FOR WRITING

1. At times Chekhov's method of filling in background information seems stiff and artificial. In part to explain why Madame Ranevsky has been in Paris, for example, Chekhov has Anya say, "It's six years since father died. Then only a month later little brother Grisha was drowned in the river, such a pretty boy he was, only seven years. It was more than mamma could bear, so she went away without looking back." The speech might seem for the reader's benefit only—gratuitous for the characters in the play since they would already know about everything Anya mentions. Later in the play Madame Ranevsky covers some of the same ground: "[M]y boy was drowned and I went abroad—went away forever, never to return, not to see that river again." Write a three-page essay that focuses on such "set pieces" (Charlotta has more than one), explaining why they are more than artistically awkward ways of filling the reader in on background information.

2. On the evening of the estate's auction Madame Ranevsky remarks, "It's the wrong time to have the orchestra, and the wrong time to give a dance. Well, never mind." Write a one- or two-page essay explaining why throwing a party at such a time is and is not an appropriate thing to do.

3. When Trofimov says, "Humanity is advancing towards the highest truth, the highest happiness, which is possible on earth, and I am in the front ranks," Lopahin replies, "Will you get there?" Trofimov answers, "I shall get there. [A pause.] I shall get there, or I shall show others the way to get there." At this point comes Chekhov's stage direction, "[In the distance is heard the stroke of an axe on a tree.]" Focusing on this moment as well as others, write an essay of three or four pages explaining how the timing of Chekhov's stage directions comments on the surrounding dialogue.

4. Suppose a politically active friend wrote you a letter saying, "I've just found the clearest statement of revolutionary [or conservative; you pick] ideals in all literature: it is Chekhov's The Cherry Orchard." Write

a reply to your friend in which you build a case against the argument that the play is entirely revolutionary (or entirely conservative). Of course, your position will be stronger if you cite specific passages.

Passages from Letters

QUESTIONS FOR DISCUSSION

1. In his letter to A. N. Pleshcheev dated October 4, 1888, Chekhov remarks that he does not wish readers to read "between the lines" of his work with an eye toward labeling him "either as a liberal or a conservative." Based on your reading of three Chekhov plays, why might a reader be tempted to label him one or the other? Does Chekhov manage to resist these labels? If not, why not? If so, why and how?

2. In a later letter to Pleshcheev (October 9, 1888), Chekhov remarks that his works do contain "the element of protest" in that they "protest against falsehood from . . . beginning . . . to . . . end." Where and how might you see this protest in the three plays you've read? How does Chekhov seem to define *falsehood* or what specific kinds of "falsehood" does he seem to explore and criticize?

3. In his October 27, 1888, letter to A. S. Suvorin, Chekhov claims that the artist's task is not to offer "the solution of a problem" but instead "to formulate the questions correctly," leaving solutions and/or answers "to the jurors" or readers. What problems does Chekhov tackle in these three plays? Does he follow his own credo by exploring questions and problems rather than answering or solving them?

READING/WRITING IDEAS FOR CHAPTER 27

ESSAYS ON THE AUTHOR'S WORK AS CONTEXT

Among my favorite assignments, one that I have found both useful and enjoyable for students, is the assignment that asks them to write about "the author's work as context" or to produce what I call "multiple-text, single-author" essays. Students find this assignment instructive and gratifying for a number of reasons, not least the sense of accomplishment they get from feeling that they have become experts on something. Requiring students to make some use of the passages from Chekhov's letters included in the anthology adds even greater depth to the assignment, because it allows students to begin to use primary source material in a relatively painless way, allowing them (and you) to focus on questions about why and how writers use such material to make arguments without getting caught up in questions about how researchers locate it.

The multiple-text, single-author essay presents a series of useful challenges for student writers, especially when it comes to theses and structure. For that very reason, I always begin this assignment sequence by having students read multiple sample student essays to address questions about why one writes such essays, about what kinds of theses and structures tend to work, and about how writers decide which structures "fit" their arguments.

I have discovered over the years that such essays tend to employ one of three types of structures, and I generally try to provide students with sample essays that represent each of these types. Though I have yet to come up with satisfying names for these three structures, I can offer the following rough characterizations:

1. *The "side-by-side" or "simultaneous" structure,* in which a writer discusses all of the works by his or her author simultaneously. Within the body of the essay, topic sentences tend to be claims about the author and his or her work in general, and paragraphs include evidence from all or most of the texts under discussion. Obviously, this structure tends to work best when the writer has one overarching interpretation that fits all of the texts under discussion, when the stories all seem to fall into a single, basic pattern.

2. *The "serial" or "one-text-at-a-time" structure,* in which the body of the essay is divided into text-specific sections; the challenge is to craft very clear and careful transition paragraphs linking one section to the next. This structure tends to work best (or only) when students can show that and how one text somehow complicates the view of an author's work that might be suggested by another text.

3. *The "lens" structure,* in which a writer focuses primarily on one text, using it as a lens through which to look closely at the entire canon of the author's work, using references to other texts merely to support or amplify points about the focal text. This structure tends to work best when students see one text as particularly typical and/or revealing of an author's work.

TROUBLESHOOTING

Careful, thoughtful discussion of structure is key to helping students write truly successful multiple-text, single-author essays because the real danger is that such essays prove to be either incredibly repetitive (again in this text we see . . .) or incredibly incoherent, rambling through a series of similarities without really making connections between them or indicating their overall significance.

AUTHOR'S WORK AS CONTEXT–FOCUSED WRITING EXERCISES

1. Identifying and Describing Patterns in the Author's Work

The following is an exercise that has proved very helpful to my students as a way to generate ideas for essays about multiple texts by a single author. Indeed students often comment on this exercise in their end-of-term evaluations, citing it as their favorite.

Read the three Chekhov plays at least once, underlining quotations that seem significant to you. As you read, work not only to understand the individual plays but also to look for patterns across these texts, similarities that link them together into a coherent whole, make them part of a unified canon. Once you have finished, think more about these similarities, working to answer the following questions as if you were trying to capture for someone who hadn't read your author the essence of that author's work. You may well also want to make notes about which of the quotations you underlined in reading the stories might serve to illustrate or support the claims you make.

- How would you describe your author's typical **hero or heroine?** What makes them alike? What (internal and external) characteristics do they tend to share?
- Which hero or heroine seems most typical in light of your description? The least typical? Why?
- How would you describe and/or categorize the **other characters** whom the heroes or heroines encounter, or interact with, in the plays? Are there similar types? Do the plays tend to present characters who are foils to the main character, clear antagonists?
- Which character(s) seem the most typical? The least typical? Why?
- How would you describe the **problems or conflicts** that the heroes or heroines of these plays typically face?
- How would you describe the typical **plot and/or structure** of your author's plays?
- In terms of plot, conflict, etc., what's the most typical play? The least typical? Why?
- How would you describe the **setting** of these plays? The significance and role of the setting or environment (social, cultural, and/or physical) in the plays?
- In light of setting, which play is most typical? Least typical? Why?
- What's the overall **tone** or **mood** of these plays—the feelings they tend to evoke? How do they do so?
- What do you think are some of the central themes, concerns, problems, or issues articulated or tackled in these plays?

Taking all of these factors into account and without referring to any particular play, use this sheet of paper to narrate, outline, script out, or draw a map or flowchart that captures the basic features, action, elements, etc., of your author's work.

2. Generating Theses and Describing Structures

Because multiple-text, single-author essays do represent such a challenge to student writers in terms of structure, etc., I almost always have students who are writing such essays do an exercise before they start drafting in which they articulate at least two different possible thesis statements for the essay, describe exactly how they would structure each essay, and say a little bit about why and how each structure fits each particular thesis or argument. I usually leave it up to the students themselves to decide whether it would be more helpful to them to write an informal discussion of the essay for us to discuss or whether they want to write actual topic sentences, transition paragraphs, etc. Though students may well complain about having to plan more than one essay, I strongly recommend requiring them do so, and I assure you that they usually appreciate it later. With any assignment, I find that students almost always write better essays if they are forced to try out different thesis statements rather than settling for the first that comes to mind. And with this assignment in particular, outlining different essays can help students really get why and how different theses suggest different structures.

Because certain kinds of thesis statements simply work better for this kind of essay, I often give the students a formula for this thesis, requiring that their thesis statement be something like, "In [titles of plays], Chekhov explores the conflict between X and Y." Though this may seem ridiculous and reductive (to you and/or to your students), it is also incredibly helpful to them, especially in terms of helping them avoid the problems described in "Troubleshooting," above.

28

LITERARY CONTEXT: TRAGEDY AND COMEDY

Each of the two plays in this chapter admirably reflects its genre. *Oedipus the King*, model for the Aristotelian definition of tragedy that was to remain the formal ideal for centuries, depicts the hero/king's preordained violation of a universal law, his vain struggle against his destiny, and his acquisition of knowledge so painful that the appropriate mark of his enlightenment is the loss of his eyes. *The Importance of Being Earnest*, in contrast, defines its characters in terms of social roles, twits convention with some of the most sparkling humor in English literature, and in the end provides a wonderfully contrived resolution that reinforces the comic expectation of a happy ending replete with marriages.

SOPHOCLES

Oedipus the King

PLANNING IDEAS

- A few days before starting on *Oedipus the King*, divide the class into five groups and have the members of each read a Greek tragedy other than *Oedipus the King*. Group 1 might read Sophocles' *Antigone*; Group 2, Aeschylus's *Agamemnon*; Group 3, Aeschylus's *Prometheus Bound*; Group 4, Euripides' *The Bacchae*; and Group 5, Euripides' *The Trojan Women*. At the beginning of the discussion on *Oedipus*, each member of each group does a one-minute presentation on some aspect of the similarities or the differences between *Oedipus* and the other tragedy. (This assignment can be done in conjunction with the third writing suggestion described below.)

• Because virtually everyone in Sophocles' audience would have known the story of Oedipus, you might use this play to broach the topic of why one should bother to see or read a play the ending of which one already knows. You might relate an anecdote about one of Flannery O'Connor's first public readings of "A Good Man Is Hard to Find," a story about a southern family out for a drive in the country. O'Connor told her audience that the story ended with an escaped convict's shooting the entire family. With the ending revealed, she proceeded to read the story. Why would O'Connor do such a thing? What point was she trying to make with her audience?

COMMENTARY

Our students are faced with an uncertain world, and we see them groping toward contemporary oracles. Time and again they are forced to choose between equally unpalatable alternatives, without being able to find comfort in the knowledge that everything is foreordained, whether by the stars, or by a Calvinist God, or by the *moira* (fate) that rules the life of Oedipus.

In a different way, Oedipus was faced with such a situation when he visited the oracle at Delphi before the play begins. Informed that his fate was to kill his father and marry his mother, he saw two alternatives—to return home and realize his *moira* or to refuse to accept his destiny. When he decided on the latter, he refused to accept the limitations of his mortality, a refusal called *hubris* by Aristotle in his influential definition of tragedy. What happens to Oedipus as a result of his choice is an education in human limitation.

Nothing in the play is more theatrical and more significant than the contrast between Oedipus as he first appears and Oedipus as he appears at the end of the play. The first scene has a ceremonial or hieratic quality. The Chorus of Theban Elders is lamenting the plague when Oedipus appears and asks what is going on. He knows the answer; he has already sent Creon to Delphi for help. The question is part of a ceremony in which the king (or tyrant, as the Greeks called him, using the word differently than we do) allows his subjects to make requests of him and promises to help them. He sees himself as a king, a god on earth. He has conquered the Sphinx; surely he can conquer the plague.

What Oedipus does not realize is that beneath his royal robes there is only "a poor, bare, forked animal," as Lear discovered. The Greek audience was constantly reminded of this because Oedipus' name, which means "swollen-footed," reminds us that when he was a baby, his father drove pins through his ankles and arranged for him to be left to die of exposure. We do not know how the Greeks represented his wound on stage, but there must have been some reminder of his physical infirmity.

Forgetful of his infirmity, the reminder of his mortality, Oedipus must learn again that he is human. Coming to Thebes as a young man, he saved the city by killing the Sphinx. He was acclaimed as king and married Jocasta, an older woman, but a queen and still presumably beautiful and sexually responsive. Over the years his reign has been happy and his marriage fruitful. He is the man who has everything, but he has come to believe that his success and happiness are the result of his own choices. The fact that the Elders want him to save the city from the plague suggests that they believe he can do so, and Oedipus also believes that he can.

The body of the play recounts the steps by which Oedipus comes to realize, as the Chorus points out at the end, that we can "Count no mortal happy till / he has passed the final limit of his life secure from pain." At first, proud and forgetful of his humanity, Oedipus initiates his own downfall with his promise to the people that he will not rest until he has brought the truth to light. At this point Creon has returned with the message of the oracle that the murderer of Laius must be punished. If Oedipus had asked the right questions, he might have discovered the truth at this point, but the dramatic movement depends on the tension between discovery and the failure to react properly to that discovery. The dramatic effect is further intensified by the use of dramatic irony, as in Oedipus' speech in which he swears, essentially, to drive himself out of Thebes without understanding the true meaning of what he is saying. The dramatic irony is intensified when Oedipus says that he must punish the murderer of Laius lest the murderer of one king should move against a second. He does not understand that his oath ensures that Oedipus, the murderer of Laius, must punish himself for that act.

The second discovery is made by Teiresias, and it is not ambiguous. Teiresias tells Oedipus that he (Oedipus) is the murderer, but again Oedipus refuses to understand. He sees Teiresias' statement as part of a conspiracy led by Creon. We see in this attack something of the insecurity that Oedipus feels in relation to his wife and her brother, who are, after all, older, more experienced, and natives of Thebes. The resulting quarrel between Oedipus and Creon brings Jocasta to the stage.

Jocasta is an interesting character: she does not believe in oracles because, as she tells us, an oracle said that Laius would be murdered by his own son. Oedipus does not make the connection with what the oracle has told him. He resists discovery again, instead focusing on the question of whether Laius was murdered by a "robber" or "robbers" at the place where three roads met.

The next discovery is that of the First Messenger, who comes to tell Oedipus that his father is dead, but instead tells him that his parentage is unknown. Jocasta understands and leaves the stage to kill herself, but Oedipus yet again resists discovery. He fears that Jocasta feels shame for his humble birth. Jocasta has tried to prevent Oedipus from searching for the truth, but he moves forward to the inevitable revelation. In the moment before the final discovery Oedipus finally understands.

SHEPHERD: I'm right at the edge, the horrible truth—I've got to say it!
OEDIPUS: And I'm at the edge of hearing horrors, yes, but I must hear!

After the ultimate revelation the play moves rapidly to its conclusion. Jocasta has killed herself, Oedipus has put out his own eyes, and Creon is left to rule, however unwillingly.

At the end of the play Oedipus appears again, deposed, self-blinded, self-exiled from the city in which he had felt himself a stranger. At the beginning of the play Oedipus was different from other people because he was happy, successful, and powerful. Now he is different because of his overweening pride and the crimes that he has committed because of it. Yet Oedipus is a tragic figure because he has learned to hate his crimes but not to hate himself. He might have chosen to kill himself, following Jocasta's example, but the fact that he does not expresses his basic dignity, his acceptance of himself, and his humanity.

QUESTIONS FOR DISCUSSION

1. Does Oedipus already know what the Priest "tells" him in the opening exchange with the Priest? If he does, why is the scene included? How might it be staged to make it more plausible?
2. How does Oedipus react to the message that Creon brings from the oracle at Delphi? Does he have any other motive for his decision to seek Laius' murderers than his desire to rid the city of plague? Why had there been no earlier search for the murderer of Laius?
3. Why does the Chorus, in its first ode, say, "I am stretched on the rack of doubt, and terror and trembling hold / my heart" when, in fact, the response of the oracle implies a solution to its problems?
4. What dramatic device is used in Oedipus' oath to avenge the murderer of Laius? How does the choice of the words used reinforce the dramatic effect? The story of Oedipus would have been familiar to the Athenian audience. How might this knowledge have affected their reaction to Oedipus' oath?
5. What is Teiresias' initial response to the summons and questions of response? What does he finally tell Oedipus? Why does Oedipus not believe him?
6. Why does Oedipus suspect Creon of plotting to gain the throne of Thebes? How is this suspicion related to Oedipus' later assumption that Jocasta is upset about the possibility that Oedipus may be of low birth?
7. Why does Jocasta tell Oedipus what she knows about the death of Laius? How does Oedipus react to the various details of her account? Does he ignore any important ones?
8. Why does Oedipus begin his account of his adventure at the place where three roads meet with an account of what happened to him in Corinth and at the oracle in Delphi? How does Jocasta react? Does she suspect anything out of the ordinary?
9. What is the reaction of the Chorus to this scene between Oedipus and Jocasta? Why does the ode end with the Chorus figuratively turning its back on oracles?

10. What news does the First Messenger bring? What revelation is brought about by this news? How do Oedipus, Jocasta, and the Chorus react?

11. Why is one shepherd both the man who escaped from the murder of Laius and the one who was to have exposed the infant Oedipus to death? Does Oedipus ever clear up the question of the number of "robbers" involved in Laius' death?

12. Referring to his self-blinding, Oedipus says, "It was Apollo, friends, Apollo, / that brought this bitter bitterness, my sorrows to completion. / But the hand that struck me / was none but my own." How does this statement also refer to the entire tragedy of *Oedipus?*

13. What elements of Oedipus' character caused him to go to Delphi after Polybus and Merope had denied the story that he was not their son? Do similar impulses inform his other actions?

14. What parts of Oedipus' downfall come from his own character? Which ones come from the circumstances of his life? Is there evidence in what we know of Laius and Jocasta that Oedipus' guilt might be in part inherited?

15. Since the opening scene is a public ceremony of sorts, how should Oedipus be dressed? Would his appearance in full royal regalia be appropriate? How would such an appearance add to the impact of the final scene?

16. This play was written to be performed by only three actors. Which roles would have been performed by each of the three, assuming that no two actors played the same role?

17. How does the actual time of performance relate to the amount of time required by the events of the play? How is the passage of time indicated?

18. What view of the gods and their decrees is presented in *Oedipus the King?* Does the fact that the oracle has said that Oedipus will kill his father and marry his mother absolve him of guilt in doing so? If not, why not?

19. The terms *hubris* and *hamartia* are frequently used in discussions of tragedy. How are they relevant to the story of Oedipus?

20. How does the account of Oedipus' search for the murderer of Laius resemble a detective story? What makes it different?

SUGGESTIONS FOR WRITING

1. There are a number of references in *Oedipus the King* to blindness and sight and to light and darkness. Find some of them and write an essay examining the role of this group of images in the play. Consider questions like these: With what *kinds* of enlightenment and darkness is the play concerned? Why is it significant that Apollo, the sun god, is also a god of prophecy? Why is Teiresias, a prophet inspired by Apollo, presented as blind? What is the relation between his blindness and that of Oedipus?

2. Write an essay that centers on the function of the Chorus in *Oedipus the King*. Consider questions like the following: Why does the Chorus consist of the elders of Thebes? Does the Chorus consistently express a point of view different from that of any of the major characters? If so, why does the play *need* to have such a point of view expressed? Why by a group rather than an individual? What part does the Chorus play in the action? How is the content of the choral odes related to the action around each ode?

3. It is sometimes said that in comparison with his younger contemporary Euripides, Sophocles in his best-known plays seems generally to favor the status quo and the powers-that-be. Choose one of the following options:

A. Read a play by Euripides (*The Bacchae* and *The Trojan Women* are good choices), and compare and contrast it with *Oedipus the King* in terms of political conservatism and subversiveness.

B. Using only the text of *Oedipus the King*, write an essay that demonstrates how it either conservatively controls a potentially subversive response by the audience (such as anger at the gods for their cruelty and perhaps anger about authority in general) or subtly invites such a subversive response.

OSCAR WILDE

The Importance of Being Earnest

PLANNING IDEAS

- Since Wilde and Shaw were both turn-of-the-century British playwrights and *The Importance of Being Earnest* and *Pygmalion* were produced within twenty years of each other (the former in 1899, the latter in 1914), you might want to have students read and discuss the two plays together. Or, if you've already assigned Shaw's play, you might instead have them read and discuss it again after they've tackled Wilde's. Allowing you to foreground in discussion the ways in which particular dramatic texts are shaped by the exigencies and preoccupations of particular sociohistorical moments, such an assignment could work well either as a preview for or supplement to the culture as context discussion coming up in Chapter 29.

- Wilde's very short Preface to *Dorian Grey* can be a real help to students who can all too easily miss the point of Wilde's humor. But I usually like to save the Preface until late in the discussion, using it to complicate and broaden our conversation rather than letting it overdetermine students' responses to the play.

- While this play is positively crackling with wit, there are those who miss a great deal of it. What is wanted can be extraordinarily difficult to teach: a sense of what is funny. Although I was at first suspicious of any kind of exercise that tried to explain jokes (nothing is less funny than such explanations), I have found that some students respond well to a sort of "find the humor" exercise. The idea is to offer certain of Wilde's favorite techniques, with examples, arranged in categories on a handout. The students then find other examples of the same types.

Examples:

A. Non sequitur

> ALGERNON: Please don't touch the cucumber sandwiches. They are ordered espe-
> cially for Aunt Augusta. [*Takes one and eats it.*]
> JACK: Well, you have been eating them all the time.
> ALGERNON: That is quite a different matter. She is my aunt.

B. Unexpected word

> ALGERNON: I hear her hair has turned quite gold from grief.

C. Parallelism

> LADY BRACKNELL: To lose one parent, Mr. Worthing, may be regarded as a mis-
> fortune; to lose both looks like carelessness.

D. Pun

> JACK: It is very vulgar to talk like a dentist when one isn't a dentist. It makes a
> false impression.
> ALGERNON: Well, that is exactly what dentists always do.

• Staged readings of scenes from this play can be quite effective; most students manage the requisite timing surprisingly well.

COMMENTARY

At the heart of the play is the basic comedic plot: a young man and a young woman wish to marry. Some difficulty is interposed that renders the union seemingly impossible, but then the difficulty is removed and all live happily ever after. The plot here is double, for there are two young men and two young women: the romance of the second pair is triggered by the complications of the romance of the first pair and resolved by the resolution of those complications. This is the heart of comedy, for the typical comedic plot is concerned with someone who is denied his or her rightful place in society, but who ultimately overcomes the denial. In comedy—as opposed to such forms as farce—marriage is viewed in its social aspect rather than its sexual one.

The concern is with the wedding rather than the wedding night, and therefore the surface unconcern with sexuality works. Many other comedies overlap into the area of sexuality but not *Earnest*; it stays strictly within the proper domain of comedy. Jack and Algernon are eminently suitable to be husbands, except that Jack has no parents and Algernon no money; and those two characteristics are important to marriage in its social aspect. As healthy young women, Gwendolen and Cecily are admirably suited for marriage and motherhood, and we feel that it is well that difficulties are so expeditiously resolved.

While it is a perfect comedy, *Earnest* also exemplifies the narrower genre called the *comedy of manners*. The comedy of manners differs from other comedies in its emphasis on life among the wealthy, with people who "toil not, neither do they spin." Their concerns are those of high society rather than of society in the general sense. Algernon, for example, is deeply concerned with such burning issues as who his dinner partner will be or what music is to be performed at a party. The values of such people may seem superficial to many people, including today's students; but if nothing else, these serve to make the play even more amusing. That Wilde himself understood this is clear in the brilliantly funny interrogation of Jack by Lady Bracknell. Throughout we are confronted with a comic inversion of values. When he hesitantly admits to Lady Bracknell that he smokes, she is delighted because she thinks a man should have some occupation.

Lady Bracknell, as a senior matron, is one of the controlling forces of society, who can change either the fashion or the side, or both, if necessary. Her values are totally consistent and totally inverted from our perspective, and their inversion gives them much of their humor.

The play is also a brilliant example of the artful use of comic stereotypes. Jack and Gwendolen are representative of such "witty lovers" as Beatrice and Benedick in *Much Ado about Nothing* and Mirabell and Millamant in *The Way of the World*. Algernon and Cecily are "sentimental lovers." Miss Prism is an old maid, anxious to marry Canon Chasuble, a slightly dim clergyman, and Lady Bracknell is the managing matron. Yet though all are "stereotypes," Wilde succeeds in giving each of them more than enough individuality to maintain our interest in them. For example, Algernon is portrayed throughout the play as being excessively interested in food, not a usual trait in a sentimental lover.

The glory of the play is as much in its language as its structure and characterization, for Wilde was a master wit. Some of the devices he uses are worth examination, as discussed in "Planning Ideas" above. One is the non sequitur, as in Algernon's remark to Lane: "Speaking of the science of Life, have you got the cucumber sandwiches cut for Aunt Augusta?" That the connection between the science of Life (whatever that is) and cucumber sandwiches is at best tenuous is the source of the humor here as in other places. A second technique is the use of the unexpected word. When Lane mentions his marriage, Algernon is shocked because "Really, if the lower orders don't set us a good example, what on earth is the use of them?" The question would not be funny if he had said "upper" instead of "lower," but the unexpected word provides the humor. Another form of humor is the use of rhetorical balance and parallelism, as in Jack's remark that "When one is in town one amuses oneself. When one is in the country one amuses other people." Puns may be the lowest form of humor (and then again they may not), but Wilde uses them brilliantly, as in the title of the play, which leads to the final line. Another form of humor is the establishment of apparently logical categories that have no real meaning, as when Algernon explains why he does not intend to have dinner with his aunt: "To begin with, I dined there on Monday. . . . In the second place, whenever I do dine there I am always treated as a member of the family. . . . In the third place, I know perfectly well whom she will place me next to." A final form of humor is the use of speeches that clearly contradict facts, as when Gwendolen, replying to her mother's command to go into the next room with her, answers, "Certainly mamma," and remains behind. As explained in the third of the planning ideas, these examples can be multiplied many times from other sections of the play.

As this commentary suggests, Wilde's play thus continues to entertain and, perhaps, to educate, despite the tremendous differences between the lives and outlooks of contemporary readers and those of the Victorian audiences who were Wilde's first "readers." But just as Chekhov's plays increase in complexity the more one knows about turn-of-the-century Russia and about Chekhov himself, so both the humor and the point of Wilde's play deepen the more one knows about both Britain in the 1890s and Wilde's role therein. To open up such issues for students, I generally start with the play itself, asking them to pick out lines that they recognize are supposed to be funny, but whose humor they might not fully appreciate. Then I supplement that list with a list of my own, which prominently features lines such as Gwendolen's remark in Act II that "home seems . . . to be the proper sphere for the man," a man becoming "painfully effeminate" when he "begins to neglect his domestic duties" (an obvious send-up, to those in the know, of Victorian "separate spheres" ideology); Lady Bracknell's insistence (in Act I) that being "bred in a handbag" indicates "a contempt for the ordinary decencies of family life that reminds one of the worst excesses of the French Revolution" (an only slightly exaggerated version of Victorian commonplaces about class); Chasuble's description (in Act II) of his "charity sermon on behalf of the Society for the Prevention of Discontent among the Upper Orders" (a typical Wildean reversal that pokes fun at Victorian middle-class efforts to "improve" the lower classes); and the exchange between Cecily and Gwendolen (in Act II) about "agricultural depression," a condition from which "the aristocracy are suffering very much" "at present" (through which Wilde sends up Victorian politics and political economy by conflating economic "depression" with upper-class mood swings).

My point in doing so, however, is not just to give students a sense of the background they might need to fully appreciate the humor of particular lines but to instead use the lines to lead students toward a characterization of the particular (Victorian middle-class) values or worldview that Wilde is mocking throughout Earnest, most often through witty reversals of its chief credos, including the separation of life into the public sphere (associated with men) and the private (associated with women); the insistence on moral idealism and earnestness; and the valorization of work and of usefulness (over beauty, pleasure, etc.). For only by having some sense of these credos can students fully appreciate both the irreverence that constitutes so much of the point of Wilde's humor and of the play as a whole, which, as Wilde himself once insisted, "has as its philosophy" the idea "that we should treat all the trivial things of life seriously, and all the serious things of life with sincere and studied triviality."

Students can also better appreciate this irreverence if their attention is drawn not only to the ways in which (as the above discussion indicates) Wilde adheres to certain generic formulae but also to the ways in which he in the process self-consciously deviates from, and thereby challenges, traditional Victorian aesthetic norms and values. Obviously the play itself embodies that challenge, but the best way to focus students on why and how it does so is to focus them first on the discussions of literature within the play. What's the significance, for example, of the fact that Miss Prism (the most conservatively and stereotypically Victorian character in the play) has written a three-volume novel? That she insists to Cecily (who, interestingly enough, finds "novels that end happily" "depress[ing]") that "fiction means" the "good ended happily, and the bad unhappily"? That the play generally endorses Algernon's view that style is much more important than substance or meaning? Once students have begun to formulate their own answers to such questions, I hand them a copy of Wilde's Preface to the novel *Dorian Grey* to continue and amplify our discussion of the conflict between the "art for art's sake" view endorsed and embodied in Wilde's play and the (moralistic or utilitarian) view to which it is implicitly opposed.

QUESTIONS FOR DISCUSSION

1. What is the purpose of the opening exchange between Algernon and Lane?
2. What do we learn about the opening situation of the play from the conversation between Algernon and Jack? How does Wilde use the cigarette case for expository and comic purposes?
3. What does Algernon offer Jack in exchange for a free dinner? How does he fulfill his share of the agreement? What plot complication results from it?
4. How does Lady Bracknell react to the news of Gwendolen's engagement to Jack? What does her maternal interrogation of Jack tell us about her values and those of her society?
5. How does Wilde make use of the fact that Jack was found in a handbag? What further information do we get from Miss Prism early in Act II that contributes to the solution of the play's problems?
6. Why does Algernon suggest that Jack's brother died of a chill rather

than of apoplexy? What use is made of this later in the play?
7. How does Algernon discover the address of Jack's country place? How has Jack attempted earlier to keep it secret?
8. What bargain does Jack offer to Lady Bracknell? How does she react? What might have happened if the problem had not been resolved?
9. Describe the steps by which the problems are resolved by the appearance of Miss Prism, including any new misunderstanding that may have arisen.
10. Are we prepared for the embrace of Miss Prism and Canon Chasuble? If not, why do we accept it?
11. What is the meaning of the final line of the play?
12. Certain of the characters in this play have names that suggest something about their characters. Of which ones is this true, and what do we learn about each from the name?
13. Why does Gwendolen insist that Jack make a formal proposal of marriage?
14. In the opening scene of Act II what conclusions does the audience reach about the attitudes and relative intelligence of Miss Prism and Cecily?
15. Why is Miss Prism shown misunderstanding the meaning of the allusion to Egeria?
16. Describe the relation between the attitudes of Gwendolen and Cecily and what they actually say in the opening scene of Act III.
17. The last part of Act II, the scenes between Gwendolen and Cecily, then between them and the two young men, and finally between the two young men, are full of examples of syntactic and rhetorical balance and parallelism. Describe the effect of this device.
18. Compare Lady Bracknell's examination of Cecily in Act III with her interrogation of Jack in Act I. What accounts for the similarities and differences?
19. A good bit of the humor in this play, and a good bit of the meaning, depends on the contrast between appearance and reality. For example, in the first exchange of the play Algernon asks Lane if he has heard what Algernon was playing on the piano. What are we to make of Lane's reply that "I didn't think it polite to listen, sir"? Can you find other examples of this phenomenon? What do they tell us about the meaning of the play?
20. There are numerous references to food and drink; find examples of them and comment on their meaning in the play.
21. How does Wilde make use of diaries as a structural and comic device in the play?

SUGGESTIONS FOR WRITING

1. Write a short essay on *The Importance of Being Earnest* that either supports or refutes the following thesis: "Wilde wrote the play strictly as

entertainment; any attempt to find a moral is misguided." (You could use a great many of the play's lines in building either case. A couple of examples: Does the behavior of Miss Prism and Canon Chasuble suggest anything about the values of conventional moralists? Do the Canon's remarks about his sermon on "the meaning of the manna in the wilderness" have a serious implication about institutional religion?)

2. After reading *The Importance of Being Earnest*, do some research on Oscar Wilde's life and literary career. Then read the play again and write an essay showing how your research changed your reading. How does the play seem different after you have learned about the playwright's troubles with the social strictures of Victorian England?

READING/WRITING IDEAS FOR CHAPTER 28

ESSAYS ABOUT LITERARY CONTEXT

As the headnote to and the reading and writing ideas for the "Evaluating Drama" chapter suggest, you might want to consider combining these two chapters, using them as the focus for a unit culminating in an essay assignment that asks students to evaluate a comedy or a tragedy by employing the generic definitions and characteristics discussed in this chapter. Such an approach is, in a sense, suggested by the anthology itself, since this chapter opens with the claim that "Classifying literary texts serves a variety of purposes for historians and literature critics who may need to . . . make a value judgment about its literary quality or cultural value."

However, if you would rather focus students at this point on interpretation rather than evaluation, the chapter also works quite well on its own. For this approach, the anthology suggests a number of workable essay assignments that focus students on analyzing *Oedipus* as a tragedy or *Earnest* as a comedy. But since those assignments all focus students on the ways in which the plays conform to generic patterns, you might want to supplement them with the following prompts, both of which instead focus students on the ways in which the plays might be seen as *not* wholly conforming to such patterns.

- The anthology suggests that comedy generally "tends to endorse the values of society." Write an essay in which you explore the ways in which this claim does and does not hold true for *The Importance of Being Earnest*. What does the play suggest about the values of Victorian society? Which of those values does the play seem to endorse and which does it seem to subvert or undermine (or simply poke fun at)? How might the very fact that Wilde's play is a comedy serve to subvert traditional Victorian values (not least the valorization of "earnestness" itself)?
- The anthology suggests that tragic characters are more individualized than comic characters and their fate more clearly the result of their personal flaws or limitations. At the same time, however, the anthology indicates that such characters are also to

some extent representative or typical when it points out that Oedipus' fate is important, in part, because he is "a king" rather than "the son of a shepherd." Write an essay in which you consider whether and how Oedipus might be seen as a type (or stereotype) of a certain kind of king rather than as an ordinary individual.

Another good option is to have students adapt either one of these assignments or one of those in the anthology to write an essay that focuses not on *Oedipus* or *Earnest*, but on a play contained elsewhere in the anthology that they've already analyzed without any reference to its genre. Or you might simply have students write essays in which they argue that and why a particular play that they've already read should be seen as a tragedy or a comedy. Assignments like this, which ask students to reinterpret a familiar text in light of their "new" knowledge about literary context, tend to work well precisely because they make vividly apparent to students exactly why and how the consideration of literary context can broaden and complicate their interpretation of a particular dramatic text.

29

CULTURE AS CONTEXT: SOCIAL AND HISTORICAL SETTING

I tell my students there are two ways of spending a few weeks in a foreign country. One way is to seek out the familiar: to find people who speak English, to spend time, as much as possible, in the way one would spend it at home, to eat familiar foods (there's a McDonald's restaurant every-where), generally to try to make the place seem less strange. The other way is to immerse oneself in the foreign culture: to try to converse in the native language; to participate in activities that seem unfamiliar; to try the local cuisine; to experience, as much as possible, the culture from the inside. Most students agree that the second way is better.

Of course I'm developing an analogy about reading plays that center on social groups or historical periods different from our own. While we can never completely negate the complex cultural assumptions that have shaped us and have made us see the world the way we do—just as we will never be natives of the foreign country—we can to a certain degree immerse ourselves in the world of the characters in the play. We'll never be Ruth Younger or Willy Loman. But we can, if we exercise some curi-osity and some sympathetic imagination, live with them for a while—not as critics whose job it is to measure their lives against ours but as fellow travelers on a journey that is all the more valuable for its oddness.

For me, however, the "foreign country" analogy can become problem-atic if and when it suggests, as it might to some white students, that plays about people of color *alone* demand an utterly different, more "culturally sensitive" reading strategy. For that reason, I find that effective discussion of Hansberry's *A Raisin in the Sun* in this context can be tricky, largely because I want students to appreciate the distinctly African-American dimensions of the play, as well as the importance of its 1950s setting, yet I am wary of allowing them to see *only* texts that focus on people of color as being informed by "cultural context" and/or as taking them to a for-eign country simply because they aren't about middle- or upper-class white people. That's why I actually tend to teach the two plays in this chapter in reverse order, having students *first* read, discuss, and contextualize *The Death of a Salesman* and only then tackle *A Raisin in the Sun*. That way, it becomes possible for students to see reading for cultural context as something one can do with any text, while also allowing us to compare these two particular texts to grapple with the ways in which they *do* suggest a difference between African-American and European-American families' experiences of "America" and the "American Dream."

LORRAINE HANSBERRY

A Raisin in the Sun

PLANNING IDEAS

- Try breaking students up into groups, assigning each group a topic or a question about cultural context to research. Then have the groups both report their findings to the class and suggest the specific ways in which those findings help illuminate the play. Topics might include the following:

A. Nigerian history and culture (starting with the reference to the Yoruba tribe in Act I, Scene 2 and to the legendary Chaka in Act II, Scene 1).
B. the African independence struggles of the 1950s and 1960s, including that of Nigeria (which gained independence in 1960, just one year after Hansberry's play was first produced) and of Kenya (whose struggles are alluded to via the reference in Act II, Scene 1 to Jomo Kenyatta [1891–1979], the immensely important Gikuyu scholar and resistance leader who was imprisoned during the Kenyan Emergency of the 1950s and then served as the country's president from independence in 1963 until his death).
C. the beginnings of the American civil rights movement in the late 1950s and early 1960s, including the emergence of Afro-centrism.
D. Lorraine Hansberry.

Alternatively, you might wait until the class has read and begun to discuss the play, encouraging students to articulate possible research topics and questions as part of that discussion and then breaking them up into research groups. (Though this strategy eats up more class time, it also allows students to practice defining such questions and topics for themselves; see "Reading/Writing Ideas for Chapter 29.")
- If your focus here is more thematic than generic, you might have students read Hansberry's play in conjunction with two short stories that deal with similar issues—James Baldwin's "Sonny's Blues," which is

included in the anthology, and Alice Walker's "Everyday Use," which is not—and/or with relevant poems in the anthology, such as Helene Johnson's "Sonnet to a Negro in Harlem," Langston Hughes's "The Negro Speakers of Rivers" and "Harlem (A Dream Deferred)," Maya Angelou's "Africa," Derek Walcott's "A Far Cry from Africa," and Ishmael Reed's "I Am a Cowboy in the Boat of Ra."

COMMENTARY

Hansberry's play is a wonderful text to discuss in terms of historical and cultural context precisely because the temporal, geographical, and cultural settings of the play are so crucial to its meaning. For the three generations of the Younger family in themselves embody three crucial phases or facets of the African-American experience at the unique point of intersection that was 1959—that moment in U.S. history when the postwar economic boon that seemed to put the American Dream within everyone's reach was ending and the very sanctity of that dream was about to come under increasingly heavy fire from the various "liberation" movements of the 1960s.

Lena and Big Walter represent a generation still close enough to the horrors of slavery and of the postemancipation South to glory in the mere fact of their family's "freedom" and survival. "In my time," as Lena puts it, "we was worried about not being lynched and getting to the North if we could and how to stay alive and still have a pinch of dignity too." As a result, Lena simply can't understand why her son—with his "job, a nice wife, and a fine boy"—shouldn't be both happy with what he has and as hopeful about the future he can make for himself and his family as she and her husband were when they moved into their Southside apartment. Despite the fact that those hopes didn't come to fruition—that the apartment she and Walter initially saw as a temporary stop on their way to better things has become, as the initial stage directions indicate, a "room" in which "Weariness has . . . won"—Lena herself has not really succumbed to, or even fully recognized, that defeat or that weariness, just as she doesn't see that the apartment has become, in Ruth's words, "a rattrap" that represents the entrapment of her own family.

Key to the hopefulness of Lena and her husband is or was the conviction that their dreams would be realized in the next generation, if not in their own; as Lena says of Walter, "he sure loved his children. Always wanted them to have something—be something. . . . Big Walter used to say, . . . 'Seem like God didn't see fit to give the black man nothing but dreams—but he did give us children to make them dreams seem worth while.' " And as Lena recognizes, her son has inherited his father's capacity to dream as surely as he has inherited his name: "That's where Brother gets all these notions, I reckon."

Yet in Walter's generation the long deferral of that dream has, in the words of the epigraph from Langston Hughes, begun to "fester like a sore": Walter vacillates between anger and bitterness—as George tells him, "You're all wacked up with bitterness, man"—and wild schemes for "[i]nvest[ing] big, gambl[ing] big, hell, los[ing] *big* if you have to" in order to achieve in a single moment all that Lena and her husband once dreamed of achieving "little by little." Simultaneously Ruth vacillates between upholding the simpler, long-term ambitions of the previous generation and giving way to despair and weariness. And if that despair is symbolized, as Lena herself seems to recognize, by Ruth's desire to give up the child who also represents the family's future, then Walter's status as a daring, but doomed, dreamer is aptly captured in George's reference to him as Prometheus, the mythological hero who suffered eternal punishment for daring to steal fire from the gods.

If this allusion and other aspects of the play encourage us to sympathize with and even admire Walter, however, the play as a whole ultimately encourages us to also see him as seriously misguided, not only because he is all too willing to risk everything the family has in the effort to achieve his dreams but also because of the way his dreams themselves differ from, and in some ways pervert, those of his father and mother, chiefly because they involve a confusion between means and ends, money and the possibilities it can buy. For whereas Lena and Big Walter dreamed of the life they could buy for their family with money—a life symbolized by house and garden—Walter's dreams focus on money alone: to Walter, as Lena puts it, "Money" itself "is life." And in a play that equates drink with self-destructive escapism (in a way that makes it very like James Baldwin's "Sonny's Blues"), the mistake encoded in that credo is to some extent embodied in the very fact that Walter's scheme centers on opening a liquor store and thereby profiting from the self-destruction of others just as surely as Willy Harris himself does when he absconds with the family's money. Thus Walter's determination to sacrifice pride and everything else for money by accepting Mr. Lindner's bribe represents a fitting climax precisely because it brings to the fore the ethic Walter has been unconsciously on his way toward adopting throughout the play, while his ultimate refusal of the money represents his return to his father and mother's more truly ethical version of the dream, an idea made clear by the fact that Walter here speaks for the entire family rather than for himself alone and that his words refer not only to his responsibility, as his father's son, to inherit and maintain what his father earned but also to his responsibility to his own son: "this is my son," he tells Lindner, "who makes the sixth generation of our family in this country, . . . and we have all thought about your offer and we have decided to move into our house because my father—my father—he earned it." Fittingly enough, it is only now that Lena Younger fully accords to Walter his status as the family's new patriarch when she avows, "My son said we was going to move and there ain't nothing left for me to say."

Obviously the character who in some ways provides us with the most

critical angle on Walter is not Ruth or Lena, but Beneatha, whose disa-
vowal of her brother culminates in her assertion that the man willing to
take Lindner's money is "no brother of mine," "not a man," "but a tooth-
less rat." Thus if Walter's schemes in some ways represent the perversion
of his parents' dream, the younger Beneatha's Afro-centrism represents
the questioning of those very dreams that would come to characterize
certain segments of the nascent civil rights movement—a vision that sees
such dreams and the Christian faith that fostered them in earlier generations as the "assimilationist" internalization of the norms and values of
"the dominant, and in this case, oppressive culture." And it is precisely
this vision that comes to the fore in Beneatha's ultimate attack on her
brother: "There he is! *Monsieur le petit bourgeois noir*—himself! There he
is—Symbol of a Rising Class! Entrepreneur! Titan of the system! . . . Did
you dream of yachts on Lake Michigan, Brother? . . . I look at you and I
see the final triumph of stupidity in the world!" Thus rather than dreaming, as Walter does, of becoming like whites—or, as Ruth puts it, *"be*[ing]
Mr. Arnold" rather than "his chauffeur"—or of marrying the rich George
Murchison, the one black person in the play who has achieved Walter's
dream, Beneatha instead dreams of abandoning the American "system"
all together and becoming, with Joseph Asagai's help, more authentically
African, "a queen of the Nile!"

Yet if the play sympathizes in some ways more with Beneatha's dreams
and schemes than with Walter's, it nonetheless also emphasizes the
ironic and even mistaken aspects of this Afro-centric dream of recapturing
a cultural identity and a "home" that has never been one's own (issues
that also come to the fore in many of the poems mentioned in "Planning
Ideas" above). Not least among these ironies is the fact that Beneatha's
very rejection of her family's values and dreams and the language that
she uses to judge them are themselves the product of the education that
their hard work, their hope, and even their religious faith purchased for
her (a point brought home by her use of a French phrase to castigate her
brother), while her judgments also entail a blindness to the fact that, as
the stage directions themselves make clear, the ostensibly "assimilated"
Lena herself embodies the best of African womanhood, "Her bearing . . .
perhaps most like the noble bearing of the women of the Hereros of
Southwest Africa—rather as if she imagines that as she walks she still bears
a basket or a vessel upon her head." (Such ironies become the central
focus of Alice Walker's "Everyday Use.") Moreover, Beneatha's dreams of
achieving authentic Africanness are in some ways as mistakenly grandiose as Walter's dreams of instantaneously becoming Mr. Arnold. As Lena
recognizes, these two ostensibly different siblings thus share a strikingly
similar "philosophy of life" in that both "think things have more emphasis if they are big, somehow."

In Beneatha's final conversation with Asagai, Hansberry brings to the
fore not only the ironic similarities between Walter's and Beneatha's
ostensibly very different "philosophies" and dreams but also the ease

with which all such dreams of immediate and dramatic transformation can turn into the despair Beneatha articulates in her vision of an endless, Sisyphean circle of struggle: "Don't you see there isn't any real progress, . . . there is only one large circle that we march in, around and around, each of us with our own little picture—in front of us—our own little mirage that we think is the future." Yet Asagai's response seems to capture the far-from-despairing vision offered in the play as a whole, with its ambivalent, but nonetheless triumphant conclusion: "It isn't a circle—it is simply a long line—as in geometry, you know, one that reaches into infinity"; "At times it will seem that nothing changes at all . . . and then again . . . the sudden dramatic events which make history leap into the future."

But if it is thus through Beneatha and Joseph that the play most self-consciously foregrounds the competing conceptions of social progress at work in the play, it is perhaps through the juxtaposition of Beneatha and Walter that we can most clearly see the extent to which the play is as much about gender as it is about race and class—or, more accurately, about the complex intersections among the three. For Beneatha's role differs from Walter's not only by virtue of the very different dreams vouchsafed to her, in part, by her education but also by virtue of the fact that she is a woman, a difference that the play foregrounds to some extent by figuring Beneatha's moral choices in terms of the choice between lovers and between her dream of being a doctor and the expectation that she should, as Walter puts it, "go be a nurse like other women—or just get married and be quiet." However problematic are Walter's admonitions to his sister and his constant complaints about the extent to which his sister, wife, and mother emasculate him by refusing him their trust and support, the play as a whole ultimately seems to endorse the assumptions about gender roles and relations those admonitions and complaints entail. And that endorsement becomes most clear, perhaps, when Lena tells Walter "I been wrong, son . . . I been doing to you what the rest of the world been doing to you," thus suggesting that this matriarchal family's refusal to accord Walter his rightful status as their leader reproduces within the domestic sphere (and thus legitimates) the disempowerment he suffers as a black man in a public sphere dominated by white men. "I'm telling you to be the head of this family from now on like you supposed to be," Lena says, affirming both that Walter, rather than she or Ruth or Beneatha, is the rightful leader of the family and that, as Walter puts it early in the play, "the colored woman" should be "building their men up and making 'em feel like they somebody. Like they can do something." And obviously the end of the play—in which both Walter and Lena once again affirm his rightful role as son, father, and family patriarch—endorses this view.

From this point of view, too, Beneatha's Afro-centrism becomes even more ironic since part of the lure of African culture as it is figured within the play lies in the status it accords to the male warrior, a lure foregrounded when Walter responds to Beneatha's Nigerian music by affirming "in my *heart of hearts* . . . —I am much warrior!" and when Asagai himself mocks Beneatha's "liberated" "New World" notions. Thus, even if the play to some extent mocks Beneatha's dreams of returning "home," it nonetheless seems to envision the ascendancy of the "colored woman" in African-American culture as a key facet and/or symptom of the tragic cultural loss and oppression suffered by Americans of African descent.

QUESTIONS FOR DISCUSSION

1. As the epigraph announces and Hansberry's text itself affirms, "dreams" are a central focus of *A Raisin in the Sun*, as is the difficulty of "expressing" or making others "understand" one's dreams. How would you characterize the different dreams represented by the various members of the Younger family, especially Lena and Big Walter, Walter, Ruth, and Beneatha? What, for example, do Lena's remarks about how she and her husband "was going to set away, little by little," "buy a little place out in Morgan Park," and create a garden suggest about the nature of the dreams she and her husband shared? What does the exchange between Lena and her son about money being "life" and Walter's references to "gambling" suggest about the differences between her dream and her son's? What do Beneatha's remarks about her brother, particularly in the final scene, and her interactions with George Murchison and Joseph Asagai suggest about her dreams and the way they differ from Walter's? How might you account for the differences among the characters' dreams?
2. How does the play ultimately answer Hughes's question, "What happens to a dream deferred?" Which, if any, of the different "dreams" in the play is endorsed by the play as a whole? To what extent is the play's ending a happy one?
3. What role is played by minor characters in the play, especially George Murchison, Joseph Asagai, and Karl Lindner? What about Willy Harris, a character who never appears, but who nonetheless becomes key to the play's plot?
4. What is the significance of the play's setting—of the fact that it takes place in "Chicago's Southside" "Sometime between World War II and the present" (i.e., 1959), that the action of the play all occurs within the Younger's apartment, and that Hansberry describes this apartment in a very particular way in the play's initial stage directions? How does the dialogue within the play add to your sense of the symbolic significance of the apartment?
5. One of the few key props in the play is the flower that Lena keeps on the windowsill. Why is that prop so key to the play?
6. What is the significance of the play's various references to current events both in America (atomic testing, for example) and in Africa (the activities of Jomo Kenyatta, for example)? What about the allu-

sions to American popular culture (Greta Garbo, for example) and to classical myth (as when George calls Walter "Prometheus")? What exactly do these various references contribute to the play—both individually and collectively? What kinds of references and allusions are most typical of particular characters, and what do they tell us about those characters?

7. Early in the play, Walter Younger complains about his wife's failure to support both him and his dreams and suggests that her treatment of him is just an example of a more general problem with the relations between African-American men and women. What do you think the play as a whole has to say about this issue—how might it be seen to agree and disagree with Walter's diagnosis? What, for example, is the significance of Lena's statement that "I been wrong, son . . . I been doing to you what the rest of the world been doing to you. . . . I'm telling you to be the head of this family from now on like you supposed to be"? Of the play's final scene? How might the play engage such questions through the character of Beneatha, as well as through the interactions of Walter and Lena?

8. One point in the play that seems especially tricky in terms of staging and tone is the scene in which Walter and Beneatha dance and sing to the Nigerian music provided by Joseph Asagai—to what extent are Beneatha and Walter's words and actions meant to seem ridiculous, as Ruth's remarks suggest, and to what extent are they meant to be portrayed seriously and/or sympathetically? How would you stage and direct this scene so as to effectively communicate either or both of these tones to your audience?

9. Part of the reason that this scene is so tricky is that both Beneatha and Walter are, in a sense, performing, a point underscored by the fact that shortly afterward George Murchison says to Beneatha, "we're going to the theatre—we're not going to be *in* it." What might these lines (and George's subsequent remarks about curtain times in Chicago and New York) begin to suggest about how Hansberry's play as a whole comments on or questions dramatic conventions and/or the nature, status, and role of the theater in American life? How might such questioning relate to the play's exploration of the African-American experience?

10. Another question about staging might arise in relation to the play's epigraph, which plays such a key role in setting the stage for the play, metaphorically speaking. If you were staging the play, would you somehow include the epigraph in your production? If so, how? One possibility would be to have an actor or actors recite the lines from Hughes's poem at the opening of the play, perhaps before the curtain rises. What would be the effects of doing so? Would you have one of the actors in the play itself speak these lines (in or out of costume) or would you have an actor not in the play do so? What would be the effects of each of these various choices?

SUGGESTIONS FOR WRITING

1. Write an essay in which you explore the character of either Walter or
   Beneatha or Lena Younger, discussing the ways in which your character does or does not develop over the course of the play. If you do
   see your character developing, when and how does she or he do so?
   Which moments in the play seem especially revealing or significant
   from this point of view? *Or* write an essay in which you explain the
   role played by one of the minor characters in the play, such as George
   Murchison or Joseph Asagai. What worldview or values might this
   character represent within the play and/or what specifically does your
   character contribute to the play as a whole (thematically as well as
   structurally)?
2. Write an essay exploring the significance of a particular moment or
   scene in the play—perhaps the final scene, the scene in which Walter
   and Beneatha's singing and dancing are interrupted by the arrival of
   George Murchison, or the final conversation between Beneatha and
   Joseph Asagai. What issues or questions are brought to the fore in your
   moment, and how exactly does your moment contribute—both structurally and thematically—to the play as a whole? (You may also want
   to consider in your essay questions about how exactly you would stage
   and/or direct this moment to make it mean to the audience what you
   suggest it should.)

ARTHUR MILLER

Death of a Salesman

PLANNING IDEAS

- Before assigning the play tell students to be on the lookout for repeated
  phrases (examples: "well liked," "the woods are burning," "I'm going
  to lose weight"). There are others. After reading the play spend some
  time discussing the purpose of such repetitions.
- A good way to approach the difference between reading the play and
  experiencing it in the theater is to focus on the stage directions. When
  we read the play we learn of Happy, for example, that "Sexuality is like
  a visible color on him, or a scent that many women have discovered."
  How do you get that across in performance? (Spray the theater with
  musk?) Is there a universal color, scent, acting style, or even appearance that would do? Sexuality or "sex appeal" may not mean the same
  thing to everyone. Most of us, no doubt, can understand why Arthur
  Miller was attracted sexually to Marilyn Monroe, whom he married,
  but can we all understand what Monroe saw in Miller?

• Having introduced students to *tragedy* earlier, you might now introduce the term *pathos* and allow the discussion to pursue the question
of whether *Salesman* is pathetic or tragic. Linda's evaluation of Willy
and his situation is quoted in the chapter: "He's not the finest character
that ever lived. But he's a human being, and a terrible thing is happening to him. So attention must be paid"; this is perhaps the basis on
which one might want to argue about the possibility of a "tragedy of
the common man," and of course the discussion would double back
to the use of common rather than elevated language. Most definitions
of tragedy also involve the protagonist's recognition of himself and his
situation, so that Biff's claim in the Requiem that Willy "never knew
who he was" would have to be evaluated in terms of the text. Finally,
the Greek gods may be here replaced by "society." To what extent is
Willy the victim of his society, that is, more specifically, of capitalism?

COMMENTARY

From the earliest scene in *Salesman*, it appears almost inevitable that
Willy will eventually kill himself. References to suicide are scattered omi-
nously throughout the play and more liberally in the latter half before
Willy actually takes his life. The play's title, together with the fact that
he does eventually commit suicide, generates a sense of tragic destiny.
Does Willy have any choice in the matter? What role do the members of
his family play in that choice—or lack thereof?

Like much previous drama, from *Oedipus* to *Hamlet* to *Hedda Gabler* to
A Raisin in the Sun and on and on and on, *Salesman* significantly, though
not necessarily centrally, concerns parent(s) and child(ren). It should not
take much to get your students to talk about parents, their weaknesses,
imperfections, responsibilities; but you may want to hang out some bait,
like the question about why Biff steals, or why Happy just can't help
seducing executives' girlfriends. Willy claims Biff ruined his own life to
spite his father; Biff claims Willy filled him with hot air. Who is right?
How much responsibility lies where?

On the one hand, Biff is surely right when he suggests that Willy led
both him and Happy astray by teaching them not only to equate success
with money and power (being a "boss big shot" and "a leader of men")
but also to see personal magnetism alone as the key to that success. In
the process, Willy does, in Biff's words, fill the boys with "hot air" by
making them believe that they alone possess this unique treasure, a treasure that makes them better than ordinary boys like Bernard. As Willy tells
the "earnest and loyal" young Biff in the first act,

> Bernard can get the best marks in school, y'understand, but when he gets out in
> the business world, y'understand, you are going to be five times ahead of him.
> That's why I thank Almighty God you're both built like Adonises. Because the man
> who makes an appearance in the business world, the man who creates personal
> interest, is the man who gets ahead. Be liked and you will never want.

By teaching Biff to see himself as better than hardworking "worms[s]" like Bernard and even encouraging him to use Bernard to achieve his own ends (by, for example, cheating off of his math test), moreover, Willy also (and, I think, somewhat unwittingly) teaches Biff and his brother both to see the end as always justifying the means and to see other people as, in a sense, means to, and/or markers of, one's own success. For that is precisely what Willy himself seems to have done by having an affair with a woman who promises to get him in to see the Boston buyers, and it is Biff's discovery of this affair that originally made Biff fully aware of the emptiness of his father's value system, an awareness that leads him to reject his father and his father's teachings but that also leaves him without anything to put in its place—in his words, "mixed up very bad."

On the other hand, however, one can see the play as also tracing the process through which Biff comes to recognize the more positive aspects of Willy's character and value system, those aspects of Willy's character that Linda seems to have always recognized and appreciated and that make Willy, as she sees him, a tragic character to whom "a terrible thing is happening." One of the things that Linda sees, I think, is that for all that he teaches his own sons to despise the kind of sheer hard work represented by Bernard, Willy himself has always worked just as hard and just as faithfully. And he has done so, moreover, out of a feeling of both loyalty and responsibility to his firm and to his family, thereby enacting an ideal far different from the kind of selfish individualism that led his own father and brother to abandon their families to pursue wealth and that Willy himself teaches the sons whom "he loved better than his life." As Linda poignantly asks, "[Y]ou tell me he has no character? The man who never worked a day but for your benefit? When does he get the medal for that?" In this way, Willy becomes the "fake" that Biff accuses him of being in a different and ironically more positive sense, espousing and encouraging his sons to adopt a value system that is, in crucial ways, a kind of perversion of the one his own life embodies. As Biff says at the very end of the play, Willy's tragedy is, in a sense, that "[h]e never knew who he was."

That irony comes to the fore in Willy's encounters with Howard, the character who most obviously embodies the kind of heartless business ethic that Willy himself has to some extent espoused, despite the fact that much of his own life enacts a quite different, less self-centered and more familial ethic. For when Howard heartlessly casts Willy aside, insisting that "business is business" and that "business" justifies and even necessitates treating Willy merely as a tool that has outlived its usefulness, Willy fittingly invokes the language of familial relationships and responsibilities, insisting not only that Howard should live up to the promises his father made but also that he should see Willy himself as a member of his family and even as a kind of father figure.

By coming to see that he can and should embrace and respect his father for "who he was," Biff eventually embraces and enacts the familial ethos that Linda has all along espoused and respected Willy for embodying and that is most fully embraced in the play by the loyal Charley. Biff also, I think, comes to see the heroism, as well as the tragedy, inherent in the life of "a hardworking drummer," a perfectly ordinary "dime." Among the many tragic elements of the ending, however, is that it is too late for Willy himself to accept or embrace this more truthful vision of himself, just as it proves impossible for him to embrace or fully respect Charley or Bernard, the two characters in the play who most obviously embody the ethic of hard work and of simple devotion to family that Willy cannot recognize as his own greatest qualities and his own greatest gift to his sons.

As Charley himself insists, drawing our attention back to the title of the play, Willy's tragic blindness is intimately related to the fact that he is a salesman, a man whose very business demands taking and encouraging others to take the shadow for the substance, the dream for the reality. As Charley puts it, "for a salesman, there is no rock bottom to the life. He don't put a bolt to a nut, he don't tell you the law or give you medicine. He's a man way out there in the blue riding on a smile and a shoeshine. . . . A salesman is got to dream, boy." It is in this context that Biff's desire to work with his hands, to actually make things rather than to sell them, takes on added significance, as does his remark that "there's more of [Willy] in that front stoop than in all the sales he ever made."

And it is, perhaps, in terms of this juxtaposition of real work with the dreamlike and dream-driven labor of the salesman that the play most obviously and directly comments on the direction American society at large was taking in the 1940s and 1950s as the country's economy began to shift into the phase that one might label "postindustrial" and/or as "consumer culture"—that is, an economy centered less on industry itself than on advertising and public relations, activities that are all about creating images rather than actual things or, in Charley's words, "a smile and a shoeshine" rather than "nuts and bolts." Such an economy is, moreover, devoted not only, as Willy himself is, to the production of "dreams" in the sense of images rather than real things but also to the manufacture of ultimately unfulfillable "dreams" in the sense of consumer desires. In consumer culture, to quote theorist Jean Baudrillard, "a need [for something like a refrigerator] is not a need for a particular object [the refrigerator itself] as much as it is a 'need' for difference (the *desire for social meaning*)" or, in other words, the need to be seen as the kind of person who can recognize and afford the refrigerator defined as best because it has, in Willy's words, "the biggest ads of any of them" (*Selected Writings*, Stanford, Calif., Stanford University Press, 1988, p. 45).

Such competitive desire for what a thing connotes about one's status rather than for the thing itself are, after all, precisely what seem to drive Happy, not least in leading him to seduce a series of executives' girlfriends: for, as he confesses to Biff in a way that makes clear just how endless and unfulfillable such desires are, "I don't know what gets into me, maybe I just have an overdeveloped sense of competition or something, but I went and ruined her, and furthermore I can't get rid of her. And he's the third executive I've done that to. . . . I don't want the girl, and, still, I take it and—I love it!" As a result, as Happy himself suggests, consumer culture traps one in an inescapable process of acquisition in which one can never simply "enjoy" anything once it's acquired (an idea underscored at the end of the play when Willy and Linda finally succeed in paying off a house that there is no longer a real family to live in). As Happy puts it, "it's what I always wanted. My own apartment, a car, and plenty of women. And still, goddammit, I'm lonely."

That ultimate and, in consumer culture's terms, unassuagable loneliness is evoked not only through the content of the play but also through its form, particularly in the way it foregrounds Willy's isolation in a world in which dreams and reality become indistinguishable from each other. For that and other reasons, the set design, lighting, and music are all key elements in the production of *Salesman*; and you may want to lead your students through a discussion of how these can contribute to the movement, effect, and even meaning of the play. Jo Mielziner, who designed the scenes, writes informatively of the problems, intent, and solutions in *Designing for the Theatre* (New York: Atheneum, 1965), and you may want either to tell your students about the initial production or to ask that one or more students read and report on the issues discussed in that book.

More readily available for full class discussion is the device of the flashback, not only the meaning but also the structure. All stories have a past, but in most plays the "necessary" past is supplied by exposition. You may want to ask your students how Miller might have used exposition to tell his story, perhaps asking them to reduce one or another of the flashback scenes to exposition of various kinds (not just the narration of a past scene, such as Willy's description of Biff on the football field). This exercise can be expanded into an interesting writing assignment; see the third writing suggestion below.

QUESTIONS FOR DISCUSSION

1. The play is set in post–World War II New York City, while the flashbacks take place in 1928. Why should Willy choose precisely the year 1928 to recall?
2. Biff seems driven to steal. Why? What personal or family reasons are there? What, if any, societal reasons?
3. Willy seems constantly badgered by machines (his cars, the washer, the refrigerator, the wire recorder, etc.), yet Charley remarks that Willy was "a happy man with a batch of cement," and Willy himself desperately wants to grow things and laments that "I don't have a thing in the ground." What positive and negative values are suggested by these details? How do they relate to the vocation of "selling"?

4. The drama never mentions what Willy sells. Why not?
5. Several characters in the play are searching for the American Dream. What is Willy's definition of this dream? Happy's? Biff's? Linda's? Charley's? Howard's? What characters appear to share the same vision?
6. Some critics have suggested that the idea that a boy would react so strongly as Biff did to his father's infidelity seems dated in the 1990s. You might ask your students if they agree with this. To what degree have we grown used to infidelity in our culture? To what degree do they think changing mores would affect their own reaction to discovering a parent had been unfaithful?
7. In Act I Willy describes himself as "fat," "foolish to look at," and a man who "talks too much," which does not fit his own philosophy of success. How does he reconcile the two? What, if anything, does he do to make aims and reality coincide? How does the contradiction reflect on his words? His beliefs?
8. Why are Willy's interview suggestions to Biff so contradictory? Does Willy follow his own advice in his interview with Howard Wagner?
9. Do the names Miller chooses for his characters have allegorical implications? If so, why would the playwright include allegory in this apparently realistic play?
10. The Requiem makes no mention of the twenty thousand dollars in insurance money. What do you think would have happened to it?
11. Miller tips us off with the title that Willy will die in the end. Why reveal the ending before the play has begun?

SUGGESTIONS FOR WRITING

1. It is hard to imagine two works more different from each other than *Death of a Salesman* and "A Rose for Emily," but a comparison of the two either as "elegies" or as stories suggesting the clash of cultures or generations makes a good paper topic. An alternative is to compare *Salesman* with "The Rocking-Horse Winner" in an essay centering on the role of money in the two works.
2. Write two or three pages of dialogue between Linda and Willy in which she confronts him about his suicidal tendencies and attempts to convince him that killing himself would be a mistake. Of course, the dialogue should be consistent with the facts and evidence of the play.
3. Choose a play you have already read, such as *Oedipus* or *Hedda Gabler*, and write a *Salesman*-like flashback. Then, in a one-page evaluative analysis, explain how adding your scene would change what Sophocles or Ibsen or Williams wrote.

COMPARATIVE QUESTIONS ON *A RAISIN IN THE SUN* AND *DEATH OF A SALESMAN*

1. Taking into account the differences in the experiences of a working-class black family and that of a middle-class white family in the 1950s (in general and in terms of these particular plays), compare Walter Younger in *A Raisin in the Sun* with Willy Loman from *Death of a Salesman*. What are their attitudes toward their responsibilities, wives, sons, jobs, other women, authority, the past? Compare the myths and values that sustain them.
2. What do these two plays seem to be saying about the American Dream? What exactly might the two plays, when compared, suggest about the differences between the experiences and values of African-American and European-American families (or of men in particular) in the 1950s? Between their relationship or attitude toward the myths and dreams so central to American culture? Even if Hansberry wasn't explicitly thinking of *Salesman* when she wrote *A Raisin in the Sun*, how might you see the later play as echoing and even commenting on the earlier one (and/or, more generally, on treatments of the American Dream by white playwrights like Miller)?
3. In what sense might you see either or both of these plays as exploring questions particularly relevant to the United States in the 1950s? In what sense might you see them as addressing issues that remain relevant today? Does one play seem more "modern" or relevant in these terms than the other, or are the two plays each relevant or "modern" in different ways?

READING/WRITING IDEAS FOR CHAPTER 29

ESSAYS ABOUT CULTURAL CONTEXT

Though this chapter suggests many possible writing assignments, one quite interesting one might involve asking students to write essays that interpret one of these two plays by relating it to its particular sociohistorical context, showing, for example, how *A Raisin in the Sun* is informed by the independence struggles that took place on the African continent in the 1950s and/or by the "Afro-centric" movement in United States or how *Death of a Salesman* is informed by changes in American culture and/or economy in the 1940s and 1950s. If you do choose to go with this assignment, you might use this as an opportunity to get students into the library (if that's a requirement or need of your particular course, as it is of mine), asking them to identify and locate both primary and secondary materials relevant to their text and/or topic. If you choose to go that route, you might want to get students started in one of the two ways suggested in "Planning Ideas" for *A Raisin in the Sun* and discussed further in the writing exercises, below. (You might, however, also want to consider saving this chapter and assignment until after students tackle Chapter 30 and assignments that follow.)

A second, less research-oriented essay assignment might instead ask students to focus on cultural issues in a more thematic and/or text-centered way by, for example, having them write about what one or both of these texts suggest about the ways in which gender, race, or class helps to shape one's identity and/or one's experience of America and the American Dream or about what *A Raisin in the Sun*, in particular, suggests about the ways in which black Americans live across or between "cultures." Since such an assignment would likely be a more focused version of the theme-focused essay assignment, you might consider getting students started with versions of the exercises described in "Reading/Writing Ideas for Chapter 6."

TROUBLESHOOTING

Obviously the first, more methodology-focused essay assignments described above will likely be much less familiar and much more challenging to student writers than the second, more thematic assignments, particularly if your assignment includes a research component. My students often tend to be both very excited and engaged by assignments that require them to incorporate source materials of various kinds and to read a literary text or texts in terms of them, but they are also often uncertain about how to go about doing so effectively. One of the biggest challenges they face in tackling assignments that involve analyzing a text in terms of information about cultural context is the temptation to let their essays turn into reports on that information or on that context, rather than crafting essays that use such information in the service of analysis. Thus from the beginning of our work on such an assignment, I simply try to emphasize the similarities between this kind of essay and the other kinds of analytical essays with which they're familiar, to insist that analysis and the text should remain the focus. I also use the exercises below to try to ensure that students approach outside sources from the very beginning with an eye toward questions that arise from, and return to, the text they're analyzing. And, again, I find that it's very helpful to start students off by having them read and discuss essays of the kind that they are being asked to write with an eye toward generating and answering questions about *why* and *how* writers successfully tackle this kind of essay.

CULTURAL CONTEXT–FOCUSED WRITING EXERCISES

Since the more methodology-focused essay assignment described above is the more challenging and differs most from those discussed in previous chapters, the exercises below are by and large meant to suggest ways to get students started on that particular assignment.

1. Identifying the Nature and Function of Primary and Secondary Sources

As with so many essay assignments, I tend to begin this one, as I've already suggested, by having students read sample essays of the type they are being asked to write, either not-too-intimidating scholarly essays or essays by students, and asking them to answer a series of questions as they read. The reading exercise for this assignment tends to look something like this:

Mark the places where each writer mentions source material of any kind. Then, when you've finished, go back and look at your markings, working to generate answers to the following questions:

- Which of these sources are *primary?*
- Which of these sources are *secondary?*
- How would you define the difference between primary and secondary sources? To what extent are the two kinds of sources materials themselves different and to what extent does the difference seem to have to do with the way the writer uses the materials?
- What function do each of the references to primary sources seem to serve in this essay? Why does this writer use primary sources? Make a short list of what you see as the primary functions of primary sources. Might primary sources serve purposes other than those for which they seem to be used in this essay? If so, add those to your list.
- What specific techniques does the writer use to incorporate primary source material effectively? When and why, for example, does the writer quote from the sources? Paraphrase? How do they introduce sources?
- Does source material ever seem to get in the way of, rather than contribute to, the argument here? If so, why do you think it does interfere? What might this writer have done differently or better?

2. Generating Contextual Questions

One way to get students started on writing their own contextual analysis of a text and to ensure that they focus from the outset on the text itself is to have them reread the text in question and to generate research questions along the way, to note when, and where, and how in the text questions arise for them about the cultural context of this story that they can answer only by acquiring more information about that context and/or about the author's particular relation to it (a technique also described above in "Planning Ideas" for *A Raisin in the Sun*). You might have students conclude the exercise by looking over their list of questions, grouping related questions together to generate a list of bigger topics and choosing which of these large topics interests them most. (Students reading *Death of a Salesman*, for example, might discover in rereading it that they want to know more about the economy and culture of America in the 1940s and 1950s, especially, perhaps, facets that are directly alluded to in the play, such as the urbanization process [as well as the suburbanization process], the development of advertising or of labor-saving devices and appliances for home and office [such as refrigerators and tape recorders], or the status and role of the salesman.) Or you might simply wait and have this "homing in on a topic" part of the exercise be part of the in-class work you do with the exercise after students have completed it.

Have them bring their list of questions and topics to class for comparison and discussion; have them discuss both the questions and topics themselves and strategies for identifying and locating sources that might help them find out the things they want to know about their topic. With this exercise, as with many others, I find it helpful to first use one student's questions as an example for the whole class to discuss and to then break the class up into small groups so that everyone's exercise gets thoroughly discussed and students leave the class with a rough idea of where to go next.

CRITICAL CONTEXTS: A DRAMA CASEBOOK

As the critical essays in this chapter begin to suggest and as George Steiner's *Antigones* confirms, Sophocles' *Antigone* seems to have an enduring fascination for readers of all stripes precisely because it provides such fertile ground for debate and disagreement. As a result, it's a wonderful text to use to teach students both just how interesting and challenging it can be to participate in such debates and just what kind of strategies one can use to do so effectively.

Obviously, however, such teaching and such writing raise a number of questions, many of which are discussed in the reading and writing ideas sections of Chapters 12 and 25 of this guide. Here, however, I've chosen to focus less on the questions and more on one particular set of techniques, strategies, and assignments that I've found useful in helping my students tackle the challenges of participating in a critical conversation as both readers and writers.

PLANNING IDEAS

- If you're not having students keep a reading journal throughout the term, you might want to have them start something of the sort now to record their responses to the critical essays in this chapter, encouraging them to use their journal as a place to pose questions about the essays as they read them, to talk about what bugs them about particular essays and/or what points they agree and disagree with, to make notes about aspects or elements or moments of and in the play that aren't discussed in the essays or that they interpret in a different way than a particular author does, and even about writing techniques used by these writers that they might want to try out in their own writing. I personally find that doing so is a way to help students feel that, even as readers, they are active participants in, rather than passive witnesses to, scholarship.

- Since the excerpt from George Steiner's *Antigones* included in this chapter of the anthology is more a general meditation on the issue of interpretation than an interpretation of *Antigone* in particular, you might want to consider having students read this piece early on in the unit, perhaps even before students actually begin reading the critical essays, using the piece to initiate discussion about how extant interpretations of a text do and can inform our reading of it.
- As Steiner (and the anthology) point out, productions of a play are themselves as much interpretations of, or arguments about, that text as are the kind of critical essays students will encounter in this chapter. And one might say the same, in the case of *Antigone,* about different English translations. For that reason, you might want to consider also having students look at filmed versions of *Antigone* and/or having them read alternative translations either of the whole play or of especially important passages.
- Since I use this chapter as part of a unit on writing with secondary sources, my class schedule and assignments for the unit look something like this:

A. Day One: I assign students two sample essays to read, along with a list of questions to pose about the ways in which secondary sources function in the essays. In class, we discuss these particular essays to generate ideas about why and how writers can effectively write about a text in terms of "critical context" (see exercise 1 in "Reading/Writing Ideas for Chapter 30").

B. Day Two: For this class, students are asked to read *Antigone,* and we spend class time discussing the play. Using the ideas in "Questions for Discussion," below, I focus mainly on helping students articulate their ideas about the play, even encouraging them at the end of discussion to define a list of possible topics, issues, or questions they might want to pursue in writing about the play. Along the way, however, I try to ensure that we touch on at least some of the major issues that will come up in the criticism, as well as some of the major issues that *aren't* discussed there (see "Commentary," below).

C. Day Three: Students are asked to read and summarize the critical essays included in the chapter (see exercise 2 in "Reading/Writing Ideas for Chapter 30"). In class, I begin by simply asking students to talk about any moments in the critical essays that confused them in order to make sure that they have a basic understanding of the various arguments. Then, I have students identify the major issues that are being debated by the critics. Once all of these are on the board, we work to define each critic's position on each of these issues, looking at passages from the essays that support our contentions about where critics stand. Finally, if we have time, I have students make another list, this time, of issues or questions that aren't addressed in the critical essays.

D. Day Four: Students are asked to come in to class with topics, questions, or actual thesis statements that they might use as the basis for their essays on *Antigone,* and we discuss a few of these in class, working to help each student construct a workable thesis and a motive that explains the relationship between his or her argument and those of critics (see exercise 3 in "Reading/Writing Ideas for Chapter 30").

E. In the last days of the unit, students draft, critique, and revise their essays.

SOPHOCLES

Antigone

As the critical essays in this chapter of the anthology suggest, *Antigone* is generally seen to revolve around the conflict between Creon, who represents the authority of the state and/or human law, and Antigone, who instead defends the laws of the gods, which she sees as superseding those of the state. Overlapping with, and informing, this conflict is another between Creon's view that political bonds, such as those between citizens of a state, are primary and Antigone's advocacy of personal, familial bonds. It is the former view that clearly underwrites Creon's order that Polyneices remain unburied, for as Creon insists, "I would not count any enemy of my country as a friend—because of what I know, that she it is which gives us our security" (lines 205–208). Equating that "security" with his own kingly authority, Creon insists, as he tells Haemon, "There is nothing worse / than disobedience to authority. / It destroys cities, it demolishes homes; / it breaks and routs one's allies. . . . So we must stand on the side of what is orderly" (lines 723–728). For Antigone, however, there is something worse than disobedience to the laws of man and the state, as well as a higher "order" that must be obeyed and/or secured, one endangered by disobedience to the divine laws that she insists are both more powerful and more permanent than those imposed by mere mortals such as Creon: "I did not believe your proclamation had such power to enable / one who will someday die to override / God's ordinances, unwritten and secure. / *They* are not of today and yesterday; / they live forever" (lines 496–501). From Antigone's point of view, then, the divine law requiring proper burial overrides the human law that decrees Polyneices should not be buried. And in burying Polyneices and defending that action, Antigone simultaneously insists on the sanctity and primacy of familial bonds over political ones: in her view, Polyneices remains her brother and her duty to him stays the same, regardless of his actions toward, or relationship to, the state.

But if the central conflicts of *Antigone* are relatively straightforward, many viewpoints emerge when it comes to questions about how the play as a whole ultimately judges the two positions represented by Antigone and Creon. Of the readers/critics represented in this chapter of the anthology, for example, Richard C. Jebb, Maurice Bowra, and Bernard Knox might be said to occupy one end of the spectrum, each of these critics basically suggesting that, in Jebb's words, Antigone is "wholly in the right," Creon "wholly in the wrong," the play on the whole insisting that "if the two [human and divine law] come into conflict, human law must yield." At the other end of the spectrum, perhaps, lies the argument of Hegel, which is not presented directly here but which does serve as a reference point for almost every critic whose work is represented. Hegel argues essentially that the play ultimately sides with neither of the two characters, instead showing both to be right in principle, both wrong in the utter one-sidedness of their adherence to that principle. To quote Hegel (via Jebb), "both were wrong, because they were one-sided, but at the same time both were right." In between these two extremes, perhaps, lies the argument of Martha Nussbaum. For while Nussbaum agrees with Jebb, Bowra, and Knox in labeling Antigone the "morally superior" character in the play, she also insists that to see Antigone as "a blameless heroine" (as they tend to do) is to neglect the extent to which Antigone herself is guilty of "a ruthless simplification of the world of value which effectively eliminates conflicting obligations." "Like Creon," Nussbaum goes on to say, Antigone "can be blamed for a refusal of vision" and for an adherence to principle that ultimately renders her as emotionless and as deaf to the individuality of others as Creon himself proves to be.

But while you may want to preview this critical argument in discussing the play with students, you may also want to steer them toward a consideration of aspects of the play that don't come in for much critical commentary here. Chief among these, for me, are questions about the role played by gender in shaping the conflict between Antigone and Creon—an issue that discussion question 7 (below) is meant to introduce and that might culminate in a question about the extent to which the play is or is not "feminist"—and (potentially related) questions about the role played by the minor characters here, especially Haemon and Ismene, characters who receive little attention from any critic except Nussbaum.

QUESTIONS FOR DISCUSSION

1. What can you discern from the play about the events leading up to the scene with which the play opens? How and why exactly has Polyneices been killed? What do we know about the parents of Antigone, Ismene, and Polyneices? What significance do these prior events have within the play? Are different interpretations of their significance offered in the play?
2. Why exactly does Creon refuse to allow Polyneices to be buried? What does this decision tell us about Creon's worldview and/or values? What other evidence would you marshal to support this interpreta-

tion? Does Creon or your view of Creon change over the course of the play? If so, how and where and why?

3. Why exactly does Antigone believe that she not only must bury Polyneices, despite Creon's order, but also "shout it out" (line 99)? What does this tell us about Antigone's worldview and/or values? What other evidence would you marshal to support this interpretation? What does Antigone mean, for example, when she says, "I shall be / a criminal—but a religious one" (lines 84–85) or when she tells Creon that "I did not believe your proclamation had such power to enable one who will someday die to override God's ordinances, unwritten and secure" (lines 496–499)?

4. Though Antigone and Creon and the values they each represent are obviously in conflict within the play, is there any way in which the two are alike?

5. What role is played by other characters in the play, particularly Ismene, Haemon, Teiresias, and the Chorus? What worldview or values do these characters seem to embody?

6. How exactly is the conflict between the worldviews and values of Creon and Antigone resolved over the course of the play? Which, if any, does the play as a whole seem to endorse?

7. What, if any, significance do you attribute to the fact that the Sentry initially tells Creon that a man has buried Polyneices (lines 268–271)? That Creon says that "I am no man and she the man if she can win this and not pay for it" (lines 528–529), or is there other evidence in the play to suggest that the conflict between Creon and Antigone is related to the gender of the two parties?

8. At one point in the play, the Chorus seems to suggest that Antigone is doomed, along with the rest of her family, to a tragic fate, saying that "No generation frees another, some god / strikes them down; there is no deliverance" (lines 647–648); at another, however, the Chorus tells her, "it is your own self-willed temper / that has destroyed you" (lines 920–921). Which, if either, of these interpretations does the play as a whole seem to endorse?

9. There is much disagreement among critics about the significance of Antigone's statement that she would not have defied Creon to bury a husband or a child (lines 954–962), some even suggesting that the remark is so out of place and out of character that it must not have been written by Sophocles. What do you think?

RICHARD C. JEBB

from *The Antigone of Sophocles*

MAURICE BOWRA

from *Sophoclean Tragedy*

BERNARD KNOX

Introduction to *Sophocles: The Three Theban Plays*

QUESTIONS FOR DISCUSSION

1. Jebb very clearly states his argument that Sophocles' play centers on "two principles which are opposed to each other. *Creon represents the duty of obeying the State's laws; Antigone, the duty of listening to the private conscience.*" What he doesn't do here, however, is present evidence to back up this reading. Is evidence to support that argument presented in any of the other essays in the chapter? What evidence might *you* draw from the play to support and develop this argument? What evidence might you use to challenge or complicate this argument?
2. Jebb is equally clear in his insistence that the play ultimately sides with the principles of Antigone over those of Creon; again, however, he doesn't provide us with evidence. Is evidence for this point of view presented in any of the other essays in the chapter? What evidence might *you* draw on to support and develop this claim? What evidence might you use to challenge or complicate it?
3. Through his references to Hegel, Jebb indicates that there is at least one critic who disagrees with him. How would you sum up Hegel's counterargument about the play? How exactly does it differ from Jebb's? What evidence might you marshal to support and develop Hegel's argument? How do the arguments of the other critics here relate to that of Hegel?
4. Jebb asserts at one point that Sophocles' tragedy considers "issues, moral and political, which might be discussed on similar grounds in any age and in any country of the world." To what extent do you think this is true? How and why exactly might the "moral and political" "issues" raised in *Antigone* be relevant today? To what extent or in what specific ways might the play and the issues it considers seem more historically and culturally specific than Jebb allows? How might

you stage the play so as to emphasize its universality? Its historical and cultural specificity?

5. In making his argument about *Antigone*, Bowra emphasizes Creon's pride a great deal more than Jebb does, suggesting that the play "shows the fall of a proud man," and that "its lesson is that the gods punish pride and irreverence." What evidence might you draw on to support and develop this claim about Creon? Is there any evidence to suggest that Antigone displays a similar kind of pride (as Bowra himself suggests at one point)? Is there a difference in the level or kind of pride each character exhibits?

6. Toward the end of his essay Knox suggests that some critics believe that the speech Antigone makes toward the end of the play, in which she insists that she would not have defied Creon to bury a husband or a child, isn't, in fact, by Sophocles, insisting that "a decision on this point is of vital significance for the interpretation of the play." How exactly do you interpret the significance of these lines? How might their removal affect the play?

7. Like Jebb and Bowra, Knox invokes, to counter, the argument of Hegel. Along the way, however, he does something the other critics do not when he urges us to see Hegel's reaction to the play as being informed by his reaction to the specific social and political conditions of his own day and age. Knox suggests, in other words, that critical responses to, or arguments about, particular texts are informed by the critic's own particular social and historical location. How, then, might you see Knox's own argument or that of any other critic in this chapter as being informed by contemporary American social, historical, and political conditions and/or attitudes?

GEORGE STEINER

from *Antigones*

This excerpt from Steiner is, in large part, less an interpretation of *Antigone* itself than it is a thoughtful contemplation of different interpretive strategies. For this reason, it may be useful to have students read this piece early in this unit, using it to initiate discussion of the way in which productions themselves constitute part of the ongoing interpretive dialogue about a text and about the way pre-existing interpretations of a "classic" text can and should affect our reading of that text.

But despite its focus on more general interpretive issues, Steiner's piece does ultimately offer an interesting interpretation of *Antigone*, though an interpretation that may prove somewhat difficult for students to readily grasp and understand. As I understand it, this interpretation involves seeing the play as contemplating the "dissociations between thought and action, between understanding and practice," its "undeclared tragedy" residing in the characters' unrelenting insistence on action, their failure to face the complexity of the situation at hand or to attempt to understand alternative views. As a result, the play may be seen to contemplate, even to question, the action-centered ethos at the heart not only of Greek drama but also—if we are to believe philosopher Michel Foucault—of the classical ethos more generally. Though Steiner doesn't say so here, such an interpretation would, I think, lead one to see the play much as Hegel did in the sense that in these terms both Antigone and Creon seem equally faulty, equally guilty.

QUESTIONS FOR DISCUSSION

1. What exactly does Steiner suggest about how we do and should read "a work of literature" when he contrasts such a work (in the first paragraph) with "a piece of sculpture"? What, for example, is the significance of the word "circumvent"?
2. In the second paragraph, Steiner continues to make an argument about how we do and should read literary texts by insisting that "we can hardly hope to reconstruct the inward process of assemblage and unification as it is experienced and reported . . . by the artist himself." What kind of reading process or strategy is Steiner implicitly arguing against here?
3. In the third paragraph, Steiner implicitly suggests that drama represents a special challenge to readers and particularly to readers reading with an eye toward "reconstruct[ing]" authorial intention. According to Steiner, what are those special challenges? How do his references to a particular Russian director help him to define those challenges?
4. How does Steiner characterize the readerly strategies of the "philologist and textual scholar"? What exactly does he suggest is wrong with such strategies? What exactly does he mean when he says that "a great poem or play" has an essentially "organic nature"?
5. What does Steiner suggest in the next paragraph about how the literary critic does and should proceed in interpreting a text? What does he mean when he says that "Honest literary criticism is simply that which makes its proposed constructions most plainly visible and open to challenge"? What kind of reading strategy does Steiner seem to be advocating here and in the rest of the excerpt?
6. What does Steiner mean when he says "there is no complete modern innocence in the face of the classics"? What is he suggesting about the relation between "text" and "context"?
7. Toward the end of this excerpt Steiner's argument becomes less about reading strategies in general and more about his particular interpretation of *Antigone*. What exactly is that interpretation? How exactly is it like and unlike those of Jebb, Knox, and Bowra? For example, would Steiner accept Jebb's argument that Antigone is presented in the play as "wholly in the right" and Creon as "wholly in the wrong"? With

Hegel's argument that both characters are at once right and wrong?
8. Leaving aside the question of whether or not Steiner would agree with the substance of the arguments made by the other critics in this chapter, what do you think he would say about their reading strategies? Might any of these critics be seen to employ any of the reading strategies that Steiner criticizes in this excerpt? Might any of these arguments illustrate what he calls "honest literary criticism"?

MARTHA C. NUSSBAUM
_____

from *The Fragility of Goodness*

Nussbaum's argument could be seen as offering students a middle ground between the two extreme views represented by Hegel, on the one hand, and Knox and Bowra, on the other. For while Nussbaum agrees with the latter that Antigone is ultimately the "morally superior" character, she insists that critics, such as Knox and Bowra, who see Antigone as "a blameless heroine" err in neglecting the extent to which Antigone herself is guilty of "a ruthless simplification of the world of value which effectively eliminates conflicting obligations. Like Creon, she can be blamed for a refusal of vision." (If we take, as I think we can, Nussbaum's "vision" to be akin to Steiner's "thought," we can see a real kinship between Nussbaum's argument and Steiner's more enigmatic and/or tentative one.) Like Knox, Nussbaum puts emphasis on the centrality of "the family bond" to Antigone's creed, but in keeping with her general criticism of Knox-like visions of Antigone, she also argues that Antigone's insistence on a family-based ethos ironically becomes as emotionless and as impersonal as Creon's state-based ethos. More interesting, perhaps, is that in the process of making her argument, Nussbaum gives much more time than any of the other critics do to the role of Haemon and Ismene, whom she suggests embody the kind of passion for particular individuals of which both Antigone and Creon are equally incapable.

QUESTIONS FOR DISCUSSION

1. In the first paragraph of this excerpt, Nussbaum insists that one can both see Antigone as "morally superior to Creon" (as Knox, Bowra, and Jebb do) and agree with Hegel's argument that Antigone and Creon are equally right and equally wrong. How exactly does Nussbaum reconcile these two opposed arguments? In what sense does she see Antigone as "morally superior"? In what sense does she see Antigone as faulty and/or as like Creon?
2. How exactly might one see Nussbaum's interpretation of the play as like and unlike Steiner's?
3. Nussbaum's argument pays a great deal more attention than other

critics to the role played by Ismene and Haemon. What exactly does she argue about their significance to the play? How might you enlarge on that argument? What might the critics who don't mention these two characters argue about their role?

REBECCA W. BUSHNELL

from *Prophesying Tragedy*

Though Bushnell's focus on speech may make it at first seem somewhat anomalous in terms of the critical conversation going on in the other essays in the chapter, her argument can easily be aligned with the "pro-Antigone" arguments of Jebb, Knox, and Bowra. For ultimately Bushnell's argument about the way in which Antigone maintains the power of authoritative speech, while Creon becomes "nothing, a voice which is . . . 'without significance' " ends with the statement that "Sophocles gives the victory to" Antigone.

QUESTIONS FOR DISCUSSION

1. How exactly is Bushnell's interpretation of the conflict between Creon and Antigone like and unlike those of other critics? Does it ultimately seem more like the pro-Antigone arguments of Knox, Bowra, and Jebb or more like the Hegelian interpretation?
2. Bushnell is the only critic to say anything about the role played by gender in the play when she says that "Antigone is denied personal and political autonomy in the city of Thebes" because she is "a woman." How might you expand on this insight?
3. Bushnell seems to make two contradictory claims when she says both that "Antigone loses this battle" and that "Sophocles gives the victory to her." Why and how, according to Bushnell, aren't these claims as contradictory as they might seem?
4. Bushnell's argument mainly focuses on the end of the play, but what evidence might you draw from the earlier portions of the play to support her argument that the play is, in a sense, about the power to speak authoritatively?

MARY WHITLOCK BLUNDELL

from *Helping Friends and Harming Enemies*

Though Blundell gives due weight to Nussbaum's argument about the likeness between Creon and Antigone, she, too, ultimately sides with the pro-Antigone faction of this critical debate, ultimately insisting that "One-sided and 'autonomous' though she may be, Antigone's obsession is less sterile and destructive than Creon's." In the process, however, Blundell offers a very different interpretation of the conflict between Creon and Antigone than that offered by the other critics, insisting that Antigone's focus on duty to family does not conflict with, or entail a repudiation of, duty to the state (as all of the other critics tend to assume that it does). In fact, Blundell argues, the idea that duty to state and duty to family are necessarily in conflict is attributable to Creon alone within the play, an idea shown to be a mistaken one that ultimately and ironically endangers the very state he ostensibly honors. In Blundell's words, "It is Creon's own scorn not just for the family but for public opinion which finally brings the *polis* 'doom instead of *soteria*' " or salvation. Also key to this argument is the fact of Antigone's royal blood (a fact largely ignored by other critics): for, as Bushnell argues, this fact renders her invocations of duty both to family and to ancestral gods simultaneously, if implicitly, an invocation of "obligations to the *polis.*"

QUESTIONS FOR DISCUSSION

1. Though Blundell ultimately seems to side with the pro-Antigone camp, she in fact sees the conflict within the play very differently than other critics do. How exactly does her interpretation of the conflict differ from those of the other critics you've read?
2. One of the facts Blundell draws on to support her argument is Antigone's membership in the Theban royal family. Why is that fact so important to Blundell's argument?
3. Toward the end of the excerpt, Blundell quotes Haemon. What might this quotation suggest about how Blundell interprets Haemon's significance within the play? How is her interpretation of Haemon's role like and unlike Nussbaum's?

READING/WRITING IDEAS FOR CHAPTER 30

ESSAYS ABOUT CRITICAL CONTEXT

In my experience, both literature-based composition courses and composition-focused literature courses tend to require students to write at least one essay over the course of a term that incorporates secondary sources, usually literary criticism of one sort or another. Such assignments have proved both beneficial and enjoyable to my students for a host of reasons, not least the fact that "research essays" are so commonly assigned in all types of courses, yet my students often feel very uncertain about their skills in this area. But such assignments can also be really rewarding to students because they sometimes suddenly begin to see their essays not just as responses to assignments that have value only in the

context of a particular classroom, but as real contributions to real scholarly debates, their chance to be part of a conversation that includes, but
extends well beyond, this particular classroom.

I personally have begun to require my students to write two research
essays, providing them with the secondary source material for the first
assignment and requiring them to identify and locate some or all of
their source material for the second. This arrangement works well for
me because it allows me to focus separately on the very different issues
of research per se and of writing with sources, focusing first solely on
the techniques and strategies involved in actually incorporating source
material into one's writing, as well as questions about why one bothers
to do so, and then and only then on actual research strategies and techniques. Thus for my purposes and for those of you who—like me—
aren't blessed with an extensive university library, this "critical contexts" chapter works well for the first kind of essay assignment, saving
me the time and labor that I usually put into assembling packets of secondary source material.

With this essay assignment, I find that two central questions I face are
when and how exactly to introduce the critical essays and how specific
to be with the assignment, questions discussed at length in the reading
and writing ideas for Chapters 12 and 25. Rather than here re-engaging
those questions or discussing the range of possible strategies and assignments they suggest, I want to illustrate one approach in more detail.

That approach entails using the materials in the chapter as part of a
unit that culminates in a relatively loose essay assignment, one that simply asks students to make an argument about *Antigone* that incorporates
material from the secondary sources. I do so because I have found that
being allowed to formulate their own topics and questions, while making
the assignment more difficult in certain ways, makes it easier for students
in other ways by encouraging them to feel that they are real scholars
participating in a real critical debate.

TROUBLESHOOTING

One of the main challenges that my students face in writing critical context essays (or research essays of any sort, for that matter) is the tendency
to let sources dominate the essay and drown the students' ideas out. I've
found that this problem tends to take one of two forms in my students'
essays: first is the essay that simply reiterates the argument of a source;
second, the essay that spends all of its time arguing with a source or
sources, yet "forgets," in a sense, that the only way to make such an
argument is to provide an alternative interpretation of the text. The main
thing I try to do is insist from the beginning that (and how and why) the
text itself has to be the focus, that even arguments with sources can only
be substantiated by interpretation of evidence from the text. Though they
don't always serve to head off such problems, the exercises described

below have proved extremely helpful to me in teaching students how to use sources to make their own argument about the text.

CRITICAL CONTEXT–FOCUSED WRITING EXERCISES

1. Identifying the Functions and Uses of Sources

To prepare students to write essays that use secondary sources, I almost always begin by having them read one or two essays that do so. My goal in having students read and then discuss such essays is to begin to ask questions not only about *how* writers use secondary sources, but also about *why* they do so, the idea being that one can't do something effectively unless or until one knows what the purpose of doing so is. In preparation for discussion, then, I ask students to read the essays very carefully and to pay particular attention to the use of sources, asking them to formulate answers to the following basic questions as they read:

- Mark the places where each writer refers to secondary sources. How does the writer introduce source material? What does the writer tell you about each source? Are there any places where you feel the writer doesn't give you enough or gives you too much information about a source?
- What function does each reference to a source seem to serve in the essay? Why does the writer refer to each source? What precise contribution does it make? Are there any places where you feel the purpose of source material isn't clear? Where source material doesn't seem to make much of a contribution?

In discussion, I allow students relatively free rein, but I make sure that at some point in the discussion we pay particular attention to how writers use sources to establish a *motive* for their essays, by which I mean the reason a writer gives the reader for thinking his or her essay worth reading.[1] In this case, motive means, more particularly, a sense of the contribution the essay makes to the ongoing critical conversation about a particular text. To facilitate this discussion, I put on the board what I see as the three main source-related motives that writers can use, and I try to get the students to identify the particular motives established by the student writers whose essays they're reading.

While this exercise works for me because I make sure to assign essays that use sources to establish one of these three motives, you could still use a version of this in-class exercise by simply giving students a handout that includes the following definitions and sample introductions (though you might want to have students match up definitions with examples rather than putting them together for students as I've done for you here, and you might also want to warn them that these examples do not all come from essays on drama).

---

1. This discussion of motive is heavily indebted to my colleagues at the Harvard Expository Writing Program, particularly Gordon Harvey, who first introduced me to the term and provided both the general definition and the definitions of particular types of motives to which I refer here.

1. Published critical interpretations disagree about a particular issue, thus suggesting that there's still a problem or a puzzle here worth investigating.

Sample Introduction

Given that Sylvia Plath's "Daddy" is a poem in which a daughter compares her father to a Nazi and herself to a Jew, it is perhaps not at all surprising that the poem has provoked a variety of unusually heated responses from readers, literary critic Irving Howe even going so far as to dismiss the poem and its author as both "pathological" and "hysterical." Yet however dismissive his ultimate attitude toward the poem might be, Howe does offer a viable interpretive framework for interpretation of the poem when he labels it a "revenge fantasy, feeding upon filial love and hatred." Building on, yet refining, that idea, many critics, including Margaret Homans and Mary Lynn Broe, have come to consider the poem as enacting what Judith Kroll calls a "ritual of exorcism" through which the female speaker seeks to "expe[l]" "the father's ghost" and to overcome her extreme "attachment to him."

Yet while these critics all agree that the poem can best be understood as a "ritual of exorcism," they disagree rather dramatically when it comes to assessing the extent to which this exorcism is ultimately successful. On the one hand, Kroll herself adopts the most positive view, at the very least implying that the speaker is ultimately successful in "finally exorcis[ing] her father as if he were a scapegoat invested with the evils of her spoiled history," her "true self . . . released . . . when the oppressor is made hateful, and thereby overthrown." On the other hand, however, Mary Lynn Broe takes the opposite stance, suggesting that the exorcism "comically backfires as pure self-parody: the metaphorical murder of the father dwindles into Hollywood spectacle, while the poet is lost in the clutter of the collective unconscious." Plath's "Daddy" thus remains a puzzle, for even if we see the poem as embodying the speaker's attempt to exorcise her father and the "false self who is in his thrall," it remains uncertain whether the speaker is ultimately successful or not.

2. Particular published interpretation(s) are faulty in some particular way and need to be challenged or complicated.

Sample Introduction

In *Othello*, Shakespeare creates one of his most captivating characters. At a time when the world perceived Venice as a playland seething with lax morals beneath a veneer of purity, his Desdemona stood out in her ability to adhere to her principles and act on what she believes right ([Virginia M.] Vaughan[, "Global Discourse: Venetians and Turks," *Othello: A Contextual History*. Cambridge, UK: Cambridge University Press, 1994,] 16). This strength, in addition to her beauty and chastity, sets her apart from Elizabethan literature's other battered and browbeaten victims of jealousy like Lady Elizabeth Cary's Mariam (Vaughan 84). The majority of critics, however, believe that as the play progresses, Desdemona, who "is initially portrayed as a spirited and independent woman . . . loses her self-confidence" and that "Desdemona abandons her ability to think for herself" (Vaughan 72). And in her essay, "Marital Discourse: Husbands and Wives" [in *Othello: A Contextual History*], Virginia Mason Vaughan explains how "many have wondered why the young woman who stood against her father before the Venetian Senate goes so submissively to her death" (73). These critics maintain that Desdemona, previously such a strong-willed character, contradicts the very nature of a strong person by succumbing to the debilitating pressures around her. A close examination of her last speech in Act IV, Scene ii, however, proves the contrary of what these critics claim. Finally aware of Othello's suspicions of her unfaithfulness after he openly confronts her in their argument, Desdemona begins in this monologue to remedy the turmoil she suddenly finds herself facing. By not giving in and staying true to her heavily Christian ideals in this pivotal passage, Desdemona demonstrates more power of free will than her husband, Othello. Once seen in this light, her final submission becomes a continuation of her strong will, not an abandonment of it.

From Jeannette Y. Louh's "Persistence in Life and in Death: Desdemona's
Strength of Character." In *Exposé: Essays from the Expository Writing Program,
Harvard University, 1995–1996* (Cambridge, Mass., Harvard University Press, 1996).

3. Particular published interpretations make a particular claim that needs to be expanded on or utterly neglect a particular and particularly significant issue in, or aspect of, the text.

Sample Introduction

Elizabeth Graver's first short story collection, *Have You Seen Me?*, attracted considerable critical acclaim upon its release in 1991. Most reviews of the collection focused on conflicting interpretations of her protagonists' tendency to face reality head-on or to retreat into fantasy worlds of their own. From Susan Heath's claim that the protagonists' "clarity of thought is what keeps danger at bay" to Roberta Schur's belief that the protagonists "rely on their private fantasy worlds to escape the pain of the real world," each critic offers her own interpretation of this reality-fantasy conflict in Graver's work. Certainly there are a multitude of possible reality-fantasy interpretations of "The Body Shop," Graver's tale of a ten-year-old boy, Simon, who lives and works tirelessly with his mother in her mannequin repair shop. Studying the story from such an angle, however, would mean treading on ground already covered by every reviewer of Graver's work and ignoring the aspects of "The Body Shop" which distinguish it from her other stories. For while Simon's internal and exterior worlds are clearly important, Graver's commentary on gender roles is equally, if less obviously, so. Through a unique parenting situation, Graver explores how difficult coming of age is for someone who lacks a same-sex role model. Without a father, the protagonist is forced to serve the dual role of husband and child to his mother and, as a result, his development as a separate individual is severely hampered.

From Paul Todgham, "Inside 'The Body Shop,' " an unpublished student essay.

2. Summarizing Critical Conversations

Because using source material requires that students can understand and effectively describe not only individual arguments but also the relationships between different arguments and because I've discovered— much to my chagrin—that these tasks often prove difficult for students, I always have my students write short summaries of source material. I usually ask them to first write very short summaries (say, three sentences long) of the argument of each source and then to write what I call a "synthetic summary" that brings those arguments together in two or so paragraphs, showing how they all fit together as parts of one argumentative "conversation." Doing so requires that they define the main issues that are, in a word, at issue in the conversation and that they essentially define a spectrum of possible stands on those issues, indicating what place each source occupies on that spectrum. Sometimes I also have students conclude their summary with a paragraph or two in which they evaluate the sources, pointing out weaknesses in the arguments, identifying questions or details ignored by critics, etc. Then, in class, I organize discussion of the criticism in the manner suggested in the last of the planning ideas for this chapter.

In the case of the specific materials in this chapter, students tend to identify two main questions or topics at issue in the critical conversation about *Antigone*, one having to do with the exact nature of the conflict between Creon and Antigone (and/or about the exact nature of the world-view and/or values each represents) and the other having to do with the way in which the play ultimately resolves that conflict. And in the above commentaries, I've tried to indicate my sense of where particular critics stand on these two issues, as well as some of the issues or elements of the text that are either utterly neglected by the critics or touched on only slightingly.

3. Developing Theses and Motives

For this assignment, I ask students to describe in writing two different possible topics or even thesis statements for their essay on *Antigone*. In class, I remind students of the possible source-related motives described above, putting these on the board. Then I have individual students present their "favorite" topic to the class, and the class as a whole then discusses both how this writer might turn that topic into a workable thesis statement or question and how he or she can use references to sources to establish in his or her introduction one of the possible kinds of source-related motives we've identified.

Students who want to write about whether the play ultimately suggests that Antigone or Creon is proved to be the "morally superior" character in the play, for example, would likely want to construct an introduction that looked something like the first sample paragraph above, whereas students writing about gender issues in the play might create one something like the second sample paragraph and students writing about Ismene or Haemon's role in the play something along the lines of the third.

Evaluating Drama

Juxtaposing a classic, and classically, American tragedy with one of Shake-speare's finest comedies, this chapter might provide you with an opportunity to revisit generic issues raised in Chapter 28, while also introducing students to the difficult task, or even art, of evaluating rather than simply analyzing dramatic texts. And, in fact, you might want to capitalize on that conjunction of issues by having students consider not only general evaluative questions about whether and why either of these plays is a good play but also more specific questions that incorporate a consideration of genre—as in, (why) is this play a good comedy or tragedy?

TENNESSEE WILLIAMS

A Streetcar Named Desire

PLANNING IDEAS

- *Streetcar* is a useful play for reviewing large contextual issues, whether historical, social, or philosophical. Besides being a characteristic Tennessee Williams play, it is also a characteristic southern play, a characteristic American play, and a characteristic modern play. You will know that, but your students are not likely to have read widely enough to know it or even to know what features might define these categories. But you have some other plays to draw on now, and a brief glance at questions of topicality will give you a chance to review some features of plays already studied, especially those by Chekhov, Ibsen, Hellman, and Miller.
- Ask your students what features, characters, scenes, or stage directions here remind them of plays they've read earlier. Get them to explain exactly what the similarities (and differences) consist in.
- Here is another specific way to get the class to consider questions of setting, character, language, and symbol, as well as social and cultural questions. Ask the class to describe the place that, although not shown in the play, is central to its conception: Belle Reve. (This exercise would also make, properly limited, a good paper topic.) List everything we

actually know about Belle Reve. What do we assume, beyond what we're told, about its appearance, size, and value? How important is it that the audience makes specific assumptions about Belle Reve? (See also the "Questions for Discussion," below.)

- Another, complementary way of approaching some of the staging issues is through close analysis of Williams's stage directions. Williams pays much more attention than most playwrights to details of production—from the appearance and clothes of actors to specific stage directions—and he gives full and precise accounts of how he expects the play to be staged. If you have spent time in class earlier having your students analyze in detail the staging of a scene from another play, have them compare the stage directions in that play with those of Williams. The Bear works particularly well as a contrast because Chekhov's directions are relatively brief and only suggestive. Even if you haven't spent class time on staging in The Bear, you can easily look back to it and invite the students to compare the two strategies. Help them notice, too, how Williams's staging—like Ibsen's—suggests visually some of the larger themes of the play. Have them walk through, for example, the end of Scene 2 in which Williams's directions, as well as the dialogue, suggest the uncertainties of Blanche and Stella while emphasizing the simpler determination of the men. Ask them to interpret the effect of having the men walk between the women, spatially dividing them. Get them to speculate at length, after they have seen classmates walk through the scene, about the effect on the audience. Have them relate the visual effects specified here to specific passages of dialogue in the play; that is, make them back up their interpretation of character and themes with specific evidence in the text. What advantages and disadvantages are there when a playwright is so visually specific about his intentions?

- Now that Tennessee Williams's Collected Stories have been published (New York: New Directions, 1985), some of your best students might wish to take on the difficult (but rewarding) task of comparing some of the stories to other Williams plays. The reading of the stories can, of course, extend the points made in the chapter (and in class) on authorial context, for the stories present many of the same themes, concerns, and character types as Streetcar and the excerpts in the text. Williams is not as skilled a writer of stories as he is a playwright, but his often more tentative art in the stories is sometimes an advantage in looking at the relationship between his life and work. Several of the stories are sort of "trial" versions of the plays and offer especially promising paper topics for students capable of independent work and longer writing assignments. The different demands and effects of narrative and dramatic art can become quite evident in close comparisons. If you can offer your students the time to do the extra reading and writing, try having them make one the following comparisons:

A. "Portrait of a Girl in Glass" with *The Glass Menagerie*

B. "Three Players" with *Cat on a Hot Tin Roof* (the story versions lacks some of the play's central characters, Big Daddy, for example)

C. "Night of the Iguana" with *Night of the Iguana*

D. "The Yellow Bird" with *Summer and Smoke*

COMMENTARY

Even for students whose only knowledge of American drama comes from their reading of the plays in this anthology, *Streetcar* will undoubtedly strike a series of familiar chords: Blanche DuBois, with her memories of the past and her inexorable descent into madness, may well and rightly remind some of Willy Loman, while others will undoubtedly be struck by the similarity between Williams's visions of the conflict between Old and New South and that offered in Hellman's *The Little Foxes*. Such comparisons may well be a productive way to spark discussion, particularly about the peculiarly American and peculiarly southern character of the play and the ways in which it is informed by historical and cultural context.

What comparison with *The Little Foxes*, in particular, may allow you to foreground is the almost Darwinian nature of Williams's depiction of the brutal but vibrant Stanley Kowalski's triumph over the fragile Blanche DuBois. From the very beginning of the play, after all, Williams goes out of his way to associate Stanley with animal brutality by having him arrive on the scene with "a red-stained package from a butcher's." (I am always reminded of Tennyson's "Nature—red in tooth and claw.") And, lest we miss the point, Williams gives us a second chance later in the play when he has Blanche herself refer back to this primal scene in explaining that Stanley is "common" not only in the sense that he comes from a socially inferior caste but also in the sense that he represents the lowest, most animal-like form of human life: "He acts like an animal, has an animal's habits! Eats like one, moves like one, talks like one! There's even something—sub-human—something not quite to the state of humanity yet! . . . Stanley Kowalski—survivor of the Stone Age! Bearing the raw meat home from the kill in the jungle!" Blanche thereby invokes an almost Darwinian paradigm to characterize Stanley, insisting that he represents an earlier step on the evolutionary ladder, a man whom "Thousands and thousands of years" of evolution "have passed . . . right by," and that paradigm reappears in Stella's reference to Stanley as "a different species."

And, as this suggests, Blanche herself is associated throughout the play with civilization and refinement or, in her own words, with "Such things as art—as poetry and music" and the "tenderer feelings" that distinguish humans from animals. Thus Blanche is not only an English teacher but also one who continually insists on reading characters and events in the world around her in literary terms—as, for example, when she compares Mitch to Dumas's Armand. Such a comparison, moreover, is merely one

example of the countless ways in which Blanche thereby insistently val-
orizes the "tenderer feelings" that reach their apotheosis in romantic
depictions of love like those of Dumas. Such depictions, moreover,
depend heavily on the kind of ritualized notion of human interaction
that is also embodied in Blanche's devotion to traditional social decorum,
a decorum which—from Blanche's point of view—is the "magic" that
beautifies and ennobles human interaction, softening our more brutal
impulses just as her Japanese lantern softens and beautifies the light of a
bare bulb. In Blanche's own words, "I don't want realism. I want magic!"
And the play encourages us, I think, to respect and even honor Blanche's
"magic," recognizing that there is something right in the idea that the
moon would be real rather than paper "if you believed in me" and something truly noble (rather than "sinful") in her efforts both to make the
world a more beautiful place and to thereby stand up, in a sense, for "what
ought to be the truth" rather than for what is. (As I jokingly ask my students, do you really think a writer wouldn't, in some sense, side with the
character he associates with literature?)

From Stanley's point of view, however, "poetry and music," like the
civilized social codes that Blanche insists on upholding, are merely "a
pack of lies" that simply disguise rather than truly change or refine the
brutal truth—in Stanley's eyes, in other words, it truly is "only a paper
moon, Sailing over a cardboard sea," and one had better simply face the
fact, just as one should face the fact the men and women are drawn
together by lust rather than love or by, in Stella's words, "what men and
women do together in the dark." And part of Stanley's strength clearly
lies not only in his sheer animalistic vitality but also in the "realism" that
allows him to stand face to face with the brutal truths of human existence
in a way that Blanche simply cannot, truths that the play ultimately
affirms, in part, through the scene in which a nameless prostitute rolls a
drunkard only to have her own sequined bag stolen by the equally nameless "negro woman"—as if human life were a brutal struggle in which one
is always either victim or victor.

In this play, of course, Stanley is, indeed, the ultimate and inevitable
victor, not only because he destroys Blanche but also because he wins
Stella (who is, in many ways, the focal point of the ideological battle
waged between Stanley and Blanche in the play). Fittingly enough, it is
Stanley's devotion to realism that, of course, allows him to destroy Blanche—much of the action of the play centering on his inevitable discovery
and revelation of the truth about Blanche, culminating with Stanley symbolically and literally "seiz[ing] the paper lantern" and "tearing it off the
light bulb." In the process, too, Stanley finally becomes the brute that
Blanche has all along accused him of being, practicing the "[d]eliberate
cruelty" Blanche herself calls "the one unforgivable thing," "the one
thing of which I have never, ever been guilty."

Despite, or perhaps because of this "drive that he has" to win at all
costs, however, Stanley is, as Stella puts it, "the only one" "likely to get

anywhere." Thus, in the end, the play turns Blanche's evolutionary meta-phors on their head, suggesting that in the struggle of the fittest that is contemporary American life, it is the "primitive" Stanley Kowalski's and not the evolved Blanche DuBois's who both survive and reproduce.

QUESTIONS FOR DISCUSSION

1. Just as *Antigone* centers on the conflict between the different ideals represented by the characters of Creon and Antigone, Williams's *Streetcar* seems to center on the conflict between Blanche DuBois and Stanley Kowalski. What exactly does each of these characters seem to represent? Why and how are their worldviews and/or values in conflict? What's the significance, for example, of the fact that Blanche teaches English ("Never arithmetic, sir")? That she is so con-cerned with her appearance? That she "can't stand a naked light bulb, any more than [she] can a rude remark or a vulgar action"? That she is compared to "a moth"? That Stanley is "a Polack" who refers to himself as "the unrefined type," "common as dirt"? That he first appears carrying a blood-stained package from the butcher's? That he is referred to as "an animal," "a pig," and "a richly feathered male bird among hens"?

2. Of these two characters, whom do you most sympathize with and/or admire at different moments of the play? When and why, for ex-ample, might you sympathize with and/or admire Stanley? Blanche? What are the admirable characteristics of each? Their faults?

3. What role does Stella play in this conflict? What, for example, is the significance of the scene in which Blanche tries to convince Stella to leave Stanley?

4. At one point in the play Blanche tells Mitch that "The first time I laid eyes on [Stanley] I thought to myself, that man is my execu-tioner! That man will destroy me." Is Blanche right? How and why exactly does Stanley "destroy" Blanche? At what point in the play do you realize that Blanche is doomed? That Stanley is destined to be her "executioner"?

5. What is the significance of the fact that Blanche is, as her name sug-gests, of "French extraction" and that she speaks French at least once during the play? That Stanley insists that he is "a one-hundred-per-cent American, born and raised in the greatest country on earth and proud as hell of it"?

6. What is the significance of Stanley's allusion in Scene 8 to Huey Long's remark that "Every Man is a King"? How might this remark resonate with the references to class sprinkled throughout the play, including the initial description of Stella as "of a background obvi-ously quite different from her husband's" and Stanley's reference to how he "pulled [Stella] down off them columns"?

7. Much of the action of the play centers on the process whereby Stan-

ley discovers and reveals what he sees as the truth about Blanche and about Blanche's past, and he more than once refers to her as a liar. Yet Blanche herself offers us a very different reading of her lies, particularly in her encounter with Mitch in Scene 9. In what sense is and is not Blanche a liar? Why is Stanley so bent on discovering and revealing the truth?

8. A key moment in Blanche's past and one that we get both from her point of view and from Stella's is the night when her young husband shot himself. What is the significance of that moment? Why do you think it figures so largely, not only in Blanche's mind, but also in the play?

9. What is the significance of the play's title? How did Williams change the play by naming it *A Streetcar Named Desire* rather than *The Poker Night?* How does the title resonate with other mentions of desire throughout the play—as when Blanche responds to Stella's reference to the "things that happen between a man and a woman in the dark" by saying "What you are talking about is brutal desire—just—Desire!" (Scene 4) or when she tells Mitch that desire is "[t]he opposite" of death (Scene 9). What different kinds or notions of "desire" are at issue in the play? What role might these different notions play in defining the conflict between Blanche and Stanley?

10. What emotional associations does Belle Reve have for Blanche? For Stella? What values for each? In what ways do the two feel differently about it? About their earlier lives? What aspects of the character of each are involved with their experiences of Belle Reve? With their memories of it? With their sense of what it stands for personally? With what it stands for symbolically? What does Belle Reve stand for to Stanley? How important are the particulars of Belle's Reve's history? Why does the play not go into more detail about the plantation? How fully does Belle Reve represent "old southern values"? What does the history of Belle Reve tell us about conflicts within the tradition? About interruption of the tradition? Who are the heroes in the myth of Belle Reve? The villains? In what specific ways might a southern audience be likely to understand the symbolism of Belle Reve more fully than another audience? How does the name of the plantation (literally "beautiful dream," of course) comment on what happens in the play?

11. Like Belle Reve, New Orleans is portrayed in ways that are somewhat stereotypical: there is ever-present music, an easy (although superficial) mixing of blacks and whites, a strong consciousness of different ethnic traditions, a preoccupation with food and drink, a lot of emphasis on play, gambling, leisure. Does this kind of "typicality" weaken the play? What advantages does such satisfaction of expectations have? What other stereotypes does Williams use in the play? With what effects? How do these stereotypes affect the themes of the play?

WILLIAM SHAKESPEARE

A Midsummer Night's Dream

PLANNING IDEAS

- This play includes a number of scenes that play extremely well when acted out, especially the scenes involving the rustics. The Pyramus and Thisby play-within-the-play in particular almost always works—even better if performed with makeshift props and costumes rather than elaborate ones.
- Students reading *Dream* are more easily confused by who is in love with whom than they would be if they watched it. It helps to sort things out ahead of time as follows: at first both men love the same woman, then each loves the wrong woman, then both love the other woman, and finally each loves the right one.
- Have the class untangle in a prose paraphrase the "tangled chain" of Peter Quince's Prologue beginning at V.1.126. A volunteer can then deliver the speech as Quince might.

COMMENTARY

At the end of *A Midsummer Night's Dream*, Demetrius loves Helena because he is still under the influence of the love potion; he hasn't had the antidote sprinkled into his eyes. The fact that his condition isn't very troubling to us is instructive. In a play that depicts erotic love as foolishness (significantly, *fond* meant "foolish" in Shakespeare's day), it doesn't really matter whether the condition of being in love is induced by a chemical from a plant or one from the lover's own glands. Either way, it's a kind of temporary insanity. The convention of ending the comedy with a marriage celebration (in this case a triple marriage) assures us that the young lovers' infatuation will develop into mature love. But of course comedies *end* with weddings because a good, stable marriage doesn't make for good theater; erotic lovers' ups and downs do.

Dreams, of course, blur the line between reality and fantasy. Although imaginary, they are based on ordinary actions in real life—and seem real enough while they are going on. If the lovers find dream and reality "strange and undistinguishable," so do the rustics. Nothing could be more real to them than what to us is pure fantasy: the prospect of their performing great theater in the court of Theseus. The rustics are hopeless dreamers, but they do end up providing very pleasurable theater at court.

In the end, of course, we enjoy the Pyramus and Thisby play every bit as much as the courtiers do. The whole of *A Midsummer Night's Dream*, in fact, is immensely enjoyable in part because of the dreamlike rapidity with which we are whisked from the company of courtiers to that of rustics and fairies. The implicit largeness of the world in which these groups can interact in a small space is something of a marvel. Puck's epilogue makes it clear that the whole play is to be thought of as a dream. Surprisingly enough, the effect is not to remind us that we are really ordinary human beings who have been watching other ordinary human beings stand on a stage and say things. It is to remind us that we have lived for a while in the imagination of one of the very best ever to give to airy nothing a local habitation and a name.

QUESTIONS FOR DISCUSSION

1. Despite the fact that *A Midsummer Night's Dream* is classified as a comedy, there is a great deal of anxiety and danger in it: Egeus threatens his daughter Hermia with death; love is withdrawn from Hermia suddenly, and for no reason; insults and mockery are perceived by Helena. What makes the play funny? What aspects or parts of the play strike you as comical, and why? Can peril be an ingredient of humor? Does some of the humor stem from the audience's recognition of irrationality in their own lives—such as the capriciousness of love?
2. Are the rustics (Quince, Snug, Bottom, Flute, Snout, and Starveling) in the play for any reason other than comic relief? How might the Pyramus and Thisby play be related to the main action of *Dream*?
3. What different views or aspects of love are represented by Oberon and Titania? By Theseus and Hippolyta? What characterizes the male and female roles in those couples? How do those roles compare with those of the four young lovers?
4. Discuss the proposition that female society is made an issue in this play. Is there evidence to suggest that Hippolyta's past, Titania's relation to the changeling, or Helena and Hermia's friendship shapes the direction of the play? Or are such things only obstacles to be overcome by the males?
5. Why do we read of Theseus' ideas about the imagination at the beginning of Act V? Why does he associate it with love? What might that indicate about his attitude toward the antics of Shakespeare's comedy? Is Theseus' conception of the imagination one the play itself accepts? Is it a comment on the position of the powerful?
6. Why does the audience keep interrupting the play-within-a-play of Act V? Are they entirely contemptuous of what they are watching?
7. Is Shakespeare talking about his own play or drama in general by ending with the play-within-a-play and Puck's closing address to the audience?

SUGGESTIONS FOR WRITING

1. Evaluate Shakespeare's *A Midsummer Night's Dream* by comparing it with a Shakespeare play generally considered inferior—such as *Titus Andronicus* or *The Merry Wives of Windsor*.

2. Choose a relatively minor character, such as Egeus or Philostrate, and explain in a four-page essay what this character adds to *A Midsummer Night's Dream*. Be careful not to focus on the level of plot; it is obvious that without Egeus' prohibition of a match between Hermia and Lysander, for example, the adventures in the woods would never take place. Focus instead on how Egeus or Philostrate reinforces the play's thematic concerns.

READING/WRITING IDEAS FOR EVALUATING DRAMA

EVALUATIVE ESSAYS

Obviously, there are any number of good ways to teach students the fine art of evaluating literary texts, and some of those ways, as well as the potential problems and questions raised by each, are discussed in "Reading/Writing Ideas for Evaluating Fiction" and "Reading/Writing Ideas for Evaluating Poetry." And there you will also find assignments that could, with some very slight revision, work well in conjunction with this chapter.

As the headnote suggests, however, the inclusion of a tragedy and a comedy in this chapter offers you and your students the opportunity of approaching evaluation and evaluative essays in a slightly different, generically specific way. And if you choose to go this route, you might want to begin by having students read or reread Chapter 28 of the anthology in conjunction with this chapter, focusing discussion on the ways in which we can evaluate plays not simply as plays, but also as plays of a particular generic kind. For, as the anthology suggests, different dramatic genres work in very different ways, especially in terms of the kinds of expectations they produce and in terms of the views of human life they tend to assume. Thus students can, I think, more effectively and responsibly evaluate particular dramatic texts when they are encouraged to do so by judging the text not against abstract standards but against standards that take some account of the conventions and challenges peculiar to a particular genre. If you agree, you will probably want to craft an essay assignment that asks students to make arguments about why and how *A Streetcar Named Desire* is or is not a good tragedy or *A Midsummer Night's Dream* a good comedy.

Since students tend to find such evaluation easier when they are allowed to compare texts, you might also or instead craft an assignment that allows or requires students to do so, an assignment that might resemble one of the following:

• Compare either *Streetcar* or *Dream* to another tragedy or comedy in the anthology (such as *Death of a Salesman, Antigone,* or *Oedipus,* in the case of *Streetcar; The Importance of Being Earnest* in the case of *Dream*), showing exactly why and how one tragedy or comedy works better than another.
• Compare either *Streetcar* or *Dream* to another tragedy or comedy by the same author that is generally considered inferior to this one (such as *Sweet Bird of Youth* or *Night*

of the Iguana in the case of Williams, or *The Merry Wives of Windsor* in the case of Shakespeare).

- Compare Shakespeare's *A Midsummer Night's Dream* to *Hamlet* (or another tragedy by Shakespeare), showing how and why Shakespeare is more successful at one genre than another *or* compare a short story by Williams with a related play [see "Planning Ideas" for a list of possibilities], showing how and why the play is better than the story or vice versa.

TROUBLESHOOTING; EVALUATION-FOCUSED WRITING EXERCISES

Students are often quite enthusiastic about evaluation, but sometimes that very enthusiasm blinds them to the real challenges involved in turning "gut responses" into effective evaluative arguments. One such challenge centers, I think, on the need to carefully establish and even defend the criteria being employed—or what the anthology labels "the grounds of judgment"—to be able both to fully communicate our judgment to others (readers) and to convince them that those judgments are reasonable and even somewhat convincing. To do so effectively, too, often necessitates, as the anthology also suggests, becoming a bit self-critical or at least self-aware about the assumptions and values that underlie our judgments and even, perhaps, about the way in which these are shaped by our particular backgrounds. And such self-awareness is seldom easy to come by, particularly—quite frankly—for people as young as many of our students are.

One technique that I've found effective in encouraging students to confront such issues is to assign the kinds of exercises outlined in "Reading/Writing Ideas for Evaluating Fiction" and "Reading/Writing Ideas for Evaluating Poetry." But I also sometimes word the actual essay assignment so that it asks students to conclude their essay with a moment of self-reflection, a paragraph or so in which they must look critically at their own evaluation and try to understand what that evaluation may reveal about their own assumptions and values. Though such self-reflective moments can sometimes turn out to be either perfunctory or embarrassingly confessional, they can sometimes take student writers to an entirely new level, adding real depth and complexity to these particular essays and, more generally, weaning students of the idea that argument is always and necessarily about resolutely occupying and defending a particular position or about ignoring complexity to achieve an aura of absolute certainty.